MUSLIMS IN SPAIN  1500 TO 1614

MUSLIMS IN SPAIN ✕ 1500 TO 1614

L. P. HARVEY

The University of Chicago Press

CHICAGO AND LONDON

The University of Chicago Press, Chicago 60637
The University of Chicago Press, Ltd., London
© 2005 by The University of Chicago
All rights reserved. Published 2005
Paperback edition 2006
Printed in the United States of America

14 13 12 11 10 09 08 07 06   2 3 4 5

ISBN: 0-226-31963-6 (cloth)
ISBN-13: 978-0-226-31964-3 (paper)
ISBN-10: 0-226-31964-4 (paper)

The University of Chicago Press gratefully acknowledges the generous support of the
Program for Cultural Cooperation between Spain's Ministry of Culture and United
States Universities toward the publication of this book.

Title page illustration: detail from Hoefnagel's engraving of Granada (1565).
Courtesy of the author.

Library of Congress Cataloging-in-Publication Data

Harvey, L. P. (Leonard Patrick)
    Muslims in Spain, 1500 to 1614 / L. P. Harvey
        p.   cm.
    Includes bibliographical references and index.
    ISBN 0-226-31963-6 (cloth : alk. paper)
        1. Moriscos—History.   2. Muslims—Spain—History.
    3. Spain—History—Ferdinand and Isabella, 1479–1516.
    4. Spain—History—House of Austria, 1516–1700.   I. Title.

    DP104.H37   2005
    946'.04'088297—dc22   2004015747

Contents

Preface

This history begins in 1500 or, perhaps more precisely, on December 18, 1499. On that day the inhabitants of what was then the principal Muslim quarter of the city of Granada, the Albaicín, exasperated with the failure of the Castilian authorities to respect certain fundamental clauses of the terms whereby the city had been surrendered eight years earlier (in particular, failure to keep the promises made to respect their right to live as Muslims), rose in revolt and took over their part of the city. In their own narrow and winding streets the populace easily established control, but theirs was a singularly ill-prepared revolt which collapsed within three days (just when disaffection was beginning to spread outside the city to the mountainous expanses of the Alpujarras, for example, where things went differently). Order was swiftly restored in the Albaicín, so what happened in Granada between December 1499 and January 1500 might well by now be remembered, if at all, as a merely local affair, an urban riot stifled by firm police action were it not that it marks a significant divide in the history of the Iberian Peninsula as a whole and the beginning of a process that led to the end of Spanish Islam altogether, 114 years later.

For centuries before the end of 1499, the Christian monarchs of the various Spanish kingdoms had ruled over Muslim as well as Christian subjects, and Muslims had had a secure and accepted place in Spanish life. It is true that in certain places and from time to time antagonism against Muslims might manifest itself, but there was never any doubt: they belonged in the land where they were born. In the great medieval *Poema de Mio Cid* the words "Moors and Christians" are to be taken simply to mean "everybody." But from early 1500 onward, there begins in earnest the process whereby Spain's Muslims were to be eliminated from Spanish society. First they were obliged to convert to Christianity— not all of them at the same time; as we will see, it was not until the mid-1520s that the last Muslims were forced into compliance, then in the rest of the sixteenth century there followed periods of persecution, and finally there came the total elimination of Muslims from Spanish soil: the Expulsion of 1609–1614. In theory, at least, no Muslims were left whatsoever after that, and in fact so few did remain that we can say that to all intents and purposes 1614 brought an end to Islam in Spain.

Some Western historians, when dealing with the communities of forcible converts who came into existence as a consequence of these events, tend to see them as exotic and strange, almost out of place in their own homeland, and marginal to the great events of the Hispanic imperial drama which was being played out over the face of the globe at this time. As for what has been written about them in Arabic, it has to be said that until the pioneering work of the Egyptian scholar Muhammad 'Abd Allah 'Inan,[1] there was very little indeed available in print on the subject of the closing phase of the long nine-hundred-year history of Muslims in the Iberian Peninsula (although there is no lack of works on the early periods, the Umayyad Emirate and Caliphate, in particular). The Arab world, not surprisingly, if it has spared any thought at all for al-Andalus (the Iberian Peninsula), has tended to be far less interested in the closing century of decline and disaster than in the periods of Islamic dominance.

Nowadays, however, Arab historians from many parts of the Arab world, and not just from North Africa, are undertaking investigations into the history and culture of the crypto-Muslims of Spain in this final period. The fact that they themselves in their studies usually employ the loan-word *moriskiyyun* ("Moriscos") in speaking of their subject is sufficient indication that their interest was in the first place sparked off by European scholarship in this field (which does not mean, of course, that these modern studies by Arab scholars do not bring important and original insights; some of the most valuable work in recent years, for example, has arisen from the explorations of the Ottoman and other archives undertaken by Tunisian historian Abdeljelil Temimi).

This volume is an attempt to look at the final period of Muslim presence in the Iberian Peninsula, making use of materials from both sides of the religious and cultural divide: both the sources in Arabic, disappointingly scant though they are for this late period, and the abundant materials in the European languages. But to books written *about* the Muslims in Spain in this final period there is a necessary complement, and one which is frequently ignored: what they themselves wrote, their own underground literature. This was in most cases in a dialect of Spanish

---

1. "Enan" is the form of his name used by the historism himself on the alternative English-language title page to his study *Nihayat al-Andalus* (1966).

(very different from the standard literary language), and was set down by them in a script adapted from the Arabic one (what bibliographers and scholars nowadays term *literatura aljamiada*).

In this study an attempt is made to listen to what the Muslims, crypto-Muslims, Moriscos of Spain, themselves had to say. To do this is no innovation, for the great nineteenth-century pioneer of Morisco studies (the term he himself used) was Pascual de Gayangos, and he made every effort from the beginning to make available to a wider public his unrivalled knowledge of the Arabic and *aljamiado* sources. His 1839 article, "The Language and Literature of the Moriscos," marks the beginning of modern scholarly investigations in English (it appeared in *British and Foreign Quarterly Review*). In more recent times, accounts that make extensive use of the Morisco material have not been lacking, as for example Anwar Chejne's *Islam and the West: The Moriscos, a Cultural and Social History* (1983), but thanks to greatly increased research activity in this field in recent years, especially in Spain itself, fresh material is becoming available in such abundance that it seems to me that the time has arrived to attempt a new synthesis for English-speaking readers.

This book follows chronologically from my earlier study, *Islamic Spain, 1250 to 1500* (1990), but yet sets out to stand on its own as a completely independent work. It is mainly concerned with events, with what the native Muslim populations of Spain did after 1500, and with what was done to them, but it is also concerned with concepts: how their Christian neighbors thought about these Muslims as well as how Muslims thought about themselves and about the Christians. Such considerations are not mere optional afterthoughts to the narrative of events, they are rather the necessary preliminaries to any understanding of them. The very different ways in which people can speak of events of the very recent past in the land that some call "Palestine" and others call "Israel" bring home to us how "what actually happened," both over the short term and over the longest of periods, may be conceptualized in totally different ways by members of different groups.

If I had allowed myself to be distracted from making the first draft of this introduction, one morning in 1995, to steal a glance at the front page of that day's newspaper, I would have found there accounts of a violent conflict in which what was at stake was whether Muslims should continue to live in a particular European city. The Christians who wished to drive these European Muslims out had never lived in the areas from which they were seeking to expel the present inhabitants, but they were entirely convinced they had the right to determine who was "at home" there and so could stay, and who, being an intruder, deserved to be "cleansed" away. I could not have failed to note that morning that when it came to the presence of a Muslim minority on European soil, the emotions that governed men's actions were as intense and as bitter as they had been among Christians and Muslims in Granada five hundred years before. As I complete the revision of these pages, well into another millennium, the newspaper headlines look much as they did in 1995, although the places where there are bloody disputes have changed. In this volume we are dealing with events that took place half a millennium ago, but with fierce emotions no less powerful today than they were in 1500.

In the Iberian Peninsula toward the end of the Middle Ages the Christians who pursued the objective of Reconquest had no doubts about the rightness of what they were doing. On the contrary, they possessed a profound conviction that they were carrying out a pious duty. They were striving to recover what had regrettably been lost by their forebears (by Roderick, the last of the Visigothic kings, as their copious ballad literature told them). For the Muslims there were no doubts about their entitlement to live in their homeland either. They no more thought that they might have some obligation to hand back al-Andalus, their name for it, to its original owners, the Christians, than do Egyptian Muslims today feel they should perhaps hand their country back to the Copts. The Muslims of the Iberian Peninsula felt as secure in their entitlement to their lands as do the present citizens of the United States in theirs.

The surrender of Granada in 1492 provoked among some pious Muslims reflections about how their sins must have brought this upon al-Andalus, but they were assailed by no doubts about their legal title to their property. As with Palestine/Israel, there are two names for roughly the same geographical space, Spain/al-Andalus, and two claims on that space. It is not so much that there are in consequence two versions of the same history as that there are two quite different histories located within one and the same geography. I do not hope to be able to conflate or reconcile those two histories. What I want to try to do is to provide an opportunity for us to listen to both sides.

Acknowledgments

A full record of my indebtedness to friends and colleagues for all their help and for their various contributions to this study would be a very lengthy document indeed. That much will be obvious if I say that already in 1956 when I presented the Oxford doctoral thesis (still unpublished) that contained the nucleus of this book, I had to be dissuaded from including what had already by then become an overlong list. To set out in full now, so many years later, all those who have been of assistance to me would mean that I might never get to my first chapter.

Yet I do not wish to convey the misleading impression that I am lacking in gratitude. One of my principal sources, an enigmatic crypto-Muslim known as the Young Man from Arévalo (*Mancebo de Arévalo*), in a preface to one of his works was at pains to point out that "this is not all my own work" (*no salió todo del trabajo mío*), but he went on to regret that "[t]o name everybody [I should thank] would be a very long task" (*Si todos se ubiesen de abocar, sería un enanto muy largo*). Most of those who over the years have been so generous with their assistance and hospitality, I must beg to accept this general expression of my indebtedness.

There are, however, a few names that I cannot fail to mention. I have no doubt that I should begin with Fr. Pedro Longás, who bears the prime responsibility for having taught me (in 1954, it must have been) to read Spanish written by Muslims in Arabic characters (*aljamia*), and for having then pointed me in the direction of some of the treasures in this field in Madrid, in the Biblioteca Nacional and in the Escuela de Estudios Árabes (where Don Emilio García Gómez proved extraordinarily helpful to an utterly inexperienced research worker). My patient research supervisors at Oxford were, first, Sir Hamilton Gibb, and then, after Gibb had departed for Harvard, Professor A. F. L. Beeston, but I became perhaps even more indebted to Samuel Stern, ever ready to make his extraordinary scholarship and breadth of expert bibliographical knowledge available to all and sundry.

I will simply add that over the years in the writing of this study (putting the names in no sort of order except a roughly chronological one) I acquired special debts of gratitude to Dr. Cecil Roth, Sir Godfrey Driver, Fr. Dario Cabanelas, Professor Thomas Glick, Dr. William Polk, Dr. and Mrs. Martín Gavira, Professor Álvaro Galmés de Fuentes, Professor Albert Hourani, Professor Alan Deyermond, Fr. Feliciano Delgado, Professor Antonio Vespertino, Professor Abdeljelil Temimi, Professor David Hook, Dr. Mercedes García-Arenal, Dr. Consuelo López-Morillas, Dr. Ottmar Hegyi, Professor Luce López-Baralt, Professor Alberto Montañer, Professor Sjoerd Van Koningsveld, Dr. Gerard Wiegers, Dr. Barry Taylor, Dr. John Edwards, Dr. Míkel de Epalza, Professor María Jesús Rubiera, and Dr. Luis Bernabé. In writing those names down, I began by indicating in the conventional way those no longer with us by the words "the late." I soon found myself too depressed to continue that practice and finally decided to make no such distinction. I hope the quick will not object to being put alongside those others whose still-lively intellectual presence animates much of what I have written.

Abbreviations

BL	British Library, London
BM	British Museum, London
BN Madrid	Biblioteca Nacional, Madrid
CODOIN	*Colección de documentos inéditos para la historia de España,* 112 vols. (Madrid, 1842–95)
CSIC	Consejo Superior de Investigaciones Científicas
DRAE	*Diccionario de la Real Academia Española*
EI	*Encyclopaedia of Islam,* 2d ed. (Leiden, 1960–)
GAL	Carl Brockelmann, *Geschichte del arabischen Litteratur,* 2 vols. and 3 suppl. vols. (Leiden, 1937–49)
GR	Fancisco Guillén Robles, *Catálogo de los Manuscritos Arabes existentes en la Biblioteca Nacional de Madrid* (Madrid, 1889)
J	Julián Ribera and Miguel Asín, *Manuscritos arabes y aljamiados de la Biblioteca de la Junta* (Madrid, 1912)
RAH	Álvaro Galmés de Fuentes, *Los manuscritos aljamiado-moriscos de la biblioteca de la Real Academia de la Historia (legado Pascual de Gayangos)* (Madrid, 1998)
SIHM	Henri de Castries et al., *Sources inédites pour l'histoire du Maroc,* 26 vols. (Paris and Leiden, 1905–65)

LIBRARIES CONSULTED

Archivo diocesano, Cuenca
Archivo Histórico Nacional, Simancas
Biblioteca Nacional, Madrid
Biblioteca Provincial (sala reservada), Toledo
Bibliothèque Méjanes, Aix-en Provence
Bibliothèque Nationale, Algiers
Bibliothèque Nationale, Paris

Bodleian Library, Oxford University
British Library, London
Escuela de Estudios Árabes, Madrid
Library, Vatican City
Real Academia de la Historia, Madrid
University Library, University of Cambridge
University Library, University of Uppsala

Muslims in Spain in the Sixteenth Century

ONE ❦ The Beginnings of Crypto-Islam in the Iberian Peninsula

In modern Spain, at the opening of the twenty-first century, there are to be found many congregations of Muslims with their own mosques and other community institutions. And scattered in many parts of the country there reside a great number of individual Muslims who enjoy those religious and political freedoms that the modern Spanish constitution guarantees to all.[1] However, between these Muslims now living in modern Spain and the Muslims living in Spain after 1500 and up to their final expulsion, there is no continuity or organic linkage whatsoever. (No doubt in the case of a few of the individual Muslims who now reside in Spain it might be possible to trace some genealogical connection with ancestors who came originally from the peninsula, but on-the-spot continuity is lacking.)

The first Muslims had arrived in the Iberian Peninsula in 711; the mass expulsion of all Muslims was decreed and carried out in the period 1609–14, nine centuries later. In this great final displacement of population some 300,000 people were forced to leave their homes and were deported from Spain: some of them went out by road over the Pyrenees, but most left by sea. The diaspora left them scattered from the Atlantic seaboard of Morocco in the west to Ottoman Turkey in the east (and possibly beyond). The following pages cover this final century of Muslim presence in the Iberian Peninsula and attempt to trace what happened from the time the first of Spain's Muslims were forcibly converted to Christianity up to the end, several generations later, when in a final cataclysm almost all of the descendants of these converts were expelled from their homeland.

Perhaps the most frequent designation in modern times—both in Spanish and in English—for these forcible converts has been "Moriscos." For this volume the title *Muslims in Spain, 1500 to 1614*, has nevertheless been preferred (to *Moriscos in Spain*, etc.) for two reasons. In the

1. See appendix I.

first place, Muslims (or *Muslimes*) was what these people actually called themselves within their own community. In the second place, "Moriscos" as we will see, although widely accepted, may give rise to confusion and misconceptions that are best avoided.

The special characteristic that marks off Spain's Muslim communities in this final period, distinguishing them not merely from their forebears in the medieval Iberian Peninsula but also from other orthodox Muslim communities in any other place in the world at any time was that they were all perforce crypto-Muslims. They were subjects of a Christian monarch who lived their true religion secretly because, during most of the period that concerns us, they were regarded by their Spanish rulers as having been legally converted to Christianity. They were, in the expression then in use, *nuevos cristianos convertidos de moros* ("New Christians, converted from being Moors") and fell under the jurisdiction of the Inquisition. (As unconverted Muslims they would not have been answerable to that tribunal, which was, in theory at least, purely concerned with internal Church discipline. Once they became converts, however, there was no doubt that they were subject to its ministrations.)

THE IMPORTANCE OF NAMES: *MUSLIM, MORISCO, NEW CONVERT*

Morisco gives rise to misunderstandings because, although it appears to be a word with a simple definition, in fact the usage governing it is by no means straightforward. The main problem arises because we have to deal with not just one sense but two related but still distinct sets of senses.

Let us start with the older semantic level of usage of the term (which, to avoid confusion, will be called *morisco* [1]). This presented no serious problems so long as it was the only sense. In the medieval Castilian of the twelfth century already, *morisco* (1) is an adjective associated with and derived from the noun *moro* (which itself might function as both noun and adjective). *Moro* meant "Moor" (in one or other of the two main acceptations of that word ([a] "North African" or [b] "Muslim," etc.). Closely associated with this noun *moro, morisco* (1) was an alternative adjectival (never substantival) form: cf. English "Moor*ish*." *Morisco* (1), just like *moro,* is to be subdivided semantically into either "pertaining to the peoples of North Africa" or "pertaining to their Islamic religion." In the history of the Castilian language, there are abundant early attestations of both *moro* and *morisco* (1). Thus in the *Poema de Mio Cid* (dating from the early thirteenth century, although some would place it even earlier), *moro* occurs meaning "Moor" (in both senses mentioned, i.e., "North African" and "Muslim"), and alongside it we also find *morisco* (1) meaning "Moorish," "having to do with Moors," as in, for example, "piel morisca" or "Moorish skin," that is, "Moorish leather" (what is called in English "Morocco leather"). It needs to be stressed (and is often forgotten) that *moro* and *morisco* (1) ("Moor" and "Moorish"), going back as they do to the oldest level of the Spanish language, have never ceased to be used and can still have these same meanings, right up to the present day, even though *morisco* (2), the acceptation to be discussed in the next paragraph, occurs nowadays with greater frequency.

To turn then to *morisco* (2) (note there is no parallel *moro* [2]), this acceptation developed much later, not until the sixteenth century, and its semantic range is narrower and far more specific. It is the sense that will concern us most directly in this study. The *Dictionary of the Royal Spanish Academy* (*Diccionario de la Real Academia Española,* hereafter *DRAE*) defines this *morisco* as:

> Said of those Muslims who at the time of the restoration of Spain remained behind, baptized. (*DRAE*, s.v. "morisco")[2]

One might out of a misguided sense of historical accuracy raise pernickety objections to that definition. In the first place, it would clearly be desirable, indeed essential, to add to those who "remained behind" (the original converts) the three or four generations of their descendants. Another key element left unstated in the Academy's definition is that these were almost all *unwilling* converts. Yet the Academy's wording deserves to be cited here, not merely because of its authority but also because the wording does convey the attitude of the majority community toward this religious minority.

In spite of what the *DRAE* and a number of other authoritative reference works imply, the word in this sense (*morisco* [2] = "convert from Islam") actually does not come into use in the Spanish sources *immediately* after 1500. It was not until later, from about the middle of the sixteenth century, that it was generalized. Before that, certainly in the early years after 1492 (the date of the conquest of Granada by the Catholic Monarchs), and in the first half of the century, it is far more usual to find expressions such as the one already mentioned, "new converts" or *nuevos cristianos convertidos de moros* (although a few early examples of *morisco* [2] may be found). "New converts" (and especially the full form, "new converts from Islam") must have been an over-long and clumsy designation, so it is hardly surprising that the single-word expression *morisco* (2), when it did become available, soon took over as the preferred way

---

2. "Dícese de los moros que al tiempo de la restauración de España se quedaron en ella bautizados." I translate literally; what is meant is "after the completion of the Reconquest."

of referring to these "converts from Islam," especially among Christians (Muslims themselves were naturally reluctant to use it, although a few examples do occur in late Muslim texts). By the end of the sixteenth century, it even became possible to make a semantic distinction between *moro* and *morisco* (2), and to say, for example, "These Moriscos are just as much Moors (Muslims) as the people in Algiers" (*Estos moriscos son tan moros como los de Argel*). In 1599, Lope de Vega could use this same distinction in his play, *Los cautivos de Argel,* and expect his audience to grasp the point immediately. One of his characters speaks of changing "from being a Moor to being a Morisco" ("desde ser moro a morisco"; Case 1993, 121). Lope presents the man in question as having been brought up in Spain under the name of Francisco, having subsequently crossed to North Africa, where he adopted a Moorish name, "Fuquer," but in the play he contemplates moving back again to Spain. Clearly by Lope's time *morisco* (2) was semantically firmly established.

A useful word, then. What is there against it?

Historians in modern times, when writing about these forcible converts, not only in Spanish but in almost all modern languages, Arabic included, have certainly employed "morisco" as a conveniently specific term and have been little troubled by the problems it poses. These are not inconsiderable.

In the first place there is the anachronism of applying this designation to people well before it was in general use. That may not be an objection of any great weight, although ignorance about the sixteenth-century limits to the currency of the word "morisco" sometimes does lead otherwise well-informed modern readers of early texts into misunderstandings.[3]

A second objection, and one of much greater moment, is the insidious ideological bias inherent in this use of the word. To accept that an individual is correctly referred to as Morisco is by implication to go along with the proposition that it was justifiable to redesignate him in that way against his own free will in the first place. It is to reclassify him, to impose a new sub-Christian identity on him without his assent. We can tell from their own writings (and, as we will see from chapter 5, there is quite a large corpus of such material) that the "converted" Muslims did not think of themselves as in any way different doctrinally from their fellow Muslims in other parts of the world (although they were,

3. Diego de Haedo, in the introduction to his *Topographia e historia general de Argel* (Valladolid, 1612) tells his readers that there are various languages in use in the city, but "la [lengua] morisca" "es general entre todos" ("the Moorish language is general among them all"). He can only mean here North African [Arabic], and those who have imagined that he meant that "Morisco" speech, whether Hispano-Arabic or Romance, are mistaken. Here in Haedo we clearly have *morisco* (1), not *morisco* (2).

of course, conscious of the special difficulties that arose from their historical situation). Their aspirations, as clearly expressed in their own writings, were not at all those of converts to Christianity. On the contrary, they constantly expressed wishes that the institutions of Islam might be restored in their native land ("the minarets raised up again," "las açomoas empinadas"). And, as has been said, they normally speak of themselves simply as *muslimes*. *Moro* and *morisco* (Morisco) were names that *other people* had for them, not the name they used for themselves. As time went by, they did perforce have to begin to accept the label, but Morisco was not ideologically neutral when employed in the sixteenth century, and it can easily smuggle an undesirable bias into our discourse today.

However limited the use of the term *Morisco* in Morisco sources of the period may have been in texts from the first half of the sixteenth century, it did come to prevail in Christian sources from the second half of the century, and it is by now so well entrenched in the modern secondary literature in Spanish on these topics, and it has spread to many of the major languages, that it would hardly be possible to eliminate it altogether or replace it systematically by something less inherently ambiguous or less ideologically skewed. Even modern standard Arabic uses *al-muriskiyyun*. Whether the Arabic of the Muslims of Spain in this final period itself adopted the word *morisco* (2) as a loanword is an interesting question. A Granadan Arabic text dateable from 1587 has the unmodified Castilian morphology of the word *moriscos* ([*sic*], with a Castilian plural termination) in the middle of an Arabic sentence, but the context is an unusual one (the word is there as a necessary component in a racist joke—see appendix II).

In my opinion, it would be quite absurd to seek totally to root out such a well-established, even if potentially tricky, word as *morisco* (2), and for the sake of tidiness in classification to set about substituting for it some newly coined term. There will be many contexts in this volume in which the word *Morisco* will be used because it is convenient to do so and, indeed, some where it is the only appropriate term in the context, for once these Muslims had been forced to pretend to be what they were not, a new situation came into being, a new, complex, and inherently muddled identity was in play. But where, as in the title of this book itself, an inclusive and ideologically neutral term is needed, it is hoped that it will contribute to clarity if we permit these folk to be what they usually called themselves in their own writings. Moriscos was what they were forced to *become,* unwillingly; Muslims is what they *were* underneath.

A further remark on definitions. The Spanish Academy, in the passage just quoted, rightly speaks explicitly of Spain. The descendants of

Peninsular Moriscos, when they arrived as refugees in North Africa, might understandably still for the time being be called Moriscos (by the Spanish administrators of the enclave of Oran, for example, who had the task of herding the refugees over the border into Muslim territory). Among fellow Muslims in North Africa they were not "Moriscos." Before long it became usual there to call them the *andalusiyyun* ("the Andalusians"), or just *al-Andalus*, and those are the names by which their descendants are still known.

THE OTHER "MORISCOS"

The Inquisition did its best to keep Moriscos out of the New World and on the whole was successful (see Dressendörfer 1971.) So there was scope for the word *morisco* to evolve semantically in other directions. *Morisco* might indicate a dark or darkish skin color (in a usage linking back, of course, to *morisco* (1), "North African," "Moor"). Sometimes, in a colonial society that developed quite elaborate terminologies to distinguish various categories of persons of mixed descent, a *morisco* (3) emerges as a technical term for a degree of skin pigmentation. Thus, for example, one Spanish dictionary (*Vox: Diccionario general ilustrado de la Lengua Española* [Barcelona, 1973]) records under *morisco* acceptation 5 in its numbering (marking the sense as both "Mexican" and "obsolete"): "said of a descendant of a mulatto man and a European woman, or of a mulatto woman and a European man." This *morisco* (3) in my numbering will not concern us in this volume.

In the Philippines there is a sense of *moro* that should, perhaps, also be mentioned here for the sake of completeness, although it has no bearing on *morisco* (2). *Moro* is there a designation attached to a specific group who are not North African at all but who certainly are all Muslims. These people mainly live in Sulu Province. *Morisco,* when it occurs in the Philippines, is a local usage, and a special application of *morisco* (1) rather than *morisco* (2). Apart from such clearly delimited exceptions, *morisco* is a peninsular Spanish designation for a historical phenomenon specific to the Iberian Peninsula.

ETHNICITY

Were these people, or were they not, aliens in the Spanish kingdoms?

That awkward racial question will never be very far away in the course of the following pages. That many Christians *felt* these fellow inhabitants of their country to be in some essential way alien, because they were the descendants of invaders who had arrived long ago can be in no doubt: the whole Spanish national enterprise of the Reconquest, as well as the events of the period under study, rested on that conviction.

Still nowadays in Spain, in dozens of towns and cities, there are enacted annually pageants of "Moors and Christians." These take a variety of forms, but one unvarying feature is that the Christians eventually triumph, not the Moors, however noble (and however gorgeous and enviable their fancy attire may be). It would be a profound mistake to see these pageants as mere opportunities for dressing up, still less as shows put on for tourists. Tourists may or may not be present, but the street theater of *Moros y Cristianos* makes a powerful public statement about the identity of Spain's citizens; an identity that was arrived at in combat with the national enemy, the Moor. Spain's national patron saint, Saint James, has the epithet *Matamoros* ("Moor Killer"). The swaggering finery in which the "Moors" are arrayed in these pageants only serves to underline the triumph of the Christians who overthrew them.

There is a tendency for Spaniards—Christian Spaniards, that goes without saying—to define themselves by their confrontation with this enemy. Nonspecialists in modern times who wish to find out about the *morisco* (2) often insist on asking the question, "Yes, but were the people who were expelled really *different* from other Spaniards or not?" By which they seem to mean, did they have any obvious distinctive *physical* characteristics, such as dark skin or frizzy hair. And such enquirers resent being put off by carefully worded politically correct even if also factually correct replies—to the effect that it is impossible to know now, at the beginning of the twenty-first century, what was the true ethnic nature of those various Morisco communities (who certainly differed widely one from another) that were eliminated from Spain at the beginning of the seventeenth century. They want to know what the genetic relationship of the seventeenth-century displaced persons was to the original Muslim invaders of 711 (or to the various groups and individuals who had arrived in the peninsula from the Islamic lands in subsequent centuries). What can we know about the "race"[4] of the Moriscos?

4. The word "race" (Spanish *raza*) first came into existence in Spain, and wherever it is used in the modern world it is in origin a Hispanism. It is not only in Nazi and Fascist terminology that it can have a positive connotation (as witness French *chien de race*, "pedigree dog"), but in Spain in the later Middle Ages, where it started out, it certainly carried a *negative* charge. *Raza* (*raça* in medieval spelling) meant a "defect" or "blemish" in the weaving of a piece of cloth. A bolt of cloth, *sin raça* ("without any defect," "with no snags") was naturally worth more, and so by extension the ethnically pure were, for the purposes of the Inquisition, "sin raza de judíos/moros": "with no Jewish/Moorish blemish on their pedigree." The transition of this word from being an objectively negative commercial term in the late Middle Ages to its shamefully positive sense in the twentieth and twenty-first centuries, is one of the most curious of semantic migrations.

Even if we were to posit two genetic stocks that started out as quite distinct, one, that of the "native" inhabitants of the Iberian Peninsula, and the other, that of the invaders of 711, it has to be borne in mind that by the time the final expulsion came, the two groups would have had nine centuries to intermingle. If the two groups had remained totally "uncontaminated," the one by the other, over such a long time span, that would itself have been a most remarkable biological phenomenon. Now, incredible as it may seem, claims by Christian Spaniards to purity of "Gothic" blood (by which they meant descent from the Visigoths who had ruled before the Muslim invaders arrived) were so frequent in the sixteenth century as to be the subject of standing jokes in the *comedias* of the period. Anybody from the Montaña, the mountainous region of the Asturias where Muslim rule was reputed never really to have penetrated, tended to claim automatic noble status on these grounds alone, and such lineage could be of considerable legal and practical importance in a society obsessed by ethnic purity (*limpieza de sangre*). Nor were genealogical fictions confined to one side. There were Muslims who would have their fellows believe that they could trace their descent back to an Arab tribe, perhaps even to a Companion of the Prophet himself (and we will see that in the late 1560s the leader of the last large-scale rebellion of the Granadan Muslims claimed to be an Abenhumeya, i.e., Ibn Umayya, i.e., a descendant of the line of caliphs of Damascus and later emirs and caliphs of Cordova).

Whatever the genetic truth was, it was certainly more complex than any simple dichotomy of Germanic Goths versus Semitic Arabs. The Iberian Peninsula at the time of the invasion of 711 had already been an ethnically varied place, and "Goths" were not the majority of the population at that time. By the same token, the largest contingents fighting on the Muslim side in the early battles were certainly not the Arabs but the Berbers. (And anybody who knows anything about the Berbers is aware that "Berber" is itself a convenient blanket designation covering a range of peoples.)

In the intervening centuries between the arrival and enforced departure of Muslim elements, even though no massive influxes of population seem to have taken place at any one time, there certainly was a constant trickle into the Iberian Peninsula—occasionally much more than a trickle—of people from the various Islamic lands, above all, of course, from North Africa. Further to complicate matters, an active slave trade existed in the Middle Ages. One of the results was that white slaves from central Europe, usually called in Arabic *Saqaliba* (Arabic "broken plural" of *Saqlaba*, i.e., "S[c]lavs") had been brought into the peninsula. (Some, but not all, of these were castrated by the slave traders to increase their market value.) A slave trade with Africa persisted much longer than that with Europe, so that black slaves were still being brought across the straits and into Granada right up to the end of Muslim times and almost certainly later.

There were decrees made by the Christian authorities against contin-ued Muslim ownership of such slaves, not, we may take it, out of any desire to stamp out slavery as an intrinsically evil institution (for owner-ship of slaves was not unknown among Christians inside Spain, as well as overseas in the plantations). The ban arose from fear that Muslim masters would be in a position to proselytize and to win for their religion souls that might otherwise have come to belong to Christ. Such concern by the Christians shows that, up to the end of the fifteenth century, there continued to be some black African contribution to the gene pool of the Muslim communities, particularly in Granada. The extent of that contri-bution may have been enhanced by the structures of the Islamic family, and these structures seem to have in part survived the enforced conver-sions. In the theory of Islamic law, Muslim females could only marry Muslim males, and in general practice Muslims did tend only to marry other Muslims, so any fresh genetic elements entering the community's gene pool from outside would tend to be retained within it. It was possi-bly the element from black Africa, even though it was a small one, that reinforced the tendency for Spanish Christian writers to characterize the "moros" as in complexion more "Moreno" (brunette, dark, swarthy) than Christians.

So it may well have been the case that in the sixteenth century the Muslims of the peninsula did tend to be darker in color than their Chris-tian neighbors (although we cannot assert that with any degree of cer-tainty). But any difference of appearance or complexion that may have been observable over the whole population certainly did not apply to all individuals. And if there *were* differences of skin pigmentation, they were not so marked that one could tell at a glance to which community a person belonged. (If the Inquisition had been able with confidence to tell from a man's face what were his religious allegiances, it might have been spared the embarrassing task that had to be undertaken during some of its trials: that of inspecting the prisoner's foreskin.)

There are engravings and drawings of Spanish Muslims from this period by artists such as Hoefnagel and Weidetz, northern Europeans who had an eye for what was exotic and likely to interest patrons in the Netherlands or northern Germany. Perhaps the artists were tempted to play up whatever they found picturesquely different? The facial types they show us (we must beware of trusting in the coloration in some of our library copies, where such tints were added later by others and not by the artist) are of an "Iberian" rather than an "Arab" cast—insofar as such epithets have any meaning in this context. The evidence is sketchy, and the truth is that we will never[5] with any scientific certainty have a clear sense of the ethnic make-up of the Muslims of the Iberian Peninsula, whether it was significantly different from that of the majority population that eventually drove them out. It is likely that whatever differences that might be visible at the level of individuals, at the level of the population as a whole they were insignificant. But what can be asserted as absolutely certain is that by the end of the sixteenth century a great number of Christian Spaniards were firmly convinced that there were indeed great differences between themselves, descendants of the populations native to the peninsula, and these "alien" intruders.

THE IMPORTANCE OF NUMBERS

It is as impossible to escape from the question of race as it is impossible to avoid the question of how many Muslims lived in Spain during this pe-riod. Here we are on slightly firmer ground, although it must be stressed that even in what was a century of bureaucracy and statistical reports, and indeed in some places of actual census returns, we do not possess exact figures that command universal assent, even after such authorita-tive studies as Nadal (1984) on the general population, Domínguez Ortiz and Vincent (1978, 75–90), or particularly Lapeyre (1959) on what he called "Morisco Spain." We are dealing with a religious group, most of which was at the beginning of our period driven into clandestinity and which had many reasons for avoiding the prying attentions of authority; a group of which many members sought at various periods to slip away illegally abroad and some to "pass" and merge into the majority. These were people who avoided registration. Nevertheless, it is necessary to form some estimate of the proportion of the total population with whom we are concerned, even if we preserve a good measure of skepticism about the reliability of any results.

We live in a world that expects to be provided with exact figures and thus accepts only reluctantly that precise population statistics will in this field always be beyond our reach. Especially in recent years, an immense effort has been put into the analysis of information available in

5. "Never" is perhaps a foolish word to use. Considerable advances are currently being made in the scientific study of the genetic makeup of various populations, and these studies are throwing light on the history of various communities. See, for example, Luigi Luca Cavalli-Sforza, *Genes, Peoples and Languages* (London, 2000). However, it would seem to me that the nature of the extant data on Muslim minorities in Spain would preclude the exploitation of such new methodologies (not least because we have available nowadays no samples of Morisco genetic material). I would be delighted to be proved wrong.

the various archives and reports. In most cases, this information survives in the form of counts of "hearths," that is, households (*fuegos, focs,* etc.). The number of households was important because it was the basis for much taxation and so is often a matter of careful record. In order to move from counts of hearths on to estimates of a global population, it is obviously necessary to multiply hearths by a factor representing the average family size—which is precisely what we do not know. With dedicated rigor specialists debate the exact size of the required conversion factor. It is quite clear that a quite tiny error in the size of the factor chosen may have an enormous impact on the size of the eventual population estimate.

Methodologically this procedure seems to me essentially flawed because it rests on the assumption that general factors may be deduced and extrapolated over whole populations from the limited areas where exact figures are known. Now we tend to know most about well-ordered communities, not about the situation during the destruction and chaos of war and social upheaval. In addition, studies of populations, both human and animal, that are undergoing various sorts of extreme stress indicate that reproduction rates, for example, may vary greatly in response to such unusual stimuli. Warfare and bloodshed obviously reduce the number of males able to start families, so tend to cause populations to fall, but sometimes, in response to the challenge of external attack, the family sizes actually increase. There may be "booms" of "war babies," and on balance the population may not fall. On the other hand, the impact of defeat at the hands of a militarily superior enemy may lead to a catastrophic fall in population when a defeated community descends into psychological depression (and sometimes falls victim to illnesses imported by the invaders). An example (among many) of this effect is provided by the catastrophic collapse in the Maori population of the islands of New Zealand in the nineteenth century after the arrival of British settlers and troops. At one time it even seemed possible that the Maori would eventually just fade away and disappear. But then, when the crisis was in part overcome, the Maori population began healthily to climb back. In Tasmania, on the other hand, in the same general part of the globe and over similar periods, there was no recovery from decline, and the native Tasmanian population first sank into a depressed shock and then disappeared altogether.

What is being argued here is that the stresses of conquest, forcible conversion, enforced relocation, illegal emigration, poverty, and persecution will have had a whole range of different effects at different times in the various regions of the Iberian Peninsula. I do not believe that any human biologist would now be in a position to estimate what those effects might have been on reproduction rates in the 1600s. The necessary experiments have not been carried out and can never be carried out. The basic data are just not available. In consequence, figures for average Morisco family sizes, among other data, are unlikely to give us more than a very rough approximation as to population numbers. We have to accept our ignorance. Wittgenstein's maxim, "About what we do not know, on that we should keep silent," would seem appropriate here. Unfortunately, total silence is not tolerated, but estimates must never be confused with demonstrable facts.

ESTIMATES

For the peninsula as a whole, one can hardly do better than to follow the prudent approximation based on research given by Sir John Elliott in another context (Elliott 1986, 86): "Like other parts of Europe, sixteenth-century Spain had seen a significant increase in population—perhaps from 7.5 to 8.5 million for the peninsula, excluding Portugal (whose population numbered rather over a million) between 1541 and 1591. Of this total population, almost 1.5 million were inhabitants of the Crown of Aragon; 350,000 of Navarre and the Basque Provinces; and some 6,600,000 of the lands of the Crown of Castile." For the Moriscos, the same historian, writing in 1989 (Elliott 1989, 225) but relying principally on Lapeyre (1959), adopts a figure of 275,000 for those who were finally expelled. This was the number of those officially known to have left the country at the end. Clearly this number is lower than the total population earlier in the sixteenth century, in the period when it was still policy to retain the converts rather than to get rid of them.

Perhaps an adjustment of some 10 per cent will compensate for, among other things, clandestine emigration and those lost in fighting and give a figure of some 300,000 to 330,000 (always bearing in mind that guesswork has played a large part in arriving at this estimate). It will be seen that some one-third of a million out of some eight million or more gives a proportion of about one to twenty-five,[6] or very approximately 4 percent. This estimate may err by a considerable margin, but even if the number of Moriscos were to need to be increased by as much as a further 25 percent, to a total of, say, half a million, the overall percentage in the country would be scarcely exceed 5 percent of the total population. These figures are substantially in line with global estimates of Morisco

6. I note that this figure ("at the level of the Spanish population as a whole . . . one in twenty-five") is also arrived at quite independently by Casey (1999, 229).

populations reached by Domínguez Ortiz and Vincent (1978, 82–83), who give 321,000 for the period 1568–75 and 319,000 for the eve of the expulsion in 1609.

In the lands of the Crown of Aragon taken as a whole, Muslim and later convert population were very dense in certain zones, particularly in the Valencian countryside where there were still, up to the end, villages that were predominantly "Morisco." Nevertheless we must put what was perceived as the "Morisco problem" into some overall demographic proportion. The major power in the world at this time, imperial Spain, felt itself under threat inside its own borders from a minority that constituted perhaps one in twenty-five of its total population. True, in certain strategically important areas (in Granada, until Granadans were deported in the 1570s, and on the sea coast of Valencia right up to the end) the Moriscos might indeed represent a military threat if they were ever to receive substantial and sustained overseas aid.

In general, we are speaking of a relatively small and powerless minority. In this, the final century of the existence of Spanish Islam, then, a key factor was not the absolute population of Muslims, nor yet the rate of increase of the Muslims, although this was a theme that preoccupied many Christian commentators of the period who often spoke of the propensity of the Moriscos to breed rapidly. The Christian communities, on the other hand, with their numerous priests, monks, and nuns, not to mention all the soldiers absent overseas, were held to reproduce themselves more slowly. (Such calculations made by Christians rarely took into account the way that persecution and clandestine emigration must have acted as a countervailing brake on population increase among the Moriscos.) The key demographic trend in the Iberian Peninsula as a whole, far outweighing all these others, was that surge in the Old Christian population to which Elliott refers in the passage cited above. It was population *growth* in Castile, above all, sustained until the plague that struck Castile in 1599–1600 (Elliott 1989, 225), that really served to keep Spain's Muslims demographically marginalized. They may have bred like flies, as some observers alleged, in some villages, but at the national level the significant trend was the growth of the predominantly Christian population of the center and the north (the source of the manpower for Spain's imperial expansion), and it is to that undoubted factor (the reasons for which cannot be discussed here) that we should ascribe the long-term demographic eclipse of Spain's Muslims. The final expulsion was a cruel coup de grâce to a community long in decline, not a measure of self-defense taken by Christian folk in any real danger of being demographically overwhelmed and outbred.

THE DRIVE FOR CONVERSION TO CHRISTIANITY

Forcible conversion of Muslims came at different times for the various kingdoms into which Spain in the sixteenth century was divided: first to suffer were the lands of the Crown of Castile in 1500–1502, then Navarre in 1515–16, and finally the lands of the Crown of Aragon (i.e., Catalonia, Aragon, and Valencia) in 1523–26. We will see that the historical circumstances were quite different in each case. Each of these conversions will be dealt with in turn in the following two chapters, but we must start our investigation by examining the theological and historical background on both sides of the religious divide. And perhaps surprisingly for these purposes, it is essential to look briefly across the Portuguese frontier.

It was not until 1500 that Muslims in Spain had to confront the problem of what to do about the threat of conversion under duress. The year 1492 had been a landmark year, certainly, but whereas the conquest of Granada brought the end of the last bastion of political autonomy for Muslims in the peninsula, it did *not* bring about any forcible conversions. After 1492 all up and down the length and breadth of Spain Muslims in practice enjoyed freedom to worship as their forefathers had worshipped before, and those rights were in most cases entrenched not just in a single constitutional instrument but also in an array of capitulations, charters, coronation oaths, and other formal guarantees. The Muslims of the formerly independent Muslim Kingdom of Granada after 1492 simply had their status assimilated to that of the Mudejars ("subject Muslims who accepted Christian rule") of the rest of the peninsula. It was for that reason that the final chapter of my study *Islamic Spain, 1250 to 1500,* covering the period 1492–1500, was entitled "All Mudejars Now."

For a few years after 1492 there was stability on the basis of the maintenance of the religious status quo: as compared with pre-Conquest days, very little seemed to change where religion (rather than politics) was concerned. The discontinuity came not in 1492 but toward the end of the decade. Yet for the opening chapters of this present volume the symmetry of a chapter headed "All Christians Now" is not possible because even though the objective cherished by the Catholic Monarchs from the outset, that all their subjects should worship according to the one true faith, continued to be an aspiration, it was no more than that. It was an underlying policy objective, certainly, but one that was to elude them and their successors right up until 1614. How did this objective come to be adopted? We need now to look at what was happening in Portugal in the closing years of the fifteenth century.

CASTILIAN POLICY ON FORCIBLE CONVERSION: THE RELEVANCE OF THE EVIDENCE OF THE PORTUGUESE CONVERSIONS OF 1497

It may seem surprising that it is to Portugal (at this point and up to 1580 an entirely independent state[7]) that we must now briefly turn. This is because it was curiously in Portugal and not in any of the Spanish realms that Spain was first able to insist on the implementation of a policy of monolithic Catholic Christian unity, with, as a corollary, the elimination of all other faiths. Castile's handling at this period of its relations with Portugal establishes beyond all doubt that religious intolerance at home in Spain was not something into which the Catholic Monarchs only drifted or were propelled by accident and circumstance. On the contrary, they and their negotiator Cisneros were so committed to a policy of forcible conversion that they were prepared to impose it in a series of difficult negotiations on their unenthusiastic neighbor, Portugal.

From the point of view of Spain's Muslims, what went on in Portugal in 1497 was a very clear warning; from then onward they must have been aware that putting an end to the Muslim presence in the Iberian Peninsula was a cause dear to the Spanish monarchs' hearts. This must have created considerable unease among Muslims on the Spanish side of the frontier, and so is not to be disregarded when we come to consider how rapidly the seeds of revolt could be propagated among the Granadan Muslims three years later.

Portugal and Castile, each engaged in bold overseas ventures, had, in the final decade of the fifteenth century, a firm and successful policy of avoiding conflict between each other within the Iberian Peninsula itself. Matrimonial alliances sought to cement and reinforce good relations, but these were bonds from which there can have been no immediate expectation that an actual political merger of the kingdoms would result. That was certainly still the situation in 1497 when Manuel the Fortunate (who had acceded to the Portuguese throne in 1495) asked for the hand of Isabel, one of the daughters of the Catholic Monarchs. There was already a male heir to the Castilian throne, Juan, when Manuel married Isabel, so there was at the time no reason to suppose that this match would lead to the political union of Portugal and the Spanish kingdoms. However, the young Castilian prince was to die that same year altogether unexpectedly, and so it did seem for a time likely that any son of Manuel and Isabel (she, with some reluctance as we will see, had accepted the proposal of marriage) would eventually rule over almost all the peninsula.

---

7. From 1580 to 1640 the Spanish monarchs also reigned over Portugal.

Such dynastic details might seem totally irrelevant to the history of Spain's Muslims, but in fact we need to pay close attention to them because out of the negotiations leading up to a marriage settlement between Manuel and Isabel there emerged, rather unexpectedly, the decision to expel Portugal's Muslims.

Diplomatic negotiations to draw up the marriage contract proved remarkably sticky, above all because of one factor: the extreme reluctance of the young lady in question. She had been married to Manuel's cousin, Afonso, heir presumptive to the throne of Portugal at the time of his death in 1491. Now in 1497 this pious twenty-six-year-old widow was still grief-stricken and resistant to the idea of remarriage. The young Portuguese king, on the other hand, pressed his suit with some urgency (some said for deep romantic reasons and not just because of dynastic ambitions). This put the Portuguese at a disadvantage in their dealings with the Castilian negotiating team (among whom Cisneros was prominent).

Castile and, indeed, all the territories ruled by both of the Catholic Monarchs, had, in 1492, just five years before, been cleared of Jews. Jews could continue to live in Portugal, however, and indeed many of the Jews ousted from Spain had taken refuge across the border. Jews had made important contributions to many aspects of the general life of the Portuguese nation over the centuries. Insofar as specifically Jewish cultural activity was concerned, it is perhaps significant that some of the earliest books ever printed in Hebrew characters anywhere in the world came from presses in Portugal in the fifteenth century. After the 1492 expulsion of Jews from Spain, it is hardly surprising that it was to Portugal that many of the refugees went, and there they were made welcome. Yet the young widow Isabel, or rather those on the Castilian team negotiating on her behalf, let it be known that she would be unwilling to marry Manuel unless his kingdom came in line with her parents' kingdoms by converting or expelling all its Jews.

For good measure, and this is what is of relevance to us here, Cisneros added in the course of the negotiations the further stipulation that the Muslims of Portugal should be eliminated at the same time as the Jews.

Isabel knew Portugal, of course, from her first marriage, but there is no indication that this extra demand suddenly added by the Castilian emissaries to their list of demands in any way reflected a need that she had perceived herself during her days in Portugal. The small and quiescent Muslim minority there posed no problems whatsoever, nor did it arouse popular animosity. To some churchmen the very presence of people of another faith living alongside them may have constituted some mild spiritual challenge, but we hear nothing of Muslim-Christian tensions.

We have a report, certainly not verbatim and no doubt highly edited but from a well-informed chronicler who inspires confidence, Damião de Gois (Harvey 1984, 50), on how the implementation of the conversion was discussed within the Portuguese Royal Council in the context of the proposed marriage. Opinion in that body was divided. Much earlier precedents for the expulsion of the Jews were adduced in the debate, but *there were absolutely no parallels to adduce for such treatment of Muslims.* That the pope himself tolerated Jews in the territories over which he ruled directly was of course a powerful argument *against* expulsion of the Jews from Portugal, but the other side in the debate, some of those speaking could list many countries from which Jews had already been driven out: England, France, Scotland, and Sweden, among others. The petulance of the speech with which Manuel cut through this inconclusive debate is striking, even when filtered through Damião de Gois's reporting: "I am not concerned with the law," the young king said: "I have made a vow (*devoção*) to do this, and my orders are to be carried out." He seems to be implying that he had made a promise to his bride-to-be, and he would not be deflected from carrying it out. Before these particular marriage negotiations with the Castilian emissaries, Manuel had not been given to displays of piety. There is absolutely no indication that he had earlier held the creation of an all-Christian kingdom as a cherished objective of his own. We can only conclude that the Castilian negotiators used the leverage provided by his desire (for whatever reason) to finalize the marriage contract in order to impose on their Portuguese neighbor a religious policy that was theirs, rather than his.

It is inconceivable that those official negotiators, Cisneros in particular, who did in this way successfully push Portugal to expel its Muslims, were not looking toward the eventual imposition of a similar policy at home in Spain, and, indeed, it is difficult to imagine that the Portuguese would have acceded to the Castilian demands unless it had been at least tacitly understood that Castile itself would be moving at some time in the future toward the same degree of religious uniformity. I therefore regard the conditions imposed on Portugal in 1497 as the first indication that Castile[8] envisaged putting an end within its own territories to the medieval Mudejar dispensation according to which Christian rulers accepted Muslims as their subjects.

8. In this context one must carefully separate Castile from Aragon. The Aragonese constitution placed constraints on constitutional innovations such as this. M. D. Meyerson (1991, 51–60) argues that Ferdinand was "forthright" in his defense of Mudejarism in Aragon, whereas he felt "wavering disapproval" for Isabel's policy in Castile. This view, which I find difficult to accept, is discussed further below in chapter 3.

In fairness, it must be said that when the conversion was put into effect in Portugal, the Muslims were given the option of leaving Portugal across its land frontier into Spain! This superficially puzzling circumstance has been used to argue[9] that Spanish policy was *not* motivated at this point by any anti-Islamic sentiment. The Portuguese Muslims, it is pointed out, were accorded not simply permission to exit through Castilian territory, but given explicit rights of permanent settlement there. I think such an interpretation is misguided.

Two key aspects of the actions taken against the Jews by Manuel are relevant here: the transport arrangements and the policy on children. (We will find these same two areas of concern arising time and again in relation to Spain's Muslims in the following period and right up to 1614.) With regard to the arrangements for the transport out of the country for those who refused the offer of conversion and who opted instead for expulsion, what was important was the question of where precisely those expelled were to embark, and so by implication what was to be their ultimate destination. Although several places were named in the first proclamations as authorized ports of embarkation, at the last moment Lisbon was made the only one. Since Jews and Muslims caught in Portugal after the set date would incur the penalty of enslavement, the chaos and panic at the docks can be imagined. There were not enough vessels available to transport just the Jews (many of whom did suffer the penalty foreseen).

As for children of a tender age, they were excluded from the expulsion orders, or to put it another way and to be more explicit, were *not allowed* to leave with their parents! Obviously such exemptions, when viewed through the eyes of the Christian authorities, looked quite different from the way they looked to the Jews and Muslims. The authorities were moved by a desire not to deprive the innocent young of their chance of hearing the gospel of Christ and so of becoming true Christians. Anybody who drove the innocents away from Christendom would bear a dreadful responsibility. (This type of argument was to be repeated again and again in Spain much later, when the expulsion of the Muslims was under discussion.) The parents of the children that were, in accordance with the edicts, to be left behind, felt the same emotions as any parents anywhere would feel if forced to hand children over with no hope of ever seeing them again. (To these universal human sentiments we must add the

9. As, for example, by Suárez Fernández and Fernández Álvarez (1969, 284–85): "Es indudable que los Reyes Católicos no practicaron una política antimusulmana: cuando en 1497 los moros son expulsados de Portugal, se les concedió asilo en Castilla." (There can be no doubt at all that the policy pursued by the Catholic Monarchs was not anti-Muslim: When in 1497 the Moors were expelled from Portugal, they were granted asylum in Castile.)

religious dread felt by pious Jews, horrified at the prospect of their off-spring being brought up against their will in such an imperfect faith as Christianity, and so unable to perform the sacred rites.) The anguish of the Jewish families caught in this cruel trap is described by contemporary observers.

The Portuguese Muslims were therefore well advised to avoid if they could a similar fate, and to keep clear of the Lisbon docks if at all possible. They opted instead to negotiate permission to leave overland. As we have seen, their probable fate if they had tried to leave by sea would have been slavery: they had no guarantee that shipping could be found before the deadline, indeed, it was unlikely in the extreme that they would all have managed to secure passages. The centuries-old community of Portuguese Muslims was in this way brought to an end overnight, but at least the children of the Portuguese Muslims were spared the dreadful fate inflicted on the children of the Jews.

De Gois is utterly frank when he comes to explain why this surprising concession was made by the Portuguese authorities. It was not out of any impulse of generosity or nobility of sentiment. His text is so revealing and has such direct bearing on the way Muslims were later to be treated elsewhere in the peninsula (particularly in the lands of the Crown of Aragon), that it must be translated here in extenso:

In case we are censured for carelessness in not explaining why the King had the Jews' children seized, whereas the children of the Moors were not, especially since the reason both of these groups were being obliged to leave the country was that they had refused baptism and rejected the teachings of the Church, it must be borne in mind that no harm could result to Christians if they took away the children of the Jews. Jews are scattered all over the earth, and have no country of their own, no lordships, cities or towns, and indeed in all the places where they dwell, they are transients [*peregrinos*—perhaps "outsiders"], and payers of tribute, so they lack the power and authority to execute their will against those who do them harm and injury. The Moors, on the other hand, have, for our sins, and in order to punish us, been permitted by God to occupy the greater part of Asia, Africa, and a good part of Europe too, and in these places where the Moors have empires, kingdoms and great lordships, there live many Christians who are subject to their tribute, not to mention the many Christians held captive by them. It would have been very prejudicial to all these peoples to take away the Moors' children, because those subjected to this harm (*agravo*) would clearly not fail, after expulsion had been inflicted on them, to seek to execute revenge on those Christians who lived in Moorish (Muslim) territory, and above all to take revenge on the

Portuguese, who would incur special blame. This was why the Moors were allowed to leave the kingdom with their children, whereas the Jews were not. May God grant out of his mercy that they may all learn the way to truth, so that they may therein achieve salvation. (Harvey 1984, 39)

This Machiavellian line of reasoning should not be forgotten when in chapter 9 we come to look at the ways in which the expulsion of the Moriscos was put into effect in the period 1609–14 under the different conditions of that later age. In terms of global strategy the Christian nations of the Iberian Peninsula at the end of the fifteenth century felt, vis-à-vis the Islamic world, that they were potentially vulnerable, but by the time the Edicts of Expulsion were eventually put into effect the combined kingdoms of Spain and Portugal were immeasurably wealthier and more powerful than any of the Islamic powers of the early seventeenth century. Fear of reprisals no longer held Christian policymakers back in the way that it had done 112 years earlier.

The Portuguese Muslims had to pay exit dues at the border as they crossed into Spain in 1497. The short-term consequence of the infanta Isabel's religious scruples about having any non-Christians at all in her new homeland, Portugal, was thus an actual increase in the number of infidels in her native land, Spain! (Not to mention a rise in revenue collected at the frontier.) None of this makes any overall sense unless we assume that there was some understanding among the Christian rulers that the anomaly thus created would be a temporary one, soon to be rectified by the implementation of the policy of expulsion where Castile's Muslims were concerned—as did in fact happen. But whereas the Portuguese Muslims had a real choice (albeit a distressing one) between conversion (in which case they could continue to live in Portugal) and expulsion (to the neighboring kingdom where they could continue to be Mudejars), as we will see, for all the Muslims resident in the lands of the Crown of Castile at the time of their forcible conversion in 1500, the choice that was available to the majority of them was in practice limited, and after that point no real choice was to be available at all.

Before returning to the story of the Spanish Muslims proper, this account of relations between Manuel and his pious wife Isabel needs to be rounded off, if only because its sad end reminds us that so far we have spoken only of the Crown of Castile and Leon (and incidentally of Portugal). We must not forget that there were very large Muslim communities, as yet unconverted, in Valencia and Aragon, where they were governed by different laws, and so at this stage in their history they enjoyed a quite different fate.

Manuel and Isabel did get married, and they went on a protracted visit to various Spanish territories. It was actually in Saragossa, in Aragon, in 1498 that Isabel presented her husband with a son. The whole of the Iberian Peninsula joined in the celebrations because the baby seemed at one time destined to unite all the Iberian kingdoms! But Isabel died as a consequence of what had been a very difficult delivery. (One may guess she may have foreseen the trauma, and perhaps that was why she had tried so hard to avoid a second marriage in the first place.) The infante, given the auspicious name of Miguel da/de la Paz (Michael of the Peace), was himself to survive only a few months. And so the tempting matrimonial alliance for which Portugal had sacrificed its whole Jewish and Muslim communities, a political alliance that had appeared for a short time to promise rich rewards for the Portuguese royal house, led nowhere after all.

The wild rejoicing at the birth of such a promising heir, Miguel and the grief for the death of first mother and then child were thus acted out against the backdrop of the Aragonese city of Saragossa, where, protected by the Crown for another quarter century from all persecution, there lived a sizeable and prosperous community of free Muslims who continued to enjoy all the Mudejar rights guaranteed to them explicitly by the coronation oaths sworn by all the kings of Aragon!

THE CONVERSION OF THE MUSLIMS OF THE CROWN OF CASTILE

If the King of the Conquest does not keep faith, what are we to expect from his successors?[10]

Those words, so full of foreboding, were spoken in Granada by a revered local Islamic scholar, Yuce Banegas, a survivor from the days before the arrival of the Castilians. They were addressed to a young Muslim student, a visitor from the center of the peninsula (from Arévalo—of him we will hear much more below). I used Banegas's words to close the volume entitled *Islamic Spain, 1250–1500,* but I repeat them here as they express the fears of those Muslims who could foresee to what was to come. The treatment they had anticipated was indeed about to be visited on Granadan Muslims. The new dispensation under which all inhabitants of Castilian territories were obliged to become Christians and were forbidden to remain as Muslims stemmed from the suppression in 1500–1502 of

10. "Si el rey de la conquista no guarda fidelidad ¿qué aguardamos de sus suzesores?" BN Madrid Res. 245 f. 87v, quoted in Harvey (1990, 339).

a rebellion that had swept through the Muslim-inhabited mountainous regions of the Kingdom of Granada. This new policy began to be implemented in Granada in 1500 and was summed up, in its definitive form, in a *pragmática* ("royal decree") dated February 12, 1502. In the preamble of this proclamation (and in the many other associated documents), the action taken was justified by reference to the rebellion of which mention has already been made.

The rebellion had wiped out, so it was argued in these texts, any rights that Muslims might have been able to claim, not only under the 1492 peace settlement for Granada but also under the many city charters, *fueros,* and other documents in which were recorded the rights (some of them very ancient rights indeed) of the various Mudejar communities of Castile. Yet it was only the fact that the terms by which they had surrendered in 1492 were not being implemented that had driven the Muslims of Granada to take up arms against their new Castilian rulers. As for the Mudejars of Castile, they had done nothing whatsoever to justify their being deprived of their protected status in this way.[11]

Clearly if the Spanish royal family induced the Portuguese to adopt a policy of religious uniformity for Portugal in 1497, then the argument that the enforced conversions of 1500–1502 in Castilian lands came only as a result of the armed revolts in Granada of 1499–1500 and would not otherwise have taken place, is not very convincing. The suspicion must therefore arise that arguments about the revolts having voided the terms of surrender of Granada were mere pretexts. A skeptic might even harbor suspicions that the 1500 revolt in Granada may have been to some extent intentionally provoked (Cisneros and his men were indeed provocative, as we will see).

In this welter of uncertainty, one thing alone is clear: each side was confident of being in the right, and each accused the other of acting in bad faith.

TWO OPPOSING VIEWS OF THE CONVERSIONS

The circumstances under which public worship according to the religion of Islam was brought to an end in the Iberian Peninsula were, not surprisingly, seen in quite different lights by Muslims and Christians. To gain an overall view, let us look at two contrasting summary general accounts of what happened, the first by a sixteenth-century Christian historian, the second by a seventeenth-century North African Muslim historian of al-Andalus, which was, as we have seen, the name that the Iberian

---

11. This final period of Islamic Granada and of Mudejar Castile is discussed in the closing chapter of *Islamic Spain, 1250–1500* (Harvey 1990, 324–39).

Muslims had for the peninsula. Neither account is contemporary, but both are by scholarly individuals with an exceptionally good array of source materials available to them. Their accounts reflect moderate, not extremist, views within each community.

The Christian historian, Zurita, annalist of the Crown of Aragon, was by no means a religious bigot (in many ways quite the reverse). This is how he saw what happened after the conquest of 1492:

> At the time of the conquest, after the surrender of the city of Granada the Moors were grouped together in the Albaicín, but within the main part of the city there had remained, separated from the Christians, a Moorish quarter of some five hundred houses, and when these people saw that the Albaicín Muslims had all turned Christian, they sent word to the Archbishop, asking him to consecrate their community mosque [as a church], and they became converts too. Following them the majority of the villages that there were round Granada were brought to the Christian faith, and thus the converts in Granada and the surrounding villages reached the figure of 50,000.
>
> The Moors of the steep parts of the Alpujarras mountains in the direction of the sea, seeing what a great number of people had been converted in such a short space of time, formed the view that if the process was not cut short, day by day the number of conversions would increase, and their own numbers would grow ever less. The rumor was beginning to be put about among them that they were to be converted forcibly, and so they began to occupy certain strong points. The men of Huéjar, in the steepest part of the mountains, were the first to rebel: the village could only be reached through narrow dangerous passes.[12]

A quite different view is to be found in the North African historian, al-Maqqari (himself proud that his family originally came from al-Andalus). Writing in the seventeenth century, and so separated from the events he was describing by a somewhat greater gap, yet still with good access to the traditions of the proud refugee community to which he belonged, he summarizes for his readers the events in the whole period covered by this present volume as follows:

> Then the Christians violated the Capitulations, and one after another voided the terms to which they had agreed. Finally in A.H. 904 [A.D. 1498–89] the point was reached of forcing the Muslims to convert to Christianity. When the Christians had established their superior strength, the priests wrote to all the Christians who had accepted Islam, telling them that

12. Fernández y González (1866), citing a manuscript, "Historia de Aragon y Cataluña," BN Madrid G 17.

they were to be obliged to turn to the religion of unbelief.[13] Although the [Muslim] people spoke out, they had no power to do anything about it, and what was commanded was done. The Christians then took their campaign one stage further: they said to a Muslim whose grandfather [possibly "whose forebears"] had been Christian, that he should return to the Christian religion. When this monstrous state of affairs became known, the people of the Albaicín rose against their rulers and killed them. This was the beginning of the conversion to Christianity [of all Spanish Muslims]. The justification was that the command had emanated from the king, and that if anyone rebelled against his ruler, he was to be put to death unless he converted to Christianity, in which case his life was pardoned. In general people did without exception accept the conversions, both in the towns and in the country areas. Yet they held back from [true] conversion, and the Christians were kept at a distance. The conversion was thus of no avail. The enemy laid siege to a number of villages and hamlets, among them Belfique and Andarax, and either killed all the inhabitants or took them prisoner. The only place that escaped was Sierra Blanca, where God gave help against the enemy, and many of them were killed, including the lord of Cordova.

The Muslims then left the places where they had lived, and went with their families to Fez, taking with them their transportable possessions but not their jewelry. From this time on the Muslims [who had remained behind in Spain], while putting on an external show of conversion to Christianity, in secret worshipped Allah, and performed their prayers. The Christians increased the persecution to which they subjected them, even burning people for that reason. Muslims were forbidden to carry short swords and other such weapons. They rose in revolt against the Christians and took to the mountains time after time, but God did not grant them victory, and finally the Christians expelled them in 1017/1609. (al-Maqqari 1949, 6: 279)[14]

CONVERSION IN GRANADA

The Capitulations by which the city of Granada had originally surrendered in 1492 must have been regarded by many on the Christian side as more than generous. The pattern for such surrender documents that had been established in the centuries-long process of the Christian Reconquest had been that if a city or fortress surrendered to its attackers, either before an attack was launched or even fairly early in the fighting,

13. Al-Maqqari, of course, is referring to those people who had in earlier times, before 1492, been converted from Christianity to Islam. They were to be obliged to return to their former Christian beliefs.

14. For the continuation and conclusion of this passage, see chapter 11, pp. 367–68.

its inhabitants could reasonably expect favorable treatment; they would be left in possession of most of their property and would be allowed to continue to worship God as they saw fit, provided they made a total military and political submission. If they resisted for a long time, on the other hand, and certainly if they held out until they were overwhelmed, they could expect harsh treatment, loss of their property, and in all probability loss of their personal liberty. That is what had happened in 1487 to the Muslim inhabitants of the great city of Malaga, who ended their lives as slaves (unless funds could be found to pay their ransoms).

The city of Granada had also put up protracted resistance, so from the Christian viewpoint it was fortunate for its inhabitants that the terms by which it was allowed to surrender were not punitive. This is not the place to discuss exactly why that should have been.[15] Nor is this the place to analyze in detail the lengthy text of the Capitulations themselves or the actions taken by the occupying forces when they took the city over in January 1492 (Harvey 1990, 324–28). For present purposes it is sufficient to note that (with many exceptions, notably the Alhambra itself, and the principal mosque) the Muslim inhabitants did not suffer expropriations and were allowed to continue to live in their old homes and to practice their own religion. The Capitulations entered into considerable detail on religious matters. Some principal religious buildings were taken over, but among the promises made was one protecting those converts to Islam from Christianity who were resident in the city at the moment of its surrender.

To a modern mind, such equal treatment of all Muslims in this way is unsurprising, but there is no doubt that to observers in the fifteenth century it must have seemed unusual, even shocking. Nowadays religious toleration means not just acceptance of the right of others to continue to believe in other religions, but also, quite crucially, acceptance that individuals may *change* their religion of their own volition. That was not the view taken in general by medieval Christians, who regarded the abandonment of the true faith as being sinful. "Renegade" was a term   *Cervantes* of opprobrium. Exactly the same view was taken by medieval Muslims (and by medieval Jews). It is still taken by many (most?) modern Muslims, too. To abandon the true faith once it has been professed is simply not acceptable. (It is, according to the religious code—shari'a—a capital offense.) It will be seen that if one formulates the rules in sufficiently general terms, the same wording covers both *medieval* Christian and Muslim societies: "in either society, whether Christian or Muslim, all believers

---

15. One major factor among many was the desire of the Catholic Monarchs to take over the Alhambra palace-fortress intact. See Harvey (1990, 310–22).

in the Abrahamic monotheist religions are to be tolerated, *but* whereas in any given place conversion into the ruling monotheist religion of that place is permitted, abandonment of that particular ruling religion, even for one of the other permitted monotheist faiths, is not." De Gois, as quoted above, makes it clear why Jews fitted uneasily into this formulation: in medieval times there was no sovereign Jewish state to exercise the sanctions the other two could bring to bear. Thus it was that the inclusion in the Granadan Capitulations of protection for people who in the past had been converted *from* Christianity gave rise to special difficulties.

It might have been predicted that there would be objections from some pious Christians. The completion of the Conquest/Reconquest of Granada and the fundamental switch of sovereignty that that entailed meant that the "inherent" religion of that place had changed. When the terms of surrender were still being negotiated, in protracted talks, the converts (from Christianity to Islam) concerned did not pose any problem in terms of the rules as just set out. They had converted to the dominant faith of the city of Granada. But once the Castilian forces had taken over there, once the frontier between Christendom and *dar al-islam* shifted and the converts now found themselves on the wrong side of the religious divide, they would not be tolerated. Yet the Catholic Monarchs had promised to leave these converts unmolested. A logical, political and religious impasse had been created.

We must assume that the Catholic Monarchs knew what they were doing when they approved the clauses of the Capitulations in question, and we can only speculate that they hoped the problem would simply go away before very long. Possibly they may have thought that the numbers of such converts remaining in Granada would not be large. And perhaps they hoped that such neo-Muslims would soon wish to leave (as they were allowed to do in the early days). Most probably they were confident that once Granada was in Christian hands, any ex-Christian in his right mind would soon decide to return to the faith of his fathers or forefathers.

But the problem did not resolve itself quietly in this way.

We do not have census statistics broken down by religions for 1492, of course, but Ladero in has provided figures for these converts to Islam resident in Granada that are surprisingly large. One explanation for this may be that as independent Muslim territory shrank, Granada would have become the sole possible refuge available for anybody who had for whatever reason wished to change his religion. And so converts concentrated there. The lists studied by Ladero give the actual names of persons (forcibly?) baptized in 1500, among whom there is a small contingent *elches - cristianos convertidos al Islam*

of "renegades." In Granada the name used in this and similar contexts for people in this category was *elches*.[16] Ladero's estimate is a maximum of 300 such *elches*, 101 of whom were induced to admit their errors and become Christians again. Although these numbers are surprisingly high, there seems no reason to reject them. Who, after all, would have had a motive to fabricate such details?

Of the various issues of Muslim-Christian relations that arose in post-Reconquest Granada, the most sensitive was what may be termed the *elche* question, even though relatively few individuals were directly involved. It was, however, not the only point of friction. The two men first placed in charge of the city in 1492 by Ferdinand and Isabella were skilled administrators, and they commanded respect on both sides of the religious divide. They successfully avoided stirring up unnecessary conflicts in the initial period while the new regime was being consolidated. A small Christian ruling class was thus able to govern a large population in a city still overwhelmingly Muslim. In military and civil affairs Íñigo Hurtado de Mendoza, marqués of Tendilla, appointed *alcaide* ("governor") and captain-general, brought with him the sound reputation he had earned in the Granadan wars. Fernando de Talavera, a religious of the Jeronymite order, was appointed to the newly created archiepiscopal see of Granada. Tendilla had great success in engaging "friendly" Muslims in the civil administration of the city, Talavera had his priests use Arabic in their religious preaching, and they were listened to. Relations on the whole were thus good, peace prevailed, but those floods of instant converts that all pious Christians desired (expected?) did not appear. As the decade passed, the free-and-easy administrative improvisations of the early days, arrangements that had worked because of the personalities involved, had to be replaced by bureaucracy, for the population of incoming Christian settlers soon built up, and the old generation of experienced frontiersmen died out. A descendant of this Don Íñigo, Diego Hurtado

16. This is, at the phonological level, no more than a straightforward adaptation to Castilian sound patterns of Arabic *'ilj*, meaning "foreigner." Semantically the situation was far more complicated. In late medieval Iberia the word had acquired a specialized sense. In Granadan Arabic, all non-Granadans might be so termed, even Muslims. *Elche* was then adopted by both sides as a convenient label when, for example, prisoners born in the north of the peninsula, whatever their religious status, came to be ransomed. It may seem strange that a word that started out as a denigratory term in use among Arabic-speaking Muslims when speaking of people of Christian origin or descent was in the period that interests us used by Christians as well as Muslims when speaking of converts to Islam, but that is undoubtedly what happened. See F. Maíllo, "Diacronía y sentido del término 'elche,'" in *Miscelánea de estudios árabes y hebraicos* 31 (1982): 79–98; and Lapiedra Gutiérrez (1997, esp. 243–47).

de Mendoza, looking back on these early days in the introduction to his *Guerra de Granada,*[17] speaks of the regime of the early days of the new regime as follows:

> They gave them [Tendilla and Talavera] companions well-fitted to found a new commonwealth (*república*), which was to be the capital of the kingdom and the defensive shield against the Moors of Africa who had conquered it in earlier times.... The city could be governed as between settlers and companions in a kind of rough and ready (*arbitraria*) justice, because they were all of a like mind, and their resolve was directed together towards the common good. This state of affairs came to an end as the older generation died out.

No doubt a Granadan Muslim might not have shared that view of a settler Golden Age of smooth and benevolent government, but it does appear to have been the case that relations not only among settlers but also between settlers and Muslims deteriorated as the easygoing ways of the early days were replaced at the prompting of newly arrived "outsiders," anxious to make their mark and introduce some bureaucratic order.

One such tidy administrative innovation that had unfortunate consequences was the sharp delimitation in 1498 of two zones within the city, one for Christians and one, the Albaicín, for Muslims (Caro 1957, 97). A year later Archbishop Cisneros (of Toledo) arrived on a protracted visit. To have two archbishops working in one city must have seemed rather strange. Cisneros could explain the time he was spending away from his own see by his need to attend on his monarchs, also present in Granada at this time, but it was his position as inquisitor-general that seems to have occupied most of his time. There is every indication that he had come primarily with the intention of giving fresh impetus to a campaign of conversion that, he could point out, was getting nowhere. In a spirit of goodwill he made his services available to the evangelistic campaign of his colleague. But rather than follow the irenic style of preaching that Talavera had made his own, Cisneros and his staff began to adopt a much more outwardly militant, even physically confrontational, approach. He was against the use of Arabic (whereas Talavera had sponsored the production of a dictionary, a grammar, and a prayer book). "Pearls before swine" was how he spoke of such an approach. Nevertheless, without backing it would probably have been difficult for him on his own to upset the modus vivendi that had been established in the city between Muslims and Christians, especially in the face of the opposition of such powerful local figures as Governor-General Tendilla and Archbishop Talavera.

17. Hurtado de Mendoza (1970, 100).

No doubt it was the attitude of the royal family that was decisive. Here we cannot speak with absolute certainty, and we have to evaluate two contradictory indicators. The Portuguese marriage negotiations in which Cisneros had acted as trusted advisor of the Crown, as we have seen, show him and the monarchs as working in concert towards the elimination of Islam from Christian lands. However, as an indicator that royal commitment to what one might call "religious cleansing" was *not* unconditional, it must not be forgotten, as has been stated above, that all his life Ferdinand never allowed the Muslims of those kingdoms over which he himself reigned (Aragon, Valencia) to be harassed in any way. It was not that Ferdinand was pro-Muslim, but he was not prepared to break his coronation oaths. There is also the paradoxical point that Ferdinand was most anxious to begin to carry crusading warfare into Islamic North Africa. And he was looking further to the east as well, for he put himself forward as protector of the Christians in the Holy Places. He realized that Spain's capacity to launch a military expedition across the Mediterranean would be impaired if there were trouble with Muslims at home. There is no certainty on this subject, but it would seem likely that Cisneros, in stirring up trouble with the Granadan Muslims, had gone well ahead of his royal masters. Perhaps he was seeking to create "realities on the ground," faits accomplis, that could not then be disavowed. When Cisneros's excess of enthusiasm created a very dangerous situation, as it did, his royal masters briefly disowned him, but that is to run ahead of our main narrative, and we must return to the *elches* of the Albaicín.

Although the 1492 Capitulations did explicitly protect the *elches,* loose drafting provided loopholes that might be exploited by anyone intent on stirring up trouble. The full wording of the clauses in question is as follows:

> Nobody may by word or deed abuse any Christian man or woman who before the date of the Capitulations had turned Moor. If any Moor had taken a renegade as his wife, she will not be forced to become a Christian against her will, but she may be questioned in the presence of Christians and Moors, and be allowed to follow her own will. The same is to be understood of children born of a Christian mother and a Moor.
>
> No Moor may be forced to become a Christian against his or her will . . .

Whereas the general clause ("No Moor may be forced to become a Christian. . . ") may appear to protect *all* Muslims, it might be possible to argue that since renegades were really, underneath it all, Christians, they were not protected by this heading. The rights of wives and children were indeed explicitly guaranteed, but the wording does not make it

crystal-clear that males were safe. However, the conflagration engendered by the failure of this legislation to provide the *elches* with security
in fact arose not from this particular loophole, but from the inocuous-
seeming provision that female *elches* might be questioned about recon-
version in the presence of witnesses to make sure whether they wanted
to reconvert or not. The clause opened the way to what the Muslims saw
as harassment of their women and children by those who carried out the
questioning, and this they were unwilling to accept. The concept of the
family as situated in inviolable space (*haram*) came into conflict with the
provisions of the Capitulations.

Accounts of the confused street fighting that broke out as a result
in Granada are not surprisingly themselves confused. Alonso de Santa
Cruz (1951, 1: 193) has it that the murder that lies at the heart of this
affair, that of one Velasco de Barrionuevo, an officer of justice (*alguacil*),
occurred because he strayed into the Moorish quarter without realizing
what was afoot. That does not seem likely, although if, as we have seen,
different groups of Christians were pursuing different policy aims, it is
not altogether impossible that there was a blunder or a misunderstanding.
Other sources (reviewed by Lea 1901, 36 n. 1) assert that a member of
Cisneros's staff, Sacedo, in the company of one Barrionuevo, intentionally entered the Albaicín to question a woman who was the daughter of
an *elche*. When she began calling out (for help?) as they traversed a public
place (*Bib al-Bunut*), a crowd gathered to release her. Barrionuevo, who
already had a bad reputation among the people of the Albaicín, was killed.
Sacedo would have died too if he had not run away and been hidden by a
woman under her bed until nightfall. The Muslims erected barricades to
protect their quarter. To say that rioting broke out is perhaps misleading,
for one of the first things done by the inhabitants of the Albaicín in this
rising was the election of a committee of forty to administer their area.
This was a rebellion that was protesting against disorders, rather than
setting out to create chaos. Cisneros, in his house in another part of the
city (the Alcazaba), fled after being attacked.

It now fell to Tendilla and to Talavera to repair the damage done by
the high-handedness of Cisneros, and this they did, gradually, calmly,
and with great courage. Talavera tried to enter the barred-off Albaicín
quarter in procession behind a cross. Stone-throwing drove the bearer
of the cross back, so Talavera took up the cross himself, but the stone-
throwing still continued, and the archbishop had to be dissuaded by his
companions from pressing forward. Tendilla then tried his hand at paci-
fying the Albaicín. After being first of all refused entry to that quarter,
he was eventually allowed in, to take up temporary residence there along
with members of his family. Presumably by putting himself at the mercy

of the rebels in this way, he was making a symbolic demonstration of his trust and good faith. He was, as it were, offering himself as hostage to his own subjects. Tendilla succeeded in bringing the whole city back into obedience to royal authority. (The murderers of Barrionuevo were even handed over by the *qadi* to the authorities!) It seemed that the old viceregal regime of the early days would be restored, but before long it became clear that it was Cisneros's new policy that was going to triumph after all and not that of Tendilla and Talavera. The basis of the deal that was offered was not a reversion to the *status quo ante*. The inhabitants of the Albaicín were not to be punished for their rebellion, it was true, and they might remain in the city, but on condition that they accepted conversion. Thus began the new dispensation.

CRYPTO-ISLAM IS BORN

Cisneros had successfully argued that the Muslims had lost all claim to continue to be treated according to the 1492 peace terms, so that now the monarchs might impose whatever terms they saw fit. Faced with the determined campaign of conversions pushed through by Cisneros, the Muslims gave up overt resistance (we will soon see that covert resistance never ceased). They converted in large numbers, 50,000 souls accepted baptism, says Alonso de Santa Cruz (1951), 60,000 said Pope Alexander VI in the letter of congratulations that he sent to Cisneros on March 27, 1500). With hindsight we can probably best understand the "success" of the drive for conversion to Christianity as something quite different: for the Muslims of Granada it marked the beginning of underground crypto-Islam, which will be discussed below.

Reference has already been made above to the survival of remarkably detailed, even if only partial, documentation of the early stages of these forcible conversions. Miguel Angel Ladero Quesada (1987) has studied "the lists of those converted" in Granada. His source, a bound volume of lists of converts, reached its present home, the Complutensian University Library in Madrid, from the institution from which the modern Complutense stems, Cisneros's own foundation, the university at Alcalá (*Complutum* in Latin). Ladero assesses the number of individuals listed as "about 8,000 in round numbers." (This estimate should not be interpreted as casting doubt on the larger numbers just mentioned. The volume was only bound up in the mid-nineteenth century from already incomplete bundles of papers, so more than 8,000 must originally have been listed.) The sheer weight of the labor of carrying out so many thousands of adult baptisms within a short space of time is well brought out by these registers. Listings are in the first place arranged under the name of the cleric who carried out the baptism, and the place and church, among other things, and within these subheadings the order is largely chronological. As Ladero points out,

> Although the chronology of the conversions was already known in its general lines, we now have much more exact information, for we can see that although the official date of the beginning was November 1, in reality nothing is recorded before the 20th, and the conversions began with those of the *elches*. They were the primary and declared object of Cisneros' campaign, and to their number were then added small groups of Muslims not of *elche* status, just enough of them to awaken the atmosphere of anxiety that led to the revolt that broke out on December 18 (the feast of Our Lady of the O). The revolt possibly led Cisneros to move to Santa Fe.[18] It did not hold up the process of baptism, but at this stage, progress was still slow. However, there is a rapid increase in the number of baptisms in January 1500, and then in February comes the final contingent: the Muslim prisoners at Huéjar, and many of the small villages (*alcarías*) of the Vega of Granada." (Ladero 1987, 296)

It is possible to see the *elche* crisis as little more than a pretext to force through the general conversion of the population. Certainly if it had not been for this issue, Cisneros and those of like mind would have found it difficult to get their campaign of conversions started. The *elche* question was the aspect of the 1492 Capitulations that furnished the issue over which it was easiest to arouse Christian public opinion. The 1492 surrender terms in effect had meant that an individual was to be permitted to follow his own judgment against the doctrine of the Church. The whole of Western Europe was about to tear itself apart over exactly that theological question. Not that the Muslims of Granada took their stand on any point of theological principle. For them it was rather a matter of the support that any one of them owed to fellow members of the community. And as has been explained above, the position was that "once a Muslim, always a Muslim."

The solidarity shown in this way by Granadans towards the small group of converts from Christianity who lived amongst them was at the heart of the crisis. If the Granadans had taken the line that in practical terms there was nothing they could do to protect the *elches,* if they had made a realistic assessment of the likely outcome and abandoned the converts to their fate, there is every chance that toleration would have continued to be extended to the established Muslims of the lands of

18. This is just outside Granada proper; Ladero is referring to the fact that the lists have 115 individuals baptized there by Cisneros on December 27, the last of them being the famous case of the noble Zegrí.

the Crown of Castile for some time, just as in the lands of the throne of Aragon Muslims were for a generation left unmolested. But the Muslims of Granada were unwilling to back away from their obligation to support their fellows, and thus Cisneros was presented with the pretext he needed: he could argue that it was a Muslim "revolt" that had brought the Capitulations to an end.

There is in the Complutensian documentation just mentioned a separate list that has as a heading: "These are the apostate *elche* renegades who were Christians and then turned Moors and now once again have submitted to our holy Catholic faith and have been reconciled.[19] From the first day of November in the year 99." There are 101 persons on folios 339–46. As well as the baptismal registers there are included no less than 219 "testimonies and depositions against the *elche* renegades and against the renegade women whom they call *romías*."[20] Ladero also published from a document in the Simancas archives the following contemporary report on this affair:

> At the time their Highnesses were about to leave Granada the archbishop of Toledo [i.e., Cisneros] arrived there, he knew that among the Moors of that city there were some *elches* (those who were once Christians), and since this was a case in which the Inquisition could take an interest, he thought he could find some way to get them to admit their fault and bring them back to our faith, so that perhaps some of the Moors would be converted to our faith, either by his preaching or because of gifts he gave them. Out of his desire to win some souls for Our Lord, he determined to stay on in Granada to set to work. He had license from the Inquisitors-General where the *elches* were concerned, so he remained in the city, and Our Lord was pleased to grant that, thanks to the archbishop's preaching, and his gifts, some of the Moors did convert. He continued with the task. Because slight pressure (*pequeñas premias*) was being applied to the *elches* to make them admit their errors and convert to our faith, as is legally permissible, and also because the archbishop's men were converting the *elches'* sons and daughters of a tender age, as is legally permissible, the Moors of the Albaicín, concluding that the same thing would happen to them all, rioted (*alborotaronse*), and killed an officer of justice (*alguacil*) who went to arrest one of them, so they rose up, barricaded the streets, brought out their hidden arms, made new ones for themselves, and set up a resistance.[21]

19. "Reconciled" here, of course, has a technical theological sense of "accepted back into the Church."

20. *Romías*—the Arabic word simply means "Christian woman."

21. Ladero (1987, 302–3).

The text, it will be observed, despite being well disposed toward the archbishop, conveys very clearly why the revolt took place. The archbishop was exerting pressure on the renegades, he was conducting a determined campaign, which included the use of bribes and moderate force, to get Muslims to convert. He considered that what he did was inside the law, but the Muslims saw his actions as outside it, and so they lost confidence in the regime under which they had hitherto lived in peace and in their desperation took up arms in a cause that they must have known was doomed.

The initial reaction of the Catholic Monarchs to the news of the insurrection was annoyance with Cisneros, who was summoned to explain himself. There is evidence that the monarchs were thinking in terms of an extension of the policy of preaching to the Granadan Muslims in Arabic, the method already adopted by Talavera with some success, but it was not to him but to someone well thought of by Cisneros that they turned. On April 4, 1500, they wrote to Barcelona, to one of the few ecclesiastics capable of undertaking the necessary campaign of evangelism in Arabic. Martin García, the priest approached, had available to him the services of a converted *alfaqui* from Játiva, Juan [de] Andrés, and so was presumably thought of as well-equipped to engage in polemics with the recent converts. (Juan Andrés was author of the treatise *Confusion of the Sect of Muhammad* that was to have a certain fame in Western Europe.) Ferdinand and Isabella wrote to him as follows:

> **Master Martin García:**
> You will be aware that the Moors of the city of Granada have converted to our holy Catholic faith. Because very few of them can speak any language except Arabic, and because there are no churchmen who know Arabic, the said converts cannot be well instructed in the matters of our faith, and there exists a great need, especially now at the outset, of churchmen who know Arabic, so as to instruct the newly converted. Because we are aware that you know Arabic, and that with your learning and preaching and good example you could be of great benefit to them, we therefore ask you, and charge you, that, seeing how much thereby Our Lord will be served, you should prepare to come and stay some time in the said city, so as to render service in the aforementioned way.[22]

This policy of attempting to convert by persuasion continued for another decade, but parallel with it went the contradictory policy of conversion under duress. The final abandonment of persuasion was marked in

22. Barcelona MS ACA Reg. Cancillería 3614 f. 105v, quoted in Echeverria (1999, 67 n. 38).

1511 by a series of decrees against the Arabic language and other distinctive characteristics of the Muslim community (Cabanelas 1993, 507–8), and there was increasing exasperation at the absence of any positive response on the part of the "new converts" to these missionary endeavors. Talavera died in 1507, but his gentle approach had effectively been abandoned well before that date.

AFTER THE ALBAICÍN RISING: REVOLTS IN THE RURAL AREAS

Resistance in the city of Granada lasted only a few days, but fighting was to spread before very long into the Vega and on to almost all the mountainous terrain of the former independent Muslim kingdom (Grima 1993). The situation would have been very dangerous indeed for the Spanish authorities were it not that the rebels, often tactically well led, seem to have lacked any overall strategic command. The Christian forces could thus proceed to put down the rebels in one area, then move on to another center of revolt, as and when the occasion arose. Such a lack of sustained and coherent control had been a common enough characteristic of Granadan resistance to Castilian onslaughts even before 1492. It is not surprising that after several years during which Castilian policy had been directed to separating the masses from their leaders (a policy in part implemented by encouraging the aristocracy to leave the country, in part by facilitating the absorption of Granadan notables who wanted to do so to pass into the Christian upper classes), resistance should have been disarticulated. It would be a very difficult undertaking to attempt to present a general account of the scattered but dangerous revolts and the piecemeal Castilian responses, and no attempt will be made to do so. Mention will merely be made of one or two of the many places where the Muslim forces came to represent a serious threat. To convey the totality of the confused and disorganized fighting spread over a period of a year would be impossible, but we can perhaps see how even in the absence of a central Muslim command, in circumstances that meant that the various local Grenadan forces ultimately stood no chance against the armies of the powerful Castilian state, the threat the rebels posed nevertheless had to be taken very seriously indeed by the forces of the Crown.

Already in 1500, Peter Martyr of Anghiera, from his vantage point at court, had to report to one of his many correspondents as follows:

> The inhabitants of the Alpujarras had scarcely heard the news that in the city of Granada everybody had been converted when they, in fear that they would suffer the same fate, but yet buoyed up by the confidence they drew from their mountain fastnesses, in places quite inaccessible, rose in revolt.

They all complained in private (*murmuraban*) against the Archbishop of Toledo, Francisco Ximenez [Cisneros], because he was the one who had recommended that the Christian religion should be imposed on them, and they blamed him for their rebellion. (Anglería 1953, 1: 409; Grima 1993, 188)

As an example of the response that the risings evoked even in the furthest eastern regions of Granadan territory (the area most distant from the Albaicín, where the troubles had been sparked off), one may cite the warning messages dispatched on January 23, 1500, to Lorca and to Murcia in the following terms: "The Moors of the Alpujarras have risen, and are preparing scaling ladders and other military devices. It is held certain that they will attack Marchena, and after that Almería," and so the local authorities were to be prepared to render necessary assistance. A week later Pedro Fajardo set out from Murcia with 130 lances and 800 foot soldiers for Almería (Grima 1993, 189 n. 13), and troops from the militia were sent from Lorca and Cartagena, too. The strength of this rapid reaction might initially have seemed disproportionate, but it soon proved fully justified when a Muslim ambush impeded the advance on Marchena, and the Christian forces had to turn back in retreat to Almería. The reports had it that no less than 5,000 rebels were besieging Marchena, and Pedro Fajardo's bands would have been quite unable to confront such a large army. Fajardo's march had achieved the effect desired, however, for the besiegers melted away when they realized that sooner or later the Castilians would be bringing in yet more troops. The places such as Alhama where the rebels were known to have received support were soon subjected to the violent pillaging that was such a common feature of this kind of warfare.

By February the Catholic Monarchs had even greater numbers of troops heading toward rebel territory: Peter Martyr of Anghiera speaks of 15,000 horses and 80,000 infantry, and by March the king himself was directing operations in the Alpujarras. It was actually troops under the command of Luis de Beaumont, constable of Navarre on the other (eastern) front, who were involved in what became the most infamous incidents of the whole campaign: the slaughter of the 3,000 prisoners taken at Andarax and the blowing up of a nearby mosque with 600 refugees, women and children, inside. Although this all took place in Queen Isabella's realms, Ferdinand's reputation in the world at large suffered as well when the brutality of this campaign of repression became known. (An Arabic lament on the subject of the atrocities was to cause a considerable impact as far away as Istanbul.) But inside the Kingdom of Granada the determined and energetic military response had the effect of convincing Muslims that there was no alternative to surrender. What was new in the situation at this time was that those Muslims who surrendered and wished to stay on in their homes were only permitted to do so if they were willing to accept conversion to Christianity. The Muslim masses seem to have done this, although it is impossible to speak to their hidden inner motivation.

THE MORISCO PERIOD BEGINS?

It is at this point that many historians would place the beginning of the "Morisco" period, using that term in its narrower (*morisco* [2]) sense of "former Muslim who after conversion lived on under Christian rule." As has just been pointed out above, in this sense the word as such was not yet in widespread use, but it is at this point in time that, avant la lettre, the phenomenon designated by the word came into existence.

A feature of Castilian policy under the Catholic Monarchs that was a continuation of what they had done successfully in the buildup to the conquest of 1492 was the recruitment of members of the Granadan Muslim upper classes by means of bribes or inducements of various sorts (see Harvey 1956). Before 1492 we have the possible case of Boabdil himself, and certainly that of Cidi Yahya al-Nayar, later known as Don Pedro de Granada Venegas, both redoubtable leaders of their people in the struggle for independence at certain stages of the fighting, both pensioners of the invaders at others. The fates of these two illustrate the choices to be made at this time. Boabdil after a short period in the Alpujarras took refuge in Morocco, and ended his days as a Muslim. Yahya, along with many other members of his clan, successfully passed over to become a dignitary of the new regime, as a Catholic, at least in his public life. It was not only such major figures as Cidi Yahya who allowed themselves to be attached by money and honors to the Castilian cause. Through the suborning of community leaders of middle rank the Christian authorities sought, with some success, to control the Muslim masses. By September 1500, for example (Grima 1993, 192), the leaders of the rebels in the eastern region round Almería, the men who had given Pedro Fajardo and the constable of Navarre such a hard time in the fighting earlier in the year, were taking part in talks in Granada and were ready to strike a deal. Zulema "el Baho" of Almería itself, in return for being made *alguacil* of the administration his own city (an office to be inherited by his offspring) and for an annual payment of 12,400 maravedís, not only agreed himself to become a Christian (with a change of name at baptism—he became Francisco de Belvis) but, what was more, he backed the policy of conversion of all the peasant cultivators in the surrounding countryside. Similar deals were struck with the local administrators of almost all the towns and villages: Pechina, Benahadux, Rioja, Tabernas. The arrival of the newly baptized ex-rebel leaders back in their home regions at the end of September provoked indignant rage: many of the young men of a die-hard persuasion once more took to the mountains, and so the Castilians had again to campaign in rough country where their *guerrillero* adversaries were at an advantage, and it was difficult to deploy heavy weapons.

And yet at the same time many Granadan Muslims, unable or unwilling to fight yet another war, did accept conversion. The sustained military action, the repeated evangelizing campaigns, above all, the absence of any significant aid from Muslim countries overseas, combined with the promptings of these local leaders who were collaborationists, must have convinced those who wished to stay on in their homeland that sooner or later they were going to have to accept the baptism that was being thrust upon them, and so they were perhaps well advised to do so on the best terms available.

In an *aljamiado* manuscript in Cambridge University Library (Harvey 1958, 335–37), in the context of the narration of a visit to an estate in the Granadan countryside belonging to a very well-to-do Granadan Muslim called Ali Sarmiento, the author tells how he had seen and copied there a document emanating from the Castilian royal chancery setting out the privileges and protection to be accorded to his host in recognition of services rendered to the Crown. Ali is described as very old ("more than a hundred"!) but extremely well-preserved. He was described as a former "catredático" in Granada (which I interpret to mean *imam* or perhaps *khatib* in the city—the *cátreda* being, in my opinion, the *minbar* or pulpit of the mosque—but I am aware that another possible interpretation is to give the term its more normal Castilian interpretation of "professor"). It is also stated that he was an *'alim* ("a learned man") and very rich, so that during Ramadan "meat was never lacking in his house, whether for the poor or for the servants." "After the loss of Granada no [other] Moor ([*sic*]; the *aljamiado* manuscript itself reads *moro* here) remained with such wealth. For as this man was *so much in the good graces of the Christian King and of his prelates, he had whatever he wished.*"[23]

This close collaborator of the Castilians is represented as at the same time a pious person full of Islamic virtues (he preached to the guests he received in his home) and possessing abundant scholarship. His Arabic-language library—books and commentaries (*alkitebes y tafsires*)—he made available to his visitors.

Alongside Ali Sarmiento we could set numerous other prominent known collaborators (a detailed study of many cases will be found in

23. Cambridge Dd. 9. 49 f. 245r (emphasis added), cited in Harvey (1958).

Galán [1991], 260–82). Galán distinguishes between the collaborators among the old Granadan aristocracy who came to have a leading role precisely because they had played a prominent part in the actual surrender and those motivated by ambition or desire for gain who appeared on the scene a little later. In this latter category he places businessmen like the members of the Mora family, Castilian Mudejars by origin (from the Kingdom of Toledo). In 1497, Yuçaf Mora, a silk factor, was appointed *amin* (warden) of the *alcaicería* (government-controlled silk market) in Granada. And in 1500 he was one of those listed as converted to Christianity in the city (Galán 1991, 270–71). Galán's distinction between the traditional leadership and a new generation of men who rose to the top as entrepreneurs is useful, but as he makes clear, these merchants also often served as political go-betweens and negotiators. In a society in collapse, rigid social class boundaries could not be maintained. We know of most of these individuals through Castilian sources, of course, and it is rather unusual to find such collaborators spoken of in Islamic works. Yahya ben Brahim al-Fishtali (el Fisteli), regarded by Galán (1991, 271) as "the most outstanding of this type," was an important man of affairs and financier who was eventually baptized as Fernando de Morales. The same historian reproduces part of a document dated 1498 to which el Fisteli appended his signature in Arabic characters alongside others who sign in Latin characters (Galán 1982, especially 47–49). El Fisteli continues to crop up over many years in documents, first from Granada itself in the 1490s, and then, more frequently, from Malaga. Although to focus on his career will take us chronologically too far ahead, he provides such a good introduction to the nature of the leadership on which the inhabitants of the territories of the former Nasrid Kingdom of Granada were beginning to have to rely that it will be useful to follow him a certain way into the future.

As farmer of the special taxes levied on Muslims he was an invaluable tool of the Castilian regime. But tax administration was only part of his activities. El Fisteli was busy with his own property dealings, was at times a money lender, and was even involved in import-export transactions. In this connection in 1508 he was in partnership to import leather goods from Morocco with such famous Christian servants of the Crown as Hernando de Zafra and Francisco de Cobos and was also involved in handling ransom payments. (Without background information one cannot be sure whether this was an aspect of the slave trade or a public-spirited enterprise directed at getting captives home and exchanging prisoners. At this time one activity could shade into the other.) It is difficult to think of two more eminent civil servants at this time than el Fisteli's two named business associates. What such high-level Castilian backing could not insure against was piracy, however, and the export business (but not el Fiṣteli's other enterprises) failed because one of its ships was captured by "Turks" (Galan 1982, 48)!

El Fisteli's powerful connections are perhaps most clearly shown in the long-running series of legal disputes that he fought with the municipal authorities in Malaga over the office of inspector of weights (*fiel ejecutor*). It hardly needs to be said that throughout the history of al-Andalus the market inspector and his special jurisdiction (that of *hisba* or *ihtisab*) was of the greatest importance. El Fisteli as *fiel ejecutor* was continuing an ancient Andalusi and indeed Islamic tradition. His paid post had been awarded to him for life after the wave of conversions, and it was presumably part of the program of inducements and sweeteners with which the Catholic Monarchs won over the acquiescence of so many of the existing dignitaries at that critical juncture. The new immigrant Christian ruling caste, what one might term the settler aristocracy, did not take kindly to having somebody from the old pre-Christian days, and what is more, an astute businessman, foisted upon them in this way. They tried to get rid of el Fisteli, but he would not back down. In 1508, the king issued a document (*cédula*) confirming him in office and restating his right to a place on the city council (*cabildo*). In the light of what was to come, we may surmise that it was this latter issue that aroused most ire. El Fisteli, like most of these convert leaders, seems to have preferred to be known by the new name he had assumed at baptism, but he characteristically continued to use his Arabic *nisba* alongside, sometimes in preference to, his new name of Fernando de Morales. That he was a hardheaded man of business is clear from the documents, but his was a voice able to speak out on behalf of his people. He had an independent mind. Already by 1510 the city fathers were trying again to wriggle out of their obligation to employ him. They had been granted a new charter (*fuero*), and they argued this permitted them to appoint a fresh *fiel ejecutor* on a monthly contract.

Again royal intervention was forthcoming to protect el Fisteli/Fernando de Morales. The city tried to tempt him with the line that he could still collect his salary (500 maravedís a month), but he was to have no share in fines imposed by the officials (an important part of the income of the *fiel ejecutor*). Yet again royal intervention on behalf of el Fisteli meant that he won the day; indeed, it took a threat in 1511 to fine the city authorities 1,000 golden doblas (an absolutely immense sum) before they would comply. In 1512, the Moriscos of Malaga, deprived of their representation in the *cabildo* by the death of another ex-Muslim notable of the old guard, Fernando de Malaga, petitioned that el Fisteli be empowered to speak for them. Later the same year the Moriscos of the whole Kingdom of Granada petitioned successfully that el Fisteli should be appointed the *alguacil* in charge of the collection of the 20,000-ducat contribution to the royal purse (*servicio*) due from them. Bitter opposition to all this came from the municipality. There had been fraud in the nominations, so the city intimated. And there was no need for representation for the new converts—there were so few of them anyway, because most had emigrated. What is more, el Fisteli, presumably because of his North African links, was alleged to be a security risk. Yet once again the Crown overruled the Christian townsfolk of Malaga and confirmed el Fisteli in his appointments! Even so, wrangling continued, and el Fisteli had to take his case up to the superior tribunal of the Royal Chancellery in Granada. He resigned from the post of *fiel ejecutor*, but not from his seat in the *cabildo:* he did not wish to leave the new converts unrepresented, he argued. The city was thus free to appoint a new *fiel ejecutor* but then proceeded to claim that the new appointee would take over el Fisteli's vote in the *cabildo.* This time the royal intervention solved the crisis by the compromise judgment of giving a vote to both men.

We thus see that the Crown gave sustained backing over many years to this new convert in the face of the stubborn and often devious campaigns of the powerful Christian leadership of this key seaport. The Christians of the municipality obviously aimed at destroying the political career of el Fisteli. One is forced to conclude that the Crown prized very highly indeed the services that el Fisteli was able to render. It is unlikely that these were exclusively financial, and perhaps his role as spokesperson for the new converts was understood as providing a desirable channel through which new convert opinion could be monitored and controlled.

With the incomplete evidence available now, it would be impossible to attempt any evaluation of the motives of those who accepted to serve the Castilian authorities in the way that el Fisteli and many other men of substance in the community did. To describe him, and Yuce Banegas, Ali Sarmiento, Pedro de Granada, and so many others as "collaborators" (as I have myself done above) or as "collaborationists" with the Castilians, is superficially accurate enough. How should we correctly describe men who, whether in a concerted way or as individual opportunists (how are we to tell?), adopted a policy to which there was no realistic alternative either in 1501 or later? For a proper understanding of their motivation one would need far more detailed information on the chronology of various interacting processes that were taking place. Did, for example, the original decision of some Muslim leaders to strike a deal with the Castilians after the collapse of the risings in the Alpujarras precede the fatwa of 1504 by which crypto-Islam was legitimated (see below), or did it follow on as a consequence, as the logical implementation, of that policy of retreating into clandestinity? In other words, did the collapse of the resistance on the part of the local leadership *create* the situation that called into being the policy of taking Islam underground, or did the authorization of such a doctrine by Ahmad Bu Jum'a in the text I am about to discuss *induce* people like one "Francisco de Belvis" to adopt a policy that was no more than a realistic acknowledgement of what was going on in any case? It is unlikely that we will ever come across evidence to establish beyond doubt where the truth lies.

What is certain is that in the early months of the new century, the inhabitants of many of the villages, of which the headmen had been subjected to strong Castilian pressure (and so became "collaborationists," "traitors"?), did convert. In late September 1500, Tabernas, Rioja, Benahadux, Pechina, among other villages, accepted baptism. Equally certain is that the inhabitants of other villages, particularly those situated in the Sierra Alhamilla and Sierra de Filabres, refused, and stubbornly accepted the consequences of their refusal. Examples are Turrillas, Níjar, Inox, Senés, Vacares, and Velefique. And among those consequences were intense and sustained artillery bombardment, such as might have been encountered in a major military campaign, rather than in a local police action. Lorenzo de Padilla in his chronicle of the reign of Philip le Bel described the assault on Velefique as follows:

> The Moors took up strong defensive positions, so that it was necessary to bring up much artillery, and attack them with determination. However, those parts of the wall that the cannons could knock down in the daytime were carefully repaired during the night by the Moors, so the Christians in the morning found the parts they had damaged in good repair. The commander found himself in a difficult situation, for the artillery was of little avail, and the weather conditions were severe, it being midwinter. Unable to think of any other tactic, he was advised that the water cistern, the only one for the whole village, might be undermined. He ordered the work to be commenced, and had such good success that within a week they had drained it completely. The Moors, finding themselves without a water supply, had just decided to surrender when it snowed very hard, and they thought they would have supplies for some time. They were mistaken, for there was only enough water for a week, so they asked to negotiate, and Fernando de Zafra came to speak in the king's name. However, all terms were refused other than surrender at the king's mercy. The siege of this place lasted three months, and the besiegers suffered great hardships because of the snow and cold, from which many of them died, and others lost arms or legs from frostbite. At the king's orders, the alcaide de los Donceles (the commander) had enquiries made as to who were the originators of this uprising, and of those accused, who were almost 200 in

number, he ordered the guilty ones to be taken up to the top of the village's mosque tower, and thrown off. Their bodies were smashed when they hit the ground. The rest were pardoned.[24]

In that account we meet a name familiar from the final stages of the negotiations for the surrender of Granada: Fernando de Zafra. It might seem that we are witnessing a repetition of the process of fighting followed by negotiations that was so characteristic of the final stages of the Granadan War. The outcome, however, was very different. In the fighting leading up to 1492, Ferdinand, through Zafra, had usually been willing to strike some deal because it served the overall Castilian policy to do so. That was no longer the case. Ferdinand held that he was not dealing with legitimate enemies but rebellious vassals who had forfeited all claims to consideration. (He had adopted the position put forward by Cisneros.) Those prisoners who had been spared the fate of being cast down from the tower were reduced to slavery and sold, as were the womenfolk and the children. The inhabitants of some rebel villages (Níjar, Inox, and others) that did not put up such a desperate stand as Velefique had done were given terms, but these simply amounted to permission to buy back from slavery the prisoners taken, and at a relatively high price (25,000 ducats for 790 prisoners). Those who refused to enter into such dealings had all their property confiscated (and they became slaves in any case). Mass baptisms continued in many areas.

Who among the Muslim lower orders had received the best advice, then, those whose local leaders made a desperate and heroic last stand that became the prelude to slavery, or those whose leaders sold out ignominiously and profitably to the new regime and thus avoided bloodshed?

What is certain is the cruel disruption occasioned in the lives of thousands of people, the led and not the leaders, when suddenly faced with a choice between Islam and Christianity, between their loyalty to their local Muslim neighbors and the bonds that bound them to the new Christian state. This state was by now established firmly in what had such a short time before been the Islamic Kingdom of Granada. The unimportant case of Pedro de Mercado, an unimportant individual, well illustrates how the old society was being torn apart by the forcible conversions.

In an official document[25] the corregidor of Ronda was instructed by the Crown to look into a certain claim for compensation. Pedro de Mercado, described as a "new convert" from a village in the mountains near Ronda, alleged that "at the time that the Moors of the said mountains

24. *Crónica de Felipe I, llamado el Hermoso*, in *CODOIN*, 8: 70–71; see also Grima (1993, 195).

25. On this incident, see also Acién (1978, especially 454, n. 35).

rebelled against our service [i.e., taxation]" and fled to Villaluenga, they had wanted to take him with them, but because "he had the wish to be a Christian" as he "came from Christian descent" (we are given no idea what the facts of the case were) "he did not wish to go with them, and they, when they saw he did not want to go, took from him his wife and one of his daughters, and bore them off, and they burned down his house, with the corn and barley and the clothing it contained, and they took his two donkeys and killed them, and two laden pack-mares, and four of his cattle, which they ate, so that he was ruined. And those that had done the above to him subsequently turned Christian, and now live in the said village, and he begs and petitions us that we order that he be reimbursed for the losses he has incurred." What the outcome of the petition was we do not learn from the documentation, but whether Pedro received compensation or not, it is clear enough that the whole framework of his life had been destroyed.

As for the figures of power and influence who had emerged within the community of new converts at the outset, few were left by the second decade. It was in the nature of things that the role of such men should be ambiguous. They served two masters (and above all else, they served their own interests). They were called into existence because it suited the incoming regime to have a way of communicating with the Muslim (and then new convert) masses. The personal prosperity of these placemen was earned by their willingness to be subservient to Castilian policies. But they did in some circumstances act as a channel, perhaps the only channel, though which new convert grievances could be brought to the attention of the new ruling class. As such useful intermediaries faded from the scene, Granada became ever more difficult to govern, and the political situation there became ever more fragile. On the Christian side there was a parallel destabilizing development. The original generation of men who had fought the wars of the Reconquest, who "knew their Moors" from long direct experience and knew the terrain of the frontier because they had fought over it so many times, came to be replaced by fresh incomers, administrators and lawyers, often quite out of touch with the rapidly changing realities of life away from the cities where they preferred to live.

TWO ❧ Spain's Muslims under a New Order

THE FORMAL BASIS OF THE NEW ORDER IN CHRISTIAN LEGISLATION: THE NEW STYLE OF CAPITULATIONS

Once they had defeated those Muslims of the Kingdom of Granada who had risen in open rebellion in 1501 and 1502, the forces of the Spanish Crown offered to accept the rebels' surrender, but on terms that were far less favorable than those available hitherto. The earlier types of capitulation, those negotiated in 1491 and earlier, had set out the adverse juridical consequences of a conquest by force of arms, but those consequences were still made to fit inside the broad framework of what Spanish historians have in modern times termed the *convivencia* of the two religions, that is to say, the necessary live-and-let-live of the Iberian Peninsula in the days before the keys of the Alhambra were handed over in January 1492. Now, after a second round of Spanish victories a decade later, things were quite different.

The new style of document in use at the opening of the sixteenth century set out the new juridical order that was being imposed. Such documents did not simply assert the primacy of Christianity. They went on to try to ensure that Islam was eliminated as soon as possible. If there were concessions to the ex-Muslims, they were of a superficial and transitional kind.

Vélez Rubio and Vélez Blanco

A good example of such a document is the one for Vélez Rubio—or the virtually identical one for the sister town, Vélez Blanco (Grima 1993, 220–23). A number of such texts have survived—including those for Almería, the Alpujarras, Cenete, and Çuhehal (see Campos 1978). It should be stressed that those who entered into this new type of agreement were in their juridical status former Mudejars, and they were being asked to relinquish the ancient rights guaranteed to them by previous "capitulations," signed in the case under consideration as recently as 1488.

Perhaps it also bears saying that "capitulation" in this usage does not, either in English or in the original Spanish (*capitulación*), connote surrender. It is simply a "statement of the heads or *chapters* (*capítulos*) of a solemn agreement." It was not because they had taken part in a rising against Spanish authority that they were deprived of their rights in this way; indeed, on the contrary, the preamble to the document makes reference to the favorable treatment that these people merited. In the eyes of the new administrators, the status was what was felt appropriate under the radically new circumstances.

The New Capitulations

The document, dated February 26, 1501 (it is noteworthy that signing as secretary of the king and queen we find Fernando de Zafra yet again), had clauses to the following effect:

1. The townsfolk were to be freed from "Moorish dues" (*derechos moriscos*), meaning those set out in Islamic law, on condition that they agree to pay standard Christian tithes and firstfruits (*diezmo y primicia*).

Quite a lot lies behind this simple clause, and some explanation is required. It is not just that the change of religion brought about by the baptism of the Muslims of the two Vélezs has the logical consequence that these people are taxed on the same basis as Christians. A papal bull of March 22, 1500 (Grima 1993, 217), had just authorized the Catholic Monarchs to keep for their own purposes two-thirds of tithes paid by the New Christians (rather than the two-ninths retention that was standard *in Spain* in the case of Old Christians). The Crown, of course, up to this point had retained for itself the *whole* of the old "Moorish" taxes (*derechos moriscos*), with the exception of the funding for certain local charities—it had taken over the taxation structure that it had found functioning at the time of the conquest, and continued to apply it. The Crown might appear to be likely to lose as a result but really might hope to gain, because its large (two-thirds) share of the relatively easily administered tithing system would yield well, whereas if it continued to rely on imposts taken over from the ramshackle Nasrid system, endless litigation might be foreseen. The Church stood to gain from the change, too, because its admittedly small one-third share was to be collected from a newly enlarged tax base: the huge number of converts, people who up to this point had provided it with no revenue whatsoever. The key administrative term here, *derechos moriscos,* is a good example of how misleading the word *morisco* is if not properly interpreted.[1]

1. It is, of course, an example of *morisco* (1) as discussed in the previous chapter.

2. The people of the town are to be subject to the laws of the kingdom. The object of this clause is obviously also to bring an end to Islamic law, although that is not mentioned explicitly. It seems also to be intended as a protection against vexatious litigation ("so that they are not to be troubled [*fatigados*] with lawsuits"). There is to be no conflict of jurisdictions. The old is replaced by the new.

3. Travelers are to seek accommodation in lodging houses (*mesones*) and not in the houses of the *alguaciles* nor "in the houses of those who were converted against their will." This seems to be a positive clause to prevent new converts being discriminated against, although I have to confess I do not grasp its full import.

4. The income from charitable foundations should all be devoted to relief for the poor, ransoming of captives, and highway repairs. This clause is clearly dealing with what had been the important Islamic institution of pious endowments (Arabic *waqf,* plural *awqaf,* or in the Arabic of al-Andalus, *ahbas* or *habices* as they were generally called in the Castilian documentation). It is intended to make sure that such local charities were to continue to be available for local use and not be misappropriated for private benefit.

5. Crimes (*culpas e esçesos*) committed before this capitulation came into force were to be pardoned.

6. To call anybody "Moor" or "renegade" (*tornadizo*) became a punishable offense.

7. The townsfolk might have their own butchers and fishmongers as before, but they were to slaughter in the Christian fashion.

8. They were not to be forced to buy new clothes until the old ones had worn out (i.e., the old-style dress of Islamic Granada was not to be banned overnight).

9. They were to be allowed "without any impediment" to move elsewhere in Christian territories. (This is, of course, *not* permission to emigrate to North Africa.)

10. Clergy were to be appointed to teach them the Catholic faith.

11. All legal documents drawn up in Arabic by their *alfaquis* and *cadís* were to be regarded as just as valid as documents drawn up by "our notaries public." (On careful scrutiny, this clause says nothing on the subject of the use of Arabic in the courts *in the future,* when, of course, there would be no Islamic officials available to elucidate these "equally valid" legal instruments.)

12. The townsfolk would not be obliged to perform labor on public works unpaid; they were to receive the same daily rates as Christians.

13. Baths were to be permitted.

For the Muslims of Spain, now forcibly converted, a new order had thus arrived. The choices were stark: (1) remain and accept baptism; (2) remain, refuse baptism, and become a slave; or (3) leave the country and become a refugee in an Islamic country. The third might appear an easy option, but it was not. In the days after the surrender of 1492 and in some earlier negotiations, the Castilians had been willing to provide transport, even in some cases free. From this point onward, in general (there were exceptions) the policy was to block emigration and certainly not to provide passages gratis. This may at first sight be puzzling, for the emigration of the Muslims, now most of them in theory at least "new converts," would have removed a political problem and opened the way for further colonization by Old Christians of the lands that once belonged to the Muslims. It would seem that the decision had been reached if possible to retain the services of the inhabitants of these recently acquired territories.

The Option of Escape

Of course, one alternative for those who wished to take the third option, exile, but who wished to avoid inflicting on their families the vexations entailed in trying to make their individual way across to North Africa in the face of Christian authorities who were disapproving or worse was to organize a mass exodus of a whole village or similar community. This was only feasible, of course, in the case of communities on or very near the sea coast, but in such cases it did happen.

Turre and Teresa are two small villages near the coast of Almería in the Sierra Cabrera. Some of their inhabitants had literally to fight their way out, but it seems that in the confused skirmishing that arose in the course of the mass escape we have to recognize not only straightforward religious motivation, a desire to live in an Islamic country, but also the desire to settle old scores and feuds as they went. Such factors not infrequently call into question a purely religious and sectarian analysis of events. It would, of course, be difficult to find any anthropological field study from any part of the Mediterranean basin that contained no reference to such bitter local feuds.

Mojácar was the largest village of this area, and Christian settlers were already beginning to be attracted to what is still today a place of great charm; their arrival, the ways in which the local administration favored them in land disputes, among other things, caused resentment. When baptism began to be forced on the Muslims of this region in early 1501, the people of Turre and Teresa decided they must after all leave, and on their way out of the country they resolved to take the opportunity to strike a blow at enemies in Mojácar. With the aid of their Berber rescuers from across the Mediterranean, the people of Turre stormed Mojácar's fortifications, but the assault ladders that they had prepared (or stolen?) for the purpose were cast down from the walls by the vigilant defenders. In consequence, the planned embarkation in boats brought across from Africa by the Berbers became a rout and a massacre. The local Christian militia turned out and was able to cut the raiding party to pieces. Would-be refugees and their North African allies alike were put to the sword or condemned to slavery.

Their neighbors from Teresa had better luck and got away, although the authorities naturally confiscated the property that they had abandoned. That was the disadvantage of such schemes for collective escape: the refugees had to go into exile with only such goods as they could convey to the small boats in which they made their getaway.

Such emigration of individuals or small groups from places near the sea is a constant feature of this early period and continued sporadically until it merged into the final flood of those who were expelled at the end. The examples just mentioned of whole villages that attempted to transfer themselves to the far shore are a clear indication of the rejection by whole communities of the conversion to Christianity that was being forced upon them.

Clandestinity as a Reaction to the Forcible Conversion

Those who did not live near enough to the coast to plot such an escape had to find other means of surviving as Muslims. It is against this background that we must understand the reaction of the Muslim masses to conversion: it was to turn their religion, always hitherto thought of as essentially a faith to be lived and proclaimed in public, into a secret and underground phenomenon.

One way in which the new converts were at times subjected to pressure to conform to Christian ways was by having forbidden food and drink forced upon them. As far as alcoholic drink was concerned, at least, there is plenty of evidence that the new ways were inculcated with some success, and that some converts readily availed themselves of what was offered. Even the most rigorist of Islamic regimes rarely succeed in stamping out the drinking of alcohol altogether, and in al-Andalus the ban seems always to have been administered with some laxity, especially in Granada in late medieval times. The new enforced freedom with which the converts had to cope (and drinking might be for some of them more an obligation than a matter of free choice) led to results that might have been predicted: drunkenness and disorder.

On August 19, 1515, we find the queen, Juana, in an attempt to deal with the public order offenses that were occurring, writing to her officials (the *corregidores*) of all the principal cities of the Kingdom of Granada (Granada, Guadix, Baza, Almería, Vera, Purchena, Malaga, Vélez Malaga, Ronda, Loja, Alhama, and Marbella) as follows:

> Know that I have been informed that some of the newly converted who are resident in the above-mentioned cities, because of the great amounts of wine which they drink, become so intoxicated that they fall down in public in the street, so that the Old Christians mock them. When they are drunk, they cause disorder (*escándalos*), and since it is my duty, as Queen, to deal with such matters ... I command you, the aforesaid officers, and your lieutenants, that on each and every occasion that you find a New Christian drunk outside his own house or garden, that you have him brought to the prison of the place where he is found, where he is to be held for one day and one night as a punishment for his misdemeanor. And I command that the officers of the watch (*alguaciles*) who arrest them, and the keepers of the jail, are not to collect any dues or any other charge from them for being held in prison in this way, and anyone who does impose such a charge will incur the penalty. (Gallego and Gámir 1968, 185)

Drunkenness among the new converts continued to be a problem. On September 2, 1521, we find the *ayuntamiento* (city council) of Baza voting to ban the sale of wine in taverns to prevent drunkenness. (Apart from its intrinsic interest, this bylaw provides a possible though not unambiguous early attestation of the use of the word *morisco* in the sense of *morisco* (2) discussed in the previous chapter.)

> It was resolved that because in this city the sale of wine in taverns (*bode-gones*) gives rise to problems of many kinds, with Moriscos and other ill-disposed (*mal vinientes*) persons foregathering in such places, and getting drunk, brawling and disputing, so that the Moriscos neglect their own affairs and spend the whole day in the taverns, and when they do go home, they beat their wives, in order to avoid these troubles, and many others which might be mentioned, it was resolved and decreed that all those in this city who have wine of their own production should sell it in their own homes, and not supply it to tavern-keepers. Nor should the aforesaid tavern-keepers sell it, nor should there be bars or taverns to sell wine not produced by the owners. If wine should be brought in from outside for sale in this city, it is to be sold only in the municipal warehouse (*alhondiga*) or the market square (*plaza publica*) of this city, and no tavern-keeper may deal in it with the intention of selling it in bars under the penalty that any person or persons dealing in wine for sale to others should pay a fine of 600 maravedís. And if anyone brings in wine from elsewhere for a citizen of this city at a time when the price of wine here is above 8 maravedís,

that is allowable, provided that the sale takes place in his house, and that permission is granted by the magistrate and his deputies, and if it is sold in any other way, the aforementioned penalty applies. (Gallego and Gámir 1968, 185)

The city fathers were concerned to make sure that their own domestic supplies were assured in periods of scarcity! But they were trying, with what success we do not know, to limit the availability of wine to the new drinking classes that had been brought into existence by the conversions.

Instruction in the Christian Religion

It was frequently asserted later in the century that any ignorance among the New Converts concerning their new religion was in part the result of inadequate instruction at the outset. That was no doubt the case in some areas, for it was not easy to recruit priests to labor in such an unrewarding mission field, especially at a time when in the New World relatively easy ecclesiastical preferment beckoned, but as early as 1514 we find Fernando de Toledo issuing the following proclamation. The document acknowledges frankly that the inhabitants of Huéscar, although already baptized, were still in need of elementary instruction. Note, too, how, as an afterthought, after signing the document, Fernando de Toledo added further regulations specifically intended to reduce the level of drunkenness:

> Whereas the Duke our master, desirous that the New Christians of this city of his should be instructed in the doctrine of our holy Catholic faith, and that they should fulfill and carry out all the obligations of good Christians, and that they should abandon their evil Moorish ceremonies, he, with the agreement and assent of certain religious, when he came here on his visitation issued certain ordinances and instructions, and since to keep and observe them is of great benefit to the souls and consciences of the said converts, we will set them out below so that they may be better known and observed:
>
> I, Fernando de Toledo, duke of Alba...lord of the townships of Huéscar and Castilléjar, out of regard for what befits the service of God our Lord, and in especial by way of provision for certain things relating to the newly converted, my vassals, resident within the bounds of the above-mentioned towns of Huéscar and Castilléjar, in order that they may be instructed in the doctrine [of the Church], and that they may abandon the uses and customs they had when they were Moors, as is my duty to do, as lord of these places, for the salvation of the souls of these said new converts, who are already united to our holy Catholic faith by conversion and baptism, do hereby command that henceforward the said new converts should do as follows:

Firstly, that their children from the age of six to thirteen should be instructed and taught to read and write, and that their parents should bring them on Sundays and holy days to Mass, so that they may learn the doctrine of spiritual things. The better to put this into effect, I command the governor by me appointed to draw up a register of those who ought to learn to read and write, which is to be handed over to the schoolmaster or schoolmasters appointed to teach them. The schoolmaster may in this way know who is absent, and he is to notify my governor, who is to inflict the following penalty: the father (or mother where there is no father) of a child sent to learn to read and write will be fined one real for every occasion when it is the fault of the parent that the child fails to attend (half the fine to be paid to the duke's office, half to the person acting as informant). (Gallego and Gámir 1968, 182–84)

There is no explicit statement to that effect, but I take it for granted that it was literacy in Spanish these schoolmasters were to impart and not in Arabic. Further sections of the regulations dealt with adults who were to be forced (*apremiados*) to attend church, with fines for nonattendance, and a quite large penalty (1,000 maravedís) for failure to memorize the Credo, Salve Regina, Ave Maria, and Pater Noster before the following Easter (the proclamation was dated in June, so they had some nine months).

Weddings were to be celebrated in the "Old Christian" way: no henna decorative designs on the skin, no cutting of the hair (it is difficult to say why this should be regulated, unless it refers to the traditional shaving or removal of pubic hair in preparation for the wedding night), "nor the other things they normally do," except that they might have *zambras* (celebratory dances) on the eve of the ceremony and on the day of the ceremony itself. An interesting concession, presumably the authorities realized they would never be able to enforce a total ban on dancing. On feast days the newly converted were to keep their front doors open so that magistrates could enter and make sure that the people there were not still working. In church, women were to leave their faces entirely uncovered.

One of the regulations at first puzzled me, for it appears to be designed to prevent a decent preparation for church attendance:

The public baths are not to be lit [or "heated"] on Sundays, nor feast days nor Fridays, and any bath-keeper who disobeys incurs the penalty of 600 maravedís on the first occasion, and 100 lashes for a second offense, the same penalties apply those making use of the bath.

It is the mention of Friday that put me on the track of what was on Fernando de Toledo's mind. The converts were to be prevented from making themselves ritually pure, so that they would thus not be able to pray the Friday *salat*. That much is obvious. The ban on Sunday morning baths is more interesting, however, for it links with the whole question of clandestine Islamic worship and tells us that the Oran fatwa (which will be studied below) or some parallel document was being invoked in Huéscar, and what is more, that Fernando de Toledo had some inkling of what was going on. The "converts" would wish to be ritually pure *according to the Islamic precepts* at mass, because they would wish their enforced attendance at the Christian service to count as an acceptable substitute for the canonical Islamic prayer. Fernando de Toledo for his part seems to have been trying to make sure they arrived at church decently unwashed, because Christianity does not make cleanliness at times of prayer a *ritual* requirement, whereas Islam does! It must have been his way of ensuring that they attended church as an act of purely Christian worship that could not be subverted so as to count as a substitute Islamic prayer. It may be amusing at this distance in time for us to note that for Fernando de Toledo there were circumstances in which for him uncleanliness was next to godliness (in a sort of perverse exaggeration of Saint Paul's teaching to the early Church that cleanliness should be an internal spiritual matter and not merely a question of some external code of ritual purity).[2] It was doubtless not amusing to the newly converted, obliged in this way to mingle with the great Christian unwashed.

To sum up the confused state of affairs that prevailed in the Kingdom of Granada in the decades immediately following the conversion, we may turn to Mármol (who in the following passage is thinking of the former Muslims of Granada rather than the ex-Mudejars of Castile proper,). His testimony is far from being contemporary to the events he is discussing, of course, but he is well-informed. He states his Christian viewpoint firmly and unambiguously but does not allow himself to be carried away by excesses of prejudice. The Catholic Monarchs, he tells us, after the conversion, extended to the converts their grace and favor.

> But it became immediately apparent how little use these kindnesses were in making them cease to be Muslims. Although they might say that they were Christians, they paid more attention to the rites of the religion of Muhammad than those of the Catholic church. They made a point of closing their ears to whatever bishops, priests and monks told them. They were now better off, and more in control of their own property, than they had been under the Moorish kings, but they were never content, and yearned after the old days. They put their trust in empty fictions, called *jófores* or prophecies, because in them they were told they would become

2. See Acts 10:15, among other texts.

Moors again, and be once more what they once had been. This state of affairs continued for so long as the older generation survived and still had some liberty for their barbarous beliefs. Those of the next generation, although they did grow less restive with time, were well aware, from their experience of affairs, that they were being less favored, and that the magistrates were treating them more firmly, and so they began to bewail their fate excessively, and to become even more entrenched in their evil resolve. Hence it was that hour by hour their enmity for the name of Christian increased. Although with feigned humility they adopted moral ways in their behavior, their forms of address and in their dress, inside themselves they hated the yoke of the Christian religion, and in secret they studied their doctrine and taught one another the rites and the ceremonies of Muhammad. This defect extended to all the common folk. There were certain of their nobles who gave themselves over to matters of faith, and regarded it as an honor to be and to appear to be Christians. Of these our history does not concern itself. The rest, even if they were not avowed Moors, were secret heretics, they had no faith, and their baptism was superficial. The more sharp-witted they became in their evil ways, the less they knew of [true Christian] doctrine. If they went to mass on Sundays or holy days, that was only for the sake of form (*por cumplimiento*), and to avoid being fined by the clergy. When they confessed, they never admitted to mortal sins, nor did they tell the truth. They observed Fridays, and washed themselves then, and behind locked doors they performed the *salat.* On Sundays they stayed indoors and continued working. After the baptism of their babies, they washed them in warm water to remove the sign of baptism and the holy oil, and they performed their own ceremony of circumcision, and gave their children Moorish names. Brides, who had been made by the priest to wear Christian bridal dresses to their [wedding] benediction in church, stripped them off when they got home, and dressed as Moorish women, and celebrated their weddings with Moorish musical instruments and Moorish food. Although some of them did learn the prayers, that was only because they were not allowed to get married unless they knew them, and many of them avoided learning Castilian so they would have an excuse for not learning them. They welcomed the Turks and the Berber Moors into their own homes and farmsteads, and gave them advice on how to commit murders, robberies and how to take Christians captive. They even took captives themselves, and sold them, so that corsairs came to Spain to get rich, just as one goes to some parts of the Indies. Whole villages at times passed over with them. One might say this was the lesser evil, and one which Christians had less cause to regret. It could happen that a Moor was in Spain one night, and the next morning he was in Barbary with his neighbors and all his friends. The Kings of

Spain undertook certain measures to put a stop to this, among others there was the decision of Queen Juana, daughter of the Catholic Monarchs, who commanded that they should abandon their Moorish dress, because she could see how effective this would be in making them forget that they were Moors. She gave them six years to wear out the clothes they already had made, and then another ten years went in dissimulation, but finally in 1518 the Emperor Charles when he came to reign in Castile, commanded that the ban should be applied, although that same year at the supplication of the Moriscos he suspended it during his good pleasure. Later the Licentiate Pardo, who was Abbot of the church of San Salvador in the Albaicín, and the canons of that church, who were fully aware of how the Moriscos lived, informed His Majesty that they were still observing the Moorish rites, and in the year 1526, when he was in Granada, he nominated ecclesiastical visitors for the whole territory, among them Gaspar de Avalos, Antonio de Guevara. (Mármol 1991, 63)   *Lib 2, cap. 1*

The decisions promulgated in 1526 take us forward into a new period that will be discussed below.

Conversion of the Mudejars of Long Standing in the Lands of Castile

It is necessary to recall here the distinction between the Muslims of the Kingdom of Granada, still Arabic-speaking, only recently incorporated into the lands of the Crown of Castile, only marginally assimilated, and the Muslims of all the other areas under the Castilian monarchy, descendants of the many generations of Muslims who had lived under Castilian rule, for the most part native speakers of Castilian, usually highly assimilated. Some Muslim areas, notably Toledo, had come under the Christians as early as the late eleventh century, but it had been in the second half of the thirteenth that the greatest expansion of Castilian-dominated territory southward had taken place. In some areas, notably in certain urban Moorish quarters (*morerías*), such Muslim communities dated back continuously to pre-Reconquest days, but it was not the case that all Muslim communities in Christian territories could trace back their history to settlements that had already existed under Muslim rule. Fresh Muslim communities appear to have been set up in some places under the patronage of Christian lords (on Palma del Río, see Harvey 1990, 71–3) or with the encouragement of Christian municipalities (Ávila, for example). Castile's Mudejars had, for perhaps three centuries (for longer in some cases) been unfailingly loyal subjects of their Christian monarchs.

There were important sociological differences between these two groups, Granadans and Castilians. When the Granadans had a Christian-dominated society imposed on them, their own social structures had been still relatively intact. Still living with them were some of their former ruling elite, so they could turn to their own men of religion, their own cultural and political leaders. The Mudejars of Castile, on the other hand, were mostly fairly humble folk, cultivators and craftsmen, and although as the years and the centuries went by they do seem to have thrown up some men of remarkable talents who provided leadership, the orthodox teaching predominant throughout the Middle Ages had been to the effect that emigration (*hijra*) to a Muslim-ruled country was a religious obligation incumbent on all those able to leave. That meant that there was a constant drain of leaders and scholars away from the Mudejar communities and southward to Granada, sometimes further away across the seas. The religious leaders who stated the case for emigration so cogently in the fatwa literature (see Harvey 1990, 56–60) no doubt had it in mind that Muslims in Christian territory would be subject to pressure, direct and indirect, and the need for emigration was preached in order to protect the religion from erosion. Yet the effect of this strict doctrine on the Islamic communities in the Christian lands must have been to weaken them and make them more vulnerable. The largely leaderless Mudejar communities of Castile had not for centuries given to their Christian rulers and masters any cause for concern. They were as docile and obedient as the fifteenth century came to a close as they had ever been.

Both groups of Muslims, on the one hand, the Granadans, conquered in 1491–92 or just before and then conquered again in the campaigns undertaken in response to the revolts of 1500 (the First War of the Alpujarras), and on the other hand, the established Mudejars, who for so many generations had lived in New and Old Castile and other areas, were indiscriminately lumped together and ordered to convert to Christianity at more or less the same time. Even so, the documentation concerning them emanating from the royal chancery and other official sources was not in all ways identical. The circumstances of the conversions of these two groups, as we might expect, differed somewhat. The capitulations as they affected places such as the two towns of Vélez (discussed above) exemplify the conversions imposed in Granadan territory. What of Castile and the ancient Mudejar communities of the *meseta central?*

The Edict Imposing Conversion on the Mudejars of Castile

Although the conversion of all Muslims is what the Castilian authorities wanted to achieve, at the very beginning of the process of imposing the New Order at least some simulacrum of an alternative to conversion was offered. Muslims who refused to change their religion were, in theory at least, to be allowed to emigrate (Fernández y González 1866, 432–34).

The relevant new legislation is dated July 1501, in Granada, but it is perhaps possible that it was not made public on that date, and in any case its main force would not have been felt in Granada itself, where there were few Mudejars of the type affected. It was explicitly in the other kingdoms of the realm ("our kingdoms and lordships of Castile and Leon") that the new provisions of July 1501 were intended to have their impact. And in these regions the key date was that of the actual proclamation of the *pragmática,* which does not seem to have taken place until February 12, 1502, in Seville. The dates of local proclamations and of implementation vary somewhat, as do the contents very slightly from place to place, but it would seem safe to treat this as one family of documents with one objective: that of changing the tolerated Muslims (Mudejars) of the medieval dispensation in the Christian kingdoms into the enforced converts of the early modern period.

The key initial argument deployed in the preamble to the *pregón* (actual proclamation) is that after the success just achieved in Granada, where not a single Muslim remained by 1501, it would be a great scandal to permit Muslims to remain elsewhere. The expulsion (*que echemos*) of the Muslims, "even though they were peaceful and might be living quietly" (this much is freely conceded, no bones are made about it), is justified by the need to protect from the malign influence of the nonconverted those who had accepted conversion. And so after careful consideration it had been decided that "[a]ll the said Moorish men and women should leave from these our kingdoms of Castile and Leon, and that they never return thence."

The edict affected males of fourteen and over and females of twelve and over, whether they were locally born or were immigrants, the only exception made being that manacled prisoners and slaves were not included. (One notes that the rights of property of the slave owners are given precedence, even over theological considerations.) Those expelled were entitled to take whatever possessions they wished, which sounds reasonable enough until one reads that, nevertheless, gold, silver, and all embargoed goods were not to be exported. The penalties for attempting to take out gold and silver were draconian (death and confiscation of the contraband). Those who framed the provisions concerning the route and destinations seem to anticipate and indeed outdo the methods of Kafka's bureaucrats. Refugees might *not* go to the kingdoms of Aragon or Valencia, or to the principality of Catalonia, or to the Kingdom of Navarre. "And because we are at war with the Moors of North Africa, and with the Turks," they might not go to Africa or to territories ruled by the Turks, either.

Where, then, on earth might they go?

"To the lands of the Soldán (i.e., of the Mamluk ruler of Egypt, who was not in conflict with the Catholic Monarchs after Peter Martyr's embassy) or any other place not forbidden by us." Since a limitation had been placed on the export of permitted goods "by any route other than the coast of Biscay," from which few ships sailed in those days to Egypt, in effect no one might leave with his luggage and possessions for any *real* destination, and so in effect virtually all Muslims would have to accept conversion. (But of course they had not been ordered to do so.) In addition, harboring Muslims after the date named as the final deadline (end of April 1502) was to be most severely punished.

Thus, and in such a summary fashion, at such short notice, was Mudejar status brought to an end after two and a half centuries of *convivencia*. Examining the history of *La comunidad morisca de Ávila* (1991), Serafín de Tapia Sánchez was surprised to find that for Ávila, "[t]here has not been preserved any reference to the massive baptism." The same is true of many other places. This momentous historical event left behind relatively few direct records, apart from the above-mentioned lists for Granada (which is a totally different case). Such absence of evidence is perhaps not entirely surprising. The Muslims themselves were not anxious to have recorded an event that ought never to have happened, to which they, in terms of their own theology, ought not to have assented in any way. As for Christians, we do know that in Ávila, for example, the development was marked by that all-purpose Hispanic public celebration, a bullfight (Tapia 1991, 140 n. 8). This was held on May 7. It does seems to have been a fairly elaborate festivity; some of those asked to contribute to the expenses objected that it was beyond their means. Unfortunately, we do not have accounts of the actual ceremonies of conversion themselves nor of how they were organized.

Even though we may be in theory well aware of the immense pressures to which the Muslims of Castile were subjected at this time, nevertheless we cannot help being in some way surprised at the speed and the apparent ease with which this far-reaching change could be pushed through. To understand what went on from the viewpoint of the Muslims of Spain themselves, to understand what their apparent assent really meant, it is necessary to look at the advice and teaching that they were receiving at this time from their spiritual advisers.

CONVERSION TO CHRISTIANITY:
AN ISLAMIC PERSPECTIVE

Islam throughout the world is a faith the organization of which is by no means monolithic—in many ways it is and always has been the opposite of that—but Islamic Spain was a land where there predominated Sunni orthodoxy according to one school (*madhhab*) alone, that of the imam Malik b. Anas. This is often regarded as being, of the four equally orthodox schools, the one that interpreted the law most rigidly, with the strictest regard to the letter. Quite how this religious uniformity in al-Andalus came about would require us to trace the history of Malikism in the peninsula over the centuries, from its introduction in Caliphal times, and that would fall quite outside the scope of this volume. In earlier times, other interpretations of the law were to be found as well, but when, in the Almohad period (eleventh to twelfth centuries) there had been an attempt by that North African dynasty to impose their form of the creed, the people of al-Andalus and, above all, their religious leaders, the '*ulama* and the *fuqaha*, perhaps in a nationalist reaction (although one should be suspicious of such an anachronistic category), came to stress their adhesion to Malikism as the form of religion proper to their community. This may be the key to the predominance of this one school of law in the late medieval period. When we come to the last of al-Andalus's native Islamic dynasties, the Nasrids of Granada, Maliki orthodoxy is all but universal, and this unquestioning desire for orthodoxy continues into the final period that concerns us here.

There certainly are features of Islam as a popular religion as it existed in the sixteenth century in Spain that might be described as "unorthodox," but such aberrant manifestations arising from superstition, from contamination by ancient folklore, or by Christian (and in some cases Judaic) beliefs and practices did not betoken adherence to any organized "heresy," nor are they evidence for the existence in Spain of any of the non-Sunni Islamic belief systems that flourished elsewhere in the Islamic world. In many Islamic regions, there are popular superstitious beliefs and local customs that cohabit more or less uneasily with the strict letter of the law (shari'a). In Spain, although the orthodox establishment of scholars ('*ulama*) may not ever have been able totally to eradicate such beliefs (and there is plenty of evidence in surviving manuscripts of magical practices and other forms of unorthodoxy), superstition was relegated to the margins and doctrinal orthodoxy was never under threat.

Thus it is all the more surprising to find that in the final century of its existence, Spanish Islam in its practice departed in one quite radical way from what Sunni orthodoxy has always regarded as the firmly binding rules of religious discipline. As we will see, this departure from right practice did not in any way imply a departure from right belief. The doctrinal innovations that we will be looking at began presumably as purely temporary expedients, in no way calling into question any of the basic obligations of all Muslims such as the requirement to observe the dietary regulations. However, as has been said in quite another context, nothing can be more enduring than the temporary and "temporary" expedients that in this case continued in use for a century and more do merit our special attention.

The Oran Fatwa of 1504

The key theological document for the study of Spanish Islam in this final period is a *jurisconsultum* fatwa—a considered legal opinion provided on request) handed down by a mufti in Oran in 1504, that is to say, very shortly after the crisis created by the forcible conversions, first in Granada and then in all the lands of the Castilian Crown as described above. There is no reason to doubt that it is a direct response to them. This fatwa sets out for the benefit of the persecuted Muslims of Spain what modifications might legitimately be introduced in the range of religious obligations incumbent on a Muslim when he is being subjected to oppression. A fatwa is usually a response to a quite specific enquiry on a difficult point of detail, so it is unusual that this consultation covers what is almost the whole range of a Muslim's religious duties, but it was a response, a *responsum* to a particular, if unusual, situation at a particular moment in time, not a reformulation of universal doctrine. We do not have the actual document that the mufti sent to the persecuted Muslims in Spain, but a copy of the Arabic text (written out on empty leaves at the beginning of an unrelated Arabic manuscript, now in the Borgiano collection in the Vatican library) survives, as well as translations in Spanish in Arabic characters. The fatwa does not indicate the persons to whom it was directed, it merely bears the discreet indication "to be sent to those living abroad/afar (*al-guraba'*)[3] yet near to Allah, if that be His will."

This mufti from Oran showed acute sympathy for the plight of Muslims living in Spain, people who kept to their religious faith even though it was the cause of so much suffering for them: "those who hold fast to their religion just as somebody might clutch to himself a burning ember." In his opening paragraph, he expressed various pious hopes: "we pray to Allah to help us and you to observe his rightful law (*haqq*)," and he exhorted the recipients "that you may adhere to the religion of Islam, and that you may instruct in it those of your children who reach maturity." "If you fear that harm will result from the enemy coming to know your inner thoughts, blessed are those *guraba'* (those living abroad, who dwell afar)

---

3. *Al-guraba': garib*, plural *guraba'*, as will be seen, was a word of great spiritual resonance in this marginalized community. See n. 8 below.

who do what is right when others fall into corrupt ways, for indeed he who remembers to worship Allah when those around him forget to do so is like a man who is alive among the dead."

The mufti thus starts by affirming in orthodox terms the obligations of all Muslims. He then turns to the heart of the matter on which he had been consulted: whether any relaxation of the shari'a requirements was permissible under the conditions of persecution which now obtained in Spain:

> Know that idols are carved wood and hard stone which can cause you no harm and can do you no good, it is to Allah that the kingdom belongs. Allah did not take to Himself a son, and alongside Him there is no other god, so He is the one you must worship, and you must display perseverance in your adoration of Him.
>
> So [you must carry out] ritual prayer (*salat*), even though only by making some slight movement (*bi'l-ima'*),
>
> and [you must contribute] ritual alms (*zakat*), even though as if apparently it is some hypocritical show of generosity to a beggar (for Allah does not look at your face, but into your heart),
>
> and [perform] ritual ablutions (*gusl*) after major pollution, even though by plunging into the sea.
>
> If you are prevented from praying, then you should make up at nighttime what you have had to omit during the day; and when ritually pure water is for practical purposes lacking, then you must wipe yourself clean [in the ritually approved fashion—*tayammum*], even if it is just by rubbing your hands clean on a wall. If that is not possible, the generally held view is that the prayer and its execution are not required in the absence of water or clean stone, although you should make some slight pointing motion with your hands or face toward clean earth or stone or a tree such as would have been ritually acceptable for that purpose (this is as taught by Ibn Naji in his commentary to the *Risala,* and is based on the Prophet's words: "Take from them whatever they can bring").
>
> If, at the hour of prayer, they force you to prostrate yourself before their idols, or make you attend their prayers, maintain it as your firm intention to consider what they do as forbidden, and have it as your desire to carry out the prayer specified in Islamic law, bow down to whatever idols they are bowing to, but turn your intention toward Allah. Even if the direction is not that of Mecca, that requirement may be disregarded, as it is in the case of prayer when in danger on the battlefield.
>
> If they oblige you to drink wine, you may do so, but let it not be your intention to make use of it.

If they force pork on you, eat it, but in your heart reject it, and hold firm to the belief that it is forbidden. In the same way, if they force you to do anything thing which is forbidden.

If they would have you marry their daughters, that is permissible, for they are people with a scripture (*ahl al-kitab*), and if they oblige you to give your daughters in marriage to them, then you should cleave firmly to the belief that that is forbidden, were you not under duress, and abhor it in your hearts, so that you would do otherwise, if you were able.

In the same way, if they force upon you the taking of usury, or some other unlawful thing, do it, but reject it in your heart, and only keep back for yourself the original capital sum invested, and if you repent, then give the rest away as charity.

If they oblige you to pronounce words of blasphemy, do what they ask, but employ whatever stratagems of equivocation you can, and if you do pronounce the words they require, continue to put your trust in the faith. If they say to you: "Curse Muhammad," then, bearing in mind that they pronounce it as "Mamad," curse "Mamad," and signify thereby the Devil, or else the Jewish Mamad [presumably the mufti has in mind the Sephardic synagogue official called the Mahamad], since it is a common name among them.

If they say, "Jesus is the son of God," say that if they force you to, but let it be your intention to say it without the words in the possessive case [i.e., "of God"], namely, that servant of Allah, the son of Mary, who is rightly revered. If they say, "Say the Messiah is the son of God," then say that, but intend it to be a genitive possessive phrase, in the same way as one can say "the house of God," without meaning that God actually resides there.[4]

If they give you the order, "Say Mary is His wife," then say that, but intend the possessive pronoun to refer to her cousin,[5] who married her in the time of the Israelites, and then separated from her before the birth (as explained by al-Suhayli in his commentary to *Al-muhkam min al-rijal fi'l-Quran*), or else mean that God out of his might and power brought about her marriage.[6]

If they say Jesus died on the cross, mean by that that he perfected thereby the mortification of his flesh, his suffering, and the publishing of

4. I am not sure I grasp the thrust of the cavilling argument at this point: I presume that the mufti means that Jesus belongs to God in the same way that a house may belong to God, without any *parental* relationship being implied thereby?

5. Meaning her husband, the preferred match being between cousins.

6. It is, of course, extremely unlikely that the Moriscos' Inquisitorial persecutors would ever have made any such demand as this one, but that is neither here nor there.

his praise among mankind, and that Allah brought this about when he raised him to heaven.[7]

Anything which presents difficulties to you should be sent to me, and, God willing, we will set you aright in the light of what you write.

I pray that Allah may so bring it about that Islam may be worshipped openly without ordeals, tribulations or fear, thanks to the success of the attack of the noble Turks. We reassure you before Allah that you have served him, and done his command. You must reply. Greetings to you all. Dated at the close of Rajab 910 [A.D. 1504]. To be sent to the *guraba*'.[8]

The use by the mufti of the word *guraba*' ("stranger," "outsider") in this general address evokes a picture of an embattled heroic remnant of Muslims clinging on to their faith in spite of great suffering. These people, the mufti may have been suggesting by his choice of vocabulary, were "outsiders" in the sense that they were physically outside the bounds of *dar al-Islam,* but they had nevertheless been entrusted with a special honorable role in stressful times leading up to Judgment Day. Much of the behavior of the Moriscos is best understood against the background of beliefs in the imminent coming of the end of all things. The very awfulness of their situation tended to confirm them in their faith.

The fatwa, it will be seen, provides detailed rulings on a whole range of points, but it was above all important because of the original solution that it proposed to the general question of whether a Muslim could fulfill his or her obligations in conditions of clandestinity. Hitherto the teaching

7. It is very likely that my translation fails to do justice to what appears to me to be a piece of unconvincing logic-chopping. Muslims do not, of course, accept that Christ died on the cross.

8. In a number of hadiths current in the Iberian peninsula, a special role is assigned to the *guraba*' of al-Andalus at the end of days. When I first came across such traditions (in a collection of allegedly ancient hadiths about al-Andalus translated into Spanish by the Morisco Jesuit Ignacio de las Casas, a man who will come to our attention in a quite different context in chapter 8), I mistakenly assumed that the texts being translated were late fabrications. Although I could not be certain whether they were intended to reconcile the defeated and downtrodden Muslims of Spain with their fate, or whether, on the other hand, they had been created by black propagandists on the Christian side, I could not conceive that they had not arisen outside the circumstances of the sixteenth century. They seemed to arise so directly out of the experiences of the forcibly converted Muslim communities at that time. I was quite wrong in my assumptions, for Dr. Maribel Fierro pointed out to me that hadiths containing prophecies substantially identical in their use of the term *guraba*'. to those current in the sixteenth century are to be found in Arabic texts as early as the ninth century. In the light of Fierro's correction, the use of the word *guraba*' is therefore even more puzzling in the sixteenth century.

was that a Muslim could not. The obligation was to leave, to emigrate from any country of which the rulers made religious observance impossible. This duty to emigrate was regarded as imperative, particularly because the Prophet himself, when his followers were subjected to persecution by the rulers of Mecca, had led them into that emigration to Yathrib (Medina) that marked a vital stage in the unfolding of Islamic history. For a mufti to explain how true religion could be served by staying put thus was a bold innovation. Recipients of this fatwa would, henceforward, not see themselves as abandoning their faith. On the contrary, it told them they might see themselves as making use of permissible temporary devices under extraordinary circumstances in order to survive so that they could fulfill the special role that had been assigned to them in the last days of history.

A fatwa is an opinion emitted by an individual scholar and has the authority of that scholar. In the case of the Oran fatwa of 1504, the scholar in question is only known to us from just this one text, yet his opinion clearly did enjoy wide currency among the Muslims of Spain, for translations of it survive in three *aljamiado* manuscripts now preserved in three libraries. One of the translations bears the date 1564 [?]. This date is certainly not the date of the original, as has sometimes been mistakenly assumed, but it is positive evidence that over six decades the fatwa continued to circulate and be of importance to the Moriscos. Unfortunately none of these manuscripts enables us to determine the geographical regions in which the text circulated. It is reasonable to assume that the mufti originally sent the opinion to Muslims in lands of the Crown of Castile, probably to Granada itself, where the shock of adjustment after the conversions of 1501–2 will have been most severe, but it is also reasonable to assume that after forcible conversion was extended to the Crown of Aragon in the 1520s, the fatwa will have been read there too.

The Oran fatwa is not to be seen as *in intention* a new departure in doctrinal terms, for, as suggested above, both sender and recipients must have regarded it as providing for temporary expedients intended to help the Muslims of Spain through a crisis of persecution. In practice, though, it was for the Moriscos the basis of their Islamic status for a century and more: until the expulsion. It is important to remember that this fatwa did not embody the only view current. Far from it. The indications are that outside the Iberian Peninsula, at least, the older unbending interpretation of the law, very far removed from that expressed by Ahmad Bu Jum'a, was still being propounded, and we can be sure that the rigorist teachings of the Middle Ages shari'a requirements will not have been forgotten overnight.

Other Legal Opinions: The Cairo Fatwas

I discussed in my earlier study (Harvey 1990b, 56–60) how the orthodox Muslim view held throughout the late medieval period was that emigration (in Arabic *hijra*, a word with Koranic resonances) from lands held by the infidel was an obligation that would continue in force right up to the end. The enormous collection of fatwas, the *Kitab al-mi'yar*, compiled by the North African al-Wansharisi (d. 1508), contains a great deal of Hispano-Arabic material on this theme, and it is perhaps the most convenient source of opinions contrary to those expressed in the Oran text. Without exception what views we find in al-Wansharisi take the strict line according to which a Muslim was called upon to leave Christian lands and emigrate to *dar al-Islam* under almost all circumstances. Very recently, a further very important source indeed has been described and discussed in articles by van Koningsveld and Wiegers.[9] They not only analyze a fatwa of the Andalusi scholar Ibn Rabi' (d. A.D. 1320), embodying teachings on the need for Muslims to escape from Christian domination, but also, and even more interestingly for our present purposes, discuss fatwas handed down in about 1510 by the muftis of the four orthodox schools of Islamic jurisprudence in Cairo, who had been consulted on various doctrinal problems with which Muslims in Spain were wrestling.

These opinions are of interest not so much for what they tell us about the praxis of the Muslims of Spain in our period (they go into little detail on such matters, unlike the mufti of Oran, and one has the impression that these scholars in Egypt had little conception of what life under Christian rule was really like), but rather because they show that the special and unprecedented situation that had arisen in Spain was exercising the minds of pious Muslims in the heartlands of the Islamic world (and not just in Spain and North Africa). And what is most remarkable about the opinions expressed (which are in broad although not in complete agreement among the four muftis) is that the rigorist line taken on emigration (*hijra*) by earlier muftis (up to the time of al-Wansharisi) is not followed. The four orthodox muftis make no reference to the Oran fatwa, but in general their thinking is parallel to what had been propounded in 1504 in that they accepted that Muslims might continue to reside under Christian role in Spain (i.e., they do *not* call for emigration).

The Leiden scholars are much to be congratulated in succeeding in gaining access to this group of fatwas and have placed this whole field

9. I am much indebted to my colleagues from Leiden for allowing me to see a prepublication copy of their study, "The Islamic Statute of the Mudejars in the Light of a New Source," *Al-Qantara* 17 (1996): 19–58. See also van Koningsveld and Wiegers (1996b).

of Hispano-Arabic studies in their debt by publishing it from the photocopy that was available to them. The original remains inaccessible in a private collection in Morocco, and there are, of course, a range of *expertises* (which they themselves are uniquely well-prepared to carry out) to which the original will need to be subjected if ever it becomes available for scientific study. There must remain some doubt about the importance we should attach in the present context of sixteenth-century studies to a text that cannot be shown positively to have circulated at that period in Spain itself (in the way that the Oran fatwa undoubtedly did). The very idea of the four muftis coming together in this way to pronounce on this subject is, to say the least, surprising. (As just stated, a fatwa is an individual scholar's opinion, not, in premodern times at least, normally the product of a committee.)

One possible explanation for the genesis of this recently discovered "Cairo" document (and I am speculating here) is that it was primarily aimed at influencing public opinion in Egypt itself at this juncture rather than at alleviating the situation of the Islamic remnant in the Iberian Peninsula. This was the final stage of the crisis of the Mamluk state, and we know (from the Granadan Ibn al-Azraq's earlier mission to the Mamluk court and Peter Martyr's counter embassy, among other sources) that at one and the same time the Mamluks were being forced urgently to face eastward to stem the Ottoman advance, southward, where the Portuguese had penetrated into seas formerly dominated by Muslims, and westward, where the Muslims of Spain were clamoring for support. Could the quadripartite Cairo fatwas have been intended to point out to opinion in the Middle East, in Egypt above all, that there was no *absolute* obligation on Muslims to attempt to do something about the plight of Spain's Muslims, because these people could still continue to worship? If the Muslims of Spain could fulfill their religious obligations at home, then the urgency with which fellow Muslims in other countries needed to come to their assistance was diminished, and in consequence the Mamluk state could the more easily excuse its expedient policy of concentrating on the more immediate problem of the Ottoman threat.

The underlying purpose of this rather puzzling, but undoubtedly extremely important, Cairo document merits further investigation. Among the many questions it poses is not only why we hear nothing of it in Andalusi or Magribi sources right up to the present day: We hear nothing of it in Eastern sources either. This may well have something to do with the special circumstances of the imminent eclipse of Mamluk power.

That the four muftis in Cairo should have made no effort closely to harmonize their recommendations is, of course, in no way surprising. In Western legal traditions, we are familiar with the delivery of divergent or minority verdicts, but one finding will nevertheless usually prevail when judgment is delivered. In the Islamic practice, each of the schools is of equal authority. In this case it has to be said that only the Maliki's findings will have been of greatest practical importance, because in Spain the other schools had no foothold. I think we must presume that the quadripartite fatwa was produced because, bearing in mind its potential oriental readership, it would have been impolitic to fail to seek the views of the other muftis. The Dutch scholars who have edited and studied the text are not, as has been explained, at present free to reveal much about the manuscript in which the fatwa may have been preserved. We must hope that eventually further studies can be carried out by them. One result of their discovery, an incidental contribution, but one of some importance, is that the Oran fatwa is no longer an isolated phenomenon, and Ahmad Bu Jum'a's was clearly not the only jurisconsult prepared to give consideration to the crisis of conscience that the Muslims of Spain were undergoing. That his had been the only fatwa during this period had seemed surprising. It remains the only such text known actually to have circulated in Spain.

The Muftis of Cairo Confront the Problems of Living under Spanish Rule

Hijra

Among the problems raised in the Cairo fatwas, that of emigration is addressed more directly than in the Oran text. The person requesting the legal opinion takes for granted (as do all the muftis in their answers) that when it is possible for a Muslim to do so, there is an obligation on him to leave a land not under the government of Muslims. This is, as we have seen, standard doctrine. It is the starting point of the thinking of the muftis in Cairo, but we soon find that what they are really concerned with are justifiable *exemptions* from that obligation, mitigating circumstances justifying noncompliance with the general rule rather than strict enforcement of the rule. What if the Christian authorities refused to countenance emigration and imposed heavy penalties on any fugitives they apprehend? Is it permissible to postpone emigration until conditions are more favorable? What if the Muslim is not in danger of losing his life, only of having his property taken from him? And, since emigration was only incumbent on those who could really *afford* to go, what precise proportion of one's wealth should one be prepared to spend on the journey? These are the sort of doubts as to points of detail that are addressed. (The original questioner had seemed to want to prevent fudging: he asks for what amounts to a firm percentage figure!)

The scholars of Cairo, as has been stated, did not offer a united front. On emigration, the Maliki mufti does not require immediate action: postponement of the decision is permissible. The maximum proportion of one's wealth that one is obliged to spend on such emigration is one-third—this being the proportion of one's estate that one is free to dispose of in a will, and the implication is that emigration ought not, in the opinion of this scholar, be allowed to ruin a family financially. In practice, this provision would have provided an excuse to stay for almost everyone.

Pilgrimage

What if the Christian authorities allow a Muslim subject to depart but before granting him exit documents, require him to provide sureties for his return? Should the pilgrim go back to Spain once he has left? Or should he risk creating problems for those back in Spain who had gone surety for him and who might be left in the lurch? If a Muslim has escaped but his children were still in Spain, should he go back in order to try to get them out?

On pilgrimage, the Maliki agrees that the pilgrim has a duty to return to Spain under the circumstances described. (This is perhaps rather surprising. One feels the mufti in Cairo can have had little grasp of the realities of life for his Spanish brethren.)

Religious Scholars

Should religious scholars whose services were required to teach Islam to those unable to leave go or stay? Could they still function as religious scholars under such conditions?

On the duties of scholars, the Maliki actually says a scholar who is needed in Spain *ought* to stay. This is at notable variance with fatwas collected by al-Wansharisi, in which a Muslim who stays on to provide help and advice to coreligionists who need his services is still said to be in the wrong (Harvey 1990, 56–58.).

The Use of Non-Arabic Languages

Was the use of some form of Romance (*'ajamiyya*) permissible for religious purposes? Either to convey the meaning of the Koran or to preach where Arabic is not understood?

On the use of a non-Arabic language, the answer is disappointingly obtuse: perhaps by design? The Maliki, in an apparently rigorist interpretation, flatly prohibits recitation of the Koran in a language other than Arabic if the person concerned can do it in Arabic, but then he goes on to say that if the person is incapable of doing so in Arabic, *'ajamiyya* ("non-Arabic language") is permissible, as is its use by students. The attitude on *preaching* in a language other than Arabic is perversely and illogically ultra-strict: it is not allowed if the preacher can use Arabic (no mention is made of whether the faithful can *understand* what the preacher is saying!). And actually to explain the sermon is rejected outright. The Hanafi *responsum* on this topic is much more ready to countenance the use of a language other than Arabic in situations where the congregation would otherwise not understand. Hanafism was (and is) the school most widespread among the Turks, and among the Turks there was a well-established tradition of use of their own language for certain well-defined religious purposes.

One wonders whether these Cairo fatwas may have been directed more to the Muslims of the Crown of Aragon than to the converts of 1502 (who all fell under the Crown of Castile). The Cairo regime had, as has been mentioned in chapter 1, a tradition stretching back at least as far as the fourteenth century of taking an interest in the affairs of Aragon's Muslims. For that reason, perhaps discussion of these fatwas should have been reserved for the next chapter, but it seemed preferable to look at all such *jurisconsulta* at the same time.

Other Reactions to the Problem Created by the Forcible Conversions
In the theology both of the victorious Christians and in that of the conquered Muslims there was agreement in that both religions required clear and unambiguous either/or decisions with regard to religious loyalty; both sides rejected compromise or fudging. The solution proposed by the mufti of Oran (that Islam should, if obliged to do so, be prepared to go underground) did not call into question the basic polarization demanded by both sides. His fatwa was simply, as has been pointed out, a "temporary" expedient to meet a specific situation envisaged as transient. In fact, following generations kept it in use for a century and more, but it was not intended at the outset as a ruling of permanent validity. On the Christian side, the type of irenic approach to Christian-Muslim relations advocated in Spain in the fifteenth century by John of Segovia was not taken up again in the sixteenth. On the Muslim side nobody called for true compromise either. Today things have been different, of course. Christians and Muslims may talk in modern times of such topics as "inter-faith relations," although their understanding of the meaning of those words may differ widely. Nothing in the way of dialogue occurs in the sixteenth century. Entrenched positions were defended.

On the Muslim side under modern conditions some have moved towards an explicit acceptance that *jihad* other than in a moral sense is inappropriate. This way of thinking seems to have emerged first in India and not in the Magrib. The literature is abundant but has little bearing on the case of al-Andalus; see Jaffar (1992). The sixteenth century was, we must remember, an age when conflicts of religion were pursued energetically, both inside each of the religions (between warring sects), and between the major religions themselves.

Preaching to the Summarily Converted

What actually happened to the Muslims of Spain after their conversion? We do not know as much as we might expect about the follow-up to the Edicts of Conversion by the Christian authorities; as for the impact on the Muslims in either Granada or Castile of the various edicts and proclamations, we can only make inferences. (We do have a graphic description of what happened some twenty years after this, when the news of the much later enforced conversion of the Muslims in the eastern kingdoms reached the *faqih* (Islamic lawyer) of a small village in Aragon, as will be discussed in chapter 3.) If the Castilian authorities were to succeed in making the nominal "conversion by decree" into a reality, it is clear that they had to preach and teach to the many instant "converts" they had just created. The "converts" needed instructing in their new faith. Writers later in the sixteenth century, trying to find an explanation for the ultimate failure of the Spanish Christian attempt to turn Muslims into Christians, besides condemning the perversity of the stubborn Muslims, also often laid some blame on deficiencies in the initial evangelization campaigns, but there is no reason to suppose that the ecclesiastical authorities did not take their new task seriously, although we must bear in mind the limited means available to them. Castile had just suddenly found itself at the hub of a world empire, and although that certainly did bring in vast new sources of income, at the same time vast amounts of money were soaked up in the administration and defense of the empire, and serious inflation was created. The surplus income available for new purposes such as evangelization was in short supply throughout the century. More important, the Spanish church suddenly had to send priests and religious to hundreds of new posts in many parts of the globe, and in particular, missionaries were needed for preaching in the Indies. Whatever the financial means available, trained manpower could not be improvised overnight. The church was under strain and could not provide enough missionaries. The Crown was aware of these needs: on October 24, 1500, a *real cédula* (royal warrant) funded a great number of ecclesiastical appointments for Granada (Domínguez and Vincent 1978, 95), and after that time most parishes in Granada had a parish priest at least, but the quality was not always high.

The record is largely silent on what happened at the parish level in the next decades. The very existence of the Oran fatwa does provide indirect confirmation from the Muslim side that in some places energetic steps were being taken to enforce the conversion. But neither the Inquisition nor the full disciplinary authority of the dioceses had yet been systematically invoked. It was at the end of the first decade of the century that the church revised its evangelistic methods and began to organize repressive rather than persuasive measures. A debate was to take place over the next sixty years between those (a majority among Christians of all ranks) who argued that Islamic beliefs would not be swept away until the whole interlinked fabric of the manners and customs of Islamic society had been banned, and those few who asserted that there was no need to deprive the Granadans of their innocent local customs, their folklore (to use a twentieth-century term).

1510

Writing toward the end of the sixteenth century but looking back on the immediate aftermath of the first conversions, Luis del Mármol described the situation. His words convey well the uncomprehending irritation and exasperation that was the reaction of many Christians to the failure of the policy of forcible conversion. It will be noted that he was aware of the strength of the Moriscos' clandestine religion. He had had access to some of the intelligence of the Second Granadan Rebellion and knew very well that by his day Islam had not faded away at all. One may doubt whether most Christian observers, writing immediately after the conversions, would have known that Islam had gone underground in the way that Mármol does.

> After the dissidence in the Kingdom of Granada had been put down, and the Moors converted to our Catholic faith, . . . the Catholic Monarchs continued to heap benefits and favors on them, and ruled over them with love, treating them well in every way. The Monarchs ordered their officers, both military and judicial, to favor these converts and encourage them. But it soon became apparent how little these kindnesses had served to get them to abandon being Moors. For although they said they were Christians, one could see they paid more regard to the rites and ceremonies of Muhammad's sect than to the precepts of the Catholic church. They zealously shut their ears to everything they were told by the bishops, clergy and friars in their preaching. . . . Trusting in those empty fictions they called *jófores* or predictions, they put all their hope in them, because they predicted they would become Moors once more, and return to their former state. (Mármol 1991, 63)

In 1511 came the first determined attempt of the Christian authorities to strike in a concerted way at the stubborn Islam of the "newly converted"—by extirpating their distinctive manners and customs. Earlier enactments such as the Edicts of Conversion themselves and the various capitulations of 1501, although they were a shock to the Muslims, were, in fact, designed to attenuate the impact of conversion in various ways. Confrontation on such nondoctrinal issues as the continued wearing of existing "Moorish" garments, the use of bath houses, among other things, had been avoided.

The objective now in 1511 was more far-reaching. It was aimed at having the ex-Muslims in Granada forget their old Islamic way of life completely (*que no ubiesen mas memoria de las cosas de moros*), and so they were to dress like Christians—and any tailor who made them new Moorish-style garments risked a heavy fine. They were to employ Christian-style butchers (and any who performed *halal* slaughtering ran the risk of having his goods and property confiscated). Arabic was still tolerated, but all books in Arabic were now to be handed in so that they could be checked. Harmless practical manuals would be returned, but works of Islamic law (*xara y çunna*) would be burned. Estates were no longer to be divided at death according to Islamic law. The former Muslims were forbidden to sell their property (clearly an attempt to *prevent* a wave of emigration), whereas in 1501 the Catholic Monarchs had been prepared to concede the right of the converts to sell their property (*vender sus fasiendas y casas, que lo pueda haser syn enpedimiento alguno*) in order to allow them to move.

One decree in the name of Queen Juana and dated 1513 was aimed in fact at Old Christians in Granada and is worth quoting almost complete because it will reminds us that in Granada and similar areas the ways of life of the Muslim (ex-Muslim?) community were still capable of exerting their attraction on the newcomers, the Christian settlers. Cultural influences were still not all flowing in a Christianizing direction.

1513

Proclamation That the Old Christian Women May Not Dress in the Moorish Fashion, or Go Veiled[10]
Whereas I have been informed that certain women who are Old Christians and live and reside in the city of Granada and in other cities and towns of this kingdom, forgetful of the general instructions to the effect that the newly converted should leave aside their Moorish dress and clothing, and should go about dressed in the Christian manner, themselves dress in the Moorish fashion, and cover themselves with *almalafas,* so that, in addition to the bad example which they set in this way to the newly converted, they, thinking that they are covered up, commit certain excesses and evil actions whereby Our Lord is ill served, and their own honor is jeopardized. From

10. The actual expression used is *traigan almalafa,* "wear the almalafa." This was an all-enveloping *outer* wrap, Arabic *milhafa,* rather like the *hayk* at present in use in parts of North Africa, and certainly not just a face veil.

this great harm results. So, because, as Queen and [Sovereign] Lady, it is incumbent on me to make provision against it, after due consultation with the King my lord and father, and with members of my Council, it has been decided that this proclamation should be sent out as I have seen fit, whereby. . . . . . I strictly forbid any Old Christian woman to dress in the Moorish style from this day henceforward, under the penalty, for a first offence, of loss of the clothing thus worn, and a hundred strokes of the whip, and, for a second offence, the same penalties together with perpetual exile from the whole Kingdom of Granada, the which sentences I hereby confirm without need of any further declaration. And I command my royal magistrates (*corregidores*), each in his own jurisdiction, to publish and publicly proclaim this my decree so that it may come to the notice of all. Given in Valladolid this 29th of July 1513. [*Countersigned*] I the King.

I Lope Conchillos, secretary to the Queen, had this copied at the command of the King her father. (Gallego and Gámir 1968, 179)

Whether any significance should be placed on the repetition of this same edict ten years later in 1523 in the *Ordenanças de Granada* (Granada, 1552) as cited by Caro (1957, 158; 1976, 163) is not clear (the earlier measure may simply have been put on record in this way, without any fresh intention to make it effective).

In 1523 in the same context of the *Ordenanças de Granada* (fol. CCCXIr) is included another curious regulation concerning female dress or, more specifically, cross-dressing: men were forbidden to wear female clothing by day or night. Does this indicate that the male transvestite prostitutes of whom we hear in Nasrid Granada (and in Fez and other cities even later—Lane, for example, describes them in nineteenth-century Cairo) still were to be found in Charles V's Granada? It seems on the face of it unlikely, but why enact such an odd piece of legislation if it was not needed?

A curious example of the ways in which "conversion" and the transition from Nasrid society to the ways of sixteenth-century Christian Spain could be a long drawn-out process is provided by the tax on minstrels or musicians (*juglares*) that came up for decision at the level of the Royal Council, no less, in 1517 (Gallego and Gámir 1968, 186).

At the time of the conversions, the Catholic Monarchs had, as has already been explained, stated they would abolish all the taxes that had existed under the Islamic regime because the converts were now to be taxed on exactly the same basis as the Christians. That was the theoretical basis of policy. In fact, there were exceptions; the *farda,* for example was a special tax levied on ex-Muslims to pay for the coastguard service—presumably because the high cost of watching out for raiding pirates from North Africa was felt in some way to be something for which the ex-Muslims were responsible. Another exception, one of far less importance, was the tax called the *tarcón,* which in Nasrid days had been levied when entertainment, music, and dancing was performed before large assemblies, *zambras,* weddings, and betrothals.[11] The right to collect these dues had been granted to an individual we have already encountered: el Fisteli, baptized as Fernando de Morales. He seems to have continued to exercise this right until 1517. Emboldened no doubt by the radical tightening up of regulations that was going on with the object of wiping out traditional Granadan practices, the city council (*ayuntamiento*) of Granada petitioned that the levy should be brought to an end (perhaps they wished to make common cause with their colleagues in Malaga, who, as we have seen, had endless wrangles with this same individual, eminent "new convert" as he was).

It was evidently being argued in defense of the levy that a proportion of the takings went to providing ransoms for captives and other good works (so it ought to be retained), but with relentless logic the members of the council replied that it did not seem just that an individual should have a claim over such contributions. Further, it was pointed out that "if it is not lawful for there to be such *zambras,* and if troubles result for such assemblies of people, it seems hardly right that that individual should promote them in order to preserve his own rights and interests." It was all very well, the city council pointed out, that there should be rejoicing on occasions like weddings, but that did not justify raising taxes on them, so it petitioned for abolition. The council attempted to cast doubt on the propriety of levying such a tax, which had only been given to Morales/Fisteli as an informant "por información del dicho Fistelí fecha a sus Altezas" (Gallego and Gámir 1968, 186). The implication is presumably that a less self-interested informant might have made different recommendations. Although the Crown did not contest these arguments, and although it promised to do away with the tax eventually, after el Fisteli's death, it did not try to do so while he was still alive. It is difficult to avoid drawing the conclusion that the *tarcón* was being used as a channel for payment for services rendered. The old gentleman was not to live much longer, and by January 1519 the *ayuntamiento* was able to issue a proclamation saying the tax would no longer be levied (Gallego and Gámir 1968, 189).

By no means the least interesting aspect of this affair is the incidental evidence it provides of the continued popularity in this period of the

---

11. It will be recalled that dancing the *zambra* was one of the aspects of the old traditional wedding festivities that was still tolerated.

zambra. The name still lives on into modern times but is now attached to the flamenco entertainments put on for tourists by the gypsies of the Sacromonte in their caves. What the sources do not tell us is the nature of the entertainment provided in 1517, but if the flamenco music of the twentieth century is still so full of Arab elements (as it clearly is), it is reasonable to suppose that what was offered in the early sixteenth century may have been even closer to what had existed in Nasrid days. In purely Islamic terms the music and dance of the *zambras* almost certainly would have met with the disapproval of pious Muslim scholars; what we are dealing with here is not a survival of Islamic culture as such, but of ancient Granadan, Andalusian folklore.

THE TWO POLES OF CHRISTIAN POLICY: ASSIMILATION/ CONVERSION VERSUS REJECTION/EXPULSION

Once the conversion had been forced through, it became increasingly difficult to prevent movement and mingling among the New Christian populations all over Spain. Tapia, for example, speaks of the convert community of Ávila as being characterized by great mobility (Tapia 1991, 145), with some of them moving to Andalusia. The Moriscos knew better than to draw attention to themselves, so we cannot hope for firm statistics (although what the diligence of an acute investigator like Tapia is able to extract from the records is remarkable). In general, we only hear about the population drift incidentally, as, for example, when the count of Aguilar uses the fact that some estates were losing essential workers to support his argument that further "edicts of grace" (i.e., partial exemption from the Inquisition's attentions) should be granted to the new converts (Tapia 1991, 223; Lea 1901, 52). The Inquisition in fact acceded to the suggestion and stressed at the same time that a ban on movement into Granada was in force (something that is not otherwise clear from the records).

The newly acquired mobility of the Muslims from north to south in Spain had varied consequences. It could be a factor tending to favor assimilation, for it brought Muslims out of the confines of their *morerías* and into contact with the general community. On the other hand, it enabled ex-Mudejar Castilian Muslims to contact their Granadan brethren more easily and so to renew their networks of Islamic education.

For the Mudejar communities of Castile, socially already well assimilated by 1500, forcing them to become in religious matters superficially identical with their Christian neighbors was in some cases counterproductive. At least some of the ex-Mudejars who had elicited little interest in religious matters were spurred on to recover in secret the religion that they had seemed likely to lose as a result of slow and insensible erosion. We will see in chapters 3, 4, and 5 how the Young Man from Arévalo scoured the peninsula for he called the "Matter of Andalusia" and the basic texts of his faith.

In contrast with the attempts to limit movement between Castile and Granada was the relaxed handling by the Aragonese and Valencian authorities of requests for travel documents from (still) Mudejar subjects. (Muslims in the lands of the Crown of Aragon are dealt with in the next chapter.)

At this stage, in the first quarter of the sixteenth century, we can thus detect two contradictory trends in Spanish policy. Contradictions and vacillations characterized the handling of the problem posed by the converts from Islam throughout the period, right up to the Expulsion, but in these opening decades of the century, before attitudes on both sides had had time to set too firmly, the contradictions are perhaps most apparent. On the one hand, there was a desire for wholehearted assimilation, and on the other, we detect a desire to contain, to build a wall round the alien element, isolating it. Contradictions of a similar sort had, of course, arisen often before. Christendom had felt itself tugged in two directions in its dealings with the Jews, perhaps from the days of Saint Paul, but its attitudes were even more confused in the sixteenth century when dealing with Muslims. In the world at large, Islam was felt as a threat, even to the heart of Europe. It could not be ignored. In the Iberian Peninsula, Christians pressed for acculturation, only to resist and reject it when it occurred.

One effect of the Edicts of Conversion of 1501–2, on the Muslims of Granada certainly, but also on the communities of Castile, was that they became subject to the jurisdiction of the Inquisition. Time had to be allowed for them to learn the new faith, but as we have seen, after some fifteen years they began to be harassed by that institution. In consequence, in about 1517 it would appear a small number of the Muslims from Rioja (by no means the majority of the local community) formed the plan of emigrating to Granada, expecting that they would be harassed somewhat less there! The idea that they would at least be living in an area where they would have the support of their fellows seems to have attracted them (Lea 1901, 51–52). The original edict of conversion of 1502 had set out to prevent Muslims from the northern *morerías* from joining up with their Granadan coreligionists: they were forbidden to leave the country by any ports other than those of the Biscay coast. It seems probable that any such internal migrants from Rioja would have been disappointed by what they found in Granada, for what had been lands with an overwhelming Muslim majority were, by 1517, beginning to be settled by Christian incomers. The Christian peasants of the north were on the move, too, and they had the approval of the regime behind them. The conquered territories were being taken over progressively by settlers who fully expected, and who usually received, backing from the authorities should conflicts ever arise between them and the original inhabitants.

The community disputes and violence that arose between 1512 and 1519 in the region of Motril stand out because what was at issue was pig farming (an activity that did not exist, of course, in Nasrid times). This may serve to close this chapter because it reminds us that doctrinal and theological differences were rarely debated in some academic void. Intertwined with religion and ideology were both ancient cultural prejudices and economic interests. Disputes arose from the need to wrest a scanty livelihood from the land. In that area on the Mediterranean coast, then as now, the fertile, but extremely narrow, coastal strip was fully exploited for the production of sugar cane and other subtropical crops, and the maintenance of the irrigation and other works was an exhausting but necessary task. Incoming Christian owners of livestock, on the other hand, accustomed as they were to the broad lands of the northern *meseta central* and to such practices as driving herds and flocks on to arable land after the grain harvest to clear fields of stubble (the *derrota de mieses,* "gleaning," as it was termed), began assertively to put their hogs into the sugar cane stubble. Complaints seem to have centered on the damage done by the animals rooting into vital irrigation channels, but one may guess that the very nature of the beasts was the heart of the problem. For years nothing was done, but with herds of several hundred being turned into the fields, the damage they caused could no longer be ignored. The council of Motril sought to regulate the practice—not, significantly, to ban it. Only registered residents (*vecinos*) had the right to such pasture, and nobody might put out more than ten animals to graze (Vassberg 1984, 177). One can see how the harmony of the old order was disrupted by the assertive immigrants from the north with their alien ways.

In Motril the incoming swineherds were obviously all Christians. But we have seen that Muslims trickled southward, too. Once in the south, those Muslims who arrived from Castile either merged into the masses of the newly converted or continued on their way into North Africa. The small illegal migration of 1517 already mentioned was a curious anticipation, in the reverse direction, of the mingling of crypto-Muslims from the former Muslim Kingdom of Granada with crypto-Muslims of Mudejar origin in various parts of the interior. This was to take place after the much larger population transfers that were *enforced* more than forty years later by the authorities in the aftermath to the Second Granadan Rebellion (such were the vagaries and fluctuations of Castilian policy, what was at one stage strictly forbidden became at a later stage obligatory).

The filtration of Muslims to the south in 1517 shows how, after the conversions of 1501–2, and after the various Muslim communities became aware of the teaching contained in the Oran fatwa of 1504, the interests of the ex-Mudejars of the center and north converged with those of their Granadan brethren. Hitherto, in late medieval times, Mudejars and Nasrids were not bound by ties of mutual interest (and Mudejars had even served in the Granadan wars on the Castilian side). In the early years of the sixteenth century, some tenuous bonds were being established between northern ex-Mudejars and southern ex-subjects of the Nasrid kingdom. The consciousness among the Muslims of the peninsula of a common cause certainly did not become marked until much later, until after the suppression of the Second Granadan Rebellion in the 1570s. At that point, the scattering of the Granadans did create peninsula-wide crypto-Muslim solidarity. Yet the merging of the various communities was never complete, even at the end, and very many factors still sustained distinctions between the various groups of Muslims, right up to the time of their expulsion, and indeed, beyond, into exile. The crypto-Muslims of Spain never became a homogenous group.

THREE ❧ The Muslims of Aragon and Valencia up to Their Forcible Conversion

The expression "Crown of Aragon" (*Corona de Aragón*) may give rise to justifiable confusion. In Spanish historical usage, it refers not just to Aragon proper but to all three contiguous political entities to the east of the Iberian Peninsula that were in the Middle Ages linked under a common monarch. Two of them, Aragon and Valencia, had the status of independent kingdoms, and the third, Catalonia, was a principality. The ruler of all these territories at the opening of the sixteenth century, Ferdinand, is usually thought of simply as the king of Aragon, but he was equally king of Valencia. Equally puzzling to the outsider is the fact that although Saragossa was the capital of Aragon proper, the administration and the royal chancery for this whole eastern political entity were normally centered on Barcelona in the principality of Catalonia.

There is also the vexed question of language. In documents emanating from this Aragonese chancery in the medieval period, one may expect to find in use either Catalan (the language of Catalonia and of Valencia) or else Aragonese. This attempt of mine to state the linguistic situation in simple terms will, I fear, provoke indignant protests, not least from Valencians, who regarded, and still regard, their language as in no way subordinate to Catalan. As for Aragonese, in earlier times it had had some independent existence, even a literature of its own, but by the sixteenth century the written form of the language was falling increasingly rapidly into the orbit of Castilian, from which it was distinguished more by a few external features of its orthography—the use of the spellings "ly" and "ny" where Castilian would have "ll" and "ñ"—and by certain items of vocabulary—than by any major morphological or syntactic differences.

This group of territories thus had no single language and no single administrative capital. Even the Muslims of the Crown of Aragon did not form one homogenous whole, although they are conveniently grouped together here because in general everywhere Muslims had to confront the same royal policy. In Aragon proper, Muslims spoke the local Aragonese;

in Catalonia, Catalan; but in Valencia most of them spoke Arabic as their first language (with Catalan or Valencian as their second). Valencia in the sixteenth century could boast the largest Arabic-speaking group remaining in the whole Iberian Peninsula, and some villages there continued to be predominantly Arabic-speaking right up to the Expulsion. There were other major differences between the various Muslim communities of the Crown of Aragon besides linguistic ones, and they rarely succeeded in making common cause, even at times when it was abundantly clear that to do so would have been to their advantage.

ARAGON

The Muslims of the Aragonese region proper (inhabitants of the valley of the Ebro and of its various tributaries upstream from Tortosa) used dialects similar to those of their Christian neighbors. If we are to judge from their manuscripts, they may have been linguistically somewhat more conservative, more prone to archaisms, than their Christian neighbors, but then the evidence may be misleading. Devotional texts the world over tend to be archaizing, so we must be careful not to base datings exclusively on elements in Morisco writings that, had they occurred in contemporary Christian texts, might have seemed outmoded.[1] (This corpus of linguistic material is in fact a rich, and still largely unexploited, source of information about early elements in the Aragonese varieties of Romance in general.)

The relatively few Muslims of the Catalan region (most of them from the diocese of Tortosa) spoke Catalan and appear to have been the group best integrated with their neighbors. They did not develop an *aljamiado* literature. The preservation of Arabic, both spoken and written, among the Valencians was no doubt in part due to the closeness of the North African coast. Muslim contacts with the Islamic world, even some family alliances, could be maintained; it is not surprising that the Valencian region remained highly Arabicized and Islamicized.

The fact that Ferdinand's kingdoms in the east of the peninsula should at the beginning of the century have been spared the anti-Muslim legislation that brought about forcible conversion in the lands of the Crown of Castile raises the question of Ferdinand's underlying policy intentions toward the Muslims of the Aragonese Crown. Mark D. Meyerson, in his very valuable monograph, *The Muslims of Valencia in the Age of Fernando and Isabel: Between Coexistence and Crusade* (1991), is quite positive about

---

1. A single example: the final consonant of the Latin preposition *ad* ("to") is lost early in all varieties of Peninsular Romance, but in *aljamiado* manuscripts from Aragon it often survives—*ad Allah* ("to God").

the king's aims. In Meyerson's view, the king did *not* intend to convert his Crown of Aragon Mudejar subjects. After referring to the expulsion of the Jews from the peninsula, Meyerson goes on to state: "This was not, however, part of a larger plan to impose religious uniformity on Castile and Aragon; rather, it was a measure meant to solve a widespread socio-religious problem, of which the Mudejars were not a part. Even though these initiatives against the Conversos and Jews might have suggested to some that the conversion or expulsion of the Mudejars was the next step, Fernando himself did not entertain such designs" (Meyerson 1991, 51).

I can understand how it is possible for Meyerson to make such an appreciation of Ferdinand's intentions: his study is a well-disciplined and sharply focused monographic investigation relying directly (although not exclusively, of course) on the archival manuscript sources that have come down to us in some abundance from the various constituent elements of the Crown of Aragon. I can well believe that Ferdinand's anti-Muslim intentions on this matter are absent from such archival sources. Against a broader canvas of the history of the Iberian Peninsula, the picture that suggests itself to me is less clear-cut. I have already argued that the Portuguese marriage negotiations of 1497 (see Harvey 1984) are a foretaste of what was to come elsewhere in the peninsula. It is not that Meyerson is unaware of the larger context, of the evidence concerning what happened in Portugal in 1497, for example, or in the lands of the Crown of Castile in 1500–2, but he gives less weight to these manifestations of Ferdinand's intentions than to the absence of discussion of the theme of conversion in the Aragonese *primary* sources. On the Muslims of Portugal, Meyerson accepts "[t]hat until 1499 the Monarchs had no intention of breaking the treaties [i.e., the Capitulations of Granada, etc.] is indicated by their permission to Portugal's expelled Mudejars to settle in Granada and Castile in 1497" (Meyerson 1991, 54), and he goes on to draw conclusions radically different from my own. My own view is that although the various Spanish realms were administered separately, Ferdinand can hardly have kept his mind divided into compartments so hermetically sealed that he could not relate events in Lisbon and in Granada—and Cairo and Istanbul—to what went on in Valencia and Saragossa. We do not expect complete logical consistency of policy across the various realms, but interaction had been going on for a long time and would continue throughout his reign.

The most acute crisis in Spanish-Mamluk relations was not that of 1489, to which Meyerson makes reference (97–98). The war in the Alpujarras of 1500–2, above all, the fearful massacre carried out at Andarax in the Alpujarras by Castilian troops, destroyed all confidence. The mission to Cairo arose from the danger of an impact on the Muslims of the Crown of Aragon of the policy of forcible conversion as implemented in Castilian territories. Ferdinand was—as we would expect—fully aware that policy was made on a Mediterranean-wide scale and that what was done in Castilian lands had repercussions on Mamluk policy toward Aragon.

Ferdinand's continuation of what amounted to Mudejar status in Aragon arose from the interplay of multiple factors and not just those specific issues that can be expected to be reflected in the archives of one particular area. The tendency of modern academic historiography to accord absolute primacy to archive materials over what is dismissed as "secondary" needs to be subjected to critical scrutiny. The absence from the archives of the east of the Peninsula of any plan on Ferdinand's part to convert his local Mudejars there comes to be interpreted as firm indication of the king's intentions not to convert them. That seems to me to give too much weight to negative evidence.

Meyerson's conclusion that "[i]n Fernando's mind the tradition of Mudejarism was still one worth maintaining," is in one sense an incontrovertible summary of what can be deduced from the king's actions, but I find it potentially misleading in this context. We cannot know for certain what were Ferdinand's long-term aims, but his general conduct of policy elsewhere points to his being anxious to move ahead with anti-Muslim measures when and where it was practical, prudent, and expedient to do so.

Even for his Aragonese subjects, Ferdinand did not reject the idea of converting them as a matter of principle. In those cases where conversion to Christianity was the clear wish of his Muslim subjects, he certainly did not oppose it, and indeed he actively looked after the interests of the converts. The city of Teruel lies on the borders of Castile and Valencia but is in Aragon. In 1502, the whole Mudejar *aljama* converted, perhaps because of its awareness of what was going on to Muslims in nearby border districts of Castile. "May it please God that all others that remain in our kingdoms do the same," Meyerson himself reports Ferdinand as saying (Meyerson 1991, 54).

If he had so wished, Ferdinand might well have chosen at the outset to bring all his diverse territories into line insofar as religious policy was concerned. Why then did he not do so? Why did he not issue a general edict of conversion in 1502? Both international relations and home affairs will have influenced his thinking. Rather than ascribe the difference between policy on religion in Castile and that in Aragon to the fact that Isabella and Ferdinand personally had different opinions on these matters, I would prefer to focus on the different constraints under which policy was made in the various realms. It may have been the case that they had differences of opinion, husbands and wives sometimes do disagree, after all, but the different course that events took in Isabella's realms from what happened in Ferdinand's would be quite satisfactorily explained by factors—demographic, social, strategic—far more likely to sway a master of statecraft such as Ferdinand than his personal predilections.

To have sought to vary the status of Aragon's Muslims circa 1500 would almost certainly have meant to stir up a hornets' nest of local patriotisms, not just within the Muslim communities but far beyond them. Even Philip II, who had a much tighter grip on centralized state power, almost failed much later in the century to overcome Aragonese pride. Ferdinand, anxious at the opening of the new century to maintain the overall momentum of conquest *and to take the war into Muslim territory in North Africa as soon as possible,* was prudently leaving the Muslims of his home kingdoms alone. For the time being.

ARAGON AND EMPIRE

Because the world empire that Spain acquired in the sixteenth century was constitutionally run as a Castilian concern, we may think of Castile as the outward-looking, ambitious, and dynamic element in the Hispanic royal consortium, whereas the Crown of Aragon may appear to us to have been lacking (or as being free from?) that consuming drive for imperial domination that took Spanish rule so far round the world so fast. Yet in the Middle Ages it had been the Crown of Aragon that was the Iberian power with a great overseas empire.

Aragonese ambitions in the eastern Mediterranean (and to a lesser extent, in North Africa) were not a thing of the past in 1500. Aragonese aspirations to act as protector of the eastern Christians in the Holy Land and even in Coptic Egypt may seem absurd to us nowadays (at no time did Aragon have the logistical capacity to sustain anything more than a short raid on one of the great ports of the Levant). Whether in the thirteenth century when these ambitious dreams first began to haunt Aragon's foreign relations, or into the early 1500s under Ferdinand, the Aragonese Crown cherished that eastward-looking policy. It is evident in the grandiloquent listing of regnal titles at the opening of documents produced by the royal chancery. (Such lists are obviously of limited significance. After all, the third page of my King James Bible tells me inter alia that he was king of France, a country where he certainly never ruled. But regnal titles may tell us something about aspirations.) Signing the peace treaty with Portugal in 1479, Ferdinand and Isabella list alongside their peninsular and western titles the near eastern ones of "Duke and Duchess of Athens and of Neopatria" (Alba et al. 1952, 7: 128). Still in 1504 Ferdinand, writing officially to the cardinal bishop of Lérida to inform him that Isabella had died, lists after his Spanish and Sicilian titles, but before Granada, that of "King of Jerusalem"(Antonio de la Torre 1966, 6: 393). It might be argued that in such a context lists of a king's realms are little more than idle boasts, but they do show that Ferdinand had not altogether expunged from the records his kingdoms' eastward yearnings. In the days when Spain's treasure came above all from the Indies, neither Ferdinand nor Charles (and certainly not Philip!) ever thought of actually treading American soil, whereas the first two of these three kings campaigned energetically in North Africa (and Philip, from Spanish soil, conducted, up to the point in time when events elsewhere forced him to abandon it, an energetic anti-Muslim foreign policy).

After Castile's successful campaigns against Granada in the 1480s, a small but influential group of Muslim refugees had chosen to make Mamluk lands in the Middle East both a place of refuge and a base from which to launch propaganda against the Hispanic enemy. Among them a former *qadi* (judge) of Granada, Ibn al-Azraq, had first settled in Cairo at the Mamluk court, later became a mufti in Jerusalem (also at the time in Mamluk territory, of course). Spanish Christian military successes against the Nasrid state, culminating in the victory of 1492, were received as unwelcome news in the Middle East, and the rapid overturning and betrayal of that 1492 settlement, the forcible conversions, and then the atrocities that occurred in the campaigns of 1500 thoroughly incensed Muslim opinion in Cairo and elsewhere. Observers feared that the eastern Christians would be made to suffer for what harm Christians were inflicting on Muslims in Spain. It may perhaps seem surprising to those not aware of the extent of Aragonese commitment to an eastern policy that Ferdinand should have dispatched a diplomatic mission to Egypt to attempt to turn aside Mamluk wrath, but in so doing he was not innovating. His advisers will have been well aware that in 1304 Aragon had successfully acted in protection of Coptic churches in Egypt by reminding the Mamluk authorities that mosques in Aragonese territory might become vulnerable to reprisals. The two powers, Mamluk Egypt and Aragon, in theory had no common ground on which to meet and work out a compromise. In practice, in 1304, the Mamluks had been prepared to accede to the requests of the Aragonese ambassador of those days (Alarcón and García de Linares 1940, 35). Nearly two hundred years later, the mission sent by Ferdinand was just as successful.

Yet from Ferdinand's point of view his diplomatic success in Cairo must have had an unfortunate consequence at home. His emissary, Peter Martyr of Anghiera, had pointed out to his Mamluk interlocutors how well treated were the many Muslim subjects of the Crown of Aragon, and this fact was used to reinforce the arguments that the Mamluks should treat their own religious minorities equally well. Ferdinand would have looked very cynical if immediately after boasting of his good record for tolerance in Aragon and Valencia he were to have adopted, in those very territories, a policy of enforced conversion. Ferdinand's freedom of maneuver at home must have been inhibited by the very success of his own diplomatic initiative overseas. No doubt the other domestic factors set out below had their bearing on Aragon's failure to keep in step with Castile over conversion policy, but the ghostly burden of the historical legacy of Aragon's empire in the east (Ultramar) cannot be ignored.

In Egypt the Mamluks, infuriated by the way the Castilian Crown had gone back on quite explicit and detailed promises to respect Islam and its institutions made only ten years earlier at the surrender of Granada, were outraged by some of the atrocities committed. From this dangerous confrontation in which both parties, Mamluks and Spaniards alike, were convinced of their own righteousness, and each stood to lose a great deal, diplomacy managed to find a way for each to back down. Part of the price that Ferdinand paid was that his hands were tied insofar as the conversion of the Aragonese Muslims was concerned.

DOMESTIC POLICY

The domestic roots of Ferdinand's continued toleration are also to be sought in the Middle Ages. Since the thirteenth century, when large numbers of Muslims passed under Aragonese rule and so came to enjoy some degree of royal protection, the Aragonese Crown had in various ways come to be a protector of the interests of these Muslims. If the Aragonese Crown were to relinquish that role, the stability of Aragonese society as a whole might be put at risk. As we will see, within five years of the death of Ferdinand, the Muslims had been converted, and society was indeed soon in social turmoil.

Those who owned the lands that were rented or cultivated by Muslims had economic motives to avoid change. Nobles in particular had often in medieval times given inducements to Muslims to come and work their lands. Little had changed by the beginning of the sixteenth century. A steady drift from royal (*realengo*) to noble estates had taken place because Muslims could be enticed to leave by the better conditions offered by some of the nobles. Muslims both in the Ebro basin and in Valencia excelled in producing high-yield crops on the good irrigable tracts that they tended for Christian lords, and also in dry farming on unirrigated lands (*secano*) to which they were themselves increasingly condemned. Their masters did not want to lose them. Muslims were a vulnerable minority who would show gratitude for a little local protection, for being left alone to live according to the religion of their ancestors. They might not drive such a hard bargain as Christian cultivators. At accession kings of Aragon had been required by their subjects to swear that they would not force Muslims to convert, and that Ferdinand had done (and after him Charles). This oath was included in the ceremony because it was in the interest of many groups to have Muslims securely situated at the base of the social pyramid. However, for those Christians also down at the very bottom, the landless laborers and the urban poor, the Muslims represented competition. The hatred felt for them by the Christian lower classes was building up and was to explode with terrible violence in the revolutionary movement of the early 1520s known as the *germanía*. Under Ferdinand such social forces were still held in check. The promises to protect Muslims made on his accession he had repeated to the Cortes (assembly of estates) of Monzón in 1510, and he kept his word until his dying day.

THE OTHER SIDE OF THE COIN

That the Aragonese Crown both possessed Mudejar subjects in greater numbers than Castile and was much more reluctant than Castile to move toward enforced conversion might be taken to indicate that in the eastern parts of the peninsula Muslims enjoyed some kind of Golden Age under Ferdinand. That would be far from the truth. As Haliczer (1990, 244–45) put it:

> [Despite royal legislation] the *mudéjares* of the Kingdom of Valencia had always lived in a changing and insecure environment marked by constant pressure from the growing Christian population. The pressure from below had been primarily responsible for driving the *mudéjares* from the fertile huerta to the dry farming and mountainous regions in the interior of the kingdom where they remained until the expulsion. The "expulsions" of the fourteenth century also had the effect of reducing the numbers of *mudéjares* in the vicinity of the larger towns, which were now controlled by the Old Christians, but this partial segregation of the population of the kingdom did little to reduce the antagonism between the two communities. To the evident differences in religion, dress, and customs was added the new economic role of the *mudéjares* as the servile tenant farmers of the hated Valencian nobility. As a result the fifteenth and early sixteenth centuries were punctuated by ugly incidents such as the massacre of Valencia's Islamic community in 1455.

VALENCIA

Against such a background of deep-seated insecurity in the not-distant past, it is not surprising that when news of the forcible conversions in Granada broke in early 1500, all Muslims in the eastern kingdoms tended to assume it would be their turn before very long. Meyerson (1991, 91) reports that the executive officers of the municipality of Valencia wrote to Ferdinand as early as February 29, 1500, to tell him of rumors in circulation in the city about an impending conversion: these were having an economically depressing effect on markets. The king accordingly wrote to places with large Muslim populations in the Kingdom of Valencia: to Valencia itself, Játiva, Alcira, Castellon, Villarreal, Oliva, Gandía, Valldigna, Murviedro, the Vall de Uxó, denying the truth of the rumors. He ascribed to "malevolent persons...moved...by some sinister and grave intentions" stories that it "is our intention and will to reduce by force to the holy faith and Christian religion all Moors of the said kingdom." Ferdinand put the blame for the rumors on those who wished to "move all the people against the said Moors, and to seek occasion to riot and rise against them" (91). He denied any intention to set about forcible conversion and took the opportunity to remind those to whom he was writing that "our holy Catholic church in the conversion of the infidels admits neither violence nor any force, but [only] complete freedom and devotion" (92). Should we read into those words that the king was distancing himself from what was going on in Castilian lands? In practical terms Ferdinand ordered his Aragonese *morerías* to be carefully protected and guarded to prevent untoward incidents. Similar reassurances were given with regard to Catalonia in September 1501, and in Valencia the same wording was repeated in February 1502. Of course it was hard to render such reassurances persuasive when everybody knew that in Castile the policy of conversion was being pursued so actively. The Valencian and Aragonese Mudejars were inevitably effected adversely by the crisis, particularly in that their freedom of movement was curtailed. Inland movement to Castile was forbidden, and travel overseas was now banned, now allowed once more (May 1501), now banned again (February 1502).

Mudejars were especially worried that the Inquisition would begin to institute proceedings against them. Even though Muslims may have been aware that they were, strictly speaking, outside the jurisdiction of the Inquisition, they knew that charges might easily be trumped up. A Muslim who tried to persuade a fellow Muslim who had become a convert to Christianity to return to his old beliefs might be subject to an Inquisition trial, for example, and it was easy to lay accusations of proselytism. In 1502, news leaked out that two Muslims were in jail (Meyerson 1991, 59) accused of having dissuaded other Muslims from being baptized. When subsequently the story spread that the two were themselves in process of being prepared for baptism inside the Inquisition building, what had happened in Granada in 1500, a conflagration, seemed about to be repeated in Valencia. In Granada, Cisneros had used the *elche* question to get round the fact that the Capitulations of 1492 entrenched protection for Islam. Proselytizing by Muslims or interference with Christian missionary endeavor might, in Aragon, provide an excuse for action in contravention of what had been promised. Such zealotry would have proved a threat to the security of Ferdinand's regime if it had provoked a rebellion of indignant Muslims in lands easily reached from the North African shore.

One piece of evidence that might be seen as pointing toward a positive will on Ferdinand's part to maintain a Mudejar-type status for Valencia is to be found in his readiness in the later stages of the Granadan War (1489 and after) to grant entry permits into Valencia to a considerable number of Granadan refugees. As Meyerson (1991, 74) reports, "Muslims from Vera, Almería and Granada were settled in a number of Valencian localities." Those fleeing their old homes who had first opted for North African destinations were permitted to switch to Valencia and become the king's vassals there. Ferdinand's willingness to accept fresh Muslim subjects from Granada for his Valencian lands in 1489 is, in my opinion, probably best understood as an easy and short-term solution to an immediate and pressing problem. Exactly as in the case of the Mudejars from Portugal allowed to settle "permanently" in Andalucía, the apparent long-term commitment entered into in Valencia proved to be of relatively short duration, for the fate of the immigrants became merged with that of the larger Muslim communities amongst whom they were placed, and they were to be subject to forcible conversion in the 1520s.

As is well known, Ferdinand was a ruler much admired by Machiavelli.

That in 1502 some of the Valencian Muslims were impelled to emigrate stealthily to North Africa (open emigration was at first forbidden) indicates that they did not trust his promises. The 170 inhabitants of Altea fled in "Turkish" ships one night in 1502 because of a police investigation into a runaway slave. Here we see in action what too simplistically is styled "piracy." As the century advanced there was an ever increasing danger to the coastal regions from small ships coming from North Africa, ships often manned or guided by former inhabitants of the region. Altea was but one early case of a phenomenon endlessly repeated until the very end (Meyerson 1991, 79, 95). What happened may be described as "piracy," because that term is well used of sea-borne raiders who arrive to carry off booty, but it might equally well be described from a different viewpoint as a rescue mission, perhaps even more bluntly as a revenge raid. From Valencia reports came to Ferdinand that a Mudejar from Oliva called Bablaguer was acting as pilot to a squadron of six ships operating out of Oran in April 1501. There has been ambiguity about Mediterranean piracy in many periods of its history, but the two mirror-image ways of looking at this type of activity were never in more acute contradiction than during these population movements of the sixteenth and seventeenth centuries.

It is not surprising that any emigrant group should feel homesickness. The nostalgic desire to return home is almost universal. In 1503, we have perhaps the first manifestation in our period (there could hardly be an earlier example!) of the phenomenon among those Spanish Muslims who had crossed to North Africa. The Christian lords of Benidorm, Polop, and Calpe petitioned Ferdinand to allow their Muslim labor force, who had taken themselves off to North Africa during the disturbances of the previous year (when the kingdom was in an uproar because it was assumed that the Granada policy would be put into force in Valencia), to come home. If they were to be persuaded that it was safe to do so, assurances would need to be given to them that they would not be prosecuted for their actions. Ferdinand did allow them back. Attitudes toward emigrants who wish to return illustrate the uncertainties of Christians toward their Muslim fellow-Spaniards (did they really want to see them permanently lost to Spain?). In the same way, the attitudes of the emigrants themselves illustrate the contradictions of their position (once in North Africa, were they to rejoice at being delivered at last from religious persecution or grieve over a lost homeland and a way of life that could not be reconstructed?).

THE INSTITUTIONS OF LATE MUDEJAR ISLAM

Although the Mudejars of Valencia after 1500 never recovered the confidence that they had had before Isabella determined to convert their coreligionists in neighboring kingdoms, they continued, until the time of the *germanía* in the early 1520s, to possess effective institutions of their own, derived from Islamic times. In describing what he found in his valuable exploration of the archives, Meyerson uses terminology such as *qadi* (judge) and *faqih* (mayor). These, by their apparently pristine Arabic form, seem to convey that in the period he is describing the officials who bore such designations filled roles that were substantially identical to similarly named officials in Islamic countries. There is a trap here. That Valencia's institutions were *derived* from those of the region's Islamic past is not to be denied, but the linguistic changes that had taken *qadi* and brought about the creation of Castilian alcalde, for example, served to reflect profound *institutional* changes in the nature of that office. In speaking of this period, it is, therefore, perhaps less misleading to use the evolved Castilian (or Catalan) designations than the original Arabic ones in the way that Meyerson does. The chief justice of the local Islamic community who was known as the *alcalde* cannot be said to have in reality fulfilled the functions of the *qadi* as they might have been exercised within any truly Islamic polity. And the same applies *mutatis mutandis* to all the other offices.

The essence of the compact on which Mudejar status rested was that the Christian ruler, in exchange for the political loyalty of his Muslim subjects, agreed to respect their separate religion and to preserve, insofar as possible, their Islamic legal system. In general, the Aragonese rulers strove to keep their part of the bargain, as they understood it, at least, but the logical flaws inherent in such a juridical compromise meant that as the years went by the Islamic law itself became eroded. The period that concerns us here, from 1500 to, say, 1520, is at the very end of that process of erosion. (It would be impossible to review the whole process here and now; see Harvey 1990, 103–14.)

Perhaps the type of change that had been taking place is best illustrated by the *hadd* offenses. These are those offenses for which a set penalty (*hadd*) is laid down in the Koran, and often this may be another way of referring to the death sentence, although, of course, that is not the only penalty prescribed by the Koran. The orthodox Muslim view is that an explicit statement of God's will embodied in the sacred text should be obeyed and not modified or "interpreted." For Christian monarchs the worst problems arose because the royal courts could find themselves, in difficult cases, taking over the function of court of last appeal, even where those cases had been adjudicated upon in the courts of first instance according to Islamic law. If the set penalty applicable for, let us say, duly proven adultery, was death by lapidation, should that be the penalty handed down by the king, if the case came up before him and the findings of guilt confirmed? The Aragonese authorities seem to have been unwilling to apply some of the penalties of the code.[2]

In capital cases in Aragon and Valencia, in an exercise of the royal prerogative of clemency, lesser penalties than lapidation were regularly substituted. And in consequence some offenders would try to get their case brought before the Christian courts in some way or other in the hope of milder treatment. In other cases a Muslim plaintiff might not object to what was effectively a switch of jurisdiction because he hoped to avoid the full rigors of the code that was ostensibly being applied. The Islamic

2. Rather as the British House of Lords, sitting in the late twentieth century as vestigial court of ultimate appeal in capital cases sent up to them from those constitutionally independent Caribbean states that still retain the death penalty, has found itself in difficulties. The death sentence is a form of punishment long since abolished in their lordships' own domestic jurisdiction, and indeed it survives nowhere in Europe. The court has in recent years been unwilling to confirm death sentences brought before it.

purist might well object that this was not really the Islamic system at all, but instead a new mixed system. And in the case of the accusation of adultery the rigorist might also point to the undesirable way the system often worked in practice. Royal justice would offer in substitution for lapidation a sentence of enslavement. The convicted adulteress (the ac-cused was almost always a woman, of course), having lost the protection of her husband and of her parents, might perhaps then be recruited into the royal brothels (strictly and centrally regulated in this society) and so became a prostitute. Whatever else this was, it was hardly an applica-tion of Koranic law! As Meyerson puts it: "The Valencian documenta-tion records a surprisingly large number of cases of Mudejar adultery in which the Islamic death penalty was normally commuted by the Chris-tian authorities to enslavement to the king." Most of the dossiers studied by Meyerson naturally belong to a somewhat earlier period, but that of Xuxa of Villamarchante is dated May 6, 1504, so within this final period.

Similar distortions of the Islamic code occurred in relation to other as-pects of the law. It was not that the Christian authorities intentionally set out to subvert the shari'a. The need to modify that law in some circum-stances had been felt already under many Islamic regimes, so that some of the modifications employed in Valencia may well have been continu-ations of preexistent local practices or customs ('urf, "customary law") and not innovations of the Christian conquerors. Nevertheless, the over-all effect was to create an ever increasing gap between the structures of the society in which these Spanish Muslims lived and the Islamic world proper.

If, as we have just seen, the *alcalde* was not exactly a *qadi* but some-thing nearer to being a royally appointed administrator, the *alfaquí* was not exactly the same as a *faqih* ("Islamic lawyer") within an Islamic so-ciety. In Spain, most villages of Muslims had their own *alfaquí* as their guide, it would seem, not only in strictly legal matters. Such lawyers at this period might well have studied outside Valencia, and there are records of travel permits being given for study in Granada, Tunis, and elsewhere. As the century wore on, such training became increasingly difficult and dangerous to arrange (hence, no doubt, the demand for the "do-it-yourself" manuals in the vernaculars mentioned in chapter 5). The appeal addressed to Charles in 1526 (Meyerson 1991, 265) after the forcible conversion had taken place makes a particular point of stressing the importance of the *alfaquíes* to the "new converts."

Alfaquíes would appear to be the word adopted by the Romance vernac-ulars for the Islamic clergy and so served to designate the class usually known elsewhere as the *'ulama*. The word *'alim* (Arabic plural *'ulama*, Romance plural *alimes*) did occur in Spain for the Islamic scholar, but it was only in use among Muslims, never among Christians. Even among Muslims the term was far less frequently used than *alfaquí*. The *alfaquí* within his home territory worked to preserve the Islamic law and must often have been successful in his endeavors, for a very great deal did live on from the past. Nevertheless, it would be misleading to suggest that the Islamic legal heritage had not been modified: it had.

ROYAL PROTECTION FOR THE MUSLIMS OF ARAGON IN THE EARLY SIXTEENTH CENTURY

If Ferdinand had wished to find an opportunity to back away from his stance of refusing to envisage enforced conversion of his Muslim subjects, if he had wished to make a public declaration bringing his own Kingdom of Aragon (and Valencia) into line with the Castilian domains of the dual monarchy, he might have taken the opportunity to do so in 1510, at the Cortes of Monzón (see Haliczer 1990, 244). But Ferdinand at Monzón continued the well-established Mudejar policy he had inherited; he did what his Cortes asked him to do and swore not to force through conversion of his Muslim subjects. The reason why the estates, summoned to legislate and settle grievances, wished the guarantees of religious freedom for their Muslim fellow Aragonese to be preserved was no doubt that nobles and others among them saw interference with the religious status quo as a threat to their material interests.

THE REVOLTS OF THE *AGERMANTS* IN THE 1520S

The curious way in which the Crown, the nobles, and the Muslims might under some circumstances find they could make common cause against other classes within the body politic is most dramatically demonstrated in the early 1520s during the popular revolt usually known as the *germanía* ("the brotherhood," a revolutionary movement which some nowadays would simplistically see as the prototype of modern popular democratic and, indeed, revolutionary movements). The rebels (*agermanats*), many of whom were drawn from the lower orders of Christian society, fought numerous battles and skirmishes with such forces as the viceroy of Valencia, on behalf of the Crown, was able hastily to muster. The Valencian nobility recognized in these *agermanats* a threat to their privileges and wealth and turned out to repress them with the armed men at their disposal. And since so many of their estates were cultivated by Muslims, the levies raised in this way included many Muslims. Muslims often fought effectively, but whichever way the battles went, they were to be the losers.

In July 1521, for example, when the revolutionary ferment was at its height, the viceroy's army was heavily defeated at the battle of Gandía, and the rebels lost no time in sacking the Moorish quarters of Gandía itself; something similar occurred in Játiva, Guadalest, Polop, and other places. It was not only in their property that the Muslims suffered. The revolutionaries regarded the religious difference between them and the Mudejar cultivators as something to be done away with as a matter of urgency now that they were in a position to act. They perceived the Mudejars as threatening their status in society, and in this respect their analysis was no doubt correct. The economic bargaining power of the Christian poor was undercut by the competition of Muslim neighbors. The tactic adopted by the Christian mobs had a mad logic: eliminate competition by making the Muslims into Christians. Such "conversion" was in these revolutionary circumstances a summary process: a mob would arrive at a settlement of Muslims and call on them to convert— on the spot. Christenings might be affected on occasion by aspersion from a bucket filled from an irrigation ditch, although in other cases priests were found to carry out the baptisms (if indeed one may use that solemn word to describe an act inflicted upon a nonconsenting adult).

By spring 1522 the political tide was turning, especially after the death of the Christian rebel leader Vicent Peris. The end of the year saw the authority of the Crown reestablished. The Muslims (now of course "newly converted" according to their tormentors) might have expected gratitude from the Crown, for in several battles they had played a crucial role fighting on the royal side; gratitude from the nobles too, for they had loyally stood by their masters. Many Muslims had been killed or injured.

Clearly a correct Christian interpretation of the situation ought to have been that since these Muslims had not freely chosen to become Christians, their "conversion" counted for nothing. Some Christians did take this view, but many did not. The necessary element of free will had been present when the Muslims agreed to be baptized, it was held: after all they could, instead, have *chosen* to refuse—and so opted for death! The Muslims thus received no reward for their loyalty to the Crown and to their lords. The *agermanats* were indeed punished for what they had done, but the "conversions" that they had inflicted on their Muslim neighbors in the course of that rebellion were solemnly declared to have been effective all the same. How after solemn deliberations this decision was reached is a sordid tale that reflects no honor on the junta of theologians appointed to look into the matter. Although Charles V[3] was ultimately

3. The monarch so well known on the international stage by his imperial regnal number as Charles V will of course often appear in Spanish documentation as Charles I, etc. In a general work such as this, the form that is more widely familiar has been preferred.

content to have the *germanía* push through the conversions in this way, constitutional decency and his respect for the sacredness of oaths demanded that there should be some formal investigation of the question of the promises he had made at the time of his accession. In 1518 he had sworn not to force his Muslim subjects into conversion. The Vatican was consulted, and on November 3, 1525, Charles was able to write to the inquisitor-general enclosing the papal brief that authorized him to retract those of his promises that concerned the Muslims (not the rest of his promises, of course! Lea 1901, 139).

The secular authorities in Valencia were informed that the Inquisition had been empowered to act in such Morisco cases (once the "conversion" had taken place, the Holy Office was deemed to have jurisdiction). The publication of the edict forcing through the expulsion of the Muslims of Catalonia, Aragon, and Valencia came on November 25, and for the Aragonese (and also Catalans) a deadline of January 26, 1526 was set (in Valencia it was December 31, 1525). I have said "expulsion," but I think it reasonable to interpret this as no more than a device aimed not at actually ridding the lands of the Crown of Aragon of its "Moors" but at putting them under such intolerable pressure that they would convert. Tactics were thus adopted in Aragon by Charles in 1525 that were similar to those used by Isabella in 1500–2 when she was dealing with the Castilian Muslims. In 1525, an apparent choice between conversion or expulsion was offered, but the expulsion option was made so difficult to achieve that it was in practice almost nonexistent. Documentation for those going into exile was to be issued at Sieteaguas on the Aragonese border with Cuenca, and the route to be followed then was across the whole breadth of inland Castile through Madrid and Valladolid until finally they reached the sea at La Coruña! And if those that opted for this insane overland deviation failed to embark on time, their goods were to be confiscated and they themselves were to be enslaved. Some very few do seem to have followed the prescribed route and reached North Africa via France (Lea 1901, 140). The wording of the initial decree did not make explicit how the only alternative offered, conversion, was to be put into effect, but all who did not leave the country by December 8 were told they would need proof of baptism.

BRAY DE REMINJO

For most of these events, which had such far-reaching consequences for Spain's Muslims (for they meant that their religion would from then onward be driven completely underground), we have to try to understand the whole story in the round on the basis of what may be learned from the various records of the Christian side only. The Spanish Christian sources are often so abundant that there is no great difficulty in constructing a balanced account, but it is none the less extremely fortunate that for this key moment, the forcible conversion in Aragon, we have a brief but moving account from the Muslim side as well. It is contained in an *al-jamiado* manuscript, now in Cambridge University Library (MS Dd.9.49; see Harvey 1958). This work will be examined in detail in chapter 5 in the context of the whole corpus of Hispano-Muslim writings, but here our focus must be exclusively on the reminiscences of one individual, the *alfaquí* of the village of Cadrete, not far from Saragossa, Bray de Reminjo by name.[4]

A marginal marker drawing attention to this particular passage in the manuscript is a pointer reading: *"When they baptized us,"* and in the main text we find:

I recall the year of our conversion, that a most honored friend of mine, someone with whom I enjoyed great friendship, a Carmelite friar called Fray Estéban Martel, a great friend of the Moors (*moros*) of this kingdom, more than other places. When he learnt that we had been sentenced to become Christians by force, he sent one of the servants of his father's household for me, for at that time I was residing in the mosque of Cadrete. I immediately did what it was my duty to do, and as I reached his house, he stood waiting for me. As soon as he saw me he greeted me warmly, and then began to sob, half covering his face. He had me sit at his table, for it was mealtime, and served me pomegranates and Valencian conserve, and next after that [or "as a final course," *a la postre*] a piece of roast meat. However, he ate nothing, because it was Passion Sunday.[5] After we had eaten, we entered the study of his father's house, and with tears in his eyes he said to me: 'Bray, Sir, what do you think of all this upheaval, and of the un-Christian way in which you are being used? For my part, I say, and it grieves my heart and soul to do so, that they have done you a great wrong (*sinrrazón*). I replied that I was horrified that His Holiness had given his consent to any such thing and decreed it. He answered me saying that His Holiness had not consented, but that we had been sentenced by the

4. I first transcribed this name as Baray, but I here adopt the form Bray (a shortened diminutive of Ibrahim) as suggested to me by Dr. L. Bernabé of Alicante, whose help with this passage I gratefully acknowledge.

5. The order of the courses in this meal I cannot explain at all, nor can any of the many specialists consulted by me! Passion Sunday is, of course, the fifth Sunday in Lent, that is, two Sundays before Easter Day, and the beginning of Passiontide, so a day for a Carmelite to exercise particular abnegation.

Mantuan decree.[6] His Holiness had signed the sentence through the deceit of certain French[7] cardinals who conspired against us. After many other things I said they had had small regard for the honor of their God, and that the offence that they did Him every year in the streets[8] ought to have been enough. He replied, showing more awareness than I had thought, saying that we were not in a period of grace, but of weeping.

This friend was so moved by compassion for us that he never ceased to argue before prelates and councils [*cabildos*—a word applicable both to cathedral chapters and to municipal councils] against all those who had given their consent to any such thing and to inveigh against them. Together with many others he issued a summons to protest and to argue strenuously against His Majesty and his ministers. He would have done so to some effect if he had not died within two months. He charged me to pray for him (*le hiciese obsequios*)[9] if he should die, for when I visited him he was sick, and I wept when he died, for he was a loyal friend.

6. I am quite uncertain about this expression. I am not aware that there is or ever was any enactment, etc., called the "Mantuan decree," and it is not impossible that "Mantuano" in the manuscript may be a garbled version of some unfamiliar ecclesiastical technicality that Bray misheard or misremembered: it must be borne in mind that we do not have Estéban Martel's own words here, but what would have been written down only later by Bray, and that Bray's record then had to be copied at least once before it was incorporated into the manuscript book called *El breve compendio de nuestra santa ley y sunna,* of which work in turn we seem to have a copy and not a holograph original. There was thus ample scope for corrupt transmission. The only explanation of the wording as it stands that occurs to me is that Martel is thinking of the deliberations of the Council of Mantua of 1459. This was the council at which Pius II endeavored to start a crusade against the Ottomans and so was a notable papal summons to arms against the Muslim enemy. But would that council have been remembered in Aragon more than sixty years later? I would have thought not.

7. Perhaps the Carmelite is here attempting to deflect blame from the pope (and the Church in general) toward the French—relying perhaps on the Spanish chauvinistic sentiments that mention of the French would evoke.

8. This perhaps refers to the processions of Holy Week, which were about to take place, and so would be in his mind. For a Christian these are a communal demonstration of piety, but for a Muslim who (a) rejects outright the doctrine of the Trinity and so rejects the idea that God had a son, and that that son was a comember of the Trinity, and (b) denies that the revered prophet Jesus himself suffered on the cross, the parade will have been at once blasphemy against God and a shocking demonstration of lack of respect for the prophet Jesus. If Muslims were forced to watch the street parades of Holy Week, they would have been distressed by what they would have felt to be a public offense (*denuesto*).

9. Possibly more specifically, "that I should say a funeral office for him," although I am not aware of the existence of any set forms of Islamic prayer available for use in this way at the death of a Christian.

From then onward our religion became ever weaker. Within three months they closed the mosques, and for this reason many of our scholars went abroad until the persecution had died down (*hasta que fue su duelo reposado*). (Cambridge MS. Dd.9.49 f. 4)

Dr. Bernabé, in addition to the correction he put forward to the way Bray's name is vocalized (see n. 3 above), also proposed that we should read Cadreita (the name of a village in Navarre) where I had read Cadrete in Aragon. This emendation would have the merit of overcoming some problems with regard to the chronology of the activities of the Young Man of Arévalo (because Navarre was forcibly converted in 1515 and not in the 1520s). Nevertheless I am reluctant to adopt the proposed emendation because the manuscript reading Cadrete is so clear. The Martel family was well known and active in the *fuerista* movement of Aragonese resistance to Castilian centralizing policies, so a mansion (with a room set apart as a study) belonging to a family prepared to make a stand against the imposition of conversion fits entirely into such an Aragonese background, whereas we know of no such Martel family in Navarre, and moreover, Cadreita is indeed an unlikely location for a residence of such a kind. Navarre's resistance to the Castilian takeover, after the duke of Alba made his display of Castilian military superiority in 1512, collapsed almost completely.

A very great deal might be said, ought to be said, about Bray de Reminjo. One of our problems is that the only source we have relating to him is this Cambridge manuscript. This work often leaves the reader uncertain whether a particular anecdote is to be interpreted as narrated about himself by Bray, or whether it is material relating to the Young Man of Arévalo. This question is discussed further in chapter 5.

Bray's friend, Fray Estéban Martel was certainly not the only one to protest against the anti-Muslim (Mantuan?) decrees. It must be borne in mind that, quite outside the context of relations between the two religions, in 1525 various interest groups from the Kingdom of Aragon were finding it necessary to send representatives to court to lobby on a great number of matters. The special mission (Colas 1988, 535; Lea 1901, 88, citing Andrés de Uztarroz 1663, book 2, 134) seeking to preserve the right of Aragon's Muslims to their old Mudejar status (as promised in Charles's coronation oaths) was entrusted to the count of Ribagorza and to Jerónimo Roda.

In parallel to these developments and in this same general period, but outside the Aragonese lands, there was an attempt being made by Christian authorities in Granada to increase pressure on backsliding converts. This gave rise to a Granadan mission to the Crown, but in that case the mission was headed from the outset by noble Granadan converts (*nuevos cristianos*).

The Christian Aragonese envoys received no satisfactory answer to their representations apart from a brief stay of execution. A further proclamation dated December 22 reinforced the conversion by banning all travel out of the kingdom by the new converts and ordering absentees back to their homes. From this point onward, Islamic public worship was illegal in Aragonese lands. Representations on behalf of the new converts achieved very little. The Aragonese envoys were instructed to point out that these particular Mudejars had never set out to convert anybody (a *nadie an pervertido*), they caused no trouble (*no son escandalosos*), and were not in touch with the Muslims in North Africa.

With the Christian nobility failing to secure any concessions for them, the Muslims of Aragon now undertook negotiations on their own behalf. Twelve religious scholars (*alfaquíes*) went to court to try to strike a deal with Charles's ministers directly. It would be naive to suppose that, at this distance in time, we will ever be able to arrive at the exact truth of transactions of this sort. What was going on was that a group of the sovereign's subjects offered to pay extra taxation (an extra "service," *servicio,* as the terminology of the period had it) in exchange for a favor. Groups other than the Muslims had struck similar deals in the past in order to achieve some political or practical objective, and others were to do so in the future. But it is reasonable to infer that the greater part of such deals, like the greater part of icebergs, has by the nature of things to be below the surface, out of sight. For a consideration (we hear of varying amounts paid over), a *concordia* or agreement was reached on January 6, 1526, whereby a stay of execution of forty years was accorded to the ex-Muslims: the anti-Muslim measures were to be shelved. Muslims were to accept baptism (however dubious were the circumstances under which they had been baptized), and they were to be allowed time to forget their old ways and learn new ones. During this time they were to be exempt from the attentions of the Inquisition.

There are indications that the willingness of the Muslims to accept "conversion" in this way is to be linked to advice they received from their *alfaquíes* that deceit in the profession of faith was permissible, and some Old Christians were by now becoming aware of this aspect of Islamic teaching (see Guevara 1956, 543). We may conclude that the Oran fatwa or some other document in a similar sense was circulating in Aragonese territories as well as in Granada and Castile.

Forcible conversion in the lands of the Crown of Aragon was thus a protracted process that was not initiated until after the death of

Ferdinand. Kriegel (1995, 144; see also Redondo 1979, 207–62) speaks of it in the following terms:

> As for the conversion of the Moors of Aragon, this was achieved in three phases. In the first, mass conversions occurred during the war of the *germanías,* 1520–1522, that is to say that the initiative did not come down from above. In the second, the commission set up by the Inquisition in 1524 made use of the distinction between "absolute" force and "conditional" force which had first been propounded in the thirteenth century in relation to forcible conversions of Jews, and it ruled that all the conversions which had occurred were valid. In the third, Charles completed the task after his victory over the French at Pavia in 1525, laying it down that all Muslims not converted after a named date would be expelled (while at the same time taking steps to ensure that in practical terms it was impossible for them to leave the Peninsula).

It is at first sight puzzling that the victory over the French came to be tied in with the fate of Aragon's Muslims. One anecdote recounted by Lea (1901, 81) from Bleda's *Defensio fidei in causa neophytorum* may provide an explanation. When Francis I of France was brought to Spain as a prisoner after his defeat, he ungraciously expressed his surprise at the Muslims he saw as he looked out through the window of his enforced residence at the castle of Benisanó. They were laboring on the Sabbath in this Christian land. As Lea reminds us, the project of having his Muslim subjects baptized was one that Charles had long cherished, so that his French prisoner's taunts cannot have been the only reason for his adoption of such a policy, but all the same it is not impossible that the incident did goad (or shame) him into action. There is some irony here if Francis took the moral high ground in this way, so shortly before cynically and openly breaking his solemn word to Charles by failing to keep the terms whereby he was eventually freed from detention.

The convocation of the parliamentary body for Aragon, the Cortes, in 1528 at Monzón (Colas 1988, 535) might have given another chance for such matters to be aired, and in more propitious circumstances that would probably have happened, since the Crown had no interest in prolonging the period of uncertainty unavoidably. All three estates petitioned Charles to exempt the converts from the attentions of the Inquisition. But the actual "conversions" as such were not repudiated.

ARMED RESISTANCE

When faced with compulsory conversion, not all Muslims quietly did what they were told. In the Sierra de Espadán (Castellón), the village of Almonacid (not to be confused with the Almonacid de la Sierra in the Morisco zone of Aragon) held out from October 1525 until February 1526, when the place was taken by assault (Lea 1990, 141, see esp. n. 11). At the village of María they hoped against hope for the appearance on their side of the legendary figure of the Moor Alfatimi riding on a green horse, and when he did not come, they surrendered. The fierceness of the resistance in this region may be explained by the confluence of several factors. The numbers of Muslims were such that in places they could fight on more even terms; the mountainous terrain made defense easy. Moreover, the Muslims of the area had long enjoyed the protection of the duke of Segorbe, Alonso de Aragón, an aristocrat who had been most unwilling to carry out the conversions as instructed. In the natural mountain redoubt of the Sierra de Espadán there gathered those Muslims determined to make a last stand: not only local Muslims but also men from other areas, even from Aragon to the north. They elected a leader who took the name of Selim Almanzó, or al-Mansur. One notes that almost invariably when the desperate Muslims did take up arms they assumed names evoking great days of the heroic past of al-Andalus.

The first Christian expeditionary force sent up into the hills was 3,000 strong, but it was the duke of Segorbe who was in command. He not only failed to drive the Muslims out of their encampments, he himself became besieged in Onda. What put some determination into a renewed Christian assault was an atrocity story that did the rounds. Allegedly communion wafers were stolen from a church at Chilches, and the scandal was exacerbated by the consequent decision to postpone the Corpus Christi processions of May 31. With their religious zeal thus aroused and with the license for pillage and murder that was provided by the plenary indulgence *a culpa et a poena* sent by the pope to those joining the army, the 4,000 local troops fought fiercely, and alongside them 3,000 seasoned German soldiers intended for service in Italy who had been diverted by the emperor and turned against the Muslims. The attack on the mountain strongholds came in September. The Spanish forces fought with cruel determination, but they were ready to accept some surrenders, probably because those who at this stage were taken prisoner could be sold as slaves. The subsequent massacre was blamed on the Germans. There are many examples in the history of warfare of atrocities occurring when elite professionals such as these German *tercios* come up against determined resistance from irregulars. The professionals presumably take it as an affront to their pride. In an assault on one hill, of the 72 casualties on the Christian side, 33 were Germans. From then on no prisoners were taken, and 5,000 Muslims are said to have been killed. The few who escaped death were those who straggled over the mountains to hide for a time in other valleys (Sierra de Bernia, Guadalest, Bernia) perhaps to slip away by sea to North Africa.

A HISTORICAL WATERSHED: "MORISCOS"

After 1526 there were certainly many Muslims in Spain, but they all had to be *crypto*-Muslims, and the public profession of faith (*idhan*), an act of such crucial importance in Islam, could no longer be heard in the land.

We would no doubt know much more of this period if official historiography had not tended to eliminate the pro-Aragonese accounts from the historical record. Andrés de Uztarroz seems to have managed to secure an exemption from the ban that otherwise affected Aragonese historians (Carrasco 1969, 58 n. 9). We have seen that Bray de Reminjo, when faced with the edict of forcible conversion, turned to his Carmelite friend Estéban Martel, who, from then until his death soon after, busied himself with arguing the Mudejars' case. One Jerónimo Martel was at the end of the sixteenth century an official *cronista de Aragon,* but in the early years of the seventeenth century he was not only deprived of his post, but even suffered the loss of the *Anales* that he had written. They were destroyed because, as Carrasco put it (1969, 23 n. 28), "he had given them a slant that was frankly constitutionalist" (*por haber dado a éstos una orientación francamente fuerista*). There were very many motives quite unconnected with the Morisco problem that might have led Aragonese local patriots to come into conflict with "Castilian" hegemony; the authoritarian attempt to control the way that history has been written has until recent times meant that access to this Aragonese side of the Morisco story has not been easy.

There continued to exist throughout the sixteenth century a linkage between the old *fuerista* aristocracy of the kingdom and the Morisco subject population, and certainly until the end of our period this region was the one in all the peninsula where conditions proved most propitious for the preservation of vestiges of Islamic culture. Regional differences as between Valencia, Catalonia, and Aragon proper subsisted. Nevertheless, the Morisco problem was handled in broadly similar ways in the various areas belonging to the Crown of Aragon. All the *nuevos convertidos de moros,* all the Moriscos, to use the modern historian's term, were now on the same legal footing, even though in some areas, it was true that various complicities might tend to alleviate the sufferings of the crypto-Muslims, and various feuds might exacerbate them.

So it came about that from the mid-1520s onward all the Muslims of
Spain, without exception, whatever their antecedents, had been subjected
to obligatory if perfunctory conversion. Their religious status was now
everywhere the same. In the eyes of the Spanish state and of the Christian
church they were all, at least nominally, Christians. It was certainly not
the case, however, that they had been reduced to uniformity, nor was the
treatment accorded to them by their Christian rulers uniform. In addition,
from the middle of the sixteenth century onward, Islam in Spain as an
underground religion was beginning to develop some characteristics that
marked it off from orthodox Islam as it existed and exists elsewhere in
the world, in the main because of the distorting effects of the enforced
retreat of this essentially public religion into clandestinity. The sustained
campaign to eradicate Islam from Spanish soil was led by the Inquisition,
but there is no reason to suppose that the Old Christian population at large
was not behind the Inquisitors in their endeavor. And to make things
worse, from the crypto-Muslim point of view, in this period when these
native-born Spaniards were denied the right to be anything other than
Catholic Christians, in the Muslim world their status as true Muslims was
by some called into question. Muslims in genuinely Islamic lands, noting
ill-defined differences, might well regard refugees, when they arrived
from Spain, as being of suspect orthodoxy. The apparently Christian
air that seemed to cling to the refugees was not welcomed. The heroic
determination of these people to cleave to the faith of their forebears, so
impressively attested in the Moriscos' own surviving writings (to which
we can add their refusal to buckle under Inquisitorial interrogation—as
we now know from the Inquisition's own archives) ought to have evoked
the admiration of their coreligionists, but did not always do so. As we
have seen in chapter 2, already at the beginning of the century the mufti
from Oran, Ahmad Bu Jum'a had been impressed by their fortitude in
adversity (*al-qabidin 'ala dinihim k'al-qabid 'ala'l-jamr,* he said of them,

"holding fast to their religion like a man clutching hot coals"), but not all approved of the retreat of the faith into clandestinity.

MUSLIMS IN CASTILE FROM THE 1520S: A POLICY OF ASSIMILATION

The earliest example of the Inquisition concerning itself directly with the converts from Islam in Old Castile, noted by Tapia (1991, 224), is in an Inquisitorial inspection of 1523 that took place in Segovia. Assimilation was to be achieved in Segovia by moving the newly converted out of the districts that had, toward the end of the Middle Ages (in the early 1480s) been designated as *morerías,* and forcing them to live only in houses where they would have as their next-door neighbors reliable Old Christians. Neither Old Christian nor ex-Muslim New Christian inhabitants liked the sound of this. Social engineering of this kind is rarely popular. It was probably doubly unwelcome among the ex-Muslims because only a generation or so earlier, in Segovia, when they had been obliged to move *into* the *morería,* they had lost money on the consequent enforced property transactions. Now, fifty years later, the Inquisition was in favor of shifting them *out* of their safe retreat—and without compensation. For Inquisitors and other Christian officials, it was virtually impossible to get information on what was going on inside the old closely knit communities such as this *morería;* there was a protective barrier of silence. The authorities wanted to force the converts out into the open. If the newly converted were made to live unsegregated lives, the Inquisition could hope that their Old Christian neighbors would be willing to give evidence against the incomers (Cardaillac 1979, 21–31).

On the Christian side, there was no unanimity on the question of how to supervise the converts. The diocesan authorities and, under them, the parish clergy, saw the catechism of neophytes as essentially a parochial task. The Inquisitors, so much of whose attention had over the years been focused on dealing with New Christians from Jewish backgrounds, were convinced that in dealing with these other New Christians, the ex-Muslims, they and not the parish clergy should play the leading role. On the Muslim side, the Moriscos (we can in this context call them that) preferred to keep the Inquisition at as great a distance from their affairs as possible. Their motives were not only the obvious ideological and religious ones but financial ones as well. Many aspects of the Inquisition's way of conducting its affairs inevitably reduced its prisoners and their families to poverty. The procedural ease with which it could order the sequestration of the property of those it detained, the absence of limits on the time a case might drag out, the financial penalties that it could impose (and, one might add, the total absence of any provision for the award of compensation for wrongful arrest or for appeal), meant that the Inquisition was able to inflict, besides physical and spiritual torment, eventual financial ruin as well.

Tapia (1991, 225) summarizes the policy differences within the Church on these questions as follows:

> The Council of the Suprema [of the Inquisition] wanted to have the Morisco question exclusively in its hands, but that opinion was not shared by the Inquisitor-General, A. de Manrique, nor, above all, by the Pope, Clement VII. The latter on 2 December 1530 issued a Brief giving the Inquisitor-General the power to regulate the parish clergy when they pronounced absolution to those Moriscos who confessed they had taken part in heretical practices, even where they were "relapsed," that is to say, had reoffended.

Tapia then goes on to point out that the Suprema postponed application of this papal brief until 1535, a policy decision that he explains as arising from a "refusal by the Papacy to back the attempt being made by the Suprema to extend its powers," and he even speaks of a "tactical withdrawal by the Inquisition (*repliegue inquisitorial*)"[1] from 1532 onward insofar the Morisco question was concerned. The situation is by no means clear. What we can say is that the various authorities on the Christian side did not always see eye to eye and that this gave to the Muslims some scant hope of respite.

THE *JUNTA* OF 1526 IN GRANADA

In 1526 under the direct impulse of the Emperor Charles V there met in the Capilla Real in Granada a conclave (*junta*) of theologians to investigate the Moriscos question: this marks an important landmark in the evolution of Castilian policy. It was, of course, primarily concerned with the converted Muslims of the former Nasrid kingdom and with ensuring that the mass conversions of the opening years of the century had been effective. There was a separate and specific Granadan problem. But it can have escaped the attention of nobody that policy was being revised and tightened up in the 1520s across the peninsula against the background of the recent forcible conversions in the lands of the Crown of Aragon. Charles, present himself in Granada in 1526, may reasonably have felt that the time had come to step back and take a considered view of what was to be done. The emperor was under pressure from at least two sides:

---

1. Tapia here identifies his source for this description of the period 1530–42 as noted in García Carcel (1980, 20). For the parish clergy and the "relapsed," he uses J. P. Dedieu in Cardaillac (1983, 519 n. 72).

from churchmen, who wished him to take more energetic action in order to transform merely superficial conversions into true ones, and on the other hand, from Granadan dignitaries, members both of the old settler Christian aristocracy and of those formerly Muslim families once prominent in Nasrid society who had opted for conversion and collaboration. These latter had, by and large, proved extremely faithful servants of the new Spanish regime, and they now sought the respect and consideration in the Christian world that they felt was their due. However, the new administrative class in Granada was less and less willing to accord this to them. At the *junta* the case for the ex-Muslims was presented to the Crown by Fernando Venegas, by Miguel de Aragón, and by Diego López Benexara. Far from displaying the contrition that many churchmen felt might have been appropriate, these emissaries did not shrink from listing the many grievances of the converts. They must have had some hope that their appeals would be listened to. After all, in the campaigns against the rebel *Comuneros* in 1524, many of the converts, Juan de Granada, Boabdil's brother included, had fought loyally on the royal side (Lea 1901, 214, citing Mármol 1600, 164). The sessions given over to the study of this thorny problem were presided over by the Inquisitor-General, Cardinal Manrique, and perhaps the key contributor to the debates was the recently appointed and energetic bishop of Guádix, Gaspar de Avalos. The outcome of their deliberations, embodied in the Edict of Granada of December 7, 1526 (Lea 1901, 215; or better, Gallego and Gámir 1968, 198 doc. 31) did nothing to redress ex-Muslim grievances. Quite the reverse: for those gathered in conclave in Granada had in mind above all else not a smooth political solution but "the extirpation of the errors in which [new] Christians find themselves." All that this document (*cédula*) offered by way of religious concessions was an amnesty for past offenses, and that can have done nothing to reassure crypto-Muslims. They will have been aware already that an amnesty was of dubious advantage to them: it was a device that, in the hands of a skilled Inquisitor, would in the longer run only serve to ensnare them. Any "former" Muslims who were so unwise as to make use of it would find they were expected to delate on all their past associates; and, if at some future time people who had benefited from an amnesty had fresh charges leveled against them, they would also be open to accusations of insincerity if not worse.

A clear warning that henceforward converts would be watched from close quarters was the message conveyed by the decision to transfer the Inquisition office, hitherto based in Jaen, to Granada. The Edict of December 7, 1526, to which reference has already been made, had set out to eliminate a range of manifestations of local culture and identity: the

Arabic language, local dress and costume, jewelry, baths. Only midwives who were Old Christians were to attend confinements. To make sure that the planned measures were implemented, it was the Inquisition rather than the parish clergy that was charged with the task of supervision. Since the Inquisition had been so effective elsewhere, "it is desirable that henceforward there should be an Inquisition in this city of Granada and in its diocese, and that . . . the Archbishop of Seville, Inquisitor-General, should appoint persons of learning and authority to administer it" (Gallego and Gámir 1968, 200). If the full and detailed measures had been enforced effectively, perhaps the Granadan identity might indeed have been extirpated. It was the whole inherited culture that was being banned, and not just the religion itself. Whether it was the ornamenting of women's hands with henna patterns or the practice of medicine as in the old days, the new measures tried to root out all reminders of the past.

In response, to attempt to organize their self-defense, the New Christians met and raised money, 80,000 ducats as some reports have it, to procure from the emperor a stay of execution. The fact that the authorities were indeed prepared to consider such a transaction cannot fail to surprise us. The justification for the actions which the Christians had taken, and were to take, against the newly converted was that Christians sincerely believed that they had an obligation of a religious nature that forced them to act. How could such an obligation be reconciled with the acceptance of what to modern eyes looks like a bribe? No doubt Charles did not see things in that way. Right until the very end, until the Expulsion, it continued to be true that money could often buy for the former Muslims some amelioration in their conditions, a respite, but equally from this point onward the ultimate policy objectives were clear: conversion together with complete acculturation for those who wished to stay, expulsion for those who did not.

Gaspar de Avalos had in this affair, thanks to his missionary zeal, enhanced his reputation and in 1528 was appointed to the archbishopric of Granada. In his place in the see of Guadix there came Antonio de Guevara. In other contexts there would be a great deal to be said about this Franciscan brought up at Court. As Redondo has shown in his study, *Antonio de Guevara et l'Espagne de son temps* (1976, especially 54), Guevara, like so many other intellectuals of his day, was himself a man with a racially dubious background, and this may help to explain some of his attitudes. A truly gifted writer, he enjoyed enormous success not only in his own day but long after. Critics in our days tend to handle an author such as Guevara somewhat gingerly. He may have been one of the foremost men of letters in the early to middle sixteenth century, but his work cannot be forced easily into the stereotype categories now in vogue.

For all his devotion to Renascence classical themes and his cultivation of a Ciceronian style, he was a court preacher in a medieval mold; and for all his courtly upbringing (he had been a page to the Catholic Monarchs), he was yet somehow endowed with the common touch. One suspects that that may explain the relative eclipse of his literary reputation in modern times. Some of his works were true best sellers. And because he does not fit easily into any politically correct modern classificatory pigeonhole, it is tempting to take the easy way out and ignore him. That is not a course open to us, for his close familiarity with the New Christian problem would make him a valuable source, even if he had not been such a very successful author.

Guevara was appointed to the Granadan *junta* of 1525–26, no doubt because of his considerable experience in the kingdom of Valencia in New Christian parishes, so that in his person he reminds us how what had hitherto been two separate policies, that of Aragon and that of Castile, were tending to come closer to each other (although even until the end they never merged completely). The policy Guevara stood out for was energetic evangelism. He boasts in his *Familiar Epistles* (*Epistolas familiares*) of having baptized 27,000 in Valencia! Manifestations of purely secular "Moorish" culture (such as the application of henna designs to the skin as mentioned above) he wished to see banned, just as he wanted to end what he saw as religious practices derived from the Islamic past. The 1526 edicts embody in their wording just the sort of vigorous measures Guevara desired. A little later, and by then promoted to be bishop of Guadix, he became responsible for translating policy into action on a broad scale. He was to find that not all the authorities wished to push ahead so fast. The powerful viceregal family of the Mondéjars, especially the then captain-general of the Kingdom of Granada, opposed change and was in a position to slow down what Guevara saw as progress. We can see the emergence of two conflicting tendencies among the Christian policymakers in Granada. The Mondéjars, already the second generation of viceregal administrators of the conquered land, had come to feel that they understood "their" Granada and its problems better than newly arrived outsiders. The viceregal dynasty was not concerned with what was by now to them familiar, even reassuring, no longer outlandish. But among churchmen and lawyers trained elsewhere, the old Granadan ways were an alien scandal not to be tolerated. One can find anticipations of such tensions right at the outset at the time of the original Conquest. We have seen that Ferdinand at first sided with his viceroy and blamed the rising of the Muslims in 1499–1500 on Archbishop Cisneros's inexperience in dealing with Moors, but that the king had then adopted that archbishop's policies. We will see in the 1560s how the jealousies and distrust between the military old guard and the new administrators did much to create the conditions which led to the Second Granadan revolt getting so rapidly out of hand, and how then the Royal Council was to adopt the most hawkish of all policy options: eviction from Granada. In 1530, however, between these two extremes, it was the relaxed approach of the settler aristocracy in Granada that prevailed. Guevara never did manage to enforce his ban on henna, and the practice was still an issue a generation later. Nor was Guevara under any misapprehension with regard to the lack of progress on more important matters.

By the third decade of the century there had emerged a sort of de facto ideological and religious truce. That is what it may look like to us as outside observers: for those caught up in the process it was never thought of that way. In 1529 (Gallego and Gámir 1968, 214) we find the royal secretary Juan Vázquez writing to the archbishop of Granada on the subject of the Granadan edicts of 1526, asking for a written report on how much progress had been made. One notes that, in general, the tone is really one of concern for the interests of the Moriscos, not of outright hostility to them. He recommends preventing the secular parish clergy from being beneficiaries in the wills of Moriscos (for example, to obviate corruption.) In February 1530 the same secretary called the Granadan church to account for attempting to ban the *zambra*—as we have seen, a manifestation of Muslim Granadan folklore. As for royal policy at this point, it would seem to have been to let sleeping dogs lie. The former Muslims, at the price of extra contributions to the royal coffers and by bold and determined lobbying, were achieving some success in warding off the attentions of the advocates of an out-and-out campaign of conversion and assimilation. But bribes could not achieve permanent security, only temporary respites.

Throughout this ill-defined middle period from the 1520s up to about 1560, there are two conflicting trends. On the one side, on the part of the Christian authorities, Church and the state alike, there were many attempts at turning the forced and empty conversions into true and sincere incorporation in the Church. There were edicts and decrees, in practical terms there was some sporadic evangelization, but there was no sustained campaign backed by high-level financial support. Such attempts as were made to evangelize the "converts" failed for many reasons. The basic reason, of course, is because the "converts" had never desired conversion. Perhaps the most important flaw in the Christian missionary endeavor was that there was an unresolved contradiction between, on the one hand, the desire that these new converts should be assimilated, made a part of Christian society (the ultimate objective being that there would eventually be no difference between the New Christians and the Old), and, on the other hand, reluctance to fully accept former Muslims, a continuing desire to *exclude* them from Christian society, a conviction that these "converts" were insincere. To put it bluntly and in modern terms: anti-Morisco prejudice.

As for the converts themselves, there were mixed motives present too. Many Moriscos were attached to aspects of the material and intellectual culture of the Christian majority. What they wanted was to participate in society on an equal footing. But others clung resolutely to their distinctive heritage. What they wanted was to be left alone. Contradictory processes were at work. With the passage of time, the minority culture, subjected as it was to increasing persecution, became weaker, but then as time passed, many Moriscos, with understandable human stubbornness, became ever more determined to resist the erosion of their traditions. Over the time span that we are studying, Islam did not ever show signs of quietly fading away.

In consequence, many among the Christian majority grew increasingly indignant when what they saw as their own patience and forbearance went unrewarded. In this middle period on the surface nothing much happened. Persecution was sporadic and on a small scale only. But it was in this period, the late 1520s up to the 1550s, that the "Morisco question" went finally sour. The initial humbug of the "conversions," which Christian apologists so made out had been freely accepted but that were nothing of the sort, and which Muslims assented to with profound insincerity, meant that frank dialogue was ever after that was impossible. The pious among the Moriscos, if they could not manage to flee, retreated into clandestinity, their culture kept safe underground beyond the reach of their enemies. The Christians, possessed of all power but yet powerless to impose their will, began in their frustration to contemplate ever more violent solutions. In the 1520s, there still survived a few vestiges of what Spanish historians have termed the *convivencia* of the Middle Ages: that relatively relaxed pattern of toleration[2] that had enabled the three Abrahamic religions to live side by side in the Iberian Peninsula for centuries. Some on either side still proceeded as if dialogue might lead to a way out of the impasse. But as early as the 1560s, violent final solutions were already being envisaged.

This phase of Morisco history was well characterized by James Casey (1999, 225) as follows:

> The problem was now one of assimilating the new converts. At first there was confidence that much could be achieved by preaching and teaching, and, symptomatic of the optimism of this period, the *concordias* of 1526

2. It is easy to exaggerate the extent of this medieval toleration: see Harvey (1989e).

and 1528 promised ... that the Inquisition would not be too rigorous in enquiring into the relics of Islamic practice ... at least for a term of forty years during which they must be instructed in Christianity. But looking back on a wasted opportunity, one observer around 1570 commented: "I do not know why it is that we are so blind ... that we go off to convert the infidels of Japan, China and other remote parts ... rather as if someone had his house full of snakes and scorpions yet took no care to clean it, but went to hunt for lions or ostriches in Africa."[3] Certainly there were constant complaints that the mission to the Arabic[-speaking] peoples of the peninsula never attracted the enthusiasm accompanying Spanish imperialism overseas.

ISLAMIC CONSCIOUSNESS AND ARÉVALO

For reasons that are in no way clear, one center of focus of the new Islamic ideological resistance in the early mid-sixteenth century was located in the small Castilian town of Arévalo. Arévalo lies about 100 kilometers northwest of Madrid, and it fell within an area where a well-established but not dense Muslim minority had lived for centuries, mainly in urban Moorish quarters (*morerías*). This was the zone that in the mid- and late fifteenth century had seen the adoption, the adaptation, of the Castilian language for use in manuals of Islamic theology. In an earlier study, *Islamic Spain, 1250 to 1500,* and in the chapter which follows this one, I have reason to discuss the life and works of the mid-fifteenth-century imam Içe from nearby Segovia. This region of Castile had thus provided leadership to the subject Mudejars in the preceding period.

Another circumstance that may be relevant to the emergence in Arévalo of Islamic leadership is that in the mid-fifteenth century Arévalo had for a time been used by the Castilian authorities as a place of enforced residence for certain members of the Nasrid royal house of Granada, among them the famous Abu'l-Hasan 'Ali (*Muley Hacén*). The prince had in 1454 come to attend the coronation of Henry IV and then stayed on in Castile as hostage. (The term "hostage" in modern usage implies almost without exception that confinement or imprisonment has been imposed on an *unwilling* victim, probably at gunpoint, but of course in late-medieval diplomatic relations a hostage might well freely accept a loose form of confinement under which he was treated as a highly respected guest—so long as he did not break bounds. The hostage resided abroad as a human guarantee that the terms of some pact or other would be

3. Casey here quotes Janer (1857, 266).

fulfilled). The Nasrid household maintained under official Castilian royal protection in this way in Arévalo might well have, for a time, provided a haven for Muslims, and perhaps a channel for contact between Mudejars and coreligionists in the wider Islamic world.

Even though we do not know why Arévalo was important, we can deduce that it indeed was so from two very different types of source. There is, on the one hand, on the Christian side, Inquisition archive material, and on the Muslim side, the writings of the so-called Young Man from Arévalo (*el mancebo de Arévalo*). We have already heard from him in chapter 3 (p. 95) from the treatise that is the fruit of collaboration between this Young Man and an Aragonese *alfaqui,* and the writings of the Young Man himself will be dealt with against the background of *aljamiado* as a whole in chapter 5. Here we must look at Arévalo during the period when he grew up there.

AGUSTÍN DE RIBERA

From the Inquisition documentation relating to Islamic activity in Arévalo, it emerges that one Ana de Fonseca, a Morisco widow from Arévalo, testified (Tapia 1991, 227) in May 1540 to the Inquisition in Priego that she had been brought to that small Andalusian town (quite far south, near Cordova) by her brother Luis. She had been moved there because her family was afraid that if she remained at home in Arévalo she might inadvertently betray to the Inquisition "many persons, Moors, who had converted and then had apostatized." Her evidence went on to do what the family had feared, and name residents in Arévalo itself and in nearby Medina and even Toledo as well. As a consequence of these allegations, Arévalo was visited by Inquisitors from Valladolid (under whose jurisdiction the town fell). And in Toledo the Inquisitors of that city succeeded in arresting (on September 4, 1540) one "Agustín de Ribera, *el mozo* (the lad)." During the proceedings it was noted that Ana de Fonseca spoke of a boy "who in Arévalo was held to be a prophet and the messenger of Muhammad."

In view of the interest evinced by the Inquisitors in what might emerge from Agustín's interrogation, it would seem reasonable to conclude that they identified him as the "prophet" in question, although that is not explicitly stated. Unfortunately, as Serafín de Tapia Sánchez tells us, "the truth is that little more is known of this affair, which bulked so large in the correspondence between the Council of the Suprema of the Inquisition and the Inquisition of Valladolid. This is one of the cases of which the complete documentation has not survived intact; all that has come down to us is a register of the correspondence on the subject" (Tapia

1991, 227).[4] This gap is particularly frustrating because the Inquisitors obviously believed they had unearthed a large-scale network. They were speaking in very hopeful terms about what had come to light: "Let us trust in God that a great deal can be discovered against the Moriscos." In anticipation of the increased demand for prison cells, the authorities in Valladolid were advised to have extra space available in their jail. In Valladolid itself, the affair (the effects of which were to rumble on over the years) struck terror into the hearts of the Muslim community. What are we to make of the Morisco who, on January 1, 1541, went to his parish priest in Valladolid and then brought an accusation against himself? He believed in the sect of Mahomet, he said; a few days later he was found drowned. What of the individuals who, nine years later, but in the same part of the city, were found killed, because, so the Inquisitors speculated in their report, "the Moriscos suspected that they had been giving evidence against them to the Holy Office"?

Young Agustín was to be interrogated (so the surviving summary tells us) "about the things which are said to have been done in Arévalo. Because if he does confess the truth about what he knows, it will throw much light, and will help to uncover what is hidden in Arévalo and other places where there are Moriscos." The ramifications of the case extended to Medina del Campo, Valladolid, Segovia, and Sta María de Nieva (Tapia 1991, 227). Agustín did eventually, one year later to the day, break down under interrogation. That much is to be deduced from the fact that the Inquisition records that he "unburdened his conscience." The reaction of Tapia, an experienced investigator who is familiar with a broad range of Inquisition material, to these particular files is worth quoting: "I think the most significant aspect is that one appears to catch a glimpse of something more profound and serious than the usual individual practice of Islamic rites; the rise of a prophet indicates that we are in the presence of a collective attempt to revitalize the faith, and the fact that this is not limited to one locality leads one to suppose that religious energies capable of organizing resistance by crypto-Islam must have survived; from this point onwards such resistance will be merely individual, or at the most, limited to the interior of the family, and only in exceptional circumstances extended to a group of families bound together in friendship."

Tapia suggests very acutely that some approximation to the ideas current among the accused may be gleaned from the terms of the Edict of Grace offered to the accused in 1543. Moriscos were told that they might profit from the edict on condition that they should not live together,

---

4. Tapia bases this on Archivo Histórico Nacional (Simancas, Spain), Inquisición libro 574.

but live separately among Old Christians; they should employ domestic servants (*criados*) who were Old Christians; they should marry Old Christians; they should be buried in churches; and they should conform to what the Church ordains in their food "and all other matters." This would seem to suggest that some of the accused were reasonably well-to-do (if they could take Old Christian servants and were likely to be regarded as socially acceptable spouses). The wealth of the Arévalo community is confirmed by the scale of the fines set as a result of the above-mentioned Edict of Grace. We know these because those concerned actually appealed to the Inquisitor-General to be reassessed (and were!). That these people were prepared to stand up for themselves and defend themselves in this way itself conveys something of their self-confidence and ability to negotiate with officialdom. The highest assessment, for 1,684,438 maravedís, payable by one Miguel Bori, was reduced to 600,000 (still, as Tapia calculates, the equivalent of the annual income of seventy manual laborers!); Miguel's son Gabriel had his fine reduced from 112,500 to 93,750 maravedís. Alongside these immense impositions, more than fifty people had to pay amounts varying between 5,000 and 15,000 maravedís.

While our focus is with good reason on Arévalo, it is perhaps justifiable to look ahead to 1572, when the Inquisition again claimed to have unmasked a Morisco plot in the same town. One Gabriel Cordero confessed that in 1570 he, along with other Moriscos, had gone to Valladolid to benefit from the Edict of Grace that had been proclaimed. The day before the absolution was granted, they got together with other Moriscos from Valladolid itself and performed the ceremonies of Islamic ritual purification (*atahor, guadoc*) followed by prayer (*çala*), and then, after receiving absolution, they did the same again! Tapia claims to detect "bitterness" in the Inquisitors' comments in the covering letter to their report (Tapia 1991, 257 n. 120). If this is not all another Inquisitorial fiction, it would indicate that the Muslims from Arévalo were stubbornly impervious to the pressures placed on them. This anecdote of organized contempt for one of the Christian sacraments is reminiscent of the way that the Young Man of Arévalo tested the consistency of the regime of penances being imposed for absolution in Jaén (for extracts from the Young Man's writings, see pp. 179–192.)

"MOZO" = "MANCEBO"?

Tapia does not suggest any link between the Agustín Ribera in his Inquisition documentation and the Young Man of Arévalo, but let us bear in mind the tentative conclusions he was able to draw from the Inquisition documents about Islamic religious prophecy and revivalism in the region of Valladolid-Arévalo when we come to look at what we can learn from the Young Man's writings in the following chapter.

That such a "prophet" (we are not sure the term is one he used about himself; it is more probable that it was applied to him by the investigators) should have emerged in the first half of the sixteenth century in the narrow Castilian environment of Arévalo is difficult to believe, for one must ask what message could be preached with any success at such a time and in such a place. It may help to set this phenomenon in perspective if we recall that elsewhere in the world, and in equally unpromising environments, prophets and preachers have led their religious communities into hopeless conflict with their rulers with as little hope of success (as this world might understand that word). The essential factor to bear in mind is that a totally unworldly calculus, *not* a worldly one, applies in such cases, especially once a dominant and charismatic preacher himself becomes convinced that the secular powers here below are about to be replaced by some supernal order.

A SEPHARDIC PARALLEL?

The most obvious parallels in early modern times come from Sephardic Jewish communities, and there one thinks of the case of Sabbatai Sevi (1626–76), the cause of such turmoil in the Jewish communities of the Ottoman world (and indeed, in many parts of Christian Europe as well). Less well-known but perhaps even more striking, is the parallel offered by an offshoot of the Sabbatian movement that arose not long after in Yemen under one Sulayman al-Aqta' (see van Koningsveld et al. 1990). So convinced was this Yemenite Jew, not that he himself was the Messiah, but that the advent of the Messiah was close, that he proclaimed his message in public and called upon the Muslim rulers of Yemen to surrender their powers. He boldly walked into the audience chamber of the governor of Sanaa, and told him to his face, "Your days are numbered and your rule has come to an end" (van Koningsveld et al. 1990, 16, 128, and 166). The Yemeni authorities were at first nonplussed by such an unworldly rebel, but eventually after due process Sulayman paid for his spiritual convictions with his life. Until the end, such was the awe that his unshakable faith inspired that it proved difficult to find an executioner! This incident, more than a century later, in 1666, and in a distant corner of the Arabian Peninsula, may help us to understand what had happened in Castile. In an extreme situation a determined (self-deluded—who can tell?) young leader, unconstrained by the gritty realities of "real-life" politics, may find the courage for the most foolhardy of enterprises precisely *because* he and his community have nothing to hope for in the here and now. Sulayman was, of course, in part borne along by the messianic fervor of the Sabbatian movement that was sweeping through the Jewish communities of his day. That sort of ideological underpinning was not, of course, available to the Young Man from Arévalo, but it was the case that Spain, and Castile in particular, in this period saw many brushes between religious enthusiasts (above all, the *iluminados*) and the appalled authorities.

THE YOUNG MAN'S "FAMILY TREE"

We have seen that for Spanish Muslims in this period of despair it was easy enough in purely Islamic terms for eschatology to take over from down-to-earth politics, but there is also a distinct possibility that in the Young Man's background there were explicitly Jewish influences at work. I have elsewhere presented what is, I think, a convincing case that his claims to know Hebrew were vain boasting (Harvey 1978, 21–47), but my Alicante colleagues María Jesús Rubiera, Míkel de Epalza, and others have, in discussion on this subject, argued persuasively that his readiness, unique among his fellow Moriscos of this period, to adduce Hebrew etymologies for the religious terms he coins, the way he speaks of contacts with crypto-Jews, and the undoubted rhetorical importance for him of the Promised Land, might well point to a Jewish (as well as the undoubted Christian) element in his upbringing.

CASTILE AND ARAGON: THE MORISCOS CAUGHT BETWEEN THE TWO KINGDOMS

After the forcible conversion of 1525–26, which, as we have seen, was accepted with great reluctance by some elements in Aragonese society, Aragon became, with the possible exception of Valencia, the region where the forcible converts were best able to protect and preserve their Islamic culture. The Muslims of Valencia continued to be Arabic-speaking, of course, and sustained contacts with North Africa, but what has survived by way of Valencian Morisco documentation does not indicate the existence there of any high level of aspiration toward Islamic scholarship. We ought to be tentative on this subject, for our judgments depend on the chance survival of papers, books, and other evidence. It could well be that some factor is skewing our perception. Perhaps the Valencians managed to carry most of their beloved books off with them into exile, whereas the inland Aragonese had perforce to leave bulky items behind, walled up in closets for future ages to discover. But the positive evidence, such as has survived, points to the existence in Aragon not just of scattered remnants but of active and creative foci of Islamic culture. Our chief witness to this culture is undoubtedly the invaluable hoard of books and papers found at Almonacid de la Sierra, the contents of which are discussed in chapter 5.

There are abundant indications that the scriptorium at Almonacid was not an isolated and aberrant phenomenon (see Fournel-Guérin 1979).

The question inevitably arises: why did Aragon maintain during the clandestine period such a good network of Islamic scribal activity when elsewhere we can only infer decline and decay? To try to understand how the middle valley of the Ebro, and in particular, the valleys of its south-bank tributaries such as the Jalón, became important places of refuge, we must make a brief excursus into the history of relations between the kingdom of Aragon itself and the kingdom of Castile and the Castile-based regimes of Charles V, and Philip II and Philip III. Any complete survey of this immense complex of issues must be ruled out, but I hope that some account of one series of disputes, arising, as we will see, from the detention of a small number of Moriscos but by no means exclusively involving them, will serve to convey the quite special, I suspect quite un-expected, nexus of relations, tensions, and affinities, between Christians and Muslims in this area.

Both the strength and the weakness of the Morisco position in Aragon (and in this case, I mean specifically the kingdom, rather than the whole of the territories of the Crown of Aragon) was that their principal pro-tectors were the Aragonese ruling classes (both nobles and the lawyers of the urban patriciate). Aragon was from the latter years of Ferdinand onward in conflict in some way with Castile, Castile's rulers, and Castile's ruling institutions. Wrangles and disputes took all sorts of forms and had as their immediate causes issues of the most diverse kinds, but under-lying everything was Aragonese resentment at the dominant position of Castile (while Castilians felt exasperation at the uncooperative stubborn-ness of their weaker neighbors). The strength of the Morisco position in Aragon depended in large measure on the fact that they could rely on the support of the local nobility and the local institutions when the Crown (or that effective servant of the Crown's centralizing policies, the Inqui-sition) sought to exercise its power against them. But this very support was ultimately a source of weakness because, when the showdown came between the advocates of local and regional independence on the one side, and royal central power on the other, it was central power that eventually won hands down.

This is not the place even to try to list the many disputes that rumbled on throughout the sixteenth century; some of them had little or nothing directly to do with the Muslims of Aragon. The following is a relatively minor and inconsequential case arising directly from the Crown's treat-ment of some Moriscos, but it illustrates how Aragonese regional liberties and Muslim religious liberties were entwined at this period. It will also remind us that in such matters the powerless are likely to suffer far more

than those who are powerful and well-connected. Those who were powerless in this case, were, of course, the crypto-Muslims.

A PETTY DISPUTE: THE CROWN, THE NOBILITY, AND THE MORISCOS OF MEZALOCHA

This incident actually was sparked off by a dispute over irrigation water
(as is the case with many stories of violence in the Spanish countryside).
But the background is the edict issued in early 1560 requiring Aragonese
Moriscos (by then the term was in standard administrative use) to hand
in all their weapons.

Juan Coscón, a Christian, belonged to a family prominent in the cause
of the defense of Aragonese rights (the *fueristas*). As lord of the villages
of Mozota and Mezalocha, he had become involved in a quarrel over an
irrigation canal (*acequia*) and decided that he would have to issue arms
to his workmen, among whom were a number of Moriscos. There was no
actual bloodshed, but Coscón's men did actually deploy bearing weapons,
which was deemed to be an infraction of the edict of disarmament (the
enforcement of which was the responsibility of the Saragossa Inquisition,
which is how that body became involved). The Inquisition accordingly
arrested certain Moriscos from Mezalocha, and arms were duly found
in their possession. Coscón took the case to the procurators of the body
that represented lords of estates with Morisco vassals, and the procurators took action by invoking a key ancient Aragonese legal procedure:
manifestación.

In some ways, *manifestación* may be compared to habeas corpus in the
English common-law legal tradition. Its effect was to force any authority
other than an Aragonese one detaining an individual on Aragonese soil
to hand him over to Aragonese justice, which would then itself hold him
in the special jail that existed specifically for that purpose in Saragossa
(the so-called *Cárcel de los Manifestados*). This Aragonese right to hold
the prisoner always took precedence if *manifestación* was applied for.
Originally, this procedure could not be contested at all, although the Inquisition, after it arrived, asserted that in matters of heresy its jurisdiction
took precedence.

It seems that when the writ of *manifestación* was granted in the case
of the Moriscos arrested, it did not at first come out in court that the
arrest had been carried out by the Inquisition. It proved difficult to get
this writ executed: some lawyers were reluctant to push the Inquisitors
to comply with it, especially because an auto de fe was due to take place a
few days later. The procurators for the lords were not intimidated, however, and successfully invoked their right to have the prisoners handed
over. Following tradition, they appeared at the gates of the Aljafería, the

great castle in Saragossa in the dungeons of which the Moriscos were languishing, and with their followers set up the time-honored cry, "Help for the King" (*Ayuda al Rey*), hardly the cry of dangerous revolutionaries! When warned that if he persisted he might find himself inside the jail, too, one of the procurators, Don Francés de Ariño, replied that he would be only too pleased, because if that were to happen, the whole kingdom would turn out to set them *all* free.

The Inquisitors were wily. They did not arrest Ariño (at least not then and there, they waited a few months), so the *fueristas* were denied their opportunity to summon enraged Aragonese patriots to their aid. But neither did the Inquisitors hand their prisoners over: the lawyers could not actually establish where the poor Moriscos were being detained, so the writ could not be executed. The procurators waited around with their writ till nightfall, and then had to go back home!

Having won round one in this way, the Inquisitors opened round two by summoning one of the notaries who had acted on behalf of Ariño and his associates, Bartolomé Gárate. In accordance with Inquisitorial procedure, they reminded him that he must not communicate the nature of his interrogation to anybody, and when they deemed that the wording of his response to this reminder was guarded, they clapped him straight in prison. The procurators once again invoked the procedure of *manifestación,* and this time even more vehemently. The Inquisition, on its side, put pressure on the court to annul both the edicts of *manifestación.*

The first edict, concerning the Moriscos (prisoners by now long forgotten while the Christians quarreled and litigated over their heads), was annulled, the reason given being that they were stated to be detained for *religious* reasons! At this their lords were indignant, for this certainly was not true. What they did not know was that in secret session the Inquisitors had decided that the Inquisition was entitled to give this reply about *anybody* who was in their prison! (Catch-22s, it will be appreciated, certainly existed prior to the twentieth century.) The second edict proved more difficult, for, of course, the Aragonese lawyers were prepared to try even harder where the liberty of one of their colleagues was at stake. The office of the *Justicia* continued to exert pressure, and the governor of the city was called in as a mediator. This irregular procedure of mediation was adopted, no doubt, because it avoided setting any legally binding precedents. The *real* issue by now was whether or not the Aragonese legal system was going to delineate a boundary to the power of the Inquisition or whether the Inquisition was going to establish that it could operate ultimately untrammeled by any local code or constitution. Arbitration by the governor simply ended the wrangle by having Gárate freed without settling the intractable point of principle. Public demonstrations would now lose their point. Ariño was actually furious with Gárate for leaving jail: "If there were any good Aragonese left, they would throw Gárate off the bridge" (Carrasco 1969).

Ariño continued the struggle. And baffling legal technicalities continued to dominate the case. For procedural reasons he needed an affidavit that an appeal against the original edict of disarmament had been duly registered. The Castilian authorities (in Toledo) first simply procrastinated, thus tying his hands, then ruled that an appeal against the measure could not be registered unless the procurators of the Moriscos' lords first requested the Inquisitors in Aragon to withdraw the decree. When Ariño and his colleague (Lope de Francia) tried to do this, they met with refined bureaucratic obstructionism. The procurators' response was to continue patiently and with all due respect for legal procedure, to turn up, day in and day out, accompanied not only by all their staff, but by a crowd of distinguished Aragonese of all sorts and conditions, not to mention numerous simple citizens. The business of the Inquisition was in consequence clogged up (and no doubt so much publicity was unwelcome to an institution whose lifeblood was secrecy). So the Inquisition for the time being gave in, and handed over the affidavit.

The Aragonese *fueristas* had won a victory: it was soon to prove a Pyrrhic one. The case was now automatically referred up to the Suprema of the Inquisition in Toledo. The strength of the *fueristas* lay in their ability to rely on unwavering and courageous *local* support from all classes of society in Saragossa. In Toledo, the unfortunate representative sent to make the Aragonese case, Lope de Francia, was isolated and powerless. The Inquisition did not waste time. The first day the Aragonese called, they treated him politely and told him to come back any time he liked. On his second visit the bailiff had him shown directly from the waiting room into the prison, where he was locked up. Once they had him inside, further charges were added to his dossier. His Jewish ancestry, for example (it was correct that he did have some Jewish ancestors, as did a very high proportion of Aragonese nobles). Then again blasphemy: there was testimony that once when playing *pelota* he had lost, and then cursed his damned luck, "proof" that he was either a blasphemer or an atheist.

Lope was too tough and too dignified to break down in detention. The Inquisition allowed his case to drag on, but they got nowhere with it. And at this stage it is clear that contacts at court intervened. He was released under sureties provided by Luis de Requesens, comendador mayor of Castile, no less. And when he was finally found guilty (on a charge of "troubling and disturbing the Holy Office"), his penalty was a fine of 100 ducats and three years' exile from Aragon. One has to admire his lawyers: they even appealed this sentence on the grounds that in Aragon the

Inquisition could only impose monetary fines in cases of heresy—and they won their appeal! (One has also to have deep respect for due process of law, which survived against the odds in this Aragonese jurisdiction.) When the Inquisition countered by increasing his exile by a year, he successfully insisted that it be noted that his offense related to his attempt to secure the *manifestación* of certain prisoners. The Inquisitor-General lifted the exile order, and he went back home.

As for Ariño, he too had been imprisoned, but in Saragossa, where, thanks to the support he enjoyed from an enormous number of people (and, above all, from the community organizations of the converts— Carrasco estimates he was representing at least 5,000 convert families), the Inquisition could be subjected to great pressure. The lieutenants of the *Justicia* of Aragon appeared in solemn procession to demand his release. The Inquisitors, following the procedure described above, testified he was being held for "religious" reasons, and the ranks of Aragonese justice had to back off. The Holy Office made its point by holding him for a few months more, but he was then released. It might appear then that the Inquisition had won, and certainly the Aragonese failed to set limits to the powers of the Holy Office as they had hoped.

However, if we look back at the issue of the disarmament of the Moriscos that had set in motion all this litigation in the first place, something had been achieved, although for a short time only. When in 1563 the disarmament of Valencian Moriscos came to be decreed, no attempt was made to include Aragon, where the opposition organized by the procurators had prevented the original decrees from being applied. It was not until 1575 that such a measure could be pushed through. (As for those Moriscos originally detained, we simply do not hear what happened to them! Clearly they mattered only as pretexts for wrangles among Christian factions.)

We have seen that the Muslims of Castile and Aragon, hitherto subjected to very different regimes, came, after the forcible conversions of the early 1520s, to suffer the same fate. All Spain's Muslims became either converts to Christianity or crypto-Muslims who were obliged to put on a pretense of being Christians. It made no difference whether the Muslims in question had been forced into conversion after participating in armed rebellion against the Crown (the case of many of the Moriscos of the Alpujarras) or came from families that over many generations had been loyal servants of Christian monarchs (the Navarrese, the Aragonese, and the Segovians, for example): all were now treated alike. Summarizing the Kulturkampf that had been taking place, Casey has said: "Certainly the Inquisition over the years managed to destroy much of the formal apparatus of Islam. But the *alfaquis,* through their knowledge of the rites, and their activity in circumcision, marriage contracts, preparation of the dead for burial and the like managed to keep alive a flourishing underground religion. It was among them that a quite extensive clandestine literature circulated, writings in either Arabic or *aljamía* (Castilian in Arabic characters).... 'In each house, in every corner, we have found even primers for children, with the commands of Muhammad written in verse,' wrote Aznar Cardona in 1610. And certainly one feature of this clandestine literature was its polemical nature—its utter rejection of Christianity" (Casey 1999, 227).

So it is necessary to examine the intellectual traditions that flourished (that word is used here advisedly) within Spain's Muslim communities in the sixteenth century. Chronologically that entails taking a step backward, and looking at Morisco writings from the end of the fifteenth century onward. This seems the right place to insert these matters within the present general study of the Moriscos, at the point when the central (Castilian) and the eastern (Aragonese) traditions came together to collaborate in the redaction in Aragon of the Aragonese-Castilian *Brief Compendium of Our Law and Sunna.*

The following chapter traces the Islamic literary productions of Spain's Muslims in this the final period of their existence. It is a subject that has in fact been well studied by specialists, but it is among a wider readership relatively unfamiliar, even those who are otherwise well-informed about Spain's majority Christian culture in this period. It is equally ignored by specialists in the Islamic cultures of the Middle East and North Africa. It deserves our attention.

FIVE ✤ The Intellectual Life of Spain's Clandestine Muslims

As we have seen, the characteristic that in the sixteenth century marked off the Muslims of Spain from those elsewhere in the world was the clandestinity of their religious beliefs. But the religion of Muslims is, always has been, and can only be, the religion of a Book, the Koran (*al-Qur'an*), God's final and perfect revelation to mankind. Islam is inconceivable without the Koran, God's word. And God's word must be proclaimed in public. That is an explicit obligation. For the Muslims of Spain this posed a problem. If they had only prudently avoided possessing books and had committed nothing to writing, they would have been much safer. But would they have felt themselves to be good Muslims if they had had no books? Clearly not. From their writings we can see that, although they might accept the need to keep the nature of their religious beliefs secret for the time being, they never forgot that as Muslims they should aspire to worship openly one day and that they had an obligation to proclaim God's message to everybody (which entailed having it available in writing).

Many of the extant files of the proceedings of Inquisition trials contain references to books and other written material impounded as evidence when the accused were taken into custody. In some cases, the written evidence was preserved alongside the rest of the dossier and so is still available to us now. This is by no means the only category of evidence that has survived to tell us about the written word as it was still cultivated among Muslims in Spain in the final underground period of their history. From the hiding places where they were secreted by their Morisco owners long ago, under floorboards or behind false walls, a sufficiently large number of manuscript books from a sufficiently diverse range of hiding places and other sources has now emerged for us to form a clear idea of the nature of their literature. The crypto-Muslims of Spain continued to be People of the Book, and they were people *with* books. This chapter presents some key aspects of what they read and what they wrote.

The victors write the history: the nature of the historical record is such that we must inevitably see the world in which crypto-Muslims lived through the eyes of their adversaries, rarely as they themselves saw it. But the literature that they read enables us to begin to reconstruct their mental world, and even though the number of works that they wrote themselves was not large, there is enough reliable evidence for us on occasion to hear their very voices. It is most remarkable that a community under the systematic persecution of the Spanish Inquisition, not to mention the other organs of the Spanish state, should have managed not merely to preserve a great deal of its religious and cultural inheritance (in a difficult language, Arabic, not spoken by many of them) but should also have gone beyond that and created a new written language of its own, in Arabic characters, for Islamic purposes. This way of writing their own Romance vernacular was not, as I will argue below, first developed in this period, but over the very short time span covered by this volume, that is to say, over little more than one century, we can watch the evolution of what had been little more than a medium for jotting down marginalia and occasional notes into an effective instrument for the preservation of a whole distinctive culture. This new written language that they created is now, of course, an utterly dead one. The community that created it has disappeared altogether, so nobody reads it, which makes it even more necessary to extract what information we can from the evidence that has survived.

THE LANGUAGES OF SPAIN'S MUSLIMS AND CRYPTO-MUSLIMS

Before looking at the books read and written by Spain's Muslims in this period, it is first necessary to deal with the nature of the languages in which they were written. In the course of describing the various communities of Muslims in Spain at this time, reference has already been made to their various *spoken* languages and dialects. Here we are mainly concerned with written texts, some in Arabic and some in Hispanic dialects written down in Arabic letters. In many parts of the world there may be a clear distinction between the spoken and written forms of language, and often that difference is much more marked even than that which exists between, say, literary English and the various English vernaculars. In the case of Arabic, the differences are also marked and have been so from early times. The reasons for this state of affairs are complex. Islamic educational systems have always devoted much effort to preserving knowledge of that form of the Arabic language in which the original revelation of the Koran was vouchsafed to the Prophet Muhammad in the seventh century and to protecting it from change and deformation. Spoken Arabic, like any other language, continues to evolve and to change, nevertheless, so that the various parts of the Arabic-speaking world now have available not only an elevated language that binds the Arab world together but also various vernaculars, some of which have moved so far apart that mutual comprehension between native speakers in the various regions may in some cases not be easily achieved.

Islamic Spain was no exception in all this. Spanish Muslims had but one written language, the written language they shared with the rest of Arab world. In the various regions of the peninsula a number of vernaculars were in use, some of them Arabic vernaculars, some of them the Romance dialects of Islamic communities. And just as one finds in North Africa Arabic vernaculars in some places and non-Arabic vernaculars (Berber languages, for example) in others, but only one literary language, Arabic, so in the Iberian Peninsula in the Middle Ages some of the vernaculars used by Muslims were Arabic ones and others were non-Arabic, in this case Romance-based. And for the speakers of *both,* there was the same one high-prestige written language: Arabic.

The Spoken Arabic of Spain

As has already been pointed out when describing the Muslim communities of the peninsula in general terms, by the early sixteenth century only two areas remained that had large populations of native Arabic-speakers: Granada and Valencia. Each of these accounted for up to a quarter of a million speakers. (Numbers did not remain stable under the stressful conditions described in this volume; because of persecution and clandestine emigration, the totals drifted ever downward.) There were other small Arabic-speaking enclaves outside Granada and Valencia, Hornachos in Extremadura. for example (see chapter 12), but in general Muslims in the rest of Spain spoke the local varieties of Romance. *However*—and it is difficult to stress this sufficiently in this context—the fact that the Muslims of Aragon, for example, did not from the Middle Ages onward speak an Arabic vernacular did not mean that during that period their written language was not Arabic. And for so long as their educated classes in Aragon could receive adequate training, usually in Valencia or one of the other Arabic-speaking regions of the peninsula itself, perhaps overseas for those who wished to advance their studies further, these non-Arabic-speaking Muslims continued loyal to the written language of their *umma* or religious community. In that language were studied the Holy Book and other works of devotion; in that language Muslims studied all serious matters. In that language self-respecting Muslims were literate, and so in Arabic characters they would in the medieval period sign their name on deeds, etc. (alongside which signatures Christians might, where appropriate, sign in "normal" Latin characters). This surprisingly stable but complex state of linguistic affairs, with each language inhabiting its own cultural spaces (and let us not forget that until 1492 there was also in the Iberian Peninsula a third religion, Judaism, and a third language of culture, Hebrew) continued at least until the date of the forcible conversions in the Castilian lands at the opening of the sixteenth century.

In the independent kingdom of Navarre, the situation was different again. This area provides us with a clear set of specimen texts, limited in number because Islam was brought to a particularly sudden end there in 1515 (see García-Arenal and Leroy 1984). We can witness fully trained *'ulama* (Islamic scholars) publicly exercising the functions of their offices, drawing up Arabic documents carrying Arabic signatures, and this almost right up to the date of the conversion. What the Muslim folk there spoke was Navarrese. Their written language was Arabic.

This medieval state of affairs where the languages of the Muslims were concerned was brought to an end by decree. The Christian authorities followed up the proclamations of forcible conversion with others banning Arabic. To eliminate the *spoken* dialects proved very difficult (in regions of Valencia, at least, they continued in use till the end), but to achieve an adequate mastery of the *written* language required long years of study, and that was almost impossible to achieve in this period. So where the supply of scholars dried up, as it did after a generation, the use of Arabic as a language of culture was no longer possible. In the early days after Granada fell, in the late 1490s and early 1500s, the onslaught on Arabic was directed in the main against theological and similar texts (this was the stage initiated by Cisneros in his well-known bonfire of Islamic books in the Plaza de Bibarrambla shortly before the first Edicts of Conversion were promulgated), but eventually bans were extended to cover anything written in Arabic. Such decrees had limited effect. Books could be hidden, and this was a community well able to keep secret what it wanted to keep secret. It was the lack of trained specialists able to carry forward the tradition of literacy in Arabic that was the most potent threat to the survival of the language. There occurred a cultural breakdown in both the Arabic-speaking and in the Romance-speaking zones, but that breakdown did not everywhere lead to the same results. In both cases the consequences of the breakdown were remarkable. Elsewhere in the Islamic world there are no exact parallels to what happened in Spain, which is all the more reason for students of Islam and of linguistics to pay more attention to the Andalusi experience.

Written Vernacular Arabic in Spain in the Sixteenth Century

In the Arabic-speaking areas of Spain at this time, in addition to the continued employment of standard written Arabic by those few still capable
of writing it, we have the emergence of the quite new phenomenon of the
use of the Arabic alphabet *for the writing of the Arabic vernacular.* This
is far more surprising than it sounds. As explained above, the Arabic
vernaculars had not before this time been widely used in a regular way
in writing (although of course failure to achieve grammatical correctness
in what was intended to be a standard Arabic text was something that
occurred very frequently!). Even in the Arab world of the twenty-first
century, the vernaculars have not yet evolved into media of expression
comparable in status to, say, the various Romance languages in southern
Europe. The use of the colloquial in novels—other than in dialogue—is
still a circumscribed and uneasy "literary" phenomenon, which at first
was largely restricted to Egypt, and is in any case everywhere of relatively
recent date.

As has been said, departures from standard Arabic orthography, reflecting vernacular linguistic features, are to be found from periods much
earlier than the sixteenth century. There are from various parts of the
Arab world, including the Iberian Peninsula, treatises[1] telling people
who were afraid that their Arabic might have been contaminated by local
speech patterns how to *avoid* such vulgarisms (*lahn*). And such treatises,
in the course of castigating substandard language, of course, have to write
it down, thus providing some early record of what the vulgar speech was
like. However, in the sixteenth century we begin to see documents no
longer obeying what the ancient grammar books laid down but simply
setting down *what people actually said.* All the texts from the region of
Valencia studied by Barceló (1984), for example, are in "nonstandard"
orthography. When in 1976 I myself set about the editing of a letter
in what I soon realized was Valencian dialectal Arabic, I at first was
unwilling to believe my eyes. I found it hard to accept that somebody
could possibly *intend* to use spellings such as those with which I was
confronted. Could I be understanding the text correctly, I asked myself?
To take a very clear example, when I found the spelling *bib* in a context
that certainly required the sense "door," was I really to believe that the
person writing the letter in question did not know, was unaware of, the
"correct" spelling of the Arabic word for "door": *bab*? In its other sense of
"chapter," *bab* is to be seen endless times at the head of the subdivisions

---

1. Treatises designed to provide a similar service are, of course, found for Latin,
and indeed they provide modern scholars with an invaluable source for the study of
Vulgar Latin.

of most Arabic books. Anybody literate in any way in Arabic cannot fail to have seen the word *bab* hundreds, thousands, of times. Did perhaps those who used "vernacular" spellings such as this *bib* deliberately reject the old conventions? *Bib,* we know, was how the word was often actually pronounced in Valencia (as a consequence of a process of vowel closure, termed *imala* in Arabic treatises of phonetics, that was a characteristic of the Andalusi dialects). *Bib* was what people actually said, there is no doubt about that, but nobody before the sixteenth century would *consistently* write the word that way. (A useful parallel might be that in North America the English word "water" is pronounced with some kind of voiced or attenuated dental medial consonant, but nobody there would ever dream of actually writing that word with a *d*: "wader.") In some regions where Hispano-Arabic vernaculars existed (in Valencia above all) we witness the emergence of what we may perhaps call "written vernacular texts" in which divergences from the old norms are *not* occasional slips and errors but are apparently intentional. *Bib* cannot be a mere mistake: it is part of a text in which the departures from the old norms are on the way to becoming new norms. I found this Hispano-Arabic phenomenon even more puzzling than the use in English of such spellings as "nite," "lite," or "sox," say, by people who otherwise give every indication of being aware of the traditional English orthography. Presumably the traditional spelling must seem in some social contexts inappropriate to those who favor these innovations in English. Perhaps by writing in a nonstandard way the author/sign-writer seeks to establish that he is not trammeled by the dead traditions of the past. It is, I suppose, just possible that in the same way, "nonstandard" Arabic spellings employed in some sixteenth-century vernacular Arabic texts from Spain might also indicate a similar *conscious* desire to break with the past, but that really seems unlikely. Innovation (*bid'a,* and equally, in Spanish, *novedades*) was in the vocabulary of these people a term of reproach, not of praise.

The Characteristics of the Written Arabic Used in These Late Texts
The innovating spellings are, as far as we can discover, an adequate representation of the phonetic realities of Arabic as it was spoken at this time and in this place. Most noteworthy is the phonological development already noted—the open *a* of standard Arabic *bab* closing to an *i*. Among the consonants, the array of "emphatic"[2] sounds merge, probably in their

---

2. I am, of course, aware that the term "emphatic" is nowadays rejected by many (most?) linguisticians. The problem is that there is no agreement as to what should replace it, and I know from experience the alternatives will be utterly opaque to the nonspecialist, who on the other hand, seems to grasp emphatic/nonemphatic instinctively.

totality, with the nonemphatics. This means that, for example, *s* and emphatic *s* are so frequently muddled in the written texts that we must conclude that the writer/author could not tell them apart. The same goes for the other pairs of consonants, the two varieties of *h*, *k*, *t*, and *z*. But although such basic phonological features of the language had been abandoned, there can be no doubt that late texts such as these from Spain are in a dialect that is correctly described as a variety of Arabic. Elements of all kinds (not just items of vocabulary) may be borrowed from Romance, granted, but these borrowings are well integrated into Semitic linguistic patterns. *Bonaboluntad* (goodwill) is adopted as one unit, so that "with my goodwill" becomes *ma'a al-bonaboluntad mata'i*. For a brief discussion in English of this new linguistic phenomenon, "written vernacular Arabic," see Harvey (1971) or, for fuller surveys of a larger corpus of material, see Corriente (1977) and Barceló (1984). What must be made clear about this development is that although it served a number of everyday practical purposes and even occurs in written messages of some political consequence, it is not to be found in religious or literary use.

The Romance Vernaculars and Romance Writings of Some of Spain's Muslims

Let us now turn to *aljamía*, the Romance vernacular speech of the many *morerías* of Castile and Aragon. In both these areas from the fifteenth century and earlier, we have evidence that the use of Arabic as the community's language of culture and written record continued for so long as there were educated men available to write it. But by the sixteenth century, we frequently find laments for the loss of Arabic, and the writing of the Romance vernacular in Arabic characters (*literatura aljamiada*) was beginning to be widespread among crypto-Muslims. Written vernacular Arabic of the kind just referred to is a significant and unusual development, but it was destined never to have more than the most limited of use because of the immense gravitational attraction always exercised by standard written Arabic. The international standard would always[3] tend

---

In the simplest terms, I refer here to those phonemes that are represented in most systems of transliteration by symbols with subscript dots: *ḍ*, *k/q*, *ṣ*, *ṭ*, *ẓ*. For a technical description of the sound system of Hispanic Arabic, see Corriente (1977).

3. The exception that proves this rule is Maltese. This is simply a variety of Arabic (an offshoot of the defunct Arabic of Sicily), but because it has been so long isolated from other varieties of Arabic, through being written in the Latin alphabet, because those who speak it are all Christian, and because the island was defended by the Knights of Malta from Islamic reconquest, it has been free to evolve in a way that would not have occurred if it had been anchored to Classical Arabic by the Arabic script.

to reimpose itself on users of any aberrant form of the Arabic language, as it still does nowadays. Spanish as written in Arabic characters, *aljamía* in the terminology of modern bibliographers, on the other hand, was a dynamic cultural phenomenon that began to evolve freely and with a momentum of its own. What brought the Arabic-character writing of *aljamía* to a sudden and total stop was the Expulsion of 1609–14. After that it is interesting that whereas the phenomenon of Spanish in Hebrew characters continued to flourish after the expulsion of the Jews in 1492 and, indeed, reached its apogee in the Diaspora (in Salonika and elsewhere), Spanish in Arabic characters proved to have no future outside Spain. If the refugees did write in Spanish, they seem to have been done so using the normal Spanish script and orthography. But rapidly most reintegrated themselves into the Islamic world of which the principal linguistic medium was Arabic.

Spanish Written Using the Arabic Alphabet (*Aljamía*)

In the peninsula in the sixteenth century, crypto-Muslim users of the new written medium, Arabic in script but Romance in language, certainly felt the attraction of Islamic culture, but those who had no spoken Arabic had no choice: this was the only form of literacy to which they could aspire. The new mode of writing, once it had emerged, became for them an important way of asserting their Islamic identity. Choosing to employ Arabic and not Latin characters was a declaration of loyalty, and a courageous one, for during much of our period the crypto-Muslim might expect trouble if it could be shown that he possessed texts written in Arabic characters.

With regard to the word itself, in its entry "aljamía" the Spanish Academy Dictionary (Real Academia Española, *Diccionario de la lengua española*, s.v. "aljamía") gives a definition that leaves two quite distinct senses to exist side by side. They do not coincide, and they need to be distinguished.

> Aljamía: the name which the Moors [*sic*] gave to the Castilian language. Nowadays it is especially applied to the writings of the Moriscos in our language in Arabic characters.[4]

There are present in that definition both the meaning of the word from the late Middle Ages up to the sixteenth century ("what the Muslims called Spanish"), and also the meaning in modern academic usage, "Spanish in

---

4. "Nombre que daban los moros a la lengua castellana. Hoy se aplica especialmente a los escritos de los moriscos en nuestra lengua con caracteres arábigos." Here the Academy must really have in mind the Moors in Spain only, i.e., Spanish Muslims.

Arabic characters." (The word "Morisco" here is clearly an example of *morisco* [2].) One might in an ideal world wish to see those quite distinct acceptations ("the name given by Muslims in Spain to the Romance vernacular" as opposed to "the name given by Christians to the Muslims they forcibly converted" clearly disentangled, but we can hardly rewrite the Spanish Academy's dictionary for it. As with the word "Morisco," the confusing usages are by now firmly entrenched. In practice all we can do is scrutinize with care this term within the contexts in which it occurs and to avoid being misled. In this study every endeavor will be made to use explicit terminology where necessary.

Some specialists in other fields, having come across the sense of "Spanish in Arabic characters" for *aljamía*, jump to the conclusion that this is the primary and *only* correct usage. And hence they are in danger of misinterpreting some early texts. When Cervantes spoke in *Don Quixote* of a *moro aljamiado de Toledo*, for example, he was not thinking of the writing of texts in Spanish in Arabic characters, he was simply thinking of a Muslim from Toledo "with a good command of Spanish."

I do no suggest here that the modern bibliographer's "scholarly" and technical sense for *aljamía* as relating to manuscripts and scripts ("Spanish in Arabic characters") should be abandoned. It is useful to have such a term available for use in a library catalog, for example, and *aljamía/aljamiado* fills that need. It would be absurd to seek to banish the word from modern manuscript catalog and replace it with some neologism, but one must never lose sight of the fact that in documents from the sixteenth century and earlier, the word normally does not refer to script but to language ("Romance vernacular").

Regrettably, one further semantic stretching of this term must be recorded for the sake of completeness, although fortunately this is an extension that does not have much impact on what is of immediate concern to us. There has been considerable discussion in recent years of the general phenomenon of the writing of languages in scripts other than those in majority use. With regard to the use of "nonstandard" scripts in general, there is some tendency in modern times to extend the use of *aljamía*, et cetera, so as to cover other similar phenomena such as writing Afrikaans in Arabic characters, or even, a further step, to the use of Hebrew characters to write Arabic (*aljamía rabínica*, Rabbinical *aljamía*). To try to outlaw such a linguistic shift would surely be to court failure. But one must question the advisability of diluting the sense of *aljamía* in this way. There is the risk that eventually it may come to mean nothing more specific than "written in an odd and unusual script," and by then we will have lost a quite useful word.

As for the debate about the beginnings of *literatura aljamiada* in the narrow sense, that is to say, the question of when people in Spain began to use Arabic to write Spanish dialects, this present study must focus on what went on in the sixteenth century, and there is scant space to deal with the uncertain and remote questions of origins. The view taken by some Spanish scholars has been that these origins are very remote indeed, and that view has been reinforced by the fact that a scholar of the authority of Ramón Menéndez Pidal in his influential 1901 edition of the *Poema de Yúçuf*[5] came down on the side of a dating possibly as early as the fourteenth century. (His arguments were both linguistic and literary—resting in part on the type of verse employed.)

With regard to the sixteenth century, one fact is absolutely beyond dispute, and that is that the great majority of the datable *aljamiado* manuscripts that have come down to us are to be ascribed to our later period (there are more than a hundred of them). Indeed, the number of manuscripts *positively* datable to earlier periods is so small as to be countable on the fingers of one hand. (In saying that, I disregard manuscripts dated by scholars relying exclusively on paleographical, etc., criteria.) The number of such early texts is in any case by any reckoning not large. It remains true that from very early times the Arabic script had been used in the Iberian Peninsula to write Romance personal names, place names, isolated lexical items such as plant names, even very short snatches of dialogue reported *within* Arabic texts. And from the eleventh century on we also have the relatively restricted use of Romance in the refrains of certain strophic Arabic poems from Spain (the *muwashshahat*). The hit-or-miss and unsystematic writing of Romance in these documents, poems, and other texts differed from the relatively regular, elaborate and accurate *orthography* of the crypto-Muslims of the sixteenth century. In particular, the later system possessed unambiguous spellings (based on the symbol known as *ʃadda* or *taʃdid*) for the characteristic palatal consonants of Castilian, sounds not present in Arabic itself (*ll*, *ñ*, and *ch* in conventional Castilian spelling). This is a type of notation unknown earlier in the peninsula or anywhere else (and independent of the systems in use for certain other languages such as Persian—which uses, for example, a triple-dotted letter for its *ch*). Similarly, this notation is independent of the system of writing used for the Romance refrains at the end of some *muwashshahat*.

5. This appeared first in the *Revista de Archivos, Bibliotecas y Museos* 7 (1901), was reprinted in book form the following year, and reproduced in a facsimile edition (Granada, 1952).

To explain the sudden arrival on the scene of the *aljamiado* script, various interesting ideas have been mooted: Epalza (1992, 280) has suggested that the impact in the West of the conquest of Constantinople would have brought to the attention of Muslims in Spain the fact that the Ottoman Turks had for their Islamic purposes their own way of writing their non-Arabic language with the Arabic alphabet. His hypothesis is that Spanish Muslims, following the Ottoman example, used the Arabic script to write their own non-Arabic language. On the other hand, Wiegers (1994, 40–46) looks further back, but within the Islamic West itself. He points to the readiness of the Almohads to use their Berber vernacular for devotional purposes, and to support his interesting thesis that Almohads in the Iberian Peninsula had used the local Romance language for certain devotional purposes just as they had used their own Berber language, he is able to point to a hitherto unrecognized translation of the Almohad devotional text, the Murshida, into *aljamía*.

I myself have preferred to see in the pioneering work of 'Isa, the mid-fifteenth-century imam of Segovia, a key initial impulse. One very weak aspect of this thesis of mine relates to 'Isa's immensely influential popular legal text, the *Breviario Sunni*. Only one manuscript survives in Arabic script, and the others, *earlier* in date, are actually in Latin characters. It is possible to argue that 'Isa's book may have been written first in a normal Spanish script and subsequently transliterated. The hypothesis that the *Breviario Sunni* was first written down in "normal" Latin characters is supported by a curious error, first noted by Dario Cabanelas (1952), that 'Isa's name is, in the one surviving manuscript in Arabic characters, grotesquely garbled and appears as *Ike*, a mistake impossible to account for if one assumes one has to start from an Arabic-character manuscript, but readily comprehensible if one starts with the normal fifteenth-century Latin-character spelling *Içe* (and then assumes that at some stage the cedilla was overlooked, and so $ç$ was misread as $c = K$). Such a mistake would, of course, never have arisen if the transliteration were taking place in the opposite direction.

In spite of the arguments against seeing 'Isa of Segovia as the principal creative and determining influence at the origins of *aljamiado* writings, there is an impressive cultural continuity to be discerned among Islamic authors from Spain writing in Romance, and 'Isa's writings were quoted, for example, by the Mancebo de ("Young Man") from Arévalo (among many others) in the sixteenth century, and who in his turn was quoted by Muhammad Rabadan and then by Ibrahim Taybili (in whom the tradition reaches its end in North African exile in the seventeenth century). This inclines me to ascribe a seminal role to 'Isa of Segovia. All Muslim writers in Spain after his date looked back to this imam.

One may note that the various hypotheses for the rise of what Wiegers has proposed calling "Islamic Spanish" literature are not mutually exclusive. It is quite possible that the Almohads' devotional use of vernaculars (his point) may have served to pave the way for the adoption of the new system of writing by removing some of the prejudice against the use of languages other than Arabic in a devotional context. But it is also possible that awareness of the example of the Turks, to which Epalza has drawn our attention, may have encouraged other language groups, Mudejars included, to emulate them. And the fact that the imam 'Isa gave to his people both a translation of the Koran and a compilation of Islamic law meant that the necessary basic texts, scriptural and legal, were, after the middle of the fifteenth century, available to serve as a foundation and a stylistic model (and they were indeed so exploited). All these factors may have come together with others, such as the *need* for devotional reading in a language other than Arabic felt by a community that had lost most of its religious elite. (Looking at the many pious miscellanies and commonplace books into which favorite devotional texts have been copied brings home to us how much such reading material was prized.) The debate about origins is a fascinating one, but for present purposes what is important is that *aljamía* (in the narrow sense of "Romance set down in the Arabic script") became almost the only mode of writing on Islamic subjects in use among the crypto-Muslims of Spain in the sixteenth century.

The great rarity of surviving *aljamiado* manuscripts from the fifteenth century and earlier I regard as of particular significance because, during that early Mudejar period there was no ban in force on the use of the Arabic script such as was imposed later. The Inquisition had no jurisdiction over Muslims in such matters, so it would *not* have been dangerous to own a manuscript in Arabic characters in the fifteenth century. On the other hand, during most of the sixteenth century, there was such a ban, so that almost all material was written under conditions of clandestinity. If the use of the script for this purpose had already been well-established early, one might have expected more abundant evidence to survive from the preclandestine years than from the sixteenth century, and that is certainly not the case. As table 1 demonstrates, from the fifteenth century (and earlier) *aljamiado* manuscripts are extremely rare, and from the sixteenth they are relatively common. My own hypothesis is that Spain's crypto-Muslims turned increasingly to writing in *aljamía* as a medium through which they could still manage to express their Islamic distinctiveness because they felt their identity so much under threat. Most of them outside Valencia could no longer express themselves adequately in Arabic. Their use of their vernacular set down in the Arabic script was the next best thing.

Table 1   Chronological Distribution of Aljamiado Manuscripts

Year	Number of Firmly Datable Manuscripts in Saavedra (1878)	Number of Firmly Datable Manuscripts in Ribera and Asín (1912)
1491	1	
1492		1
1494	1	
1495		1
1496	1	
1499		1
1500		1
1501	2	
1514	1	
1517	1	
1518	1	
1539	1	
1540	1	
1551		1
1552	1	
1554	1	
1559		1
1563	2	
1567	1	
1572		1
1574	1	
1577	1	
1585		1
1587		1
1588	1	1
1589	1	
1595	1	
1597		1
1598		1
1601		1
1603	1	
1606	1	
1608	1	
1609	2	
1610	1	

Table 1 *(continued)*

Notes

MS GR 92 is not dated at all by Guillén Robles (1889), but Menéndez Pidal (1952) places the poem as possibly of the fourteenth century, mainly on metric grounds. The other five manuscripts possibly to be dated before 1490 are MS GR 62 (1429); MS GR 80 (1424; but Guillén Robles indicates 1521 is more probable); also an item not listed by Guillén Robles (1889), Gg. 177 in an older classification at the Biblioteca Nacional, Madrid, had various documents from 1467 onward, MS Galmés de Fuentes (1988), 11 is from 1474; MS J 1 is dated 1462 but this is most probably the date of the original from which this copy was made, not that of the manuscript in the catalog. So only two manuscripts and some loose papers have positive fifteenth-century datings.

In addition, there are the manuscripts dated only by paper, script, etc. Of these, Galmés de Fuentes (1998, 39) places one in the "fourteenth or fifteenth century," and Ribera and Asín (1912) place part of their MS 9 in the first half of the nineteenth century.

From the fifteenth century generally, twenty-four manuscripts are listed in Saavedra (1878) and twenty-three in Ribera and Asín (1912).

Ribera and Asín (1912) assign three MSS, 8, part of 9, and 14, to the seventeenth century.

Scriptures in the Vernacular

There is a pan-European dimension to the rise of *aljamiado* literature that has been hitherto ignored, perhaps because Islamicists[6] are little given to seeking European origins for the phenomena they study. It is difficult for some to accept that Spain's remnant of Muslims were indeed Muslims, *but were also indeed Europeans of their age.* There is a tendency to regard "Muslim" and "European" as being somehow mutually exclusive categories. The European dimension that I can see in this literature is that the fourteenth, fifteenth, and sixteenth centuries were an age when many, almost all, of Western Europe's peoples acquired versions of their scriptures and religious texts in their own languages. (Not for the very first time in all cases, admittedly.) This is no place to discuss why in such diverse areas as the Basque country, Bohemia, England, Germany, Hungary, Spain, and Wales, to cite but a few examples, this should be

6. I am using this word in the older sense of "students of Islam," whether they are themselves Muslims or not. The word has in relatively recent times acquired another quite distinct and unrelated sense, and it will often be found as an alternative to the English expression "Islamic fundamentalist." That is not what I mean here.

so.[7] There is no point in attempting any exhaustive listing. From the examples quoted that from the late fourteenth to the sixteenth centuries there was under way a Europe-wide process of acquisition of scriptures and devotional works in the various vernaculars. What lay behind this Europe-wide rendering of the scriptures into the vernaculars is by no means clear, and none of the explanations commonly adduced fits all cases. The spread of printing, and the ferment of the Reformation (or the reformations) certainly played their part, but the trend to translate had begun in some parts of Europe (England in particular) very early, before the Reformation, before printing, and independently of it. That Spain's Muslims should also have wished in this general period to acquire *their* own holy books in *their* own mother tongue, and have in the process created a new written language (just as Luther set for German a new standard) is, in such a perspective, hardly surprising at all; and it is very European. Spain's Muslims need understanding as Muslims with a distinctive culture they inherited from the East, but they also need to be understood as Europeans participating in many aspects of the common culture of the lands where they were born.

A New Style, a New Language

The formative stylistic influence of Luther's Bible translations and hymns on German, and of the various English Bibles and of the Book of Common Prayer on English, are well known. Out of the process of translation was created the elevated style of the Western vernaculars.

The other source of elevated styles in the European languages came from the Classical (i.e., Greco-Roman) heritage. For Muslims, Classical antiquity signified little.[8] So an important background factor causing the language of Muslims to drift apart from that of the Christian majority was that, whereas under the influence of the predominant culture of the period the vocabulary of the Christians was becoming ever more Latinate, as we will see, among Muslims that old Arabisms were preserved at a

7. On the Basque example, see the translation of Juan de Lizarriga (La Rochelle 1571); for Czech, the Bible of Kralice (1579); England, as ever, fits into the European pattern untidily—the very much earlier Anglo-Saxon Bible translations were, of course, no longer accessible, and Wycliffe, in the late fourteenth century, worked from the Latin. The real comparison here is with Tyndale, translating the New Testament from the Greek for the first time in 1525. For Germany, there was Luther's New Testament 1522; in Hungary (actually the first book ever published in Hungarian), the Pauline Epistles (1533); Spain, Encinas (1543); and Wales, first printed edition of the New Testament in 1567.

8. The Young Man from Arévalo tells us he read Homer: he is an exception, and in any case I do not believe him. See Harvey (1978a).

time when Spanish Christian stylists tended to eliminate them as old-fashioned, and the preferred source for neologisms was Arabic and not Latin and Greek.

The Muslims of Romance-speaking Spain, on the basis of both their Koran translations and their struggle to make available some of the wealth of Islamic scholarship to those who could not read Arabic, created what was effectively a new written language. Of course at its simplest level the new "Islamic Spanish" literature consisted predominantly of words that, for all their Arabic-character spelling, were none the less wholly Spanish. Yet it would be profoundly misleading to think of *aljamía* as a matter of mere external presentation or transliteration. In our days, we are still familiar with the model of a stenographer (there are a few such still surviving, once a quite common species) who is capable, using a system of writing totally different from normal orthography, of writing down a text that *will not be in any way modified* by the special system of notation in use. That is *not* what happens in *aljamiado* literature. In *aljamiado* texts, although it is true that the medium is the message (the use of the Arabic alphabet was in itself a powerful message), almost always it was also true that *the message modifies the medium* (to turn MacLuhan on his head). From a basis that was linguistically largely Spanish, a new Islamic written language was being created that rapidly distanced itself from standard "Christian" Spanish in Latin characters.

An illuminating parallel to bear in mind here, and one that has survived (just) into modern times, is that of written Judeo-Spanish, to which some allusion has already been made. Sephardic Jews, in writing their Spanish vernacular, turned to the Hebrew alphabet as a banner of their cultural and religious distinctiveness. The parallel is far from perfect, because the fifteenth-century Castilian that Sephardic Jews took into their exile has, over the half millennium they have passed outside the Iberian Peninsula, continued to evolve in highly interesting ways, partly in response to the internal linguistic dynamics of the Romance dialects in question, partly as a consequence of fresh contacts outside the Iberian Peninsula with the languages of their hosts, partly as a result of the cultural influence of French on them in the nineteenth and twentieth centuries. To these various non-Hispanic, exotic features of the modern Sephardic vernaculars there are no Islamic Spanish parallels, of course. Morisco Spanish was an exclusively peninsular phenomenon, and it died off very soon after it was exported to North Africa, but what is relevant for us here is that the Jews both in Spain, before their expulsion, and in the Sephardic diaspora after it, also employed their new written mode of expression in translations of the scriptures, for some devotional purposes, and above all in Bible commentaries (as in that great Biblical enterprise, the *Me'am Lo'ez*). Parallel with *aljamía*, this "Biblical" variety of Judeo-Spanish (for which the term "Ladino" is best reserved) is a new Hispanic Romance language reconstructed on Semitic models. Ladino is preeminently a language of linguistic calques, but they are calques based on Hebrew on the imitation of Hebrew grammar using Spanish materials, whereas Islamic Spanish (*aljamiado*) texts were built on Semitic but Arabic models. Ladino also would provide a further illustration of the phenomenon of linguistic divergence motivated by cultural isolation. It is an example of the rejection by non-Christians of the cultural hegemony of "Christian" (Latinate) Spanish models. We see among the Sephardim a similar desire to cultivate a distinctive community identity through their control of their language and literature. (There is no space for us to enter into a proper comparative study of these matters here.)

Because Western Europe has, by and large, had a history in which one religion (Christianity) and one set of high cultural references (Classical antiquity) expressed itself through one alphabet, the Latin alphabet, we have seen little of what I may term "planned divergence." On the eastern fringes of Western Christendom we have had, in recent years, bloody fighting over the alphabet to be used to write what is basically the same South Slav language. In the former Yugoslavia cultural loyalties, not linguistic difference, determine the script to be used. A slightly different example of divergence was furnished by German. It long clung to distinctive letterforms (black-letter Gothic) that were already archaic in the sixteenth century when they came to be used by printers. In the twentieth century, Gothic script was, for a time, associated with the more extreme manifestations of German nationalism. It was a way of asserting identity. In the other direction, on Europe's furthest western fringe, efforts have been made, mainly in the twentieth century, to use a distinctive alphabet as a marker of Irish identity—although the archaizing script in question, being yet another Latin one, has to work very hard in order to manage to stay impenetrable to the outsider. In Europe in general, and with these few exceptions, the written manifestations of our high cultures tend to bring us together. There are many more tokens in common between *written* English, French, German, Italian, Spanish, among others, than there are between our *spoken* languages. But with minority languages the opposite may be the case: *aljamía* and Ladino (and Irish) show how in some circumstances the written manifestations of cultures can have the intention of marking boundaries, of creating a space within which the members of the minority can feel less threatened. A minority that experiences a threat to its continued existence tends to use whatever means it has available to defend itself.

Linguistic Differentiation

To begin to illustrate just one of the ways in which the new written medium, *aljamía*, rapidly diverged from standard "Christian" Spanish, let us take the theologically fundamental word "created." The normal Spanish word for "created" is, of course, *creó,* and God the Creator is *el Creador* (in early texts often *el Criador*). Now these words did not cease to be part of the vocabulary of the Muslims (who, in our period, often speak of *el Criador* in ways that to anybody familiar with early medieval Spanish literature sounds to be very reminiscent of the Christian usage of the *Poema de Mio Cid*). Yet to convey the full resonance of *Allah as Creator* these Muslims clearly felt in many contexts that an Arabic-based word was preferable to one with a Latin etymology. So in their *aljamiado* usage the word *khalaqó* is found much more frequently than *creó/crió. Khaleqó* is the Arabic verbal root *kh-l-q* ("create"), provided with a Castilian verbal third person past termination, *-ó.* That is an example of the simplest type of Arabic linguistic influence undergone by this new medium of expression, and very many more such loan words from Arabic were indeed introduced into the language. As noted above, this process of increasing the Arabic content of the vocabulary ran directly contrary to the de-Arabizing trend of the Spanish language in general at this period. The Arabizing vocabulary of the Muslims thus moved in the opposite direction to the general drift of languages in the West, and emphasized the fact that, for Muslims, the language of culture was Arabic and not Latin.

Perhaps the most disconcerting way in which Arabic modified the vocabulary of the emerging written language was not through straightforward and obvious loan words such as *khaleqar* ("to create") but through the less obvious channel of what some linguisticians call the translation loan word or calque. A translation loan word may superficially not be recognizable as a loan word at all. On the surface it appears to be, it *is,* a normal word drawn from the familiar ancestral common stock of the language in question. What is transferred in this type of borrowing from one language to the other is not sound, a word as a phonetic entity, but an underlying semantic structure. To those who have not encountered it before, this concept may at first be nebulous and hard to grasp, but the process in question is a simple one. In the cases that concern us here, an Arabic semantic structure infuses a Spanish word. Let us take a relatively straightforward example. In Arabic one word for "to go down" or "descend" is *nazila.* The derivative causative form from this ("to bring down") is *anzala.*[9] The corresponding verbal noun is *inzal* ("causing to

9. Following the established lexicographical practice, I am here and elsewhere giving as the Arabic "dictionary form" (corresponding to the English infinitive) the semantically quite distinct Arabic *madi'* or past tense form.

go down"), but in Arabic, since Allah "brought down," "sent down" the Koran to the Prophet, *inzal* also has as a secondary sense of "revelation." One Castilian word to render "to go down" is *descender* (which can in some contexts function also as a causative). In Islamic Spanish texts this verb *descender* acquires the full range of the senses of *anzala* and *inzal,* and in consequence the verbal noun derived from *descender, descendimiento,* can mean "[divine] revelation (as in the Scriptures, etc.)." In this way a word that *externally* seems entirely Romance—there is nothing un-Romance either in the phonology or morphology of *descendimiento*—acquires an inner non-Romance semantic content. Arabic, as the background language of culture makes its presence felt *without appearing on the surface at all.* And a Spanish-speaking Christian, unless he could guess from the context, would fail totally to understand what was meant by it. But then a text was not written in Arabic characters in order to communicate with Christians; on the contrary, it was *intended* to be kept secret.

This process of the creation of translation loan words is by no means the only way in which Arabic colors the Romance language of the Spanish Muslims. The morphology and the syntax of Arabic do also mold the language, and fully to illustrate the special features of Muslim Spanish would really mean giving an account of most features of Arabic grammar. I will not attempt to do that.[10]

Two questions troubled me when I first began to explore this strange linguistic world, and I suspect they will have been present in the minds of many of my readers. In the first place, are not the ways in which Muslim Spanish imitates or mimics Arabic merely examples of incompetent translation? In the second, are these cases of linguistic mimicry limited to translations from Arabic? What, for example, happens in texts that are the original compositions of the Muslim Spanish authors themselves? Do we find similar linguistic peculiarities in them?

The modern reader, if he reads a book that has been translated into his language from another one, generally expects it to read as if it were an original composition. Modern English book reviewers, resolutely monoglot as most of them are, still feel themselves competent to judge whether a novel has been "well translated" or not, even when they have no knowledge whatsoever of the original language. What they usually mean by a "good translation" is one the English of which sounds

10. A pioneering study of great value because it relates the Morisco linguistic phenomena with what happened in the Alfonsine translations, is A. Galmés de Fuentes, *Influencias sintácticas y estilísticas del árabe en la prosa medieval castellana* (Madrid: R. Academia Española, 1956); see for a survey of more recent bibliography, Bernabé Pons (1992).

idiomatic. Alien features carried over from the original text into the translation are accounted blemishes. It has not always been thus. The translators of the King James Bible Old Testament carried over into their resonant English translation many linguistic features of the original Hebrew. These Stuart translators, consummate masters of their art and able to exploit patterns of calquing already established in earlier Biblical translations, chose to mimic in English some of the Semitic structures of the Hebrew original. The Spanish Muslim translators were taking this process of linguistic mimicry many stages further, making their "translation" mirror the original as closely as possible in every way. It might be objected that what they produced as a translation would not be readily comprehensible to a native speaker of Spanish, so that it was not a translation at all. To say that would be to miss the point. If one regards the Koran as untranslatable, and that is indeed the orthodox Muslim doctrine, then what an approximation to a translation (the best that one can hope for) into any other language must do, above all else, is to adhere as closely as possible to the original. The translator does not hope to present *all* aspects of the original to his readers. He knows that is impossible, so he is making available to them the means whereby they can have access to a great deal of what is in the Arabic. And this attitude toward the Koran, bolstered by Islamic theology, inevitably has consequences for other translations from Arabic religious texts, from Arabic texts in general. The Arabic "feel" of the translations must have been seen as a positive, not a negative, characteristic by Morisco readers. It was their guarantee that the translator knew what he was about and was working inside the established tradition.

If we then turn to original texts written by Morisco authors, texts that are not translations, we find many of the same Arabizing features that first arose in the translations. Clearly, the Arabisms have become positively valued stylistic features, thoroughly acclimatized in the new "Islamic Spanish" style, now models to be imitated. In contrast, for Christian authors of the Spanish sixteenth-century Golden Age, the stylistic models admired were those of Classical antiquity, or from slightly more recent times, those writers, Petrarch, for example, who belonged squarely inside Europe's classicizing tradition. Such attitudes toward Europe's heritage had little meaning to Muslims. They were busy creating their own style, based on completely different models. The two traditions were not converging but diverging: Muslims made every effort to be different. And they succeeded. These literary and stylistic considerations must have some relevance when elsewhere in this book we examine questions related to assimilation. The writings of Spain's crypto-Muslims are clear evidence of their determination to be different and to stay that way.

Perhaps we can understand what was beginning to happen if we look at the parallel cases of Urdu and Hindi. These languages arise from the same North Indian vernaculars, and they differed in the first place merely in the scripts they employed. Urdu, like *aljamía,* is written by means of an adaptation of the Arabic script. For Hindi, the cultural and linguistic models that are admired are provided by the Hindu scriptures, and look back toward Sanskrit. For Urdu, the languages of culture are Persian, and behind that, of course, Arabic. So the source for the learned terms and cultural allusions of Hindi is Sanskrit, whereas Arabic and Persian fulfill that function for Urdu. Time, religious divisions, political history, can all tug one language apart into two.

In the case of the Islamic Spanish of this Morisco period, there was hardly time for a great deal of development and evolution to take place; indeed, it is remarkable that differences of such magnitude as we do find became fixed so quickly. Writers such as the Young Man from Arévalo built a distinctive style that could never be confused with the work of their Christian contemporaries. After the final expulsion of 1609, the refugee community from Spain was free to pick up the threads of Arabic culture once more; because *aljamiado* literature did not live on into modern times, we should not underestimate the tremendous effort that the crypto-Muslims of Spain in the sixteenth century had put into developing it. In spite of all the limitations inflicted upon them by the persecutions of the Inquisition (for whom any manuscript in Arabic script was liable to be condemned as a Koran), a new literature was created. It was paradoxical that considerable innovatory ingenuity was deployed in the service of cultural and religious conservatism.

Books

We have thus far been concerned largely with languages and writing systems, not with actual books and their contents. We must now address the question: how much of the great corpus of Islamic literature was accessible to the Muslims of Spain at this date? What did this persecuted minority have available as reading matter? And did they make any contribution of their own to the corpus of Islamic literature? In other words, what was the degree of cultural isolation from the Islamic heartlands from which these crypto-Muslims suffered?

First to be surveyed will be books available to Moriscos in Arabic or in direct translation from that language, and we can then proceed to look at the contents of new compositions, all of which are in *aljamía.* (The Sacromonte books are sui generis. I hope chapter 8 below will make clear why these last Arabic books to be written in Spain need to be presented as a phenomenon apart.)

Books in Arabic Available to the Muslims of Spain in the Late Period: Sources

Of the books that can be identified as having once belonged to the Moriscos, clearly what has survived until the present day in libraries and archives must be a small remnant of what once existed. It is remarkable that we know as much as we do about the banned reading matter of this underground minority. Prudent Moriscos will have destroyed many volumes before they could be used in the courts as evidence against them. Particularly in the opening years of the sixteenth century, when refugees could leave Spain more easily, prized codices would be taken out of the country by those emigrating. Nevertheless, it is possible to speak with considerable confidence of the range of written material available to Spain's Muslims after 1500.

Our sources are first of all those surviving books containing evidence (marginal and other annotations, jottings on the flyleaf, etc.) of their Hispano-Arabic provenance. As one would expect, it is in Spanish libraries above all that the richest of such collections are to be found, but the survey on which this chapter is based was extended to other libraries outside Spain wherever the catalogs permitted necessary identifications to be made. Sadly, detailed information about provenance is often lacking (particularly in the earlier accessions to the Biblioteca Nacional in Madrid). Even where the place of discovery of the volume in question is not now known, notes on inside leaves may give clues as to whether the work was once in Morisco hands, and that is what is relevant here.

Very fortunately, dating from the late sixteenth or early seventeenth centuries there is one large and virtually intact manuscript collection of unimpeachable crypto-Muslim provenance now preserved in a Madrid library (the Almonacid hoard, long housed in the library of Escuela de Estudios Árabes, and now in the headquarters of the Consejo Superior de Investigaciones Científicas (hereafter CSIC) in the Calle de Medinaceli in Madrid). There have also been other, smaller finds in recent years. These are reliably genuine sources of information, and act as useful cross-checks where items of more doubtful provenance come to light. In addition, from internal references in Morisco writings in *aljamía* we can glean a great deal of information about the Arabic reading matter generally available. The picture that emerges from all these sources is a remarkably coherent one, and it is indeed possible to form a judgment as to what might have reached the crypto-Muslims through their underground cultural networks. There is a very large measure of agreement among scholars attempting to interpret this evidence.

As we might expect, the books used by the Moriscos were predominantly works of devotion intended for the pious. If the very fact that one possessed an Arabic book at all might put one and one's family in mortal danger, one was more likely to run that risk for a religious manual than for a collection of secular poetry or a study of history. And under such conditions multivolume works of heavyweight scholarship of any sort were unlikely to survive. Among these collections, anthologies of short pious texts and commonplace books of meaningful extracts abound.

The Koran itself, of course, is by far the most frequently found book (more than fifty manuscripts contain the complete book or excerpts), but rarely does one find large opulently copied codices. Sometimes the crypto-Muslims had to content themselves with an abbreviated selection of *suras;* presumably such little volumes could be secreted with greater ease.[11] It is not unusual to find bilingual texts, usually Arabic with interlineal *aljamiado* versions or commentaries (on *aljamiado* Korans; see below).

Commentaries on the Koran usually are bulky and voluminous, and it is perhaps for that reason that among what has survived there is only one such work, and even that is incomplete: the *Tafsir* of Ibn Abi Za-manin in a manuscript from the Almonacid hoard (Ribera and Asín 1912 [hereafter J], 51). A manuscript in the Borgiano Collection in the Vatican Library (no. 132 [3]): al-Sijistani, *Tafsir garib al-qur'an* [A study of difficult terms in the holy text]) is also a work that was in Morisco ownership. Bound up with this (MS. no. 132 [4]) is the fundamental treatise by Ibn Salama on those verses of the Koran that were abrogated (*mansukh,* that is, had been replaced and rendered obsolete by subsequent revelations). The crypto-Muslims were clearly aware of the existence of a complex critical and scholarly literature on this subject, even though a very limited selection of works was available to them. Although among them full commentaries were few and far between, that should not lead us to conclude that they were unaware of the subtleties of this and other branches of Koranic studies.

One such specialist field in Arabic is called *qira'a,* "reading." This technical term refers mainly to the usually quite minor differences in the vocalization of the agreed consonant outline of the holy text. The

11. Saavedra (1889, 238), lists the following as the usual selection of *suras* found: I; II, 1–4, 256–59, 284–86, III, 1–26; IX, 129–30; XXVI, 78–89; XXVIII, 88; XXX, 16–18; XXXIII, 40–43; XXXVI; XLVII; LXXVIII–CXIV. This was not as universal a choice as Saavedra supposed, but it may serve as an example of the sort of drastically reduced text that the Moriscos sometimes employed. At the other extreme, Cristina Álvarez Millán (2002) recently reported the discovery of an immense Arabic Koran (425 × 295 mm) in the library of the R. Academia de la Historia, Madrid. It was copied in 1597 by a Morisco, Muhammad Ballester, but interestingly, possibly not in Spain but in North Africa (Álvarez Millán 2004, 367–83).

subject had early been codified into seven accepted "readings," but Islamic Spain, in this as in other respects rigid in its doctrinal orthodoxy according to the school of the imam Malik, restricted itself to the method of *Nafi'* ("the reading of those who dwell in Paradise," as its proponents styled it), and within that to the two subsystems of Qalun and Warsh. There is a manuscript now in the Biblioteca Nacional in Madrid (Guillén Robles 1889 [hereafter GR], 591) of fifteenth-century origins that probably passed through Morisco hands. Most remarkably, some crypto-Muslim must have thought it worthwhile to render this into the vernacular as *La contradición y deferencia que hay entre Guarx y Qalun* (Disagreements and differences between [the readings of] Warsh and Qalun [J 12]).

Hadith

After the Koran, there is probably no part of Islamic literature more important to believers than what is known as "tradition" (hadith). The word in its more general sense signifies "tale" or "narrative," but here it has a technical sense, and refers to narratives about the sayings and actions of the Prophet Muhammad himself and of his Companions as handed down according to rigorous criteria. Such material has immense meaning to Muslims in that it provides information supplementary to the Koran. It does not have authority equivalent to the Koran, but a story from a hadith, which, after an elaborate process of authentication and criticism of the transmission (*isnad*) is adjudged to be sound (*sahih*), may serve as a basis for preaching, teaching, and legislation (so long, of course, as it is not in conflict with the positive legislation already derived from the direct word of Allah). The problem for Spanish Muslims living in clandestinity must have been that this corpus of material is quite voluminous (even the slightest actions or preferences of the Prophet or his Companions might be recorded, and at length, and to those texts was vital that there should be added a complete record of the stages of textual transmission).

   In early centuries, hadith had been collected into what were regarded as the "six books" of unimpeachable authority (which is not to say that other sources might not contain genuine material); above all, two collections were esteemed, those of al-Bukhari and of Muslim, often referred to as "the Two Sound ones" (*Sahihan*). To have all this at hand would have meant owning a bulky library indeed. It is hardly surprising that we find no indication that any heavyweight works were in Morisco hands. Probably the weightiest item of hadith scholarship known to be in Morisco hands is one manuscript (J 10) of the Almonacid collection, *K. fihi tafsir mukhtalif al-hadith* (Book elucidating various traditions) by Ibn Qutayba.

This ninth-century author did much to create the basis for serious hadith scholarship, the critical study of chains of transmission, for example. The copy in question is described in the catalog as "full of notes, explanations and marginal markings drawing attention to interesting points." It is reasonable to assume that the copy is roughly contemporaneous with the other work bound up with it, which is dated A.H. 846 (A.D. 1443), so that the annotations are likely to be earlier than the Morisco period. It is, all the same, of significance that the Morisco who walled up the Almonacid hoard judged scholarship of this quality worth retaining.

The rest of what we find are short anthology-type collections of hadith. Selections of *Forty Traditions* were popular in many parts of the Islamic world, and not least in Spain. In a late manuscript from Spain now in the Borgiano manuscript collection at the Vatican Library (Borgiano arabo 159) there are the *Forty Traditions* of al-Ajurri, and we know of no less than three copies of the work with the same title by the great al-Gazali, two in Madrid (Biblioteca Nacional, GR 84 and 86), and one in the Vatican (Borgiano arabo 162).

A favorite work in the field of hadith was by the Egyptian scholar al-Quda'i (d. A.D. 1062), *Kitab shihab al-akhbar* (Book of the resplendent light of stories concerning the parables and teachings related by the most excellent Prophet). Al-Quda'i was indeed read all over the Islamic world. There are four Morisco-associated manuscripts of his work, one solely in Arabic, two bilingual, and one in *aljamía* alone (three of these from Almonacid), and in addition, there is a commentary on it by al-Warraq al-Babi in the Vatican Borgiano collection (see Brockelmann 1937–1949 [hereafter GAL], suppl. 1, 585[4] Cmt.). This last seems to consist mainly of brief aphorisms allegedly derived from hadith literature such as "The Koran is the remedy" (f. 5r), "The finest death is that of the martyrs" (f. 128), or "He who brings a man into Islam will enter Paradise" (f. 50v). Some would not recommend themselves to a modern taste: "A woman is like a bent rib: try to straighten her out and she will break; just take pleasure in her, even though she is bent." A similar collection, and conceived by way of a supplement to that of al-Quda'i (not one of whose traditions is repeated in it, so the author tells us) is the *Book of the Star* by Abu'l-Abbas Muhammad al-Tujibi of Denia, known perhaps more often as al-Iklishi because he lived for some time in Uclés (J 54). Yet another work in this category by an Andalusi scholar is the *K. anwar al-saniyya* by Ibn Juzayy (J 37 [10]).

Temimi (1993b, 61–68) has studied two of the Morisco manuscripts of al-Quda'i and al-Tujibi. As he puts it (63), "Reading them offered the Moriscos not only a haven of peace but also a flame of hope, something to restore their confidence, to tighten community bonds, and to give them the strength to sacrifice and to struggle." With this positive assessment of what Moriscos got from such books I would not disagree. I am not sure that Temimi is entirely fair in the strictures that he heaps on the state of these Arabic texts: "We have collated the reading of this manuscript [he is looking at this point at Almonacid J (29)][and found] a long list of errors in the copy. . . . The errors and grammatical, verbal and linguistic mistakes are proof, if there were any need for that, of ignorance of the elementary rules of the language. Often indeed the copyist forgets a word, or makes additions without realizing it. The simplicity and rhythm of the sentence are profoundly affected."

Temimi is judging this Morisco manuscript by standards he would apply in dealing with texts printed and edited by himself in modern times. To reach a fair comparative evaluation of copies executed by Morisco copyists, one ought to compare like with like. One should compare Morisco books with the productions of rural scribes at this time in other Islamic lands where Arabic was not the vernacular. In addition, al-Andalus did have some spelling conventions of its own, and departures from oriental norms that now have become standard throughout the Arab world may actually not arise from ignorance. Most important, it is necessary to bear in mind that the base text on which the Morisco copyist was working almost certainly did not correspond to whatever we may have available for comparison as a modern standard edition. The sort of relatively free treatment of the copy text that Temimi condemns was, I suspect, widespread at this time (not only in Islamic Spain, but elsewhere in the Islamic world, and not only in the Islamic world, for much the same sort of thing would have been going on in Christian Europe).

In preparing a much earlier version of this chapter, I began to attempt a close comparison of various versions of a section of the *aljamiado* translations of *Tanbih al-gafilin* (Warning to those who are forgetful) by al-Samarqandi with a printed edition (no Morisco Arabic version being extant). Although I was able to learn a great deal about how the Moriscos must have set about their task, I soon came to see that I could not sensibly pursue that particular type of enquiry further, precisely because of the complexities arising from multiple textual variations at all levels. We who live in the world of the Xerox Corporation naturally think that any copy other than one that reproduces the "original" in all its detail is a very imperfect one. In our age even clandestine underground books produced for samizdat publication can be letter-perfect. It is difficult for us to imagine ourselves into the situation of the dedicated individuals who were struggling to preserve the literature of their persecuted faith in Almonacid by laboriously copying every dot and diacritic of their

Arabic-character copy texts. It is hardly surprising that they sometimes produced imperfect copies.

I am certainly not seeking to deny that the productions of the clan-destine scribes in that up-country Aragonese village, Almonacid de la Sierra, often look like the work of clandestine rural scribes. I am only surprised at how professional their work at times can be. It is good for a scholar of Temimi's caliber to remind us that these texts have their limi-tations, but is it fair to write off the work of these scribes as worthless? As for hadith literature among the crypto-Muslims, one is forced to the conclusion—and it is hardly a surprising one, given the circumstances under which they lived—that in this field the serious scholarship of the highest order necessary to sustain studies was no longer possible. But then how much scholarship of the requisite degree of accuracy existed in the 1590s anywhere in the Islamic world outside a few favored specialist centers? Almonacid was a small village up in the hills south of Saragossa, not a major seat of learning.

The reason why some of these traditions may have been perceived by the Moriscos as speaking directly to them in their condition may perhaps not be clear from Temimi's excellent translations into French but are obvious from the Arabic originals he supplies. In translation, the special resonance for the Muslims of Spain at this period of certain words cannot always be heard. We may take as an example *garib* (plural *guraba'*). This word is rendered by him, according to context, as *étrange* and *étranger,* words with negative connotations ("strange," "stranger"). As has been explained in discussing the Oran fatwa, there was an interpretation of the word *garib* that was *positive,* and this interpretation certainly was current among Moriscos. In an eschatology from which they obviously drew much comfort, when the Prophet referred to the role of the *garib* at the end of days, they saw a promise of an ultimate favorable outcome for themselves. In this way, the ancient literature of hadith, which, so we would assume, could have nothing to communicate to crypto-Muslims about the daily tribulations of life in Spain in the sixteenth century, was felt by them to refer directly to their particular condition.

The Lives of the Prophets
In writings intended in the main for popular edification, much atten-tion was accorded to the lives of the Prophets, linked in some forms of presentation to the biography (*sira*) of Muhammad himself. Under this heading we cannot fail to mention the earliest work in circulation among the Moriscos of which we have firm evidence: the final volume of *Bad' al-khalq wa-qisas al-anbiya* (The most outstanding of mankind, and the stories of the Prophets) by al-Farisi (d. 902) (Borgiano arabo 165), with

which was associated a similar work by an otherwise unidentified Ustadh Abu'l-Qasim, *Lata'if al-Anbiya, wa-fihi Kitab qisas al-anbiya.* Also in the same group of manuscripts (they are now in the Vatican Library) are al-Qazwini's *Rai' al-durar* (see GAL, suppl. 1, 198 [6]); Borgiano arabo 132 (7), and al-Tarafi's *Qisas al-anbiya* (GAL, suppl. 1, 393) Borgiano arabo 125 [2]). In this subject area, however, it is the *Kitab al-anwar* (Book of lights) by Abu'l-Hasan al-Bakri al-Basri that appears to have been the favorite manual. We have no less than four *aljamiado* manuscripts of this one work, and an Arabic text (the latter bound up with the work by al-Tarafi just mentioned in Borgiano arabo 125). From the way in which the subject matter is set out, it is virtually certain that this particular book was the principal source of Muhammad Rabadan's *aljamiado Discourse of the Light and Lineage of Muhammad* (see below). The Arabic narrative opens with Adam, first of the prophets, who is instructed by Gabriel to give homage to the Prophet yet to come. This view of the prophetic succession (*varonía de la luz,* "the heroic succession of light," was the *aljamiado* expression) is handed on from prophet to prophet. The earlier figures are passed over rapidly to leave more space for a full development on Muhammad and his immediate forebears.

All these various works on the earlier prophets and on Muhammad are reasonably accessible, one might say even popular, compilations, of which the primary purpose was to instruct, also to exhort, even to entertain. One thing is clear from this literature: the devotion accorded to Muhammad, the celebration of the feast of his birthday (*mawlid/mawlud*) was a well-established feature of popular Islam in Spain. In much earlier times and elsewhere in the Islamic world, the marking of the day by special ceremonies may have met resistance from those who regarded it as an undesirable innovation, but clearly Spain's crypto-Muslims saw such practices as an integral part of their religion, something to be preserved under conditions of adversity along with other more central doctrinal features.

Alongside such prose narratives, compositions in verse on the prophetic line of descent deserve mention. In the period immediately preceding the one we are studying, in Nasrid days, poems were written in Granada for Muhammad's birthday and were performed on that occasion (see Salmi 1956). In Granada, such poems, in classical Arabic, were embellished with a rhetorically conventional introductory section (*nasib*) and rounded off with a panegryric (*madih*) dedicated to the ruling sultan. Nothing of all this was handed on into our period, and no new compositions sustain the tradition. It is probably to vernacular Arabic verse (which certainly existed in North Africa and presumably had done so in Granada) that we must relate the *aljamiado* compositions on this subject (discussed below).

The theme of the *nur Muhammadi* (the light of Muhammad), in the hands of some earlier writers had been a vehicle through which neo-Platonic and even Gnostic illuminist ideas might be transmitted, but there is nothing to suggest that this was behind the importance of poems on the *mawlid* among Spain's Muslims in the sixteenth century. The motive seems to have been simple and sincere pious devotion to the Prophet.

Sufism and the Moriscos

Al-Andalus was the homeland of one of the best-known writers on Sufi themes in Arabic, Muhyi al-Din Ibn 'Arabi (born in Murcia in A.D.1165). We might therefore have expected Sufism to make a strong contribution to the underground literature circulating in Spain. However, whether we look at the books in Arabic available to Spain's crypto-Muslims or at their own original writings, the Sufi element, so important elsewhere in the Islamic world at this time, is relatively absent. Moriscos had access to few Sufi religious texts of any level of intellectual sophistication, almost the sole exception being the *Minhaj al-'abidin* by al-Gazali (discussed below). Of course, some of the pious anecdotes and stories contained in the lives of prophets would not be out of place within a Sufi framework, but the unpretentious literature that has survived from the Moriscos is characterized, above all, by straightforward Sunni orthodoxy rather than by mysticism. It is perhaps not surprising that one of the steps that had to be taken (largely at the initiative of "Citi Bulgaiz," their great benefactor) in order to integrate Morisco refugees into society in Tunis when they eventually arrived there in the early seventeenth century (see chapter 11), was to put them into contact with the Sufi craft guilds (*tariqas*). One might well have thought that already in the Iberian Peninsula such guilds would have provided a highly suitable social mechanism to enable Muslims to cope clandestinely with the persecutions to which they were subjected in the sixteenth century, but we hear little of their existence. The regulation of the silk trade in Granada, the sort of milieu in which we might expect to find Sufism flourishing, was economically certainly most important, based as it was in the Alcaicería (*al-qaysariyya*), but it appears to have been a municipal concern and dealing principally with craft matters.

It is dangerous to base too much on an absence of evidence, but the lack of signs of Sufi literature is striking. The great "Ben'Arabi" was certainly remembered by the Young Man from Arévalo, but rather as a sort of thaumaturge, and within the present context it has to be said that although the name was bandied about in order to impress, not a single book of all his enormous production can be shown to have circulated among Moriscos. This is, frankly, surprising.

Pious Miscellanies

Among the books owned by Muslims in this late period were many pious miscellanies, usually arranged in a loosely thematic way and designed primarily for religious edification (although often including many items that one might classify as popular narratives designed primarily for entertainment). Because we lack a convenient name with which to designate the genre, it is difficult to discuss them, but the type is indeed easily recognized if one has any familiarity with Morisco manuscripts. I did in the past (Harvey 1958, 164ff) suggest the designation of "paraenetic works" for such volumes, but I now find that to be an absurdly overerudite term, quite at odds with the popular nature of the texts in question. Perhaps "exhortatory miscellany" would be preferable. We may certainly relate the genre to those later devotional (rather than scholarly) developments of hadith literature to which reference has already been made (anthologized *Forty Traditions*, etc.), but it is perhaps best understood as an offshoot of popular preaching (*waʿz*). The formal *khutba* or Friday homily, usually short, is something distinct; what I have in mind here were extended popular sermons, at times addressed to large multitudes, and ranging over a broad span of moralizing, admonitory, and edifying material. Those who are familiar in medieval Castilian with, for example, the lively Christian sermons of the archpriest of Talavera (with their frequent warnings of hellfire) may form some idea of the tone of this parallel Islamic genre. We can be quite sure that preaching of this kind continued among the crypto-Muslims, for the works of the Young Man from Arévalo contain eyewitness accounts of occasions when the faithful assembled (presumably in secret) to listen to sermons (sometimes given by females!).

It is instructive to compare these "anthologies of short pious texts" that we find in collections of Morisco manuscripts with a type of book in circulation in present-day Sudan as reported by Holy (1991, 25):

Most *fugaraa* [i.e., *álfaquíes*] keep a small library which consists of a few printed books and an *umbatri* ("that which mentions everything"). *Umbatri* is a collection of handwritten papers which form a loose-leaf book held together by a string, and carried around wrapped in a piece of cloth. The writings contain extracts which the *fakii* copied from printed books, from the handwritten books of other *fugaraa*, and which he has inherited from his father or some other close kinsman who was a *fakii* himself. The extracts contain descriptions of religious rituals, different methods of divination, descriptions of the precise content and form of various amulets, the use of Koranic formulae for curing diseases, protecting crops from birds and locusts, bringing on rain and for numerous other benevolent as well as malevolent purposes.

The *umbatri* is not identical to the Morisco "miscellaneous" volumes. The Sudanese do not seem to anthologize entertaining narrative passages in the way that the Moriscos did, for example. And the Morisco books were often quite well bound, not left in loose-leaf form. But there are very many points of similarity. One must presume that similar pressures have led to similar outcomes in two very different places.

There is no doubt whatsoever that among sixteenth-century Muslims in Spain the most successful work of general pious instruction, if we are to judge from the manuscripts that have come down to us, was the *Tanbih al-gafilin* (Warning to those who are forgetful). This collection of moral tales and pious teachings was not assembled by a Morisco anthologist, but by the central Asian author Abu'l-Layth al-Samarqandi. There is no copy of the Arabic text extant that can be proved to have been in Morisco hands, but the *aljamiado* translations (linguistically of unquestioned sixteenth-century provenance) provide evidence enough that the original must have been available to them. There are two magnificently executed codices containing complete translations (apparently not identical) of what is a long book, and the number of fragments from it, copied into other exhortatory miscellanies, is large.

Extensive studies of this group of manuscripts were carried out by Manzanares de Cirre, but unfortunately her transcription was not published. One of the codices on which she worked is in the National Library in Madrid (GR 1) and the other is a manuscript (J 6) in the Almonacid collection of the CSIC. There are fragments in Madrid (GR 72), in a manuscript in the National Library, Paris (Arabe 774), and in one of the Gayangos manuscripts now in the Real Academia de la Historia (old classification T 19, a manuscript that was once owned by Gayangos). In the Almonacid collection, besides the volume already mentioned, there are fragments in manuscripts J 3 (3), 4(13), and 8 (31).

Some idea of the way in which this author's name had become a byword among Moriscos is to be gleaned from the phonetic corruptions it suffered: we find Samarqandil (or, as it was written in Latin characters, Çamarqandil, and even with loss of the cedilla by oversight, Camarqindil). In a Latin-character manuscript (now in Paris) written by one Mohammed (*sic*) Devera of Albarracín, this latter form of the name puzzled even that great early nineteenth-century orientalist, Baron Silvestre de Sacy. In a reference to this manuscript, he (Sacy 1828, 311), produced an uncharacteristically wild speculation. This must be a word meaning "a disparate mixture of things: *qamar-qindil* ('moon-lamp')," he ventured. Delighting in the discomfiture of others is an entirely unworthy sentiment, but anybody who has ever struggled in vain with some *aljamiado* manuscript (as I often have) will find it hard not to take unworthy pleasure at the spectacle of one of the greatest of orientalists fumbling in the dark, too.

It may seem odd that "the man from Samarqand," a scholar working in central Asia at the end of the tenth century, should have had such success with a very different readership—the persecuted Muslims of sixteenth-century Aragon and Castile, and that these Muslims should have lavished such efforts on the study and translation of his work and have been willing to risk so much by owning such large volumes. What had he to offer? A combination of ethics and piety, suggested Joseph Schacht, in the entry for this author in the *Encylopaedia of Islam* (2d ed.).

Let us examine another example of this genre in search of further indications of what the Moriscos looked for in their pious reading.

Ibn al-Jawzi did not live quite so far removed geographically from Spain as al-Samarqandi, but far enough away in all conscience. It might seem that there would be few points of intellectual contact between the culturally isolated and mostly rural-dwelling Moriscos and al-Jawzi from urban Bagdad, capital of the revived Abbasid caliphate, in the late twelfth century. There, as a teacher in institutions of higher learning and as a preacher who not only held an official appointment to deliver the Friday *khutba* before the caliphs but who also was a successful popular preacher to the urban masses, as an author responsible (according to Ibn Taimiyya) for more than a thousand works on mainly Islamic subjects, he may be said to have lived with his finger on the spiritual and intellectual pulse of the Islamic world of his day. By him we have *Salwat al-ahzan* (Consolation in times of sorrow), J 38 in the Almonacid collection. This Madrid manuscript is in Arabic, and there is no *aljamiado* translation extant, but the copy of the Arabic text found at Almonacid was, according to Asín (in the catalog to the collection), made in the fifteenth or sixteenth century (i.e., it is *not* one of the many books of greater antiquity preserved in this library). Placing it in what he calls the "homilectic" genre, Asín describes it as a "collection of narratives designed to move to devotion" (Ribera and Asin 1912, 148). Beginning with an account of Abraham's worship at the Ka'ba, and going on to accounts of Old Testament prophets incorporating material of patent Haggadic and Christian origin, there are stories concerning Muhammad and his Companions, and the incomplete volume as we have it ends with Judgment Day and details of resurrection. Such a bare indication of the contents cannot convey the work's ideological slant. As a model of righteous Sunni orthodoxy, ibn al-Jawzi stood against anything that smacked of heresy: against Shiism, against the platonizing Brethren of Purity, against Sufism, against philosophy and philosophers. To call the author of so many books an anti-intellectual would obviously be absurd, but his life's work was to try to hold together the narrow old Sunni consensus (*ijma'*) and to resist innovations of all kinds. The strictly pious, observant, nonspeculative non-Sufi Islam for which he stood, of which he was a principal spokesman at the heart of the caliphate, was likely to appeal to the persecuted crypto-Muslims of Spain living beyond the boundaries of the Islamic world. Ibn al-Jawzi's writings in no way reflected the realities of the Iberian Peninsula of his day, nor yet did they foreshadow the tribulations to come for the people of al-Andalus. What he dealt in was straightforward doctrinal certainty, and it was for that precisely that so many confused crypto-Muslims in Spain yearned.

The school of Islamic law to which Ibn al-Jawzi subscribed was Hanbalism, but all Spain's Muslims at this time, indeed most of them at any time, followed in *fiqh* (Islamic law) the teachings of the imam Malik Ibn Anas (Malikism). (It was not until refugees found themselves living in lands where the other schools of law flourished that some late Spanish Muslims began to take some interest in them.) Ibn al-Jawzi's work was valued for its religious preaching. When it came to the law rather than general religious instruction, in Spain the textbooks Muslims wanted were Maliki ones.

Fiqh: Islamic Legal Texts

The legal texts available in Spain at this time are best divided for our purposes into two groups, early works inherited from the "classical" period of Islam and later studies, many but not all of which were written in al-Andalus itself. In the first group we have basic short manuals produced during the great age of Maliki legal activity at the end of the tenth and during the eleventh centuries. Of these, perhaps the most important text was the *Risala* (Treatise) of Ibn Abi Zayd al-Qayrawani (d. 996). This standard textbook has remained in use into modern times, so it is hardly surprising that Muslims in Spain should have valued it. It is not so much a manual for the profound student (it is too succinct), as a reliable introduction to law for the general reader. Not surprisingly, we have several manuscripts attesting to the esteem in which it was held: one in the National Library, Madrid (GR 42, in Arabic, and 62, in *aljamía;* see also GR 114, in Arabic). In the Almonacid hoard, manuscript C (*sic*) is entitled *"This is the commentary on the* Risala *and its explanation, translated from Arabic to Romance, word for word."* In the same collection, manuscript J 3 has a short *aljamiado* section (f. 205ff) extracted from it.

Muntakhab al-ahkam (Selected legal sentences) by Ibn Abi Zamanin (already mentioned for his Koranic commentary) is an ancient work that survived in only one copy (GR 39, Arabic with *aljamiado* annotations).

The *Kitab al-tafri' fi'l-fiqh,* dealing with the systematic elaboration of the branches of law by Ibn Jallab al-Basri (d. 1007), is another ancient work that enjoyed wide currency still: one Arabic manuscript and at least three translations, one written in normal Latin characters and two in *aljamía* survive. The Arabic text is in Madrid (GR 102), of the *aljamiado* versions one is in the same Madrid collection (GR 2), one in the Almonacid collection (J 33), and the one in Latin characters is in Toledo. This is an author from whom the Young Man from Arévalo quotes frequently and at length. There can be no doubt as to his fame among the Moriscos. 'Abd al-Wahhab ibn 'Ali al-Bagdadi wrote in the same field (on "the branches" of the law) the *Kitab al-talqin fi'l-furu'* of which the Madrid manuscript (GR 43) is in Arabic with *aljamiado* annotations.

The final two texts of this early period that must be mentioned are both by authors from Spain, who both died in 1070. 'Abdallah al-Fihri (born at Alpuente in A.H. 462) produced not a legal textbook but a collection of specimen notarial acts (J 11). As may be imagined, this is of great use for the study of the society and institutions of al-Andalus of al-Fihri's own times, for he uses documents that he presents as genuine. (Of course, they may not always be exactly what they purport to be, and have, I fear, misled some, but that is a matter outside our present concern.) He states at the outset that his sources are the earlier compilations of Ibn al-'Attar and 'Abdallah Ibn Abi Zamanin. What is to be noted from the point of view of the study of late Spanish Islam is the tenacious conservatism that preserved in use legal formularies relating to a totally different society five hundred years earlier. These legal formularies were put together in the first place for the practical purpose of making life easy for busy notaries, who could rapidly find in them specimen documents relating to the sort of business likely to come their way. Notaries in Spain living clandestinely under Christian rule can hardly have preserved these collections for the same practical reasons. Nostalgia would perhaps not be exactly the right word to use for what they felt, but the collections were to Spain's crypto-Muslims a token that a functioning Islamic society had indeed once existed in their land (and might one day be revived?).

Ibn 'Abd al-Barr al-Namari's Maliki treatise entitled the *Kitab al-istidhkar* (i.e., *Memorandum*) J 7 survives in a thirteenth-century manuscript, but we can be quite certain that this was in Morisco hands, for the fly-leaf contains calendar notes relating to A.H. 911–920. The work takes the form of a commentary to the famous *al-Muwatta'* of Malik Ibn Anas. Malik's manual of hadith enjoyed enormous respect.

By 'Ali Ibn 'Isa Abu'l-Hasan al-Tulaytuli we have two *aljamiado* fragments of his *al-Mukhtasar al-masa'il* (Resumé of case law) in manuscript

J 9 from Almonacid and in another manuscript found subsequently in Sabiñán. About this lawyer, who studied and practiced in Cordova before returning to his native city, al-Faradi (*Biblioteca Arabico-Hispanica,* VII: 259, entry 921) relates the anecdote that his fellow Toledans became so thoroughly tired of the way this jurist continually laid down the law to them that he was obliged to retire to a small farm outside the city and live on its produce. Al-Tulaytuli's work was also the basis of the *Kitab manzum al-durar* (The book of arranging pearls on a string) by al-Fakhkhar al-Judhami, who died ca. 1323 (J 14).

Of about the same period was al-Khalil Ibn Ishaq (usually known as Sidi Khalil) who lived in Egypt and died in 1365. Confirmation that his work circulated in Spain is provided by the copy of the *Mukhtasar* (Resumé) produced by another Egyptian, al-Damiri (d. 1452; J 50 from Almonacid).

Abu'l-Hasan 'Ali ibn al-Qasim (d. 1189, see Ribera and Asín 1912, 32) was a North African who served as *qadi* of Algeciras; he compiled a collection of specimen notarial documents that was not so entirely archaic, for there are some references to twelfth-century Algeciras, but certainly nothing close to the realities of sixteenth-century crypto-Islam. This volume, *al-Maqsad al-mahmud fi talkhis al-ʿuqud* (J 5), had, from its worn appearance, seemingly been much consulted by Moriscos in the final period.

The last Islamic scholar formed in the old mold who lived in Granada under the Nasrids was Muhammad al-Mawwaq. I have written elsewhere (Harvey 1989, 71–75) of how this scholar remained in Granada after its occupation by the Catholic Monarchs. He boasts of having been called in to give medical treatment to a Spanish dignitary, presumably the archbishop Cisneros or perhaps Talavera, although he does not actually name his patient. He wrote several works, none of which survives in a Morisco copy, but in fragments of paper found in association with the Almonacid collection (J 64 [1]) there are notes of fatwas issued by him, thus confirming that there was continuity between the close of the great tradition of legal studies in Granada and the efforts of the Aragonese, as crypto-Muslims, to preserve the Andalusi heritage.

Theology

Mention has already been made above of the genre of the formal *khutba* or homily. By Ibn Nubata, preacher to Sayf al-Dawla of Aleppo (d. 984) we have among the Almonacid manuscripts (J 17) Arabic homilies. In addition there are fragmentary *aljamiado* translations of works by him (Almonacid manuscript B), so that we can be quite sure that attention was being paid by the Aragonese Moriscos to this early theologian.

Theology is rather an elevated term to apply to the simple, practical devotional material we frequently find, as for example, al-Jazari's *Al-Hisn al-hasin min kalam sayyid al-mursalin* (Stronghold of the sayings of he who is the Lord over all those sent as prophets). Al-Jazari, who died in 1427, provides prayers for all occasions: "from morning till night, and all through life until death." Of a quite different order of theological sophistication were the writings of the great al-Gazali, perhaps the most eminent of those writers in Arabic whose works were available in the sixteenth century to crypto-Muslims. With the exception only of the Koran itself, al-Gazali's is the work most frequently mentioned in Morisco texts, and by him there survive many manuscripts of Morisco provenance. Nevertheless it has to be recorded that what we have that can be shown to have been used by Spanish crypto-Muslims was hardly the most substantial of his treatises. Of the great *Ihya 'ulum al-din* (Rebirth of theological sciences) we have merely a fragment of some six folios in the Almonacid hoard. As for the *Jawahir al-qur'an* (Jewels of the Koran—there is a single Borgiano manuscript) and as for the *Kitab al-arba'in fi usul al-din* (The forty on the foundations of religion) we have a manuscript in the same collection and also one in the National Library in Madrid; there related works together make up a treatise giving what sets out to be an abridged but complete account of Islamic theology on the basis of forty key Koranic texts (the "jewels" referred to in the title). A work intended to be widely accessible, al-Gazali's *K. maqsad al-asna sharh asma Allah al-husna* ("Commentary on God's Holy Names"; Borgiano collection, no. 166), is a complete enumeration and commentary of the ninety-nine names (or attributes) of the Divinity (and al-Gazali rather disarmingly points out that the reader will not find *exactly* that number, for in some cases the substitution of synonyms would be possible, but at all events the number is not an even one because "God is uneven [one hesitates to translate this as "odd"] and loves whatever is uneven."

There is in the Almonacid collection a mere fragment of the great work entitled *K. al-iqtisad fi'l-i'tiqad* (rendered into Spanish by Asín as *El justo medio en la creencia* [The mean or midpoint in faith]. Al-Gazali argues interestingly in this work that the study of theology itself is a *fard kifai,* that is to say a universal obligation, although one that rests on the community as a whole, not necessarily on absolutely every individual personally. The works by al-Gazali mentioned so far are in the main of orthodox theological content. Of the remaining ones to be listed, *Bidayat al-hidaya* (Beginning on the right track) might, from its the title, be taken as conducting the mystic initiate at least a short way down the Sufi path, but the master's teaching was precisely that initiation was to be sought beyond and after the accomplishment of all the straightforward religious duties and did not in any way justify neglecting them (as some Sufis were accused of doing): it is then an elementary manual of orthodox rituals relating to these duties, and so is a work of a sort that might have been written by somebody with no interest in Sufi mysticism at all. Under the heading of "obedience to divine precepts," he deals with such utterly mundane matters as, for example, awakening from sleep, entry into the latrine, ritual ablution (in case of need to be replaced by wiping oneself clean with clean sand), entry into the mosque, a Muslim's duties all through the day from sunrise to sunset, ritual prayer, the imam, Friday services, and fasting. Even the closing sections do not really take the neophyte along the mystic path. After dealing with abstinence from what Allah has forbidden (as a means of discipline of the body, organ by organ), it does go on in a third section to deal with what might be called the social problems of the religious student: his relations, under Allah, with his spiritual masters, fellow pupils, his family, his friends. The epilogue points out that this work is a mere introduction to the path and that the student who has reached the end of the book must then seek instruction elsewhere: in the *Ihya*.

Among works available to the crypto-Muslims it is really only the *Min-haj al-'Abidin* (The highway for those who worship) that truly deserves the description of mystical treatise. Of this work there is one reasonably complete Arabic copy in the National Library in Madrid (GR 58) that may have passed through Morisco hands, one incomplete copy in the same library (GR 160), and in the Almonacid collection a short fourteen-folio fragment translated into *aljamía* (J 8 [34]). The colophon of the first of these manuscripts records that the task of copying it was completed on January 30, 905/1500, and so we can place it at the very opening of our period. The second has copious *aljamiado* annotations, and so it, with the Almonacid fragment, which Ribera and Asín (1912, 44)) assign specifically to the *seventeenth* (*sic!*) century, so these provide convincing proof that some Sufi aspects of al-Gazali's teachings did continue to engage the attention of Spain's Muslims throughout the final period. The *Minhaj* was, in fact, al-Gazali's own very last work. It is certainly not his most advanced treatise of *tasawwuf* (Sufism), but it does provide a complete outline of the stages of mystical initiation, subdivided as follows: (1) knowledge, (2) penitence, (3) obstacles on the path, (4) the time of hesitation, when the soul alternates between celestial delights and spiritual anguish brought on by the impediments decreed by God, (5) free impulse toward God, (6) "the canker and the worm" (eating away at the heart of the mystic, but leaving his exterior apparently sound), and (7) true praise and thanksgiving to God.

It is clear, then, that some Sufi works by the greatest of the mystics writing in Arabic were available during this period, but at the same time it must be stressed that such treatises do not by any means predominate among the books that can be shown to have been available. Overwhelmingly, we find works of simple piety.

Polemical Literature

One might well suppose that there would be no place at all for religious polemic for Muslims living their religion in secret. Open defense of Islam, open criticism of Christianity, any kind of scoring of points at the expense of the adversary, was likely to expose the polemicist, however discreet he might be, to the attentions of the persecutors. And yet we do find such texts. Louis Cardaillac (1977) entitled his study of them *Morisques et chrétiens: Un affrontement polémique, 1492–1640* (Moriscos and Christians: A polemical confrontation) and did not lack for material. That title, while well conveying the focus of Cardaillac's line of investigation, may perhaps mislead some, for the "confrontation" between Christianity and Islam of the sixteenth century was in the main not "polemical" in the sense that the two sides directed arguments against each other *face to face* or that they set out to win a debate in the sort of open forum that elsewhere and at other times had taken place. We do not find learned scholars pitting themselves against one another, with one side seeking to vindicate its own religious doctrines and to demonstrate the failings of those of its rivals. Very rarely, and in disregard of all the risks, it would seem that some Muslims did argue back openly, and as I will discuss below the Young Man from Arévalo claims to have done just that. There are even apparent references to cases of alleged conversion, although it must be said that it is difficult to accept them at face value. Longás (1915, 307) gives us extracts from the Inquisition trial of one "Juan Pepí, francés de nación," an immigrant French shepherd in the service of a rich Morisco farmer in the region of Valencia "who testifies how his master Faquinet [a diminutive of the Arab name Hakim, presumably] had persuaded him to become a Muslim, and had initiated him into Muslim practices." This shepherd, Jean Pepin from Rouen, a "simple man," as we are told, does not seem to have yielded to complex argument but to have been worn down by his master's insistence (if, indeed, we are to believe the evidence adduced in the trial—which, one suspects, may have been a mere Inquisition subterfuge to get access to the rich farmer's fortune.)

No, in this period, "polemical" texts were not consulted by Muslims in order to marshal arguments to convince Christians in open confrontations. They existed, rather, in order to confirm Muslims in their own existing beliefs, to remind them that open discussions in which Islam had

prevailed had once taken place. (Perhaps that has been the primary purpose of religious polemical writings at most points in history?) Polemics,
whether religious or ideological, serve to confirm prejudices; they are
inward and defensive, rather than outward and active tools to convince
the adversary. In the Islamic underground of sixteenth-century Spain,
the old arguments from centuries past were cherished because they told
these oppressed Muslims why they were different and why they should
hold out against conversion. This polemical literature did not serve to
convert the Moriscos' adversaries.

Islamic polemical literature in earlier times had been directed against
Judaism as well as against Christianity. Because all Jews had been expelled in 1492, the only Jews remaining were the *conversos,* trapped like
the crypto-Muslims themselves by the forced conversions to which their
ancestors had been obliged to accede (some of them as long ago as 1391).
One might well expect little attention to be paid by our crypto-Muslims to
arguments against Judaism. Yet anti-Jewish texts continued to be cherished alongside the anti-Christian works. The reason for this is clear
enough. In Islam, the seeds of the later polemical genres are to be found
in the text of the Koran itself. To ignore and omit this theme would be
to ignore a theme not without prominence in the holy book. "Bring the
Torah, and read it, if you are speaking the truth," is the direct polemical challenge to the Jews of Medina made there. In amplification of the
Koranic narrative, the later commentators developed full accounts of
how the Jews came to Muhammad, questioned him on matters of religion, and how these Jews had to retreat, satisfied in every particular by the
replies they received. These were the "Questions of the Jews," to be found
in both Arabic and *aljamiado* versions among Morisco manuscripts. A
prominent treatise in this vein was entitled *Ta'yid al-milla* by al-Raqili.
Asin (1909) argues that this text was the basis of the later *aljamiado*
polemical works. Most of what circulated in the sixteenth century was,
in the last analysis, a prolongation of disputations of the seventh century
in Arabia and did not mirror any contemporary reality in sixteenth- and
seventeenth-century Spain.

A polemicist in whom we might expect the Moriscos to take an interest
is Fray Anselmo Turmeda, alias 'Abdallah ibn 'Abdallah al-Tarjuman.
The fascinating story of Turmeda's life (born a Christian in Majorca in
1352, a successful writer in his native Catalan, he went as a Franciscan
missionary to Tunisia, where he became a convert to Islam, a successful polemical author in Arabic, and the object of a pious cult) has been
thoroughly studied by Míkel de Epalza (see Epalza 1971). Turmeda's
polemical treatise entitled *Tuhfat al-adib fi'l-radd 'ala ahl al-salib* ("The
man of letters' contribution to the refutation of those who follow the

Cross") was written in 1420, and has the violent tone that one finds so often in the writings of recent converts to any religion. Attacking the irrational mysteries of the Christian faith, he storms as follows: "What doubt can there be that any man whose mind is sound will prefer anything which is not absurd to having to believe in this festering, imbecile, crass and calumnious faith, which would not commend itself even to the intelligence of a child, which evokes laughter from people of intelligence who know anything about it" (Cardaillac 1977, 241). The *Tuhfa* has been among the most enduring of anti-Christian polemics, and as Epalza has shown, it even has a certain currency nowadays. One cannot imagine insults on those lines being deployed openly in any real interfaith discussion in the sixteenth century. It is not absolutely certain that the whole work was available throughout the period under study here, but it can be asserted that one of the manuscripts found at Almonacid certainly contained the polemic of Muhammad al-Qaysi, accompanied by a section of a treatise by one 'Abdallah, who is very probably Turmeda ('Abdallah is very often the Islamic name adopted by converts, so it really is less useful as a mark of identification than might at first sight appear). Unfortunately, this particular manuscript is one of the few items found in Almonacid that did not find its way into the custody of the Madrid School of Arabic Studies (and then to the CSIC). It was sold separately to a private collector by the widow of Pablo Gil (through whose hands the whole collection had first passed), and its present whereabouts is unknown.

Grammar

We might expect Muslims, who were experiencing difficulties in maintaining their capacity to read the Arabic religious texts, to devote considerable effort to the study of Arabic grammar, but that does appear to have been the case. Grammar (Arabic *nahw*) had high prestige among them, and indeed in the vocabulary of the Young Man from Arévalo we find a word *nahwe* (presumably from *nahwi*, "grammarian"), elevated to mean something like "scholar" in general. Some of the works of grammar studied by the Moriscos were very ancient ones. A great favorite seems to have been *Kitab al-jumal fi'l-nahw* (Book of grammatical propositions) by al-Zajjaji, a tenth-century writer. In one of the no less than five manuscripts known to have passed through Morisco hands (GR 80), there is a note made by Muhammad ibn Ahmad ibn 'Ali al-Lakhmi al-Sharifi who owned it in 1579. (Other members of his family inserted their grammar notes in the book, so we can be sure that this really was a copy used for study and not just something preserved as an antiquarian curiosity.) The *Kitab al-jumal* is in prose and aims to present systematic coverage. The work known as *al-Alfiyya* is a versified grammar intended to help students to memorize the rules. The great bibliographer Brockelmann remarked that there is a copy "in almost every library" (GAL, 1: 298). One copy now in Madrid (GR 6) contains a note at the end of the first part saying that the task of copying it was completed in Paterna in Dhu'l-hijja 906 (June/July 1501). Perhaps equally frequently to be found in North African and Andalusi collections is the work known usually as *al-Ajurrumiyya,* from the name of its Berber author, Ibn Ajurrum. To the present day, this serves for elementary grammar studies in North Africa. In the Almonacid collection there is not only the Arabic text (J 12) but also a translation, admittedly an unsatisfactory one, into *aljamía* (J 59; to render the technical vocabulary of Arabic into Romance can have been no easy undertaking).

Dictionaries

Bilingual dictionaries are not to be found. Not surprisingly, Christian scholars had none, either. In medieval times even extended glossaries are rare, and it is not until Pedro de Alcalá that we have a true bilingual dictionary—but one that did not use the Arabic script and was intended for use by Christian missionaries, not by Muslims or converts. What we do find—and it is rather surprising—is that in the Almonacid hoard there are two volumes (J 35 and J 49), of a very early lexicographical work indeed, the so-called *Kitab al-'ayn* by al-Khalil, both copies in the abridged version of al-Zubaydi. This dictionary is one of the great classic works of Arabic linguistic scholarship, still a basic work of reference today, and its presence in Almonacid would seem to point to its owner being a sophisticated student of the literary language. Just to consult this particular dictionary would have required some linguistic specialization and training, for it is arranged not in the conventional order of the alphabet with which we are familiar today and which was already in use in the sixteenth century. The arrangement is phonetic rather than alphabetic. It begins with sounds produced at the back of the mouth (hence its title, since 'ayn is the first of the guttural consonants to be listed) and works forward to the dentals. Not surprisingly, the Almonacid volumes in question are provided with a key index to assist consultation! More than any other book, this dictionary demonstrates that the owner of the Almonacid collection was a serious student.

Literature of Entertainment

I have grouped together here a wide range of classes of writing that in other contexts one might well have expected to see treated in separate categories: history, poetry, *adab* (belles lettres), narrative prose, all the genres that in modern times in English get called "literature." The reason for my classification scheme is frankly convenience: we find so relatively few such works that can be proved to have circulated among the Moriscos that it would be absurd to list them under separate heads.

Most striking is the relative (although not complete) absence of verse and poetry. The place of poetry in the culture of the Arabic-speaking peoples has always been high, and such collections as al-Maqqari's *Nafh al-tib* and *Azhar al-riyad* are there to reassure us that respect for poetry and for poets continued among the Andalusi refugees who found their way into North African exile. These books by al-Maqqari are, in their framework, prose works, but are so copiously interlarded with verse quotations, specimens of all kinds of composition, that they constitute one of our best sources of information on the continuity of the poetic culture of al-Andalus. Verse compositions from the days of the Caliphate onward are recalled and cherished, the flow is reduced to a trickle for the final period, but it never dries up altogether. Al-Maqqari was a member of a family from Spain that settled in Tetuan. His compilation of these verse anthologies in the seventeenth century has something of antiquarianism about it, but leaves us in no doubt that poetry continued to be a living reality to Arabic-speakers from al-Andalus.

In those manuscripts that we know to have been in crypto-Muslim hands in Spain itself in the sixteenth century, hardly anything of this poetic wealth survives. On strophic poetry (*muwashshah*), so characteristic of al-Andalus from the period of the *taifa* kings onward, evidence is inconclusive. There are one or two isolated fragments listed in the catalog of the Almonacid hoard. However, these texts may well not really have been in circulation in our period. They occur among paper fragments extracted by the assiduous twentieth-century editors from inside manuscript bindings. Such material may well be of very much earlier date, and reused simply as packing or padding by the bookbinders. The only poems that we can say did circulate freely were of a religious nature, and above all, we find the well-known devotional poem entitled *al-Burda* (The cape) by al-Busiri, a text used in the celebration of the birthday of Muhammad, and so to be associated with the literature centering on the Prophet to which reference has been made above.

Just as remarkable is the relative absence of ornamental rhymed prose (*saj'*). Again it was not that *saj'* was unknown in al-Andalus in Nasrid days: Granada had boasted some consummate practitioners of this mode of composition, not least of them being the great Ibn al-Khatib. But nobody carried the art form on into the sixteenth century. Some of the religious works surviving from earlier times into our period are in *saj'*, the homilies of Ibn Nubata, for example (and, of course, the Koran itself, familiar to everyone, makes striking use of this rhetorical ornament), but *saj'* was not cultivated by the Moriscos themselves. In the Arabic-speaking world the great stylistic model for the study of *saj'* was provided by the genre of the *maqama,* especially the brilliant compositions of al-Hariri. There is just one single *maqama* by this author, of which we can say it was almost certainly read by Moriscos because it is copied out in the very Vatican manuscript (Borgiano arabo 171) that contains the key Oran fatwa. The verbal extravagance, the pyrotechnics, of *saj'* seems not to have suited the somber situation of Spain's Muslims at this period. (And perhaps the recondite vocabulary so beloved of some of those who used the form, al-Hariri among them, placed the texts beyond the limited linguistic ability of many.)

Prose Narrative

Within Arabic studies the fables of *Calila and Dimna* have always been sure of a place because the translation of the collection *into* Arabic by Ibn al-Muqaffa' played an important part in the initial development of Arabic prose. Perhaps because it springs from such a distant courtly milieu, *Calila and Dimna* does not seem to have been popular among Moriscos, but there is one manuscript, probably from the period (Borgiano arabo 172), containing a single isolated story.

Long historical works are not known to have been owned by Moriscos. At best we have fragments and anecdotes. The accounts of the battles and conflicts of the early days of Islam were clearly of great importance to them, but such material is probably best classified together with pious and religious literature. We would expect that the conquest of the Iberian Peninsula by the Muslims would hold great interest for communities on the eve of their expulsion. Manuscript J 43 from Almonacid does contain a fragment attributed to 'Abdallah ibn Rushd entitled *Kitab futuh al-Andalus* (Book of the conquest of Spain), but the scholar who contributed this section of the catalog (probably García de Linares) was moved to characterize it as "brief and fabulous." The famous historical and geographical compilation entitled *Muruj al-dhahab* (Meadows of Gold) does exist in one of the Vatican's Borgiano arabo manuscripts that is one of a group likely to have belonged to Moriscos, but it is noteworthy that the copy omits the general introduction (which contains most of the general historical information), and turns immediately to the life of the Prophet and to the specifically Islamic material that was what the Moriscos will have wanted to read. Noteworthy, too, is the fact that nothing of Ibn al-Khatib, the last of the great historians writing in Arabic in the Iberian Peninsula, seems to have survived into Morisco days. On the Moriscos' own experiences, as we will see, the best source is in *aljamía,* and not in Arabic (the writings of the Young Man from Arévalo). There is one work in Arabic of some interest and merit, although, as the title indicates, it is not a long one: *Nubdhat al-'asr fi tarikh Bani Nasr* (Short treatise[12] of that time on the history of the Nasrids). This was apparently written by a Morisco refugee in North Africa. We have no indication that such Arabic texts circulated in the peninsula itself. In the scale of priorities of the Moriscos, what they considered to be of vital importance was what had happened in the early days of Islam, what was going to happen at the end of days (and many of them believed that the end was very near); they had little time to spare for more than brief anecdotes of the more recent past, especially if it was not a specifically Islamic past. Between the days of the Companions of the Prophet and the present, apart from fragmentary and largely fictional references to the great days of the Caliphate of Cordova, apart from some slight reflection of the drama of Nasrid history, there is a void. Nothing on the *muluk al-tawa'if* or on the Almoravids or Almohads at all! In this connection it is to be noted, as we will see in chapter 6, that when the last Granadan rebellion broke out, its leader, Fernando de Valor, assumed the Arab name of Ben Umayya, harking back to the great days of the eighth to tenth centuries, not to any nearer historical milestone. "History" for the Moriscos meant the early days of Islam and the early days of an Islamic regime in al-Andalus, not the totality of time elapsed.

Short Narrative Works

We do find quite a number of short prose narratives in Arabic, mostly works of pious edification, although many of these tales shade away into pure entertainment. Some have their origin in the pious literature of the lives of the prophets to which reference has already been made; no doubt it was a religious motive that led to them being written down and preserved, but many possess considerable narrative power.

Alongside "orthodox" works on the lives of the prophets, we find in Arabic (as in medieval Latin and in rabbinical Hebrew) all sorts of edifying apocryphal tales and legends. A good example of this type of narrative is provided by the story of Abraham (Ibrahim), which I published from both Arabic and *aljamiado* manuscripts in a special number of *Nueva Revista de Filología Hispánica* in 1981 (a Morisco died in an Inquisition jail for possessing a copy of a version of that text, so it was for him no idle amusement.)

The exploits of 'Ali Ibn Abi Talib were a favorite narrative subject. His tragic heroism is celebrated in a style closely parallel to the chivalric romances of medieval Europe. There are other such tales, too numerous to

12. This has been translated misleadingly as "Fragment."

mention, that include *Qasr al-dhahab* (Castle of gold), *Hisn al-gurab* (The fortress of crows), *Hirz al-wazir* (The minister's amulet): many of these are in manuscript J 27 of the Almonacid collection. Our view of the Arabic corpus of material of this kind has been distorted by the low esteem in which such "nonliterary" storytelling was held within Islamic cultures. The teller of tales (a figure much romanticized by some modern writers on the culture of Islam) belongs on the market square along with other hucksters and entertainers rather than in the mosque. Narrators of serious matters may well wish to distance themselves from the literature of entertainment. The *Thousand and One Nights,* which belongs to this category of entertainment, has in modern times (but not in earlier ones) perhaps begun to escape from these constraints, and may by now be in danger of being taken very seriously. Its immense success in translation has forced it back on the attention of Arab literary critics. Such a narrative tradition is only a hair's breadth away from pure oral narrative and the ever living tradition of the storyteller/entertainer working the crowds in public places. We should be careful not to project backward our modern admiration for the folk tale onto the Morisco past. The case of Román Ramírez, discussed below, is evidence of the continuity of such an oral storytelling tradition among Moriscos and of the hold that their narrative skills could have over the Christian public of their day. We can in the nature of things expect no direct information on the performances given by Arabic-language storytellers in Spain during much of our period. The Arabic language was banned, there was nobody to record narrative performances, and indeed it has never been the custom so to do. That the Inquisition archives tell us something of how a Morisco entertainer, Román Ramírez, presented his performances in Castilian is invaluable information.

Ephemera

Arabic survived in use in the sixteenth century for some day-to-day purposes among Muslims, even though the very act of writing the language might be used in evidence against the writer. Barceló (1984) published an extremely useful series of documents from the region of Valencia. The first 135 documents are of medieval date, but documents 135–270 (with the exception of nos. 265 and 266) are from the sixteenth and seventeenth centuries, all in the strikingly "ungrammatical" Arabic of the period and full of Romance (Catalan) elements. Up to the date of the forcible conversion, Arabic was still in some places used for all purposes, as witness document no. 157, dated 1518, which is part of the testimony in a police enquiry. The affair in question is a murky one involving the burning down (presumably in an arson attack) of a dwelling belonging to one 'Uzayyar, and a lost (presumably misappropriated—or perhaps stolen?) gold collar fished out of an irrigation ditch! Not surprisingly, the single document that survives from this trial does not permit us to reconstruct the crime with any clarity, but the important point for our present purposes is that at this date Arabic could in this region (Valencia) still be a working language for practical purposes of administrative and police work.

That there is only one Barceló document from the 1520s presumably reflects the turmoil of the period of the *germanía,* but in the 1530s there resumes a trickle of brief practical communications in Arabic (about, among other things, debts, and remittances). As late as 1594 we find one al-Gazi (presumably the Luis al-Gazi of document no. 270) keeping a note of his travel expenses in Arabic: "For shoes for myself I paid 7s. 6d.; I paid the lodging-house keeper £1.5s. . . . gave back to Alexander what he had lent me: £1.18s 4d."[13] (Barceló 1984, 340–341). As Barceló points out (1984, 355, doc. no. 233 [dated 1600]), al-Gazi is probably this same man: he had by 1600 been condemned to serve as a galley slave. In document 270, we read that in 1595 he was involved in the purchase of arms for which licenses had been obtained from that notoriously corrupt minister of the Crown, Pedro Franqueza (see Harvey 1971, 81–115). Whether al-Gazi's custom of keeping his personal records in Arabic helped to incriminate him we cannot say. On the eve of the Expulsion, in 1608, Arabic was being used by the brothers of Francisca Balaguer in drawing up a document (Barceló 1984, 366, doc. 246) relative to the settlement of her estate. We can thus assert that written Arabic continued in practical use until the very end.

Original Writings in *Aljamía*
In 1848, Serafín Estébanez Calderón, whose reputation as a writer rests nowadays on his Andalusian "regionalist" prose (for example, *Escenas andaluzas* (1847)), was appointed professor of Arabic at the Madrid *Ateneo.* One suspects that for broadly cultural and social purposes, he hit the right note (and got a larger audience) by devoting his inaugural

13. When the companion volume to this study—*Islamic Spain, 1250 to 1500*—was being edited for me by a very efficient Chicago-based editorial assistant, sums with the units £, s, and d in my medieval sources had those symbols changed so as to read "pounds," etc., instead. Presumably, £.s.d. was thought to be a British quirk that I had by oversight injected into my material, something extraneous that needed eliminating. These are in fact the symbols that occur in Valencian sources, Christian and Muslim alike, and were still in regular use in the sixteenth century. I preserve them here because they convey very directly the cultural and economic continuity of the Mediterranean world to which Luis al-Gazi, and the Valencian Moriscos in general, fully belonged. We must remember they were heirs to the ancient civilization of the Romans—with its *librae, solidi* and *denarii*—as well as being heirs to the civilization of Islam.

courses not to Arabic, in which his qualifications were scant, but to *aljamiado* literature. His opening lesson was more of an advertising prospectus than a lecture:

> If anybody wishes to explore regions that are unknown and yet still Spanish, and would like to discover inexhaustible springs of new ideas, unusual thoughts, marvels, and wonders like those of the *Arabian Nights*, all he has to do is to open up, thanks to some notions of Arabic, the rich portals of *aljamiado* literature, which is, so to speak, the Indies of Spanish literature, there waiting to be discovered, with treasures to offer to the first Columbuses to sail that way.

Quoting those words in his *Orígenes de la novela*, the great scholar Marcelino Menéndez y Pelayo observed sardonically: "Things did not work out quite in accordance with those optimistic expectations" (1905, 1: LXVI.).

There never was an unopened treasure house of secular writings in this medium. We have seen that *aljamiado* literature developed in the shadow of Arabic religious and devotional literature. Even where this "Hispano-Islamic" Arabic-character script was employed for texts originally written in Romance and not translated from Arabic, those texts were usually religious ones, too. The one apparent exception to this is the prose tale *Paris and Viana* (see below). The principal Morisco author, the Young Man from Arévalo, wrote what were primarily religious treatises (if we read them now in part for their nonreligious content, that is none of his doing). Of the original *aljamiado* books that were not devotional tracts, there were hardly any that were completely devoid of some Islamic aspect (although for the pious Islamic scholar some of the superstitious elements would have been unacceptably unorthodox).

Entertainment
It does not take long to review the extant writings in *aljamía* intended solely for purposes of entertainment. The long fragment of the prose romance *Paris and Viana* stands alone, and is really just a version, little modified for Morisco consumption, of a story known in Castilian and French versions (see Galmés de Fuentes 1970). It is perhaps best classified alongside the narratives intended for purposes of entertainment of Román Ramírez (see below).

Morisco Medical Medicine
Even after Christian Spanish rejection of the Islamic culture of Spain had brought about the blackening of the reputation of most aspects of the

Andalusi heritage, Morisco medicine continued to be respected. Morisco medical men (and women) tended some very highly placed patients, King Philip II included. A few medical men trained in the old ways clung to vestiges of their professional status through the century. Those with powerful connections such as Alonso del Castillo, Philip II's Granadan doctor (who is discussed in another connection in chapter 8), could continue their practice, but Morisco medicine came to be pushed lower and lower down the social scale. A good example of this sort of semimarginalized but still sought-after practitioner is Román Ramírez, who figures for other, nonmedical, reasons here in this chapter, or the two female healers, *curanderas,* who are mentioned in the section on the Young Man from Arévalo. To judge from some of the medical notebooks that have survived, it is clear that the line between medicine and magic or sorcery is hard to draw. But as much could be said of some aspects of medicine among Christians at this time.

The following notes are to be found in one Morisco medical text:[14]

How I saw Master Miguel prepare basilikon ointment...
How to attend to any wound from a sword or dagger...
How to deal with a wound when the bone is showing through the flesh...

Alongside these we find:

How to deal with a child thought to be suffering from the Evil Eye.

An interesting Arabic-character manuscript with much medical material of this sort was sold in 1995 by Quaritch's, the London specialist antiquarian bookseller, but that volume was more of the sort of "book of spells" that one might imagine witches or magicians to have carried with them. This manuscript was particularly interesting because it was thought to have come originally from Tunisia (the provenance was probable but not beyond all doubt). Since its spells and medical material were clearly of peninsular origin (rather than North African), it had probably been carried into exile by some Aragonese "healer" (*curandero*). It is worth noting that the pious old lady called Nuzay[ta] Calderán who will be found below preaching so earnestly in the presence of the Young Man from Arévalo that the shari'a should be carefully observed was also known as the Antesihra (*ante-* is presumably for *anti-*, and *sihr* is "magic," so one night render the name as "the White Witch."] Pious adherence to Islam could, in the practice of these people, coexist with medical superstition (so long as Satan was not directly involved). We also find other

14. MS T 16, at one time in the possession of Gayangos and now in the Real Academia de la Historia.

manuals purporting to be of use in fortune-telling such as the *Suertes de Dhu'l-Qarnayn,* the Fortunes of the Islamic Alexander, who is more of a magus figure than a conquering hero. And we find various other manifestations of superstitious beliefs: horoscopes, instructions on the interpretation of dreams, indications of propitious days to begin activities, among others.

Travel

There are a few scattered Morisco jottings, not whole books, giving itineraries and travel directions.[15] These notes were intended as practical aids for those seeking to escape from Spain (we must presume the attempts were *unsuccessful,* if the lists ended up in our Western libraries!). The longest travel text is from a slightly earlier period, the early years of the sixteenth century, and is a straightforward work of Islamic devotion. I refer to a versified account of his hajj by an Aragonese pilgrim (writing in his own Aragonese dialect): he travels all the way to Mecca from Puey Monçón in Aragon (J 13). This pilgrim does note down some secular phenomena: he was very impressed by the artificial street-lighting he found in Mamluk Cairo, for example. As his account ended up plastered inside a hollow wall in Almonacid (Aragon), he perhaps did get successfully back home to tell his tale. Also, although it was written in Arabic outside Spain and some time after our period (in the 1630s), we cannot fail to mention here a fascinating travel narrative written produced by a refugee who had fled from Andalusia to Morocco in 1599, al-Hajari (see al-Hajari 1997). His full *Rihla* ("travel narrative") is not extant, but from the surviving abridged *Kitab nasir al-din 'ala'l-qawm al-kafirin* we can see that if given the opportunity (he received royal patronage in Morocco) a Morisco author was quite capable of picking up the threads of the tradition of travel-writing that had flourished earlier in Islamic Spain.

THE YOUNG MAN FROM ARÉVALO

Of those who produced original works in the new medium of *aljami-ado* prose, there is no doubt that the most productive was *el mancebo de Arévalo,* the "Young Man from Arévalo." One of the earliest comprehensive studies of *aljamiado* literature, and certainly the earliest in English, was the pioneering article entitled "The Language and Literature of the Moriscos" contributed by Pascual de Gayangos to the *British and Foreign Quarterly Review* as early as 1838. In it Gayangos already gave considerable attention to this author, and the Young Man has figured in all the major studies on Morisco writings since then. The fact that he is singled

15. Paris, Bibliothèque Nationale Arabe 774; Madrid, R. Academia de le Historia T 16.

out for special attention here is scarcely a bold innovation on my part. Yet over the years this author has contrived to keep at a distance those who wished to penetrate his secrets. In recent years considerable progress has been made. The time has come to sum up what has been achieved and to set out what remains to be discovered. I aim to present some of the surprising conclusions of recent research carried out by investigators in Spain, Puerto Rico, and elsewhere, and to these add relevant texts from manuscript Dd.9.49 in the Cambridge University Library, "El brebe compendio de nuestra santa ley y sunna."

My first attempt to elucidate some of the problems posed by that particular manuscript appeared as long ago as 1958, in an article in *Al-Andalus,* but I am afraid I am still far from having resolved all its difficulties. Reference has already been made in chapter 4 to my hypothesis that the Young Man in question may be identifiable with one Agustin de Ribera *el mozo* ("the lad"), a Morisco from Arévalo who met his end as a prisoner in Inquisition custody in 1540. In this chapter, I prefer not to erect any superstructure of further conjecture on the basis of what remains speculation. In consequence, I will have to continue to use the admittedly awkward designation of "Young Man" or *Mancebo* rather than a personal name such as Agustin. Even setting the trial of Agustin de Ribera on one side in this way, and ignoring any possible links with an extensive conspiracy based on Arévalo, the works of the "Mancebo de Arévalo" by themselves still furnish us with an exceptionally privileged entry into the underground Morisco society of the first half of the sixteenth century. They take us, as we will see, directly into the secret assemblies and debates of this community of perplexed souls, people trying to cope with persecution and isolation. I know of no other source that conveys so well their preoccupations, obsessions, and follies.

As Gregorio Fonseca, the investigator from Oviedo who probably made the most important and startling single contribution to the elucidation of the Young Man's works of recent years, was reduced to asking despairingly about him:

> El Mancebo de Arévalo: who is this writer, this enigmatic personality? What was his real name? What was his date of birth? How did he die and where? We know little or nothing about him, and what we do know is simply what is to be deduced from the books he wrote, or at times is the fruit of conjecture." (1983, 6)

I would see no reason to disagree with any of what Fonseca says here. Let us piece together an outline of this Morisco's life. He came from Arévalo, and we know that "de Arévalo" was, in his case, not just part of his personal name, but really did indicate his home town. His mother, he tells us, was still living there (to which fact he adds the puzzling information that she "had been a Christian for 25 years"). As a young man he traveled very widely in Spain (including Alcántara, Astorga, Ávila, Gandía, Granada, Jaén, Ocaña, Requena, Ronda, Saragossa, and Segovia—all the parts of Spain except the seaboard provinces, it would seem, presumably because those would have been barred to a Morisco), visiting (crypto-)Muslim notables, and collecting in such places the teachings and traditions of his religion. On his travels he tells us he transcribed documents and texts, and some of these he copies out in his book.

Since he reports things said by people who remembered Nasrid times and the Christian conquest of Granada, and since he repeats a complaint that "the king of the Conquest" (i.e., Ferdinand) was not keeping his word, these early travels must have taken place some time between the very end of the fifteenth century (when the Capitulations of 1492 were being broken) and 1516, when Ferdinand died. (The Young Man presumably really was still "young"[16] at this time, because old ladies he met usually addressed him as "Son.") He was at some stage invited by Aragonese Islamic notables to collaborate with an Aragonese *alfaquí* called Bray de Reminjo in the production of the religious manual entitled *Brebe compendio de nuestra santa ley y sunna*. We have already met Bray in the previous chapters as an important witness to the impact of the forcible conversions. We may surmise that the manual is a response to the challenge of this new situation that arose after the completion under Charles V of the conversion of all Spain's Muslims. The crypto-Muslims of Castile and Aragon, groups that had hitherto not made common cause, must have established contact in the 1520s in order to collaborate on the production of this manual. It seems reasonable to assume that the Young Man from Arévalo was invited to collaborate because he already had an established reputation as a writer, but we do not in fact know which of his extant works was written first. Work on the collaborative volume began, we are told explicitly, eight years after the conversion. We do not know exactly what the division of responsibilities was between Bray and the Young Man in writing the work that is now preserved in the Cambridge University Library. It seems altogether reasonable to assume that all those many passages where one of the informants addresses the author as "Son" are passages contributed by the Young Man rather than Bray (and the fact that some of these passages also occur in the works in which Bray does not figure at all backs up this supposition).

16. I once proposed that "Mancebo" might not be intended to be taken literally, but be a semantic calque on '*abd* ("devotee"; see Harvey 1967). Without abandoning that hypothesis altogether, I now accept that his writings point to him having been something of a young prodigy.

Apart from this shadowy outline of a biography, we know virtually nothing about him except what may be deduced from his own writings. As for the Young Man's personality and character, we can see he was boldly disputatious, deeply convinced that his faith was the only right one. In his system of beliefs, a predominant feature was the conviction that Judgment Day was near.

We know that he, with others, was planning to go on the hajj pilgrimage to Mecca: he speaks in the Cambridge manuscript of his departure as being imminent. We do not know that he actually set out, still less do we know whether he even managed to leave Spain. One cannot help wondering whether the preparations for the hajj that he made (see below) were a trap that would allow the authorities to pick up at some convenient moment, and in a convenient way, a whole group of religious activists ready assembled for them.

The Three Manuscripts

Three works have come down to us. *Breve compendio de nuestra santa ley y sunna* (in the Cambridge University Library) may seem an odd epithet for a substantial work of some 250 ff. The Arabic term *Mukhtasar* ("*Abbreviation*," "*Compendium*") figures as an element in titles of many elementary manuals of Islamic law, etc. (that of al-Khalil, for example), that circulated among the Moriscos, and perhaps that may have had its influence on the choice of title. More specifically, the title *Breve compendio* calls to mind the treatise by the imam 'Isa of Segovia, usually referred to as the *Breviario Sunni*. Long passages from 'Isa are indeed incorporated, sometimes word for word, in the Young Man's writings, so there can be no doubt about that link. He is the heir to a tradition of works in Romance on Islamic subjects going back at least to the mid-fifteenth century. The Young Man from Arévalo's writings were read and made use of after him by Muhammad Rabadán, whose poem in celebration of the life of the Prophet was carried by the refugees to Tunisia (where we are told it was performed to music). There is an excellent modern edition of Rabadán's poem by Father José Antonio Lasarte, priest of the actual village where Rabadán lived: *Poemas de Mohamad Rabadán*. It could be said that the Young Man is a link establishing cultural and religious continuity through the period of clandestinity between the days in the fifteenth century when free Muslims lived in Spain openly and the days in the seventeenth century when their descendents were able finally to resume the free practice of their religion in North African exile. There is much in what we learn about him from his own works that does not reflect well on him: the high-handed way he misleads his readers over sources, for example. The key fact about the Young Man is his importance to *his own people*. They needed leadership, and with the exiguous means at his disposal, and in dangerous circumstances, he provided it.

The second work of the Young Man is the *Tafsira*. Belonging to the Consejo Superior de Investigaciones Científicas (CSIC) in Madrid, *Tafsira* comes from Arabic *tafsir*, elucidation, commentary, especially commentary on the Koran. This word had come to be used in Morisco speech to indicate almost any explanatory work on a religious subject. That is presumably the sense in this case.

The third of the Young Man's extant work is the *Sumario de la relación y ejercicio espiritual*. In the National Library, Madrid, the second part of this title surprisingly brings to mind Ignatius de Loyola's *Spiritual Exercises,* which were written at Manresa in the early 1520s, and so were roughly contemporaneous with the Young Man's activities. (That a Morisco author really should have had close acquaintance with Loyola's work as early as ca. 1530 is difficult to accept. Whether the similarity of the titles is due to explicit influence, something vaguely in the intellectual atmosphere, or mere coincidence, is as yet uncertain.)

The study by Fonseca mentioned above (1980) covers a number of aspects of the text in the National Library, including linguistic ones, but Fonseca's outstanding contribution is to have established beyond doubt the startling fact that the Young Man from Arévalo was deeply influenced by the *Imitatio Christi* of Thomas à Kempis, and to such an extent that long sections of the *Sumario de la relación y ejercicio espiritual* are direct transpositions of that Christian devotional manual. Apart from the systematic Islamization of such passages, the changes made in such sections are slight. Such extensive indebtedness might point to the Young Man's attendance at some school or college where the *Imitatio Christi* had been in use as a textbook (as it was in several centers at this time). It is not necessary to assume that the Young Man needed Latin to read Kempis, for the book was by this time available in a Castilian translation. The Young Man claimed to know Latin, as well as Greek and Hebrew, but the garbled state of the Latin tags that we find in his works inspire us with no confidence as to his ability to read even Latin (although perhaps the copyist of the Cambridge manuscript is to blame). As for the other two languages, Greek and Hebrew, he gives us no reason to suppose that he knew them at all. There were at least two Castilian translations of Kempis widely available (Burgos 1495, Saragossa 1510, Burgos 1516).[17] One is reluctant

---

17. That there was an early link between Loyola himself and the *Imitatio Christi* was firmly established by Father Bernard-Maître (see Bernard-Maître 1956, 30–31), but to report his demonstration in full would take us too far away from the subject of the Young Man from Arévalo.

to accept that someone like the Young Man, a staunch if clandestine Muslim, someone clearly keen to appear to his fellow crypto-Muslims as a pious believer, would have thought of exploiting his memories of Kempis for Islamic purposes, but the evidence assembled by Fonseca admits of no doubt. Since so much hangs on this aspect of Fonseca's thesis, I will endeavor to present his case briefly and in a form accessible to readers of English. Fonseca, of course, in his original presentation of his case, finds it sufficient to place selected passages from Kempis alongside the text of the *Sumario del la relacion y ejercicio espiritual*. Little further demonstration is called for. The task of presenting the same argument for English readers is much more demanding. The indirect method adopted here is to give an English version of one of the relevant passages from Kempis alongside Fonseca's edition of the Young Man's *aljamiado* text and my own English translation of the *aljamiado* text. Even with the added layer of translation into English intervening in this way, the similarities between some individual extracts are striking. One or two cases of correspondence might be put down to chance, but where similarities occur throughout very many examples, the case for a direct textual link between Kempis and the Young Man's writings becomes a very strong one indeed.

KEMPIS: If you could empty your heart of all creatures, Jesus would delight to dwell with you. (Bk 2, ch. 7)

YOUNG MAN: Dice Almuraba'i: Ya fijo de Adam, si acertaras a desocuparte, Allah morará en tu corazón. [Almuraba'i says: O son of Adam, if you manage to empty yourself, Allah will dwell in your heart.] (13r)

KEMPIS: Happy and wise is he who endeavors to be during his life as he wishes to be found at his death. (Bk 1, ch. 23)

YOUNG MAN: Dice Almuraba'i: . . . cuán bienaventurado es quien vive de tal manera cual desea ser hallado al tiempo de su morir! [Almuraba'i says: . . . How fortunate is he who lives just as he desires to be found at the time of his death!] (14v)

KEMPIS: Always keep in mind your last end, and how you will stand before the last judge, from whom nothing is hid, who cannot be influenced by bribes and excuses, and who judges with justice. (Bk 1, ch. 24)

YOUNG MAN: Dice Algazeli. . . . ¿por qué no catas el fin de tus obras, y el fin que habrán todas las cosas, y de qué manera estaras delante aquel no habrá cosa encubierta, ni se amansará con dones, ni admitirá escusación a ninguno de los annabíes. [Al-Ghazali says: why do you not look to the end of your works, and to the end that all things will have, and to how you will stand before Him from whom nothing will be hidden, who will not be softened by gifts, and who will accept no excuses from any of the prophets.] (15v)

KEMPIS: All things are passing, and yourself with them. (Bk 2, ch. 1)
YOUNG MAN: Dice Ben 'Arabi: todas las cosas pasan, y tú con ellas. [Ibn 'Arabi says: all things pass away, and you along with them.] (20v)

KEMPIS: If it seems to you that you know a great deal, and have wide experience in many fields, yet remember that there are many matters of which you are ignorant. (Bk 1, ch. 2)
YOUNG MAN: Si te parece que sabes muchas cosas, ten presente que es mucho más lo que ignoras. [If it seems to you that you know a great deal, keep it in mind that you don't know a great deal more.] (62r)

KEMPIS: In the holy Scriptures, truth is to be looked for, rather than fair phrases. (Bk 1, ch. 5)
YOUNG MAN: En nuestro honrado Alqurán se ha de buscar la verdad y firmitud. [In our honored Koran is to be looked for truth and firmness.] (66r)

The technique of transposition is simple and it is systematically applied. The basic moral, etc., teaching is left intact, but any mention of a specifically Christian feature is eliminated, often replaced with something Islamic. For example, mentions of Jesus often become mentions of Allah. The Christian Scriptures become the Koran. Moral and spiritual teachings are attributed in a less systematic way to various Islamic teachers, sometimes well-known names such as al-Gazali and Ibn 'Arabi, but sometimes a strange personage called Almuraba'i is brought to bear. (This same name, or one resembling it closely, also turns up elsewhere in the writings of the Young Man—particularly in the Cambridge manuscript—as an "authority" to add weight to statements. Considerable effort has been expended by myself and by others to see whether the quotations could be traced, so that this author might be identified: we have all failed. Almuraba'i appears to be an invention. I am forced to conclude that we are being misled, and quite deliberately.)

One purely hypothetical explanation for these textual parallels is that the Young Man, when obliged to attend missionary sermons, may have been attracted by aspects of the teachings of Thomas à Kempis. Presumably the antidoctrinaire spirit of this style of direct piety, the *devotio moderna,* based as it was on the cultivation of spiritual inwardness, was what the Young Man found acceptable, but its Christian outer forms he naturally rejected. Because he recognized so much of true moral and devotional worth in this book, the Morisco wished to incorporate as much as he could of it into his own tradition, into his own preaching: to make it his own. He did so by attaching, as it were, a series of Islamic brand names to the systematically de-Christianized contents. It must have been relatively easy for the Young Man to carry off the deception. Few of the Moriscos who read his works or who listened to him preaching in clandestine houses, would have had access to Ibn ʿArabi, for example, and so been in a position to check on his scholarship or point out the deception.

The moral sentiments and the religious teachings selected for Islamization were usually safely universal ones: before God man must be humble; this life will soon pass away; Judgment Day will come only too soon. Was the Young Man setting out to deceive his readers by ascribing such ideas to alleged Islamic sources? Or was he in some curious way deceiving himself? We will never know. One lesson to be learned from Fonseca's discovery is that any statement with regard to the sources made by this Morisco author himself must be treated with the utmost suspicion. Since we know for certain now where so much of the *Sumario de la relación* comes from, and it is certainly not from any of the Islamic ʿulama he claims to be quoting but rather from Kempis, it is at least possible that similar tricks are being played on us elsewhere (although not necessarily on the basis of the same Christian model). We should beware.

Nobody likes to be duped, and I fear that the Young Man's reputation will have suffered enormously as a result of this and other recent research. María Teresa Narváez of the University of Puerto Rico, besides her other investigations, has done work similar to Fonseca's, but on the *Tafsira*. Narváez has been able to show that one passage (a very much smaller proportion of the book than the Kempis-based sections of the *Sumario*, but still not inconsiderable) depends directly on the Senecan passages at the opening of that seminal Castilian best seller of the early sixteenth century, *Celestina*. The Morisco author had read and internalized what all literate people in Spain literate had read. I regard Narváez's findings as of the greatest interest. After all, it is possible to imagine that the *Imitatio Christi* was forced unwillingly down the throat of a schoolboy from a Morisco background and had somehow lodged in his memory without him being fully aware of the extent to which his stock of ideas had been molded by his reading. But that cannot have happened with a work such as *Celestina*. One was not obliged to read this work in class in those days; one read it because it was so popular. We therefore have evidence here of the young Morisco's free choice of reading material. Narváez's investigations provide yet another demonstration of the degree to which Moriscos were attracted by the literature of the Spanish Golden Age and appreciated its masterpieces. Their Islamic culture did not necessarily mean that they were cut off from the mental universe of the Christian majority alongside whom they lived. If I do not devote more space to Narváez's important work on the *Tafsira* here, that is solely because in the present context I wish to focus on information bearing on the Young Man's religious education, and that is provided conveniently by evidence coming from the *Sumario* and the *Breviario*.

Reminiscences from the Morisco Underground

The time has come to examine some longer passages of what the Young Man wrote himself. Two points need to be made at the outset. In the first place, the extreme difficulty of the Young Man's style must be stressed. I am not alone in finding it at times opaque. Any attempt at a near-literal translation would have merely produced extremely rebarbative jargon. I have certainly aimed at faithfulness, and I hope accuracy, in my translation of him, but where I could understand him myself (and that was not everywhere), I have tried at all times to remain comprehensible and readable. That may not always have been the Young Man's own intention, perhaps, so in that respect translator and original may not always be in harmony.

The second point concerns deceit. What is at issue here is not the systematic deceit (*taqiyya*) that was forced on the Muslims of Spain by the forced conversion, but the way that the Young Man himself and some of the individuals in the circles he describes (Nuzaya Calderán, for example) set out to deceive their Morisco readers and sometimes to deceive one other. For example, how should our knowledge that he pretends to be citing an Islamic author called Almuraba'i who simply did not exist affect our judgment of him? One could multiply examples. To denounce him as a fraud and a cheat does not take us very far. He clearly does at times seek to deceive his readers, just as one of the most striking of the characters he describes for us, Nuzaya Calderán, clearly was seeking to deceive her audience when she told them that in Mecca she had seen a book of the law inscribed on silver plates and protected by an iron grille under a marble dome—which is all nonsense. Why these lies?

There is no more poignant demonstration of the insistent demand of the crypto-Muslims of Spain to be Muslims than these fictions. The policies of the Spanish authorities had been to cut off from their religious roots those they had forcibly converted. An educational and a spiritual vacuum had been created, and so from those religious leaders such as the Young Man, such as Nuzaya, were constantly being asked by those who wanted to believe—but no longer knew exactly what that belief should be—detailed teachings that were positively "Islamic," to replace the Christian material that was being rejected. For the most part, what these ill-prepared, improvised, latter-day prophets told their faithful to believe was as near to Sunni orthodoxy as they could manage. The "articles of faith" that the Young Man preached were taken from the writings of the fifteenth-century imam of Segovia, 'Isa, and were sound and orthodox enough. I think it would be wrong to place too much stress on the fact that many details in the Young Man's writings were indeed clumsy embroidery. In the Morisco underground, there must have existed a powerful demand for information about Islam. Whenever the Young Man (or his informants) did not have the wherewithal to respond adequately to that demand, they were under temptation to invent. It will have been hard for them to admit that they just did not know something. And of course a liar, once he has started to lie, is on a slippery slope.

Extracts from the Writings of the Young Man from Arévalo

Undoubtedly the most surprising aspect of the writings of the Young Man from Arévalo is the way that he entwines into his theological writings his personal reminiscences. And since these reminiscences are of his travels in search of Islamic learning almost all over Spain (see map 1), and since he often gives us accounts of his visits to his coreligionists, we have here a historical source potentially of some importance. But can we trust this witness? As has been established, no, we cannot. We will catch him telling us things that patently were not true. That means that we must read him and interpret him with close attention, but it does not justify our ignoring him altogether.

1. The Young Man states his motives for writing a religious tract

Thus we will state truthfully that the greater part of this compendium came from the aforementioned verses [of the Koran], and not from my own work. I found commentaries in many serious books, in Arabic and in Spanish, explaining many of the things included in this compendium, and although some of the things said may be off the track (*descarriados*), that should not be attributed to lack of care, for this is the first translation, and a first reading will not always prove satisfactory. Nevertheless with middling knowledge and understanding one can make the necessary enquiries and find a solution, for there is no need to rake together specialist knowledge; it is all a matter of natural understanding, although at times the expressions may not always blend well together, for this is the first such compilation, and it includes words from many regions. May it please God to grant me grace to teach and demonstrate it to every Muslim, so as to sing His divine praise, and in the hope that it may be understood by all. May criticism not turn back against me, however [*awdita* (?) perhaps

The Travels of the Young Man from Arévalo

"bold"] it may be, for my intention was only to serve Allah and to be of service to every Muslim. Even though the things said may be off the track, and the sections concerning ritual prayer and fasting and alms-giving may be [scattered] in several places, when all is said and done the book has been put together as solidly as I knew how, and if perchance I have failed to complete some simile, the reader will accord forgiveness, because I did not commit the fault out of vice.

In the same way there will be found [rules for] inheritances and how to divide them up,[18] wills, third shares, alms given voluntarily, sins, insults pronounced by children against their parents, and by adults against minors, interest payments, pledges, weddings, marriages and divorces, waiting periods [for the divorced] before remarriage, novenas, pardons, and other additional teachings, each one of which would deserve a compilation devoted to it alone. (Preface, *Breve compendio,* Cambridge MS Dd.9.49 f. 2v)

18. This is an important aspect of Islamic family law.

2. At a Muslim assembly in Saragossa, the Young Man is given alms to help him to make the hajj; heated theological debate ensues.

It was one of the seven holy days of the year, the twenty-fifth day of the month *Dhu'l-qa'da*.[19] A whole company of honored Muslims had gathered in Saragossa, twenty Muslims, among whom were seven learned and renowned scholars [*alimex* in Ribera's 1912 transcription], and after the noon prayer they began to discuss our sufferings, and each of them made a speech (*arenga*). Among the things said, many lamented the immense loss we had suffered, and how small were the good deeds we had done. Another scholar said that all the sufferings we underwent and those that awaited us day by day, would all stand to our credit [i.e., on Judgment Day]. Those present there repudiated what he had said, because the sufferings would not count toward making up for anything missed out from the regular obligations of the Law. If the heart of the matter is missing, and that is the summons to prayer, no good deed would be acceptable [to Allah], and the things we suffer here below are no more than a short rest before the life to come. However, where there are no good deeds, there would be no exchange of excellence (*canbiança de eçelençia* [?]). This led on to many disagreements and discussion concerning sins and other debts we owe, past and to come.

In the midst of all these unpleasantnesses (*dixguxtox*), another scholar said something that was extremely harsh and haughty (*enpinada*). There in the presence of them all he said that each one of them ought to gird up his loins (*puxiexe haldax en çinta*), and if any of them wanted salvation, then they should go out and look for it.[20] Everyone there disagreed, because it caused great ferocity [*fieça*, amended to *fiereça*], and would not be to give a good Muslim example. There were different opinions expressed, and because each one of them felt the harm, which was general, as it affected him personally. I was not surprised that each one said what he really thought, for this was no time to indulge in exchanging conventionally polite remarks (*donaires*) or irrelevancies. At the end of it all, they drew up no written decision, although a lot had been said about our merit, because, as was said, good deeds when there is no imam and nobody to make the call to prayer was like having rain after the end of the growing season, for the earth soaks it up and gives little yield. Ritual prayer not performed at the right time is like that. May it please God to grant us pardon for such great trespasses (*fieros pertrechos*). *It was not yet eight*

19. Disappointingly, no year is stated explicitly, but we can assume that it is eight years after the conversion in Aragon [or 1526 + 8 = 1534.]

20. I interpret this as meaning that salvation was there for those who really wanted to make the effort, but what is being recommended? Emigration? Holy war?

years from our conversion [emphasis added.] and already one disaster was following on the heels of another.

We performed the evening (*'asar*) prayer as an assembly, and were led in our prayers by Don Manrique de Segovia, who was at that time in Saragossa with certain merchandise. As everybody wanted to do him honor, they set him at the front [i.e., made him imam] with the agreement and assent of everyone. I pronounced the homily (*khutba*) as the servant and least of those there. Since [the time for] my pilgrimage was drawing near, we were simply waiting for the company that was already assembled in Ávila la Real, and since Don Manrique knew about the difficulties of my travel plans, he provided for part of what I lacked, and gave me 10 Moorish *doblas* [presumably North African coins], and all the other scholars who were there made a contribution in my favor. May Allah award them such merits as I will beseech for them if Allah grant me grace to reach Mecca (may Allah exalt it).

At this point some of these honored scholars, who had noted how much our religion had fallen into neglect, asked me to set to work, while I was waiting to depart, and to revise a substantial part of the commentaries on our honored Koran, as briefly and compendiously as possible. I accepted the task of drawing up this *Tafsira,* so as to fulfill my obligation as a Muslim, at the request of these honored scholars. May it please God that it be acceptable to all, at least until such time as I can put together a more complete *Tafsira,* after this land has been freed (*con libertad dexta tierra*). Let no Muslim lose his faith, for Allah created us out of even less, and we are His. Let us hope for His divine mercy, which is even greater than all created things put together, for if, as a result of our sins, we are suffering now, a time will come when, out of his ineffable love, He will grant us the favor of burying (*cavernar*) the state of the unbelievers, and of restoring the throne of Islam, to the benefit of the Muslims of this peninsula. So let us not cease to call on Him, for he has promised to us more than He has yet given, mighty and powerful as He is. (*Tafsira,* J 62, ff 1–3)

The only comment that needs to be added here is to point out the author's firm conviction that the cause of Islam will triumph in the end: he expects to see that day himself. One notes the important role in the community of rich merchants and the extreme mobility of these people: they think in terms of movement between Segovia, Arévalo, Ávila, Saragossa, and even Mecca. Also evident is their determination to reinstitute the full discipline of Islamic ritual law as soon as possible. The underlying concern is whether one can fulfill one's obligations as a Muslim under these present conditions.

3. The Young Man from Arévalo is given sponsorship in Saragossa.

At this point I would have left off my work, had it not been for the great insistence of certain scholars, some of the honored nobles of the Muslim community (*aljam'a*) of Saragossa. They all made a contribution in my spiritual support, and if I failed in some blameworthy way, they all joined in bearing my burden, while I performed the task of honest scribe. Entrusting my will to His divine goodness, I proceeded with the task. May it please his nobility that my good intention does not go astray. (*Breve compendio*, Cambridge MS Dd.9.49, f. 148v)

4. Market research in Jaén on Christian penitential tariffs

For this reason a Christian scholar (*'alim* [!]) said to me in Astorga: "Why do Muslims (*moros*) deny confession since they give absolution just like Christians when a sinner comes to tell about his sins?" I replied that nothing like that ever happened among Muslims, because there was no sin that was classified as needing absolution, rather was it that every person had to absolve himself. The blessing of the *alfaquí* was not intended to deal with the sins of others; each one has to strive to put his own sins right, and if he did not know how, then the *alfaquí* gives the pardon of the one who committed the sin [(?) *el alfaquí da la parçida del que hizo el pecado*], and if the sinner does what the imam tells him, then he is redeemed should God (*Dios*)[21] so please, and not in a legal sense [*a finis juro,* which appears to be garbled Latin]: as certain Christian scholars put it: "I absolve thee in God's name from blame and penalty, as free as the day thou wert born." [The manuscript here has a number of unvocalized Arabic characters that defy interpretation.] This is the way they give absolution scot-free; even though the sinner were to go back to commit the same offense a hundred times, they would absolve him all the same.

It happened to me in Jaén that in order to put this to the test, I tried three Christian priests in the same day, and for the same sin, and each one of them gave me his own kind of absolution. Muslim scholars give out penances that are set to the measure of the sin, according to how serious it was, and if anybody commits the same sin twice, they do not set a penance, but the sinner himself sets it, with good works secured by repentance.

We went over other things, from the Old Testament to the New, it kept me busy for three days, and then I wrote up all our disputation, which was very curious, as I put it together from his intent. (*Breve compendio*, Cambridge MS Dd.9.49, 217r)

21. The Young Man uses the Christian name for God rather than Allah, presumably because that was the word used in this conversation with a Christian.

Unfortunately there is no trace of this "disputation" in the extant works of the Young Man.

5. *Permissible dissimulation (taqiyya)*

A scholar (*'alim*) of this kingdom[22] when speaking of the sufferings [*ençerramiento,* which I would interpret as a calque on Arabic *diq*] we are undergoing, said: "I know very well that we are going through a period of terror, but Allah will still not fail to punish us if we neglect the service of his kingdom insofar as our legal obligations are concerned. As for hiding our true intentions, we can all make use of this as is our privilege. [We can worship through] the singing of the foreigners whereby the Christians seek salvation, for it all may be classed as allowable dissimulation, for what is good doctrine may not be forbidden by any law, however harsh. They will not neglect our words if they are good. When one gives his will by his hand, good faith is not far away. This is what he said in his homily one Friday, along with other things of great concern for our souls, and of great consolation to us in our afflictions. May His goodness give ear to our complaint and allow us sufficient time for us to repent.

Seeing scholars so respected [here], I was pleased to stay and rest in Aragon, although I was distraught to see the land so poisoned in all directions, and to see our religion so powerless, with the law not honored. Most people simply got by with a simple belief and a simple faith. That, so they thought, would suffice to save them, so they disdained the *fisima* [?] of the service as in old times, and with little protection. (*Breve compendio,* Cambridge MS Dd.9.49, f. 126)

This passage is an example of the Young Man at his most obscure, but it cannot be omitted from this short series of extracts because the homily (*khutba*) provides us with the clearest reference to *taqiyya,* or permissible hiding of one's true beliefs, in the Young Man's writings. The key word, here translated as "hiding our true intentions," is *l'amonestança.* At first sight, this may appear to bear no connection with the meaning, and we might assume the primary sense would be "warning." The view I take is that we have here to deal with a semantic calque on the Arabic root of *taqiyya,* which is w-q-y. Although most of the words grouped under this root convey senses such as "preserve," derivative forms like *tawaqqa* mean "being forewarned against" (*amonestança*). Wishing to render the difficult Arabic term *taqiyya,* Morisco translators made use of *amonestança,* giving to the Romance word the technical sense of the

22. Presumably Aragon; see below. This seems to be the Mancebo speaking of his visit to Saragossa.

Arabic one. Such a procedure, so far removed from modern translation procedures, was *not* unusual when dealing with Arabic terms for which a translation had to be found. That *taqiyya* is indeed the subject is confirmed for us by the use of the expressions *buena disimulança* and *via privilejada* in the same paragraph. The puzzling reference to singing may be to compulsory attendance at mass, which could, according to the fatwa from Oran, be counted as replacement for the regular Islamic ritual prayers, where these could not be performed at the correct times.

The core of the argument of this passage is that banning true religion can never be a just policy and that therefore the Spanish Muslims were justified in employing dissimulation. It is clear that the preacher thought the End was very near—perhaps so near that it would come before there was time for these oppressed people to repent and so cancel out their ritual irregularities.

6. *The Young Man describes la Mora de Úbeda*

The Moorish lady (*Mora*) from Úbeda, who is mentioned so frequently in this commentary and who was so famous in Andalusia and other parts, lived in Granada, near to the Elvira gate. I paid her a visit on the Prophet's birthday. She was very old, and she could not make out the letters[23] of the alphabet, but she could argue cogently and with much sense, so it is hard to convey with what agility she moved within our honored Koran. Although her great age had had its effect, I could not outdo her, for her mental powers were too great. She was at the time some ninety-three years old. Her body and her limbs were amazingly large, I never saw anybody like her, nor have I heard of anybody who ever saw a woman of such proportions. I am not referring to her unusual appearance, but to the fact that her little finger was above my [? *nequisco*; this puzzling word does not occur elsewhere]. She always wore serge and sandals (*alpargatas*) of esparto. She was well provided with food and had no heirs; her family had all died at the time of the conquest of Granada. She did have a niece, the daughter of one of her sisters, to whom she had left her third share and no more, because she said that a woman could not dispose of more than one third of her estate if she was in good health and was more than eighty years old. She added that such women could always leave their property to those who maintain schools. She told me that if I wanted to stay and

23. Manuscript reads *no conocía las letras*, which might alternatively be interpreted as "she did not know her alphabet." That would seem unlikely, since she speaks, for example, of the various "readings" of the Koranic text in a way that would surely be very difficult for an illiterate person.

keep her company, she would bequeath me her books and money, but because I did not have a Spaniard's covetousness, I did not accede to the suggestion. She then said: "Son, if perchance anybody should be fated to offend against himself, once, or many times, what he should do is to make [*excomo* (?)] against himself, and exchange his sins for good works, and for those sins of which he was not aware, he should perform a penance of four months, this is whenever his time comes, which will be Judgment Day in the presence of the mercy of Allah."

Granada and all the country round were governed by the word of this *Mora*. She never married and was said never to have known any man. The ordinary people of the region said that this *Mora* had more credit in matters of our religion and sunna than anybody. She was a great follower of Muhammad Algazel. She was well known by all nations, because she showed me letters from all four of the legal schools, besides others from great muftis and scholars. She never allowed herself rest because she said that the highest form of jihad is to propound our Religion in lands not ruled by Muslims [*tierra de gribeçax,* namely, land that is *garib,* i.e., outside *dar al-islam*]. The sufferings undergone in support of the Religion will be natural clothing [?], and if anybody should die in such defense, all his sins will be of no effect, and his soul will be exalted.

I remained with this *Mora* until the twelfth of the month of Rabi II, and I later regretted not staying a year, because talking to her was an education for any Arabic scholar. Her way of expressing herself was not very elegant, her sayings were rustic and somewhat down to earth, but insofar as the substance of what she said was concerned, there was not her equal in all the harmony of scholars. This *Mora* used to rubricate all the missives of the kings of Granada, and the scholars used to call to greet her on the great religious festivals and on special days. What made her great was the affection she showed to everyone, and this must not have been a matter of natural inclination, but of divine providence. She no longer kept the fast of Ramadan, nor did she perform her prayers except sitting down, and she never left home for any reason. As times were so bad for Muslims, this *Mora* withdrew into the shade of her poverty, and wept for the fall of the Muslims. She said to me: "Son, may it please the Almighty that this suffering is not as long drawn out as I imagine it will be, because this Last Age is a payment for good deeds, and for all the transgressions that have gone before." (*Tafsira,* J 62, f. 440)

7. Morisco customs relating to newly born children

The *Mora* of Úbeda, when explaining the protection that adults owe to the young, said, "There is no greater responsibility to care for a child than to one who was consecrated[24] in holy grace, meaning "at the due time." Muslims also have the custom that at forty days a child's hair is cut, and they give away the weight in silver as alms. Now, for our sins, we do not go so far as to have circumcision, may His goodness grant we achieve it before forty years are out." (*Breve compendio,* Cambridge MS Dd.9.49, f. 108)

Is the author hoping to be circumcised himself before he is forty, or is he hoping for the custom to be restored generally forty years from the time he is writing? Both interpretations of the wording of the manuscript are possible.

8. Old age is a pilgrimage.

The *Mora* of Úbeda was more than ninety years old. And she said to me, "Son, all that a woman lives past eighty counts as Pilgrimage (alhaj)." (*Breve compendio,* Cambridge MS Dd.9.49, f. 192)

9. Nuzay Calderán puts the Young Man in his place.

I had a *tafsir* in Gandia, Valencia, which was more than one hundred folios, most of it dealing with the excellence of the month of *sha'ban*. In it I said this excellence had the power of securing remission of sins in advance, so that I began to hanker after visiting the *Mora* of Úbeda, and I would have done so if I had not had news that Nuzay Calderán was in Alcántara, so I did not waste time, and before the day was out I was with her, and I told her all about what I had found.

She laughed a great deal, then said, "As you eat your bread with the crust cut off, I thought you must be three years old, and you were in the first stage, and speaking through your milk teeth. Don't you know that the law in the Koran can't be measured in quantity against all the works of holy men in the past and still to come? In this book all he had in mind was his devotion, and was more inclined than us for abstinence during *sha'ban*. He was not condemned for less or for more, and he ended with nothing to reproach himself for."

There I passed a novena with great pleasure, going through the Koran, to work up certain passages that I did not know according to [the reading of] Qalun. May Allah reward her, because she never disdained my requests, nor was I any trouble to her, beyond what she was pleased to do. Indeed she invited me to go to Málaga with her, where they were awaiting her arrival to treat a woman who was suffering a difficult pregnancy

24. "Se fadó"—the reference here being the well-attested naming ceremony widely in use among Spanish Muslims.

(*condolida de parçión*). She was very keen to set out, but I could not accept her invitation, because at that time my mother was in very poor health, and I could not fail to return to Arévalo. (*Breve compendio,* Cambridge MS Dd.9.49, f. 174r)

The name Nuzay seems at first sight a strange one, but it occurs in Morisco communities, and is repeated here many times, both in this form and, in the other parallel manuscripts, with variants. There are forms with a -*ta,* "Nuzayta," an ending that must be a diminutive (in spite of the fact that the -*t* in use here is the Arabic emphatic). In the Cambridge manuscript this same lady is called Nuzaila, also presumably an alternative -la diminutive. The suffix of the surname is indubitably -an and not -on, as one might expect (Calderón being a common surname, and Calderán, not). Tapia (1991) mentions one María la Calderera as active teaching Islamic lore, and describes her as "clearly immanentist" in her beliefs. The resemblance of names is not sufficient evidence to assert that this was one and the same lady, but it would be a strange coincidence if both a Calderán and a Calderera were active at the same time in Castile. The editorial principle of giving preference to the more difficult of two readings might lead one to conclude that Calderán was what she was really called, and Calderera, a misreading or an understandable attempt to normalize an unusual name.

10. Nuzay[ta/la] Calderán, midwife and Islamic theologian, settles a theological dispute in Segovia.

On this subject Nuzaya Calderán made a notable pronouncement in Segovia one day in the presence of many people who knew Arabic well. They were talking of the importance of ritual purification (*alwudduwe*), and by way of a question addressed to everybody in general, she asked, "Which of the two is more important, what provides us with our shrouding[25] or what takes away from us our ritual impurity?" This left everybody in doubt, and everybody had his say, at the end of which she concluded with the most lofty expressions that my ears have ever heard. Her power of scholarly expression left us all silent. She ended by saying that the freedom (*sufrajio*) that is given to us by our shrouding is not of greater weight than what is able to save us from ritual impurity, each according to its merits. All the people standing around agreed with what she said. (*Breve compendio,* Cambridge MS Dd.9.49, f. 25r)

25. *Alqafania,* a term that does not occur elsewhere and is absent from *Glosario de voces aljamiado-moriscas.* Presumably it comes from the Arabic root k-f-n, "winding sheet," etc.

11. Nuzaya Calderán is called in to settle an argument in Avila: when is prayer valid?

Because it is relevant I will tell you what occurred in Avila la Real on one of the seven holy days in the year. Between honored Muslims there arose an argument (*porfía*) that was more serious than I might have expected from the important people that were present.

Some of them asserted that if anybody had made proper preparations and had a sound intention to perform ritual prayer (*assala*), he would be accompanied by angels. Others said that those who performed the obligation of ritual prayer at the wrong time were not accompanied by angels, and that such prayer would not be registered alongside prayer performed at the right time [*en sin ora* amended to *en su ora*], but put down apart, because its quantity was not equal. The first group argued back that since it was all prayer, it could not fail to be pleasing to His divine goodness and that no distinction would be made between one prayer and another, even though one was not as noble as the other, and that for His goodness there was no need for anything extraordinary, since for Him all things were present.

The other group said that all that might well be true, but they would demonstrate that the two sorts of prayer were not counted as the same, and they would prove this from Arabic texts. At the end of many altercations (*altercanzas*) they decided to send and call for Nuzaya Calderán, who at the time was there in Ávila, looking after a case of stillbirth. When she arrived at the assembly (*cabildo*) where the disagreement was taking place, they all honored her a great deal. They calmly explained the case to her, and she replied in the presence of everybody, speaking with a severity the like of which I have not seen, as follows:

"I fear that whatever way I go about it, I will be blamed, but what I have to say is that all the sentences in our honored Koran are extremely clear, if only we know how to understand them, because it states that what is most to be respected is the literal sense, for our Koran is such that it will challenge a scholar just as easily as it will [a person of] average understanding, each of them on his own question.

"As to whether there are angels or not, I say that you are all free [of blame] as I understand it. Anybody who performs ritual prayer cannot but be accompanied by angels, whether he is doing so at the right time or not. I will say that anyone who performs his prayer at the right time, as the Koran ordains, will have his angels very well prepared and effective. That was why the angels saved the murderer who had committed thirty murders, with the corresponding sins. They wanted to carry him off to hell, but the angels defended the soul, because the summons arrived at the time of prayer. This shows to Muslims how important is the time assigned for prayer. It is also quite possible for a prayer to be performed at the right time, and yet be so irregular that the angels do not give it that full protection they accord to those who carry out prayers correctly.

"As for those who pray outside the correct time, the angels will not accompany them with the same brilliance as when prayer is at the right time, and if the call to death were to arrive, as it did to that murderer, Allah knows best what would happen.

[*After further considerations, Nuzaya concludes as she began, carefully balancing both viewpoints.*]

"There are cases where a prayer out of the right time would be pleasing to His divine goodness, and when the angels would come to accompany it. But let us try for prayer at the punctual time, because that avoids all doubts and [special] preparations. Let us in general avoid being in disagreement with our honored Koran, because that is the same as disagreeing with His divine goodness. And since what you all wanted above all else was for me to bring you into agreement (*comotanza buena*) and to confirm your esteemed customs, may it please His goodness to grant us all forgiveness so we may achieve salvation. Before Allah shaped the heavens (*al-'arsh*), two thousand years [ago], His divine goodness established the hours of prayer, and dedicated them for the sons of Adam, and blessed them with essential grace. These hours are the keys to the offices in heaven, where all good deeds are registered, for evil deeds are registered in the depths of another world. (*Breve compendio,* Cambridge MS Dd.9.49, f. 34)

12. In Ávila, Nuzaya Calderán claims to tell her audience about Mecca.

In Ávila la Real Nuzaya the Wise Woman said, and proved it to be true with our honored Koran, that the *tiaber* of the sunna was in Mecca, inscribed on metal plates whiter than silver, inside a marble dome, protected by an iron grill. And when one of the muftis died, they all assembled there. (*Breve compendio,* Cambridge MS Dd.9.49, f. 94)

What is translated as "Wise Woman" reads in the text *maga.* It would be misleading to translate this as "witch." The word is still in use in Andalusia in speaking of a *curandera,* a practitioner of popular and especially herbal medicine. This old lady was present in Ávila in order to attend a patient. The story about Mecca is obviously invented nonsense with no foundation. The word *tiaber,* where in other of the manuscripts of the Young Man we find *ti'aber,* is unexplained, and may well be a mere invention, too. Corriente (19XX, personal communciation) has suggested it derives from root *th-w-b*, *thiyab* + *ero*, "chest for clothes" or "ark," but it is not, as far as I know, attested outside the works of the Young

Man. This passage illustrates the totally unreliable side of the Young Man and/or of the Young Man's sources.

13. The Young Man describes his final preparations for the pilgrimage: purchase of swords instruction in Koranic languages ("stylistic levels"?).

One Monday [*no other dating is given*] I left Alría [read Almería, perhaps?] to go up to San Climente where Bray Gonçáleç de Ávila was waiting for me, because they were having a great master craftsman called el Perrillo make two sword blades for us, and they cost us a doubloon (*dobla*) each blade.[26]

In the lodging house where we were staying, I found Nuzzayta Calderán. I was very pleased about that, because we remained there nine days, and one day we went out to the Huerta del Almirante, and I initiated a conversation with her that I thought of using, for I said to her openly that she[27] was not on the road to salvation. She cut me short, making herself quite clear: "Son, you have given me a little nip twice already, if it happens a third time, we won't be friends any more. I have already told you what my constellation indicated. I have left what I was born to, and for that I am hated by my people, and I get by (*paso*). Faith is won, if Allah so grant, in foreign lands. In some cases people have pity on me, and in others I am in agreement, and I place my trust in Allah that I will be beneath His judgment seat. I always acknowledge that it was with little effort that the prizes were won, but on the other hand I have made my contribution in matters of the highest importance, worth more than the treasures of the Indies. If you don't know this now, you will, if you go abroad, for the doubloons there turn into reales, and reales into maravedís."[28]

At this juncture, to pacify her, I turned the subject of our talk to the language of our honored Koran, and she, being somebody who knew Arabic very well, said, "Our honored Koran has three [forms of] language. One is literal, beautiful to hear, [and is] for those who are still suckling, who

26. This is puzzling. The author here may be under a misapprehension, but an understandable one. El Perrillo was not the name of a swordsmith, it was indeed a very well-known brand—in the shape of a dog, "perrillo"—to be found on some high-quality swords. A dobla was a gold coin. Perhaps the author had heard the weapons referred to as "*hojas del perrillo*," and had wrongly thought that "*perrillo*" ("dog-brand") swords were swords actually made by a man called El Perrillo. I now feel confident that *hocha* (i.e., *hoja* "blade") is the correct vocalization. I had at first taken the word to be *hucha* "case."

27. Or "I"—either is grammatically possible, but the context seems to demand the third person.

28. The sense of this is that valuable, gold coins turn into less valuable, silver ones, and the latter in turn become worth even less.

will take pleasure in attractive wording adjusted for such understandings. Because there are beginners with so little power of reason that they need the language itself to be attractive, and the world is full of places where people get bogged down. This plain language of the Koran is not employed by the scholars."

"The second [form of] language is documental. It is a source of great security, and hearts swell, and belief plunges deep, and all ends up being as agreeable as one can desire, just like land when the water from the clouds rains down on it. This documental form of language allows the natural being to ripen in the same way as natural fruits that a temperate autumn brings to maturity, so they are not green on any side. In the same way, no part of those who are bathed by the waters of our honored Koran will remain unripe, because what brings them to maturity, what leaves its impression on them, is the substance of the honored Koran, and it is for this reason that Almorabey said, 'Our honored Koran has so satisfied my appetite and left me so full that my ears are deaf, and my eyes dazzled, and my whole power of expression is obscured. All that remains is dryness in my mouth, and a fluttering of my heart and body, and the mortification of the warmth of my belly; my natural being is very altered, and I [feel as if] I am much in need of sleep (*sobrevelada*).' It is to these heights that the second language of the honored Koran rises. It is not demanded by gravity, but in a substantial amount, because its expression rises up to what is infinite. It has fourteen steps upward, each one of which must be explained by a scholar. It was for this reason that Muhammad al-Gazali had to leave off, and Almorabey grew tired, for after twenty-five years he desisted, and refused to write commentaries any more, even though he had been granted grace so to do. He was no longer engaged by the princes of Cordova, but took his leave, saying, 'The princes do not know what they are asking of me."

"The third type of language of our honored Koran is transcendental. This is for scholars and all those who have an understanding elevated above what it natural." (*Tafsira,* J 62, f. 243)

Some Final Comments on the Writings of the Young Man from Arévalo

In some parts of what the Young Man wrote (particularly passage 13), one is conscious that an attempt is being made to blind the reader with science or pull the wool over his eyes. But the negative reaction created by the pretentious jargon and deception is in part counterbalanced by the admiration evoked by his desperate attempt to improvise in Romance a religious vocabulary to replace the one that Spain's Muslim community had once possessed, and of which they had been deprived.

In his article of 1839 mentioned above, Gayangos mentions a work entitled "The Pilgrimage of the Young Man" that he had seen in the "Royal Library" in Madrid. I and a number of others have, at various times, attempted to trace this work and failed. Professor López-Baralt of the University of Puerto Rico has been particularly active in this connection. I think there is a good measure of agreement among colleagues that Gayangos may have been referring to the manuscript now in the Biblioteca Nacional (*Sumario de la relación y ejercicio espiritual*). However, there was another library that in Gayangos's day might have been referred to as the Biblioteca Real: the Biblioteca Real Particular. This, now the library of the Royal Palace—Palacio de Oriente—did in the past have *aljamiado* manuscripts in its collection, but apparently not now. In any case, the library appears never to have possessed a work by our author. There is a puzzle here that has not yet been solved.

MORISCO WRITINGS NOT IN ARABIC CHARACTERS

Roman Ramírez: A Morisco Medical Man Who Also Made Up Stories and "Read" Them to a Christian Public

Thus far we have looked only at Muslims who wrote and composed in *aljamía* for their own closed community. In a very few cases we hear of Moriscos whose compositions appealed to a Christian public. It is Inquisition documentation (Cuenca, cathedral archive, *leg* [*ajo*] 343, no. 4876: see Harvey 1975) that preserves for us striking evidence about one way in which a Morisco professional storyteller, Román Ramírez, made a successful career for himself across the cultural and religious divide, performing even in the upper reaches of Christian society (and indeed, if we are to believe his deposition to the Inquisition, he was heard by Philip II himself). He must have been born in about 1540 in Deza (in Castile, close to the border with Aragon), was married in about 1558, and settled first at Teruel. He was "about 30" when he first ran foul of the Inquisition in 1571. From his maternal grandfather, Juan de Luna by name, a man with some local reputation as a medical practitioner, he may have inherited his undisputed medical skills. His father farmed (was a "*labrador*"), but also seems to have earned a living from the medical practice he had taken over from Juan de Luna (who had also been a professional narrator of stories). So in the family background of this Morisco Román Ramírez there were generations of practitioners of some form of medicine and of some form of storytelling.

Although it was his powers as a healer (which were used by his Inquisitorial accusers as evidence of his pact with the Devil) that first got him into serious trouble, it was, curiously enough, his innocuous work as a storyteller and public entertainer that was the immediate cause of his arrest by the Inquisition in 1595. Not that anything in his tales was found doctrinally objectionable, for he had simply been booked, on the basis of his well-established reputation as a successful public entertainer, to "recite" a novel of chivalry for the delectation of what sounds to have been an entirely Christian audience (and a highly respectable one at that—many of them were distinguished lawyers).

What happened was that the poor entertainer became caught up, against his will, in a feud in which he had no interest, between two powerful Christian clans. As a Morisco he was vulnerable, and it was he who ended up in jail. What makes the case of particular interest in the present connection is that, under interrogation, the Morisco was moved to reveal some of his professional secrets as a "reader" of novels of chivalry.

Román Ramírez had been summoned to the small town of Soria in 1595 by a local worthy there called Pedro Ramírez (no relative of his, it would seem) in order to provide entertainment for a distinguished visitor, Gil Ramírez de Arellano (yet another Ramírez!), a legal official (*oidor*) from the city of Valladolid. However, when the *corregidor* (the royally appointed magistrate of the place), Íñigo de Orozco, got to hear that the storyteller was coming to town, he tried to insist that the first performance should be put on in his house, not in that of Pedro Ramírez. The ensuing squabble over precedence between the lawyers had nothing to do with the Morisco or with anything he had done, of course, but he realized that if he recited for one faction he would incur the enmity of the other, and either of them would then be well able to cause him trouble in the future. So he tried to run away. Before he could get clear of the town of Soria, Orozco had his officials pick Román up and hand him over to the Inquisition on a convenient charge of witchcraft. The Morisco was thereafter never released from prison, and four years later, in December 1599, he died in custody. It was actually only after his death that he was formally condemned to be burnt at the stake: as was the way, the prisoner's death could not be allowed to cheat the executioner's pyre of a victim. The sentence was carried out, but "in effigy," at a magnificent *auto de fe* celebrated in Toledo. Present was not only Inquisitor-General Niño de Guevara, but also the king, Philip III.

Román Ramírez had claimed in evidence at his trial that he had in the past given performances of novels of chivalry to Philip II. The assertion was not contradicted, as would have been easy to do, so perhaps we should accept it at face value, although it has to be said that, thus far, no record of any such royal entertainment has come to light. If the claim was correct, then Román provided a spectacle for both Philips, one when he was alive, the other after he was dead.

The Inquisition proceeded against Román Ramírez (without informing him of the nature of the charges, of course, which was standard
procedure) on several distinct counts. On the purely religious front, the
inquisitors were able to show that he had years earlier been included
in the "general pardon" accorded to the Moriscos of Deza in 1571. This
would have been part of the evangelistic effort that ensued after the
Granadan War of 1569–70. The point of such a "pardon" was that, in
exchange for the expunging of past offenses (and Román had confessed to
having fasted Ramadan, etc.), the person concerned, although let off with
little more than a caution, became much more vulnerable to prosecution
in the future, should he be caught in the Inquisition's net again. Once a
person had received the "benefit" of a pardon, he could not then plead
ignorance on future occasions. The excuse that Román tried to produce
for relapsing into his Islamic ways was that he had indeed continued as a
good Christian for some eighteen years until, in 1588 in Deza, he met up
with a Turkish slave who tempted him back to Islamic practices. We may
suspect that this "Turkish slave" may have been a fabrication, a device
thought up by Román to protect his family and associates. By pointing
the finger at an outsider (conveniently not available for interrogation), he
probably had it in mind to save his own folk from detention and perhaps
torture. Presumably the information already available to the Inquisitors
about Román himself would have, in itself, been enough to lead to a conviction, but once the Inquisition were seized of a case, what they wanted
to achieve above all was to make their prisoner implicate others.

Among the offenses they investigated was Román's alleged reliance
in the public performances of his storytelling on the aid of the Devil.
The evidence carefully piled up on this charge tells us nothing, of course,
about Román's own religious faith (the Devil will have been a projection
of the Inquisitors' own fears), but it incidentally leads to the revelation
of a surprising amount about Román's narrative techniques and his craft
as an entertainer. We need first to attend to the words of the deposition
of a priest (Pedro Díaz de Carabantes) who told the court he had been
standing in the street in Soria one day when the head of the town watch
came up and pointed out Román to him and to his companions:

> "Just look at that man down there," he said, pointing out a man who was
> standing by a lawyer's office about thirty or forty yards away. He had a
> gray cloak on, . . . and the aforesaid officer said he was called Román, that
> he came from the town of Deza, and was a Morisco.
> The night before, when Román was in the house of Antonio de Río,
> certain gentlemen who were amusing themselves and taking their ease
> [*jugando y folgandose*] in the house of the *oidor* [a legal official] Gil Ramírez

de Arellano, some of them who recognized him said "Hey, tell us a bit of a novel of chivalry" which they then specified, including the chapter. The said Román took a sheet of paper from his pocket, and he looked at it as if he were reading, and spoke a long passage of the book and chapter that they had asked for. And he would have been able to do the same, as was confirmed by most of those who had been present, if he had been asked for part of the Bible or Holy Scripture." (Cuenca, cathedral archive, *leg* [*ajo*] 343, no. 4876)

Not all the witnesses called to testify by the Inquisition were hostile to Román. One Licentiate Bonifaz stated that he had heard Román read chapters from novels of chivalry:

"Taking as a matter of form a piece of paper, whatever he might be handed, he would read from memory the book and chapter that was requested. However, he [Bonifaz] had never felt scruples about listening, nor did he suspect there might be anything evil about it, because having a good memory was a natural thing."

What is more, this witness stated that he had been present on occasions when Román's memory had faltered, and he had got things wrong. Was the implication that the Devil would not have made such mistakes and that the memory feats of this Morisco fell safely within the normal range of fallible human and not infallible supernatural performances? The heart of the charge against Roman was that his ability to "recite" long passages from various books without actually reading from the pages arose because he received some form of diabolical assistance.

What was probably going on in Román's performances was that he was using props like a piece of paper as a simple device to help him concentrate. Similar practices are reported by those who have studied performers of oral epic poetry in the former Yugoslavia. Oral performers might hold a book or sheet of paper while improvising in public. Such recitals were (are?) termed *z kniga,* "out of the book." The performer is not reading from the book, he is using it as a mnemonic device.

Román, in his testimony, not knowing what exactly had got him into this trouble, of course, must have guessed, from the line of questioning to which he had been subjected, that he needed to deal with the dangerous suggestion that his ability to reproduce orally long stories just as they appeared in books came from some supernatural—and so diabolical—power. He therefore provided a rational (truthful?) explanation of how he worked:

"He said he wished to reveal the secret of his affairs, and how he set about reading, which was something that he had never told a living soul before, nor ever thought to do. If there is anything more to it than this, may he be consumed in the flames. What he did was to memorize how many books [i.e., subdivisions] and chapters there were [in the volume in question], and the substance of the adventures, the names of the cities, kingdoms, knights and princesses which occurred in them. Afterwards, when he was reciting he could extend or abridge the wording as much as he wanted, but he always took care to reach the end where the adventures did, so that all those who were listening to him had the impression that he gave all the details, and that he did not alter the wording of the books in any way, but the truth of the matter was that if anybody looked in the book at the passage while he was reciting, it would be seen that although he was faithful to the adventures and got all the names right, he departed a great deal from the actual wording and added in things not there at all. What he did was something that anybody with intelligence, ability, and powers of memory could do too, and there was no mystery in it." (Harvey 1975, 97)

Román Ramírez was obviously an exceptional and odd individual, and it would be foolish to extrapolate too far from his case, but he does illustrate how enmeshed some Moriscos were in the culture of their Christian contemporaries. He obviously had a large repertoire of the Spanish novels of chivalry (he mentions quite a number), and his public in Soria expected him to be able to "perform" at will from those they named. (They shouted out their requests.) He seems to ascribe to his maternal grandfather his memory training, as well as his powers as an herbalist, and that would presumably place the medicine he practiced within the folk tradition. However, Román told the Inquisitors that he had owned a copy of *Dioscorides,* a work on botany and *materia medica,* the publication of which in a Spanish translation (in a magnificent edition that was by no means cheap) was an important manifestation of Spain's Renascence culture. Some Moriscos could and did keep in contact with the intellectual life of the general community. Román even claimed at one point to have received what amounted to a publisher's advance for the beginning of a new novel of chivalry of his entitled *Florisdoro de Grecia* ("he had been given 300 reales for what he had written")! There is no indication that the book was ever completed, much less published.

Román was a Morisco working in a fantasy genre, that of the novels of chivalry, and he was not, as far as we can judge, reflecting the reality of life as it was experienced by his community, but it is in this context of interaction between Morisco entertainers and the literature of entertainment for the Spanish general public that we must look at other prose romances in which Muslims ("Moors," etc.) do figure. The intellectual world of the Moriscos and that of their Christian neighbors were not separated from each other by any impermeable seal.

The "Moorish" Genre and Popular Entertainment

The short prose romance entitled *Abindarraez and the Beautiful Xarifa,* often simply referred to as *The Abencerraje,* was a work that enchanted Spanish readers in the sixteenth century and indeed continues to charm readers everywhere up to the present day. Following the appearance of this novel, there followed a whole genre of "Moorish" novels, the vogue for which spread throughout Western Europe and continued strong right up to the Romantic period (to the time of Chateaubriand's *Dernier Abencérage* and even later). The action of such works is usually set in the closing decades of the history of the independent state of Granada or in the early years of the sixteenth century. The novels have a "Moorish," that is, Muslim Spanish, hero (and often heroine), and the Muslims are depicted as being fully as noble and magnanimous, fully as humanly attractive as the Christians who face them, if not more so. *Abindarraez and the Beautiful Xarifa* appeared anonymously, first as an independent short narrative, but was to achieve wider dissemination when it was inserted into book 4 of the 1561 (Valencia) edition of Jorge de Montemayor's pastoral novel *Diana,* one of the great best sellers of the day, and so reached the widest of publics. How are we to explain the strange contradiction that tales about noble Moors proved so popular precisely in a period (let us say 1560 onward) when energetic measures were being put into effect to make sure that the Morisco New Converts abandoned everything reminiscent of their Islamic past, when the last social vestiges capable of reminding Spaniards of medieval tolerant coexistence (*convivencia*) in the peninsula were being dismantled?

Such "literary Maurophilia," as it was termed by Georges Cirot, who documented it comprehensively in a series of articles published between 1938 and 1944 in the *Bulletin Hispanique* ("La maurophilie littéraire en Espagne au XVIe siècle"), has given rise to an enormous secondary literature, of which one might mention, among very many others, the excellent studies by F. López Estrada, for example, *El Abencerraje y la hermosa Jarifa* (Madrid, 1957), and in English, M. S. Carrasco Urgoiti's work, *The Moorish Novel, "El Abencerraje," and Pérez de Hita* (Boston, 1976). Claudio Guillén confronted this paradox in "Literature as Historical Contradiction: *El Abencerraje*, the Moorish Novel and the Eclogue," a section of his volume *Literature as System: Essays towards the Theory of Literary History* (Princeton, 1971, 172ff), and Francisco Márquez Villanueva of Harvard brought the whole problem into clear and more specifically historical focus in a collection of essays published in 1991 (Márquez (1991, 21–27).

While I have the deepest admiration for the pioneering work of Cirot, who at a difficult time during the war years managed to assemble an impressive mass of information, I would agree with Márquez, who criticizes the exclusively "literary" approach Cirot brought to this field (and, it has to be said, most of the others who have seen the "problem" as belonging exclusively to literary history). The "literary" cult of Moorish themes, when studied in Cirot's way as a purely literary phenomenon, is liable, as Márquez (1991, 184) puts it, to be

> taken as a product of the vagaries of fashion, no more than a chance upsurge of taste for what is picturesque, and analysis cannot go much beyond summarizing plots, because we literally do not know what is the subject about which we are being addressed. Rather than allowing texts which are of the greatest value to remain silent in the limbo to which they have been relegated, we should consider them as an intellectual facet of a historical problem, and assess their value within that context.[29]

The alternative explanation proposed by Márquez himself is as follows:

> Maurophilia is the voice of a coalition of forces and groupings engaged in a struggle against the policy of duress and violence. This coalition was made up of the nobility, the Moriscos, the bourgeoisie, the [Jewish] conversos, the "political" intellectuals, clerics of an irenic persuasion, "liberals" as we would say nowadays. It is a whole opposition contingent that we would hardly expect to come across if we were to judge solely from the bibliography available to us. (Márquez 1991, 187)

With that bold formulation I would in no way disagree. I would simply add in clarification what is clear enough in the context of Márquez's writings as a whole: that none of the groupings he mentions was in any way *exclusively* aligned in support of a "liberal" policy, and that even goes for the Moriscos themselves.

Certainly the nobility and the bourgeoisie provided some of the principal advocates and implementers of the policy of repression. It is important to note that in the literature of the sixteenth century there were these manifestations of respect and admiration for the people who were at that

---

29. "La maurofilia se pone entonces a cuenta de las frivolidades de una moda, es un sencillo brote de caprichoso pintoresquismo, y su análisis no puede ir mucho más allá de resumir los argumentos, pues literalmente no se sabe de qué nos hablan. Como alternativa a que unos textos de máximo valor hayan de continuar mudos y relegados al limbo, es preciso considerarlos como faceta intelectual de un problema histórico y valorarlos desde el interior de éste."

very time being demonized and driven out of society forever. It is probably not a matter of chance that the pattern of what I would call piggyback publication inaugurated by the *Abencerraje* story and the *Diana* was repeated in almost every case for these "Morisco" novels. By that I mean that the "Maurophile" narrative rides on the back of some other work of unimpeachable acceptability and is conveyed to the public in that way.

Another example would be the story of Ozmín and Daraja, inserted by Mateo Alemán into his moralizing picaresque novel, *Guzmán de Alfarache.* The exception that might be said to prove this rule is the second part of Pérez de Hita's *Guerras civiles de Granada.* In this case, the pretensions of the author, Pérez de Hita, to be writing a completely accurate historical narrative (in fact, it is something quite different, of course) that perhaps makes the piggyback strategy unnecessary and, in any case, inapplicable. In Vicente Espinel's *Vida del escudero Marcos de Obregón* (1618), after the completion of the Expulsion, the neatly inserted story of the Valencian Morisco refugee-turned-corsair, under whom Marcos de Obregón finds himself serving as a captive, conforms to the general pattern described and is of direct relevance to the whole Morisco question. The Morisco in this work gives voice to the resentment felt by the generality of Moriscos at their exclusion from society. In Spain, he explains that

> "I felt hurt, like all the others, because I could not aspire to honors or to appointment as a magistrate or higher dignities, and because I realized that such deprivation of honor (*infamia*) would be everlasting, and that being a Christian, whether in outer appearance or inner truth, would never be enough. Some fellow who, whether by birth, inheritance or acquired qualities did not stick up above ground level more than two fingers' breadth could still dare to call a very Christian man and a true gentleman by insulting names. Above all, I saw how far distant was the hope of any remedy to all this. What have you got to say to me about all this." (Translation by the author; discussed at Márquez 1991, 189)

Here we reach the heart of the matter. Moriscos aspired not merely to better treatment, to the absence of persecution and to protection from insults. They would have been satisfied by nothing less than fair access to honor, that bedrock on which their society, their Islamic society, just as much as the Spanish society of their Old Christian fellows, was based. The Old Christians were determined to exclude them from honor, yet many Moriscos were not disposed to settle for anything less. It is surprising, perhaps, to find within Christian Spanish literature such a forceful articulation of the Morisco case, but in some of these texts, the voice of the Morisco is certainly to be heard, loud and clear, and for that reason mention of these works has to be included here.

Whether Moriscos themselves actually had a hand in the creation of such writings is another matter. Perhaps in the case of *El Abencerraje,* that seminal text, which first came to light anonymously under the good auspices of a noble Aragonese family, the Ximénez de Embum (lords of estates where there were many Moriscos), it is not impossible that the literary creator was himself a Morisco, or at least that a Morisco provided some helpful input. However, we know that other texts of this type were produced by non-Moriscos. Cervantes, Pérez de Hita, Alemán, Espinel, none of them have been shown conclusively to be Moriscos (though, to be sure, doubts have been expressed about the pedigrees of some of them).

It is just as possible for a good writer, by the exercise of empathy and imagination, to find adequate literary expression for the state of mind of a persecuted Morisco as it is for a male author to render the state of mind of a woman (or vice versa), or for a white writer to convey life as seen through the eyes of blacks (again, or vice versa). This Moorish genre *within* the literature of the Christian majority deserves, demands, our attention, not just because some of the stories and verses may have been created by Moriscos themselves (although I would not exclude that possibility in some cases), but because these literary creations of the sixteenth century force us, as readers, to begin to enter imaginatively into the life the Moriscos lived. To rely exclusively on imaginative fictional constructions would be dangerous, and such conclusions as we may draw from such sources need to be checked constantly against information available from less dubious texts, but without "literary" assistance we will be hard put to know a world so different from our own as what we find reflected in the Moriscos' own writings.

Morisco Influence on Mainstream Literature

Before concluding this rapid survey of the intellectual productions of the Moriscos and of derivative and associated literature, we should pose the question whether Moriscos, apart from feeling the influence of the majority culture (which they undoubtedly did), may have in some way exercised influence on the literature of the national mainstream. In the last half century or more, and thanks above all to the writings of Américo Castro, there has taken place an ideological reevaluation of Spanish literature, both that of the Middle Ages and that of the sixteenth century. Spanish literature, long viewed as essentially the product of a Christian culture that was exceptionally monolithic, has been reinterpreted as the outcome of the confluence of three religious cultures, Jewish Islamic, and Christian. In the light of what has been demonstrated by Castro and others about the Jewish antecedents of many of the greatest writers of what Spaniards consider to be their Golden Age, Spanish literature has taken on a different aspect. To the list of those whose Jewish background came as only a small surprise, say, Luis de León, were added other major figures such as Saint Teresa of Ávila, and the hunt for the crypto-Judaisers was then on with no holds barred. This investigation into family trees has sometimes been pursued by modern scholars (as politically correct and as antiracist as our modern world demands), with an inquisitorial zeal that rivals that of Torquemada himself. In some very few cases, the authors thus tracked down and "outed" appear to have been, in some active sense, Jews, but many more were converts who did not waver in their allegiance to their new Christian faith. Authors in whose writings a Jewish identity still showed through in spite of their own intentions. It is only reasonable to assume that if many Spanish authors of this period have turned out under close scrutiny to be Christians with a Jewish past or with Jewish forebears, some others at least might prove to be Christians with a Muslim background. Less effort has so far been expended on the search to "out" crypto-Muslims, and so it is not surprising that fewer have come to light.

It has to be said that the Muslims who contributed in this way to the majority culture were in all probability not as numerous as the Jews, but it would be wrong to pass over in silence this aspect of the newly discovered cultural diversity of a society that has for too long now been seen as monochromatic. An early pioneer in this line of investigation was Jaime Oliver Asín, and in more recent times significant contributions have been made by Luce López Baralt[30] and, of course, Francisco Márquez Villanueva.[31]

The fact that there was no watertight bulkhead separating Moriscos from Christian Spaniards culturally and that influences seeped in both directions, is a necessary corrective to the overly simplistic view of a purely Christian majority facing purely Jewish and purely Morisco alien minorities. Yet that connection must not itself be allowed to distort the general conclusions that incontrovertibly emerge from the survey of the

30. See López-Baralt (1985; 1990).

31. "Even a summary listing of intellectuals of Moorish or Mudejar origin before 1501 has yet to be drawn up. One might recall cases like the notoriously obscene poet, el Comendador Ramón, whose 'demonstrably Arab' pedigree comes out in the course of his violent verse polemic with Antón de Montoro. Or there is the early humanist Fernando Valentí, a Granadan converted under the protection of Fernando de Antequera, according to F. Vendrell de Millás, "En torno al humanista converso Ferrando Valentí o de Valencia," *Sefarad* 28 (1968): 309–12, cited in Márquez (1991, 19–20 n.).

Moriscos' own writings made clear in this chapter. From the Moriscos' books, those they owned, those they wrote, we have seen that their Islamic culture was, up to the very end, still alive, still evolving. The threat represented to it by the decline of Arabic scholarship among them, by the scarcity of people with the requisite command of the language of culture of the Islamic world, was to some extent remedied by their creation of an *aljamiado* literature as an alternative and substitute vehicle for what they needed to preserve. There is evidence of the desire of the crypto-Muslim minority to engage intellectually with their Christian fellow Spaniards, but there is also evidence of a Muslim determination not to be swamped, to defend and maintain their individuality, even when that meant they had to perform the near-impossible feat of crippling intellectual contortion involved in remaining creatively distinct and yet keeping their creativity a secret.

SIX ❧ Crisis and War: Granada, 1567–1571

In the closing period of the history of the Muslims of al-Andalus, there were three key crises, three times of suffering and bloodshed that stood out among the many others. The first, as we have seen, was the first revolt in the Alpujarras of 1500 (which was followed by the original forcible conversion of 1501); the last such crisis was, obviously enough, the trauma of the Expulsion of 1609 and after. Between these liminal dates, beyond any doubt the event of the greatest importance, not only for the Moriscos of Granada but for all of Spain's crypto-Muslims, was the second revolt in the Alpujarras of 1568–70, sometimes referred to as the Second Granadan War (see map 2). The outcome of the fighting of 1568–70 was the elimination of all but a remnant of the Granadan Muslim community from the area where, up to then, the traditions and glories of the past of al-Andalus had survived best. Once the Granadan community had virtually ceased to exist, all over Spain the Christian majority and the crypto-Muslim minorities began to relate to each other differently. The whole peninsula felt the consequences of this war. After the military defeats inflicted on the Muslim rebels, the Granadan Muslims, whether they had taken up arms or not, were all scattered by decree over much of inland Spain in an endeavor to accelerate what in modern terms we might style their acculturation.

Paradoxically, what came of this movement of populations of 1570 was not acculturation or the wiping out of sentiments of Islamic group solidarity but what (in equally modern terms) we might call a process of "consciousness-raising" among the hitherto politically inert Moriscos of the regions into which the Granadans were transferred. After the second war in the Alpujarras, marked as it was by great cruelty and unprecedented atrocities on both sides, the last vestiges of the comfortable medieval Mudejar-style accommodation between the religions and the races was wiped away by blood. Henceforth, the only "solution" envisaged by Christians to what they saw as their "Morisco problem" was the outright,

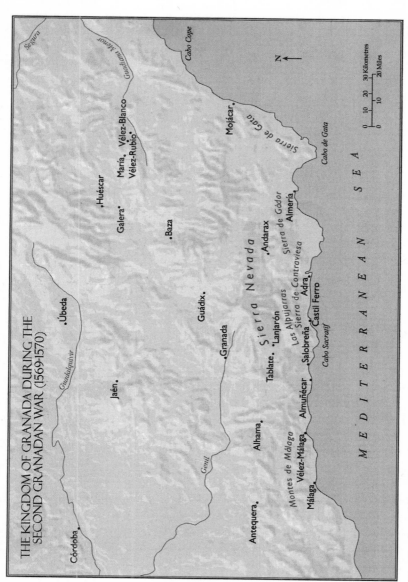

The Kingdom of Granada

total, and final Christianization of what they now felt to be an utterly alien element within the body politic. The final four decades up to the Expulsion are black ones indeed, not just for the Granadans but for their coreligionists everywhere in the peninsula. It is therefore a matter of some importance for the history of Islam in the whole peninsula to understand how within such a relatively short space of time—two or three years at the very end of the 1560s and beginning of the 1570s—localized conflicts in the kingdom of Granada brought about such a rapid deterioration in the relations between New Christians and Old all over Spain.

TENSIONS MOUNT

There had been tensions earlier in the sixteenth century between Granada's Muslims and the Christian settlers who were being encouraged to move into the conquered kingdom. The "former" Muslims, now of course nominal converts to Christianity, had always hitherto been able to purchase a respite from the attentions of the evangelizers, thanks to the payment of special financial contributions ("services") to the Crown they had been able to secure exemption from the Inquisition and from the harshest of the repressive legislation to which they were exposed. They had been able to do so with such regularity that they had almost begun to take the "system" for granted (Gallego and Gámir 1968, esp. 206–59).

The situation might be summarized broadly as follows: in the first half of the century the spokesmen of the Granadans (many of whom were members of the former Islamic aristocracy of the Nasrid kingdom), argued tactfully, even boldly at times, that their people should in general be left undisturbed so long as their local ways did not run blatantly counter to explicit Christian doctrine and the interests of the Spanish state. In opposition to this policy of minimal interference, two (partially overlapping) groups emerged in the Christian ruling classes as proponents of a hard line. These were, firstly, the new bureaucratic class of lawyers brought to Granada when new Christian administrative structures were set up there and especially after the transfer there of the Chancillería from Ciudad Real in 1505 (this tribunal had wide responsibilities for legal matters not only in Granada, but over all the southern half of the realm). The second group of proponents of a hard line was the Inquisition, especially after the Inquisition of Jaén was transferred to Granada in 1526, thus locating both supervisory administrations in the same city. These two groups were, of course, each in its way the instrument of the centralizing policies of the Crown and the Church, but each had, as bureaucracies will, its own agenda as well, and at times sectional interests could run counter to the general interest of the Crown. For example, if a special "service" was paid to the Crown by the new converts to secure exemption from the attentions of the Inquisition, that body was thereby deprived of the expectation of the various sources of income (confiscations, fines, etc.) on which it relied and was obliged to rely, in order to defray its running costs. Is it surprising that it did not favor such deals?

We can see such Inquisitorial disapproval of the granting of special concessions to the Moriscos being expressed in the "Opinion of the Inquisitor-General and of the members of the Council of the Inquisition concerning the various headings of the petition submitted [to the Crown] by the new converts of the kingdom of Granada" (Gallego and Gámir 1968, 254).

> Insofar as the second heading [of the petition] is concerned, in which it is requested that in future the property of those who are condemned should not be confiscated, nor should they have to pay financial penalties, this with the object of putting a stop to the complaints (*cavilaciones*) of those who say these things are done in order to take their property away, and to avoid legal proceedings.

This request ought not to be granted, said the Inquisitor, pointing out that it was not the first time that he had heard it, because

> what they have had conceded to them already by Your Majesty, whereby they are not subject to confiscation of their goods for offenses committed up to the present time, is already a very great act of mercy.

In short: no more concessions.

On the other hand, writing on January 11, 1544, Mondéjar, defending the old viceregal ways, characteristically supports the proposal that the new "service" should be negotiated with the Moriscos, but he tries to avoid crossing swords directly with the Inquisition (whose comments have just been cited). "If His Majesty agreed," wrote Mondéjar, "perhaps a few years more than the thirty could be granted [to the Moriscos], and I think this would satisfy them" (Gallego and Gámir 1968, 259). One can see that if this extra concession had been granted, it would in effect have negated the new tough policy. Mondéjar is acting as broker, is effectively negotiating in the interest of his crypto-Muslim subjects. His aim was to see that the policy of granting to the Moriscos exemptions from Inquisition jurisdiction was not ended.

Of course even though "services" had been paid, not all Moriscos in Granada had managed to escape the attentions of the Inquisition before this date; enough of them knew from bitter experience how important it was to keep out of the clutches of the Holy Office. For various offenses some of them had found themselves in Inquisition jails, where the increasingly harsh treatment accorded to them might be illustrated by many acutely distressing accounts. But perhaps the most revealing testimony is that of Bartolomé de Lescano, whose testimony is completely reliable because he was simply an efficient Inquisition prison administrator attempting to carry out some intelligent (and to an extent, compassionate) forward planning. His goal was not the easing of conditions for his charges but for his own convenience he was arguing for some minor administrative adjustments. Bartolomé de Lescano was *alguacil* and governor of the Inquisition prison in Granada, a bureaucrat whose function it was to make the system work. In 1557, he testified as follows in a lawsuit (see Garrad 1965). In the case in question, the Inquisition of Granada was attempting to get possession of a property, a yard adjacent to their prison building, and they were being opposed by the owner of the freehold of the piece of land, himself a lawyer and *oidor* of the Audiencia of Seville, one Melchor de León. The Granadan Inquisition thus had its own reasons on this occasion to want to bring out in court how cramped were conditions for their detainees. The depositions are convincing precisely because what comes out is revealed quite incidentally. The administrator is doing what administrators always do—asking to be allocated more space:

> In the jail there is no yard to bury any prisoner who dies inside. It has often (*munchas veces*) happened that prisoners have died in the prison, and although [I] with the assistance of others have taken them to the Santiago cemetery, even at midnight the whole neighborhood gets to know about it, for straightaway people look out of their windows, making it impossible to keep it secret. [I] also know that in all the said prisons there is nowhere to put a sick person in the sun to recover, and nowhere to put an old man with poor eyesight so he can see to delouse himself. Such things are not possible in the aforesaid prisons because so little light enters them. (Garrad 1965, 76)

Secrecy was an essential feature of all the proceedings of the Inquisition—utter secrecy until it was judged that the moment had come to make everything public in that apogee of planned publicity, the auto de fe. The prison administrator in Granada felt indignant when circumstances prevented him from maintaining a blanket of secrecy. But in spite of all the Inquisition's preoccupation with security, the Moriscos did usually know very well what was going on inside the jails. Marmol (1991, 86) preserves for us a description of the horrors.

How we come to have this forceful expression of the Muslim viewpoint in this Spanish Christian source is as follows: Mondéjar, accompanied by his son, the count of Tendilla, had set out on a tour of inspection of the sea coast near Adra, always a danger spot because of the proximity of North Africa. The Muslim leader from the Albaicín, Aben Daud, was, it so happened, by coincidence at that very time en route to Algiers (illegally, of course). Aben Daud was betrayed by the fisherman who had provided him with a boat, and he and his companions were forced ashore near to Adra. Once ashore, they were pursued by the coastguard, and in the confusion of their flight they dropped a bundle that proved to contain "a large book in Arabic letters." The Licentiate Castillo (who will figure prominently in chapter 8) was summoned from Granada to translate it. Castillo, a Morisco himself, was also an agent in the service of the Spanish authorities, directly employed at times by Philip II, no less. He someone involved in intelligence operations, not merely as a language specialist but active also in creative campaigns of propaganda and disinformation. We know he was not above actually planting forged documents when required, so we must be suspicious in this instance. The fact that this dubious figure was involved in the affair should warn us to beware of accepting at face value everything that Mármol conveys to us about the incident. The book, so Castillo told Mondéjar, was one that "dealt with the sect of Muhammad," and it included "many authorities from ancient histories." Its author's name, so Castillo stated, was "Lollori." One needs to allow for the fact that Arabic names almost inevitably suffer severe garbling when transmitted through Spanish, but even so it is impossible to guess what Arabic author this might be, and I harbor the unkind suspicion that Castillo may have been pulling the wool over Mondéjar's eyes. Tucked in the pages of this captured tome were, allegedly, two loose documents, one of which proved to be a letter written by Aben Daud (Castillo—a fellow Granadan—conveniently recognized the handwriting!). The other document, in Arabic verse, was a lamentation—"complaints sent to the Moors of Africa in the hope that they would be moved to pity and send help," as Mármol surmised. To accept as unvarnished truth this story of how the text came into Spanish hands would be naïve, but whether it was in fact written by Aben Daud or whether it was yet another of Castillo's fabrications, the text still articulates forcefully the sufferings of the *nuevos convertidos de moros* (we may even surmise that it may have been Castillo's indirect way of bringing before the viceroy and, ultimately the king, the depth of Morisco alienation.) A fairly long text, inter alia it laments that

> Anyone who praises God in his own tongue is surely lost, for if it comes to be known, they hunt him down, and catch him even if he is a thousand leagues away. They cast him in the great jail and terrorize him night and

day, saying to him "Beware!" The miserable prisoner is left with only his tears, with nothing but his power of endurance.[1] They cast him into a terrible chamber, where he lies for a long time; a thousand ocean deeps open below him, and no swimmer, however strong, can make his way up out, for this is a sea that cannot be traversed. Thence they take him off to the chamber for torture, and they tie him down to administer it, and inflict it on him until his bones break. Next they set up in the Hatabin Square a scaffold like that of Judgment Day. If any are delivered, they are dressed that day in yellow, and the rest are borne off to the flames, with effigies and frightful shapes.[2] This enemy has tormented us terribly in every place. We have been surrounded as by fire. We are suffering an oppression that is unbearable. (Mármol 1991, 86)

By the late 1560s, then, Granada, both city and kingdom, were again smoldering hotbeds of discontent. General conflagration came as a consequence of new measures implemented at the local level by the lawyers of both the Chancillería and the Inquisition. The aim of the administrators was to turn the nominal converts at last into true and observant Christians. Pressure in favor of taking more energetic measures to extirpate Islam had originated in the Church at the highest level. There is a report of conversation between Pope Pius IV and Archbishop Guerrero that the latter took care to pass on to the king: In 1560 as the sessions of the Council of Trent were being drawn to a temporary close the archbishop had gone to see the pope to take his leave, and the pontiff had been insistent that a solution must be found to the Morisco problem.[3] From the earliest days of the Christian regime in Granada, policy toward Muslims and converts had had two faces, those of the two archbishops, Talavera (of Granada itself, the gradualist) and Cisneros (of Toledo, the protagonist of energetic measures). The gradualist policy had, in practice, if not in theory, on the whole prevailed because of the continuity of the influence of the Mondéjar/Tendilla family, hereditary captains-general of Granada. Over the period from 1492, four members of the family succeeded one another without interruption in the post of *Alcaide de la Alhambra* (the Alhambra being the residence of the captain-general) and were in overall command on the spot. However, the easygoing old ways

1. The Spanish version has *paciencia*. This may render Arabic *sabr,* a more forceful concept.

2. This puzzling wording presumably arises from some allusion in the original to the Inquisition practice of burning "in effigy" condemned persons who could not actually be paraded in person.

3. Luis Cabrera de Córdoba, *Filipe Segundo, Rey de España* (Madrid, 1876), as quoted in a footnote to Hurtado de Mendoza (1970, 107, footnote 40).

were coming into conflict with a tough new attitude, a determination to make the conversion real, which emerged in the course of the decade of the 1560s. It is perhaps not too much to see it as one more manifestation of the general Tridentine affirmation of rigor in doctrine and internal reform in ecclesiastical discipline.

The new policy for Granada became manifest when, in 1567, on January 1 (a date of special significance in the city because it is the anniversary of the conquest of 1492), Pedro de Deza, newly appointed to the presidency of the Granada *Audiencia* (a position that, although strictly within the civil jurisdiction, enjoyed preeminent status in Granada in legal matters in general), proclaimed that he would set about enforcing the recent decision of a specially convened junta held in Madrid, namely, a ban on the use of Arabic, the wearing of Moorish dress, the use of Arab names, the use of Moorish baths, and a range of other measures all designed to wipe out even the memory of the Islamic past and to make sure that all Granadans became good Christians. Of course, we have heard all this before: the crypto-Muslims had heard it before and no doubt assumed that once more they would be able to find some way round the problems.

We are fortunate to have an authoritative statement of the Morisco reaction to the new policy in the shape of the text of a *memorial* ("memorandum") on the subject that was sent by Francisco Núñez Muley to Deza (Garrad 1954, 199–226). Núñez Muley claimed to be one of the oldest men living in Granada at the time, and he links back in a fascinating way to the very beginning of the Christian regime at the end of the fifteenth century. He was a member of that part of the Muslim aristocracy termed by some modern historians "collaborationist": those who had decided to throw in their lot with the new rulers but who in some way had continued to serve as the voice of Granadans whenever they found themselves in trouble with the authorities. He had actually served as pageboy in the household of Archbishop Talavera, so was familiar with the inner workings of Church and state. Over the years he had acted as the Moriscos' spokesman in a very effective way. As early as 1513 he was a member (a very junior member, but that indicates the high social status he possessed) of a group that had an audience with Ferdinand the Catholic on the subject of the attempts being made at that time to push ahead with the policy of cultural assimilation: "because in the said year of [15]13 I went with other gentlemen, natives of this kingdom, to business which concerned His Majesty the Catholic monarch, may he rest in glory" (Garrad 1954, 205). Núñez Muley claims that the delegation secured enactments "in favor of those born in this kingdom" and cites details favorable to the converts that he claims to remember from the proclamations made in Granada. Was the old gentleman's memory letting him down at this point? Such legislation does not appear, for example, in the appendix of documents to Gallego and Gámir (1968, 176–182), where we find for 1513 "that what has been decreed on the subject of Moorish clothing *should be observed,* and that within two years no newly converted woman may wear the *almalafa* [the all-enveloping outer female garment]." However, if we look at the regulations that Núñez Muley was opposing, they were of such bizarre and comical impracticality that they can in any case never have been enforced in any sustained way. Slaughter of cattle for meat, for example, where possible was to be carried out by Old Christians (even if they were not qualified to do so). If necessary, if there were no volunteers among the Christians to carry out the task, the authorities should attempt to force people to do so. Where there were no Old Christians at all, slaughter should be carried out in the presence of the parish priest, and only after a license setting out the conditions for slaughter had been obtained from the *corregidor* of the whole district! One may guess that these regulations were more honored in the breach than in the observance.

One can understand how Núñez Muley might remember in his youth participating in negotiations leading, as he saw it, to a favorable outcome. This had been the pattern for the first half of the sixteenth century: sporadic attempts to enforce ill-drafted anti-Islamic legislation that rarely got anywhere because of the stubborn reluctance of the *nuevos convertidos de moros* to change their ways and the unwillingness of the viceregal authorities to take the unpleasant measures that would have been necessary to secure change. In 1518, Núñez Muley himself had been one of the delegation that went with the marqués de Mondéjar to negotiate with Charles V the payment of special taxes by the Granadans in exchange for the suspension of some of the strict legislation, and again in 1523 he performed a similar function. This latter intervention in the public affairs of his native city is reflected in a document dated in Valladolid on August 25, 1523, from the Royal Council instructing the *corregidor* of Granada to provide a report on "the petition submitted by Francisco Núñez Muley in person and on behalf of the newly converted with the object that they may be godparents in baptisms and witnesses at weddings" (Gallego and Gámir 1968, 190–91, document 25).

It will be seen that here was a leader who was not afraid of speaking out for "his" people. He was someone to whom the very highest authorities in the land paid heed. It is interesting that by 1559 we find him representing to a committee convened annually in the Alhambra to assess taxes levied on the new convert communities that he was entitled to financial compensation for the expenses he had incurred in the course of all his work for the community (Garrad 1954, 201 and n. 8).

This is the voice of somebody who had lived through all the vicissitudes that the Granadans had experienced thus far. His 1567 *memorial* is almost the last that we hear of him, and perhaps at his age he felt he had little to gain by mincing his words. The Pragmatic that Deza was seeking to enforce rested on the assumption that when the Granadans had converted originally, they agreed to the condition that they were to abandon such things as their Granadan style of clothing (*en el tiempo que los dichos naturales deste reyno se convirtieron a nuestra sancta fe cathólica, asentaron que auían de mudar el ábito....* [Garrad 1954, 204]). This assumption the old gentleman roundly denies: "I do not believe that anybody in this kingdom has any memory of such a pact or agreement. There was no such thing, and I do not believe that any written record of it will be found, for the conversion of those native to this kingdom was by force, and against what had been agreed to by the Catholic Monarchs in the Capitulations with King Boabdil (*Rey Muley Boabdili*)... that they were to remain in their religion, and with their mosques, judges, muftis, and that they were not to be converted to Christianity." (Núñez Muley even scathingly tells Deza where he can find a text of these Capitulations, so he can go and look the point up, and have a copy made if he needed one. One can imagine how *that* piece of sarcasm was received!)

Thus we have two opposing truths with no possibility of compromise between them. Núñez Muley was stating the position as he and his fellow Granadans perceived it: the Capitulations of 1492 had been infringed by the Castilian Crown, and his generation had not freely accepted conversion. Deza adhered to the official Spanish line: the first revolt of the Alpujarras of 1500 had wiped the slate clean, so that conversion, when it came, had been offered as a generous concession to people who otherwise would have had to accept expulsion or slavery as the condign punishment for taking up arms against their sovereign. Of course, Núñez Muley's attempt to reopen the question of conversion got nowhere. I will not analyze the main body of his *memorial* in any detail. He argues effectively, as he had done throughout his life, the case for continued toleration by the authorities of Morisco ways and customs. His arguments may be summarized as follows: what the authorities sought to condemn as Islamic practices and customs were no more than regional distinctive features (what in modern terms we might call folklore). Other Spanish provinces had their regional characteristics, too, and they were not seen as representing any threat. Then he pointed out the waste of resources that would result from unnecessary change and the loss that the royal treasury would suffer from the disruption of trade and commerce. Such arguments had been successful enough in the past, especially when backed up by financial inducements. This time they got nowhere. At the end of his life, Núñez Muley was encountering the new Tridentine ideology, and the comfortably fudged accommodations of the early years of the century were no longer available. His *memorial* is of the greatest interest, but as a retrospective guide to the mentalities of the first half of the sixteenth century. He was able to achieve nothing for his people to stave off the bloody crises of the late 1560s and early 1570s.

The shift from a Granada that was securely pacified to a Granada given over once again to the cruelest forms of strife was disconcertingly rapid. We have seen that there were many antecedents to the conflict, but without doubt we can place the actual beginning of the acute stage of the crisis as occurring on January 1, 1567, after the proclamation of the new legislation intended to end Granada's cultural distinctiveness and to wipe out the last vestiges of Islam. Other emissaries besides Núñez Muley were sent to the royal court (among them Juan Enríquez of Baza) to try to negotiate a delay or some modification of the harshest of the new provisions. To no effect, even though the Council of State appears to have shown some sympathy. The banning of Moorish-style clothing (with the date of January 1, 1568, set as the deadline beyond which old-style clothes had to be replaced) was a requirement that had great symbolic impact, but undoubtedly what preoccupied the people most were reports (that as far as one can discover at the time were unfounded, although parents were, as we will see, well advised to be watching out for such proposals) that they might have their children taken from them so as to facilitate the process of indoctrination. The city of Granada became a hotbed of rumor and panic. Prophetic texts (*jófores*) full of obscure predictions circulated. There appear to have taken place secret assemblies at which the Moriscos debated the options before them, and reached the decision to resist.

We have unfortunately no record of such gatherings from the Muslim side (it would be surprising if we did) and so have to rely on reports in the Christian sources, doubly suspect because of the practice common among historians writing in the sixteenth century of inventing rhetorical speeches (often cast in a Tacitean mold) to put in the mouths of leading figures. The contents of such "speeches" (as opposed to the surface detail) is not necessarily totally unreliable as general background information: the presentational device was well understood at the time, and not intended to mislead. Nevertheless clearly we must be wary.

Janer (1857, 141–45) reproduces from Antonio de Fuenmayor, *Vida y hechos de Pío V, Pontífice Romano* (Madrid, 1595), speeches allegedly contributed by "a rich and prudent Morisco called Cárdenas" to the debate in Granada. These set out the case against rebellion—from the Morisco viewpoint (above all, stressing the hopelessness of trying to take on the military might of Christian Spain, a country dominant in all parts of the world). Was Cárdenas's speech a genuine expression of the views of a moderate party among the Moriscos? After the Expulsion, a particularly rich merchant called Cárdenas was to play a prominent role in the setting up of Morisco settlements in Tunisia, and he went on from there to Istanbul (see chapter 11). (Cárdenas was also a prominent name on the Christian side, of course: for example, Alonso de Cárdenas was the son-in-law of Mondéjar himself. No firm conclusions can be drawn from a single name.) One would be surprised if any individual, however independently minded, had dared at such a juncture, when tempers were so inflamed, to speak up so tellingly against the perils of the defiant course of action on which the Moriscos were embarking: "By the hope of what aid are you moved to rebel? Will it come from Africa, where [the Spaniards] have more forts and more garrisons than there are in Granada. Or from the Turks? They are so far away, that you will be gobbled up before they arrive." Cárdenas is made to argue that all the sufferings of the war will not be justified: "Consider, by God, how much less of a loss it is to have to change your language and your style of dress, because it is not the Arabic language that makes you Muslims...." On balance it is more probable that this is all the invention of a Christian author and that it reflects Christian propaganda in favor of peace at any price. But the argument is still forcefully presented, and in it are embedded facts that do not reflect credit on the Christian side: "Are there not as many Muslims as Christians in Aragon and Valencia, and are they not as deeply offended as we are, and as desirous as we are of revenge?" It is not altogether impossible that we have some indirect reflection here of the real debates that must have been going on.

Some inkling of all this seething unrest probably leaked out at the time. Before the outbreak of the revolt proper there were rumors and false alarms in the city of Granada, one of which, on April 16, 1568, had the good Christian townsfolk so convinced that the Albaicín (the Morisco quarter) had already risen that some looting of Morisco premises took place elsewhere in the city.

When open revolt really started at Christmastime, it was something of a damp or rather snow-sodden squib. The whole opening of the campaign was ineptly mishandled by the Morisco leadership in Granada. Allegedly eight thousand Moriscos from the surrounding districts were ready at Christmas 1568 to enter the city (making use of the bridgehead provided by the Albaicín) and to sack the Christian quarters (by then already the major part of the central built-up area). At the last moment, Morisco leaders canceled the attack (the weather was indeed very bad, and there had been heavy snowfalls in the mountains). Nevertheless, one Farax aben Farax, with one hundred fifty determined men, went ahead all the same, broke in at one of the city gates, and tried to summon the people to rise. They would not, and Farax and his men had to slink away ignominiously the next morning. They had achieved nothing inside the city, but their futile action served as a declaration of war, and elsewhere, in the mountains, many villages rose in revolt.

What was unleashed now was a wild upsurge of enthusiasm for all the external symbols of Islam that had been repressed in the generations after the forcible conversions of 1501. "The first thing they did was to proclaim the name and the religion of Muhammad, and they declared themselves to be Muslims[4] who had nothing to do with the Catholic faith which their fathers and grandfathers had professed for so many years. It was something to be wondered at how well instructed they all were, old and young, in this accursed sect." And not surprisingly, there was a chaotic and anarchic series of violent incidents in which the crypto-Muslim mountaineers paid back grudges against the scattered Christians who lived among them. Priests were particular targets.

> At the same time, devoid of respect for anything human or divine, as enemies of all religion and charity, full of cruel rage and diabolical wrath, they robbed, burnt, and destroyed the churches, they hacked venerable images to pieces, they pulled the altars down, and laid their violent hands on the priests of Jesus Christ who had taught them the faith and administered the sacraments to them. The priests were dragged through the streets and public squares, barefoot and naked, and held up to mockery and insult. Some they shot with arrows, others they burnt alive and exposed to various kinds of martyrdom. They treated with the same cruelty those Christians who were not priests who lived in their villages. A neighbor had no respect for his neighbor, nor did a *compadre*[5] respect his fellow, or a friend his friend. If anybody wanted to be merciful, it was not allowed; so great was

---

4. Our source, Mármol (1991, 95), says *moros,* "Moors," in this text, addressed by a Christian to a Christian readership. This was one of the few terms available to express the concept of "Muslim."

5. *Compadre* might be rendered "companion," but that is far too weak a term to use of a form of bonding still familiar to anthropologists who study modern rural Spanish societies. The reported dissolving of the bonds between *compadres* is possibly the most shocking of the manifestations of social upheaval that are listed here. If one man became linked with another in this way, it was accepted that the two *compadres* would in normal circumstances afford each other total and unconditional help and assistance. It is interesting to note that in 1568 such bonding across the religious divide must sometimes have taken place.

the wrath of the evil men who killed everyone they set hands on, that they would not spare anybody who stood in their way. They robbed houses, and if people took refuge in towers or strongholds, they surrounded them with a ring of flames, and burnt many of them. All those who gave themselves up were killed, too, because they wanted no Christian above the age of ten to remain alive in all the land. This pestilence began in Lanjarón, infected Orgiva,...and then Poqueira,...and the smoke of sedition and evil soon spread over the face of that land.[6] (Mármol 1991, 95)

THE CAMPAIGNS

It would be impossible within the scope of a one-volume history such as this to give a complete account of all the fighting in which the Muslims were involved during a war that ravaged many parts of the Kingdom of Granada for almost two years, from the end of 1568 until November 1570. A great deal is in fact known about the details of the campaigns. This was no minor police operation, it was a war the operations of which spread from Galera on the borders of Murcia in the north to Adra on the Mediterranean coast in the south, from Serón, Huércal, and Tabernas in the east to Coín and Monda in the west—virtually all of the Nasrid Kingdom of Granada as it had existed a century earlier. The forces involved on the Spanish side were royal troops, the renowned battle-hardened *tercios* on whom Spanish policy in Italy and the Low Countries relied, plus feudal levies and urban militias assembled under more than half a dozen generals, the most illustrious among them Don John of Austria, half-brother of Philip II, and including the duke of Sesa, the marqués of Los Vélez, and many others (their very number has its relevance).

On the Muslim side we have not only the last Umayyad (or Umayyad pretender) to rule on the soil of al-Andalus, Fernando de Válor Aben Humeya, but other native Granadan commanders, not to mention foreign military experts sent across from Algiers by the Turkish authorities. These "Turks" came to train and lead a rebellion that, if successful, would have established for them a Muslim bridgehead in the West (hardly an unimportant enterprise when the Ottoman forces were so heavily committed to a drive in that direction). Lepanto was to come in 1571, no great success for either side. What in the end halted a seemingly relentless Ottoman advance westward was not the force of Spanish arms there or

---

6. Such an intense effusion of blind communal hatred and blood lust was difficult for me to comprehend when I began to study these matters in the mid-twentieth century. Now in the early twenty-first century close parallels could be found reported in the daily press from many parts of the world.

elsewhere but the unexpected appearance of a radically new phenomenon to the east of Anatolia: Safavid Shiism. With their land frontiers directly menaced, the Ottomans were no longer free to undertake adventures far afield. In 1568–70, there had occurred a brief window of opportunity, but soon after that the Ottomans became too distracted. Much was at stake during the Granada campaign.

If we cannot trace every battle of this Granadan campaign, it is necessary to grasp the principal phases through which this strange conflict progressed. I have said "strange" above all because if ever there was a war that could have been over easily in three months, this was it. After that period of time the Christians under Mondéjar were already in a position of relative strength, and the rebels were willing to negotiate surrender. Why, then, did the Spanish forces embroil themselves in two years of expensive and potentially dangerous, at times disastrous, further campaigning? In various ways the answer that is given both by chroniclers and commentators contemporary with the events and by modern historians is the same: divisions and squabbles within the Christian camp meant that promising early negotiations foundered. That is an explanation with which I am not going to disagree, but beyond it lies the deeper and more interesting question of why the disagreements were allowed to get out of hand and why they were never resolved.

Divisions were present in the Christian camp from the outset, but are such squabbles a sufficient explanation for the inept handling of several aspects of this policy? In the background was a long-standing feud or disagreement, to which allusion has already been made, between, on the one hand, the viceregal Mondéjar regime and, on the other, the lawyers and clerics of the Granada-based new bureaucracies, administrative innovations that had been instituted largely by central royal initiative. In the foreground, in 1568, that division took the form of bickering between Deza, newly appointed by the king to push ahead with reforms, and Mondéjar. Deza's remit was to revive the long-stalled process of effective conversion of the "converts." Mondéjar pursued the policy to which his viceregal family had been committed since the beginning: to rule the Kingdom of Granada effectively on behalf of the king.

When on Christmas Eve 1568 representatives of the crypto-Muslims from Granada, from the Alpujarras, and from elsewhere clandestinely assembled in the Valle de Lecrín to acclaim Fernando de Válor as their king under what he claimed was his Muslim name of Aben Humeya (Ibn Umayya), what had at first been a spontaneous and anarchic rejection of imposed Castilian ways began to take a constitutional form. We may doubt whether Fernando de Válor's claim to such a noble descent was securely founded in genealogy, for the Nasrids of Granada had not in earlier days based their legitimacy on Umayyad descent.[7] Yet the adoption of the name Ben Humeya by Fernando de Válor as an act of self-promotion was clearly successful within his community. There could be no doubt that what was being conveyed by him to the masses, through the symbolism of the name, was that his claims to rule legitimately antedated by several centuries any right to which the recently arrived house of Austria might pretend.

This initial act of defiance committed by the rebels evoked a rapid response by Mondéjar. Operating over terrain in which he was as much at home as Aben Humeya's forces were, the viceroy was on the road to the mountains with his troops by January 3, 1569, and by January 11 his men had, with great bravery, secured the vital river crossing at Tablate. The bridge had prudently been wrecked by the rebels at the beginning of the revolt precisely in order to prevent Mondéjar from advancing in force up into the mountains, but over the few remaining bare beams straddling the stream that had unwisely been left in position by the Muslims, and in the face of deadly fire, a few individuals managed to get across. This enabled the viceroy's men to secure the bridgehead. They then pushed ahead, and in a series of bold operations they reestablished control over the mountains. Before long Aben Humeya and a second leader, El Zaguer (*al-Sagir*, "the little one"), were no better than fugitives on their own terrain. Exercising his inherited Mondéjar skills, the viceroy, from a base in Órgiba in the Alpujarras, was able by a mixture of military élan and diplomatic blandishments to bring the rebels to the brink of surrender as early as March 1569.

At the same time and on the other side of the mountains, the marqués de los Vélez was moving up from his bases in Murcia. This was emphatically not a concerted pincers movement. What had happened was that Deza, in Granada, without consultation with Mondéjar, called in help from outside the city. Deza thus gave to the marqués de los Vélez justification to penetrate into territory over which his command did not properly extend. The advance was not made into lands that Aben Humeya's forces had occupied, and there is no indication that it had been marked out as a base for resistance. Of course there were Moriscos enough for the troops of the marqués to fight whenever they turned aside toward a Morisco village.

7. Since the fall of the Caliphate in the eleventh century, al-Andalus had not been ruled in the Umayyad name, and indeed that name might not be well received in many parts of the Islamic world. The Shiite lands were not the only regions that regarded the Umayyads as more worthy of execration than of respect. During the great days of what we now think of as the Umayyad Caliphate of the West, it was in any case the name Banu Marwan (Marwanids) that was in current use, rather than Banu Umayya.

One might have thought that Mondéjar's ability to reduce the rebels in the western Alpujarras so rapidly to the point of potential surrender would vindicate him, but this was not the case. Deza and the Granadan lawyers denigrated the viceroy's willingness to negotiate, representing it as a manifestation of his deep-seated predilection for his Morisco subjects. The settlement that could have been had on terms satisfactory to the Crown in March thus slipped out of Mondéjar's grasp. Aben Humeya went from being a fugitive who was finding it difficult to survive to seeing recruits flocking in eager to avenge the sufferings inflicted by the invading troops of the marqués de los Vélez on their villages. Understandable tension and disagreements between Mondéjar and the marqués de los Vélez were blamed on the former. And this opened the way for Philip to send in from outside his half-brother, Don John of Austria, appointing him as supreme commander over both. From this point on, from March 1569 to April 1570, we may distinguish a yearlong middle phase of the conflict.

The new supreme commander was a young man of twenty-four; this was his first serious independent campaign. For Mondéjar it must have been a great humiliation to have to pass from being a captain-general in virtual sole command, and what is more, on what was very much his home terrain, to being one member of an ill-structured Council of War consisting, besides himself, of the duke of Sesa (admittedly an experienced soldier), Luis Quijada (a professional soldier but someone who obviously owed his position to the fact that he had been Don John's tutor!), Deza (not a soldier at all, but a lawyer and, as we have seen, the architect of the confused military situation that had led to Mondéjar losing sole command), and finally, Archbishop Guerrero of Granada. Whereas Mondéjar had been starved of resources, Don John was now kept amply supplied by his half-brother the king. Under this command structure, the fighting did not go well: there were all sorts of further motives for dissension and discord. Sesa was the nephew of the marqués de los Vélez, but there was a profound rift between them, so that even they could never operate well together. One might almost suspect that the direction of operations was entrusted to such a divided Council of War in order to ensure that the campaign would be long drawn out. Certainly the prospect of an end to fighting receded ever further as the Spanish armies blundered around through the rest of 1569. Often the Spanish troops seemed more concerned with booty than victory.

The Muslims soon seized the opportunity to regroup and to go over to the offensive on their own ground. Even in the *vega* (cultivated valley) of Granada their forces could move freely up to the city gates. Meanwhile the revolt, at first limited to Granada and the parts of the Alpujarras near to the capital, spread to the mountains of Almería in the east and those behind Málaga in the west. The surgical excision of the focus of insurrection, something that might have been possible at the outset, became no longer feasible, and a massive and bloody campaign of repression was the only way ahead. This present volume opened with the Castilian forces obliged to undertake after 1492 a *second* conquest of Granada in 1500 as a consequence of ill-considered policies as a consequence of which Cisneros had driven the Muslims into a rebellion they had not sought. The year 1569 now brought the need for what amounted to an expensive *third* conquest of the Kingdom of Granada within three-quarters of a century. And it was Philip himself who authorized this third conquest to be executed in such a destructive way. On October 19, 1569 (in circumstances at Galera that will be described below), he had declared *guerra a fuego y a sangre* ("war with fire and blood"), that is to say, war without quarter (in Clausewitzian terms "true war"). Philip proclaimed for his troops *campo franco*—he removed all restrictions on plunder and rapine, and he suspended the levying by the commander of his one-fifth share of any booty taken. Small wonder that many Moriscos preferred to fight on to the death with desperate courage rather than ever surrender. The countryside became littered with smoldering ruins.

One is driven to ask a question to which there can obviously never be a satisfactory answer: was it incompetence on Philip's part that led to the creation of such an inept command structure, or was it by design that the Moriscos of Granada came to be driven into ever more desperate revolt, thus furnishing Philip with an excuse to deport them from their homeland? Of course, there are many other examples of Philip setting up command structures leading to conflict among his generals, the best known being the disaster that befell his Invincible Armada. Perhaps like many other autocrats in history, he preferred to have his military commanders in rivalry one with another, never in potentially menacing harmony.

It is remarkable that the most significant developments in this middle phase of the war in Granada came not because of the success of Spanish initiatives, but from dissensions within the Morisco camp. They were themselves deeply divided. They had rarely, even at the height of the campaigning in the fifteenth century, been able to overcome that tendency to divide into factions, and they would often prefer the settling of scores to the prosecution of overall objectives. (Pérez de Hita's account of feuding between Abencerrajes and Zegríes in his *Guerras civiles de Granada* may have been largely a romantic fictional construct, but the tragic myth of the feuds that destroyed Granada continued to maintain its hold on the Western imagination into the Romantic period—Chateaubriand, Washington

Irving—and beyond, perhaps because it reflected an underlying anthropological and historical reality.)

Aben Humeya maintained intelligence contacts with his Christian enemy, as he was surely bound to do. Short of securing effective overseas aid from Algiers, and behind Algiers from Istanbul (aid that the Granadans were indeed actively soliciting), the Muslims had to place their hopes on some new accommodation with Philip. But a leader who entered into negotiations with the enemy ran the risk of being thought to be plotting a way of saving his own skin by selling out. Too often in the fighting of the fifteenth century the Granadans had seen this happen; it is not surprising that their descendents were suspicious in 1569.

The situation inside the Muslim camp was further complicated by the "Turks" (we may doubt whether most of them were actually ethnic Turks) who had been infiltrated in small numbers from Algiers through small southern ports such as Adra. Some of these "Turks" were officially appointed military experts sent to train the Moriscos and perhaps to provide some professional military stiffening to forces that owed much to the loose *monfi*/bandit tradition. The term *monfi* (*Ar.* "denied," "banned," i.e., "outlaw") was at this time applied to rebels who did not accept Castilian rule and preferred to take to the hills, surviving there by whatever means they could find. The bandit life provided excellent training in how to live off the land but was a poor preparation for the sustained and disciplined prosecution of a protracted campaign. Others among the "Turks" were the sort of freelance adventurers who still in modern times get attracted to such conflicts. The mountain terrain of the Alpujarras has throughout history, in Roman times, under the Caliphate, under Franco, provided a refuge for outlaws and bandits, and one would be hard put at times to say whether the more famous of these bandits were primarily political dissidents or common criminals.

The "Turks," seasoned fighting men who arrived from Algiers, soon became contemptuous of the unreliable rabble they had been sent to help, for when the *monfis* were needed in battle they were liable to vanish. Moreover, the "Turks" soon tired of the pretensions of Aben Humeya, who seems to have possessed many of the characteristics of the worst sort of Andalusian *señorito*, touchy and conceited. Aben Humeya in return distrusted the Turks. Mármol (1991, 199) describes the relationship as follows:

> Because he had no trust in the Turks and got on with them very badly, and possibly so as not to have to pay them while they were remaining idle, he sent them away from himself to the frontier outpost at Orgiba under the orders of Aben Abóo. Since these evil (*viciosos*) men were almost all

pirates, thieves, and murderers, wherever they went they behaved disgust-
ingly and offered insults, raping the women and stealing the property of
the local Moors. Complaints about them poured in to Aben Humeya, and
he wrote on the subject to Aben Abóo, telling him to put matters to right.
Aben Abóo's reply was that the Turks were doing no harm to anybody,
but if they were guilty of disorder, he would punish them.

Mármol now winds two further complicating strands into his account
of the murderous dissensions within the Muslim camp: sexual jealousy
and drug taking. A prominent Muslim from Albacete de Ujíjar called
Diego Alguacil/Alguazir was said to harbor resentment against Aben
Humeya for having abducted a widowed cousin of his. The woman was,
it was said, held against her will, and then he made her his mistress.
("Others," Mármol tells us puzzlingly, "thought that [Diego Alguacil's]
attitude did not arise from sexual jealousy but from concern for family
honor," for he was affronted "because Aben Humeya kept the woman
as his mistress, when with her social status he might have taken her as
a wife." But perhaps something of the real truth of this matter emerged
later. Six years after the end of the war, in Tetuan, she was "married
by their cursed rites to Diego Alguacil.") Diego Alguacil played on the
latent tension between Aben Humeya and the Turks, and then at a critical
moment, when Turkish tempers were running high, produced "a herb
which they call *haxiz* (hashish), which the Turks have the custom of
taking when they are going into battle because it makes them inebriated,
happy and somnolent. He said that he had supplied it to Aben Humeya so
he could give it to the [Turkish] captains, to put them to sleep so they could
be killed that night." Alguazir suggested they should take the opportunity
to get rid of "such a cruel man" and promote one of the Turks (Husein
or Caracax) in his place. The Turks refused the offer, explaining that
'Uruj 'Ali (i.e., Barbarossa) had sent them "not to be kings, but to assist
the king of the Andalusians, so that the best course was, after securing
approval from Algiers, to put power in the hands of a local man of noble
descent in whom one might have confidence, someone who would serve
the interests of the Muslims."

So the choice fell on Aben Abóo. As for Aben Humeya, they got rid
of him by strangulation on October 20, 1569. Some Christian sources
(Mármol among them) have the story that with his dying breath Aben
Humeya declared himself a Christian and said that what he had done had
been in prosecution of a family feud. One is reluctant to accept at face
value what is a narrative cliché: Christian accounts tell of Muslim leaders
making dubious deathbed conversions to Christianity from the days of
the Caliphate ('Umar Ibn Hafsun) in the ninth century onward.

GALERA

The most outstanding single episode in this period, a battle involving twelve thousand Spanish troops with accompanying heavy artillery and military engineers under the command of Don John of Austria, was the siege of Galera. It took place in January and February 1570. As a feat of arms, it is remembered in Spanish history, principally because here Austria established the reputation for military leadership that was to be confirmed at the naval Battle of Lepanto against the Turks in the following year. When examined critically, the accounts of what occurred can be read as revealing aspects of Don John's generalship that were less than glorious.

Any piece of terrain can be taken if only the attacking army is willing to expend sufficient lives and munitions in the attempt. In the case of Galera, the force deployed was utterly disproportionate to the prize, bearing in mind that the task was to eliminate resistance in a large village that had no outer defensive wall (although it did have an abandoned castle near its center). A place, frankly, of no great strategic importance. Facing John of Austria's twelve thousand men (plus ancillary troops) the Morisco defenders had some three thousand local men, stiffened by a few Turks and Berber professional soldiers who had come from outside. They had few weapons (apart the small arms carried by the soldiers). Women (backed up by children supplying them with improvised missiles such as rocks and rubble) helped to hold off the assault forces that were endeavoring to breach the walls. The attackers, besides cavalry and infantry, brought up several batteries of cannon. However, such success as they achieved was thanks not to these unsuitably ponderous weapons, but to their military engineers, who drove a sap under parts of the village, and then blew up the buildings that had been undermined with charges of gunpowder. These explosions actually failed to take the attackers into the heart of the defensive area (which was on bedrock, so could not be undermined), but did open up great breaches in the walls.

An incident during the first of these assaults recounted by Mármol conveys the ferocity with which the battle was fought on each side. One Juan Pacheco, a gentleman who had the honor to be a member of the order of Santiago, arrived at the last moment, in haste to join the battle. Within two hours of arriving at Galera and reporting for duty to Austria he was in action, and had volunteered for the assault party that was planning to break through the village defenses in the stunned moment immediately after the first mine was exploded. The mine went up, and Juan Pacheco rushed impetuously in through the gap thus created, only to find himself trapped, because the gap created by the explosion in fact led nowhere. Many of his companions managed to scramble back, but he was trapped and taken prisoner. When the Muslims noticed the cross of Santiago he was wearing (as was normal in this military order), they became infuriated. He was hacked limb from limb in a great demonstration of hatred.

Such was the general fury on both sides that when, in the final stages of the fighting, Don John of Austria caught some of his men making off with female prisoners and children (from whom they hoped no doubt to make some profit by selling them into slavery) he ordered his personal escort (*escuderos*) to slaughter all these prisoners:

[T]hey killed more than four hundred women and children, and would have finished off the lot if they had not been moved by the complaints of the soldiers, who were in this way being deprived of the fruits of their victory, and he only agreed when he knew that the place was already in our hands, and even so he would not spare any male over the age of twelve. He got so angry thinking of the damage which those heretics [*sic*] had inflicted without ever being willing to humiliate themselves by asking for terms.

The words quoted, it must be made clear, are from the account given by Mármol (1991, 220), a writer in no way hostile to Don John who, in fact, unwaveringly presents loyal servants of the regime in a favorable light. Mármol was, moreover, if not actually present during the assault, certainly at the very least close by at the time, for, most unusually in this *Historia,* he allows the first person to obtrude into his narrative, and tells us, for example, that his commander, finding that it was necessary to shift some tents and vehicles into store in Güéscar, "left it in *my* charge" (220). It might be argued, in Don John of Austria's defense, that drastic action was necessary at that juncture at Galera if he was to prevent his force from disintegrating in a chaos of anarchic looting. The means that he employed to stop the riot was quite simply not the exemplary punishment of his guilty men but the massacre of the soldiers' victims: more than four hundred prisoners, women and children. To speak plainly, a gruesome atrocity. Mármol makes it clear that he at least thought that Austria's underlying motive was rage (*ira*) at the humiliation of suffering terrible casualties in fighting against a largely civilian "enemy" who resisted unbowed right to the end. Mármol begins to give the names of all the famous soldiers who lost their lives at Galera, but the list gets too long, and he simply desists for fear of tiring his readers ("y otros muchos que por excusar prolijidad no ponemos aquí").

However, the most telling criticism to be made of Don John's conduct of this aspect of the campaign must be a technical, military one: his deployment of heavy artillery and mining engineers was wasteful and quite unsuited to the task in hand. The Moriscos were confronted with a quite massive display of military might. Mármol gives a good description of the geographical situation of Galera. On a rocky outcrop the shape of a boat (*galera*) was the village center (including the old castle), and down the sides of this outcrop the houses with their flat roofs clustered together. At the bottom was a church with a tall tower that made an ideal emplacement for harassing fire. In the military history of this period the early advantage in attack of cannon over defensive castle walls (the base of the walls could be battered till they fell down) was eventually overcome by military engineers who began to construct surrounding protective earthworks placed so as to absorb and deaden the impact of the cannon shot. By forcing the cannon to fire upward, such protective earthworks further diminished the destructive effect of artillery. Galera did not need to construct such buffer earthworks. Its outer houses formed, quite naturally, an ideal defensive position capable of neutralizing much of the advantage accruing to the Spanish forces from their lavish deployment of artillery. The village had no outer defenses as such, but the houses piled one over the other up the hillside were largely built of *tapia,* that is to say, had earth walls. *Tapia* does not at first sound a very useful material in fortification, but its effect seems to have been exactly the same as what might have been achieved by a skillfully constructed outer earthwork: "Artillery could not inflict damage on them, nor could our men make progress," and then, "The artillery had little effect on the houses, it simply drilled holes (*solamente horadaba*) in these walls, and did not even dislodge enough earth to allow the attackers to clamber up" (217).

One can understand (but not, of course, condone) the murderous rage of the young general when he found that he was able to employ to such poor effect the mighty military machine placed in his hands by his half-brother. To avoid losing face he was finally obliged to buy at such a disproportionate cost victory over an unfortified village.

From Galera, after razing all the houses ("and sowing them with salt," adds Mármol in what I take to be a classicizing rhetorical flourish, although can we be sure?), Don John of Austria took his army off southwest toward Baza and turned his attention to the Morisco strongholds of Tíjola and Serón. His success here was no greater, and indeed whereas at Galera he had until the end contrived, at such cost, to keep tight control over the operation, at Serón discipline did break down very badly, and the Moriscos as a result were able to inflict a severe defeat on him, a defeat that must have been felt the more bitterly because, in the confusion, his admired mentor and former tutor, the respected soldier Luis Quijada, received wounds of which within a few hour he died.

As I have said, no complete account of the campaigning can be attempted here, but just as the attack on Galera needed to be recalled because of what it tells us about Don John of Austria himself and about the courage and determination of the villagers in their defense of their own homes against overwhelming odds, at Serón, where numbers were more balanced, we can see the ability displayed by the Moriscos in the coordination of the movement of bodies of troops to outmaneuver the enemy.

The Serón operation started out as a kind of reconnaissance in force to test Morisco strength and to determine the dispositions necessary to conduct an eventual siege. It was not intended to be more, because, as we have seen, the attackers did not actually have their baggage train (or artillery) with them: those were still too bogged down in the winter mud round Galera itself. Don John went on toward Serón with just two thousand elite (*escogidos*) harquebusiers and two hundred cavalry. What went wrong at Serón was partly that this armed reconnaissance in a foolhardy way, presumably out of contempt for the organizational capacity of the enemy, attempted more than such a force could safely do, but mainly the trouble was rank indiscipline.

The Muslims made smoke signals to call in help from their neighbors, and then prudently withdrew to high ground. The Spanish forces thus found they could enter the village unopposed and, discovering there were women in some houses, discipline broke down (*comenzaron a desmandarse*). Some of the troops took women prisoners, and then shut themselves inside the houses with them "to protect the prize they had taken." At this point those Spaniards who were still at their military posts noticed that more than six thousand Muslims under the leadership of el Habaqui and el Maleh (names of which we will hear more before long) were hastening up in response to the smoke signals. The light forces that the Spaniards had in position had to beat retreat, and counterattacks failed to halt the Muslim advance. There ensued chaos, with some of the looters fleeing in disorder, abandoning their weapons as they went (*otros arrojaron vilmente las armas y dieron a huir* [222]), quite uncertain in which direction to run. "In such disorder Don John came down from the hillock [where his advisers had insisted he remain, away from the more perilous fighting] and showed himself courageously to our Christians, to persuade them to face up to the enemy, or at least to retire in good order." Mármol even claims to report some of Don John's own words, but we may be pardoned for our suspicions as to their authenticity. These may convey a poetic truth but are unlikely to be based on any verbatim report: "What is this, Spaniards? From whom are you in flight? Where is the honor of Spain? Have you not in front of you Don John of Austria, your commander? What are you afraid of? Retire in an orderly fashion, with your faces to the enemy, and before long you will see these barbarians are repulsed by your arms" (222).

The Muslims, following at a safe distance, saw Don John and his men off their land and then turned back to where the remnant of looters were by now trapped in some of the houses and churches. Fighting went on round these buildings for three days, and then the Muslims ended the matter by setting fire to the buildings with the soldiers still inside. In this engagement (at one unimportant village) the Spaniards lost more than six hundred men and more than a thousand swords and harquebuses. The Muslims by report (*fama*) lost four hundred, and many Muslim women were captured. (A short while later, Don John's army, duly reinforced, was to return prepared to besiege the village, but when the inhabitants saw what was afoot, they set fire to the castle and principal buildings and withdrew.)

The Muslims in this confused series of campaigns (with others beside Don John of Austria leading punitive columns into various zones of the mountains) gave good account of themselves and showed themselves able to put up surprisingly effective resistance in spite of their lack of firearms. The Spaniards, for their part, displayed their determination to reduce the Muslims to submission at whatever cost. Not surprisingly, given the enormous numbers of troops deployed, more and more of what had been the Muslims' mountain strongholds came to be occupied or abandoned by their inhabitants.

Spanish policy now took the form of schemes for the enforced relocation of Muslims. The justificatory arguments for this policy sound very similar to the arguments for the setting up of the British concentration camps during the Boer War or the various movements of population undertaken during communist insurrections in Malaysia and then elsewhere in Southeast Asia:

> In order to reduce the rebels to extreme want, nothing would be more effective than to deprive them of the peaceful Moriscos (*moriscos de paces*) who remained in the Kingdom of Granada. For if these could only be moved inland, that would completely deprive the rebels of their easy source of recruits, of intelligence, arms, and provisions that were secretly supplied to them. (229–30)

In the Royal Council, those behind this policy of relocation were the duke of Sesa and Pedro de Deza, but as all earlier policies had had such poor success (and since the ultimate solution, wholesale expulsion, was as yet not being openly considered), it was not difficult to find supporters for what they proposed. As early as February 24, 1570, Philip II had written to his half-brother instructing him that before undertaking further military actions he must assemble the Moriscos of Guadix and Baza as discreetly as possible, "giving them to understand that it was being done for their own good" (230), and move them out (with their families and their property).

This order Austria ignored: at the time, he was too deeply engaged at Serón. Philip's response, dated March 5, was to repeat the instructions, only this time making the measure applicable to all peaceful Moriscos in the whole kingdom and charging Deza, not Austria, with the task. Philip is obviously here employing his favorite tactic of setting one of his officials or ministers against another (and it is amusing to see Deza, who had in 1569 been used against Mondéjar, now being used against John of Austria himself!). Austria continued to make difficulties. Like any other general in history, he told his commander-in-chief he simply could not spare any of his men to carry out the task. On March 21, Philip said that the problem of the lack of royal troops could be avoided by having Deza carry out the job of policing the deportations using the city contingents (the Hermandad, etc.) and the retainers of those noblemen present in Granada. Philip instructed Austria to pass his orders on to Deza. Clearly Austria was in this instance completely outmaneuvered by his father's control of the machinery of government. Deza got on with the task.

At first, special detachments as indicated by the king undertook the relocation of a small number of key Morisco communities (the villages in the *vega* round Granada itself, such as Ugíjar and Atarfe), then a general proclamation went out affecting the whole kingdom. The groups of deportees were moved northward via Alcalá la Real and on to Linares, Almagro, and Ciudad Real, where they were handed over to local authorities. Others went via Jaén and Baeza to the region of Montiel. In the various regions of the Kingdom of Granada, the carrying out of the order of expulsion of noncombattant Moriscos was entrusted to a number of commanders, and of course the success of the operations differed from place to place, as did the degree of administrative smoothness (or of violence) with which this great movement of population was pushed through.

What happened in Torrox (in the west, near Malaga), a hitherto largely quiet area and no rebel base, is worth examining because it illustrates the type of problem that was inherent in any such operation. It was to the commander Arévalo de Zuazo that this particular task was entrusted, and he tried to do what had been done in many other places: assemble the people and shut them up in the church (one guesses it would have been the only available building that was large enough) under guard while final arrangements were being completed. Not surprisingly, some of those shut up decided to slip out and try their luck in the mountains. Thereupon the small guard left by Arévalo de Zuazo to watch over property in the village (under one Juan de Pajariego) took it upon themselves to set off in pursuit of the fugitives, no doubt hoping to appropriate for themselves some of what the refugees were trying to carry with them. The Moriscos turned back on their would-be pursuers, and if it had not been for reinforcements sent out from Malaga, they would have prevailed over them. In despair, some of the Moriscos who had tried to escape then returned to the village, and burnt it, determined not to leave anything for their tormentors. What happened at Torrox underlined the dangers of trying to push through a drastic measure like expulsion if overwhelming force was not available to police it. As we will see, the final expulsion of all Muslims from the whole of Spain was only attempted, more than thirty years later, when large additional contingents of troops could be brought in from outside the peninsula.

AN END TO OPEN RESISTANCE

The stage was now cleared for the final act of the drama. In Granada were left only those Moriscos classified as *moriscos de paz* ("peaceful Moriscos"), people whose forebears had been granted some permanent rights of residence. It is obvious that once the generality of the community had been sentenced to expulsion, the dividing line that had formerly marked off those prepared to take up arms against the government, *monfís* (the bandit-style rebels who had taken to the hills) from peaceable noncombatant villagers who before the war had not been active adherents of any political cause, became blurred. One of the reasons for the urgency with which Philip was treating this whole matter was the information he was receiving about Morisco diplomatic contacts with the Turks of Algiers and Istanbul. And ever present was the direct threat of a Turkish naval expedition and landing. There is perhaps a tendency for those liberal historians who have little sympathy with Philip II to deride both these potential threats as almost imaginary, but as Ottoman policy with regard to the West becomes better known, it becomes increasingly clear that Philip could scarcely ignore what was indeed going on. The Turkish threat was far from being an empty bogey thought up to justify action against the repression of the Moriscos. It was real. The two sides were becoming more and more polarized.

For Don John of Austria, the link between the crisis at home and the crisis abroad would have been very clear as 1570 advanced. His nomination as supreme commander of the allied fleet sent to face the Turks made him naturally anxious to have done with "Moors" at home so to free his hands to deal with Turks in the eastern Mediterranean. On November 5, 1570, he was able to report to the Royal Council that he had completed his assigned part of the deportation, in Guadix.

If the Moriscos had been handled differently in the course of the three-quarters of a century since the conquest of Granada, they might perhaps have remained what they were at the outset: predominantly unwilling to come into conflict with the Spanish authorities. To assert that the alienation of the Moriscos might have been avoided is as impossible to prove as it is to demonstrate that Boronat and other anti-Muslim publicists were right and that the final, tragic accelerated rush toward complete polarization of the communities was "inevitable." Both views are mere speculation. What is important to note is that by 1570 polarization had indeed proceeded so far as to affect relations between Moriscos and Christians in *all* those parts of the peninsula where Muslims were to be found. Things were only to get worse, very much worse (by which I mean more sharply polarized), and nothing, with the possible exception of the strange ideological maneuvers to be described in chapter 8, offered from this point onward the remotest reason for optimism. The year 1570 marks the clear divide between crisis and black despair. From then on, all that remained was to hope for a miracle (again, see chapter 8).

The final stages of the crushing of the Granadan revolt did not come until 1571. By then we are concerned not with the general population, many of whom were by then already far away in enforced exile, but with a stubbornly determined nucleus of the Granadan fighting men, holding out in the hills.

In the hope of clarifying an inevitably confused narrative, I will, until the end of this chapter, present events only from the point of view of the rebel leaders themselves and leave to one side the intricate shifts of politics of the Christians.

We must now turn back and take up the story again, from the Muslim side, at the point in October 1569 when Aben Abóo replaced Aben Humeya. As his lieutenants he appointed Hernando el Habaqui and el Maleh. Presumably as a consequence of the damaging, if costly, campaign of John of Austria against Galera and Serón, among others, el Habaqui in April 1570 put out diplomatic feelers and came to a meeting with his Spanish adversaries at Fondón de Andarax. He was heading a delegation that included not only Aben Abóo's brother but also the Turkish leader el Hoseini and others. The Muslims opened with reproaches directed against the Spaniards on various subjects ranging from promises broken to the expulsions from Granada already carried out, but when real negotiations began, it emerged that what el Habaqui had in mind was a settlement that included (1) guarantees to the rebels that they would not be pursued or legally prosecuted, (2) the return to their homes of those expelled, and (3) general reconstruction with the object of returning to the situation as it had existed before the outbreak of hostilities. In addition, freedom to migrate to North Africa was to be accorded to those who wished to go. Such were, no doubt, the opening bids of these tense talks that seemed always about to break down because one or other party was offended, was distrustful, or was experiencing difficulties with hardliners within his own camp. By May 22, matters had so advanced that, according to Mármol, el Habaqui was able to report substantial progress to Aben Abóo. What the Spanish were willing to offer was peace, but on condition that Moriscos should henceforward live far from the coast. The Turkish and North African troops were to be allowed to withdraw unmolested. On May 28, Alonso de Granada Venegas (a Christian but of the respected aristocratic Granadan Morisco family) set out as Don John of Austria's emissary to Aben Abóo. He was really rather an unwilling participant because he feared for his own safety. In Cádiar Aben Abóo came to see him and was reported to be ready to bring fighting to an end (though he was unwilling to hand over weapons— always a sticking point, that, in such negotiations, as we know). It was clear that Aben Abóo, too, was anxious to arrange passage out for the Turks (on whom he cast much blame for what had happened). This was granted, and most of them were taken off from the beach at Castil de Fierro.

According to Mármol (1991, 254)—and one is reluctant to accept his story without confirmation because of the coincidence involved— that very same day a small contingent of fresh volunteers from North Africa (*mujahidin* is not a word he employs, but that is obviously what they were), arrived on the same beach, and they, with their news of the imminent arrival of further aid from abroad, succeeded in changing Aben Abóo's mind. From his previous stance of being more than ready to strike a deal if the right terms could be found, he shifted to being prepared to fight on. This change undermined the position of el Habaqui, who continued confident that the outlined settlement he had reached with Don John of Austria could be implemented (Mármol 1991, 255). El Habaqui was an astute man but so full of self-confidence that he thought that the favor he enjoyed from Don John would protect him and that nobody would dare do him any harm. As he arrived at Yegen, after traveling two days from Andarax (where he had gone to see Austria), he noticed the village square was full of men. He went up to them and haughtily asked them what they were waiting for and why they had not gone to make their surrender in the places agreed, as others had done. One of them replied they were waiting for Aben Abóo to give the word. El Habaqui replied that the arrangements for surrender were right for all, and if Aben Abóo did not willingly come in, he (el Habaqui) would bring him in "tied to the tail of his horse." News of this reached Aben Abóo, who sent his new bodyguard to surround el Habaqui's house in Bérchul. El Habaqui did manage to slip out of the back gate but was picked up the next day on the mountainside, identified by the scarlet tunic and white turban he was still wearing. Aben Abóo accused him of treason, which he denied, but the next day he was strangled in secret, and his corpse was tipped onto a dunghill.

Aben Abóo was determined to continue the struggle. He wrote insistently to Algiers begging the authorities there to send more help. This is known to us because some of the letters were intercepted and translated for Don John of Austria and other Spanish leaders by Alonso del Castillo. Mármol incorporated some of them into his narrative, but the great source we have is the notebook in which Castillo himself made a copy of "all that has been translated into Romance by me," which survives in the Biblioteca Nacional, Madrid.[8] Aben Abóo was not without his own contacts on the Spanish side, notably one Hernando de Barradas, and in the final stages these channels were opened again, but after the arrival of the fresh contingent of mujahidin, many of the people were genuinely prepared to make a stand against all odds. Those unfortunate individuals who had become identified with the policy of negotiated surrender paid with their lives.

The various Spanish emissaries charged with continuing the negotiations must have judged that Aben Abóo would hold out as long as possible. Spanish troops were already operating in the high country, and before long Aben Abóo was a hunted fugitive there, too, "hiding himself in one cave after another" (*escondiendose de cueva en cueva* [Mármol 1991, 269]). The last members of his band to remain with him were (and the names deserve to be recorded) Bernardino Abu Amer (his secretary) and Gonzalo el Seniz (famous in his own right as a *monfí*). El Seniz had served time in prison for murder before taking to the mountains and adopting the life of a bandit. Mármol has a story, on what evidence it is not clear, of him bearing a grudge of long standing against Aben Abóo. After many obscure negotiations el Seniz wrote (in Arabic) to Deza making an offer to surrender Aben Abóo to him, dead or alive, in exchange for a promise of pardon. The proof el Seniz required of the genuine nature of the acceptance of his offer was that the reply he received should be *written in the Licentiate Castillo's own handwriting,* with which he was familiar (Mármol 1991, 270). Once again, the Licentiate Castillo and close familiarity with a person's handwriting in Arabic figure in the secret-service plotting amidst which this war coiled toward its messy end.

Aben Abóo had some wind of the treachery, and went at midnight to el Seniz's cave, in the mountains between Bérchul and Mecina de

---

8. This was published by the Royal Academy of History in *Memorial Histórico Español* [Madrid] 3 (1852): 1–164.

Bombarón. In the ensuing altercation and affray el Seniz struck Aben Abóo's head with the butt of his gun, then finished him off as he lay there, and threw the corpse out of the mouth of the cave down a steep slope. This was on March 15, 1571. Aben Abóo's few remaining followers seem to have gone over to el Seniz, who promised to have them included in his pardon. The only follower to remain faithful to Aben Abóo to the very end was his secretary, but the authorities soon caught up with him, and he was disemboweled and quartered.

The corpse of Aben Abóo, last Muslim ruler of any part of al-Andalus, was taken in to Granada (on a pack animal, of course), no doubt to secure the reward that might be expected. The body did begin to stink as it was being transported, and they had to remove the entrails and pack the corpse with salt to preserve it. El Seniz handed the Muslim leader's scimitar over to the duke of Arcos and to Deza. Arcos, however, had just been appointed to a post in Valencia and had to leave hurriedly, so the glory of making the public announcement about the rebel leader's death fell to Deza. Thus, in the end, it was the bureaucrat and not the military man who garnered the glory.

A remnant of a few hundred rebels tried to hide away in mountain caves but were soon smoked out and put to death. Resistance in Granada was at an end.

SCATTERING THE INHABITANTS OF GRANADA

As early as March 1570, well before the ending of the fighting, the deportation of the entire Muslim population of the Kingdom of Granada had been decided. Since this required careful planning and coordination, the province was divided into seven zones, in each of which the Morisco inhabitants were rounded up before actual deportation. The plan further envisaged marching the expelled groups to assembly points outside the province, and their subsequent distribution, broken down into much smaller groups, throughout the Kingdom of Castile. The object of splitting the Moriscos up was, of course, to make sure that they assimilated and to make it unlikely that they would upset the political balance in the areas where they were sent. The first part of the operation went off more or less as initially intended: 5,500 reached Seville; 6,000, Toledo; 12,000, Cordoba; 21,000, Albacete. But the second stage of this operation, the breaking up of the groups of deportees, seems not to have been put fully into effect, partly because of the reluctance of the local authorities at the reception centers to make arrangements for the transports of prisoners. For this reason, there was some tendency for numbers of exiled Granadans to build up in the southern parts of Castile. Nevertheless, many were marched quite far north; the excellent study by Serafín de

Tapia Sánchez of *La comunidad morisca de Ávila* (1991, 148–157), which gives perhaps the most detailed account of the impact of the newcomers on the northern cities obliged to take them in.[9] Henceforward in Castile, we find Moriscos are classified either as "granadinos" or else as "los de Castilla." Both Moriscos themselves and administrators who had to deal with them do not seem to have been in any doubt as to the group to which an individual should be assigned. They knew. These were two quite distinct groups.

I will quote from Tapia (1991), whose study is sharply focused on Ávila—where he is able to specify how many newcomers went to each parish—but he provides a clear picture of the overall situation:

On November 1, 1570 there began the operation of dispersal of the *granadinos* throughout the lands of the Crown of Castile, and this included both those who had taken part in the rising and the so-called *moriscos de paz*. In a series of cities outside the Kingdom of Granada, Seville, Albacete, Córdoba, great contingents were assembled, and from there were sent onward to other places. The majority of those who [eventually] reached Ávila came through Albacete, and had reached Toledo on November 26, in a transport of 4,500 individuals. There they had been subdivided into two groups, one which went to Segovia, Valladolid, and Palencia (leaving behind in those places 500 and 216 persons, respectively), and another for Ávila, Salamanca, and Zamora (1,000, 950, and 128). Those sent to Valladolid reached there on December 16, whereas those for Ávila reached their destination much earlier, on December 5, in two columns, one led by the commissary Antonio de la Hoz (600 people), and the other under Rodrigo de Monsalve (400). This last detail is known because Captain Juan de Cañavate asks the notary Juan Valero to draw up for him an attestation that he had faithfully executed the task assigned to him: to bring 567 Moriscos from Albacete. He adds that he took twenty days on the way, which implies that the rate of progress was a little slower than the original stipulation that "journeys are to be kept to a moderate distance each day, some four to five leagues,[10] so that the said Moriscos can endure it, especially the women, children and old people.

If they had indeed covered the distance as originally planned, they would have reached Ávila from Albacete in fourteen-and-a-half days. Probably

9. Tapia Sánchez (1991) himself relies in part on B. Vincent, "L'expulsion des morisques du Royaume de Grenade et leur répartition en Castille (1570–1571)," in *Mélanges de la Casa de Velázquez* 6 (1970): 211–55.

10. The Castilian league was a little more than 5.5 kilometers, so they were walking up to 27 kilometers, or about 17 miles, a day.

they stopped in Toledo for a day or two while the columns in question were being reorganized.

The travel arrangements suffered from having to be improvised, and this, together with the normal harshness of winter in Castile, brought about great suffering. The authorities showed more goodwill than foresight when they issued instructions that the deportees were to be treated as humanely as possible, "the families of the said Moriscos being kept together, namely, fathers, mothers, and children or at least with infants left with their parents, not split up or sent to different places." As they made their way, the local town criers made proclamations to the effect that nobody should rob the deportees of their property.

In what state did these people arrive in Ávila? In other towns there is precise information to the effect that, during the journey, as a result of the hardships they had endured, many contracted typhus. This happened with the people sent to Cáceres. According to the administrators in Burgos, it also happened in Toledo, Palencia, and Salamanca. Tapia suggests that since those arriving in Ávila had traveled through Toledo, they too were probably infected, but that the city authorities suppressed the information for fear of having the whole city placed in quarantine. At all events, we have the report that "there are many sick people, and many are dying of so much snow and cold, which have been excessive" (Tapia 1991, 150).

It is clear that some local Castilian Moriscos did take on the task of looking after the sick: "there was one man who took four or five sick people into his home." All the same, some hundred of those who reached Ávila died. Once they had arrived in Castile, the *granadinos* might meet resentment from Christian manual laborers who foresaw dangerous economic competition. "Many folk who used to earn their living as laborers can no longer do so because the scattering of the Moriscos over the whole kingdom has brought the daily wages down. The Moriscos take the work and leave the local people with nothing" (Tapia 1991, 152). The very fact that local Moriscos were ready to receive their brethren charitably was perversely regarded as suspect by the Inquisition: "We understand that they have welcomed them so as to learn Arabic better from them" (153).

The way that the arrival of the Granadans may have increased the self-confidence and assertiveness of the "convert" community as a whole is indicated by an attempt made by one of them in 1571 (the first time ever) to purchase a municipal office, because that would give a vote on the Consistory of Ávila. The authorities took care to block the plan as "not conducive to the service of His Majesty or public order in this city." Attempts were made to force the immigrants to be registered and to prevent them from moving about, but probably with scant success.

Ávila was, of course, but one destination among hundreds, and those who were expelled from their homes in Granada and sent there might well have counted themselves fortunate, for their coreligionists already living in some other destinations, Segovia, for example, seem not to have extended such a warm welcome to the fresh wave of refugees in the way that the Moriscos of Ávila did. The experience of the various groups in the various parts of Castile and Extremadura was not uniform, but it does seem safe to make the generalization that the sort of living that these displaced persons could make for themselves in their new, more northerly homes was hard and precarious compared with what they had known before the war disrupted Granadan society once and for all.

It must be stressed that what was going on at this point was the total relocation of the entire Muslim population of the Kingdom of Granada. Exceptions were made only in the case of a very small privileged elite. (Alonso del Castillo, for example, a useful servant of the Crown, could stay behind.) To secure permission to stay and avoid confiscation of one's property, it was not enough just to prove that one had not taken part in the fighting, still less that one had surrendered promptly when summoned to do so. Nevertheless, those charged with the expulsions clearly felt the need to justify to themselves what had been done. One tactic they adopted was to impugn the good faith of the "enemy." All Moriscos, whatever their record, were by now perceived as a threat. Moriscos are, under the surface, in league with each other. There is no indication in the records of this or any similar group being granted an exemption. The expulsion from Granada to selected locations in the rest of Spain went ahead.

THE CHURCH AND THE MORISCO PROBLEM

The impact of the exiling of the Granadan Moriscos (that term by now was in general use) from their native land was eventually felt not only by their fellow converts everywhere in the peninsula, but also by the Old Christian majority as well, even in those many areas that had been able, up to that time, to regard the Morisco problem as something about which they need never worry. All Spain was now obliged to confront the unprecedented situation that had been created by the expulsions.

What did the Christian majority want of the Moriscos? To answer that question was easy, so Christians would have said. These Moriscos must become sincere Christians and good Spaniards just like everybody else. But at the same time there was the widespread conviction that the converts were insincere and that all of them at heart were Muslims. (This was, of course, probably true.) And so there continued into the last three decades of the sixteenth century and even after conversions and then expulsions those forms of social exclusion that had grown up during the Middle Ages, when many Christian towns and cities had their Moorish quarters (*morerías*). Under the medieval dispensation these cities had provided the Mudejars with the public institutions of a separate, subordinate, but tolerated way of life: mosques, baths, and their own shops. In our Morisco period the "converts" were still set apart, more or less as they always had been. Gone, however, were the mosques and the baths. Conversion had not brought assimilation and the benefits of belonging to the national community; neither side really wanted that. So it was that each side could, with justification, accuse the other of insincerity. On the Christian side, there was a great theoretical longing to have the conversions become a reality and, at the same time, no practical desire to have these people in any but a menial place on the margins of society. The crypto-Muslims, for their part, became ever more firmly entrenched in their underground religion. (We have seen in chapter 5 what an enormous effort they put into developing a literature that would sustain this clandestine culture.)

Assimilation or Rejection

The policy of scattering the Granadan Moriscos had two distinct objectives that were not necessarily incompatible, although neither had been thought through properly. The objectives were strategic, on the one hand, and religious and cultural, on the other. The strategic objective was simply to uproot the Granadans, who had given ample proof of the enmity they felt for the Spanish state, and to relocate them as far as possible from the coast of Granada. Algerian and other raiders from across the sea had always hitherto been able to land to foray for booty or, during the years of open conflict, to bring in or take off troops and advisers from the small harbors of the Mediterranean coast. Christian Spain had long maintained a surveillance operation, on the high seas, in inshore waters, and on land, making use of the coastguard and the militias. After 1570, Christians along the coast could feel much safer, now that marauders no longer had ready-made beachheads available. The improvement in military security was obtained at significant social cost: the final polarization of society.

The Church and Islam in Spain in the Sixteenth Century

With regard to the religious and cultural objectives there was a muddle. The ultimate religious objective could be summed up as "full conversion," and no Christian ever spoke against that aim, but on the methods whereby that ultimate goal could be reached, disagreements abounded.

It was very obvious that specially trained clergy were needed to tackle the indoctrination of the "converts." We have seen that at the outset in the 1490s Talavera had worked hard in Granada to create parish priests capable of preaching in Arabic. The same policy of Arab-language evangelism was at first adopted in Valencia, too. Later, when the use of Arabic in the services of the Church was abandoned, there was no less need for specially trained priests. It cannot be said that the Church responded adequately to the challenge with which it was faced. Perhaps that is not surprising. By imposing on unwilling converts the self-contradictory nonsense of a forcible baptism and never subsequently facing up to that fundamental error, still less recanting it, the Church effectively made its own task impossible. The task of the parish clergy, conscious as they will have been that no substantial progress had been made over the course of several generations, must have been quite disheartening.

The Society of Jesus and Islam

The Society of Jesus was, of course, a new creation to help the Church and, more specifically, the papacy, to meet the needs of a new age. There were no Jesuits when our period opens in 1500, for papal authorization for the formal constitution of the Society of Jesus was not given until 1540. From his early days, from well before that date, the founder, Ignatius of Loyola, had been moved by a desire to bring about conversions, although his focus then was on Muslims in the Holy Land itself and not those of his own homeland. The Society of Jesus was, however, soon actively at grips with the "Morisco problem" in the peninsula, especially in the field of education. In the initial two decades of its history, the Society of Jesus was quite open to converts from Islam (as well as from Judaism). There was nothing of the Old Christian exclusiveness that came to characterize Jesuit practice by the end of the century, and although we cannot say that Jesuits with Morisco blood were ever numerous, there was nothing exceptional or unusual in the early history of the order about such members as Ignacio de las Casas and Juan Albotodo. The society, through its colleges, deliberately set about fostering vocations among Moriscos. Albotodo from the school in the Albaicín was perhaps the most famous of its products. (When in 1568 the Morisco mob was running riot in the Albaicín, they had tried to hunt him down to kill him.)

The Church's policy of selective recruitment of priests and leaders from among the Morisco population failed to produce the desired results. For their own safety, in the tense period following the Granadan War, Ignacio de las Casas and others were removed from Granada and sent to Rome (where thought was given to making use of their special linguistic capacities in the service of the Church in the Middle East, but that is quite another story, although a fascinating one). The Jesuits had taken over the policy of fostering assimilation initiated by Talavera and for a time had made an intelligent and determined attempt to make it succeed.

Missionary Activities in the Dioceses

It would be quite wrong to say that the Church abandoned hopes of achieving assimilation after the Granadan rebellion obliged it to acknowledge failure, but the missionary campaign necessarily took on a different character from 1570 onward. The decision to expel Moriscos from the Kingdom of Granada in the aftermath of the Second Granadan War was still based on a premise that was basically assimilationist. The assumption was that if New Christians were forced to reside away from their ancestral homes, moved to inland areas from which it was no longer easy to keep in contact with Muslim North Africa, they would eventually adopt Christian ways. Reliable Old Christians, among whom the New Christians were obliged to live, would keep them under observation, so that before long the New Christians would come to be true Christians: in modern terms, become assimilated. The implementation of this final phase would thus be a matter of joint action by the secular and ecclesiastical authorities. The deportation program may have appeared to have some prospects of success, for the experience of the fifteenth century had shown that those Mudejars who had lived away from formally organized *morerías* and had mixed with Christian neighbors had not caused problems; they had adopted the local speech and local ways. But enforced scattering nevertheless failed as a policy.

The Other Tendency: Separate Development

The Church could not ever settle on a coherent and realizable policy toward non-Christian Spaniards any more than could the state. On the one hand, its duty to preach the gospel of Jesus Christ to *all* men was clear. But it also was moved by a desire to eradicate from Christian society all heresy and evil. Eventually, in the Edicts of Expulsion, it came to see the physical eradication of the agents of heresy, the removal from contact with Christians of those who were resolved to cling to non-Christian beliefs, as being more important than the hope of making converts. This policy of separation (which in sixteenth-century Spain was not covered with any fig-leaf theory of "separate development," apartheid, such as was to be elaborated by part of the Dutch Reformed Church in mid-twentieth-century South Africa), must not be seen as the product of the special stresses of this Morisco period, for already in medieval times and in relation to the Jewish question as well as to Muslims we can find abundant examples of theologians arguing, urging, indeed demanding, that believers should not mingle with unbelievers. The most specific with regard to Spain were actually ordinances issued in the early fifteenth century by an Englishwoman, Catherine of Lancaster, during her regency (Fernández y González 1866, 400–5). From this period before the forcible conversions, one might cite several segregationist tracts (Echevarria 1999, esp. 176–78). It is doubtful whether there is any Christian theologian who nowadays would mount a reasoned defense for the action that was eventually taken in 1609, yet it is important to bear in mind that the Expulsion was not a measure rushed into effect with unthinking haste or pushed through against ecclesiastical or public opinion. It was the end term of a debate that had been taking place over the centuries, and with particular intensity during the previous third of a century—that is to say, from the time when it became clear that the conversions (forcible conversions for the most part) of the early sixteenth century had not "taken."

Conflicting attitudes thus existed side by side, and even within the same individual. If conversion should be a matter of free will, and that was what sound doctrine proclaimed unhesitatingly, then preaching ought to be a matter of peaceful persuasion. But if it was felt a Christian missionary had a duty to bring about conversions or to turn nominal conversions into spiritual realities, then zeal too easily led those in direct contact with stubborn recalcitrance to go beyond energetic preaching and to decide either to keep the unbelievers isolated in a sort of spiritual quarantine or even to resort to brutal force in order to bring the problem to an end.

The policy of scattering the dangerous (as they were seen) inhabitants of the Kingdom of Granada over other parts of inland Spain was intended to facilitate assimilation. Scattering did not, however, have the desired effect, and it sometimes, as we will see, alienated the hitherto inert Castilian ex-Mudejars.

It would not be possible to follow what happened to all the deportees in their various reception areas. Some of the groups endured long marches from Granada across testing terrain with, as we have seen, many dying on the way. Other journeys were less stressful, and those who were sent westward into Extremadura, above all to Hornachos, found themselves living in an Arabic-speaking concentration, an autonomous enclave almost, where the process of assimilation, far from being accelerated, seems to have gone into reverse (see chapter 12).

Even where the Granadans were in a minority vis-à-vis the Christians of their new place of residence, the outcome was not always the reeducation that had been hoped for, and might be the opposite. Once again, Tapia's well-documented study of the fate of the Moriscos of Ávila is instructive here, for we can see that there were many dimensions to the situation other than the purely religious ones.

The Tax Called the "Situado"

The destabilization of a community that had hitherto given no trouble is what emerges clearly from the analysis in Tapia (1991, esp. 245–67) of the local tax known in Ávila as the *situado*.[1] The *situado* was a payment made annually by some (not all) local Morisco communities to the Inquisition. It had been paid by the ex-Mudejars of Ávila up to the early 1570s. The ready acceptance of this by the city's Mudejars and new converts who were descended from Mudejars was upset by the advent of the deportees from Granada. The payment of the *situado* had purchased an understanding whereby the Inquisition desisted from the more vexatious of their programs of action against the Moriscos, especially from the

---

1. It is to his account that I am chiefly indebted in what follows.

sequestration of property. There was no one set form of such agreements: terms might vary from time to time and from place to place. Nor was it a blanket arrangement applying to all Moriscos; only to those who had signed up to pay their share of the contributions stood to benefit.

It may appear strange that an institution with such immense powers as the Inquisition should have been prepared to strike messy exemption deals of this kind. From the point of view of the Inquisition itself, what recommended the *situado* and similar arrangements was that they went some way toward relieving and evening out the financial stresses that arose from the policy demands made on it by Church and state alike. When the Inquisition moved from being a small agency disciplining a few delinquent heretics to being a relatively large organization running large jails and meeting a range of staffing costs and other administrative overheads, such as any bureaucracy has to face, it began to need to assure for itself a *steady* source of income. Since one resource it had was the money coming from its prisoners (from sequestrated possessions, from fines and penalties imposed, among other things), it could easily pay its bills when sinners and backsliders were in good supply, but of course when they were not, the same fixed administrative overhead still needed to be covered. The Moriscos soon grasped that the Inquisition had a strong motive to continue to harass them and create ever more victims unless it could be bought off and assured a steady source of revenue. After delicate negotiations, deals might be made. Thereafter, many groups of Moriscos paid their joint quota, the *situado*, and were left alone so long as they caused no scandal.

How the *situado* was actually raised then became a matter for the Morisco group's own officers or leaders. (As a result, there might well be considerable variations in the per capita contributions made by individuals.) A *situado* agreement had been made in 1558 by a consortium of Castilian towns (Valladolid, Medina del Campo, Arévalo, Ávila, Piedrahíta, Segovia, and Palencia) who were to pay 400,000 maravedís each year. Some of those who had hung back and not signed up to the original deal must have seen it as worthwhile paying the relatively high annual premiums involved (they varied from just over 500 maravedís a head in Palencia to well over 1,500 in Segovia) because, in later years, fresh places actually applied to be allowed to join.

This was all before the Second Granadan War. After the war, things changed because the displaced persons who arrived from Granada were not participants in the payment of the *situado* in their new place of residence. What is more, the Inquisition hung back from pursuing these incomers or imposing fresh vexatious charges on them. Special permission had to be secured before the Inquisition could institute action against the Granadans. (Presumably it was judged that an extra imposition might be enough to push the impoverished Granadans into rebellion, and the intention was to allow them a chance to settle into their new homes.) The local ex-Mudejars then noticed that their new neighbors from the south were paying no *situado* and yet were not worse treated than they were. What was the point of paying an imposition that yielded no benefits? The ex-Mudejars, the local Moriscos, therefore became reluctant to pay their own *situado* dues.

In 1573, twenty-two of the better-off of the Moriscos in Ávila instituted legal proceedings aimed at having their names struck off the list of those contributing towards the *situado* (Tapia 1991, 261). They argued that they had never empowered anybody to make the agreement in the first place. Most had their pleas thrown out, but in 1577 one Isidro de Chaves el Mozo, a tinker by trade, managed to have his name removed, as did Hernando de Cuéllar, a merchant, in 1584. He no doubt was to regret calling attention to himself in this way. From 1605 to 1607 (by which time he can no longer have been young) he was in an Inquisition prison for failure to pay and in danger of having all his property seized.

The fact that the individual petitions for exemption were rejected by the courts surprisingly did not lead the Moriscos to desist. These were men who had grown up in Ávila, confident of their position in Castilian society and of the rule of law. They must have thought that it existed for them as well as for the Old Christians. They do not seem to have grasped the fact that times had changed. From 1584, all those Moriscos concerned joined together, gave powers of attorney to three or four of their number, and jointly petitioned the king himself to intervene. In this way we get to know the names of their spokesmen, Diego de Fontiveros in 1586 and Diego Monge el Cuervo in 1590 (Tapia 1991, 263). The arguments presented are in general the poverty of the Moriscos and also the death and absence of many of those who originally had agreed to contribute. The assessment of 400,000 maravedís had been levied on a more numerous community than existed in Ávila in the 1580s, and that meant that the reduced number of those remaining in 1584 or later paid proportionately much higher contributions. (All this was at a time when the *total* Morisco population of Ávila was swollen by the Granadan incomers, all of whom enjoyed, for the time being, tax-exempt status.)

Philip II on March 12, 1592, gave orders that those who had originally struck the *situado* agreement and their heirs and successors should still pay. As Tapia (1991) put it, "Philip II could not accept the weakening of what was one of the fundamental instruments of state policy, the

Inquisition" (264). The problem of the reluctance of the Moriscos to pay the *situado* was to continue right up to the time of the Expulsion. And of course, the sudden cessation of this source of income was then to mean that the Inquisition itself was to feel the economic consequences of solving the Morisco problem even more severely—but that would take us outside the framework of this study.

Tapia (1991, 265–67) understandably devotes a section to the case of Hernando de Barahona, the only member of the community to be burnt at the stake in an *auto de fe* in Valladolid in this final period. It was on April 3, 1588, that Hernando, a dealer in iron, took a business trip to Segorbe, where in fact he had lived. (He had taken his wife, Ana, who had been born and raised in Ávila, to live in Segorbe in 1570, when they were first married, but "she could never get used to Segorbe (*no se hacía a Segorbe*)," and after two years they had come back north. Segorbe was, of course, in the Kingdom of Valencia, so Hernando's movements no doubt attracted cross-border surveillance at a time (the 1580s) when the fear existed that there would be some form of Turkish incursion carried out with the help of a Valencian Morisco fifth column. No complicity with the plotting that was undoubtedly going on could be proved against him, but Hernando was condemned for "dogmatizing," the catchall charge used for those who allegedly had preached a faith other than Catholic Christianity. In his case, even the fact that he had actually paid the *situado* was used against him! It was put forward as an admission that he was aware of his religious obligations. It followed that if he had, as was charged, told women "to be Muslims (*moras*) and to give up the Christian religion" (Tapia 1991, 266), he could not plead ignorance and hope for a lighter sentence.

The outcome of his trial is surprising. All those burnt at the stake had their property confiscated by the Inquisition, but the leader of the Morisco community, Diego Monge el Cuervo already mentioned above, instituted proceedings, not directly on behalf of Hernando but on behalf of the poor of his neighborhood. Diego Monge was able to produce a royal rescript (*cédula*) stating that all property confiscated from the Moriscos should be applied to help toward the *situado* payments due from the poor of the locality. And so, it would seem, the Moriscos won their case (although Hernando de Barahona and his family still lost their possessions).

Meanwhile, the expelled Moriscos from Granada who had been sent to Ávila were apparently living quietly in the Moorish quarter, and the records studied by Tapia show none of them in trouble with the Inquisition. Of great interest is a report on them provided by the local Inquisition at the request of the Crown in 1583, when there were once more fears of threats from overseas in which they might be implicated. These people from Granada, the Inquisition said

> are well accommodated in the neighborhood of the original Moriscos who were born here. These are very numerous, and rich, so that for this reason there are more Moriscos in the city than in any other city of Old Castile. These people from the Kingdom of Granada make their living from the food trade, and have food stalls and shops, and cultivate market gardens. They make things of esparto grass, and the rest of them are day laborers and are in service to private individuals. Among themselves they speak their own language[2] although most of them are very fluent in ours. They meet together at the slightest pretext, and even if they have none they go seeking one another out. They make themselves rich. Three or four or more [families?] live together in one house. They try to manage to live among the original Moriscos in streets that are out of the way, except, that is, for those who are shopkeepers in the main squares. To sum up, they have and enjoy such liberty that they go where they wish, with or without the pretext of their business needs, and it is most exceptional to see among them any glimmering of being Christian. There is no respect here for Your Majesty's Pragmatic or Instruction, nor for the enactments of the Royal Council with regard to these [Granadan] Moriscos.

We can see that what has happened is that whereas under the old dispensation the Ávila authorities could rely on the members of the former Morisco community to know their place, be subservient, and pay special taxes, after the newcomers had arrived, Moriscos began to be assertive and difficult to deal with. The effects of the deportation of the Granadans was to change attitudes everywhere.

Slavery

The policy of scattering, of course, only applied to Muslims who were being sent out of the Kingdom of Granada in organized groups to live in various places and, in theory at least, to live among Christian neighbors. Those Moriscos who formed a part of actual Christian households because they were held as domestic slaves escaped the mass exodus. They lived where their owners and masters required them to live.

There were slaves of various kinds in sixteenth-century Spain (and they were certainly not all black slaves). Through most of this period Muslim slaves were being brought into Spanish ports as a result of corsair activities. Most would be North Africans, but some might well have actually been born on the northern shore of the Mediterranean and so would

2. This must mean Arabic.

be coming back home. But some slaves born in Spain as free Moriscos would have passed into servile status in the peninsula not as a result of being taken captive at sea but as a result of the terms of surrender granted at several periods. Readers of my earlier volume, *Islamic Spain, 1250 to 1500,* will recall that most of those captured in the seige of Malaga in 1487 (with the exception of the "peace party" led by 'Ali Durdush) became slaves, some of them being sent as a gift to the pope. The end of the Second Granadan War saw very many more reduced to slavery in this way (prisoners taken at Galera, for example). Slaves were only a minority of the Morisco population: until the end most of the Moriscos, although occupying a very low rung on the social ladder, were in legal status not slaves but free cultivators or urban laborers. These crypto-Muslims might, under the Mudejar status, which most of their forebears had had in the Middle Ages (and which continued until the 1520s in the lands of Aragon), effectively be debt slaves, tied to the land by obligations set at levels they were unable to meet, but the mechanisms that kept them in subservience were rents and dues rather than shackles and chains. So it was that the enslavement of many Moriscos at the end of the Granadan rebellion of 1569–70, while not creating a totally new situation, did significantly alter the balance. Some Moriscos were slaves of the sort that could be manacled if their masters so desired. The Morisco was consigned to a level in society even lower than before.

We can see how the depressed and impoverished Morisco was regarded by Christian society to a certain extent from literary sources such as the picaresque novel. But more reliable is the information waiting to be extracted from the sixteenth-century notarial archives (*archivos de protocolos*) that survive in many cities and towns. To exploit the confused profusion of information hidden in the crabbed legal scripts in such sources is extremely difficult and time-consuming, but where an intelligent exploration has been carried out, we learn a great deal. Aranda Doncel (1984) is thus able to furnish us with detailed information about Morisco slaves in Córdoba such as is rarely available elsewhere.

One aspect of the lives of these Moriscos that may appear to be in conflict with the simplistic view of them as oppressed in every way is the fact that their fate is subject to the law and its provisions (as we have already seen in Ávila). That should not be taken to imply that their personal status was satisfactorily secure but that the oppression to which they were subject was not utterly arbitrary. (An injustice that is not the consequence of personal tyranny but is systematically embedded in the juridical structures of society, is, of course, not in any way easier to bear, perhaps the reverse.) A good example of the impact of the law on the Moriscos is provided by the numerous legal proceedings that arose from the fact that the enslavement of the Morisco prisoners was held not to affect their children. An adult could be held responsible for his/her own rebellion and punished for it, but the penalty of enslavement could not be inflicted on minors. The fate of the children immediately after capture was not in any obvious way different from that of the adults. Children were deported from Granada in 1570, and most of them were set to work for Christian masters either as domestics, farm laborers, or workers in various trades. The significant difference was that they were placed under supervision (and subject to indoctrination) until the age of twenty, at which point the masters were obliged to free them. Thus it was that over the next decade or so there was a trickle of cases in which the courts had to rule on various ensuing problems.

It does seem that it was not unknown for the authorities themselves to take the initiative of looking into the status of such minors. The Licentiate Guillén del Castillo, *corregidor* of the city of Córdoba (and so a royal official, of course), turned up thirty-six cases of children, girls and boys, in 1579. They were not freed, but when they were returned to the custody of their "owners," it was explicitly stated that this was "in order that they keep them in their service, bring them up, give them religious instruction (*dotrinen*), see that they are fed, clothed and shod."

There was a silversmith in Córdoba called Andrés Mártinez who had a Morisco lad in his service called Lorenzo. The *corregidor* instituted proceedings to have Lorenzo set free. Against the manumission it was argued that "[t]he said Lorenzo is older than he looks, he is *rebexido* ([prematurely] "aged," "stunted"), and at the time of the rebellion he was more or less the same size as he is now" (Aranda 1984, 169). We do not know the outcome of these proceedings—that is a problem that arises frequently with such notarial archives, they often tease us with fascinating fragments—but the important thing is that we see how the *corregidor* was prepared to try to intervene, however ineffectually. In other cases Moriscos themselves had to institute proceedings and actually to put up money in advance to cover legal costs! A Morisco baker called Martín Rodríguez undertook to cover costs of 10 ducats in a suit undertaken by one of his cousins against Pedro de Ángulo (170). Costs frequently were very much higher than that, and so it is not surprising if Moriscos and Christian masters alike were inclined to settle out of court—yet another circumstance that makes it impossible at times to glean information on how matters finally turned out.

Some of these notarial documents do appear to bear witness to good basic human relations between the groups. Wills may show us Moriscos being named as beneficiaries by Christians: Doña Francisca de Velasco, for example, left to three Morisco maids "10 ducats each, and whatever clothing, drapery, and bed linen they may have." Sometimes we may suspect that beneath the pious and generous formulae of the wills may lurk other motives. When Andrés de Paniagua set María Sánchez free "bearing in mind the good service she has rendered to me, the love of God, and other just reasons which have moved me," should we admire him for allowing this seventy-year-old lady to end her days as a free woman, or suspect that he was concerned to save his heirs from the burden of giving her a room in their house and looking after her in her old age? Is one being unpleasantly cynical when one doubts the real motives of Diego Rodríguez when he manumits a fifteen-year-old girl "because you were born in my household and I have much love for you"?

The freeing of a fifty-year-old slave called Juan de Agudo in 1610 obviously arose out of the maelstrom of events narrated in chapter 9 but I discuss it here as it illustrates the complex personal status of the Moriscos at this period, some of them slaves, some not. The document (found by Aranda 1984) tells the following story: Martín de Argote freed the slave Juan de Agudo at the instance of Juan's wife, Constanza Ximénez, also a Morisco, but a free woman:

> Because on the seventeenth day of the month of January of this year, a proclamation from His Majesty was published in which it was ordered that all those who had been born in the Kingdom of Granada, both male and female, were obliged to leave, with the exception of slaves, in conformity with this proclamation, the aforementioned Constanza has to leave. So as to avoid certain awkwardnesses (*yncombinyentes*) that would ensue from this, and because Constanza has asked me to give Juan de Agudo his liberty, so that they can leave together for this journey and crossing.... (Aranda 1984, 171)

That is, the master decides to let his slave go. No mention is made here, under the exceptional circumstances, of a ransom payment. In earlier years, it was frequent that a payment would be made for the freeing of Morisco slaves. The price would vary according to the age, sex, and skills of the slave. The money might come from a variety of sources, mainly from fellow Moriscos. Presumably those who provided the money were generally relatives of some sort, who might have to travel considerable distances to conclude the business, but there are other cases where it appears that it was straightforward religious solidarity that inspired those who donated the funds. Sometimes, less frequently, the slaves bought *themselves* out (Lorenzo de Robles had begged in the street to collect his ransom, Angela de la Pastora in a sort of system of installments, made a down payment and was allowed to go "wherever you like to work" in the following year in order to earn what was required). Aranda (1984, 172) notes that such "ransoms" were in general at well above the going rate for the purchase of slaves at the time. Whereas males under ten years of age might fetch 20.5 ducats on the open market, the ransoms paid to masters averaged 46 ducats; for males between 30 and 39 the respective prices were 46.2 and 84.7 ducats, respectively; for female slaves there were similar differentials.

There is obviously a conflict between the economic motives that might lead Christian owners to release their Morisco slaves at a good price and other quite different religious considerations. The purpose of the placement of Moriscos in Christian households and establishments in the first place had been to facilitate their indoctrination and assimilation. Manumission would probably be a prelude to the return of the slave to an Islamic environment, and so to Islam. A cleric like the Licentiate Juan Merino, in drawing up his will in 1580, might endeavor to salve his conscience by enjoining the parents of children in a captive family to whom he was bequeathing their liberty that they should not "themselves teach the children the Arabic language, nor should any others acting on their behalf do so, in order that it should not be an impediment preventing them from becoming good Christians." Such concerns are rarely expressed: presumably at this late stage there were few illusions about the likelihood of evangelization ever being successful. Not surprisingly, having to live as a slave rarely served to bring about the eradication of the Islamic identity of a Morisco.

Assimilation

Our evidence, made up of documents of almost exclusively Christian provenance, is—and it is important to realize this—biased toward a view that the Moriscos were an unassimilated and unassimilable minority. Evidence adduced in sources like trials will tend not to show us fully integrated Moriscos living and working within the larger Christian community. This is because nobody on either side had reason to record the activities of the assimilated. And many people had some reason for suppressing such information. Besides which, at the end, at the time of the Expulsion, the received view on both sides was that the Moriscos were unassimilable. (It is rare to find this received truth being questioned, which is what makes the authoritative study by Márquez Villanueva [1991] so welcome.)

A group that formed a conspicuous exception to this generalization about the rareness of assimilation is the small sector from the very highest levels of the Granadan (Nasrid) ruling class who sided with the Catholic Monarchs after the completion of the conquest and who "passed" into the Christian aristocracy (some of them, even before 1492). As converts to Christianity, they were accepted as members of the Christian nobility. Such aristocrats do seem to have achieved direct entry into Spanish society, and this without the need to renounce their noble identity under the previous regime. We find a noble such as Francisco Núñez Muley still able as a Christian to act as a forceful spokesman of the Moriscos of Granada. There seems little reason to doubt that he was a sincere convert.

This one class apart (whose special status in this respect arises from the highly privileged position of the noble within Spanish society at this time), any ex-Muslim had good reason to keep silent about his or her own Muslim past or, in later generations, about the Muslim past of his forebears. The Inquisition had procedures designed to ferret out information about individuals with a Muslim background, and against these the only effective form of self-defense and of defense of the local community was absolute silence. The modern investigator has to rely almost exclusively on written documents—there are hardly any useful techniques able to exploit other evidence. So we know about Muslims and crypto-Muslims because of what they wrote themselves or because of what others (almost always their enemies) wrote about them: *aljamiado* manuscripts on one hand, the contents of Inquisitorial processes, on the other.

But fully assimilated Moriscos dared not allow information about themselves to get about, so we can expect to learn little about them. It would be naive to suppose that absence of evidence means that assimilation, "passing" from one community to another, never occurred. Márquez Villanueva (1991) has written much manifest sound sense on this subject. We have to recognize that the idea that no Muslims ever entered Christian society arises from the defensive myths of both religions. The Christian apologist justified what was done to the Muslims, and in particular justified the Expulsion, on the grounds that Moriscos were always and in every way a totally distinct entity. The Muslim, writing from North Africa or from some other base in an Islamic country after the Expulsion, had no reason to celebrate the memory of former brethren who had avoided the trauma of exile and had remained behind and quietly merged into the majority. The exiles faced criticism from some North African Muslims who rationalized their own unwillingness to welcome these awkward refugees into their society by accusing the newcomers of being bad Muslims, more than half Christians. It would have done no good to the Morisco cause in the lands where they were seeking to make new homes to have it trumpeted abroad that back in Spain that there were former members of the community who had survived, not by becoming mere false converts to Christianity but by assimilating totally.

Yet there were at least a few such cases of apparently genuine conversions. Recent investigations (e.g., Ferrer 1994, 42–53) have brought to light information about the way in Tortosa the bishop made it his business, when the end came, to save from expulsion a number of families held by their neighbors to be good Christians. Inquisition material from Granada similarly throws up information of trials as late as the eighteenth century affecting families who had somehow managed to live on there as nominal Christians after 1609. Too much must not be made of sketchy evidence, but it is reasonable to assume that other individuals remained uncertain where they belonged.

Rich Moriscos

That there was a well-to-do class of Moriscos in many regions, a class able to operate successfully within the economic system of the day, may not fit with a stereotype of the Morisco either as successor of the noble Moor of the past or of the Morisco as marginalized near-pauper and victim. The former, the noble Moor stereotype, belonged by the sixteenth century to the realm of literature (*Abindarraez y la hermosa Xarifa*). During much of the century there was little scope for chivalric display in practice. An unheroic view of the Morisco is certainly to be found in literature, too: Góngora's mockery of Morisco *buñuelo*-sellers (the sort of little people who run small fast-food stalls) is but one example among many. Between these two extremes the wealthy Morisco may sometimes have gone unnoticed, especially by liberal historians, who after all have some interest in showing how ill-used the whole minority community was. Anti-Morisco publicists of the sixteenth and seventeenth centuries were ready enough to speak of prosperous Morisco businessmen: Janer (1857, 317, document CVI) reproduces from the Archivo de Estado in Simancas a *memorial* sent to the king in 1609 arguing the case against the lenient and over-generous (!) treatment being accorded to those to be expelled. This particular *memorialista,* in line with the economic theory of his day, is worried by the outflow of capital that will result from the expulsion and argues that perhaps the Royal Council has failed to take into account the wealth of some individuals.

> In order that the amount of cash that the Moriscos may carry off with them may be gauged, it must be borne in mind that there are thirty thousand households of them, more or less[3] and although among them there are many who are very poor, there are others who are extremely rich, with some of them having an estate of 50,000 ducats, even 100,000 or 150,000.

3. The writer is, of course, concerned with the Kingdom of Valencia only.

No Morisco has ever invested heavily in land, their whole trading activity is devoted to investing in rents[4] and in buying and selling. They have always been very much given to accumulating money, even in the days when they were Muslims, before they were baptized.

Here we get a picture of Moriscos as accumulators of capital that accords ill with the Islamic ban on usury. One might be inclined to dismiss such allegations about profit-seeking rich Moriscos in the *memorial* as ill-founded, and arising from that hatred for this minority that is so transparent throughout the text. However, there is abundant confirmation of Morisco participation in money-lending, speculation, and in small-scale banking. When the final expulsion came, one of the effects was to leave a number of Morisco creditors unable to claim money that was owed to them (Ciscar 1993, 50), and by the same token there were Christians whose Morisco debtors disappeared. The matter had such serious implications that a report was drawn up on the subject. The Crown was particularly concerned because it was hoped that debts due to Moriscos could be collected after they left by the agents of the Crown and the proceeds applied to give some compensations to Christian creditors. In consequence quite a lot was recorded concerning the financial activities of Moriscos in the immediately preceding period, and although it is not possible to extrapolate backwards with confidence, nevertheless a remarkably detailed picture of Morisco economic activity does emerge, and from this and similar sources it is even possible to identify some leading figures by name. Lea made a start at such investigations as early as the beginning of this century, but Císcar Pallarés (1993) has completed researches that take us far beyond that early stage.

It must be a cause of some surprise to find some Moriscos were professional moneylenders, but such was undoubtedly the case, as Císcar (1993, 60–95) has documented. Obliged as they were to participate in the emerging capitalism of the late sixteenth and early seventeenth centuries, some seem to have been able to play the system to their advantage. As in so many other parts of the world, members of a despised minority emerge in the role of providers of credit. From the little that is known as yet about the integration of Morisco refugees into the societies of Islamic lands after the Expulsion of 1609–12, it is clear that some such rich ex-Moriscos took their entrepreneurial skills with them overseas and brought the economics of the plantation system to Tunisia (and perhaps elsewhere). To explore this subject further would be well beyond the remit of this volume, but it is important that it should be established that

---

4. That is, investments yielding an income.

among the many diverse strands that made up the Morisco community in Spain itself there were men who were active in the economic sphere.

The evidence that comes down to us about the Moriscos tends to be skewed in various ways that lead us to form a view of them as all pious men committed to their religion. Both the Inquisition evidence, gathered with the object of proving that the accused were guilty of Islamizing, and the writings of the Moriscos themselves, surviving *aljamiado* and other Morisco documents that tend to be on religious subjects, might well lead us to conclude that Moriscos were all exclusively concerned with religious matters. Indifference in matters of faith was no doubt more rare in such a polarized society than in any modern one; the evidence of Morisco economic activity gathered by Císcar Pallares (1993, 60–103) is a useful corrective to the picture of an exclusively devout community that might emerge from the other sources.

In thinking about the class of rich Moriscos we must be careful not to jump to the conclusion that these well-to-do crypto-Muslims were necessarily already half-inclined to join the society of the Christian majority or that they were collaborators. There were clearly rich Moriscos firmly attached to their ancestral faith, as well as pious poor ones. We have seen in the memoirs of the Young Man of Arévalo that wealthy merchants assumed the responsibility of funding the travels and studies of poor students and pilgrims.

POPULAR VIOLENCE: THE LAY INTERVENTION OF LUPERCIO LATRÁS IN THE MORISCO PROBLEM IN ARAGON

Before 1570, for almost all Spain's crypto-Muslims, it had been important to have reliable local protectors among the local aristocracy, or indeed, for those who were really fortunate, at the level of the Crown itself. In Granada, in addition to the lords of the place of a Morisco's residence, in a general way the viceregal dynasty of the house of Mondéjar, counts of Tendilla, had, from the 1490s onward, helped all those who were willing to submit to the newly introduced regime, and in return the viceroys had spoken up for "their" subjects and endeavored to look after their interests. In other regions, there were other aristocratic families who performed similar functions—and who sometimes ran into trouble themselves in consequence. The most outstanding of such aristocratic "patrons" who had suffered persecution for being too well-disposed toward Moriscos was probably Sancho de Cardona, the admiral of Aragon. He was accused of allowing the construction of a mosque in Guadalest, and in 1569 (when he was seventy-three years old) was tried by the Inquisition and condemned. Evidence was given (Boronat 1901, 1: 445) that when Bartolomé de los

Ángeles went to Concentaina to preach and baptize, the admiral's men had hindered him. The implication was that the admiral wanted the people on his estates to remain Muslims.

Related to Sancho de Cardona was Rodrigo de Beaumont, of the family of the constables of Navarre, who had already been in trouble with the Inquisition in 1542 (Boronat 1901, 1: 473) for favoring the Moriscos in such ways as providing them with travel documents (*guiatges*). With a document from such a powerful noble saying "I, Don Rodrigo de Biamont, procurator-general of the valleys of Seta and Guadalest, so that you may come to live there," a Morisco might travel freely. That sort of medieval-style protection still continued in many areas in the 1530s–1550s, particularly in Valencia. The pious Valencian historian Boronat reported in the following terms what his researches in the Valencian archives had revealed (Boronat 1901, 1: 473–580). "There is not the slightest room for doubt about the evil consequences of the protection afforded by the lords of Cortes to their vassals, in contravention of what had been set out in edicts from the Holy Office and the Crown," he raged indignantly.

So in general feudal or quasi-feudal relationships provided Moriscos with their security system of last resort. As can be seen from the fate of Sancho de Cardona, the effectiveness of that system of protection, the willingness of nobles to look after "their" vassals or other clients, could antagonize the Inquisition in the sixteenth century (and even in the twentieth century it could still shock a pious Catholic like Boronat). But what if effective protection were not forthcoming? What if the protection required was not simply a word in the right quarters to resolve some bureaucratic delay? What if *life* was at stake? One of the many interesting aspects of the affair of Lupercio Latrás that we need to examine now is that it shows us that at this stage, in the period after 1570, the old ways (the offering of protection by the Christian nobility—both secular and ecclesiastic—to Morisco tenantry) were beginning to break down. We must examine the response of the Moriscos for their part, and of the Crown and Church on the other, to the new situation.

Banditry?

One dimension of this affair of Lupercio Latrás, one that is incidental but necessary to bear in mind if we are to comprehend the plight of the Moriscos, is the prevalence of various forms of banditry in Spain at this time. Banditry was in no way a specifically Morisco phenomenon, nor was it limited chronologically to this period. Lawlessness of kinds that in English might loosely be classed as banditry had been a problem in Roman times, and was to be under Franco. Some might regard it as endemic in the terrain.

In our period, the readiness of some desperate/desperado Moriscos (*monfíes* was the term in Granada) to take to the hills and defy the Christian authorities meant that the borderline between criminal outlaws and heroic freedom fighters is not easy to draw. That among Moriscos in the sixteenth century some dissidents should take to the hills, adopt a life of banditry, is scarcely surprising. But as we will see, there was banditry, too, on the other side. And the old order, which had provided some form of security to crypto-Muslim populations, ceased to function.

One of the consequences of the enforced depopulation of Granada that had just taken place was that it became easier for the authorities to suppress lawlessness in the mountains of the Kingdom of Granada in the south. But after Morisco banditry was extinguished there in Andalusia, it came to life again further north. From 1577 and up to the end of the century, Morisco outlaws committed a series of outrages outside Granada as impressive as any ascribed to their predecessors of earlier generations inside former Nasrid territory. It was difficult to capture those responsible in Castile and Aragon because of the complicity of the local Morisco communities. The regions of Valladolid, Pastrana, Úbeda, Seville, Badajoz, and elsewhere suffered from attacks. Finally Francisco Hernández de Liévana (Boronat 1901, 1: 301–2), president of the chancery of Valladolid, was given the special mission of eradicating such banditry. He established that some two hundred people had been killed between 1577 and 1581, and by 1582 he was claiming to have the situation under control (Domínguez and Vincent 1978, 144n.).

There were considerable differences of opinion between the various advisers to the Crown on this problem. For any course of action, advantages and disadvantages could be foreseen. This debate about the possible remedies is preserved in the official papers of the Consejo de Estado and of the other state bodies engaged in trying to settle the question. In addition, alongside such state papers some position papers (*pareceres*) volunteered by "experts" have survived, too. We must beware of taking all these *pareceres* seriously. "Projector" used to be the term in English for such self-appointed consultants and purveyors of projects—it is a pity that the word has unfortunately fallen out of use, as we need it in the twenty-first century as much as it was needed in the sixteenth. Such *arbitristas* (that was the Spanish word) might be mere cranks, or people pushing some sectional interest, or even well-informed specialists. Thus Pedro Ponce de León, knowing from his long service to the Crown that galley slaves, the motive power of Mediterranean naval fleets, were always in short supply, put up the bright idea of pressing *all* Morisco males between 18 and 40 (Domínguez and Vincent 1978, 70).

The Status of Aragon within Spain

The long historical process whereby Aragon moved increasingly under Castilian hegemony began well before the period covered in this volume and did not end with the Expulsion (indeed, it is felt by some still to be going on today). The primary motive force driving that process in no way arose from the conflict between Islam and Christianity. Yet the Moriscos' fate was intertwined with that of Aragonese political liberties, and we cannot fail to note that the constitutional crisis through which Aragon was living in the late medieval and early modern periods actually affected Aragon's Muslims perhaps more vitally than any other group within the kingdom. We have already had cause to note this in connection with the forcible conversions of 1526. Muslim communities on the estates of the Aragonese nobility, geographically isolated as they were, might persuade themselves they were still living under powerful protectors in safe havens and in refuges where the fear of hostile prying eyes was much less than elsewhere. That protection had been worth making sacrifices for in the past. Now Lupercio Latrás and the violent men he led were about to demonstrate that the old days were, indeed, over.

The principal enemies of the Muslims in the region of Aragon were to be found in two very different social groups. If many of the Aragonese upper classes were well disposed toward Muslim/Morisco cultivators, much lower down the social scale Christian hostility made itself felt (just as we have seen that in the early 1520s in Valencia during the *germanía* troubles, it was the Christian laboring class that was moved to take violent action). But the most dangerously hostile body that crypto-Muslims had to fear was, of course, the Inquisition. And the relationship of the Inquisition to the community at large in Aragon was not at all the same as that which existed in Castile. Although it is true that the Inquisition was an institution that was first introduced into the peninsula via Aragon, in our period, for political rather than religious reasons it came to be perceived by many Aragonese as a threat to their regional identity, a political tool in the hands, ultimately, of the Crown.

The Inquisition was very often an instrument in power struggles in which religious factors were of only marginal relevance and in which the interests of the Muslim/Morisco communities were not at stake at all. We risk distorting reality if we see the Inquisition's policies as solely, even primarily, directed toward the solution of a "Morisco problem" (or a "Jewish problem"). Yet in the Aragonese political arena, where the Inquisition, acting as the instrument of the new royal bureaucracy, was tending to play an ever more active role, the Moriscos, the crypto-Muslims, were of course particularly vulnerable to Inquisition action.

The Inquisition might well also be highly active against some of the Moriscos' enemies too, but nevertheless in our period, as we are about to see, it was the Moriscos that in the end came off worse. The general outcome of the power struggle was that Aragon was effectively deprived of many of its ancient liberties, a serious enough matter for the Christians. But the outcome for the Morisco community of Aragon was that it lost not just its liberties within the state but also the homeland in which Muslims had long felt comfortable.

To remind us of the special vulnerability of the Moriscos we may cite an edict of 1558 whereby the Inquisition attempted to bring about by decree the disarmament of the Moriscos—not of any other group—and not because of anything the Moriscos had done, but because their noble patrons were, so the Inquisition believed, planning to use them, alongside other forces, in the campaign to defend the ancient Aragonese institutions.

> It has come to our attention that under the pretext of your pretensions in certain legal disputes in which you [namely, the Aragonese regional patriots, under the leadership of Old Christian families] are engaged, attempts have been made to muster an assembly so as to achieve the effect you desire by the armed strength of your supporters, and to this end to bring together the Converts of this kingdom, drawn up in battle order like an army, and bearing arms. . . . which if done would cause notable harm to Catholics and their property . . . so let none of the said persons or municipal corporations or lords, *nor the said converts,* make so bold as to assemble nor respond to the said summons either with their arms or without them. (Colas and Salas 1982, 499, quoting Carrasco 1969, 129)

The crisis involving Lupercio Latrás was by no means the only one that might be cited in this connection, but because attitudes became crystal clear during a whole series of violent events, it may serve to illustrate the new state of affairs. In a struggle between regional nobility and the centralizing monarch in which the Inquisition was the Crown's chosen instrument, the Moriscos were to be the losers.

Lupercio Latrás
The extraordinary climax of anti-Muslim violence that Aragon witnessed in the 1580s is difficult to explain by reference to any one coherent pattern. What one can say is that the solidarity/complicity between nobility and Moriscos, which had subsisted for so long, now disintegrated. Effective protection for the Moriscos concerned disappeared. And bloodshed was the result.

Lupercio Latrás was the disgruntled younger son of a family of the lesser nobility (they were ranked as *infanzones,* a lower level of the nobility with no exact equivalent in English: "baronets," perhaps) from the backward region of Ribagorza. He carried out a campaign of atrocities and violence as cruel as any committed anywhere in the peninsula in the sixteenth century. Christian cattle drovers, usually referred to as the *montañeses* ("mountain men"), provided him with his fighting force. His outstanding leadership skills enabled him to turn such herdsmen into a peril to public order in general, and to the Moriscos in particular.

What happened might seem incomprehensible if one were to leave Latrás's violent personal character out of account. He was so altogether extraordinary a man that there is a risk his story will take over and stand in the way of any analysis of the Morisco tragedy in Aragon, but one cannot omit all mention of his personality. It should be made clear that his anti-Morisco campaigns were by no means his only crimes: in his long career there were infamies of all sorts.

A historical novelist might for the sake of verisimilitude feel the need to water down Lupercio's story, which is full of action and color. In essence a mere petty lordling turned leader of a crew of Pyrenean mountain bandits, his tireless pursuit of Fame (in this he was a child of his times) led Lupercio to travel far and wide. Born early in the second half of the sixteenth century in the Hecho valley, as early as 1576 he had acquired a local reputation as a hard man involved in violent feuding. Soon after that he had to flee to France from Aragon where a death sentence had been pronounced against him. The Spanish authorities were thus in a good position to exert pressure on him and succeeded in having him act as a spy against the Huguenots in France. And so he began a curious switchback career in which we find him now back on his home ground and engaged in banditry, now in royal service in Sicily as a captain of infantry (1582), now in the Azores on naval escort service in the Atlantic (where he lost, dismasted in a violent storm, the principal ship entrusted to him, and was thereafter pursued by the Spanish authorities for dereliction of duty). He was a second time engaged in espionage in France, then in 1589 in England on a secret mission to the court of Elizabeth I in London (with the "cover" that he was a refugee from Spanish royal justice). After making his way back to Spain on an English pirate vessel that landed him near Santander, he was arrested almost as soon as he got ashore and was subsequently put to death secretly in the Alcázar of Segovia (Melón 1917). Little of his work either for the intelligence services of Philip II, archenemy of local Aragonese liberties (and for Spain's enemies, France and England?) would have been known to his fellow mountain men. By some of them he came to be seen as an outstanding leader of the local resistance to the royal onslaught on their autonomy; his actions against the Moriscos were in Aragon the deeds that brought him fame.

The Destruction of Codo and of the Morisco Quarter of the Village of Pina

Latrás's anti-Morisco atrocities must be understood against a background of long-standing communal violence that saw the settled cultivators of mainly lowland regions of Aragon confronting transhumant cattle drovers from the mountains. The ancient conflict between nomads and settled farmers here had a religious dimension, too. The settled cultivators in some (not all) of the regions affected were Moriscos; the cattle men from the Pyrenees were all Christians. Twice a year the drovers needed to guide their herds and flocks on the sometimes quite long journeys from winter to summer pasture and back again, and as they made their way their animals inevitably did some damage to arable cultivations. Bitter conflicts of interest, and so legal disputes, arose. At times, these were settled without recourse to the courts in the form of affrays and murderous attacks.

To follow the stages of the buildup of one such feud is instructive. We learn from a memorandum drawn up in 1586 by the abbot of Rueda (an interested party, for this ecclesiastic was the feudal lord of Codo) that a Morisco called Calvete killed a mountain man called Oliván somewhere between Belchite and Codo as Oliván was grazing his beasts. A revenge attack was launched on November 4: five mountain men with flintlocks attacked five unarmed Moriscos working in the fields; two were shot dead. The Moriscos brought the matter before the prior of the monastery of Rueda, but he told them they should take their complaint to the noble on whose lands the attack had taken place. The Moriscos, fobbed off in this way, must have concluded that justice was not to be had through the courts. The system of protection by the nobility in which they had trusted was not working for them. They must have taken the law into their own hands, for on December 17 the corpses of two mutilated mountain men were found in the fields.

The feuding now got out of hand, but the Aragonese authorities in Saragossa were still reluctant to become involved, and deaths continued. Orders came down from Madrid that something must be done, but little was, and each side began to muster its forces. The Moriscos of Codo called in outsiders who had a reputation as strong-arm men: Agustín el Falcero, Pedro el Ferrero, Joanet de Mequinenza, and others. The royal authorities now did intervene, taking over some of the local judicial powers, but still in 1588 violence and murder continued. The mountainmen (*montañeses*) were assembling their forces and were now extending their attacks and harassment to settlements other than Codo, which was where the dispute had started. On Easter Sunday 1588, three hundred and more of them attacked Codo itself.

Somewhat to their surprise they were beaten off.

All this time the authorities in Saragossa still dithered. Troops were assembled and marched toward Codo but held back short of the village and did nothing decisive. The *montañeses* must have felt this was their chance to get their blow in first. They and other outside forces under the governor (*alcaide*) of Belchite found the village of Codo evacuated by its terrified inhabitants: they set it on fire and pillaged the ruins. The abbot of Rueda in his memorandum alleges that the *alcaide* of Belchite had been encouraged ("tuvo aliento" [Melón 1917, xiv]) to do this by the viceroy of Aragon and that the *montañeses* had been tipped the wink (*se les hizo del ojo*) that they had backing. The authorities had effectively stood by while a whole village had been destroyed, and the news of the great booty taken at Codo was leading to an influx of fresh recruits to the anti-Morisco cause. The Saragossa authorities now became seriously worried, because the Latrás's camp at Quinto was really not so far from their city. Law-abiding Christian folk could see that the attacks of the wild men might soon turn against them. The evil genie needed to be put back into the bottle.

At this point the cattlemen set about negotiating a way out of the chaos, a deal that would guarantee them exemption from prosecution for their actions and leave them in possession of their booty. They even added an offer to go away peaceably—if only the Moriscos were disarmed!

The terror created by the rampaging *montañeses* had led many Moriscos, not only those who had abandoned Codo, but others who lived in hamlets where they felt exposed, to take refuge in the village of Sástago. They must have judged themselves safer there because the village belonged to the viceroy himself, Artal de Alagón. The *montaneses* were not in the least overawed by titles. Sastago was a natural stronghold, where Moriscos could hope to put up stiff resistance. And they did indeed have to fight for their lives, for by now the *montañeses* were in an aggressive mood. Then, when the Christian attackers failed to collect easy booty at Sástago and became enraged by the casualties they suffered, they turned against Pina. This was a nearby village inhabited by both Moriscos and Christians. Each community lived in its own separate quarter, but there was reasonable amity and both shared the center of the village. At first the local Christians were unwilling to cooperate with the *montañés* outsiders, but by now a regime of terror and intimidation prevailed.

Latrás's men forced their way into the village through the Christian quarter. Before long, the streets of Pina were literally running with blood,

and the central square witnessed a horrific scene. The male Morisco inhabitants were herded there, and the bandit forces competed to see who
could deal the prisoners the most tellingly lethal blows. Other Moriscos
were simply taken up to the top of a nearby monastery tower and cast
down to the ground. More than three hundred corpses littered the centre
of Pina by the time the *montañés* onslaught was over. The attackers then
withdrew to Castejón de Monegros, where they set about the necessary
task of dividing up the spoils. That this organized bloodshed should all be
taking place on the soil of part of the realms of Philip II, in the heartland
of perhaps the greatest empire in the world at that time, cannot fail to
amaze.

Latrás and the men of his household (*lacayos*) appear to us as an
anachronistic revival of the society of the medieval peninsula: Christian
lords versus Taifa princelings, just as we find in this same region back
in the eleventh century and earlier. Through this same region, Rodrigo
de Bivar, the Cid, had led the men of his household (*mesnada*) and, after
the sack of many a Moorish village, he too had presided over the division
of the booty. It is counted to the honor of the Cid's statesmanship that
when it came to dividing the spoils, he pleaded with his men not to put
the captured Moors to death but rather to enslave them or sell them off.
Perhaps it is only fair to the reputation of Lupercio Latrás to record that
at the share-out in Castejón de Monegros he tried, *but failed,* to persuade
his men not to take the law into their own hands. He asked them to

> leave the whole Morisco business to him, he would give the Moriscos such
> a scare that not a man of that descent and name would remain in this
> Kingdom [i.e., of Aragon]: they[5] should go back home to Ribagorza. When
> that day's work was brought to an end they would destroy all the Moriscos,
> and everybody would help them, as had happened at Pina.[6]

It is clear that Latrás realized that his mountain men, with their blood
up, might extend their murderous rampage, and although he does not
say so, he must have feared that their outrages might at long last provoke
an effective reaction from the government troops. So he wanted his men
safely away from the rich lands of the valley, up in their mountain lair,
where government forces would never be so unwise as to venture—and
where he was no doubt confident that he could slip a bridle on this wild

5. He must mean his *montañeses.*

6. These words, as reported by Blasco de Lanuza (Colas and Salas 1982, 609) deserve
to be set down in the original: *dexassen el negocio de los Moriscos a su cargo, que él les
escarmentaría de manera que no quedasse hombre de aquel linaje y nombre en este Reyno;
que acudiessen a Ribagorça, que en acabando aquella jornada destruyrían los Moriscos, y
que todo el mundo les ayudaría, como en Pina había sucedido.*

stallion. But we must note that he hoped to persuade them to go home by *a promise to achieve by terror the total ethnic cleansing of Aragon*. And also note that he was able to remind his men that what had been done at Pina had been done with general complicity. Of course, it would be naive to twist these alleged words of an accomplished double agent and manipulator and to pretend that they tell us the whole truth and nothing but the truth. But Latrás could never have made this claim if his men had received no assistance whatsoever from the settled villagers during the massacre. From the general tenor of his speech we can see that the elimination of everybody of Morisco descent (and he speaks in racial and not religious terms) was a political program with some demagogic appeal among the Christian lower orders in Aragon.

What was the impact of all this on the many Moriscos in the rest of Aragon? The depredations and murderous attacks of the *montañeses* were restricted to the clearly defined area: where the routes used by the transhumant drovers impinged on settled cultivation. Elsewhere Morisco villages were unaffected directly. Yet in the whole of the kingdom it cannot have gone unnoticed that when Morisco cultivators had need of them, their lords were unwilling or unable to do anything to save them. And the Aragonese authorities, and likewise the forces of the Crown, held back from decisive military action when it might have achieved something: they preferred to see whether the dangerous rabble might be coaxed to calm down and go back up to their mountain valleys in the Pyrenees. Some Moriscos must have drawn the conclusion that their status had shifted, and for the worse. The massacres perpetrated by Lupercio Latrás and his men had shown that the bonds that had held this society together were no longer functioning effectively. The Moriscos everywhere in the kingdom, and not just at Pina, were now on notice that they were no longer effectively protected either by the aristocracy or by the law, the *fueros*. Their special status once lost could never be regained.

It is not surprising that from now on some Aragonese Moriscos placed their hopes in intervention from abroad. They were probably well able in their day to see how unlikely it was that such intervention would ever come about, or succeed if it did, but there was nothing else for them to look for: apart from the trumpet blast with which the angel Israfil would announce Judgment Day. As their literature makes clear to us, it was on the End of All Things that many fixed their gaze.

EIGHT ❦ The Last Books Written in Arabic in
al-Andalus and the Question of Assimilation

The story of the Granadan Sacromonte forgeries might seem on the face
of things of such marginal importance to the history of the Morisco people as not to be worthy of inclusion in this study. On the other hand, if
we recognize the fundamental theme of the history of this community as
being whether, after the end of the sixteenth century, any crypto-Muslim
community would continue to exist at all within the Iberian Peninsula
(to which, one might add, whether any significant cultural elements inherited from an Arabic-speaking past would survive), then to examine
the affair of the Sacromonte lead books becomes vital. This is not a mere
side issue. It is an integral part of the main narrative, as witness that so
many of the major actors in the drama elsewhere in the peninsula also
have important parts in what happened in Granada: Alonso del Castillo,
al-Hajari, Philip II, and Philip III, the Mondéjar dynasty in Granada, not
to mention the popes.

Evidence for what follows, in the form of documents and contemporary published works and of surviving material objects, is overwhelmingly strong. I say that because what did happen does at times strain our
credulity. By and large until modern times there has been little open discussion of the problems posed, but in the second half of the twentieth
century scholarly investigations did much to clarify at least the main outline of the story, and recently a major exhibition (under the title *Jesucristo
y el Emperador Cristiano* mounted in Granada in the cathedral between
July and December 2000[1]) put many key items on public display.

Briefly, in the final decade of the sixteenth century, there were perpetrated in Granada a series of forgeries in the course of which ostensibly
Christian sacred books from the first century A.D. (the days of Nero) written *in Arabic* were dug up from the ground on the outskirts of the city.

1. For the excellent illustrated catalog, see Francisco Javier Martínez Medina, ed.,
Jesucristo y el Emperador Cristiano (Córdoba: Publicaciones Obra Social y Cultural
Cajasur, 2000).

These were very soon investigated by the local ecclesiastical hierarchy and, before long, enthusiastically accepted as genuine Christian relics by the then archbishop of Granada, Pedro Vaca de Castro y Quiñones. The religious devotion accorded to them flourished not only in Granada itself, where it was centered on shrines on the Sacromonte itself (the hill where the discoveries had been made), and in the city's cathedral, but also extended to many other parts of Spain and beyond. A cult grew up that was only suppressed (as heretical) many decades later. It flourished in spite of the fact that, almost from the beginning, the Holy Office was fully apprised of developments in Granada and was anxious to bring the cult under its control. We can still today see in Granada monuments (above all, the Sacromonte abbey itself) that bear witness to the success that these forgeries once enjoyed.

The principal motive for the eventual anathematization and condemnation of this cult by the Church was that it was "tainted by Islamic heresies," and no reader of such of texts as have come down to us could deny that this assessment made by the Holy Office was, from the Church's own viewpoint, entirely correct. The Sacromonte texts are superficially Christian in the sense that they purport to deal with the early Christian church in Jerusalem and then early missionary activity in the Iberian Peninsula (they form a sort of supplement to the Acts of the Apostles). The texts do not deal with events in the history of Islam, but the Jesus that they present is never referred to as the Son of God (for example, he is, in words that are perfectly Koranic, *ruh Allah,* "the Spirit of God"). And there are very many "Islamizing" features. How was it possible for such heretical texts to penetrate in this way such a powerful bastion of post-Tridentine Catholic orthodoxy as the Spanish religious establishment?

This chapter would rapidly expand to fill a volume if there were any exhaustive attempt made to discuss here all the sources for the study of the phenomenon in question. For a dispassionate and full survey of the primary materials available, readers are referred to *Los apócrifos del Sacromonte (Granada): Estudio histórico* published by Father Carlos Alonso (1979) and for a penetrating yet urbane brief summary in English of the main events, one could still hardly do better than consult the relevant chapters (5–7I) of *Saint James in Spain* by Sir Thomas Kendrick (1960). When he was writing his study, Kendrick was director of the British Museum (as it still was then), and so enjoyed full access to its library with its not unimportant holdings in this field (not to mention his own private collection on the subject).

The events described in this chapter meant utterly different things to the various parties concerned at the time; among whom we must count the hierarchy of the Church in Granada, the remnant of Morisco intellectuals still living in Granada, the Spanish Crown, and the papacy. Getting at the truth is not always straightforward.

WHAT HAPPENED

In the mid-1590s, on the Sacromonte hill, a number of "lead books" were dug from the ground. This puzzling expression, "lead books," *libros plúmbeos,* is the term that occurs in most early descriptions. (For a list of the Latin titles of the "lead books" and sample translations thereof, see appendix 3.) The "books" were indeed bundles, packets, of small lead tablets or disks, and on them were incised Arabic texts. To many at the time these were miraculous manifestations of early Christian, certainly not of Islamic, spirituality. They were unearthed in the proximity of bones and ashes that were identified as relics of Christians martyred in Granada in the first century of the Christian era. The relics and the texts they contained were identified, after scrutiny by the Granadan ecclesiastical authorities, as dating from the earliest Christian missionary activities in Spain. The texts included, inter alia, words spoken by the Blessed Virgin Mary, by Peter, and other apostles. If genuine, they would surely have come to figure as a kind of supplement to the Acts of the Apostles, and that is how they were used in Granada in the years immediately following the discoveries, as a basis for sermons and evangelistic work.

Those who have written about the Moriscos and Morisco history, if they mention the Sacromonte affair at all (and not all of them do), include little more than a summary mention of these happenings. These were, after all, ostensibly Christian and not Islamic antiquities, and most of those principally involved were Christian dignitaries. The principle beneficiary of the discoveries at the outset was the Christian church in Granada. On the principle of cui bono, the main person or persons responsible would surely be Christian, not Muslim. As for the Moriscos of Granada, they had already been expelled from the Kingdom of Granada more than twenty years before the first discoveries were made, and so it is not at all obvious that they should bear any of the responsibility for these forgeries. The Moriscos were, twenty years and less after the Sacromonte discoveries, to be consigned once and for all into exile from the whole peninsula—long before the controversy about the meaning of the texts had been settled by the Church in Rome. Although the expulsion of all Moriscos from Granada had been decreed in 1570, there were actually present in Granada at the time a small number of people of Morisco descent, almost all of them "collaborators" with special protected status, Alonso del Castillo, whom we have met in chapter 6, among them. (There were also clearly some individuals who had filtered back into the city illegally.)

The discoveries caused a great religious sensation, and not only in Catholic Europe. Protestant scholars in the Netherlands took an active interest in the texts, too. One can only compare their impact with that of the Dead Sea Scrolls on twentieth-century biblical scholarship. Much of the copious literature on the subject was published after the Expulsion of the Moriscos had taken place, but nevertheless the Sacromonte affair needs to be understood in its origins as a desperate last-resort attempt on the part of members of the small group of "protected" Moriscos to salvage something from the shipwreck of Spanish Islam. For a time (the late 1590s and the early years of the new century) what the discoveries did undoubtedly manage to bring about was a change in Granada in the status of the Arabic language and of people of Arab descent (contempt now yielded to respect). Arabic speakers were no longer automatically identified as enemies of Christianity. In the present state of our knowledge, it is not clear what the longer-term and ultimate objectives of the plot were. What at first blush was the discovery of texts of importance to Christianity may well have been underneath it all something quite different.

The texts are unique in many ways: because of their startling contents, certainly, for, as has been said, they provide extensive supplements to the Acts of the Apostles, but also because of their format, language, and script. The latter, the script, certainly does not correspond exactly to anything we have from any other source in Arabic, Morisco or otherwise. Detailed philological investigation of such issues would be out of place here. Some of the evidence was published in Harvey (1983). In this chapter, I will mainly limit myself to arguments of a nonlinguistic nature, based on the contents of the books, and on parallel events in Morisco history. I suggest Moriscos were using ostensibly Christian vehicles to convey essentially Islamic messages.

Ideologically the Sacromonte texts do not occur in complete isolation, although in so many ways they are unique. There are other cases of Moriscos seeking to exploit apocryphal Christian texts for their own purposes (although, not surprisingly, investigators are not in entire agreement as to what those purposes were). Independent research projects have been in progress for some time now in Alicante and in Leiden on some of these aspects of Morisco writings. Míkel de Epalza and his colleague Bernabé Pons[2] at Alicante, and Sjoerd van Koningsveld, Wiegers, and others[3] at Leiden, have opened up in a most interesting way new perspectives on texts where one suspects a Morisco hand. A summary

2. See Bernabé Pons (1998). 3. See Wiegers (1993b).

examination of the problems posed by one such text, the Gospel of
Barnabas, will be found at the end of this chapter.

RELIGIOUS SYNCRETISM?

Because the Sacromonte texts combine elements that are undoubtedly
Christian (e.g., the primitive Church in Jerusalem, the preaching of the
Gospel by Saint James [Santiago] and his disciples in Spain) with credal
statements very close to those of Islam ("There is no god but God [Allah],
and Jesus is the spirit of God,"[4] I have myself in the past employed the expression "religious syncretism" in speaking of them. I still do not feel the
expression entirely inappropriate, for they do indubitably in some ways
blend things from each side of the religious divide, but I have come to see
that the term "syncretism" may mislead, or at least may fail to convey the
full significance of what I believe was going on. There is in the terminology of modern politics a term that fits much better, but I fear it is unlikely
to be adopted for use in our field for it came into being against the background of murky incidents in the history of the British labor movement.
The word I am thinking of is "entryism." It achieved some currency in
politics in the days when there took place a determined Trotskyite bid to
win control of the British labor movement (the phenomenon it describes
is certainly not a specifically British one). "Entryism" refers to a type
of infiltration whereby a concerted (and usually clandestine) attempt is
made to take over and subvert a movement (a party, a trade union) or an
ideology. A small but well-organized group of individuals who are really
opposed to the aims of a movement or party nevertheless *enter* it, join
it, and proceed patiently to win positions of power and influence inside
it, eventually transforming it into a tool serving the ends of their own
ideology. The Sacromonte affair might best be described, so it seems to
me, as a case of religious "entryism," rather than of "syncretism."

"Syncretism" is usually reserved for situations where there is ultimately some measure of coexistence, leading to partial *fusion* of hitherto
differing systems of religious belief and practice. Syncretism does not
necessarily imply exactly *equal* participation in the contributions made
toward the ultimate outcome, but to say a system is "syncretistic" usually does suggest something in the nature of a merger rather than a takeover. What the political entryist seeks to achieve is not to share power
at all but ultimately to achieve complete control (soon followed by the
excommunication/exclusion/elimination of the leaders of the vanquished majority). I wish to put forward the hypothesis that a program of

---

4. Both halves of that credal statement are to be found in the Koran (although not
side by side).

that sort may be discerned in the Sacromonte texts. Although we do not know for certain how far the creators of the Sacromonte cult planned to go in their takeover nor how fast (because in 1609 the Expulsion overwhelmed them after only fourteen years, and so masked the desired outcome), the direction in which the texts were attempting to shift religious life in Spain—toward Islam—is clear enough. That was the considered view of the authorities at Rome when all further discussion of these texts was banned in 1682.

The vigorous Sacromonte cult was certainly initially perceived as profoundly Christian, not at all Muslim, by the thousands of worshippers who flocked to the Sacromonte shrine to show their devotion. There is nothing, for example, in the solemn sonnet that the poet (and canon *racionero* of the Cathedral of Seville) Góngora composed on the subject of that holy hill to indicate that he in any way suspected that the "discoveries" he celebrated might be heretical or that they had an Islamic dimension (see appendix 4). The new cult (not new but "rediscovered," of course, in the eyes of its adherents) centered on Granada. and flourished there in the first place as an adjunct of what was the central and overarching cult of all loyal and patriotic Christian Spaniards, that of Spain's patron saint, Santiago or Saint James of Compostela. Saint James, of course, was pictured in Spain as leading Christians in their resistance to the Muslim invaders, so a cult of this nature is the last place where one would expect to find Islamic heresy lurking. One of his epithets was *Matamoros*—"Moor Killer." He had rallied Christians against the Moorish enemy on the battlefield. The ostensibly patriotic credentials of the cult could not fail to recommend it to many Old Christians and so helped in the obfuscation. The texts did come eventually to be officially condemned, anathematized, by the Church in Rome, as has been stated, but that was not until very much later. In the early days, in the 1590s, opposition to the cause of the new discoveries, such as it was, was muffled. Very few spoke up against the new cult. Among them was the Jesuit Ignacio de las Casas. He had actually been one of those who had initially endorsed the new discoveries with enthusiasm, but perhaps because of his own Morisco antecedents he soon came to see the lead books as Islamic rather than Christian, and said so. He thus became an embarrassing dissident and was hustled away from Granada, assigned by his order a place of residence elsewhere.

DRAWING THE LINE

The "Morisco Question" or the "Morisco Problem" begins and ends as a matter of delimitation, of the drawing of political, intellectual, and religious boundaries, of who belongs on one side of a line, geographic and ideological, and who on the other. The conversions, far from creating a tidy situation, had an outcome that was ambiguous and muddled. The ambiguous Morisco community, who were Christians in outward show as the law of the land demanded but still, most of them, Muslims in their hearts, were systematically hypocritical as Christians saw it, heroic resisters as they saw themselves. What ultimately brought an end to the de facto acquiescence by the Moriscos themselves in this state of affairs (i.e., crypto-Islam) was the brutally enforced movement of populations that followed on the end of the Granadan War in 1570. Thousands were killed in the fighting, and thousands expired on forced marches across the *meseta central* in winter. In the whole of Spain Muslims had it brought home to them what the reality that faced them was. The easy compromises of the past were no longer available.

For Spain's crypto-Muslims, there were now only two paths of escape from the intolerable clandestine lives in which they were trapped. They could seek actually to leave the country (but that was, of course, forbidden); or they could take refuge from the harsh realities of their lives in eschatology. They could escape from the trials of this uncertain world here-and-now by clutching at the certainties announced by their religion for the next. Morisco writings are full of texts relating to the End of Days. The Moriscos' suffering was made perhaps marginally more bearable because they had trust in the ultimate justice of Allah, who would, sooner rather than later, come to judge all men and set everything to rights.

The Moriscos had to face the reality of their situation: they were for the time being going to have to live, externally at least, as Christians. Christianity was their problem, but perhaps it could be changed *from within,* to make it, in the first place, at least less grossly offensive to a Muslim, by cutting out or avoiding references to doctrines to which no self-respecting Muslim could ever subscribe. These would be, centrally, the doctrines of the Trinity and of Divine Sonship. There would also need to be eliminated a number of other beliefs, perhaps not of the same central importance, but quite unacceptable to a Muslim all the same because they ran directly counter to explicit Koranic prescriptions (an example being the use of wine in the Mass). Such corrections of the major "errors" of Christianity were not conceived in any spirit of ecumenical compromise. The underlying intention is eschatological. The changes were to be part of the upheavals that would be a necessary preliminary to Judgment Day and the establishment of God's kingdom.

The movement to effect a doctrinal transformation of this kind was certainly *not* widespread in the Morisco communities at large. It seems to have been the creation of a small, inner group or elite (which is precisely how "entryism" operated in twentieth-century politics), and it appears to have been propagated at the outset not in those milieux that had generated the most active resistance to Christianity, but, quite the reverse, by a very few members of the highly privileged class of "collaborationist" Moriscos still present in Granada at the end of the century.

In addition to the success that this project to enter, penetrate, and subvert Christianity had among some, many Granadan Christians (the newly unearthed texts were soon placed on the altar of the cathedral), it must also have had some acceptance among Muslim new converts, for copies of the Sacromonte books were eventually carried to North Africa by refugees from Spain. Understandably the orthodox *'ulama* of North Africa soon repressed what they immediately recognized on their side too as a dangerous heresy. In Tunisia the Morisco traveller al-Hajari (Al-Hajari 1997, 68–90, 227–262) found in circulation in the refugee community copies of certain of the lead books, books he had last encountered in Granada. He was sufficiently impressed by what he read to copy out in full one of the texts and incorporate it into his autobiographical *Kitab Nasir al-Din 'ala'l-qawm al-kafirin.*

It was the Christian community in Granada who greeted the new holy texts with most enthusiasm at the outset. That may have been what was planned by the forgers. The texts were thereafter eagerly promoted by the ecclesiastical establishment of that city, notably by the archbishop, Don Pedro Vaca de Castro y Quiñones. That the support of the new message came from the local hierarchy explains how this cult took hold so rapidly and how it was sustained for so long, even though the Church in Rome (thanks to the reports of the papal nuncio) and elsewhere was aware of its "true" nature more or less from the outset.

HOW THE CULT TOOK HOLD

The time has come to trace how the forgeries were launched with such success. A preliminary lesser discovery had helped to build up expectations. In March 1588, as part of building works carried out in the Cathedral of Granada, an old tower had been knocked down. As they worked, the demolition crew came across objects that were interpreted as ancient relics dating back to pre-Islamic times: a fragment of the Virgin Mary's veil; the bones of the protomartyr Stephen; a parchment. (How relics from the days of the original evangelization of the Iberian Peninsula came to be in a structure that had formed part of the mosque complex in Nasrid times is one of the many unexplained aspects of this affair. Presumably the tower was supposed to have been part of a Christian church on the site dating back to long before the mosque was ever built.) The demolished building in which these objects were found is named in the contemporary sources as "the Turpian Tower" (*Torre Turpiana*). I am not aware that that particular name had ever been mentioned in earlier texts, but no doubt Turpian (*turpiana*) had the ring of Roman antiquity to it.

The parchment, when studied, proved to contain texts in clumsy Latin but also in Spanish and Arabic. These very languages, especially when taken together with the Arabic of the main Sacromonte discoveries that were to come seven years later, would be more than enough to convince us immediately in modern times that these were not genuine ancient relics. It would be a gross linguistic anachronism to claim that Arabic was ever spoken, whether in the Holy Land or in Spain itself, in the first century C.E., yet that is what these texts implied. In defense of the scholars of the sixteenth century, it needs to be said that some of them, among them the venerable and respected Semiticist Arias Montano, articulated these very objections, but the hysterical enthusiasm with which the discoveries had been greeted at the outset meant that cool evaluation of evidence was not subsequently on the agenda, and skepticism was simply ignored.

The barefaced ingenuity of the arguments brought forward by the promoters of the discoveries almost compels admiration. There is a difference, so the argument ran, between erudite classical languages such as Latin and Arabic, on the one hand, and the vernaculars, the Romance languages and the spoken forms of Arabic, respectively, on the other. This difference had always existed, so the apologists argued, and the texts discovered were simply very early manifestations of the vernaculars that had been written down.

Then the Sacromonte discoveries proper started to emerge from excavations undertaken in February 1595, not as before in the cathedral precinct, but this time just outside the Granada city limits. They were not all made at once, but by the end, in December 1599, there were some two dozen "books" inscribed on plates of lead dating, so it seemed, from the first Christian century. They had been written, so it was believed, by disciples of Saint James.

In the first place, because the Sacromonte discoveries, like the Turpian Tower parchment, contained references to the evangelization of Spain, they were welcomed as "proof" of the ancient status of the Christian diocese of Granada, which up to that point had labored under the disadvantage of being the youngest of the Spanish Church's foundations (its records, relics, and indeed its history, went back no earlier than 1492, of course). Suddenly from being the junior foundation in the peninsula, the Church in Granada found it did not fear comparison with anybody. Very many pious Christian folk in Granada, especially but not exclusively the ecclesiastics of the cathedral, were delighted. No local patriot in Granada wanted the new evidence discredited.

Immaculate Conception

There was more to the discoveries than local patriotism, however. Debate within the Church at large (and not just in Spain) on the subject of whether the Immaculate Conception of the Blessed Virgin Mary should be officially defined as dogma or not had, of course, begun centuries earlier. Early opponents of the doctrine had included Bernard of Clairvaux and Thomas Aquinas; in the other camp, Duns Scotus had been a supporter, and the Franciscan order, in general, had so consistently championed the cause that it was often referred to as the "Franciscan" doctrine. In the sixteenth century, the debate still remained unresolved. Catholics were free to make up their own minds on the question of the Immaculate Conception. Much earlier on in the century, it had still been possible for Peter Martyr of Anghiera, admittedly in a private letter to Luis Hurtado de Mendoza (dated from Burgos, June 4, 1515), when passing on ecclesiastical gossip, to adopt quite a mocking or sardonic tone about this aspect of Marian devotion: "In the last session it was decided, to my mind very piously, that an end be put to the ancient debate between Dominicans and Franciscans about the Conception of the Virgin Mary. Silence has been imposed on both parties, and it has been declared that it is not impious to believe in it piously." As years passed by, we hear flippant remarks of this sort much less.

As an indicator of the strength of Marian sentiment in Granada at about midcentury, we may note that Vincent (see Cortés and Vincent 1986, 203) found already in 1560 that 25 percent of girls in Granada were baptized María. That was before the discoveries. By the early seventeenth century the case for the "Franciscan" doctrine had triumphed in Granada at least. In 1615 (December 7) the custom of going in procession to accompany the *Inmaculada* from the convent of San Francisco was instituted, and in 1618 (September 2) *all* members of the cathedral chapter and the city council swore to defend her, an oath that all new appointees were obliged to take. (That the city *continued* devoted to the Immaculate Conception was manifest in civic disturbances in 1640, provoked by alleged libels against her.)

In the course of the sixteenth century, then, the doctrine of the Immaculate Conception had acquired increasing support, not least in Granada; by the early years of the seventeenth century many were convinced that a final decision about making the related doctrine incumbent on all believers would not be long delayed. (It was, in fact, delayed, perhaps as a consequence of the ignominious outcome of this Sacromonte affair. It was not until much later, until December 8, 1854, under Pius IX, that in the bull *Ineffabilis Deus*, formal "definition" was accorded and that day elevated to the status of a feast day; although, eight years before that, in

1846, the Immaculate Conception had already been declared patroness of the United States of America by the American Catholic bishops assembled in council in Baltimore, and their decision was confirmed by the pope in 1847.)

This debate, of course, did not hinge on whether Jesus himself was without sin (that indeed was doctrinally clearly established in the orthodox creeds), but whether His mother had been born in a similarly immaculate state. The Sacromonte lead books provided very many texts to back up the "Franciscan" doctrine, hence the attraction they exercised over many of the faithful. There were, for example, in these texts such welcome statements as one allegedly uttered by Saint Peter himself to the effect that "Mary was not touched by sin" ("Lam darakaha al-dhanb al-awwal").[5] So these ancient local relics did not only flatter the vanity of local historians in Granada, but they also supplied proof texts that, if genuine, would make these books of absolutely primary theological importance throughout the Christian world. It is not going too far to say that the Sacromonte excavations claimed to yield up what appeared to amount to long-lost but vital supplementary scriptures.

To a certain extent, the books were a counterbalance to aspects of the canonical New Testament. In the Acts of the Apostles we have a Christianity that is Pauline, whereas in the Sacromonte texts what is striking is that Paul does not appear. Paul, of course, taught very clearly that the strict regulations concerning ritual purity and diet that Christianity had inherited from its Judaic, Semitic, past no longer applied. Among the aspects of Christian practice that distress Muslims is the fact that the formal regulation of ritual purity has been abandoned. (Jesus in the Gospels is very scathing when a Pharisee tells him he ought to have washed his hands before a meal.) Any move toward reintroducing concepts of ritual purity, etc., of disregarding Paul, would have pleased the Moriscos.

What perhaps strikes the modern reader of these texts most is the unambiguously Islamic impact of the credal statements to which reference has already been made: "There is no god but Allah and Jesus is the Spirit of Allah."

THE MUTE BOOK

All the books discovered were difficult to decipher and translate. An extreme example of the ambiguities inherent in this form of writing is that the same consonant outline, when unpointed (i.e., without *nuqat*), could represent either *b, t, th, n,* or *y.* The permutations of uncertainty in

---

5. For a photographic plate of this passage from British Library MS Harley 3507, see Kendrick (1960, plate 8b, facing page 77).

even a short word containing several such letters are immense. A number of translators were over the years called in to produce their versions of the Sacromonte texts. In addition to the books that were translated in this way, there still remained one book that resisted all their efforts. Its script and its language were even more impenetrable, and defeated all comers. For that reason, it came to be known as "the book that did not speak" (*El Libro Mudo*).[6] *Mudo* was by way of a nickname, of course, and its real title (known from references to it elsewhere) appears to have been *Kitab haqiqat al-injil* (Book of the Truth of the Gospel), a title rendered by some translators into Spanish as *Certificación del Evangelio*.[7] To the modern skeptic (and no doubt to the sixteenth- and seventeenth-century skeptic as well) this undeciphered text waiting in the background must appear as a sort of religious blank check, to be filled in when the occasion demanded by those who controlled the process of translation/interpretation.

THE MORISCOS AND THE LEAD BOOKS

If the texts contained what many Christians wanted to hear, what of the Moriscos? What was in the "lead books" for them? The Islamizing tendencies for which the Church eventually condemned the books were really obvious enough. "There is no god but Allah and Jesus is the Spirit of Allah" may be doctrinally unexceptionable from a Christian viewpoint, but a Muslim will find himself on familiar terrain with it, and welcome it positively: "Ruh Allah," "the Spirit of God" as an epithet of Jesus is present in the Koran. Jesus is never at any point in the Sacromonte texts described as "the son of God." In the book on the sacrifice of the Mass, no mention is made of communion wine—and so one might go on. The Sacromonte presented a Christianity purged of what was unacceptable to Muslims.

In addition, there are passages in which the excellence (*fadl*) of Arabs and of the Arabic language are praised, and at the end of days (eschatological elements abound) the Arabs have assigned to them a preeminent role. Thus not only does the pride and self-respect of the Christian church in Granada emerge enhanced after the discoveries, the Arabic speakers of the Kingdom of Granada could rejoice, too. From being ashamed of their language and culture, persecuted for it, at a stroke they found themselves courted precisely for their ability to read the hitherto banned language. To elucidate holy texts that explicitly spoke of their own high status was a profitable exercise from several points of view.

6. To translate this as "the Dumb Book," as is done by some, is surely not acceptable now that the colloquial American English sense of "dumb" ("stupid") has become so widespread as almost to have ousted the word's original English meaning, "mute."

7. Van Konigsveld et al. (1997, 249) have "essence."

It will have occurred to many readers to object that the expulsion of the rebellious Moriscos from Granada in 1570–71 ought to have left the city devoid of Muslim inhabitants. These Moriscos still available in 1588–95 to act as translators were members of a very small "collaborationist elite." Any study of the principal such personage, Alonso del Castillo, must take as a starting point the invaluable biography written by the late Father Dario Cabanelas Rodríguez (1965), *El morisco granadino Alonso del Castillo*. Castillo had, as we have seen in chapter 5, provided outstanding service to Philip II's forces in the Granadan War by translating intercepted dispatches and even forging documents and false prophecies to serve as black propaganda and sow confusion on the Muslim side. Here is an experienced specialist in propaganda and psychological warfare.

This scholar of Morisco origin had been called in to help catalog the Arabic manuscripts of the first collection that Philip II formed in the Escorial and so had direct contact with the monarch. He had also been employed to transcribe and translate the inscriptions on the walls of the Alhambra. He was into the bargain a medical man and well connected in every way. It is not surprising that he was one of the first of those from whom the archbishop of Granada sought advice on what were proving to be horrendously difficult texts to translate. There were many others employed subsequently as translators; some invited to attempt the task turned the invitation down. The archbishop, faced with what from the beginning seemed to promise great things, was anxious to secure cross-checks, to make sure that the books really did say the extraordinary things that Alonso del Castillo and the other early interpreters were reporting.

Was Alonso del Castillo the actual forger, as well as being the translator? Was the forger putting into Spanish what he had originally composed himself in Arabic? I am tempted to draw that conclusion, but until closer textual studies of the lead books can be made based on the Arabic originals—rather than the Latin and Spanish versions produced by contemporaries—investigation of the question of authorship must proceed with caution. One possibility that I will mention but take no further here is that we may have to deal with more than one forger and more than one point of view. The lead books were not all dug up at the same time. The discoveries on the Sacromonte were spaced out over a considerable lapse of time (February 1595 to December 1599). Some books were found with very few witnesses present at the time. On May 11, 1599, for example, two brothers, Domingo and Bartolomé de Villa, came across two "books" in a spoil heap of waste from previous digs. That sounds very suspicious. It is obvious that anyone wishing to slip in an additional text to his own liking would not have found it difficult to do so.

THE EVIDENCE OF AL-HAJARI

In the history of the study of these lead books it has not hitherto been possible to know how the Moriscos themselves viewed this whole matter. It is extremely fortunate for our present purposes that in 1997 a largely autobiographical work by a man born as a Morisco (although he made his career in North Africa) was edited in Arabic with an accompanying English translation by Koningsveld et al. (1997).[8] The Morisco-born author of this work went under a number of names: Ahmad Ibn Qasim (Bejarano) al-Hajari by no means is an exhaustive list. I had first became aware of him as a Morisco scholar—although not of what he had to say about the Sacromonte texts—as long ago as 1959 when publishing extracts from a treatise on gunnery written by another Morisco refugee in North Africa (Harvey 1959). Until Razouq and then van Koningsveld et al. produced their editions I could make no further progress.

For our immediate purposes, it is of great interest that the *Kitab Nasir al-din* tells us how the archbishop of Granada attempted to recruit the Morisco al-Hajari to work on the lead books for him. Al-Hajari's account of his interview with the archbishop permits us to see for the first time what was happening in Granada in 1595 through the eyes of a Spanish crypto-Muslim and to appreciate how sudden and how complete was the switch in Christian attitudes toward the Moriscos themselves and toward their Arabic language after the discoveries had been made. One moment literacy in Arabic was knowledge to be hidden from the Christian authorities at all costs, the next to read Arabic well became a valued and sought-after accomplishment. I will therefore quote extensively from the relevant sections of the *Kitab Nasir al-din*. For the translation that appears, here I rely on van Koningsveld et al. (1997, 68–91), but I have felt free to make some minor changes and to dispense with a few of their annotations, so as to keep the focus in the present context on Sacromonte material. What al-Hajari tells his readers is not to be accepted uncritically, of course. He is, among other things, attempting an apologia for his own actions, defending himself, now that he was living in Tunisia once more, against possible accusations coming from his fellow-Muslims of direct collaboration with the Christian enemy.

In 1595, so al-Hajari tells us, he had been living in Granada in the house of one of the well-connected elite community of Moriscos allowed to remain in that city. He was clearly not the only Morisco to have returned to the city. We find him having dealings with other "illegal immigrants" (they are even more anxious than he is to avoid calling attention

---

8. Of the Arabic text alone there is a serviceable first edition by Muhammad Razouq, ed. (Casablanca 1987).

to themselves). The passage on which I wish to focus finds him in the company of one Muhammad Ibn Abi'l- 'Asi (a member of a very distinguished Granadan family). Muhammad was actually giving an Arabic lesson to a priest in the archbishop's entourage, and this was taking the form of reading aloud in Arabic from a printed book. The priest receiving instruction is named as "Maldonado." Since Carlos Alonso (1979, 22) tells us that Diego de Maldonado, abbot of Santa Fe, had, in 1588, a role in arranging for the inspection by the cathedral authorities of the Torre Turpiana discoveries, that makes it highly probable that the Maldonado who was taking an Arabic lesson in 1595 was the abbot.

> I was in their company, but I had not revealed to the Christian that I could read Arabic, because of the sentence of punishment which they usually passed upon those who appeared to do so. While he was reading the book there was hesitation at the correct reading of some words. So I said to them: "Maybe it means this!" They found that this was true. Thereupon the priest looked at me and said, "You know how to read Arabic? Do not be afraid [to admit it], because the archbishop is looking for someone who knows something of reading Arabic, so that he may explain something written in that language that has come to light."
>
> He took me to his house. He had books of every art and language. He brought me books in the Arabic language. I read and translated for him some words which he was unable to read. Then he met me another day and told me: "The archbishop has ordered me to bring you with me to his presence." I said to myself, "How shall I save myself, as the Christians kill and burn everyone on whom they find an Arabic book or of whom they know that he reads Arabic?" (al-Hajari 1987, 72–73)

[Al-Hajari here realized he had a problem. Whereas the senior Morisco interpreters who had already been engaged to work on the project could account for their command of the suspect language (there was no reason why men of their age should not have learnt their Arabic in the old days), he, as a young man, might have some awkward explaining to do. And, of course, the danger was not only for him personally, but for his teacher, whom he must at all costs not betray.]

> "What shall I say when he asks me about my teacher?" On the way the priest said to me: "Tell the great master that the interpreters do not know anything." [I.e., tell him the existing translators were not up to their task.] I said to myself: "I shall tell him exactly the opposite, because anyone who puts forward false claims will certainly be put to shame."
>
> When we had entered into his [i.e., the archbishop's] presence, he approached us, and said to me: "Father Maldonado has told me that you

can read Arabic very well." I answered: "I am not well versed in it!" He said: "Where did you learn [this]?" I answered: "You should know, my lord, that I am an Andalusian ... " (73)

[The Arabic term here is "andalusi," which does not, of course, only signify "from Andalucía" but also more generally "from al-Andalus." What al-Hajari means is that he is a Spanish Arab. He continues]

...I am an Andalusian from al-Hajar al-Ahmar.[9] Our spoken language there is in fact Arabic. Then I [also] learnt to read Spanish. Later on I went to Madrid—the residence of the Sultan[10] where I found an Andalusian man, a medical doctor, from the country [region] of Valencia.

Al-Hajari here is interrogated about his Arabic teacher and invents what sounds like a cock-and-bull story, no doubt intended to obscure the identity of the real man.

... Everything I told him as an answer to his question about the physician from the country of Valencia was a lie. But [I did this] because the reading of Arabic [books] which had no connection with the Islamic religion was permitted to the inhabitants of Valencia, whereas this was forbidden to the other people of the country of Al-Andalus. Thus I protected myself from their evil by lying. This is an acceptable thing to do, as can be established by the words of al-Ghazzali—may God allow us to profit from his scholarship—who has said in his book *Al-Ihya,* "If an upright man crosses your path who is followed by an evil person looking for him, who asks about him to hurt him, you should tell him: "He went in that direction," viz. the direction opposite to the one he actually took..... Lying in such a case is permitted, nay even recommendable, even though the giving of right guidance is obligatory [in principle]. Thus it appeared to me that who is wont to speak truthfully, his words will be accepted even though he is sometimes forced to lie in a situation in which lying is permitted.

The archbishop then ordered the parchment to be brought forward. He was extremely pleased with my translation, for he knew it was truthful. He gave me 300 riyal (reales), as well as a letter granting me a license to translate from Arabic into Spanish and vice versa. The news spread among the Christians, until they pointed at me saying, "There is the man who understood the parchment which was found in the tower, while already some ten years have already passed since it was found!" Thus the archbishop ordered me to write down a copy of the parchment and sent it to the pope in the City of Rome. (72–76)

9. Van Koningsveld et al. (1997, 18ff) discuss their identification of this place as Hornachos.

10. I might prefer simply to translate this as "King."

[Al-Hajari devotes considerable space to the contents of the 1588 parchment, then tells us of an encounter he had with certain Arabic-speaking people from his hometown who had come to Granada on a visit. He went to call on them.]

After greeting them in the customary way, I opened the book. But when they saw that it was written in Arabic they became extremely afraid because of the Christians. I told them: "Do not be afraid. The Christians honor me and respect me for my ability to read Arabic." But all the people from my town thought that the Christian Inquisitors who used to sentence and burn to death everyone who manifested his adherence to Islam in any way, or was reading the books of the Muslims, would condemn me as well. Driven by this extreme fear, the Andalusians used to be afraid of each other. They only spoke about religious matters with someone who was "safe," that is, someone who could be trusted completely. Many of them were afraid of one another. Some of them, who would have loved to learn something of the religion of God, did not [even] find anyone to teach them. After I had decided to emigrate from that country to the country of the Muslims, I used to teach every Andalusian who wanted to learn, both in my own town and in the other towns I visited. Thus, when the Andalusians saw in what situation I found myself, they used to say to each other: "He will certainly fall into the hands of the Inquisitors!" This situation developed to such an extent that when I stopped by a group [of them] to have a talk, I saw that every one of them slunk away, until I was left completely on my own.... (81)

[Al-Hajari then passes on from the 1588 discovery to write about the discoveries of 1595 and after (i.e., about the lead tablets). He names the place where the finds were made as "Khandaq al-Janna." This Arabic place name corresponds to what we find in the Spanish sources: Valparaiso.]

As for the books found in the cave in *Khandaq al-Janna,* they were 122 in all. Their leaves were, as I said before, of *asrab.*[11] One of the books was called *Book of the Maxims of Saint Mary.* It was transcribed from the copy of the *faqih* al-Ukayhil, the Andalusian interpreter.... It was said that there were 101 maxims in the book. The precise wording of the third maxim was as follows: "After the Spirit of God, Jesus, a light from God will come to the world whose name shall be the Obliterator, the Brilliant One (and in the foreign language the Paraclete), the Seal of the Messengers who [comes in] confirmation [of them], the Seal of Religion, the Light of

---

11. That is, lead. The term "lead books," "libros plúmbeos," etc., frequently occurs in the Christian sources. The word here vocalized by van Koningsveld as "asrab" is an unusual one, the more common term being *rassas.*

the Prophets. Apart from this there will be no light for them, nor for any one of the inhabitants of the universe. Those who will be truly enlightened by the clear illumination which comes from God [only]. But whoever does not believe in him will not have a share in Paradise. But surely most of the people are unbelievers!" The pious mystic and religious leader, the *faqih* Muhammad Ibn ʿabd al-Rafiʿ al-Andalusi said to me in Tunis— may God preserve it—"The maxim quoted contains seven of the names of the Prophet—may God bless him and grant him peace! These are 1) Light from God, 2) the Obliterator 3) the Brilliant One, 4) the Paraclete,[12] 5) the Seal of the Messengers, 6) the Seal of Religion, [and] 7) the Light of the Prophets...." (83)

As for the book of which good tidings are hoped, in accordance with the statement to be found in the *Book of the Gifts of Reward* by Saint Mary— peace be upon her!—which will be dealt with, God willing, at the end of my present book, where she said: "The people will adhere to one religion only," this is the writing entitled *The Essence*[13] *of the Gospel,* consisting of seven leaves of lead, and written in a kind of letters which are unknown in our time. All the kinds of alphabet circulating nowadays among the inhabitants of the world were brought to the archbishop, but the letters used in the book differed from all of these. The translators used to call it the *Dumb Book,*[14] as nobody had been able to decipher it. At the beginning there was the seal of Solomon—peace be upon him—with an Arabic legend. But apart from the seal the text was written in a script which will not be read until the end of time in the island of al-S.b.r. in the Small Sea, east of Venice.[15] .... I said to the archbishop: "I would like to read the book which has not yet been deciphered entitled *The Essence of the Gospel.* Perhaps I will be able to figure out something of it." He answered, "The time has not yet come for this book to be deciphered." He knew this from the book entitled *Book of the Gifts of Reward* by Saint Mary.

12. This assertion by the Morisco author will be puzzling to readers both Christian and Muslim alike. Obviously in Christian theology "Paraclete" is a Greek term, "the Advocate," and is the third member of the Trinity, not an alternative epithet of the Prophet Muhammad. However, what al-Hajari must have in mind is that some (most?) Muslim theologians regard "Parakletos" as the result of the textual corruption (*tahrif*) of an original, "periklytos," interpreted by them as a reference to Muhammad (= "praised"). The New Testament text is thus regarded as foretelling or foreshadowing the coming of the Prophet of Islam.

13. Rather than "Essence," which is the choice of the Dutch translators, here and throughout this text, I might prefer "Truth"—the Arabic is *Haqiqa*.

14. See 275 n. 6 above.

15. A footnote by van Koningsveld appears here: "The meaning of this sentence remains obscure."

Of this work I found in Tunis—may God preserve it—a copy in Arabic and another one in Spanish. An Andalusian who used to translate brought these two copies, but I found in the Spanish [copy] nonsense and lies not to be found in the Arabic version. (85–87)

At this point, van Koningsveld informs us that "the author blotted out the following 16 lines of his text, which have thus become illegible." This appears to suggest that the Leiden scholars think their base text derived from a holograph. That seems to me not proven. We do not, incidentally, have the Spanish text to which reference is made, but in the British Library (Harley 7507) there exists a completely independent transcription of the book. This particular London manuscript was the work of Bartolomeus a Pectorano, one of the translators employed in Italy on the texts when they were under study in Rome. A complete edition of the London manuscript will be found in the appendix to Harvey (1956). In a great number of places where the copyist in Tunis, whoever he was, had to mark "blank in the manuscript," the scholar working in Rome records a plausible reading. For my translation of key sections of this British Library manuscript, see appendix 3.

This chapter of al-Hajari's book closes with a fascinating account of how he took his leave from the archbishop.

When I wished to go to the city of Seville to leave the country of the Muslims, I went to the priest[16] and told him: "I am planning to go to my town. My father wrote to me to come to him, and it is obligatory to obey one's parents." He answered: "In some matters this is obligatory, but in others it is not." I said: "I really must go." So I asked him to support the Andalusians because they were held in contempt among the old Christians. He told me: "You should know that I am at their side, always. They rose up against the Sultan while I was chief judge in the city. Then the brother of the Sultan[17] came, and he took 140 men from among the notable Andalusians and killed them. All this to take their properties. But he should have left them alone because they were not among those who revolted. Rich and prosperous people are only well off when tranquility prevails among them, so that they can enjoy their possessions, in contrast to others. But you, Andalusians, follow a discreditable custom!" I asked him: "And what is that?" He said: "You always stick together. You do not give your daughters to the old Christians, and you do not marry women from among the

16. We might hesitate whether he means Maldonado or Vaca de Castro, but the reference below to the priest's service as "chief judge" in Granada makes it probable that Vaca de Castro is meant.

17. John of Austria.

old Christians." I told him: "Why should we marry women from among the old Christians? In the city of Antequera there was a man from my family who had fallen in love with a Christian girl. On the day they went to church with the bride in order to conclude the marriage, the bridegroom had to wear a coat of mail under his clothes and to take with him a sword because her family had sworn they would kill him on the road. Even years after he had married her, none of her family had visited her, but [still] wished [to see] him and her dead! Marriage is not meant for man to make enemies, but friends and family!" We said goodbye, wishing each other well, and I went away. What I told him about the Andalusian and the Christian woman was correct. She [in fact] converted to Islam with His help. She became an excellent Muslim; with her help her mother, an old woman, converted to Islam as well! (90–91)

Al-Hajari's attitude toward the lead books is, it should be noted, to accept them as genuine. That must have been the attitude of many of the Muslims of Andalusi origin he came across in Tunis, especially of those who owned the copies from which he in turn transcribed. What are we to make of the portrait of the archbishop of Granada that he gives us in the *Kitab Nasir al-din?* Kendrick (1960: 73), writing before the *Kitab Nasir al-din* became available, quoted Richard Ford's characterization of the archbishop as a "relico-monomaniac whose hobby was holy bones." There was obviously more to him than just that. Was al-Hajari exaggerating the closeness of his own contacts with the prelate in order to make himself sound important? It seems unlikely that he would choose to do so, for he must have been aware that the story he told was quite likely to get him into trouble with his coreligionists in North Africa. If al-Hajari's report of the archbishop's final words is to be regarded as basically reliable, and that is the view I myself take, then Castro comes across as a man sincerely committed to a patient policy of eventual assimilation through intermarriage, and I am not aware that this side of the archbishop has been remarked upon before.

The subject of marriages may appear to be introduced into al-Hajari's account of this conversation illogically, it seems to come almost out of the blue, as it were, but it is possible to spot the association of ideas in the archbishop's mind. The whole Sacromonte affair was about the ultimate feasibility of a real and permanent merging of the two communities. Could the two religious systems find a common frame of reference (perhaps common scriptural ground) was the underlying theme of the lead books. But in daily life the one acid test of good and mutually satisfactory community relations would be intermarriage. Would it be acceptable to Muslims? Could there ever be true reciprocity? The archbishop was quite right to raise this particular question. Without some intermarriages in the longer run the communities would never merge. But equally al-Hajari was quite right to give the honestly negative reply, which he did.

What of the archbishop's attitude toward the lead books themselves? Was he taken in by them, as al-Hajari clearly was? Or was he aware of their nature, was he even, in some way, promoting, stage-managing, the imposture? (That he financed the digs and facilitated the process of authentication is beyond doubt, but that is not the same thing as convicting him of active forgery.) Was the archbishop a manipulator or was he being manipulated? To suggest that he might have been a promoter of the cause and not its passive victim is not necessarily to impute to him base motives. The human mind is at times adept at persuading itself that what ought to be true is.

It is hard enough to penetrate the mental processes of the archbishop, even though a great deal of evidence survives from a number of sources. To do the same with al-Hajari's mind is harder, for our sources are fewer, and they are largely restricted to his own writings. To understand his attitudes, indeed to understand Morisco attitudes toward the Christian scriptures in general, it is necessary to look briefly at a technical point of Islamic doctrine from which Christians usually shy away: the doctrine of *tahrif.*

TAHRIF

Tahrif relates to the status of the Christian scriptures. It means literally "alteration," especially "changing the text." Christians who are hostile to Islam tend to impute unworthy motives to the Prophet Muhammad, and medieval polemicists regularly present Muhammad as an imposter or as someone suffering from some mental or moral aberration or physical affliction. Medieval polemical writings were full of such attacks. Christians who are well disposed toward Islam, on the other hand, stress the toleration toward Christianity that is built into Islamic law. The focus in interfaith discussions is thus on the Prophets rather than on the actual text of the scriptures. The attitude of Muslims, not toward Christian people, but toward the Christian scriptures, those present in the hands of Christians, is a subject that is usually avoided. Probably because it is hurtful. Muslims revere the founder of Christianity, the virgin mother, and also His Gospel, in the Koran referred to as *al-injil* (*evangelion*). But the *injil* to which Muslims refer is the Gospel as *originally* revealed, perfect and uncontaminated. The Gospel that Christians actually possess is *not,* in Muslim eyes, that perfect Gospel (any more than the Jews' scriptures are the uncontaminated original Torah). What has taken place, in the view of Islamic theologians, is a process of corruption (*tahrif*) of the original message, and this is how *Muslims* explain the presence in the Christian scriptures of those Christian doctrines that are unacceptable to Muslims, such as the mention of Jesus as the son of God. *Tahrif* (which may variously be held to be corruption of the actual text, or the twisting of the meaning of the text), explains how it is possible for Muslims to respect the religion of the peoples of the book in theory, while disagreeing with many Jewish and Christian doctrines and practices.

AL-HAJARI AND *TAHRIF*

Al-Hajari refers to this doctrinal point toward the very end of the *Kitab Nasir al-din 'ala'l-qawm al-kafirin* in a passage where he has been dealing with the Sacromonte texts:

> I say: the statements of the *Book of the Gifts of Reward* about the Essence of the Gospel are apparently *contradictory to the Gospel they possess nowadays*, and to the unbelief and to the trinitarian doctrine of the Christians. But it is in harmony with [...] the noble Quran. (261, emphasis added)

What recommends the Sacromonte text to al-Hajari is that he recognizes it as being in harmony with the Koran. Al-Hajari seems to have been much more perspicacious than many of the Christian theologians in Granada at the time: they had failed to grasp the importance of the way these texts diverged over some doctrines from the Christian Bible but coincided with the Koran.

THE LONG-TERM OBJECTIVE OF THE FORGERIES

We know that these apocryphal texts were taken very seriously in Granada at the end of the sixteenth century. What might have been the next stage, had they been fully admitted into the scriptural canon of the Church and not just approved by a local synod in Granada (convened by the archbishop in the teeth of papal disapproval), is mere speculation. Only fourteen years were to pass between the 1595 discoveries and the Expulsion. If the lead books had had a longer period in which to operate, one may wonder whether the outcome in the long run would have been that more Muslim people like al-Hajari, after being attracted to texts that said things with which they could agree, would subsequently be attracted to mainline Catholic Christianity itself. Or would the opposite have taken place, and would those people who were Muslims at heart (the Moriscos) who "entered" the Church, bringing with them these new apocryphal scriptures, have succeeded in changing ("reforming" or "subverting," according to one's point of view) the institution they had "entered"? Would Islam or Christianity have benefited? We can only speculate.

It is far more likely, of course, that the two originally conflicting religious groups would have continued locked into endless internecine doctrinal disputations. There are, after all, plenty of other cases in the world of insoluble deadlock maintained against all the dictates of common sense. Our central problem as we seek to understand the Sacromonte affair is this: was this as originally conceived a subterfuge thought up by Christians who were anxious to present their message in a guise acceptable to Muslims; or was it quite the opposite: a subterfuge thought up by Muslims seeking to penetrate Christianity and change it from within? Who was the duper and who the duped?

The subterfuge was certainly not the creation of the central agencies of the Church such as the Holy Office, for as soon as Rome heard of what was going on, it took cautious steps to halt the advance of the heresy. That is clear from the reports of the papal nuncio. (Although he proceeded with deliberation, he was not deceived.) Few Christians would have had necessary expert knowledge of Islamic susceptibilities to fabricate the Sacromonte forgeries. On balance, it seems more likely that this was, at its inception, in some sense a Morisco enterprise, the enterprise of a minority, a Morisco minority. Further research is certainly needed on the subject.

What might possibly settle the question regarding objectives would be an analysis of the so-called *Mute Book*. Was its eventual decoding and interpretation intended to bring Christians into the Islamic faith or Muslims into the Christian fold? In which direction did it face? One can hardly believe that this textual witness would continue to keep mute and refuse to testify, if subjected to the *peine forte et dure* of modern cryptographical analysis. Until recently it has been under lock and key in the archives of the Holy Office, whither it would have been consigned when the lead books were anathematized in 1682. The recent exhibition in the cathedral in Granada would seem to point toward the possibility of more material coming into the public domain. If the *Mute Book* were to emerge into the light of day, then there is a major research task to be undertaken.

The Arabic text of the *Kitab Nasir al-din* edited by van Koningsveld et al. (1997) has a final section stating that the Blessed Virgin Mary herself copied out the text of the book entitled *The Truth of the Gospel* (they opt to translate *Haqiqa* as "Essence," as noted above), and sent it to Saint. James and his disciples (i.e., to Spain):

The leaves of the *Book of the Truth of Religion* were thicker than those of the other books, as thick as a large *real* coin, and [possibly] thicker. It contained the secret of all the books, because after it had been read, *the people would follow one religion.* End. (194, emphasis added)

Whatever the contents of the *Mute Book* turn out to be, these Sacromonte texts, because they are beyond doubt the last works written in the Iberian Peninsula in the Arabic language, do not deserve to be ignored in the way that they have been. In one way or another, Moriscos must have had some hand in their creation, and it would be surprising if the books did not yield up yet more information after further study.

THE GOSPEL OF BARNABAS AS A MORISCO TEXT

We must now turn briefly to a work that, although in the period after its creation in the sixteenth and seventeenth centuries went virtually unnoticed by the world at large (there were just a few isolated early references by Western scholars, among whom one might mention the Dutch scholar Adrian Reland and George Sale in London in the eighteenth century), it has, in the twentieth century, probably achieved wider dissemination than any other originating from a late Morisco background, and that not only in the West, but especially in the Islamic world. It is indeed the only book to come out of this Morisco milieu to attract a large Muslim readership in modern times. I refer to *The Gospel of Barnabas,* which I will cite with that English title, not least because its twentieth-century success undoubtedly stemmed from the Oxford (Clarendon Press) edition brought out by L. and L. Ragg in 1907 under that English title. Besides their edition, based primarily on an Italian text of the Gospel itself (the only early text available to them at that time), the Raggs provided an English translation. This became the basis of further translations: into Urdu, Persian, Turkish, and Arabic, and it was in this way that *Barnabas* began to be widely known in the Islamic world in the course of the century. (Presumably its success owed something to the doctrine of *tahrif.* If one believes that the Christian scriptures are textually corrupt, and then one is confronted with what appears to be an alternative piece of Christian scripture, outside the orthodox Christian canon, in which are articulated some—not all—of the things that Muslims feel should be in a genuine gospel, then one might well be tempted to welcome the new text.)

The entirely unsuccessful attempts that I myself made in the 1950s to trace the Spanish version (which I assumed, and still assume, to have been its original language) were sparked off by the mention of it in the introduction to Sale's translation of the Koran (London, 1734; viii). Sale told his readers that in his day it was in the possession of the "rector of Hedley in Hampshire." I attempted to pick up its trail in Hampshire and got nowhere. In 1976, however, a Spanish text resurfaced in Sydney, Australia (see Fletcher [1976]). Scholars in general are still far from seeing eye to eye on the *Barnabas*, but following Epalza (1963, 1982), there is emerging among many specialists in the study of the Moriscos a view that a Morisco hand may be discerned to be at work. Of course, scholars in other specialist fields may take a different view.

To pursue this complex question in detail might take us well outside the confines of Morisco studies and require an examination of its possible "pre-Morisco" aspects—whether the Barnabas text that turned up in the sixteenth or possibly the seventeenth century in the form in which it is available to us today has a prehistory. Does it in some way, however imperfectly, preserve ancient anti-Pauline Judeo-Christian teachings? Readers would do well to refer to the bibliographical surveys of the literature provided by Epalza and by his Alicante colleague L. F. Bernabé Pons for such "pre-Morisco" aspects of the subject (and for its "post-Morisco"[18] aspects as well). As the title of Wiegers (1995), "Muhammad as the Messiah: A Comparison of the Polemical Works of Juan Alonso with the Gospel of Barnabas," indicates, one of the strangest and most puzzling features of this family of polemical writings is their presentation of the Prophet Muhammad as the Messiah. That is in flat contradiction, of course, with what the Koran itself tells us. The idea is also at variance with the bulk of Morisco literature as described above in chapter 5 (totally orthodox in this as in so many other ways). Significantly in the present context, the idea that Muhammad is the Messiah is also at variance with the Sacromonte "lead books," in which Jesus, not Muhammad, is the Messiah (*masih*). *The Gospel of Barnabas* disagrees with the lead books in a number of other particulars, too, as for example in that it omits John the Baptist from the narrative of the life of Jesus, whereas John is present in the Sacromonte *Acts of Jesus and Mary*—"Chapter of His baptism in the River Jordan."

What then is this idiosyncratic *Gospel of Barnabas?* I would not disagree with Bernabé (1998, 23) when he characterizes the *Gospel of Barnabas,* in the form that has reached us, as claiming to be, not "the Gospel (*injil*) that God sent down to Jesus according to the Koran (and according to the *Gospel of Barnabas* itself). That gospel has been totally lost, and in textual reality the Koran has taken its place." What the *Gospel*

18. By that I mean the uses made of it in later Islamic polemical writings, first in North Africa, and more recently in worldwide Islamic missionary publications.

of Barnabas claims to be is at least "a witness both to the true teachings of Jesus" and "confirmation that the canonical Christian scriptures have undergone alterations."

In spite of the very different interpretation of the Messiah in the two sets of texts, the lead books and *Barnabas,* Bernabé sees a link between them. The Sacromonte initiative, he suggests, failed, and *Barnabas* is the next Morisco attempt to carry the ideological campaign further. Those are my interpretation of his words. What Bernabé actually says is:

> [The *Gospel of Barnabas* was] the last fruit of a secret and ambitious long-term plan that was drawn up and set in motion from Granada. A group of highly educated Moriscos conceived a strategy that, taking advantage of unusual circumstances, set about infiltrating into Christian society texts couched in ambiguous language that were intended to deliver the Arab people and the Arabic language (and by extension, the Hispanic Morisco community) from the extreme depths of intolerance and contempt to which they had been condemned by the mentality of their rulers. They started with what we may term "kite-flying" exercises (the *Verdadera Historia* of Miguel de Luna, or the parchment in the Turpian Tower), which permitted them to calculate with precision what effect these texts might produce on society, and they then went on, still sheltering with delicate prudence behind the story of the discoveries, to launch (or more exactly in this case, to bury) one text in succession after another. . . . As more and more lead books appeared, with the various relevant commentaries, these Granadan Moriscos must have gone further and further ahead with their plan to launch texts with ever more ambitious objectives, and finally they reached the "Truth or Verification of the Gospel" as spoken of by the Blessed Virgin Mary. But perhaps from the reaction which this evoked, they must have drawn two conclusions that they bore in mind in planning their final text, their last coup. In the first place, [they concluded] that there was no point, after all the hostile comments that had been evoked in Spain and the skepticism of learned circles elsewhere in Europe, in persisting with yet another book attributed to Saint James. In the second place, [they saw that] there was in the New Testament someone else who could be inserted to play the role that had been occupied by Saint James. What is more, someone to whom an ancient ecclesiastical decree had attributed an apocryphal gospel that bore his name: Saint Barnabas of Cyprus. (Bernabé 1995, 250–51)

Bernabé presents those ideas as a hypothesis. I do not share his view of the final stages of the Sacromonte cult, and so I do not go all the way with him on the *Gospel of Barnabas* itself either. On the Christian side, I think we can detect little falling away of general Marian enthusiasm or of specific support for the Sacromonte texts, right up to the time of the Expulsion and beyond. For example, in 1609, that fateful year, a royal commission on which there served, among others, the Inquisitor-General Cardinal Bernardo de Rojas y Sandoval, Juan de Velasco, constable of Castile, not to mention Luis de Aliaga, the king's confessor, met seven times, heard the archbishop Pedro Vaca de Castro state his case and found in favor of the relics. On the books the report was more guarded ("they did not seem to contain anything contrary to the faith"), and it called for yet more work on translations. One might indeed see this as in a way a tactful beginning of the end for the Sacromonte cult, for the pieces of lead were now being made subject to critical judgments passed outside Granada, and so, once deprived of enthusiastic local support, they were likely eventually to be rejected or at least downgraded. But since this commission did not make any recommendation *against* the king assuming the role of patron of the Sacromonte, the cause continued well protected and was still very much alive. Among the Moriscos both in Granada itself and also in exile, support cannot have faded altogether either, and of this Bernabé is aware. As he mentions, al-Hajari returning from the pilgrimage found in Tunis a group of Moriscos, pious Muslims like him, but men still devoted to the cause of the Sacromonte texts.

The Sacromonte forgeries were launched on the world well before the Expulsion, and we can be reasonably confident that the process of their elaboration took place *inside* the Granadan crypto-Muslim community. About the *Gospel of Barnabas,* doubts still abound, and as Bernabé suggests, in one of the alternative hypotheses he presents, the *Gospel* may have assumed its present form *outside* Spain. Whichever explanation we opt for, that *Gospel* is still evidence of the enormous ideological pressures to which this Morisco community was being subjected. And together with the Sacromonte lead books, it demonstrates the ingenuity (ingenuity more than wisdom), determination, and persistence with which the Morisco intelligentsia continued stubbornly to fight back, even when anyone conducting a realistic assessment of the probable outcome of their ideological campaign might have concluded that the cause was already lost, that the last vestiges of Islam would soon disappear from the Iberian Peninsula.

NINE ⚜ Expulsion

THE SEEDS OF THE POLICY OF EXPULSION

When we look for the beginnings of the policy of systematically expelling all Muslims from Spain, how far back should we search? Some might say, some did say, that we should look as far back as the Arab/Muslim Conquest itself. In this view, expulsion would be regarded as the final stage of the long process of reversing the invasion of 711: what in Spanish is generally known at the *Reconquista*. That is what a reading of the Spanish literature of the fifteenth and sixteenth centuries might suggest. The theme of the original "destruction of Spain" (*destruicción* [sic] *de España*), as brought about by the Muslim invasion (an invasion allegedly facilitated by the treason of one Count Julian who, in pursuit of a feud of his own, encouraged the national enemy to cross over from Africa), is endlessly restated with variations by authors at every level of sophistication, from the anonymous creators of Spain's popular ballads to the most erudite of poets. Such writings, and earlier ones from the medieval period, bear witness to an ideology of manifest national destiny. The Islamic conquest, by this view, was an aberration that had needed one day to be corrected. And then, when the Reconquest, completed in 1492, proved unsatisfactory to the victors, left as they were still with the insoluble problem of an insubordinate minority, thoughts turned to the Expulsion. The intention was to bring the peninsula back to the status quo ante, to how things were before 711.

It may help to bring some sense of perspective to our thoughts here if we reflect that if after nine hundred years (1611 − 711 = 900), it was justifiable still to regard the *Moros*/Moriscos as interlopers in the Iberian Peninsula and to throw them out, then a similar drive to put back the clock of history might with greater force be advocated in very many other parts of the globe. The European conquest of the Americas is in some areas separated from our present day by a mere one-third of the chronological gap that stretched between the Spain of the Expulsion and the Arab conquest. Yet the Americas as we know them are felt as a firm fait accompli of history, an omelet that nobody ever expects to see unscrambled. Nobody imagines America's white and black inhabitants will one day be eliminated in favor of the peoples of the First Nations.

And when did the Reconquest of the Iberian Peninsula begin? In the eighth century already, as patriotic Spanish legend would have it, or did the process really get under way in the eleventh century, in the period of Alfonso VI and of Rodrigo de Bivar, the Cid? That was when profound Christian penetration into Muslim territory was first achieved, and when the push southward began in earnest. However, the policy of those early conquistadors toward their Muslim adversaries was not to expel them all from the peninsula. Reconquest did not in its earlier phases imply systematic ethnic cleansing (although it was often accompanied by some movement of populations). The *Poema de Mio Cid,* that we may take as the articulation of ideas current when it was created in the twelfth century, certainly did not envisage that the conquered Muslims would be driven out. The great Christian national hero, the Cid, is represented in that epic as allowing conquered Moors to remain in occupation of their lands, either with him as their lord, or else under some form of tributary relationship. The historical record shows us that in such early days, although vanquished Muslims might well be expected to vacate their homes, might be driven off their lands, even enslaved (where, for example, they had in the judgment of the victor failed to surrender in time after being invited to do so), they were not driven out of Spain or Portugal altogether.

Throughout the Middle Ages, Reconquest was a distant objective toward which some looked forward, the ultimate triumph of Christianity. What precisely would happen then to defeated Muslims was not specified. Perhaps this was because the prospect was, even for those who were optimistic, felt as very far in the future. Even when in the later fifteenth century it did begin to look as if final and total victory might soon be achieved, a poet like Juan de Mena, whose great epic poem *El laberinto de Fortuna* takes as its overarching theme the need to complete the Reconquest, spares no thought for what would happen if conquered Muslims wanted to stay but did not want to become Christians. One can only presume that there was an unspoken supposition lodged in the minds of Christians that the Iberian Peninsula would somehow eventually revert to being what it had once been, an entirely Christian land; that Islam would conveniently disappear. And so when Islam did not disappear, even after the victory of 1492, Spain's rulers, secular and ecclesiastic, were at a loss. The long-term military aim, Reconquest, had at last been achieved, the battles had been won, the land had been occupied. There then followed the botched conversions described in this volume. The country was made Christian at last: nominally Christian at least. Yet everybody knew that Moors were still Moors. That phrase cited so often before comes back again: *Tan moros como los de Argel.*

To the modern mind, the obvious conclusion to draw at this point would be to acknowledge the failure of the ill-conceived policy of forcible conversion and simply to accept Muslims as fellow subjects. That would not have been a leap into the unknown, it would simply have been a return to the familiar medieval model of Mudejarism, to a regime under which Muslim subjects were accepted as subjects of a Christian monarch. Yet that course of action does not seem to have been considered in council at all. The alternatives that were considered were either intensifying the program of evangelization so as to make conversion to Christianity a reality (i.e., just trying harder); or ending the perceived anomaly created by the existence of thousands of false Christians within Spanish society by getting rid of them (in which case, how?). On the whole, the advocates of persisting with the process of conversion were to be found among the clergy, while those who called for radical surgery and amputation of the offending member were those preoccupied by military and strategic considerations. But as we have seen, there were many cross-currents. The resentment felt by poor and landless Christians obliged to compete economically with hard-working Muslim neighbors at the bottom of the social scale might lead them to want to get rid of their rivals, whereas some members of the Christian aristocracy might fear that the departure of their Morisco cultivators would spell ruin for the rural economy, and so they wanted to keep them.

If Christian Spaniards were no longer willing to share their state with Muslims, why, we must inevitably wonder, did they not simply allow such unwelcome neighbors to leave, to go away to live as Muslims elsewhere? That briefly had been the policy when the Granadans were first forcibly converted in the early years of the sixteenth century. It had run up against two types of objection, one strategic and the other theological, and so had been abandoned. In strategic terms it was argued that one should avoid strengthening the Islamic countries by presenting them with extra population (with people, moreover, who would take with them Spain's secrets). As for the theological arguments, they were complex, but they centered on the impossibility of allowing the Moriscos to leave with their children.

It will be recalled that the expulsion of Jews and Muslims from Portugal at the close of the previous century (see chapter 1) had served as a testbed for the policy of expulsion. Although the Muslims of Portugal had in the end been allowed to leave with their children; it had only been fear of reprisals (on Christians in Muslim lands) that had led the Portuguese to agree that Muslim families would not be broken up. (Jews, unable to carry out reprisals, were made to suffer in this way.) Now, toward the end of the sixteenth century and at the beginning of the seventeenth, such considerations weighed less heavily. The strategic balance in the world had shifted. Christendom no longer felt so exposed to retribution from the Islamic world. Expulsion might be a feasible option.

It would be quite wrong to imagine that Christian opinion in Spain on the question of the Expulsion was unanimous. Until the end there were those who argued against such a policy, not usually on grounds of natural justice, certainly not of religious freedom, but usually because it was hoped that true conversion could still be achieved in one way or another. Christian duty required one to try again; to be persistent. What is probably an early example of this point of view is stated in a document in the archive of the Colegio de Corpus Cristi, Valencia (Boronat 1901, 2: 493–99). This argues that the attempts at securing the conversion of these people had failed because of the unsatisfactory methods adopted and because of the incompetence of those charged with the task (2: 495). The task might be difficult, very difficult, for the Moriscos were more stubborn than the Moors in Barbary, but it was not impossible. The false converts had become hardened by all their sacrileges and the sins against the Christian faith in the past. For this reason, it would be necessary to undertake much more efficacious measures than those employed hitherto, but that did not mean that the missionary endeavor should be abandoned.

As another example of such determination not to give up, one may cite the "Discurso antiguo en materia de moriscos" printed by Janer (1857, 266–68), unfortunately undated, but certainly later than 1584 (it incorporates a reference to the construction of the Escorial). The document articulates the case for deferring expulsion and for persisting with attempts to win the Moriscos' hearts: "It will be impossible for us to convert the Moriscos unless we first of all tame them and take away the fear, the hatred, and the enmity that they feel for the name Christian."

THE DECISION REACHED AT LISBON 1581

The problem of what to do about the Moriscos was studied by Philip and his counselors, and with some urgency. During time they spent in Lisbon on the occasion of the solemn ceremonies of his accession to the throne of Portugal. In April 1581, Philip had for the time being transferred his center of administration there. With the whole Iberian Peninsula now under one monarch, it is not surprising that a fresh impulse should be given to the drive for achieving effective religious uniformity as well.

Lea (1901, 296) describes some of the more extremist proposals under consideration at this point as follows:

> In 1581 when Philip II was in Lisbon, regulating his newly-acquired kingdom of Portugal, a junta of his chief counsellors, including the duke of Alva, the Count of Chinchón and Juan de Idiáquez, concluded to send the Moriscos to sea and to scuttle the vessels, reserving only those who could be catechised and those who desired to stay, for it was not deemed wise to add to the already numerous population of Africa. It was resolved that when the fleet returned from the Azores the matter should be executed by Alonso de Leyva, but it was abandoned, because when the fleet arrived it had to be sent to Flanders.

As Benítez Sánchez-Blanco (1990, 309 n. 7bis) correctly points out in an annotation to his Spanish translation of this passage, Lea is here actually going beyond what is said in his immediate source, which was a document published in Danvila (1889). The document had reported (long after the event) someone's recollection of discussions in Lisbon during which the idea of scuttling ships in order to get rid of the Morisco refugee passengers had been mentioned. It is quite unreasonable to take it for granted that such a proposal, if discussed, would in fact have been approved by the full council, let alone put into execution at that time.

The following alternative proposal for a Final Solution, made a few years later in 1587, in the course of the further consultations that ensued after these Lisbon discussions, was mercifully never put into practice either. This proposal shrank from sentencing the Moriscos directly to death by drowning, but what makes it more horrifically fascinating is that it had a North American dimension. It came from Martín de Salvatierra, bishop of Segorbe. In a report on the solution of the Morisco problem that the bishop submitted to the king on July 30, 1587 (Boronat 1901, 1: 633–34), the bishop reviews, toward the end of his recommendations, various objections likely to be made against the radical line, expulsion, which he proposes:

> It is no valid objection to say that if [the Moriscos] go to Barbary they will join up with the Muslims there, and descend on Spain, because in any case there are more than enough people [to do that] in North Africa already. They do not refrain from attacking for lack of numbers, but because, as is well known, they are in fear of Your Majesty's forces.

But in case expulsion to North Africa (which is what he seems to have in mind) is still not acceptable, he offers the king an alternative:

> These people might be transported to the Coast of the Cod and Newfoundland (*las costas de los macallaos* [*sic*] *y de Terranova*). These are very broad lands and are quite uninhabited. They will die out there completely, especially if the adult and young males are castrated and the women [are sterilized]. One year the Valencians could be transported to one destination, the next the Aragonese to another, the next the Castilians to another.

Exactly what the bishop had in mind one prefers not to imagine in too much detail. The term he uses—"capando"—in the phrase "capando los masculos grandes y pequeños y las mugeres" certainly means unambiguously "castrate" speaking of males; I have not elsewhere come across it used of an operation on a female, but whatever the prelate did mean by that (one hopes he was not very clear), he envisaged placing the Moriscos in such a physiological—and geographical!—situation as would make it quite certain that they did not breed. This was an extreme position, but not an isolated one, among Christians. The following year Alonso Gutiérrez, addressing the king from Seville on the same subject, shrinks from actually recommending castration but yet cannot bring himself to abandon the idea altogether as a policy option:

> It is not advisable that those who are born in excess of the number[1] should be castrated (*se castrasen*) although this is done in the Indies to slaves without thinking too much of it (*con muy pequeña ocasion*). I am not giving it as my recommendation, but to draw it to your attention for careful consideration.

Thus the most radical of measures were already being debated at this point, some thirty years before the final expulsion. It is to be noted that already in the 1580s the "Morisco Question" was by some perceived as having a solution outside Spain itself. (The international dimensions of the "Morisco Question" are discussed in the following chapter.) What had begun as an entirely internal matter, a domestic issue, now was to be solved in some way overseas. And so the powerful Spanish monarchy found that in order to deal with this "domestic" matter, it needed to involve its experts in foreign as well as home affairs. It cannot be a coincidence that when at last in 1609 the final decision was made to put the Expulsion into effect, it was done on the very day that a twelve-year truce with the Netherlands was signed.

---

1. He is actually proposing measures to limit population growth mainly by taxation.

Images of bizarre violence seem to have haunted the minds of those appointed to the think-tanks of those days. Boronat (1901, 1: 24), in a chapter in which he looks at the evolution of policy under Philip III, picks up a version of the proposal to get rid of the Moriscos by drowning them at sea (scuttling them) and defends it as reflecting views widely held. Boronat was referring to papers submitted some twenty years after the initial debates of the 1580s for consideration at the councils of 1601 and 1602, at which point a decision to expel the Moriscos was actually reached but not put into effect. Among these papers on the table were two letters written by Juan Boil de Arenós, dated August 13, 1601, and January 24, 1602, describing the "obvious danger in which the Kingdom of Valencia finds itself because of the Moriscos." Boil adds that Doctor Fidalgo, the prior of Calatrava and a "great theologian and man of religion," advocated "that they should all, without exception, men, women, and children, be sent to sea in boats without oars, steering gear, rigging, or sails, and scuttled, and sent to Africa like that."[2] Boronat is a historian who gives the impression of not having much of a sense of humor, but in reporting this poisonous outburst he remarks dryly that "surely these scuttled boats would have sunk before reaching their destination." He goes on to excuse what he grants are "harsh words" by asserting that "public opinion was demanding radical measures," and even goes on to claim that it would be wrong to blame these ideas on the individual informants, as "the whole nation, with rare exceptions, desired to see coercive remedies adopted."

The debates in council in Lisbon in 1581 and after had ushered in the final period of Morisco history, thirty years or so when the Spanish authorities felt an ever increasing urgency to settle this matter. But obstacles stood in the way of practical action. In the first place, there were powerful strategic considerations, such as a lack of military force to police the operation within Spain. Beset as it was by its troubles overseas, the country would have to wait for a window of opportunity before exposing itself unnecessarily at home.

Then there was the question of finance. This may seem strange in the case of a realm disposing from the 1580s onward of the treasure of not one but two world empires, but there was never enough money for everything. Another factor was the reluctance of many members of the nobility (especially the nobility of Valencia) to accept what they saw as a potential threat to their prosperity. Finally, there were theological scruples (in the main, as has been said, scruples about the fate of infant children). Objections to any radical anti-Morisco policy thus continued strong, but

2. Boronat (1901, 2: 24 n. 31) gives as his source the reference Archivo General de Simancas, Secretería de Estado, leg. 212.

nevertheless what had at the outset had been quite unthinkable thoughts were now being entertained.

The statesmen assembled in Lisbon in 1581 had wanted to do something effective but had not been able to. That gave time for sounding out opinion. We have the text of the response made in late April 1582 by Jiménez de Reinoso, Inquisitor of Valencia, to the enquiries sent to him (Boronat 1901, 1: 596–602 from Simancas, Consejo de Inquisición libro 110.) The Valencian Inquisition had been asked to set out those disadvantages and those advantages that might ensue if the Moriscos (and this is the term in fairly regular use by now, *moriscos*) were expelled from Spain, and in particular from the Kingdom of Valencia. Among the disadvantages the Inquisitor listed were the loss of one-third of the population of the kingdom and the loss of two-thirds of the income accruing to public funds ("because they"—presumably the Moriscos—"are the ones who pay most" [por ser aquellos los que mas pagan], Reinoso adds, revealingly). Other disadvantages included a shortage of foodstuffs to be foreseen in the years immediately after the Expulsion ("because the Moriscos as a whole are the ones who provide supplies") and a decline in the incomes of the Valencian nobles because the productivity of their lands depended on the Moriscos. (This was judged by Reinoso to be the greatest drawback to a policy of expulsion.) A last point against this was the expense of carrying out the expulsion and the risk that the Moriscos, if they got to know the secret in advance, would put up resistance.

Reinoso argued that these were nevertheless all disadvantages that could be dealt with. To fill the gap created by the loss of "the 19 or 20,000 Morisco households in this kingdom," settlers [presumably Christian immigrants?] could be brought in from La Mancha, etc. (although he warned they would have to be better treated than those Galicians who had been taken to Granada after the Second Granadan War). As for the loss of income, since the Crown derived relatively little income from Valencia, this was not a matter of great concern, although loud protests might be expected from the local interest groups, who did stand to lose a great deal. Regarding food supplies, the staples (of a Christian diet is not what is said, but that is clearly what is meant), bread, wine, and meat could be brought in from outside. Reinoso suggested that negotiations should be undertaken with the local nobles, and possibly some inducement be offered to offset from Morisco land and property the losses to be expected. (It was thought incomes might rise again after about five years.) Last, he proposed that the Expulsion might be funded from savings on the local defense budget, from confiscations of Morisco property, and in any case "such a great benefit, and such a necessary thing, cannot be got on the cheap (*no puede costar poco*)."

As for the danger of a rising, Reinoso did not think the Moriscos would dare, especially if the expulsions were carried out in wintertime, when they could expect no help from overseas. The report goes on to insist on the need to eliminate heresy: "And this cannot be achieved by any means other than by expelling all these unbelievers from Spain."

Copious precedents from Scripture and ancient history are adduced to justify what might have to be done: "examples of the transportation and the expulsion of peoples to foreign kingdoms and lands (*exemplos de la translacion y expulsion de gentes en reynos y tierras extrañas*)." The ancient parallels cited here may surprise us: Publius Cornelius Scipio driving the Carthaginians from Spain; Sisebut the Visigothic king expelling the Jews; and, a parallel to be found in the proceedings of the seventeenth council of Toledo, Egica's expulsion of those Jews who had accepted baptism in order to stay on after the expulsion decreed by Sisebut. Chronologically the closest parallel adduced is the action of Ferdinand and Isabella in expelling the Jews.

Reinoso is so anxious to see the policy of expulsion put into practice that he argues the Moriscos might as well be sent to Africa. He doesn't actually say so, but one suspects that he wants to get the whole unpleasant business concluded just as soon as possible, and he was not inclined to spend too much time over details.

> Nobody reasonably acquainted [with the matter] could have any cause to complain, and if the Moriscos had to be sent to Barbary [i.e., Morocco or Algeria] or to Africa [i.e., Tunisia], it would cost a lot less than if they had to be embarked on the other sea [i.e., from an Atlantic port].... Just let them leave Spain, and they will not be able to do it harm thereafter." (Boronat 1901, 2: 601)

Reinoso closes cryptically and enigmatically: "In the matter of the children, new orders could be given."

How drastic the action was that Philip II himself had been prepared to contemplate may be deduced from one of the specific pieces of guidance he gave to the Junta when it convened in Lisbon in 1581: "I think that among other ideas it would be good to order that children not be brought up with their parents."[3] Philip is still unwilling to surrender what he sees as the souls of innocents; he was prepared to break up Morisco families to save the souls of the little ones.

His conscience could in any case remain clear on this score, for he was actually not able to take any substantial initiatives on this question

3. I here gratefully adopt the translation provided by J. Kamen, *Philip of Spain* (New Haven and London, Yale University Press, 1997, 131) of British Library MS Add. 28357 f. 302.

before he died in 1598. The subject had not disappeared from the Council of State's agenda in the 1590s, far from it. In 1590, after looking at various alternatives, the council came down in favor of taking action to deal with the problem, but Philip's secretary, Francisco de Idiáquez, in 1594 was not impressed. He remonstrated that the subject was constantly being debated but never actually resolved (Lea 1901, 302). Philip II continued nevertheless to dither, and by 1595 he was again inclining to step up the attempts effectively to convert his Morisco subjects. Why did he not act? Why did he return instead to an approach that had proved, over all but a century, to have no probability of success?

We have to bear in mind at this point that the affair of the Torre Turpiana, followed by the beginnings of the Sacromonte discoveries in the mid-1590s (see chapter 8) did not go unnoticed at court—quite the contrary. If the Sacromonte texts were genuine, then that meant Philip II had in his realms relics of the greatest importance not just to Spain but to the Christian world at large. And since they were in Arabic, they might be expected at last to move Morisco hearts. In that case, 1595 was hardly the moment to cast out Moriscos who might hold a key to the interpretation of scriptures that had surfaced so opportunely!

DISENGAGEMENT

The accession of Philip II's son, Philip III, in 1598 brought a new atmosphere. Not totally new, for it was Philip II who had already that year negotiated the Peace of Vervins with France and so initiated a policy of disengaging from the endless, widely scattered wars and conflicts that had so drained Spain's resources (and morale). By 1604 came the Treaty of London with James I of England. And by 1609 was to follow the Twelve-Year Truce with the Netherlands. Philip II, for all the military might at his disposal, had found his military resources overstretched. A policy of peace in Western Europe now left Philip III's ministers free to contemplate new initiatives. What is more, until 1618, Philip III's chief minister was the duke of Lerma. Lerma was a Valencian noble, initially with all the reluctance of his kind to give up the profitable services of the Morisco cultivators who worked his lands. But if Lerma were to change his mind, he was in a position to negotiate effectively with his Valencian peers and strike a deal.

Policy toward the Moriscos in the very early years of the reign of Philip III seemed a direct continuation of that of his father: renewed support for missionary campaigns directed at the Moriscos (who were, of course, by now so well inoculated with ideological antibodies that they withstood such blandishments). In 1599, as the follow-up to the missionary endeavors begun at the end of Philip II's reign, there came the proclamation of yet another edict of grace. It was largely ignored, as had been the fate of all such initiatives. Once again most Moriscos held back from securing "grace" and future immunity for themselves at the price of delating on their past Muslim associates.

LERMA CHANGES HIS MIND

The most important development at the end of the century was the espousal by Lerma himself of the policy of expulsion. On February 2, 1599, he submitted a paper on the subject of the Moriscos. Morisco males between fifteen and sixty as Moors (Muslims) were liable to the death penalty (for their treason), and so might legally be enslaved and their property confiscated (Lea 1901, 307, citing Danvila 1889, 233–40). Although Lerma was already Philip's favorite (*valido*) and so was inundated in a flow of royal munificence, he was always greedy for more. Contradicting the established view that Moriscos meant profit for their landlords, he could see the potential *short-term* gains that might accrue from getting rid of them. To enslave able-bodied males would provide either useful galley slaves or, where relatives outside Spain were prepared to negotiate them, ransom payments in exchange for manumission. To a man like Lerma, a minister who enjoyed the services of such skilled fraudsters as Rodrigo Calderón, or at a lower level, Pedro Franqueza, dealings with the Moriscos during this crisis offered scope for all sorts of underhand operations. A number of years ago, when I came across in a Valencian archive a document about the illegal purchase of arms and weapons written in 1595 in Arabic by a Morisco who was informing his associate that he had obtained an arms permit from Franqueza, I was at first not certain how to interpret what was written. The Morisco had written in Arabic characters *ifranqizza,* and I puzzled for hours, trying to make sense of this as some garbled Arabic word, before I yielded to the obvious, and saw it as a reference to Lerma's subordinate. I now have no doubt at all that this notoriously venal government servant was involved in supplying arms to the other side (Harvey 1971, 81–115). (It is possible, of course, that Franqueza was operating behind his master's back: if so, that would have been a dangerous game.)

In the background to these policy debates was the major question of municipal indebtedness. As has been explained above, a class of rich Moriscos had emerged who in some cases (in contravention of Islamic bans on usury of course) held income-yielding investments (*censos,* etc.). If Morisco creditors were shipped off abroad, Christians who had taken out loans from them would never be required to pay them back. Kamen

(1991, 220–21) appears to take a not dissimilar view of Lerma's motivation at this point to mine:

> Lerma's own personal role was also important: he changed his mind, and presented to the council a proposal that the lords in Valencia—of whom he was one—should be compensated by being given the lands of the expelled Moriscos. The element of personal profit, as in all his policy, was crucial to the duke, but it is clear that he could not have proceeded had the lords in Valencia, who all along had bitterly opposed the move, not also changed their minds. And their position was getting desperate. Productivity rose during the good years of the sixteenth century, giving those lords who received tithes (such as the Church), a satisfactory income from their Morisco tenantry. But where seigneurial rents were fixed, the nobles were barely able to cover their debts. In the area of Turís, part of the duchy of Gandía, in Valencia, seigneurial rents during the sixteenth century rose four-fold, but tithes increased sixteen-fold. Meanwhile the principal of the duke's debts in *censos* rose thirteen-fold between 1551 and 1604. By 1600, the Valencian nobility were paying one third of their income in *censo* debts and were unable to make good their losses from the fixed tenancies of their Morisco vassals. They stood, therefore, to gain from dispossession and expulsion.

Lerma's new ideas as presented at the level of the Council of State did not lead to an immediate change in what was happening in the villages, on the ground. Any abrupt change would hardly have been possible, for a renewed edict of grace had already been secured from Rome,[4] and that could not be set on one side high-handedly; the Church might resent that. Lerma was presumably too skilled a politician to think that the course of the ship of state could be altered overnight. So efforts to implement the program of evangelization apparently continued. But the council was at the same time beginning preparation for drastic action against the Moriscos. And the archbishop of Valencia, Ribera, an immensely influential figure, someone who had earlier in his career seen himself as the one to guide these people to true conversion, had by now despaired of ever eliciting from them a "sincere" response, and so, from being something of a protector of the New Christians or at least one who stood against the adoption of energetic and un-Christian policies, was becoming the outspoken

4. The papal policy on the Morisco problem was, not surprisingly, complex. See Pérez-Bustamente (1951, 219–33), also Boronat (1901, 2: 35). That the papacy was kept fully informed of what was being discussed and that it was more than a mere interested observer, is not in doubt, but that is not the same as saying that the papacy participated in the final decision.

enemy of a people who in his opinion had now had their last chance and squandered it, who once and for all had spurned Christian charity.

Ribera in fact went too far even for the king. He ran into trouble over a printed pastoral letter containing a warning that unless the Moriscos responded positively to the current offer of the edict of grace, they might run the risk of expulsion. The royal authorities understandably did not like that at all. The danger was that the Moriscos in their desperation might be driven to offer violent resistance or otherwise to cause trouble. Lerma preferred to take the Moriscos by surprise. Ribera was persuaded to withdraw his pastoral letter, though no doubt in Valencia at least the damage had been done. By late 1601, Ribera had ample evidence that the edict of grace had been ignored. He now came out firmly—but in a memorandum (*memorial*) to the king (not in a public statement)— in favor of expulsion. He still wanted to adhere to something like due legal process, however. The Crown should employ the clergy to collect evidence of the Moriscos' apostasy and treason, he advised, then have the Moriscos formally condemned and their property confiscated, before sending them into exile.

Seen from the point of view of an administrator or a soldier rather from that of an ecclesiastic, to expel hundreds of thousands of people was going to be difficult enough under any circumstances. To hold preliminary trials for heresy, as Ribera and others wanted, would risk more than delay. Desperate individuals might take up arms. (As we will see, some few eventually did, but the amount of military action required was small, and limited to certain specific areas.)

Viewed from the religious point of view, it was essential that things should be done in due form. The moral responsibility for driving away potential converts, particularly innocent children, would be dreadful to contemplate. In the event, expediency and other political considerations prevailed, and theological niceties were laid to one side. (Hence the eventual need for the voluminous literature of apologetic self-justification that was to appear *after* the expulsion had been completed.)

WAYS AND MEANS

Thus the Morisco issue came up for consideration once more at a committee (*junta*) held on January 2, 1602. The committee consisted of Lerma; the count of Miranda, Juan de Idiáquez (providing continuity with the deliberations of 1581); and the king's confessor, Gaspar de Córdoba (Boronat 1901, 2: 48). It would seem that on the fundamental matter of whether or not to expel, there was now agreement. Under discussion were not principles but ways and means. Of the Moriscos, those of Valencia and if possible Aragon should go first.

J. H. Elliott (1973) gives what is the generally accepted, and no doubt correct, view of Philip III's character: "Philip III (1598–1621) was incapable of any personal initiative, and depended for most of his reign on the services of a favourite (the *valido* or *privado*), Francisco de Sandoval y Rojas, Duke of Lerma 1553–1625." Yet paradoxically it appears to have been the king himself who cut short discussion of the various bloody (*sangrientos*) means that might have been adopted, excluded "the measure of killing them or scuttling them" (*darles barreno*—that ghastly alternative had not been forgotten, we can see), and came out crisply in favor of shipping them to Barbary. Idiáquez and Miranda had favored this solution of deportation to North Africa; Lerma and Gaspar de Córdoba had held that because the Moriscos had been baptized they should either be "finished off or treated really well" (*acabarlos o regalarlos*—one wonders what that meant exactly.) Philip concluded that "[i]f with good conscience they may be expelled, that is what is most suitable, most easy, and the swiftest" (Boronat 1901, 229). That certainly does not sound like indecision, but perhaps Philip was really acting in character all the same. The truly idle are at times capable of surprising decisiveness where it will spare them future trouble. Philip III wanted this item off the agenda once and for all.

The operation should start in late summer, it was decided, and galleys and contingents of troops (the dreaded *tercios* among them) should be summoned from their bases in Italy. "Let this be done, and with all possible haste" (*con todo el calor posible*) was the royal command. Again, those do not sound like the words of the dithering monarch of whom we hear so much elsewhere.

But "all possible haste" were royal words that failed to secure action in 1602. On December 3, Ribera briefly took over the office of viceroy of Valencia, adding it to his responsibilities as archbishop. And the Morisco question was not tackled. It was not that he was doing nothing at all. On December 14, he issued a proclamation against bearing firearms and swords by night, and in January 1603 there followed further decrees against bandits "and other malefactors." Perhaps these were intended as preparatory measures to strengthen the hand of the authorities without alarming the Moriscos by mentioning them explicitly.

In January 1604, Ribera was relieved of his post. We must assume that the churchman's year in actual government had not been a success. In 1605, we find his successor, Juan de Sandoval, once again issuing decrees against banditry and against illegal arms, as Ribera had done. Given the way that government initiatives had of running into the sand, perhaps no real explanation for the lack of action over the Expulsion is needed, but behind this particularly apparent dither-and-delay was what was going on in the arena of international relations (see chapter 10). There were good reasons for delaying action against the Moriscos until a full appraisal of the global situation had been made.

Valencia was, at the close of the sixteenth century, the one region capable of providing leadership to the Morisco cause (with the exception of the small and inward-turned Extremaduran town of Hornachos, discussed below in chapter 12). A Valencian rebel leadership did emerge that in the 1590s sought to enlist the help of Spain's enemies in France and England. But after the trial and execution of the Valencian Morisco leader Alamí and his fellows in 1605, even this resistance collapsed.

A FINAL APPEAL FROM SPAIN'S MUSLIMS
FOR HELP FROM NORTH AFRICA

There was just one further attempt made by Spain's Muslims to save their homeland. There never was any real chance that it might succeed, for it was predicated upon large-scale assistance being provided by the Moroccan sultan Muley Zaydan, and this appeal was made at a time when he was embroiled in the bitter internecine warfare that weakened the Magrib. We may not think that this final démarche posed any serious threat to Spain. Given the state of internal Moroccan politics, there was absolutely no hope that the peninsula could be invaded, as seems to have been the plan. The important point is, however, that this last conspiracy was taken very seriously by Philip III himself.

We know about this affair, shrouded under a veil of security at the time, of course, from a text Janer included in his *Condición social de los moriscos en España* under the heading: "What His Majesty has commanded to be put forward in the Council" (Janer 1875, 274–7; also Lea 1901, 289–90). Janer is normally careful to tell us where the documents of his "Colección Diplomática" were to be found in his day, but he gives no information on the location of this source. The status of this piece of evidence is therefore less than satisfactory. It purports to be a position paper drawn up as a background to the discussion that was held on the subject of the Moriscos in the council and would seem to have been drawn up by the principal proponent of action on this front (Lerma or somebody working under his orders).

Conveying as it does the atmosphere of panic prevailing in the council chamber, the text is worth translating complete. We must inevitably tend to see the Expulsion as the measured action of a great world power contemptuously tidying away an unimportant minority. If the document is to be taken at something near its face value, however, we have to see the Expulsion as not at all such a manifestation of confident imperial might, rather as the worried reaction of an insecure ruler who felt himself unable to control a rapidly deteriorating crisis. (Of course, there is in the background the question of the possibly corrupt personal motivation of Lerma and his circle. They had reason to push the king on to commit himself to the policy of expulsion, playing on his insecurities and inadequacies.)

The text printed by Janer is stylistically cryptic: it is designed to be read by those already immersed in the issues:

His Majesty has received reports that the 50 Moriscos who crossed over to Barbary went to Marrakesh and asked Muley Zaydan forcefully why he was expending his strength making war on his brothers when he had the chance to regain Spain, which had been conquered in former times with the ease that is well known. Although there had at that time [i.e., in 711] not been a single Moor in Spain, and although King Roderick had had no enemies compared with the many that His Majesty now has to face, and even though Roderick had mustered 70,000 men, the Moors beat him, and won the war in less than eight months. Now there are less people [living in Spain], because they have been consumed by the plague and the war in Flanders. One has to grant that in those days [711], trained men and arms were few [in Spain], but nowadays there are even fewer, and they are less bold and courageous. As for arms, they are in the hands of the Moriscos, who have managed to procure them in secret. They will find him 200,000 men just as formidable as he is, ready to lay down their lives and their property. It would not be necessary [for Muley Zaydan] to cross with such a great host as that brought across by Miramolin: merely by landing 20,000 men, any port could be seized. Inland there would be no resistance, especially if use were made of the Rebels [the Dutch?] and other peoples of the north who are the king's enemies, and who would join in at low cost, because they want to do him harm. This was an advantageous opportunity that they should seize for Spain was a spent force (*consumida*), quite unable to offer resistance. He [Muley Zaydan] is said to have responded that he could not abandon his bid to recover the kingdoms over which his forebears had reigned [in North Africa], but he gave [to the Moriscos] his word sworn on the Koran that once this was done, he would not rest until he had conquered Spain. He had spoken to some Hollanders who were there and had explained his intentions to them, and asked whether with their ships they would assist him to cross with 20,000–22,000 men if he paid them well to do so. The Dutch had replied that they would not just help, they would establish a bridge of ships over which he could pass in complete safety.

His Majesty [King Philip] has taken this all into account (especially now that Muley Zaydan, ever our principal enemy, has achieved what he desired [i.e., won the war against his rivals in Morocco]), and he [Philip] has borne in mind that in these kingdoms [i.e., Spain] things are going badly, as is well known. *What is to be feared is the multitude of Moriscos* among whom are men so anxious to throw off their subjugation and so stubborn in their adherence to their beliefs (*secta*). He has also taken into account that the Turk, according to the latest reports, is disengaging himself from his conflicts with those in rebellion against him, and with the Persians; also that the disaffection that has become apparent among even those Italian princes who have been most committed to our cause, because the resources of the kingdoms His Majesty possesses there have been exhausted and used up, and his subjects there have become discontented, so that there is reasonable cause to fear that once they see His Majesty occupied in the defense of these realms against attacks from enemies who are so many and so powerful, they may move against His Majesty in a way that cannot be resisted, so that everything will be in peril. This is especially so because Our Lord must be very offended at the way that over such a long period heretics and apostates of such a pernicious and obstinate kind have benefited from our lack of resolution.

His Majesty's view is that there is now no time to be lost in seeking a remedy to these enormous evils. He is resolved to finish off these evil people by whatever means seem best and most speedy, and he will not shrink from putting them to death ["sin reparar en degollarlos," literally "slitting their throats"]. For, as those who have been engaged in the conversion have discovered, it is not just that nothing has been achieved, but that every time some effort has been made, their stubbornness and ill will has only increased, without a single one of them ever being converted, in spite of all the hopes. The patriarch archbishop of Valencia is quite in despair, [as are] all the others who over the years have striven so hard. The process has been so long drawn out that it is now quite out of the question to leave the security of the realm dependent upon it, for on the security of this realm depends [that of] the rest of Christendom.

His Majesty desires that the Council should once again review the reports submitted on this subject. He would draw to their attention in relation to Valencia that after the bishops of that kingdom assembled to provide for a further campaign of instruction and conversion of the Moriscos there, the Moriscos have displayed even greater disaffection and obstinacy, a clear demonstration of how fruitless are such attempts.

Let the Council take this matter in hand, and keep to this task to the exclusion of everything else.

When it comes to individual nominations, consult His Majesty as to how and when for whatever needs to be provided for, at home and abroad.

Secrecy must be preserved, for bringing what we intend to a successful conclusion depends on the Council.

Attention should be paid to setting up the militia, as has been discussed for so long.... [the document goes on to list other areas needing attention].... to what persons are to be employed in carrying out this task.... to what help is to be sought from the councils and subjects of these kingdoms. It should be borne in mind that for reasons of secrecy they are only to be informed when the time to carry out the action has come... to the raising of troops.... [the procurement of] arms and munitions.... For this will be of great service to us and to Christendom and will bring renown to His Majesty and to these his realms, and will strike a blow at his enemies. (Janer 1857: 274–76; emphasis added)

It will be seen that the memorandum reflects fears about the vulnerability of Spain; indeed more than merely reflecting them, it seems designed to reinforce them. It is for that reason that it would seem likely that we have here a text, possibly an incomplete text, drafted by someone seeking to bring about an urgent resolution of the Morisco problem at any price, possibly Lerma himself.

On the subject of the Moriscos, the question that we tend to ask in modern times (with our modern viewpoints) is how Spain ever came to undertake such a course of action as the Expulsion. The memorandum suggests anxiety and fear as strong motives contributing toward this decision.

THE FINAL DECISION TO EXPEL

On April 4, 1609, the Royal Council met, and on April 9, 1609, a truce was concluded with the Dutch, the so-called Twelve-Year Truce. On that same date, the king did finally proceed against the Moriscos. The idea of a linkage between the two events is obvious enough. Voltaire observed, "Philip III could not get the better of a few Dutchman, and unfortunately he could drive out 700,000 Moors from his dominions" (Voltaire quoted in Caro 1957, 248). The unstated implication of Voltaire's sarcasm seems to be that for the frustrated monarch the decision to do something that did lie in his power was a substitute for what he would have wished to do elsewhere but could not. Lynch (1969, 2: 42) has remarked that "Spanish statesmen of the time measured out their policy by calculation, not by accident, and Spanish policy was never more calculating than it was in 1609." Where I would not follow this historian is when he says, "Ironically, the war with Islam had lost much of its urgency, and by 1609 was no longer a major preoccupation" (2: 43). It is true, we now know, that North African Islam was settling into decline, but *fear* of war with the Islamic world and what that might mean was still a powerful motivating force.

IMPLEMENTATION

The decision as to how precisely to begin the implementation of the policy of expulsion was governed by considerations of broad strategy. The Valencian Moriscos were the largest coherent group, the only one in a position to threaten to take over a port or landing zone. They had already been discovered to have been in contact with England and, above all, with Henry IV's France. And in the early seventeenth century, just as nowadays in the twenty-first, the Valencian coast was wide open to clandestine contacts with the Magrib. (The crossing near the Straits of Gibraltar would be shorter, of course, but effective coastguard surveillance was far easier to maintain.) Militarily, the first priority for Spain in any operation to carry out the Expulsion would be to deprive its enemies of the possibility of establishing a bridgehead to supply a counterattack. Inland Moriscos and others might safely be left to be mopped up later. Valencia was the strategic key.

But secrecy was essential, and that was difficult to achieve since the Moriscos were fully alive to the dangers that threatened to overwhelm them. It was perceived by Lerma that it might betray the fact that something was afoot even to have the selected military commanders reconnoiter the terrain. The officers appointed were Agustín Mexía, in command of the land operation, and Pedro de Toledo, marqués de Villafranca, who had special responsibility for the naval implications (which were, of course, considerable). For Lerma and the king to see the two commanders on July 24 in Segovia posed no special problems, but unusual precautions were necessary to get Mexía down to his command in Valencia without arousing suspicion. The king's orders to the two local dignitaries who had to be informed—to the viceroy of Valencia, Caracena, and to the archbishop, Ribera—were carried by Mexía himself and not by dispatch riders or special agents. Ribera was told, "Because in this matter secrecy is so important, so that until it has been carried out no one should know about it or even be able to imagine what our intentions are, I have arranged that Don Agustín's journey to the city and Kingdom [of Valencia] should be under cover of inspecting the present condition of its fortifications and reporting what is needed to bring them up to the highest standard" (Boronat 2004, 2: 159 and n. 2)

THE FIRST OF THE DECREES OF EXPULSION: VALENCIA, 1609

The decisions that had for so long been discussed among administrators and senior soldiers behind tightly closed doors under a thick blanket of security were finally made public in a decree (Boronat 1901, 2: 190) issued on behalf of the king by the marqués of Caracena, and directed to all the king's subjects in Valencia. The proclamation was made on the authority of a "Royal Letter of August 4, 1609, signed by his royal hand and confirmed by his secretary of State, Andrés de Prada," and the proclamation was itself dated September 22, 1609.

The preamble in the normal way was given over to justification of the enactment. Every effort had already been made to convert the Moriscos (and this is the term actually employed here), but "their stubbornness has only increased" and they were "heretics, apostates, traitors guilty of lèse-majesté both human and divine," and because they had sought by their "ambassadors" ("por medios de sus Ambaxadores," a term that seems unwittingly to concede to the Moriscos near-sovereign status) to secure "the harm and the upset of our realms," out of obligation to his good and faithful subjects because "the peril is evident," the king announced, "I have resolved that all the Moriscos of this kingdom should be expelled and sent to Barbary."

The clauses that followed stipulated the following:

1. *Firstly* all the Moriscos of this Kingdom, men and women with their children, should within three days from the publication of this proclamation in the places where they live, leave their houses and embark wherever the Commissar orders them to do. They might take with them "such goods and chattels as they can carry" and embark on the ships prepared to take them across to North Africa, where they would be landed "without suffering either in their own persons or in what they are carrying with them, any ill-treatment or harm by word or by deed." They are told they will have provisions supplied on the voyage, and are advised themselves to bring what they can with them. Disobedience to the proclamation was to be punished by death.

2. Any Morisco found away from home and unsupervised (*desmandado*) in the period from three days after the proclamation until the embarkations had started might be arrested and be stripped of all his possessions (*desvalijarle*), and anybody (presumably any Christian) who performed this act of confiscation would incur no penalties at all. If the Morisco offered resistance, he could be killed.

3. All Moriscos were to wait where they were until the commissar came to collect them (and were threatened with similar treatment if they failed to do so).

4. If there were any attempts to hide or bury property or to burn houses, crops or other property, all the inhabitants of the village in question became subject to the death penalty.

5. In six houses out of every hundred the Morisco inhabitants were to remain behind to show those who took over the properties how to work,

among other things, the sugar mills and irrigation systems. These were to be chosen from among the most likely to convert. As far as one can discover, this incredibly insensitive clause remained inoperative: nobody would stay.

6. No Old Christian, whether soldier or native of Valencia, might make so bold as to ill-treat the Moriscos by word or deed, nor touch their property, or their wives or children.

7. Nobody was to hide any of the Moriscos or to help them escape. The penalty for this was six years in the galleys.

8. To reassure the Moriscos that they would not be molested, ten of the first group to arrive in North Africa were to be allowed to return to reassure their fellows that they would be well treated (and so on with future transports). This also was largely but not entirely a dead letter. Some did return from the first transport.

9. Children of four and below who wanted to stay (how their wishes were to be ascertained is not stated) might with their parents' agreement remain and not be expelled. We can see here and in the next clause that this issue of "innocent children" continued to be fudged. This went on until the end, and beyond.

10. Children of six and below with a single Old Christian parent might remain, and the mother as well, even though she was a Morisco woman. But if the father were a Morisco and his wife were an Old Christian, he should be expelled, and children under six should remain behind with the mother.

11. Those who for a considerable period, as might be two years, had lived among Christians and had not attended Morisco meetinghouses (*aljamas*), might remain.

12. Those who with license of their bishop received the holy sacrament (from the rectors of the places where they reside) might remain.

13. His Majesty grants and agrees that if any of the said Moriscos should wish to leave for other kingdoms, they may do so, so long as they depart from their place of residence within the time limit laid down, and do not enter any part of his Spanish realms.

It is the firm will of His Majesty that the penalties of this proclamation should be enforced without allowing any remission.

To be proclaimed in the accustomed form, Valencia September 22, 1609.

The decree is a curious mixture of a number of brutally functional clauses (nos. 1, 2, 3, 4, and 7), and others that can have had little or no practical effect (nos. 9, 10, 11, and 12), possibly inserted in the document to salve the conscience of Philip or his administrators. Other clauses propose quite impractical solutions (5 and 8) for problems that seemed likely to arise. As for clause 13, it is difficult to see how a Morisco family could have organized its own journey to some destination other than North Africa if it had only three days available to do so, especially bearing in mind that Moriscos were not told in the first place where they were being sent!

The decree clearly envisages more than one relay of shipping (all the Moriscos of the Kingdom of Valencia could not conceivably be embarked at one time): in the event there were broadly three phases from various ports. The first deportations were in late September up to late October. The Spanish fleet escorted a motley array of ships of many nations from Denia. Well protected by the galleys that had been brought across from Naples, some 5,300 souls embarked on September 30th, and the galleys set out on October 2, arriving off the Spanish *presidio* of Oran on October 5.

WILLING VICTIMS?

It may seem strange that such an enormous movement of population could be set in motion so easily. Why was there not more resistance? (We continue to ask similar questions about such movements in our times.) As we will see, there was armed resistance in a few places, but many went joyfully. This was for some what they had longed for all their lives, what they had been prevented from doing by legislation forbidding emigration to Muslim lands. Bleda (1618, 1001–3) reports an answer allegedly given by one of the *alfaquíes* asked on the docks at Alicante why they were acting in obedience to the letter from the king. Perhaps Bleda invented the story to suggest that the Spanish authorities were not to be blamed for the expulsion, that it was all a favor done to the Moriscos, but the words are worth reporting:

> Do you not know how many of us bought or stole boats in which to cross to Barbary with much danger? Then why, when we are offered safe and free passage[5], should we not avail ourselves of it, and go to the land of our ancestors under our king the Turk, who will let us live as Moors and not as slaves, as we have been treated by our masters?

A LAST STAND

The realists among those being expelled may simply have understood that resistance was hopeless and would only lead to increased suffering

5. The old man, or possibly Bleda, was mistaken here! On the naval ships the deportees went free, but on the vessels belonging to private owners, a charge was made, as we know because in order to prevent fraud, special arrangements were made whereby the passage money was held back by the Spanish port authorities on trust and not paid over until certificates of disembarkation in Oran had been presented.

by the noncombatants. The Spanish forces included some of the best and most experienced troops in the world at the time, and they were well armed, more than a match for a rabble of Moriscos with improvised lances and such cutlasses as they could find. The Spanish military deployment, intended to ensure that those deported went quietly, was sufficiently powerful to crush any stand made by the Moriscos, if one were undertaken, but the authorities wanted above all to prevent any risk of trouble developing. To that end, Pedro de Toledo, with 550 of the best troops brought across from Italy at an early stage, set about occupying strong points in the Sierra de Espadán, places where, in the past, rebels had been known to seek refuge. The move was ill-advised: what happened was that those Moriscos determined to make a military stand chose other inaccessible mountain fastnesses instead.

What did the Moriscos who took up arms hope to achieve? Hard information is lacking, and it is difficult to penetrate the minds of those caught up in such an unparalleled disaster. Some seem to have thought that if only they could hold out for sufficient time, help might reach them from across the seas, or from some supernatural source (there were prophecies of "the Moro Fatimi" and his green horse). Two mountain valleys were chosen by the Valencian Morisco resistance to set up camp. One was the coastal region near Guadalest: Val de Aguar. The other, at Muela de Cortes, was in the hills looking down on the Júcar River. In each case, we are told by our Christian source (Bleda 1618, 999–1016) that a "king" was chosen. "King" (*rey*) in such a context should not be taken to imply that the individual had any pretensions to general monarchy. Rather, it signified no more in such a context than "important Moorish leader" and is to be found already in this sense not infrequently in the late-medieval Castilian ballad literature. In the case of the revolt centered on Muela de Cortes, there had been preparatory propaganda by one Pablillo Ubcar (presumably a local form of the name Abu Bakr), but the "king" actually elected was Vicente Turixi, who set about collecting supplies, for men did come in large numbers, certainly in thousands. In the barren terrain they were occupying, and in the winter months (November 1609 onward) there was no question of living off what was available in the immediate area. In the forays carried out, cattle and grain were lifted. Fonseca, another Christian source (Fonseca 1612, 236–48), from his ecclesiastical viewpoint, in his account speaks of atrocities against churches and clergy. There seems no reason to dismiss these reports as fabrications. The military response when it came in November was under Pedro Mexía, who deployed considerable additional forces, so that he eventually had 6,000 men under his command. He did try at first to negotiate with the insurgents, but, conscious of his greatly superior strength, soon lost patience with the rabble that opposed him.

He first dealt with the Val de Laguar, where the castle at Azabara was surprised, then later in a bloody action the castle at Pop was tackled. Mexía, on November 21, drove the Moriscos back, inflicting on them enormous losses (Bleda speaks of 3,000 killed on the Morisco side, and in Mexía's force only one man, Bautista Crespo, killed by his own weapon when it blew up.) The main body of the Moriscos (estimates vary, 11,000–22,000) simply retreated higher up the mountains, where in the midwinter they were easily starved into surrender, and the miserable remnant was escorted to the coast. The debacle is hardly surprising; ill-equipped untrained volunteers were pitted against well-trained, well-supplied, well-led professionals.

Mexía's military successes no doubt had its effect on the other center of resistance, at Muela de Cortes. The Moriscos seem in general to have avoided pitched battle. Some 3,000 did surrender in late 1609 and were expelled, but a remnant (2,000?) held out in this infinitely difficult terrain (the last of them not being rounded up until 1612). Turixi, with a price on his head, was caught in a cave, then taken down to Valencia, where he was mutilated and executed on December 18, 1609. He allegedly died as a "good Christian," whatever that may mean in such a context. His adherents were hunted down, and in these final stages the authorities were paying a bounty of 20 escudos for each head brought in. Any prisoners were taken off to be galley slaves. Those who surrendered without putting up a fight were still enslaved but were spared the galleys.

There were, of course, other incidents and violent confrontations, but in general the eviction of the Valencians, by far the largest group of Moriscos, went ahead as quickly as was feasible. These were the Moriscos who would have been best able to cause trouble for the Spanish authorities. Many of them were still speakers of Arabic, and they often lived in large Morisco communities in remote rural areas: in such circumstances their sense of group solidarity was strong. It was for this reason that they had been singled out to be dealt with first. Once they had gone, it became much easier to deal with the rest piecemeal. In a sense the die was cast by December 1609. The Valencia clearance had not been completed altogether, but what remained to be done was a tidying-up operation well within the capacity of the forces available.

ON THE FAR SHORE

What was the reception of this huge influx of refugees in North Africa? The experience of the first contingent at Oran did not provide much guidance to what might happen elsewhere at other points on the

Mediterranean coast, because Oran was a fortress (*presidio*) in Spanish hands. Landing the poor people there was easy; it was getting them across the land frontier into Muslim territory that presented problems. The galleys could achieve a swift turn-round in the Spanish-controlled port, and when they reported back to Denia, they were even able to display some Moriscos ready to tell their coreligionists still in Spain that those who had already made the crossing had arrived safe and sound. From Alicante there departed another flotilla under Luis Fajardo, with more than 8,000 Moriscos in ships of various shapes and sizes, some of them ocean-going vessels from the Atlantic fleet. Bad weather drove them back, and it was October 11 before they finally reached Oran (where the Atlantic sailing ships, not ideally suited to such a task in coastal waters, had to be towed into harbor by the Mediterranean galleys).

In the very north of Valencia (Vinaroz in modern Castellón) the commandant of the whole seaborne operation, Pedro de Toledo, was assembling contingents who had had a long hard march inflicted on them before they could reach the allotted point of embarkation. On October 14, 3,300 more refugees were brought to Oran, and smaller groups of ships soon arrived with 2,500 more. Meanwhile, privately owned ships were also operating alone or in convoys, so that by October 20, 32,000 people had been transported. This part of the expulsion, in merchant ships and largely based on the port (*Grao*) of Valencia, continued throughout.

The transfer of population thus began with what was from the Spanish point of view a considerable logistical success. Possession of Oran was the key. But whereas the first of these human waves had been allowed across the land frontier out of the Oran enclave into the territory of Tetuan, the vast numbers soon arriving, many unannounced, posed problems on both sides of the frontiers. The Spanish commandant in Oran, Aguilar, had begun to ask for relief when the figure of 22,000 had been reached. Let the rest go elsewhere! On the Tlemcen side of the frontier, some unescorted groups were treated by the desert dwellers in a way that might have been foreseen: they were robbed. To cross the territory of a desert tribe permission should be sought, tolls negotiated. Aguilar did what he could, which was very little. The local Muslim authorities must soon have realized that without being consulted they had been maneuvered into acting as unpaid agents facilitating an odious policy of ethnic cleansing that they would have opposed if they had had any voice in the matter. The flood of refugees must have presented them with a host of awkward problems.

The news that things were after all not going altogether smoothly in Oran must have got back to the peninsula, and now some villages began to calculate that they might as well fight near to their homes rather than on unfamiliar and inhospitable terrain elsewhere. From Teresa and other villages some made for the mountains, where, as we have seen, ill-organized resistance was attempted.

The second wave took place in very late October. The urgency with which the operation was now being prosecuted can be judged from the fact that, in spite of the heavy fighting in the mountains described above, embarkations continued. The risk was that bad winter weather might force a halt to the expulsion campaign, and no doubt that would have been disastrous for the whole Spanish timetable. Momentum must be maintained. The generally fine weather at sea in fact favored the Spanish fleets, and as October came to an end, further contingents sailed from the ports already mentioned.

THE FINAL CONTINGENTS FROM VALENCIA: WINTER SAILINGS

By November, some ships were being driven back by the weather, and on November 13 Luis Fajardo had to report from the safe harbor of Cartagena that three small vessels (*saetas*) with one hundred Morisco passengers on board had gone down in a storm. One has to remember that in those days it was quite normal for Mediterranean shipping to be laid up for the worst of the winter. Whereas the early sailings had in general carried groups from places near to the coast on a relatively short crossing to an unproblematic destination, Oran, as the year wore on the deportees were coming from further and further inland, and so arrived at the Spanish coast exhausted after difficult journeys. Then, sometimes from awkward small anchorages, sea voyages had to be endured that were often longer than the earlier ones. Several times ships were driven back or suffered buffeting in storms. The privations of the refugees were severe. And at the far side, the captains, anxious to return to safety, afraid of trouble from the local inhabitants, in some cases chose to unload their human freight wherever they could find a spot: at Arzeu, for example, or at Cap Falcon. And the local inhabitants now were indeed showing such open hostility to the Spanish fleets that shots were being exchanged.

Some of the bigger ships, designed for the Atlantic, were now withdrawn from this coastwise service. As for the merchant vessels that were only participating for profit, many were prudently switched by their owners to other trades. And there were cases of desperate Moriscos managing to capture and make off with the vessels on which they were being transported. Things were no longer going at all as smoothly as they did at the outset, but all the same the greater part of the task, insofar as Valencia was concerned, had been accomplished. The statistics assembled by Lapeyre (1959) show 116,022 transported from the Valencian ports and roadsteads in this massive movement of population.

THE EXPULSION OF THE MORISCOS OF ARAGON
AND OF CATALONIA

Since Aragon and Catalonia were grouped with Valencia under the same "Crown," it might reasonably be expected that the circumstances of the expulsions in all these realms would be similar. That was not the case. The differences arose partly because the relevant decrees for places such as Aragon were issued much later than those for Valencia, partly because only some of those expelled from Aragon were consigned to North Africa, and so for the first time land routes over French frontier were used.

It is not entirely clear why there was such a relatively long gap between the Valencian decree of September 1609 and the decision relating to Aragon of April 17, 1610, which apparently was proclaimed publicly only on May 29th (and so in fact after the proclamation dated January 10 relating to the lands of the Crown of Castile). The Spanish authorities in Oran had made it quite clear that the flood of refugees with which they had to cope in late 1609 had given rise to difficulties of all sorts, so that there were sound logistical and operational reasons for taking a little more time before increasing the total of persons displaced. Against that had to be set the fact that the Aragonese Moriscos knew that they were almost certainly the next in line to be driven out, even if they did not know exactly when. Not surprisingly, they began abandoning the cultivation of fields from which they were to reap no benefit and sought to make such preparations for their journey as were permitted. The situation in the Morisco villages was thus very unsettled. And, as the Christians saw matters, there was always the danger that the Aragonese Moriscos might seek to take up arms as some of the Valencians had done. The proximity of the French border and the fact that these Moriscos of Aragon (along with the now-expelled Moriscos of Valencia) had already had active contacts with the representatives of Henry IV of France (before that king was assassinated) made this a daunting prospect.

Another and quite separate factor leading to delay in the promulgation of the decree for Aragon was local Christian opposition. We have seen how in the course of the sixteenth century Aragonese liberties had been eroded, but in spite of this some Aragonese nobles and some legists had the courage to voice their disquiet. In the case of the Valencian nobles, bald self-interest was widely seen as determining their stance in this matter. In Aragon, nobles also stood to lose money by losing good cultivators, but in this kingdom, ideals of independence were strong. The rhetoric of loyalty to the ancient liberties enshrined in the constitution was available to inspire spokesmen, so that for them to speak up was easier. The count of Luna and the canon of Saragossa, Doctor Carrillo, went to Castile first in November 1609 to make their case, which was mainly an economic one. The king listened but paid no heed to what was said.

There was also the question of the Morisco children, as we have seen, an encoded way of raising in its most acute form the whole issue of whether baptized Christians might be exiled beyond the confines of Christendom. There was an assembly of theologians to discuss the problem in Valladolid on April 25, to clear the way for a session of the Council of State on May 11, but these bodies were being asked to deal with faits accomplis. Philip III had in fact already on April 17 decided to go ahead with the expulsion from Aragon and had sent Agustin Mexía, fresh from his experiences in Valencia, to Saragossa, with dispatches for the archbishop, the viceroy, and other dignitaries. When the Council of State on April 25 handed over to Agustín Mexía the task of deciding what to do about the children, he must have known what was expected of him.

Across the frontier in France, Henry IV had, on February 22, 1610, already issued an *ordonnance* offering to the Moriscos a place of refuge, on two conditions, the first being that they should *not* settle to the south of the Dordogne (presumably the security risks that would have been created by having in the frontier regions people so easily manipulated by Spanish agents were felt to be too great). Henry's other provision was the Moriscos must become Catholics (he had, of course, himself decided seventeen years earlier that Paris was worth a mass).

> His Majesty has every good intention toward them—of treating them with humanity, receiving them in his realms, where those willing to make a profession of the Roman Catholic Apostolic faith may reside in all security. Those others who do not wish to do so will be granted right of passing freely as far as his ports for the Levant so that they may thence arrange transport to Barbary, or elsewhere, as they may wish. (Lapeyre 1959, 145)

That generous offer might have been seen by Philip III's ministers as a potential threat. Spain's enemies were being offered asylum in a place where they might sooner or later turn into a danger to their former homeland. The assassination of Henry IV on May 14 by Ravaillac immediately put in doubt whether the promise would be fulfilled. Some Moriscos did cross the land frontier taking advantage of Henry's *ordonnance,* but when the proclamation was made on May 29, Henry was already dead.

Essentially, the expulsion from Valencia had been by sea and was directed to Oran. Although numbers of Moriscos in Aragon were smaller, this time those driven out were being scattered in various directions. Some were to go by sea from an embarkation point on the Ebro delta (Los Alfaques). But others were to enter France using the pass at Canfranc.

From the speed with which columns of refugees arrived at the Pyrenean border, one suspects they must have been mustered in advance. However that may be, they were not allowed to across immediately. The French viceroy of Navarre, the duc de La Force (whose memoirs survive and constitute a valuable source) insisted on consulting the queen regent, Marie de Médicis. As he must have expected, her views did not coincide with what had been decided by Henry. It was July 9 before he received his new instructions, which were as unclear as those given by Philip III to Mexía on the subject of Morisco children had been: the duc de La Force might let the refugees enter, he was told, if he had to. This he did, setting an upper limit of 8,000–10,000, and these would have to pay an entry duty (10–12 *reales* a head). The crossing at Somport remained open until September 4. Other mountain passes were used as well, and some 10,000 exited through Navarre.

Other Moriscos who had at first been heading for the French border were redirected to Los Alfaques, an embarkation point that was also handling Moriscos in large numbers from Saragossa and Teruel (38,000) and from Catalonia (3,600) also. The destination of these ships is not known. Lapeyre (1959, 104) contends that they went to Oran, but in view of the length of the voyage to the African coast, I suspect that many captains found some way of discharging their cargoes in southern France. Once in France, the Moriscos were routed to Agde, with a view to taking ship once more, this time to Tunis.

The vice-chancellor of Aragon was able to inform Philip III in 1618 that his kingdom was "cleaner than any other of this breed" (Lapeyre 1959, n. 7), an assessment that Lapeyre accepts. I know of no evidence that would prove or disprove it. There must always have been a temptation to tell the monarch what he wanted to hear.

In Catalonia, on the other hand, although some areas had been subjected to wholesale clearance (such as Lérida, Ascó, and Benisanet), others, especially villages near to Tortosa, were protected by the bishop of Tortosa. He declared them to be good Christians, and so they were allowed to stay. Enemies would have it they were "as much Moors as the people in Barbary" (*tan moros como los de Berbería,* a minor variant on the familiar old wording) and even insisted in pursuing the matter as far up as the Council of Aragon and the Council of State. Philip III would have none of such troublemaking and in 1614 ruled in favor of the bishop of Tortosa: the ex-Moriscos were to be allowed to stay. The total number of the Catalan Moriscos who in this way escaped the expulsion is given by Lapeyre (1959, 113) as 397 households; according to how one estimates the average size of a household, that would make 1,600–2,000 individuals.

THE CROWN OF CASTILE

The nature of the Morisco settlements and the way in which the expulsions were organized in Castile differs here again. There was a lack of homogeneity about the Moriscos of the Crown of Castile. There were the well-established and integrated ex-Mudejar communities of Old and New Castile and other areas of the *meseta,* where small urban Moorish quarters housed generally small groups of craftsmen and laborers. In addition, we must not forget the Granadans, who, after the deportations of the early 1570s, had been settled wherever room could be found. The intention had been to place the Granadans in small communities where they would be more rapidly acculturated, but this had rarely happened. These people were often only poorly integrated. Many had subsequently found their way to such urban centers in Andalusia as Seville, where work was to be had. A few had even illegally slipped back into their old Granadan homeland, where their local knowledge helped them to remain inconspicuous. Granada itself once more had a Morisco population, albeit a small one.

To deal with this diversity there were several decrees of expulsion made at various dates, and not just one. With the expulsion in Valencia in 1609 advancing reasonably in line with expectations in the east, the decision could be taken in September of that year to deal with the potentially equally dangerous inhabitants of Hornachos in the west. That rather exceptional township is the subject of chapter 12.

EXPULSION FROM THE LANDS OF THE CROWN OF CASTILE

After the first proclamation of 1609 (as described above—which for convenience I have termed "type 1") the rest of the peninsula outside the lands of the Crown of Aragon was covered by at least four distinct proclamations or enactments of expulsion affecting different geographical areas, each slightly different both in the justificatory preambles provided and in the actual provisions, although, all agreed, that Moriscos had to leave. I have grouped the other proclamations as follows:

Type 1: First in a proclamation dated September 22, 1609, and then in subsequent proclamations in October and November the Valencian Moriscos were expelled by sea from a number of ports on the Valencian coast and sent to the Spanish enclave of Oran.

Type 2: on January 5, 1610, affecting Old and New Castile, was issued in Valladolid (see below "self-administered expulsion");

Type 3: dated January 12, 1610, affecting Granada, Murcia, and Andalusia (see appendix 5 for the Spanish text);

Type 4: July 10, 1610, affecting Old and New Castile, Extremadura, and La Mancha, and was issued at Aranda (see appendix 7 for the Spanish text).

Finally, under type 5, I group a miscellany of further edicts of more restricted scope that attempted to grapple with various remnant groups that had, in one way or another, avoided the effects of the first four types of decree, or had been overlooked, or had attempted to defend themselves by litigation and thus had managed to stay on after the deadline set for their area, or had simply slipped back into Spain after being cast out. This protracted " tidying up" process may be deemed to have reached its close in 1614.

The decision to proceed against the Morisco inhabitants of Andalusia and Murcia was made, and the relevant decrees were signed on December 9, 1609, although they were not published until January 12, 1610, for Andalusia proper (it appears to have been January 18 for Murcia). These expulsions were enforced deportations more or less on the Valencian type 1 pattern of the previous year. However, one of the commissars, Alonso de Sotomayor (he was actually in charge of the Murcian operation) put forward a highly intelligent suggestion specifically with regard to Old and New Castile. He proposed that some of the Moriscos should be allowed to banish themselves, take themselves into exile. He was thinking above all of the well-assimilated Moriscos, the ex-Mudejars, of Castile. Given that the Spanish authorities were here dealing with people often living in relatively small and geographically dispersed communities, the logistical problems of assembling them and escorting them would have been immense. If the overstretched forces of order could transfer some of the burden of administration onto those being expelled, a near-impossible task might become feasible. Sotomayor's suggestion might be seen as growing out of the final, thirteenth clause of the original edict affecting Valencia. That did allow individuals to opt for a different destination, but the arrangements had to be made from scratch within the impossibly short time then allowed: three days. It seems to have remained a dead letter. The expulsion from Castile gave those departing thirty days' notice.

PARTIALLY SELF-ADMINISTERED EXILE: CASTILE
Sotomayor's scheme as it was eventually put into effect contained what were from the administrative point of view two refinements. In the first place, an element of bureaucratic order was injected into the system by requiring those electing to remove themselves from Spanish jurisdiction to make a formal report of their intention to the count of Salazar in

Burgos. Most of the Moriscos in question lived in Old and New Castile and in the province of Toledo, that is to say, to the south of Burgos. In the second place, it needs to be borne in mind that these particular Moriscos were only allowed to leave via the French frontier. It will be appreciated that this had them moving in the opposite direction from that taken by the Andalusians, who would have to go generally southward, to Seville or other Mediterranean ports.

A copy of the *cédula* in which the conditions attached to this "self-expulsion" option were set out was edited by Boronat (1901, 2: 288, n. 17)[6] from what he described as a "very badly printed" handbill. This phase of the expulsion is less well known than the large-scale clean-sweep expulsions affecting other regions, and it is perhaps desirable to give a fairly full extract from the text.

The King
Whereas for just and necessary reasons I have been moved out of consideration to the service of God and the safety of these realms of Spain to command that the Morisco New Christians resident in Valencia should leave and go away from these said realms of Spain for the reasons set out in the proclamation which has been by order made there, now, seeing that those of the said nation who inhabit the kingdoms of Old and New Castile, Extremadura, and La Mancha have become disquieted and shown signs that they may wish to depart and live outside these realms, and have begun to dispose of their property, selling it for far below what it is worth, and *whereas* it is not my intention that any should against his or her will live here, I therefore allow and give permission in virtue of these presents to all those who may wish to depart from these my kingdoms and realms of Spain, to live outside them wherever they desire, to do so without incurring any penalty within the space of thirty days counting from this proclamation. I grant that during this time they may dispose of their goods, chattels, and livestock but not their real estate, and they may take away the proceeds, not in coin, gold, silver, jewels, nor letters of exchange, but in the form of merchandise purchased from native inhabitants of these kingdoms, and from no others, and also in fruit and produce from them. I nevertheless permit them to take such money as they will need for the journey they have to make. And in order that they may do all this in security, I hereby take and accept under my royal protection those who wish to leave this kingdom and guarantee them and their goods, so that during this period they may go about and be safe, sell, exchange, and alienate all the above-mentioned goods, chattels, and livestock of theirs and make use of the money, gold, silver, and jewels in merchandise the export of

6. The copy edited by Boronat was certified in Valladolid on January 5, 1610.

which is permitted by the laws and decrees of these realms, without suffering unjustly any harm during the said period ... they may export the said merchandise after paying the normal customs dues ... and I command all the officers of justice of my kingdoms, governors of my frontiers ... that they see to it that the above is observed, and that they do nothing against it ... under penalty of loss of office. And I command that this my *cédula* be proclaimed so that it may be known to all. Delivered in Madrid December 28, 1609.

It is my will that those who wish to leave my realms should not pass through the province of Andalusia nor the kingdoms of Granada, Murcia, Valencia nor Aragon, under penalty of death and confiscation of goods.

I, the King

What is conceded by the document proper is little enough: whereas the Valencian expulsion proclamation gave only three days, here the Moriscos have a month during which they were not confined to their home villages: they could travel about freely to realize their assets. The ban on export of money or bills of exchange was, of course, very harsh to our modern minds, but it was a provision that stemmed from the mercantilist economic theory of the times.

More important, together with the *cédula,* one needs to read accompanying instructions regarding the implementation of the edict sent by the king to the count of Villanueva de Cañedo (Boronat 1901, 2: 290, n. 20; also in Janer 1857, 340–41):

My cousin,

In order to avoid such fraud as might occur as the Moriscos leave the country by virtue of the proclamation that I sent to you, I have resolved that in addition, the following should be proclaimed and carried out:

Before any Morisco may leave his place of birth or residence to go abroad, he must go to the officer of justice of the place to inform him and to have registered officially what persons are traveling, with descriptions and details of everything of any kind they will be taking with them. They should be given confirmation of this registration, with a list of the things registered, to avoid problems on the road or in places through which they pass. Send me as soon as possible a copy identical to that handed to those leaving, addressed to Andrés de Prada, my secretary of state. *All Moriscos leaving for France* [emphasis added] are to be obliged to pass through the city of Burgos and to report with their certification and with their property to the count of Salazar of my Council of War, whom I have instructed to go there to check the documentation and ensure the smooth passage of these people, who are not to be ill-used and who should be accorded the necessary attention.

They may spend their money, gold, silver, and valuables while traveling between their place of residence and the city of Burgos on those things authorized in the proclamation, for from Burgos onward they are not to be allowed to take with them more money than is, according to the fixed scale, required for the journey, and the rest must be used for purchases as permitted in the proclamation. Infractions are to be punished by confiscation.

I charge you to publish this where you are and to instruct the officers of justice to carry it out without fail. The registers and certificates are to be sent to me punctually. Any offenses are to be referred to the said count of Salazar. Madrid, January 19, 1610.

I, the King

And so in January 1610, Salazar began supervising the exodus of the long-established communities of the towns and cities of the center of the peninsula.[7] These Moriscos, particularly those from the prosperous ancient communities such as Toledo, traveled in some style. The wealthy ones even came in their carriages, and Salazar reports to the council that his inspections had revealed one fraud: jewels and money were being hidden in the axle trees. Within three months, some eight thousand individuals had left by this route. One reason why the scheme functioned so well was that on the French side there were positive arrangements to cope with the influx. A French official, M. de la Clielle, had been sent to deal with them as they came across the border, and indeed the *Mercure françoys* reported that the governor of Saint-Jean-de-Luz was there to wish them well (Lapeyre 1959, 160 and n. 1). Perhaps this is why Saint-Jean-de-Luz became something of a staging point, and its temporary population of Moriscos grew considerably. It seems to have persisted for some years as a center for Morisco refugees to judge by the reminiscences of al-Hajari.[8] Most of these Moriscos, once in France, made their way to Agde to take ship for Tunis, but a few may have gone northward into France in line with original concessions. The success of this route was great, to the

7. Somewhat confusingly, these people are often referred to in the contemporary documentation as *moriscos viejos*. Any attempt by a modern historian to create a standard terminology with long-term validity for all these communities is doomed to failure. They were, in the nomenclature more usual in modern historical studies, descendants of the "Mudejars of Castile."

8. See his memoir of his travels in France, and of his meetings with such refugees, *Kitab Nasir al-Din* (Al-Hajari 1997, 118ff).

alarm of the Spanish military men, who presumably feared they might lose control at the frontier. On March 28, 1610, Salazar was told to close the operation down, but so numerous were the groups already near to France that it was decided to let them through, and it was late April before a total ban could be imposed on the traffic. Between 16,000 and 17,000 had passed that way, to the profit of the Spanish Crown, which had taken above 100,000 escudos from the refugees (who had to pay to the Crown half of what they had with them!). Salazar nevertheless warned his royal master against what was going on: his letters to the king show that by late March Salazar was very anxious.[9] Could it really be wise, he asked his masters, to send out "so many people of a good class, men of property, to a country so unfriendly" (*tanta y tan buena gente y con hazienda a un Reyno poco amigo*; Lapeyre 1959, 160 and nn. 2, 3)? Salazar meant, of course, unfriendly toward Philip III, not unfriendly toward the refugees themselves!

Two quite unconnected deaths seem to have precipitated the closure of this French route, for some months at least. In the first place, the death of Sotomayor, who had been charged with the supervision of the Mediterranean port of Cartagena as a point of exit from Valencia/Murcia, led to Salazar being cross-posted to replace him in early May. It is unclear whether anybody was nominated to replace Salazar in Burgos. Then, as already mentioned, the assassination of Henry IV on May 14 meant that the authorities on the French side had to consult the queen regent, who adopted a quite different attitude toward the tides of refugees. So the authorities on each side had their reasons not to favor this land route. But as with so many other aspects of this tragedy, there was indecision and muddle. By August 17, the French route was resumed, with Vitoria (much nearer the border) as the inspection point instead of Burgos. Were these later crossings in August and September of the "semivoluntary" kind? Perhaps not, by this phase.

ENFORCED EXPULSIONS

By no means all the refugees who made their own way to the land frontier with France were wealthy, but some were. The vast majority of the Moriscos were expelled willy-nilly in organized groups through the seaports. As we have seen, the ports of the Valencian coast were used in 1609. In 1610, in addition to the land frontier, a much wider range of sea routes were in use, with Moriscos leaving by ports from Seville in the west to Los Alfaques on the Ebro delta in the east. (Mention is made

9. These letters are extant. See A. G. Simancas, Estado leg. 220.

in some of the documents of authorization of use of ports on the Biscay coast, but at the present time reliable information on attested cases of such routes in fact being employed has not come to light.)

The Edict of January 12–13, 1610: Affecting Andalusia (Including Granada Whither Some of Those Expelled Earlier Had Returned)

To justify its harsh provisions aimed at subjects who had not been guilty of rebellion, the preamble to this edict finds it desirable to blacken the reputation of these Moriscos; it was not just that they "were or preceded from those who concurred with the rising in the Kingdom of Granada" (and that was not true in all cases), they had, so it was alleged, subsequently had treasonable dealings with the Turks and with "other princes to whom they offered their persons and their possessions." They had failed to reveal the plots that had been launched against Spain, "a clear sign they are all of the same opinion." In order to silence those who might claim that *individual* guilt had not been demonstrated, the edict then adduces an argument based on group responsibility: "When some detestable crime is committed by members of some corporation or college, it is only right that the body should be dissolved, and that some should be punished for the offenses of others." Thus, *without exception,* the Moriscos were all to be expelled (no exceptions being made for infants) and were obliged to leave within thirty days. The procedure with regard to property is as above: money in the form of coin might not be exported, but nonembargoed goods could be (this is represented as a merciful dispensation, after all, the king might "justifiably" have confiscated everything).

After dealing with these categories of deportees between January and May, by July attention moved to the other groups who remained: those Moriscos from the non-Andalusian parts of the lands of the Crown of Castile who had not thus far taken advantage of the chance to leave of their own volition as provided in the edicts of January (presumably some had hoped that by simply staying put they might avoid expulsion; others may simply have lacked the resources to pay their own travel expenses).

The Edict of July 10 Issued in Aranda (Affecting Old and New Castile, Extremadura, and La Mancha)

This edict, while following the earlier ones, shows some minor but significant differences. It refers to those who had "not made use of the permission" granted to those who had left earlier. It seems to justify action against any who remained by "inferring their mind and intention" to leave from the fact they were already known to be disposing of their possessions! It would hardly be worthwhile commenting on the humbug of this argument were it not for the fact that it reveals an uneasy conscience.

Once again, the assertion is made that alleged conspiracy and treachery would have justified inflicting the death penalty "without scruple," so that what is being done is represented as "mercy" (*piedad*), and that the king's obligations to assure the "conservation and security of my realms" force him to act.

Once again, the idea of collective responsibility is brought forward. All the Moriscos must pay the penalty for what some are alleged to have done. Sixty days is stated as the time granted for the Moriscos to prepare to leave (but in fact only thirty were given). It is spelled out that Moriscos who are members of the clergy, such as monks and nuns, are exempt. The point of exit was to be the southern sea ports (later, those living in the north of the peninsula were again allowed to leave by France). Curiously, the wording of the ban on the export of currency and valuables is repeated unchanged from the earlier edicts, but then the text closes, "But although it is forbidden to them by the laws of these realms, if any of them should wish to take out their property in money, silver and jewels *they may do so, so long as they register it, and hand over half of it to my treasury* [emphasis added] to the person appointed to receive such things, as the other Moriscos who left have done, but in this case they may not take goods with them." This, then, allows those expelled to follow a similar procedure to that briefly in place on the Burgos-Canfranc route, although on less advantageous terms. The former Mudejars of Castile people who had never given any trouble to the Crown whatsoever, were given this reward: they only had half of their money confiscated, instead of all of it, and they lost all of their chattels!

AWKWARD AND EXCEPTIONAL CASES

The edicts frequently contained such words as "without exception," but of course there were exceptions. There was a desire to get rid of all Moriscos as tidily as possible, but various categories were generally recognized as posing special problems. (This was quite apart from such individuals as enjoyed the protection of those powerful enough to risk helping them, in spite of the edicts. Mention has been made of the protection afforded by the Church within the diocese of Tortosa to local Moriscos.) The authorities saw that there was one category that would have suffered a great deal if they had been sent to Muslim lands, and that was the very small number of individuals who had in the recent past entered Spain as converts from Islam to Christianity. (In the Mediterranean world of piracy and corsairs, such cases were not unknown.) These people would themselves have realized that in Islamic terms they would be classified as *murtadd* (perhaps "renegade"), and for them under Islamic law the *hadd* penalty was death. Presumably the Christian authorities had some inkling of the fate that would await any such converts if they had been rejected as dubious and sent back. The proclamation issued at Aranda in July 1610, for example, made provision for these cases and explicitly exempted "Moors from Barbary" who had come to be converted (see appendix 5).

The proclamation in question had opened by dealing with another difficult borderline category: mixed marriages in which an Old Christian man had married a Morisco woman. (The opposite case, that of a Morisco man married to an Old Christian woman, would be covered by the 1609 edict and other parallel enactments under its clauses 11 and 12 whereby Moriscos who had lived among Christians and could be certified so to have done, might be exempt from expulsion.) An Old Christian man's household would by definition be Christian, so his wife would not be expelled, whereas a Morisco man's whole household would be suspected of Islamic heresy.

Slaves

Yet another awkward category is one that has already been mentioned: slaves. In general, the Muslim slave belonging to a Christian master was allowed to remain, because he was the property of his master. But then within this category was the even more awkward subcategory of Morisco refugees from Spain taken captive in North Africa (as, for example, in skirmishes round the Spanish *presidio* enclaves such as Oran). As we will see, the fear here seems to have been that they would have children who might eventually be manumitted, so that the Morisco problem might start up all over again. A proclamation made in Seville by Luis Méndez de Haro y Sotomayor, marqués del Carpio, on August 4, 1610, addresses these problems:

> *Whereas* it has pleased His Majesty to determine the procedure to be followed in the case of such Moriscos as have left this country and then have been captured in Barbary, commanding that they be held as slaves, just as with other Moors ["Muslims"] taken in Barbary, nevertheless, in order to avoid the problem that would arise if they had children, they are to become galley slaves, and the Royal Treasury will pay those who have taken them captive whatever price may appear to be fair .... so that all such slaves taken in Barbary are to be declared, collected and handed over .... (Bauer [1923], 166)

Galley slaves were kept chained, and so presumably the marqués del Carpio considered there was no danger that they would breed in the way that domestic slaves might!

THE FINAL REMNANTS

In a *cédula* addressed on March 22, 1611, from Madrid to this same official, the marqués del Carpio, the progress made up to that point with the program of expulsions was summarized by the king as follows:

> Marqués del Carpio, my cousin, and my resident in the city of Seville, you are already aware of the proclamations that I have ordered to be made in my kingdoms about the expulsion of those Moriscos that used to reside there, but because it is understood that many have never left, and others who did go have returned and have managed to hide, it is fitting that this operation should be brought to a perfect conclusion to the service of God and of myself... and so I charge you that immediately upon receiving this you have it proclaimed that within two months from the date of its publication all the Moriscos within your jurisdiction must leave my realms, and that this is to include both the Moriscos who came from Granada and those who failed to leave when summoned to do so in previous proclamations, and those who left and have now returned, with no exceptions, even if they have an affidavit that they have lived as good Christians, because such documents are extremely suspect.

Those with such papers were at least to be allowed to sell their property (including real estate) and leave with what they could realize. Also obliged to leave were former Granadan Moriscos who had been slaves but who by the time the proclamations had been made had become free men, and included in this expulsion were

> the Moriscos known as "Moriscos Antiguos" [i.e., descendants of, among others, the former Mudejars of Castile] who have been living in isolated villages, quarters, or streets and have been treated as such, and have had to pay the *farda* or other special taxes levied on Moriscos to which the Old Christians did not contribute.

Exemptions in line with the subcategories already mentioned were listed: Christian men married to Morisco women, together with their wives and children; any who have come from Barbary to convert to Spain's holy faith; any Moriscos, even from the Kingdom of Granada, who were priests, monks, or nuns; and those who at the present time were slaves.

The provisions of the proclamation were to be carried out without fail, and a list was to be drawn up and submitted to the Crown of all those who had benefited from the exemptions.

In the same year, 1611, in various areas, officers were given the mission of investigating and rooting out Moriscos who had slipped through the net. Success rates varied. The bishop of Tortosa continued to defend his Moriscos (should we say "ex-Moriscos"?) tenaciously. In Denia, the investigator turned up fifty persons liable to expulsion and seven to send as galley slaves. By 1612, the main focus was on Moriscos who had quietly returned, some to their home regions, where some were aided by their old neighbors.

One thinks of the way that in *Don Quixote* Cervantes showed Sancho Panza as very sympathetic to his old Morisco neighbor Ricote. Cervantes had Ricote reenter the country under the guise of being a German pilgrim. One rather gathers that Ricote was going to leave again to join his wife and daughter, who were in Algiers. But these womenfolk are represented as being fundamentally Christian, so that one wonders about his real intentions. The name Ricote, which in *Don Quixote* is a personal name, must surely have been intended to recall the place name of the Ricote Valley, Val de Ricote.

The Val de Ricote was in fact one of the very last areas to be cleared. The reasons for this are puzzling. Perhaps there was some uncertainty as to whether this mountain fastness in the south east of the peninsula had been caught by the edicts of 1609 and January 1610. More likely, it was being protected by powerful interests. The redoubtable reputation of these independent mountain folk may have helped to save them for so long. Whatever the cause, 1611 found the inhabitants of the Val de Ricote still residing on the land of their ancestors. Here again, that faithful servant of the Expulsion, the count of Salazar, was given the task of tidying up the anomaly. By now there was an enormous number of troops available, and the problem would be deploying them effectively in the terrain rather than obtaining their services. The royal galleys under Philibert of Savoy brought across 280 men of the dreaded *tercio* of Lombardy. Nor was money for the operation lacking. A royal *cédula* dated October 13, 1613, repeated the expulsion order to make the king's intention clear. With Salazar at Cieza, just outside the valley, the mountain folk knew that there was little hope left. They tried to impress him with their right to live where they always had done by conducting impressive Christian religious processions. To no avail. The only concession accorded to them was that as they were being hustled out with so little notice, they were allowed to appoint agents to sell their property for them *after* they had left, and then have the money remitted to them.

And so they went, in late December 1613. "About 15,000" of them was the figure given by Lea (1901, 256), certainly far too large an estimate, even if we assume this last redoubt would have become overpopulated. Lapeyre reminds us (1959, 196) that Bleda (1618, 1060) had given a figure of 2,500, and he also reports other figures much at variance with these. The discrepancies presumably arise because it is not clear whether the Val de Ricote proper is intended, or whether the surrounding area with nearby villages is to be included. Lapeyre concludes: "There are doubts, but the figure of 7,000 will not be far from the reality."

This, then, is probably the last area to be inhabited by Muslims in al-Andalus, the last area to undergo "cleansing." The indefatigable Salazar was back in Madrid by early February, and on February 20, 1614, the Consejo de Estado advised the king that the Expulsion might be deemed to be complete. The king gave his approval. Although there crop up after this date cases of individuals, and even small groups, who were being accused such things as Islamic practices, there seems to be no reason to dispute the assessment of the council. The religion of Islam, brought to the Iberian Peninsula in 711, was driven out in 1614, 903 years later.

The Muslims of Spain after 1500 had no state of their own. And they had been forced to change their religion, so their religious status was not their own either. What is more, the change that had been forced on them was, by the canon law of the Church that now claimed them as its members, a step that could never be reversed. Yet both they and their Christian neighbors knew very well where their true religious loyalties lay. In consequence, their political loyalty could easily be impugned. The catchphrase "Tan moros como los de Argél" ("Just as much Muslims as the people in Algiers") was not just an accusation relating to their religious faith, although it was that. Algiers was the enemy across the water: the place that corsairs came from. The words stigmatized the Moriscos as the Enemy Within: in league with the enemy overseas (Perceval 1997, esp. 87–124). They were under suspicion of being traitors.

International relations should be what the words say: the study of relations between nations. By this definition Spain's Muslims could have no "international" relations during the period covered by this book. But is the definition appropriate in their case? For there is a dimension of the history of the final phase of the existence of Muslims in the Iberian Peninsula that cannot be understood adequately unless, alongside their community life inside Spain, we take into account the Spanish Muslims' network of relationships with the rest of the Islamic world and with other states in Europe, too: a distinctive network of *international* contacts.

In the eyes of the Old Christian majority, the Moriscos, as new converts, ought to be subject, were subject, to rules laid down for them both by the Church (especially by the Inquisition, but not solely by that body) and by the Spanish state. Either the Moriscos were, after the conversions, subjects of the Crown, in which case unauthorized contacts with other states, especially with Islamic ones, were treasonable, or else, if they were not true subjects, they were rightly to be treated as enemies.

These "newly converted" ex-Muslims were thus trapped by the system in which they found themselves. There can be no doubt that they were much in need of someone to speak up for them. It is hardly surprising that they made efforts to get their views heard.

The representation abroad of the interests of the Muslims of Spain was, of course, an activity that had been going on before the surrender of Granada in 1492 and before the forcible conversions. This continued after those conversions and through the sixteenth century, which is hardly surprising, since the need was greater. It was an activity that even continued after the last Spanish Muslim had been deported and the last vestige of al-Andalus had ceased to exist (indeed, it became more urgently important at that stage). Representations relating to the interests of Moriscos never ceased although they had no state. There was certainly no centralized institutional continuity, no equivalent of a "Morisco Bureau," but that did not prevent a series of diplomatic maneuvers that endeavored to enlist the help of foreign states. This chapter concerns itself with those attempts.

The focus of much of this work has necessarily been on events within the peninsula, often events on a geographically and chronologically very small scale, perhaps what happened in one small village or on a given day. The forcible conversions need to be felt in all their detail or else they remain abstractions. But now the international relations of the Moriscos require us to step back and review what happened with a broader, in part geopolitical, perspective, and over a much longer time scale.

Before 1492, when the Muslims of Nasrid Granada were free to conduct international relations in the true sense of the term, they had looked to three potential allies within the Islamic world for help and support. At the greatest distance from Spain, but already, by the late fifteenth century, after the capture of Constantinople in 1453, the leading Islamic state, was the Ottoman Empire. Scarcely nearer at hand, but with a much more firmly established, indeed centuries-old, nexus of relations with the Iberian Peninsula, were the Mamluks of Egypt. And nearest of all, just across the water, in what Spain's Muslims called *al-'udwa* or *allende,* "the other side," was, of course, North Africa, the Magrib, which, in the latter part of the fifteenth century and after, was undergoing a period of great instability. In Tunisia, culture under the Hafsids might flourish, but in terms of military power the regime there was weak, too. Further to the west, immediately across the narrow Straits of Gibraltar, lay al-Magrib al-Aqsa, Morocco. There the empire of the Banu Marin had long since collapsed, and various groupings were to dispute that legacy. The Sa'adids only emerged in Morocco as the clear successors in the course of the sixteenth century.

The Nasrids of Granada brought their plight to the attention of the Muslim states in all three of these areas, but as I had said at the close of my study of the period 1250 to 1500: "When Granada's hour of need came, no assistance was forthcoming from any quarter whatsoever" (Harvey 1990, 267). In the period studied here, responses were feeble when compared with the massive aid that had in earlier centuries come from North Africa in the day of the Almoravids and the Almohads.

Representations on behalf of the Muslims of the Iberian Peninsula made in the pre-1492 period had not been limited to those coming from Nasrid Granada. Muslims living in the Christian states, the Mudejars, had also tried to enlist assistance from overseas. As Meyerson argues (1991, 67), "It is very much within the realm of possibility that Mudejar-Ottoman contacts had in fact been established" in this period. His explorations of the Archivo de la Corona de Aragón turned up reports reaching Ferdinand about suspected contacts between Aragon's Mudejar subjects and Istanbul. In 1487, for example, two Mudejars, one a man from Paterna called Pecoret, were reported to be in the Ottoman capital. We need to be aware that an unverified confidential security report such as this is not the same thing as an established fact, and such Aragonese archive material is proof of no more than the extent of Ferdinand's preoccupations, of his fear that assistance from overseas might reach his subject Muslims. However, Andrew Hess, in the course of his investigations into Ottoman sources, has shown (Hess 1968–69, 1970, 1972, 1973, and 1978) that Christian Spain had indeed good reason to be worried. The threat was distant but real. Among Ottoman policy objectives, action in aid of the Muslims of al-Andalus was not a primary concern, but nevertheless the eastern empire did concern itself with these Muslims in the far west, and over the years it sustained a patient drive westward by its own forces and associates. Although the story that Mudejars from Valencia were in Istanbul seeking allies against Ferdinand may have been a mere scare story in its day (when Ferdinand was alive there was no immediate likelihood that the Ottomans would ever be able to put troops ashore in Spain), yet slowly, relentlessly, the Ottomans did develop the necessary seapower (see Hess 1970) to create an effective threat. Eventually, the Turks advanced along the North African littoral. Egypt came under Ottoman rule by 1517, and North Africa as far west as western Algeria was to fall within the Ottoman sphere of influence. Hess was able to demonstrate (1978, 60–61) that Nasrid appeals in the late fifteenth century evoked practical responses. A naval mission was entrusted to Kemal Reis, and he, from bases on the southern shore of the Mediterranean (Bijaya/Bougie, Bône), was in contact with the Muslims of Spain until he was recalled in 1495. That was certainly not the end but the beginning of Ottoman involvement.

The Spanish view of how things turned out is that eventually, in 1571, at the Battle of Lepanto, Spain and its allies heroically stemmed the tide that had been flowing westward. Is that the right way to look at these events? Both fleets suffered grievous losses in that battle. Lepanto was a disaster for both sides, although the Christian naval forces claimed the victory. But the Turks were able to replace their losses within a relatively short space of time, whereas the concentration of Spain on the Enterprise of England meant that its buildup of ships in the Mediterranean was not as rapid. What caused the westward progress of the Ottomans to falter was rather that, unexpectedly to the east of Turkey, on the land frontiers of Anatolia itself, the Ottomans had to direct their attention to the Safavid threat.

To return to the beginning of our period, parallel to the approaches to the Ottomans made by the Nasrids at the end of the fifteenth century were those made by their envoy to the Mamluks of Cairo, Ibn al-Azraq. These contacts have been dealt with in chapter 3 in relation to Ferdinand's internal policy toward the Muslims of his Aragonese realms. The consequences of this diplomatic activity were not inconsiderable, for it provoked a response from Spain. There were Muslims in Spain, in Valencia, and in Aragon who would inevitably suffer if the Mamluks were to yield to Granadan requests that retaliation for their Granadan woes should be inflicted on the Eastern Christians. There was a danger of a spiral of vengeance, which did not occur. The outcome of this round of negotiations was mixed but positive for both sides. The diplomatic offensive initiated by the Granadan Ibn al-Azraq was stymied by the counter-embassy of Ferdinand's Peter Martyr. The Muslims of the Crown of Aragon were left unmolested for another generation, until the 1520s in fact. And the Eastern Christians escaped persecution, too. They did not have to pay the price for the actions of the rulers of Spain.

In commenting on the original Granadan embassy to Cairo that elicited the counter-mission led by Peter Martyr, Meyerson (1991, 290 n. 22) examines the question as to whether it was sent by Boabdil or by al-Zagall—and comes down in favor of the latter. This is perhaps to assume that procedures with regard to things like accreditation were as formal then as they usually are now. It was quite normal for use to be made of travelers or others who happened to be present in the country in question. The "ambassador," Ibn al-Azraq, was a Maliki scholar of distinction. After the surrender of Granada in 1492, Ibn al-Azraq could scarcely return home. He stayed in the east and had no reason to cease to make representations, in Egypt and elsewhere, on behalf of his fellow Granadans. His "accreditation," such as it was, had been to the Mamluks. It will have become increasingly clear to him that no real help would come to his homeland from that quarter. The power of the Cairo regime had not yet in his day collapsed, but the superior vigor of the Ottomans was apparent to all. The only hope that the Muslims of Spain had of securing effective help in the long run was, as we can see clearly now, from the Ottomans, but there is no reason to regard the efforts made by Spain's Muslims to make representations to Cairo, or indeed the efforts made by Ferdinand to neutralize such anti-Spanish propaganda, as being in any way idle exercises. Both parties, Aragonese and Mamluk alike, were relying on long experience stretching back over centuries that told them that these particular diplomatic channels could in some circumstances be effective, particularly in crises when religious feelings were running high. It would seem logical to infer that the restraint shown toward the Muslims of the Crown of Aragon so long as Ferdinand was alive was in some measure due to the skill of the diplomats in keeping open these well-established pathways.

THE IMPACT OF THE TURKS LATER IN THE CENTURY

How different things were forty years later is demonstrated by a letter from archives in Istanbul published by the Tunisian historian Temimi (1975, 100–5). By then the Turks had made themselves into a major naval power, had extended their sphere of influence westward as far as Algiers, and were still pushing steadily ahead, encountering, and usually overwhelming, Spanish outposts as they went. With our knowledge of how things eventually worked out, we are tempted to regard what went on in North Africa at this time as a mere byway of history. We know it led nowhere eventually, but that was not how monarchs saw things at the time. A letter published by Temimi is dated that year, and is addressed in 1541 to Sulayman al-Kanuni ("The Law-Giver"), urging him to send his general Khayr al-din to Spain to lead the Muslims in their struggle: "The whole community joins to present this our petition to our Sultan, may he ever be victorious. Let him come to our aid and send that warrior in the holy war Khayr al-din Pasha from Algiers, the man best fitted to bring us victory, feared as he is by the infidel."

It might on the surface appear that the appeal of 1541 had little more effect than those made to Istanbul in the previous century. Khayr al-din certainly did not start operations inside Spain itself, but his establishment of what amounted to an advance Ottoman base in Algiers was of immeasurable strategic importance from then onward. No longer was *el Gran Turco,* the Great Turk, so far away that no Spanish Muslim could realistically hope for his help. From the Ottoman garrison in Algiers, Valencia was within easy reach. What could be achieved by Algerian seaborne raids was limited, but *¡Moros en la costa!* "The Moors have come ashore!" became a dreaded cry, and the need for Spain to defend its Mediterranean coastline was a considerable drain on resources.

A MORISCO DIPLOMATIC MISSION TO ISTANBUL

When the Spanish legislation of the 1560s set about effectively eliminating all vestiges of Islam from Spain, as we have seen, those Andalusians who took up arms in the Alpujarras could now turn with confidence to Algiers for help: Algiers was by then their safe channel of communication with Istanbul. Once the Morisco revolt in the Alpujarras was under way in the late 1560s, something like normal diplomatic relations between the tiny Muslim enclave and the mighty Caliphate could be maintained.

Mármol (1991, 192) tells the story of the establishment of contact at this period with the Ottoman world as follows. It is interesting to see him so anxious to blacken the reputation of those who came forward in Algiers to volunteer for service in Spain.

How Hernando el Habaqui crossed over to Barbary to seek help, and how Aben Humeya reestablished the position, thanks to the aid sent from Algiers and other places.

Hernando el Habaqui set out from Spain on August 3 [1569] (which was the very day that Aben Humeya was defeated at Válor). It took him a week to reach Algiers, and he presented an urgent request to 'Uluj 'Ali to send him ships and troops. As intercessors he had certain marabouts who pressed his case on religious grounds. He ['Uluj 'Ali] had a proclamation made that any Turk or Moor who wished to cross over to help the *Andaluces* (that is the name they give in Africa to the Granadan Muslims) were free to do so. But when he saw that many men of good quality had been attracted by the reputation they would gain from such an expedition, he concluded it would be better to take them [into his own service] to Tunis, and so that is what he did, granting a free pardon to all fugitives from justice ready to go to help the *Andaluces*. From such people el Habaqui selected 400 harquebusiers under the command of a treacherous and evil Turk called Husayn. He set sail with them in eight foists [a type of small ship] freighted by some private persons with arms and munitions to be sold to the Moors, and he brought them all to the Alpujarras. With this assistance, and with what arms and munitions were being brought in other ships from Tetuan by Muslim and Jewish merchants, the enemies of God took new heart to continue their evil course. . . . Husayn puffed them up with hope by telling them that 'Uluj 'Ali had sent him on the orders of the Grand Turk to discover how the land lay, and how many Morisco men there were there able to bear arms. He asked to see the Almanzora and Alicante valleys, the Sierra de Filabrés, all the villages in the Alpujarras, and then entered Granada in secret and Guadix and Baza too, and reconnoitered those places. He found out everything he wanted about the inhabitants, and told them he would like to have had wings to fly to render account to the Grand Turk, so that he would straight away send a powerful expedition, and he then went back to Barbary laden with presents, jewels, and prisoners....

Mármol goes on to tell us that

Our galleys captured a foist on its way to Barbary, in which they found, among other things, a letter written in Arabic that appeared to be from Aben Aboo to certain Turkish commanders, friends of his, who were in Algiers.

"Praise be to God, who is One. From the servant of the one God to the commanders Bazquez Aga, ... and to all our Turkish friends and confederates:

We would have you know that we are well, praise be to God, and if only we might see you in person, we would lack nothing to content us. You should know that Nebel and commandant Caracax have destroyed us, and the whole kingdom, because they came to tell us they wished to return home, and although we did not wish to permit them to leave, for we still hope for help from God, and from you, still they insisted, and left. If anybody tells you that I gave my permission to the people of al-Andalus to make peace with the Christians, do not believe them, they are heretics and do not believe in God. The truth is that el Habaqui and Muza Cache with others went to the Christians, and made a deal with them to sell the land to them. They then made an agreement with Caracax and Nebel [and others], and they and other merchants gave them sixty prisoners, to enable them to obtain ships to cross safely to Barbary. When he had made this deal, el Habaqui went to the people, and told them all to surrender to the Christians and to leave Castile. I thought they had in mind the good of the Muslim community. I subsequently discovered that what they were doing was selling us all out. For this reason I had him arrested and had his throat cut.[1]

Later in his account of the fighting in the Alpujarras, Mármol (1991, 223) gives us the text of what he alleges is another such letter, from Aben

1. The version of this letter in Castillo 1852 has simply "detained and imprisoned" in the place of "arrested and had his throat cut."

Aboo to the mufti of Constantinople this time, asking him for help from the Great Turk.

> We have heard of your lofty state, and your great generosity, and of your compassion to those who are forlorn and downcast, of your interest in our affairs and your sympathy for our suffering. The lofty king sent us a missive sealed with his seal and promising us help from many armed men in his fleet and everything we may need to sustain this land. Because we are now suffering so much, we once more have recourse to the Sublime Porte and ask for help from you and for victory for you. Help us and the God of Hosts will help you. My Lord, inform the mighty king of what is happening to us, and tell him about us, and of the great war we have on our hands. Tell His Highness that if he should deign to aid us, may he do so swiftly, and with haste, before we perish, for two powerful armies are coming against us, and if we are lost he will have to give account for us on Judgment Day. Much more could be said, and I only cease because a man has no more strength to speak. May God's salvation and benediction be with you. Shaaban 11, 977, corresponding to February 11, 1570.

This dispatch was allegedly captured and translated for Don John of Austria. We know from the register of state papers translated by Alonso del Castillo that the falsification of "captured" dispatches for propaganda purposes certainly took place in this war. There is thus every reason to be distrustful of texts such as the one printed by Mármol, but even if we reject it as wholly spurious, it would still show that there existed a suspicion on the Christian side that such correspondence arising from contacts between Moriscos and Turks was probably taking place. And we know from the documents from the Ottoman archives edited by Temimi and others that such suspicions were well founded.

The crucial decision *not* to give further Turkish military support to Granada came in 1570. The moment of greatest need for the Granadans coincided with a pressing call for all available Ottoman military forces to be assigned to the capture and occupation of Cyprus. The Morisco cause did not lack advocates at Court, the most highly placed individual to speak for them was probably the powerful Sokollu Mehmet Pasha, a Bosnian by origin. Viewed from the perspective of Istanbul, however, the choice between Cyprus and Spain can surely never have been in doubt: a rich and strategically important prize near at hand and easily taken against an expensive and hazardous distant enterprise almost certainly doomed to failure. The following year did see a great naval expedition heading westward, but, as we have seen, it got no further than Greek waters and terminated in the Battle of Lepanto. What is relevant about that battle for our present purposes was that it caused the Ottoman westward advance to pause, and a pause was at that juncture enough to settle the fate of the Moriscos. The outcome of Lepanto could thus hardly have been more disastrous for the Moriscos if the Turks had lost outright. Since help of any sort was not going to come *in time,* events at Lepanto spelled the end for them.

A NEW DIPLOMATIC ORIENTATION

The eventual defeat of Granada's Moriscos by Don John of Austria, followed by Lepanto (Don John again), led to a realignment of power among the Moriscos. Up to that point in the late history of the Muslims in Spain, the heartland of resistance had been in Granada: not the city, but the mountains of the kingdom of that name, especially the Alpujarras. From 1571 onward, after the completion of the expulsions from Granada, the only remaining substantial concentrations of Muslim population with a surviving effective leadership were in the east of the peninsula, in Valencia and in Aragon (the *Levante,* in Hispanic terms). In consequence there took place a realignment, or rather a double realignment, affecting both Christian Spain and the Muslims of Spain. To cite Hess (1972, 66) once more, on the surprising switch effected by Philip II:

> Following the Ottoman victory at Tunis in 1574 and the state bankruptcy [declared by Spain] of 1575, Philip II made a dramatic new effort to resolve the manifold pressures bearing on his enormous empire. Sensing that the Turk had reached the limit of his ability to expand in the west, the Habsburg ruler launched another secret attempt to secure a treaty with the Ottomans; at the same time a succession crisis broke out among the heirs to the Safavid state in Persia.

In addition to the obvious general desirability of securing the disengagement of Spain from its long series of conflicts with the Turks, we must add specifically, the motive of the Battle of Alcazarquivir (or Battle of the Three Kings) of 1578. The sympathies of the Spaniards might on that day have been on the side of the Portuguese against their Muslim enemies, and indeed some Spanish military aid came to Sebastian's cause, but since Sebastian of Portugal had led his army into a defeat in which such a very large proportion of the Portuguese ruling classes, Sebastian himself included, were killed or captured, the opportunity for Philip to take over in Lisbon presented itself. And that opportunity was seized.

And so the configuration of "international relations" was changing radically and rapidly. In these radical realignments, the Moriscos had no primary role to play at all, but, as we will see, they were much affected.

Suddenly, in the 1580s, the way was open for Christian Spain to unify the whole Iberian Peninsula. The Turks, or rather the particular Moroccan prince they sponsored, had lost at the Battle of Alcazarquivir, and so their westward advance was halted. But more important in their Anatolian homeland itself, extreme instability on their northern frontier, engendered by the Safavid menace, indicated that it was prudent for them to desist from overseas adventures. And since Granada, the channel through which Ottoman aid for al-Andalus had hitherto passed, had been so conclusively eliminated after 1570, the Turks no longer had a functioning network of sympathizers within the Iberian Peninsula.

In the background to all this was a surprising, even shocking, fresh development: Turco-Spanish contacts and eventually negotiations that led to the conclusion of a truce between the two former enemies in 1580. As Braudel pointed out (1973, 2: 1143–1185 and especially 1165), there is a tendency of Spanish historians to pass over the truce of 1580 as a mere aberrant development, whereas in fact it was the culmination of diplomacy that had been going on for some years; it was a development of primary importance:

> The 1580's mark a turning-point in the history of Spain's relations with Islam. . . . After Margliani's embassy [i.e., to Istanbul in 1580] a *de facto* peace reigned. The 1581 truce seems to have been renewed in 1584 and even in 1587. And later hostilities when they occurred bore no comparison with the mighty confrontations of the past. The truce was more than a clever expedient of Spanish diplomacy. (Braudel, 1973, 2: 1165)

After commenting that the reasons behind these developments were not altogether clear, Braudel continues:

> But the phenomenon itself is visible for all to see: the Hispanic bloc, and the Ottoman bloc, so long locked together in a struggle for the Mediterranean, at last disengaged their forces and at a stroke the inland sea was freed from that international war which had from 1550–1580 been its major feature. (2: 1185)

Braudel was of course thinking at this point in terms of broad global strategy. Yet what occurred had enormous implications within the Iberian Peninsula for the Moriscos.

It may have seemed that in the early 1580s Philip was presented with a chance to settle his Morisco problem once and for all, because the fear that the Turks would seek to intervene to rescue them had suddenly receded. How much the Moriscos knew of the way that they had been abandoned by the Muslim power on which they had built such hopes is not clear. Philip's negotiations were largely secret. Hess translates the terms of the Turco-Spanish accord of August 1580 as follows. The sultan addresses Philip:

> It is necessary that your irregulars and corsairs who are producing ugliness and wickedness on land and sea do not harm the subjects of our protected territories, and that they be stopped and controlled. . . . From this side also no situation will come into existence at all contrary to the truce. Whether it be our naval commanders on the sea, our volunteer captains (corsairs) or our commanders who are on the frontiers of the protected territories, our world-obeyed orders will be sent, and damage and difficulty will not afflict your country or states, nor the businessmen who come from that area. (Hess 1972, 69)

The abstractions of the high style of the Ottoman chancery muffle the impact of a really astonishing alliance. It was not an alliance that was destined to last, but what alliances ever do? At this moment in Mediterranean history, suddenly all bets were off. The Ottomans had acquired the time to organize themselves better against the dangerous Safavids. Philip had time and space to digest the prize of Portugal that he had just swallowed. He might also have proceeded against his fractious Morisco subjects. He chose instead to confront not only Protestant dissidence in the Low Countries but to plan action against Elizabeth of England.

That policy option took some time to emerge as his preferred path. We have seen in chapter 9 that almost as soon as he arrived in Lisbon he had set in motion policy studies made with a view to bringing the Morisco question to a conclusion. The Moriscos were beyond doubt high on the agenda. If the planning undertaken in Lisbon in 1581–82 did not lead to rapid action, that was because Philip allowed himself to become embroiled in conflict in the north. Why he made that mistake (for it clearly was from the Christian Spanish viewpoint a mistake) falls far outside the scope of the present study. The consequence of that option was that Islam subsisted in Spain for a further three decades.

REALIGNMENT OF THE MORISCO ALLIANCES

Moriscos could not know in 1580 that events overseas, the Dutch wars and the English defeat of the Spanish Armada, were soon to limit Philip's capacity to act against them at home. Far from being reassured, they must have become aware that the international realignment meant they could no longer expect such help from the Turks as they had received in the recent past. And they could see that in Morocco Ahmad al-Mansur was more concerned with keeping the Ottomans out of the northwest Magrib than attempting to help them.

Time had come for the Moriscos to look for allies elsewhere. In a quite new direction, closer to hand, in the north, where Philip had his greatest enemies: the Dutch, the English, and just across the Pyrenees, the Protestants of France. The new orientation at first served them well. Philip, with such enemies abroad, could not risk putting into action any of the anti-Morisco schemes that had so recently seemed feasible. The new importance in Morisco politics of the French frontier meant that it was the Morisco communities of the northeast, Aragon and, to a lesser extent, Valencia, those who were in a position to maintain contact with Europe north of the Pyrenees, who took over the leadership of Spanish Islam.

We now know that turning northward and seeking Christian allies (Henry IV, Elizabeth of England, William of Orange) in the long run did the Moriscos little good, no good at all, in fact, but the attempted realignment was a rational step. Turkey had left them in the lurch, and in any case was too far, would always be too far away. If anything was to be achieved before it was too late, it would have to be thanks to forces nearer to hand.

The Spanish security services seem to have managed to keep up with the evolution of Morisco policy. There were in this period several trials in which Moriscos were condemned as agents of foreign powers. In 1575 in Saragossa a Huguenot called François Nalias, a man allegedly linked to the Moriscos of Navarre and with the representatives of Henry IV, was convicted as a spy. We know from the *Memoirs* of the duke de La Force that these alleged diplomatic contacts were not the figments of the imagination of Spanish agents. Henry of Navarre was indeed promised by one Miguel Alamí large forces (60,000 fighting men from 76,000 families divided into five tribes!) if only his troops would cross the frontier into Spain and provide the Moriscos with arms. They could easily take Valencia and proclaim Henry king, it was alleged.

Throughout his life, Henry was nothing if not a political realist, and he and his advisers will have had no difficulty in scaling these absurd Morisco offers down to size. But contacts there were, and until the end Henry seems to have been sympathetic to the Morisco cause.

In this northward-facing final phase of the Morisco pursuit of overseas assistance, possibly the greatest mistake committed by the Moriscos was their attempt to find allies in England. The consequences for them were disastrous. But to follow what happened at this stage we must first look southward across the Mediterranean to the North African power that has thus far largely been ignored in this survey: Morocco. Morocco, the Islamic land nearest to hand to the Iberian Peninsula, had been the source, from the days of the Almoravids onward, of vital assistance to Spain's

Muslims; it was destined to be the land that, along with Tunisia, was to provide a place of refuge for the largest proportion of the Muslim refugees. In any survey of the Moriscos' international relations it must occupy a key position. If it has been left until last that is solely because it has been convenient to focus on the East. Morocco's complex history was certainly not static during the sixteenth century, it was at this time evolving rapidly.

Many eminent historians ascribe only a marginal role to Morocco in the history of the Islamic world at this period. Bernard Lewis (1982, 118), for example, gave the following evaluation: "In the world of Islam Morocco, in Arabic called *al-Maghrib al-Aqsa,* the Far West, was a remote and isolated outpost and a comparatively small and weak country at that." Remote it certainly was from the power centers of the Middle East, but small and weak was not how the English queen or the Dutch *stadhouder* perceived this giant of the Islamic West.

The power vacuum and political chaos in northwest Africa that had certainly persisted since the collapse of the Marinids was at this juncture brought to an end by Ahmad *al-Mansur* ("the Victorious"). In the course of his long reign (1578–1603), he succeeded in establishing a firm grasp on power. He had reason to be apprehensive about the westward expansion of the Ottomans. He also had reason to be worried by the fact that certain coastal fortresses and even restricted areas of the hinterland were dominated by Iberian garrisons. But paradoxically, Ahmad's greatest military enterprise was to send a column of troops marching not east or north but *south.*

The direction of advance may have been away from the Iberian Peninsula, but it is nevertheless an event of direct relevance to the history of the Moriscos. This expedition, to Timbuktu and the bend of the Niger in search of gold, stands as a curious African counterpart to the far better-known Spanish exploits with an identical objective in the New World. (Not to mention Sir Walter Raleigh's fruitless pursuit of El Dorado.) What is more, Ahmad's bold expedition was a feat of arms executed in large measure by men born in Spain, most of them Moriscos.

Following up a first expedition, a sort of reconnaissance in strength across the Sahara toward the lands along the Niger [in modern Mali] in 1584, Ahmad in 1591 ordered into action a powerful column equipped with small arms and even artillery, under the command of a general born in Spain, Jaudar, Jaudar Pasha as he came to be known. The objective was the wealthy (and Muslim) Songhay empire.

Jaudar had risen to his command through posts in the royal household (at first in Ahmad's harem: he was a eunuch). The generally accepted view on his origins and early years is that he was born in Spain at Las

Cuevas de Almanzora: the bibliography of those who have taken this view will be found ably and honestly presented in a chapter entitled "The Pasha Jawdar's Cuevas de Almanzora Years" in Haïdara (1993, 17–33). Haïdara gave this chapter the subtitle "Archeology of a Silence" to indicate that he was able to dig up no positive evidence connecting Jawdar to Cuevas (although he seems still to accept it as his subject's birthplace).

A communication I received from the present Moroccan ambassador in London, His Excellency Mohammed Belmahi, contradicts this view. The ambassador has just completed a survey of all his predecessors ever in post in London (an impressive sequence stretching back to 1588). Number 7 in his list is Caid Jaudar Ben Abdallah, identified as the victor of the expedition to Timbuktu. And he is described as being of Portuguese origin. Possibly the failure up to now of anyone writing on the Jaudar Pasha who marched across the Sahara in 1591 to link him with the London ambassador is to be explained by an error of transliteration. In England, as for example, in the caption of a contemporary engraving, I note the misspelling "Jaurar" occurs. In Arabic, the letters *r* and *d* are very similar in shape, so it is easy to see how this happened. Such an ambassador not surprisingly caused quite a stir in London society, and reports survive about him in the *London Gazette*. The fact that this Jaudar served in London as late as 1637 might at first sight cast some doubt on his identification with the conqueror of Gao and Timbuktu, but if we assume that the Jaudar was in his mid-twenties when he was entrusted with command of the Sudan expedition, then he would have been in his seventies in London. We tend to take for granted that our modern practice of requiring senior servants of the state to retire on their pensions in their sixties has always prevailed. That was not the way things were done in the seventeenth century, and there is no reason to reject the evidence from the Moroccan embassy that Jaudar served in London.

Although Jaudar's small contingent of cavalry for the expedition to Timbuktu was Moroccan, the core of his little army of 5,000–6,000 men were Moriscos and other soldiers of European origin, among whom the *corps d' élite* were specialist Morisco troops trained in the use of the harquebus. (The words of command in this expedition across the Sahara to the bend of the Niger were given in Spanish.) That there was such a strong Morisco element in the expedition to Timbuktu should not be taken as necessarily indicating that Ahmad was well inclined toward the refugee community. A certain wariness on his part would have been justified. In internal Moroccan politics, refugees from Spain threatened to upset the social and political balance in some areas where they had settled, and there were even towns (Rabat/Sala) where they threatened to become a dangerous destabilizing element, particularly because they proved themselves quite prepared to negotiate independently with non-Moroccan powers, with the Ottomans on the one hand, the English, the Dutch, even the Spaniards, on the other. One wonders (and this is purely speculation) whether for Ahmad one of the merits of his Timbuktu enterprise may not have been that it removed so many rootless fighting men far from the heart of his empire and busied them with tasks far away in the south. (And there indeed, after Jaudar's return, they proceeded to fight one another in wars that recall the internecine strife that took place in the sixteenth century in Peru between equally insubordinate factions of conquistadors.)

With his firearms Jaudar had no difficulty in slicing through the proud medieval-style armies of the *askiya* of Gao. One might argue that such a battle between soldiers and military technologies effectively from quite distinct historical and technological ages (late sixteenth-century, i.e., early modern, vs. fourteenth-century, late medieval) ought to impress us no more than the fighting in Mark Twain's fantasy *A Connecticut Yankee in King Arthur's Court.* That would be to ignore the terrain over which he had to operate. Jaudar's victory was a triumph, above all, of logistics and military discipline under appalling conditions. He marched his men for some seven hundred miles across some of the worst desert in the world. The sixteenth-century exploits of the Spanish conquistadors in the Americas are remembered still because for the nations of modern Spanish America the epic stories of how they came into existence help define their national identity. Jaudar's march, and his conquest of Gao and of Timbuktu in 1591, are almost completely forgotten nowadays because after he himself returned north in 1599, his conquests soon fell into chaos, and the *pashalik* he had commanded eventually faded away. Yet the determined generalship of his march might more properly be compared with Alexander the Great's renowned expedition to the Saharan oasis of Siwa: an unsupported column striking across the North African desert and far into the distant unknown.

There is still in Mali a small remnant of the descendants of the largely Morisco army that had marched south with Jaudar. Nowadays they have fallen on hard times. In Arabic one name for an harquebusier was *rami,* of which the plural is *arma'.* The word in the first place in Arabic signified "archer," but as frequently happens with military terminology, an old name was reused for a later technological innovation. In modern times in statistical lists, "Arma" is however a label attached to a particular ethnic group, the descendants of the families founded by the men who marched with Jaudar. Once a dominant military aristocracy on the whole bend of the Niger, they are now a small, marginalized remnant who keep themselves to themselves.[2] A sad human monument to a curious Morisco adventure.

Morocco failed to keep control of the vast territory Jaudar and his largely Morisco harquebusiers had subdued for it. Perhaps it lost interest when he heard that the gold mines that had attracted its army southward across such inhospitable country could not be found. (They were, as we know now, very much further away.) But although there were no mines, the local treasuries were full of gold, and this was captured. Jaudar ordered the transport northward of a great quantity of it (described as *tibar*, "gold dust," i.e., "alluvial gold," a clear indication that it had not been produced by smelting from any mine). A train of sixteen camels brought the booty north, sufficient to earn for Jaudar's master the epithet of *al-dhahabi*, "the man of gold," "el dorado," as the Spaniards would have said. Ahmad got the gold he so desired. And by stripping in this way the assets of the kingdoms of the blacks, accumulated by them over many years, he now had the means of buying the military, naval, and scientific equipment for which he hankered. Dutch and English merchants, arms dealers (among others) hastened to his court to offer to satisfy his needs. The Barbary Company had been set up in London in 1585 at a time when Morocco was already awash with funds derived from the ransoms the Portuguese aristocracy had paid after Alcazarquivir. Its great days were those of Ahmad's affluence.

THE MORISCOS AND FRANCE

In 1604, Henry IV's agent in Valencia, Panissault (Lea 1901, 287), had allegedly been present at an assembly in Toga at which 64 representatives (syndics) elected one Luis Asquer (perhaps *al-'askar*, "the soldier"?) as their "king," to lead a rising to take place on April 7, 1605. The details as given by the duke de La Force, Henry's viceroy in Navarre, do not sound very convincing. If they had emerged in confession extracted in the course of a trial, one might assume that the witness in question was simply blurting out to his interrogators what he thought they wanted to hear. But it is difficult to see why the tale as we have it in de La Force's *Mémoirs* should have been fabricated by him. Ten thousand men were

2. The University of Granada in 1984 sent a scientific and anthropological expedition to this area and published a report, with copious photographic illustrations, under the title *Andalucía en la curva del Niger*, ed. M. Villar Raso et el. (Granada, 1987). Among their many and surprising findings is that the Arma firmly classify themselves still as white men, even though their skin color is no lighter than that of the blacks among whom they live. The cover of the volume in question uses an impressive photograph of the noble and tragic black face of the Arma leader with whom the Granadan expedition had most contact: Zakariya Touré.

to gather near Valencia and under cover of darkness burst into the city, where they would set fire to the holy sepulchers (?) in the churches. The Spaniards could be expected to rush to put the flames out, and the Moriscos, identifying themselves by shouting "Francia!" would be aided by the many French residents of the city to take over and capture the arms stores.

This all sounds profoundly ill-conceived, scarcely credible, frankly ludicrous. The *Mémoirs* assert that French agents and Moriscos did discuss plans along these lines (the Moriscos are even reported to have paid over 120,000 escudos, presumably for arms and assistance). The set date came and went with nothing happening. What did ensue was the arrest in Valencia of the Morisco leaders Alami (already mentioned above) and Iriondo, along with a French agent, Saint Etienne. One suspects that another of the Morisco leaders, Pedro Cortés, may have struck some sort of deal with his captors, for he was spared, while the others were executed. We can guess at the explanation for Henry's lack of success when we learn of what the English were up to.

THE ENGLISH AND THE MORISCOS
The English, thanks to the navy created for the nation by Henry VIII, were an Atlantic power. Under Elizabeth I, the English were in conflict above all with Spain. English interest in Morocco was not merely as a market for English products. The idea of a military and naval alliance between Elizabethan England and al-Mansur's Morocco seems far-fetched now because we know that in practical terms nothing was ever achieved, but there were certainly serious negotiations, their objective being the launching of a military expedition against Spain. In these Anglo-Moroccan talks, the Moriscos were interested parties. Among the emissaries from the Moroccan side were Moriscos.

Ahmad had taken care to contact Elizabeth as soon as he came to power. He wrote in October 1576: "Now I have reached my country and succeeded to my estate, I have held it to be one of the most important and urgent matters to inform you and write to you so that you may be aware of this affection for you" (Hopkins 1982, 1). The two states had a number of interests that helped to bring them together. The English lacked a friendly harbor near the Straits of Gibraltar to use to harass the Spanish fleets (and especially the Silver Fleet). If only a port on the Atlantic coast of Morocco could be made available! The Moroccans needed timber, iron, ropes, and tackle such as could be procured in trade with the northern nations. Toward the end of the century, it looked as if a deal could be struck. Then suddenly, in 1603, two deaths changed the outlook completely: those of Ahmad and of Elizabeth. Ahmad's death was grave news for the Morisco cause. Morocco was again plunged into a civil war, this time among his three sons. There was little hope of mobilizing help for the Moriscos in Spain at such a juncture. Of Ahmad's three rival sons, one, Muley Zaydan, did eventually emerge victorious, but the secure predominance enjoyed by Ahmad was not reestablished, nor was his adventurous foreign policy continued in quite the same form.

The death of Elizabeth was even more disastrous for the Moriscos, and for reasons that can hardly have been foreseen by those who had participated in the initial Anglo-Moroccan talks. During the 1590s and up to the death of Elizabeth, talks (and trade) seem to have continued, but always with some distrust on each side. Since Spanish was the negotiating language, Spanish-speaking Moriscos often served as intermediaries. But out of these contacts the grand anti-Spanish alliance that would have lined up Morocco, England, Henry IV's France, and perhaps the Netherlands, was not achieved. Why?

Elements in the extant diplomatic correspondence between the Sa'-adids and the English court give strong indications as to one reason. First we may look at a letter dated 1601 from Ahmad al-Mansur to Elizabeth. It is intended to let her know that the Moroccan ambassadors who had been engaged in talks at her court (at the palace of Nonesuch in Surrey and elsewhere) had returned safely home to Morocco, but the following sentence hardly demonstrates boundless trust: "As for the excuse offered by Your Majesty for not sending our people on toward Aleppo, we have been pleased to accept it, have understood it in the most generous fashion, and interpret it by the best standards of affection and esteem" (Hopkins 1982, 5). Ahmad had explicitly requested that his envoys, after completing their business in London, should be put on a ship from England to the Levant (not at all a direct passage, but presumably a relatively secure one). The English had failed to do this. The reason is not clear, but an underlying motive slips out in a remark by John Chamberlain (*Sources inédites*, 1900–65, 2: 204): "our merchants nor mariners will not carrie them into Turkie because they thinck yt a matter odious and scandalous to the world to be too frendly or familiar with Infidells." At the highest level, as between monarchs, Anglo-Moroccan diplomatic relations between royal courts might be possible, but at the popular level the basis of trust essential was simply not present. English public opinion might not accept such an alliance, even if England's leaders conceived of this as a way to strike against England's principal foe, Spain. The common folk in England, in naive enactments executed by their Morris (Moorish) dancers on village greens all up and down the land, were used to cheering on Saint George as he fought the Turkish (i.e., Muslim) knight (as they still do nowadays, although they may have forgotten quite why).

At a courtly level, Spenser's *The Faerie Queene* cast the Saracen knights, Sans Foy and Sans Loy and others, as dangerous enemies. English people knew what side they should be on.

After Elizabeth's death, relations deteriorated, and the consequences for the Moriscos could not have been worse. By 1609, Muley Zaydan was forced to write in very firm tones to James I of England, complaining that the English authorities had allowed Castilian emissaries to sequestrate Moroccan goods (sugar) and pointing out that commercial confidence would evaporate if this sort of practice was allowed to continue. "We have addressed you concerning their rights [those of Moroccan merchants who claimed they had unfairly been deprived of their goods] so that you may know that your persistence in this sort of act concerning the rights of merchants will upset the well-being of your country . . . but this is a matter for your own right judgment, so do what you consider to be in your interest." This, dated in 1018/1609, is of course some five years after James had initiated the reverse in English policy that brought such harm to the Moriscos. It was the eve of the expulsion of the Moriscos from Spain.

There were many reasons tending to pull the anti-Spanish powers apart, but the most important new element in the situation was the identity of the monarch himself: James VI of Scotland/James I of England. In his address to his new Parliament at Westminster, James described himself as "an old and experienced king," and so he was, a man of considerable intellectual powers but already set in his patterns of thought from his long years on the Scottish throne. And when he learned of some of the English enterprises that he was taking over, he was deeply shocked.

King James was proud of being an author of independent stature, and among the not inconsiderable list of books to his credit there are two, *The True Law of Free Monarchies* of 1598 and *Basilikon Doron* of 1599, in which he had just set out with clarity his thoughts on the divine right of kings, a doctrine of which he was an unconditional supporter. In the long run, Stuart ideas about the nature of kingship were to cost England (and Scotland) a great deal. James's rigid conception of what should be the relationship between monarch and subject were more immediately disastrous for the Moriscos. Subjects owed complete and unconditional allegiance to their monarch. On learning that Elizabeth and her officials had been toying with the idea of supporting the Moriscos, subjects of the king of Spain, against their divinely appointed monarch, Philip III, James made it clear he would have nothing to do with such scandalous dealings. Subjects had no right to oppose their ruler. That was axiomatic. He was not content simply to withdraw support from rebels and traitors, he insisted on going further and handing over to his divinely appointed opposite number in Spain information about what had been going on. So, in the terminology of modern espionage and subversion, the cover of the English agents and of their contacts was "blown." We may guess that the security of France's contacts with the Moriscos will have been compromised, too. By June 23, 1605, arrests had been made in Spain, and suspects tried and condemned. It is quite likely that the Spanish authorities would have found out what was going on in Valencia and elsewhere without the help of James, for Spanish intelligence had not been without its successes, but what happened will have been a devastating blow to the Morisco cause.

Perhaps even more important is the fact that the accession of this Scottish king to the English throne and his decision in 1604 by the Treaty of London to put an end to the long period of hostilities between England and Spain had disastrous implications for the Moriscos. In the absence of externally generated dangers, Spain could now safely switch resources from its overseas commitments to deal with its internal problems. Very soon another peace, or rather truce, sealed the Moriscos' fate. In 1609 was signed the Twelve-Years Truce between Spain and the Netherlands. The decks had now been cleared. A solution, a Final Solution, was now possible in Spain. No state in Western Europe was at this juncture willing to befriend Spain's internal enemies. The only real help the Moriscos secured was from the Muslim states. Muley Zaydan made representations to the French authorities on behalf of Morisco refugees who had been cheated and ill-used. (What is more, he secured some compensation for them.) And the Ottoman sultan, as has been mentioned, sent out an imperial rescript (*firman*) urging his governors and officials to facilitate the resettlement of the Moriscos in various parts of the Ottoman Empire. But that was not the sort of military intervention from North Africa that, in the Middle Ages, had time and again rescued the Muslims of the Iberian Peninsula from disaster.

THE MORISCOS AND HOLLAND

Al-Hajari, in his *Kitab Nasir al-din 'ala-l'qawm al-kafirin,* appends to his account of the mission that he undertook to France in 1611 a short but fascinating section on the further journey that he undertook, from the Atlantic port of Le Havre in a Dutch ship sailing to Amsterdam. A meeting was arranged for him with the *stadhouder,* the head of state, Prince Maurice of Nassau (and al-Hajari claims he actually had four meetings with the ruler in The Hague). The encounter deserves mention here because we are told how Maurice asked the Morisco for his opinion on soundings he had received about possible Dutch participation in an invasion of Spain from Morocco. This is, of course, precisely the story

Philip III's intelligence services had picked up and that had figured in the position paper that was on the table in 1609 when the actual decision to expel had been reached. By this stage in 1611, of course, most of the potential members of the fifth column who might have been envisaged as assisting the proposed invading force were refugees or had been killed. That detail is not mentioned in al-Hajari's text, but he does tell us how diplomatically he gave a cool response to the scheme: the Moriscos had no land of their own, he reminded the Dutch. It would be necessary to consult the Ottomans and other Islamic rulers, etc. Maurice proposed that they should remain in touch, and indeed he provided al-Hajari with a code to use in such communications! (Of this we hear no more, but that is hardly to be expected.)

Al-Hajari tells us that as official interpreter (and presumably in 1609) he had had the task of translating for Muley Zaydan the Spanish documents relating to the Expulsion (no doubt communicated to the king by Morisco intelligence). Morocco was in no position to act at that time. When the Edicts of Expulsion were published, the Moriscos had no friends or allies in a position to take any action to save them. And so it was that Philip's seasoned troops, with for once no work to do overseas, no foreign enemies to face even on Spanish soil, were fully available for "duties in aid of the civil power" in the Iberian Peninsula itself.

The conduct of international relations by the Moriscos was not the sole or even the primary cause of the catastrophe that befell them. It is difficult to see how things might have been handled differently at the various stages of this tragedy. ("Tragedy" seems a wholly appropriate word, the tide of misfortunes seemed to advance inexorably). It is perhaps remarkable that this acephalous community, devoid of constitutional structures except at the local level, still did manage to make sure the world was not wholly unaware of what was going on and to enlist widespread sympathy and some practical help.

The declining effectiveness of the international relations of the Moriscos mirrored the community's decline. Still, in the late fifteenth century and into beginning of the sixteenth, Ibn al-Azraq and other Spanish Muslim envoys had been able successfully to use the Mamluks of Egypt as a means of putting pressure on Ferdinand and restraining him from acting against his Mudejar subjects in Aragon and Valencia. Something could at that time still be achieved through astute diplomacy. By the end of the sixteenth century and the first decade of the seventeenth century, there were simply no diplomatic levers left sufficiently robust for the Moriscos to hope to use them to hold back Philip III from his objectives.

ELEVEN ❦ Aftermath

Muslims had been leaving the Iberian Peninsula from the eleventh century onward, or else leaving the reconquered northern areas and moving southward as the Christian kingdoms took over more territory. In the later Middle Ages, for some, this meant crossing the seas, usually to North Africa; for others, internal migration meant going to Granada or Valencia. The outflow to North Africa continued even after, in the early sixteenth century, such movements of population had been forbidden. Those determined to leave had to plan their illegal escapes in small boats, but they still went. Sometimes individuals, sometimes whole groups, left clandestinely, even a whole village at one time. This flow of people, usually a mere trickle, at times became a flood and added up over the centuries to a massive Andalusi diaspora. Since the refugees moved outward in so many directions, the labor of collecting information about their varied fates once outside Spain will entail tracing obscure events in perhaps a score of countries. Although we are relatively well informed concerning some reception areas, such as Morocco and Tunisia, little can be said with confidence of others like Turkey, Greater Syria, or Egypt. We have only a few sparse indications. This chapter certainly cannot hope to give a full account of the Muslim diaspora from Spain, yet it is hardly satisfactory to recount what befell those expelled as far as the quayside and then say no more about them.

To study the diaspora of Spain's Muslims will be a major research project.[1] This short chapter aims only to sketch in some indication of the sort of things that happened to some of the exiled Moriscos. Interesting details are beginning to come to light, but a full and coherent general picture has yet to emerge.

The eventual task of tracing the Moriscos into their exile will be complicated by the fact that in some cases the destination of the vessels

---

1. The University of Leiden has begun a major project in this area.

taking the refugees overseas was not correctly stated on the manifests of the ships (in the unlikely event that such documentation has survived). There were various reasons to account for obfuscation with regard to the real destinations of some of the ships. Surveillance of contraband was likely to be less severe for ships ostensibly sailing to Christian ports, for example, but above all there was, still and always, the question of young children. Initially during the Expulsion from 1609 on, it had been the intention to keep back infants (as in Portugal with the Jews). Lapeyre (1959, 153), in his discussion of this topic comments that "[i]t does not seem that these instructions [i.e., about taking children away from their parents] were known about, or at least it seems that they were not applied from the beginning of the embarkations." Nevertheless, as he goes on to say: "One is struck by the great number of the ships which were freighted for Christian ports, and for Marseilles above all. Did they all really go to these places?" Clearly, Lapeyre supposes that some ships apparently sailing to Christian ports were diverted after leaving Spain and sailed into Muslim harbors. In addition, of course, the masters of some ships might well suddenly take it into their heads to offload their passengers in places other than the destination as originally fixed. They might simply have wished to save on sailing-time, and so increase their profits. They might have been genuinely afraid to venture into corsair-infested waters. Or they might have had criminal intentions. In addition, the refugees rarely stayed put long in the port where they had disembarked. A destination relatively near at hand, such as Marseilles, would usually be only the first staging post of an odyssey that might end in Istanbul or beyond.

Pirates would not be put off by the knowledge that most of the passengers in a ship full of refugees would be mere impoverished outcasts; there was a good chance there would be among them a few rich men with as much wealth secreted in their effects as possible. Pesciolini, an agent of the Medici, reporting to his masters at home on departures from Marseilles, speaks of a ship setting out from that port for Constantinople carrying wealthy Moriscos, among them one "Lopez Estalavella," and merchandise to the value of 350,000 crowns (Temimi 1993, 57, doc. no. 15).

As compared with the Muslim world, European countries took in few of the refugees. In northern Europe, indications are sparse indeed. For Germany, the only evidence is from fiction, but ought not to be discounted totally. When Cervantes had Sancho Panza meet his former neighbor Ricote, Ricote had returned to Spain in order to dig up his buried treasure under cover of being a member of a group of German pilgrims. Ricote's wife and daughter were supposed to have ended up meanwhile in Algiers. That is a destination to which many Moriscos really did go, but maybe Germany did also function as a haven of refuge for at least a few.

Both England and Holland were countries that had some contact by way of trade and diplomacy with Moriscos from the 1580s onward. Moriscos in Moroccan service came to London on official or private business, but there is no indication that refugees ever arrived to settle there, nor in Holland, in spite of al-Hajari's visit to the Hague mentioned in the last chapter. In France, and especially in the region of Bordeaux, it is clear that Pesciolini did meet a not inconsiderable number of refugees. Of France, what he tells us coincides with what we can learn from numerous sources, that some did settle, especially in the south. Al-Hajari and his traveling companions were given a friendly enough reception in the capital, Paris, and elsewhere in the north, but the only settlements of Moriscos to which he refers, long-term or temporary, were near places like Bordeaux and Saint-Jean-de-Luz. Henry IV, it will be remembered, had given orders in February 1610 for preparations to be made for the Moriscos' arrival. And those willing to accept conversion to Catholicism were to be permitted to settle beyond the Garonne and Dordogne. Others were to be transported on to North Africa.

Even if Henry had not been assassinated, we can only guess whether his scheme would ever have been implemented in full. Certainly, there are indications of local objections. But of course after Henry died there was a change of policy as described above. Nevertheless it would be strange if no displaced Moriscos finished up in France. There is plenty of evidence (Cardaillac 1971b) that there were some places where relatively small groups managed to find a new permanent home, but the very large numbers that might have hoped to benefit from Henry's offer of hospitality had to find a new life elsewhere.

If France was unwilling to solve the human problem that Spain had created, it seemed at the time of the promulgation of the first decrees of Expulsion that Tuscany was going to provide a home to a substantial number of those stranded at Marseilles. Ferdinand I de' Medici, grand duke from 1587 to 1609, had long been active in building up his domains, and especially the port of Leghorn, by encouraging immigration. But what he really wanted was people with the capital and the skills to develop new enterprises. Already many Spanish Jews had found their way there. Ferdinand was succeeded by Cosimo II, and in pursuit of the grand design to expand trade based on Leghorn he had his agents set about actively attracting Morisco immigrants. Some Moriscos did go to this part of Italy; Temimi (1993, 48) adopts Jean Pignon's estimate of three thousand, a not inconsiderable number. Nevertheless, the very large numbers of Moriscos who seemed at one time likely to cross to Leghorn did not materialize, and above all the very wealthy merchants on whom the grand duke's agents had set their sights preferred to go elsewhere.

Mention has already been made of the interest that the Medici agent Pesciolini took in the movements of Lopez Stalavella. This rich Morisco changed his mind about settling in Italy and sailed past Leghorn and on to Turkey. It does seem probable that the desire of Cosimo to attract some Moriscos was genuine. His correspondence with agents attempting to headhunt suitable people for him in Marseilles confirms this. The reluctance of the Moriscos to commit themselves was understandable. They must have asked themselves whether they were genuinely wanted After all, they had thought they were wanted in France. The sorts of immigrants that the Medici were looking for were, on the one hand, *entrepreneurs* with available capital; on the other, laborers prepared to work the land and carry forward the program of public works. The capitalists preferred (perhaps mistakenly, we will see) to seek their fortune in an Islamic country. Perhaps those three thousand who did accept Cosimo's invitation were the simple folk he also needed. We do not yet know, and it is to be hoped that further investigation will inform us on this fascinating—and surprising—episode.

OUTSIDE EUROPE

So much for Moriscos in Europe, or rather Christian Europe. In the Balkans, in Ottoman territory, we know that individuals reached Belgrade, and we may guess that some went to Sarajevo (where there were also Sephardic Jews). But these are small side-eddies: the main stream took large numbers of Moriscos to Ottoman Turkey, on both sides of the straits, in Istanbul and also Brusa (Harvey 1962). Recent publications by Temimi make it clear that the choice of Turkey and other lands under Ottoman suzerainty was not merely prompted by individual preference but was the Morisco response to positive offers of support and sponsorship emanating at the highest level.

The Ottomans had by now emerged more clearly than ever as the sole Islamic power in the Middle East likely to fulfill the responsibilities of the Caliphate. There were reverses (Lepanto) as well as successes, but with the exception of Morocco (see below) there was nowhere else for the Moriscos to turn when they were faced with the final disaster. The Ottomans had other troubles in their now vast empire, but recent research has shown that their response to the appeals made to them for help were much more generous and far more practical than has hitherto been realized. The full story will not come to light until the vast archives of the Ottomans (who were paper-loving generators of official reports almost to outdo the Habsburgs) are fully available. The exploratory work done by Temimi has already brought startling results. He has been able to publish *firmans* (imperial rescripts) addressed not only to administrative officials in Turkey itself but also to Tunisia, setting out a program of assistance to the displaced Muslims. Thus far, the most valuable document is actually one addressed to the authorities of Tunis in 1613 and directly concerned with the settlement of refugees there.

No doubt in order to place the Tunisian initiatives within a wider perspective, the document informs the beylerbey, the head of the Tunis authorities: "We have permitted them to settle near to Adana, Azir, Sis, Tarsus, and Kars." Before Temimi made this document available, I myself had thought that the only parts of Turkey where we could be certain that Moriscos did in fact find refuge were Istanbul and Bursa (Harvey 1962, 1964). Apart from his discoveries, no independent references to Spanish Muslims in any of these places had come to light. One can see that there might well be a good reason for the Ottomans to wish to strengthen the reliably Sunni element in southeastern Turkey, where the politically dubious Alavi Shi'is were numerous (and perhaps there was also the thought that Arabic-speaking Muslim cultivators from some low-lying areas of intensive agriculture such as the *huerta* of Valencia might rapidly adapt to the life of a partly Arabic-speaking rich agricultural zone such as the neighborhood of the coastal plain of Adana and Tarsus). Those considerations would not have applied in the case of Kars, of course. High in the mountains, that city had only fallen under Ottoman rule in 1580. Its extreme climate would have made life very hard for the newcomers. Presumably it was thought that as Sunnis and as safely subservient clients of the Ottoman regime, the Moriscos might help to stabilize the difficult Safavid frontier. As has been said, we lack independent confirmation that these Anatolian projects were ever put into effect. That such policies were even envisaged shows us how efforts were being made to turn the crisis of the Expulsion to positive advantage.[2]

Of equal interest to this contribution by Temimi to the study of Ottoman policy is what he and others, especially Míkel de Epalza, have shown

2. That in various regions round the Mediterranean basin administrators hoping to facilitate development and innovation should have looked to the specialist manpower and the entrepreneurial expertise made available by the Expulsion was quite logical. There is a natural tendency, certainly apparent at the present time, to look down on displaced persons and refugees as almost by definition underqualified. It is not incorrect in some respects to see the Moriscos as a survival of medieval structures into modern (post-1500) times. But the opposite is also true: some Moriscos were innovators and modernizers. See Thomas Glick, "Moriscos and Marranos as Agents of Technological Diffusion" in *History of Technology* 17 (1995) 113–25. With regard to Tunisia, the classic study of Morisco immigration is, of course, Latham (1957).

us about the Tunisian side of things. Here there is no doubt at all that there was very extensive immigration of refugees from Spain, and these people went both to the capital, Tunis, where among other activities they successfully manufactured and traded in textiles, notably the well-known red Tunisian "bonnets," *chéchia;* they also went to the countryside, above all, to the region of the Cap Bon peninsula. There they participated in extensive agricultural developments (see Epalza and Petit 1973). The efforts made in Tunisia under the Uthman Dey (ruler) to provide the Moriscos with new homes were the largest-scale and the most generous of the various schemes put into effect to solve the grave problem created by the Edicts of Expulsion. The tax holidays that the Moriscos at first enjoyed in Tunisia were part of the package of incentives that the Ottoman authorities had devised, but the local Tunisian authorities added further support and help of all kinds. Efforts were made to integrate these strangers into the structures of Tunisian life, and here Uthman could count on the enthusiastic collaboration of a wealthy Morisco merchant who had already made his way in Tunisian society: Abu'l-Gaith al-Qashshash (Epalza and Petit 1973, 186).

Besides his studies of the positive aspects of Tunisian policies toward the Moriscos, it is one of the merits of Temimi's investigations that he has also documented the existence in Tunis of a counter-current, of the resistance to the pro-Morisco policy of the Sublime Porte that local interests in Tunisia eventually mounted. The Ottoman regime was not a closely integrated centralized empire, but the complaints coming from Moriscos in Tunisia to Istanbul prompted a *firman* dated July 9, 1615, in which Ahmet I, reproving the beylerbey Yusuf, wrote: "The situation [of the Morisco minority] has grown considerably worse because new taxes have been imposed, including some from which local people are exempt. Their situation is even worse than it was under the unbelievers. . . . How are we to accept these injustices committed against those who had to flee from the unbeliever to seek refuge in our territories?" (Temimi 1993b, 36). Istanbul in this way sought to ensure good treatment for the refugees, but if in Tunisia the local powers came to perceive some of the Morisco leadership as a threat to them, it was obviously the Moriscos who had to yield and not their hosts. Central Ottoman backing was of limited use, for it was among local Tunisians that the Moriscos had to make their new life. Under Uthman's successor Yusuf, local impatience with the immigrants surfaced.

The type of agricultural settlement set up by the Moriscos in some areas of Tunisia has similarities with the Spanish colonial exploitation in the Caribbean and elsewhere in the New World. Large-scale cultivation of crops for international rather than local markets (sugar, cotton, grain) on lands granted to the newcomers by the central Tunisian government (grants at the expense of the existing Beduin populations who had been engaged on low-intensity farming on the same land). There were, of course, important differences between plantations in Tunisia and those of the Caribbean. The Beduin displaced by decree in Tunisia were perhaps in a better position to make their resentment of these European immigrants felt than were the Caribs and Arawaks in the Americas. As far as can be discerned at present, and this is one of so many areas in need of investigation, the Moriscos themselves constituted the greater part of the workforce and did not depend in any vital way either on existing local labor or on imported slaves. Nevertheless there is much of the plantation economy about the Morisco settlements of Tunisia—and perhaps elsewhere.

Perhaps even more interesting than the social and religious tensions that arose when local Tunisians found themselves having to compete with large numbers of these energetic and able immigrants is the fate of the individual *entrepreneurs* themselves. We have seen how keen Cosimo II had been to attract such Moriscos to Tuscany. In Tunisia, the role of Mustafa Cárdenas might well be described as that of a venture capitalist. He brought capital from outside and invested it in the development of activities, agricultural and industrial, intended to produce goods for sale for profit on the Mediterranean market. Over the initial period of development, the Tunisian administration was willing to grant extensive tax concessions, presumably in anticipation of eventually broadening its tax base so as to secure increased tax yields in the long run. But this style of imported capitalism seems to have accorded ill with the type of society into which it was implanted. Cárdenas was driven out by the dey who followed after the Moriscos' initial benefactor, Uthman (Temimi 1993, 32–3.). Yusuf Dey seems to have sought to retract the tax advantages at first conceded to the Moriscos. He himself had some interest in the trade in exporting grain. Perhaps the competition that the well-connected Moriscos could offer was troublesome to him. Cárdenas took himself (and his capital?) off to Istanbul.

The bulk of the immigrants remained. They assimilated to the host society but still nowadays keep some of the ways and customs they brought with them from Spain. Some even retain their Spanish surnames, obvious enough in cases such as Blanco or Castillo, well disguised in others by phonological change. Who but a specialist would recognize behind Zbiss (as it so happens, the surname of a distinguished Tunisian researcher into Morisco history), the familiar name *López*, or more specifically, the Valencian form *Llopis*, transformed into its modern Tunisian form by palatalization of the initial consonant; the medial p, s sound nonexistent in Arabic, was replaced by the nearest equivalent, *h*; and, by an altogether typical Magribi shift of the stress, the disyllabic name is reduced to a monosyllable with an initial consonant cluster. The name *Zhiss* might stand as an emblem of how in North Africa the Hispanic heritage is not lost but is adapted to quite different circumstances (and may at times become unrecognizable in the process).

Although the memory of the settlements of the "Andalous" (the name by which the descendants of the immigrants are still known in North Africa) is alive after nearly four hundred years, the impulse that they were at the outset undoubtedly able to give to the economy does not appear to have been sustained for more than a few generations. It is not surprising that an Islamic society like seventeenth-century rural Tunisia should have rejected the alien implant, but the subject deserves far more attention than it has received from economic historians. Perhaps the discredit into which the Marxist concept of an "oriental means of production" has fallen discourages investigators from looking into this interaction. The Morisco phenomenon has been ignored because it fails to fit smoothly into schemata designed to account for quite different realities. In Tunisia, the European and the Islamic economic systems, for so long in external contact through the machinery of international trade, now became intimately enmeshed in a new way as a consequence of Morisco immigration. Plantations were set up as speculative ventures to provide agricultural produce for Europe's markets.

As a destination for the refugees, it is Morocco that comes first to mind, and it did indeed take many thousands in the period 1609–14 (let us not forget it had, for many centuries, been accepting such refugees). It is probably in Morocco that the destructive potential of the enormous movement of population represented by the Expulsion made itself most keenly felt. In modern times we have seen how the tensions generated by the condemnation of very large numbers of Palestinians to exile without hope has led to conflict and war in very many of the countries that found themselves acting as hosts to them. Seventeenth-century Morocco, too, saw not dissimilar destructive fighting, with the Moriscos at times setting up a city-state (Sallee, as it was known in Western Europe) within the host state, at times even *against* the host state, and going to the lengths of negotiating at a diplomatic level with Morocco's enemies.

Mention has already been made of the circumstances that led Timbuktu in modern Mali to become a place where some Morisco soldiers settled. One of the most enduring of the centers of refugee culture in North Africa was Tetuan (see Gozalbes 1988, 1992). This became the important city it is today thanks above all to the leadership of Sidi Ali al-Mandari, who at the end of the fifteenth century and the beginning of the sixteenth made use of forces that had just been obliged to abandon Granada in order to secure a hold on the new settlement. Al-Mandari had once been *alcaide* of Píñar in Spain, and at some time before 1485 led a group of some hundred fighting men across the straits. Those Muslim refugees later were to make their way to Tetuan. They were crossing into a land already imbued with Andalusi culture. In some cases they were rejoining members of their own families.

At the time of the Expulsion of 1609–14, the Naqsis family dominated Tetuan. We do not know whether the Cacimi de Cárdenas who served as secretary to this family was related to that Mustafa Cárdenas we have already met in Tunisia and Istanbul. In Tetuan, Cacimi de Cárdenas, who claimed to be a "*moro andaluz*," was concerned in negotiating ransoms on behalf of his masters, the governors of Tetuan, in their dealings with the Redemptorist Fathers in Tangier in 1625. In Tunisia, Moriscos earned their living in agriculture, manufacturing, and trade. In Morocco, too, they were engaged in trade and production, but at the heart of this commercial activity were all the transactions associated with piracy, including the ransoming of captives. Exiled from their home and resident in another land that, particularly after the death of Muley Zaidan, was torn by strife both inside and outside the circle of the ruling dynasty, many Moriscos turned to the profession of arms dealing.

We have seen how at home in Spain the fighting powers of the formidable men from Hornachos had imposed, if not respect, circumspection. Those same Hornacheros were now employing their fighting skills for the part-Morisco communities of Tetuan and Sallee. In Tetuan, one Hamed Tagarino, "who said he was one of the Moors expelled from Hornachos," traded prisoners with the Redemptorists. There were others from Hornachos: men with such names as Bonito, Carpintero, Blanco, Volcacin (Bu'l-Qasim?), Abrahen Cacin (Ibrahim Qasim), Ali Galán, and many others (Gozalbes 1988, 115). The Moriscos engaged in corsair activities sailing out of many other bases in the Mediterranean, from Algiers, for example. Tetuan was not itself an actual pirate center, of course. It is not, after all, a seaport at all, but it was close enough to various small ports from which piracy could be organized. Its distance from the coast meant it was safe from surprise enemy landings. Effectively, it was the great Morisco place of settlement inside the Straits of Gibraltar.

Outside the straits, on the estuary of the River Bu-Regreg, near Rabat at Sallee, a second Morisco nucleus could launch ships that ventured far out into the ocean—and even on occasion to the shores of England and Ireland. (There are even stories of Moriscos reaching Iceland.) The English, of course, were at the time their prey, but at times they were trading partners, and the refugees-turned-sea-wolves would have had the association become closer. One English agent, Harrison, reported back in 1625 that he had been approached by the *almocadenes* of Tetuan, presumably the Naqsis brothers, who had sounded him out on a projected alliance. In a land divided between contending factions, they explained, they recognized no king but God. Muley Zaidan, whom they had served so well up until that time, had become a cruel tyrant, and they now aspired to a free state such as the Netherlands or Venice. They offered to assemble 10,000 men to attack a Spanish *presidio* such as Ceuta, if only England would provide the powder and help with the recasting of their cannon. Harrison appended a note (*SIHM* 1 [II]: 573–82) written by the Moriscos: "With God's favor, Moors and Englishmen will take Spain, and we will cook our food with their crosses and saints. We will all be brothers and God will assist those who followed his commandments. God before all else." Harrison was later to relay an offer of 40–50,000 men, and to tell how the Moriscos had bemoaned their exile and said how they longed to live under a Christian government. He may in this instance simply have been reporting what he felt his London paymasters wanted to hear, or alternatively his Morisco interlocutors may have been telling him what they thought *he* wanted to hear, but it is not surprising that some of these Moriscos with whom he was in touch should in their exile have had ambiguous and vacillating attitudes. The Moriscos of Sallee even at one stage went so far as to have negotiations with the Spaniards themselves, to see if it could be arranged for them to return to Spain. Were either of the parties serious in their intentions, or were they sounding each other out?

Readers of *Robinson Crusoe* may recall that before Defoe's hero ever reaches his island, he has a completely separate adventure in North Africa and is for some time held captive in "Sallee." Robinson Crusoe would never have escaped from slavery there without the help of a boy called Xury, about whom we are told that he was a "Maresco." I have no doubt that Defoe meant to convey that he was a Morisco, and perhaps the form arose at the outset out of no more than a graphic confusion between the letters *o* and *a*. (Defoe has the boy sold off by Crusoe when they reach Brazil, which seems a very poor reward for the services he had rendered!)

THE ECONOMIC CONSEQUENCES OF THE EXPULSION IN SPAIN ITSELF

If this volume is unable to provide an adequate survey of the history of the Morisco diaspora itself, it is even less able to cover adequately the negative aspect of that diaspora: the impact of the loss of so many inhabitants on the country they left behind. That would be the story not of the Moriscos themselves but of the void left by their departure, and that is an entirely different subject. The subject has certainly aroused a great deal of interest and is in part dealt with in such speculative (I am not using that as a term of disapproval—quite the contrary) works as Américo Castro's *España en su historia* and the many other studies from varied points of view written on what in Spain has been called the *cuestion de España*— how did Spain come to evolve in the way that it did? To what extent did the reduction of the tripartite religious structures (Christian-Muslim-Jewish) of Spanish society to the monolithic post-Tridentine religion of the late sixteenth century and after affect that evolution? At the other extreme, another approach has been to eschew speculation and investigate objective economic facts: how did the peninsular economy react to the traumas to which it was subjected? Was the Expulsion a disaster in practical economic terms? Some studies have shown that some sectors of the economy displayed remarkable resilience and a capacity to bounce back.

This volume is not an economic history, and I certainly make no claim to be in a position to evaluate the various findings of those who have investigated this difficult subject. I would only say that in another area, where an even more remarkable rate of economic recovery was certainly achieved very rapidly, the twentieth-century postwar Western Germany of the "economic miracle," nobody would expect a study of that to yield much information on society in the Nazi period preceding it, and by the same token what we can learn concerning Morisco history up to 1614 from the long-term behavior of the Spanish economy after 1614 is limited. The determining factors governing success or failure lie quite outside the purview of this volume.

THE IMPACT OF THE EXPULSION ON THE SPANISH ECONOMY: A CASE STUDY

It may however be worth looking at what happened in just a single, small locality to demonstrate that the Moriscos did not depart from the peninsula without material consequences for the Christian communities there. If we focus on the case of Letux, a village near Belchite in the Ebro Valley east of Saragossa, that is mainly because there an excellent short study by Plou Gascón (Institución Fernando el Católico, 1988) is available that addresses the question. I have not selected Letux as a "typical" case; quite the contrary, in my view its location in an intensively farmed irrigated zone meant that the crisis created by the loss of skilled labor was particularly acute there. What studies of the immediate short-term impact of the expulsions can do is to reinforce what is already known about the close involvement of the Morisco communities in economic and political life at a local level.

Letux was an almost exclusively Morisco village where the inhabitants had enjoyed a good relationship with the Christian Bardají family who had owned lands there since 1409. Relations between lord and villagers were excellent into the sixteenth century. In 1520, when one of the noble family came to make his will, he commended to his son the vassals on his lands, and "principally those of Letux, who have behaved very well toward me" (Plou Gascón 1988, 294). As was the case in most cultivated areas of this kind, the local people were collectively indebted in the form of bonds (*censos*) committing them to make future payments against their crops. The obligations had had to be entered into in order to pay dues exacted by the lords and other authorities. And no doubt because it was in the interest of the Bardají family that the Moriscos should have the cash to pay these debts, the landowner allowed *his* lands to stand as a guarantee of last resort should the *censos* go unpaid. Presumably the Bardajís felt they could safely do this, as the outcome of nonpayment was likely to be a further rescheduling of Letux's debts, thus placing cultivators even more hopelessly in his power. Such a system created what in effect were debt slaves. The cultivators were free men even with some real estate of their own, but the degree of their indebtedness was such that the fruits of their labor all went to paying *censos*, dues to the landlords, and other local levies and taxes. Unless crop yields and market prices were high (logically a rare combination of circumstances, of course) the cultivators would probably sink further into debt.

The Edicts of Expulsion caused this particular financial house of cards to collapse. The *censos,* of course, went unpaid, and those who held them took legal proceedings against the lands. The upshot was that since the owners of unpaid *censos* would have first call on any produce of the lands in question, no newcomers could be found foolish enough to attempt to take over the actual cultivation of fields formerly held by Moriscos (because they would see the fruits of their labor disappear in paying back the vast debts incurred in past times). And since in such an area of intensive agriculture as the Ebro Valley any period of neglect causes long-term damage (silted-up irrigation works, unpruned trees and vines that were good for nothing) things grew rapidly worse as the years went by. This is not the place to describe in detail the financial wheeling and dealing and the endless negotiations between unsatisfied debtors and all the other interested parties. The problems of this one small village seem as intricate and insoluble as those of some modern third-world state unable to get the banks to reschedule in a realistic way its crushing burden of debt. Half a century later the problem was still far from being resolved.

The foolhardy Christian settlers who had been persuaded to take over were still in 1654 having to plead extreme poverty:

> It is not only the case that the situation in this village has not improved since the last rescheduling (*Concordia* is the word actually used), indeed, things have got worse, and grown quite impossible, so that the village is on the brink of being abandoned because there are not enough villagers and inhabitants to carry the burden.

In this case, the settlers were able to secure a reduction of the amounts payable by 60 percent, together with other concessions, but the problem was not at an end.

GENERAL CONSEQUENCES

The views of economic historians may at first sight appear contradictory on the general question of whether the impact of the Expulsion was harmful to the Christian majority. The contradictions may be deceptive, for it must be borne in mind that the total expulsion of this sizeable minority was an action that impinged in different ways in different places for the very obvious reason that in some places the Muslims represented a significant proportion of the population, but in other places not.

Attempting to grapple with overall statistics, E. J. Hamilton (1978) played down the economic consequences because the price indices showed no changes after 1609. On the other hand, Chaunu (1961) deduced from the fall in trade with the Indies that the economy did suffer. (An objection to both these economic historians is that they analyze statistics that are accessible rather than statistics that are informative.) Domínguez Ortiz (Domínguez and Vincent 1978, 203) took a more radical approach, and even called into question the permissibility of generalizations implying the existence of a "national economy" in Spain at this time. Whether or not that particular objection is valid, it was certainly the case that those cities and regions with large Morisco populations felt the impact strongly. Aranda Doncel (1984, 373), looking at Córdoba, judged the impact to be "limited to the city of Córdoba itself and specific *señorial* estates in the Campiña and sub-Betic region." He singles out as particularly affected the town of Priego (where the influence of the noble Aguilar family was predominant), one presumes, because Moriscos there had constituted about a quarter of the population and had dominated the silk industry. On the other hand, where few Granadans had been settled, as on the royal (*realengo*) estates in the north of the province, there was little impact.

The Spanish state, then, with its policy of Expulsion, had created economic problems for some of the Christians of the areas from which the Moriscos had departed. And it did little to resolve them. In the modern world we are familiar with the concept of whole communities burdened with debts they will never ever be able to meet, and we know how unwilling institutions may be to confront the facts of long-term indebtedness. Our creditors at the present day may prefer, by such devices as rearranging the interest rates or the length of time over which payments are to be made ("rescheduling"), to postpone the days of reckoning in the hope that things will somehow eventually, mysteriously, get better, even when it is patently obvious that things are more likely to get worse. To uphold the principle that debts should be paid is taken as the first priority. Much the same often happened in Spain in the aftermath of the Expulsion. Yet at the same time, many landowners, Lerma and others of the Valencian aristocracy, must have perceived that in the upheaval there would arise opportunities for them to better their position. In any profound economic crisis, the astute and the powerful may turn the chaos to their advantage, while the weak and undercapitalized may well lose. And where there are bankruptcies, as there were after the Expulsion, it is often difficult to get accountants to agree on the correct interpretation of the figures. But these are all problems for Christian Spain in the seventeenth century: in this new crisis the Moriscos were no longer involved in any way. They were elsewhere, across the sea, trying to build a new life.

THE MORISCOS AS REFUGEES AND DISPLACED PERSONS

The Morisco refugees who arrived in various countries outside Spain were Muslims (or at least most of them were), but they were also Spaniards of the early seventeenth century, attached to many features of Spanish life and culture. After the trauma of the Expulsion and the stresses of their search for a place to live, faced with the unending struggle of finding the means to survive in a new society that they did not always understand and that did not understand them, it is not surprising that at times some were visited by desires to return, to be Europeans again. Some of them looked into possible ways of converting those desires into reality; and a few did actually manage to slip back. They had been rejected by Spain, but did they belong in Morocco? Some of them were in doubt about their true identity: it would be astounding if they were not. At the heart of the tragedy of the Moriscos was a choice that was forced on them that many of them would have preferred never to make; a choice that was conceptually beyond them.

The Muslims of Spain in the end lost their homeland, and so lost their own history. Let us close with some brief and sad indications of the profound crisis of identity that inevitably beset them on whichever side of the Mediterranean they found themselves. The following case of one, very confused Morisco is reported by Haliczer (1990, 269):

> A native of Benillup, [Amet] Moro had gone to Algiers at the time of the expulsion, where he had lived for three years. During that time he turned corsair, and served on several corsair boats engaged in raiding Spanish shipping. He was eventually captured and made a slave in Valencia city. At the outset he pretended with some success to be a Moor, but was finally brought before the Holy Office after he was captured, along with several other slaves, trying to escape. In his testimony before the tribunal he admitted his Valencian birth and baptism, but showed clear signs of repentance and a desire to receive instruction in Roman Catholicism. Seemingly unimpressed, the tribunal handed down the relatively severe sentence of perpetual imprisonment with the first three years to be spent in galley service.

In an account written by the English Jesuit William Atkins of his captivity in Sallee (Murphy 1994, 246–47) we read:

> Though manie of the Mores of this place were brought up in Spaine, and are therefore of a well-tempered naturall disposition, and Christian-like behaviour, yet the great infection which this place receives from the Alarabes or wilde Arabians that much infest this barbarous cuntrie hath brought a generall corruption into their manners and an utter disorder into their civill government.

That is a former captive (and a religious) speaking here, of course. Against Atkins's account we may set the following words of the Moroccan historian of Andalusi descent, al-Maqqari.

> When the Christians in 1017 [A.H.; i.e., A.D.1609] expelled them, thousands of them left for Fez, and as many again went to Tlemcen through Oran, the great mass going to Tunis. As they made their way, in the region of Fez and of Tlemcen, they were harried by the [nomadic] Arabs and others who have no fear of God, who robbed them of their property. Only a few escaped this disgraceful scandal (*ma'arra*). On the other hand those who went to the region of Tunis were, for the most part, safe, and they still to this day inhabit villages in the countryside there. This was also true of those who went to Tetuan, to Sallee, and to the Algerian Metija. A great number took service with the sultan of the Magrib and settled in

Sallee, conducting the holy war against the enemies of the faith by sea, as is well-known at the present time. They turned the castle at Sallee into a fortress and built there palaces and baths and houses, and there they live at the present time. Some groups reached Constantinople and Egypt and Syria and other Muslim lands, where they live in the way described: "Allah, as the most generous of all, has granted the earth to those who dwell thereon as an inheritance." (Al-Maqqari, *Nafh al-tib* 1949, 5: 279)[3]

It is obviously no more possible to make easy generalizations about the fate of the Moriscos once they were outside Spain than it was to present a straightforward account of what happened to them while they were still in their Spanish homeland. Most endured hardships on their journey into exile. Some perished. Some eventually flourished. And everywhere the surviving generations have tenaciously kept alive the memories of al-Andalus, the land from which their ancestors were excluded.

3. This continues the brief passage from the same source cited on pp. 23–41.

TWELVE ✤ Hornachos: A Special Case

Hornachos had never, even in the great days of al-Andalus, been other than what it was at the end of our period (and indeed still is today), a small settlement in a hilly region of Extremadura: in the sixteenth century a quite a densely populated large village or small township of some 4,500 inhabitants (Lapeyre 1959, 152). Yet in the final stages of the existence of Islam in the Iberian Peninsula it played a role disproportionate to its size. It came to be important in our period because it afforded a relatively inaccessible place of refuge where Muslims might live away from the constant surveillance of Christian neighbors, and in our period its population consisted predominantly of Muslims. Its special, exceptional status is evident from the way it is named in its own right in the proclamations relating to the final expulsion, de facto acknowledgement of the measure of independence that the Moriscos of Hornachos had carved out for themselves. (It was the only town to be singled out in this way—all the other edicts refer to kingdoms or other major administrative areas: see appendix 5.) The privileged treatment accorded to the Hornacheros during their journey into exile (they were allowed to travel in a group and with their own weapons) is to be explained not by any desire on the part of the authorities to do them favors, but by the reputation that the inhabitants had gained of being tough, awkward adversaries. We will shortly see why.

As will already have become apparent in chapter 11, the cohesive sense of group solidarity of these folk was to continue after they arrived in North Africa. Just as they had imposed themselves on their Christian neighbors in Extremadura, so they proved ready to deal violently with those of the Moroccan host community bold enough to stand in their way. It is because the story of the Muslims of Hornachos differs in so many respects from the historical experience of all other Morisco communities of the Iberian Peninsula that an account of events there has been assembled here separately in a single, chronological sequence (even though to do that it will be necessary to turn back, briefly, to the beginnings of the history of the crypto-Muslim communities of Spain).

HORNACHOS AT THE END OF THE MIDDLE AGES

In 1494, a report made to the Order of Santiago (the principal landowner of the whole territory) on the subject of Hornachos ran as follows:

> Your inspectors went to the town of Hornachos, and after their visit to the castle and to the *comendador* [the Order's official on the spot] they found that within the whole town, and indeed within the entire municipal limits, there was not a single church or hermitage, for the people there are all Muslims, the only exception being the miserable chapel (*capillejo*) within the castle where the *comendador* and his men hear mass. (González Rodríguez 1990, 70)

It may at first sight seem strange that a place so firmly under the administration of one of the great military orders, and in that sense a religious establishment, should have so little that was openly Christian about it. Although this was no doubt an extreme case, it was not an isolated one. In the north, in Aragon, as much as in the south, the institutions of the Church (such as the military orders, but not them exclusively) had often shown themselves more than ready to have Muslims as their tenants or as cultivators of their estates. The presence of Muslim cultivators on Church-owned estates enabled lands to be kept in profitable cultivation that might otherwise have been difficult to exploit. The military orders were in no way special in this respect, although the organization of their estates into *encomiendas* (concessions), and the fact that they tended to have charge of establishments on what had in the recent past been on depopulated frontiers (in places like Hornachos) meant that they often did become particularly dependent on a Muslim workforce: free Christians might well prefer to seek to farm in their own right and on easier and more profitable land.

After the proclamation of conversion of 1502, there took place a certain initial outflow of population from this area of Extremadura, and this we can reasonably interpret as emigration to North Africa, which at this stage was still permissible. Presumably to balance out the consequent fall in population, an effort was made by the authorities to bring in Christian settlers from the north, thirty families "well known to be of descent clear of any defect as far as their Christian faith and morality were concerned" (González Rodríguez 1990, 73). We can, of course, decode this wording as signifying that they would introduce an ethnically more desirable element. This policy of colonization by Old Christians appears to have had little effect, for when, in 1526, the decrees were issued relating to conversion of the Muslims of the Crown of Aragon (decrees that had no *direct* bearing on the status of the inhabitants of Extremadura, of course, but which stirred up unrest among all Spain's Muslims for the good reason that this legislation closed the door finally on any form of coexistence within Spain between Islam with Christianity), rioting and disturbances of such extraordinary violence broke out in Hornachos that, in consequence, the old center of the town actually had to be demolished (González Rodríguez 1990, 73). It is true that the local historian to whom we owe this piece of information, Mateo Ortiz de Thovar, was not a contemporary of these events. His work, *Discourse concerning the most wonderful and miraculous image of Christ of the Rosary of Hornachos* (see González Rodríguez 1990, 73, esp. 12–17) was not composed until the end of the eighteenth century, and as a source it does not inspire unquestioning confidence for various reasons. On the other hand, it is difficult to see why someone writing out of local pride should have invented this particularly shameful story. Whether there was a revolt in 1526 or not, Hornachos as a center of Muslim population continued to grow, and rumors were rife about its sullen hostility to Christians. Franciscans in the convent that had been founded in the town complained of being intimidated by harquebus shots (the Hornacheros were skilled in the handling of this weapon, a reputation that was eventually to stand them in good stead in their North African exile).

In material terms the town seems to have prospered. The yield of the *encomienda* to the coffers of the Order of Santiago was 6,000 escudos annually (González Rodríguez 1990, 53). At the same time, a shift took place whereby the municipality was demoted in official status: from 1575 the castle was no longer occupied by a *comendador*, and eventually administration was moved out to Llerena. Hornachos cannot have been a pleasant posting, lonely and exposed. It is not only the reports that come to us from the Franciscans of the town that indicate that the place was rapidly turning into a near no-go area for non-Moriscos. One rumor had it that the town had its own paid assassin who carried out death sentences for it. Certainly it was the alleged lawlessness of the Hornacheros that led at the close of the century to a prominent judge, López Madera, being sent there on a special mission as described below. In our present age it is perhaps easier for us than it was for historians of confident imperialist times to understand how, by ruthless determination, a small isolated population may have been able to demarcate its own space and defend that space with remarkable success, against apparently overwhelmingly strong forces.

One of the factors that helped the people of Hornachos to achieve such a degree of de facto independence was that many of the menfolk earned their living in running transport businesses, which meant some of them owned strings of pack horses and mules. They were *arrieros* ("muleteers"). Long-distance commerce in many regions of the Iberian Peninsula depended until well after the end of our period on pack animals rather than on wheeled transport. An *arriero* who drove his beasts over wild tracks and dangerous terrain that he knew like the back of his hand was accustomed to making his own decisions and acting on them. His business gave him a certain independence of means, as well as a network of friends and associates over a wide area. Without mentioning the illegal harquebus that he probably had secreted in his saddlebag, he certainly had to have available the tools of his trade, which perforce included the knives and sharp instruments necessary to keep his pack saddles and other tack in working order. He could thus never be effectively disarmed. Perhaps most important, he was used to breathing the air of freedom. Here was no easily intimidated and poverty-stricken member of an urban proletariat, neither was this an oppressed rural cultivator such as the authorities had to deal with elsewhere. Small wonder that until the end the policy to deal with Hornachos clearly was not to stir up such a dangerous nest of hornets unnecessarily.

The spirit of the place was well conveyed by Lope de Mendieta reporting to Philip II from the town itself on May 17, 1569. He describes the busy air of preparation after receipt of the news of the troubles in Granada. The children were practicing the use of weapons, while their elders were in contact with the Granadans.

> [S]some of them come here, and some of these people travel to Granada: they have their own secret track which allows them to avoid entering any village. Bearing this in mind, they might be of considerable disservice to Your Majesty, keeping their relatives provided with an abundant supply of tipped darts ... what is more, they are in much more frequent contact with the Moriscos of Magacela and Bienquerencia than they were before the rising. (Domínguez Ortiz and Vincent, 1978, 48 and n. 34)[1]

The one major initiative taken at the government level at this stage with regard to the Hornacheros in fact made things—from the Christian point of view—much worse. We have seen (chapters 6 and 7) how, in the aftermath of the Second Granadan Rebellion, the Granadan Moriscos were uprooted from their ancient homeland and resettled inland. That policy was a failure everywhere, but at least in inland Castile it might have made some sense in that, if sensibly implemented, it might have speeded up the process of assimilation. In many cases, the Granadans

---

1. This is cited from a manuscript in the Instituto de Valencia de Don Juan dated May 17, 1569.

were settled in fairly small groups in areas with a clear Christian majority and where the Muslim minority was Castilian-speaking; areas therefore where contact with the ingrained customs of the Granadan countryside and with the old language, Arabic, was terminated. But to send Muslims from Granada to Hornachos was, on the contrary, to send them to an area where they could live their lives as Muslims in greater security and isolation than ever before, where, as far as can be ascertained, Arabic still survived until the end. Assimilation did not take place.

Hornachos received in 1571 displaced Moriscos from areas in the Kingdom of Granada, but we do not know how many in all. Approximately 5,000 (González Rodríguez 1990, 64) were moved out of the Sierra de Ronda and the area around Malaga, and after a march via Antequera, entered Extremadura and were sent on to Medellín. The road lay close by or through Hornachos, but probably the displaced Moriscos would still have had to go on to Medellín, where allocations were made to the various towns and villages. In other parts of Spain, the Granadan Moriscos came to constitute a large proportion of the Moriscos in any area, and because of their cohesive group spirit, they were perceived by the Christians as particularly difficult to deal with. In Hornachos, the existing Morisco settlement was already causing difficulties. And there was no Christian population of any consequence. The deportation to Hornachos of people from the Ronda region simply brought together two groups of dangerous malcontents.

What makes it so difficult to get to the bottom of what was going on in Hornachos in the final period is that all the individuals or groups who played a part in this very involved drama can be demonstrated not to be trustworthy, so that all evidence is suspect, and all motivation probably underhand. This goes for both sides, Christians and Muslims alike.

An equal lack of trustworthiness in one of the leading Christians involved, Alonso de Contreras, is so obvious that his autobiography, *Life of Captain Alonso de Contreras,* has been taken by some as no more than a piece of picaresque fiction (and viewed as such it has very considerable merits and deserves to be much better known by students of literature). It is true that *The Oxford Companion to Spanish Literature,*[2] commenting on these memoirs, grants that they have been authenticated "enough...to prove their general veracity," but the fact that this autobiography was written down in the first place at the urging of that master weaver of plots, Lope de Vega, makes us reluctant to take them as unadulterated truth (though it may at the same time make us anxious to read them: Lope was impressed by their quality). Even the most uncritical of readers,

2. Philip Ward, *The Oxford Companion to Spanish Literature* (Oxford, 1978), 131.

taking note of the accelerated switchback of fortune that allegedly took Contreras at such breakneck pace from Flanders to Tunisia and from Greece to Puerto Rico in a series of fantastic adventures: a switchback from abject poverty up to vast wealth (amassed in piracy against the Turks, etc.) and back down again to destitution, will realize these are tales to be taken with more than a grain of salt. So we will scarcely be inclined to accept as unvarnished truth what allegedly happened to Contreras in his dealings with the Moriscos in Hornachos. Yet can the narrative be ignored altogether?

Alonso de Contreras, so he tells us, at the lowest point of his many misfortunes, was imprisoned and tortured (by Christian jailers) in an attempt to make him confess to being the "King of the Moriscos" of Hornachos. This was in 1609 (chronological exactitude is not what we can expect in this literary genre, but as we will see, what Contreras alleges that year of all years might just have been true). Contreras tells his readers that some five years earlier (in 1603) he had arrived at "a place called Hornachos" (*una tierra que llaman Hornachos,* he says, apparently vaguely—he seems to wish to avoid suggesting that he made his way there on purpose), at the time "entirely inhabited by Moriscos, except for the parish priest" (words strongly reminiscent of those used in that report from 1494, "Todos son moros salvo un capillejo" [All are Muslims except a miserable chapel; González Rodríguez 1990, 70]), and there, allegedly by chance, he stumbled on a large cache of arms.

To explain how he came to make this discovery, he tells an unconvincing yarn of feeling hungry and looking in an outbuilding for chickens to eat, and there, discovering by chance a secret chamber where "against one of the walls there were three whitewashed tombs under an equally white vault." Using his hunting spear (*venablo*), he tried scraping at the top layer and found that the plaster came away to reveal the side of a wooden box. This contained a number of harquebuses and harquebus ammunition. All this he reported, so he tells us, to the local authorities, who represented to him that it was "in His Majesty's service" (*por mejor servicio de Su Majestad*) that he should keep the whole affair secret. He respected this advice, and so, he tells us, he went on his way. In Contreras's book, what follows next has no connection whatsoever with the Hornachos episode—the ex-pirate has a spell as a hermit far away on Mount Moncayo—but eventually, so he tells us, he was arrested on charges of plotting a rebellion and being "King of the Moriscos." Of all the highly colored incidents narrated, this is perhaps the one most difficult to accept at its face value, and yet can it be that we may have here some approximation to facts that Contreras himself may not have been in a position fully to grasp? He claims in his narrative that he did not waver under interrogation and was eventually released when some soldiers turned up who were able to confirm what he was saying about his really having reported the arms discoveries in Hornachos.

Another side of this same murky affair involves a senior law officer in the service of the Spanish government, Gregorio López Madera, the man who had Contreras arrested. Now thus far it is possible to dismiss the Contreras narrative as part of a novel. But this official, far from being a fictional personage, was a well-known judge (and, incidentally, the author of a book on the Granadan lead tablets, *Discursos de la certidumbre de las reliquias descubiertas en Granada desde el año 1588 hasta el de 1598* [see chapter 8]). Given his extremely distinguished career (*alcalde de Casa y Corte,* knight of the Order of Santiago, corregidor of Toledo), one might assume López Madera to be a much more trustworthy witness than Captain Contreras, but we will see that there are good reasons for not necessarily accepting all he says without question, either. Nevertheless, the fact that the name López Madera should crop up in the Contreras account tends to confirm that it contains some truthful elements.

López Madera became involved in the Hornachos affair in October 1608 when he was given the task of investigating the murders and other lawlessness that was being reported from Hornachos. He had orders to launch prosecutions as necessary. Law officers of his rank were from time to time given key assignments in the provinces, and if an *alcalde de Casa y Corte,* a special rank of law officer, took charge of a case, the general belief was that he would deal with it firmly and with expedition.

Why, then, did he (allegedly) arrest and torture Contreras? We have to bear in mind that López Madera was expected to produce rapid results, particularly because he and his masters would have been aware that the proclamation of Expulsion was imminent. They would have wished to unmask the plotters before it was too late. To break down the notorious Hornachero wall of silence would have required more time than was really available. López Madera may have calculated that if Contreras was poking about in some outbuildings in Hornachos, it was because he already knew something was likely to be found there. So Contreras was the possible weak point, a man on whom pressure might be exerted more effectively than on any hardened local *arriero.* One of the charges against Contreras was that he accepted bribes from the Moriscos of Hornachos to keep quiet about the arms he had discovered. That would have been a natural assumption to make: the Hornacheros were skilled in getting what they needed by means of bribes. The *alcalde* can hardly have thought it likely that a man with Contreras's background would really lead a Morisco rising, or be asked to do so by the local people! But by the same token a man with his odd and dubious reputation would serve very well as a scapegoat, if it turned out that a scapegoat was needed. There must also be the possibility that Contreras went to Hornachos in the first place as an agent of the authorities and that the prosecution opened against him was either intended to mislead the Moriscos or was a mistake. Such things have been known to happen in the history of intelligence and counterintelligence, but further speculation will obviously take us nowhere.

The government may well have feared that the weapons held by the Hornacheros would be used by them in some form of armed resistance to deportation, a last stand in the south perhaps, similar to the mountain-top campaign in the east, in the Kingdom of Valencia, which was mounted by Vicente Turixi. The reputation that the Hornacheros had of being able to bribe or buy their way out of trouble will have led the authorities to select López Madera to be in charge of action against them, he was somebody tough enough to stand up to them. As we will see, he may have resisted Morisco bids to corrupt him (nothing has come to light to suggest that he really took bribes from them), but he was all the same guilty of abuse of his office.

López Madera soon let the Moriscos know how he intended to handle his mission: he arrested eight men he thought might be ringleaders and hanged them all. Others arrested were condemned to service in the galleys or were flogged. When the Edict of Expulsion affecting Hornachos followed in September 1609, it was López Madera who was entrusted with the task of putting it into effect. On January 16, 1610, a public proclamation gave the townsfolk just sixteen days to wind up their affairs and leave.

It so happens that there has survived an estimate of the value to the lands and other real estate belonging to the Moriscos there at this time. Domínguez Ortiz and Vincent published it from a document in the Simancas archive (Consejo y Juntas de Hacienda 503). The numbers are clearly round ones: 1,000 dwellings are estimated as worth 30,000 escudos, and 10,000 fanegas of land have the same value, land under special cultivation (vines, etc.) are given as worth 41,000 escudos, 150 beehives are estimated at 8,000 escudos, and other items (dovecotes, mills), 6,800 escudos. As Domínguez says, this is an underestimate, but it gives some idea of what the Hornacheros had at stake: a great deal.

López Madera supervised the departure in early 1610 of the column of refugees (some 2,500–3,000), and their embarkation in Seville. At the cost of a special payment to the Crown of 30,000 escudos (i.e., the same as the estimated value of all 1,000 houses in the town!) the townsfolk had bought the right to take their arms with them (Boronat 1901, 2: 283).

From Seville they went to Ceuta, and thence on first to Tetuan, and only later to Rabat.

In this confrontation between royal power and Hornachero rebelliousness, royal power prevailed in that the Crown finally did rid itself of rebellious subjects. But in many ways, particularly with regard to the bearing of arms, we may note that these singular Moriscos always got what they wanted. Since López Madera had been sent to Hornachos with the task of imposing the law and suppressing insurgency, one must wonder whether what his mission brought to light impelled the authorities to hasten the exit of the Hornacheros on their own terms, to get rid of these troublemakers as soon as possible and at any price.

The connection of the *alcalde* with Hornachos did not end in 1609. He was assigned the follow-up task of arranging for the town to be resettled after the Moriscos had departed. In general in this volume we cannot look at the process whereby Christians took over the former Morisco properties, a broad subject that does not always bear directly on the Moriscos' own story, but in this particular instance it will be as well to mention López Madera's role because of what it conveys about his general reputation and reliability. He was accused by the Christian settlers of peculation, and so it was that the *alcalde* himself was subjected to investigation by a special inspector (*visitador*). In January 1614, he was sentenced to pay a heavy fine, and although not formally dismissed, he was relieved of his functions (Lea 1901, 348). His son felt he owed it to his father to raise with the king the harshness of the treatment meted out to such a very loyal servant of the Crown. The son was accorded an audience in the Escorial (presumably with the king himself); we do not know what was said on that occasion, but we may form some idea of the tone of the interview from the fact that the poor son, after he came out of his audience, sank on to a bench and expired on the spot.

Appendix I

The following extracts are from two articles of the Spanish Constitution
that deal with the religious freedom of the individual. The Spanish Constitution was approved by the Spanish Parliament (*Cortes*) on October
31, 1978, and that vote was confirmed in the national referendum of
December 6 of that year.

Article 16

1. Liberty of ideology, of religion, and of worship, are guaranteed to
all individuals and communities, and no limitations will be imposed on
public manifestations other than those made necessary by considerations
of public order as laid down by the law.

2. Nobody may be obliged to make any declaration with regard to his
or her ideology, religion or beliefs.

3. No religious denomination will be designated as the religion of
the state. The public authorities will take into account the religious beliefs of Spanish society, and will in consequence maintain relations of
cooperation with the Catholic Church and with other religious faiths
(*confesiones*).

Article 27

3. The public authorities guarantee the right of parents to ensure that
their children receive religious and moral instruction that is in accordance with their own convictions.

Appendix II

"MORISCO" AND "MUDEJAR" IN GLOSSES BY ALONSO DEL CASTILLO

In 1994, Federico Corriente and Hussein Bouzineb published an excellent edition of a sixteenth-century collection of Arabic proverbs from Granada (*Recopilación de refranes andalusíes de Alonso del Castillo*). As the editors pointed out (Corriente and Bouzineb 1994, 8), one of Alonso del Castillo's remarks provides a very precise dating (June 20, 1587 or later), so we can safely conclude that he continued intermittently to add to his compilation until he was quite old. This short work is an invaluable source of information on many different subjects, among them the state of vernacular Arabic in the Iberian Peninsula in the final period. Personal revelations about the psychology of this enigmatic Morisco scholar come not so much in his choice of proverbs as in the brief explanatory glosses that he occasionally volunteers. It is in one such gloss on another word that the term "morisco" rather surprisingly turns up, and in another we have his treatment of "mudajjal," his version of Mudejar.

Morisco

I begin with proverb no. 104 (Corriente and Bouzineb's transliteration of the proverb reads "hubb + alashari wajamal lal'attari wasaxá almustári ma fihum xáyr." The editors translate this as "Amor por hechizos, belleza por obra de perfumista y generosidad producida por el vino, no valen." I would translate this into English as "Love brought about by magic spells, beauty created by cosmetics and generosity arising from wine: none of these count." Alonso del Castillo's uncharacteristically long gloss here interests us: "ay alladina yuriduna nawala + lhubbi bi a'mali + ssihri 'asa an yuhabbu walmuriskus yasxu ida sakiru waya'maluna + ljamal bizayyi l'attar." ("Es decir, los que quieren lograr el amor haciendo hechizo a veces son amados, y los moriscos son generosos cuando se emborrachan, y hacen hermosura con adorno de perfumista." "Those who want to obtain love by the effect of magic, perhaps are loved, and the Moriscos, when they get drunk, are generous, and they create beauty by means of cosmetics.") Now clearly at some stage (probably as Alonso del Castillo was copying out his own notes) something untoward happened to the text here, because it will be seen the order of the three elements in the proverb (love, beauty, generosity) does not match the order of the gloss. I will not attempt a textual reconstruction. All that actually concerns us are the words (and they are unambiguous): "walmuriskus yasxu ida sakiru" (And Moriscos are generous when they are drunk.) What is remarkable is (1) the use of the Spanish word *moriscos* in Arabic; (b) its Castilian plural form (*-s*), retained within the Arabic text (it is treated as an imperfectly assimilated loanword); and (c) the fact that a Morisco such as Alonso del Castillo should cite a proverb that disparages the members of his own community.

Gossip to the effect that the "newly converted" could not hold their liquor would not have been surprising in Old Christian circles, but that Alonso del Castillo should record for us the reputation of the Moriscos for drunkenness I do find puzzling. It is almost as if Alonso del Castillo, by using this word, "Moriscos," is seeking to distance himself from his own background. It is as if he were not in his own mind a real Morisco but something else. From his highly privileged and safe vantage point in society he must have developed very confused attitudes toward both his vulnerable fellows and his own identity.

Mudejar

Perhaps we can discern similar attitudes in his handling of the word "Mudejar." The proverb in question (1309) tells us, "If you see a Jew in tears it will be because he has been cheated by a Mudejar, and if a Mudejar is in tears it will be because he realizes he has been cheated by a Genoese, and if the Genoese is in tears it will be because he will have been cheated by a Catalan."

This last proverb is a series of sneers at various groups. Among some Arabic-speaking Granadans this seems to tell us there was a hierarchy of distrusted noninsiders, and in this ranking the Mudejars occupied only the third position. They were not even the top fraudsters; that honor went, in this ranking, to the Catalans.

As for the form of the word, the *d-j-l* root that he attributes to Mudejar is not an error of his own invention. As the historian Andrew Hess points out (1968, 3 n. 6), in the Ottoman Turkish sources one finds *mudaccal* as well as *mudaccan* and *müdeccir* (in transliterating from his sources Hess is, of course, using *c* with the value it has in modern Turkish orthography. The Ottoman scribes will have been reflecting the uncertainty present in the Arabic missives that were reaching Istanbul from Granada.

Appendix III

THE SACROMONTE TEXTS

The following section lists the Latin titles of the lead books found during the excavations undertaken on the Sacromonte hill near Granada. It is derived from the chapter "The Second Sequence of Apocrypha Found on the Sacromonte (1595–1599)" in Alonso (1979, 104–15). To each Latin title (which Alonso tells us are derived from a BN Madrid 6.637) I append the page number in the Spanish version as given in Hagerty (1980). Hagerty edits various manuscripts on the subject by Adan Centurion, marqués de Estepa, which at present are preserved in the Secret Archive of the Abbey of the Sacromonte (see Hagerty 1980, 51, for details). Neither of these sets of titles is, of course, "original" in the sense that they do not (as far as is known) figure on the original bundles of lead tablets. We have information about some—most—of the Arabic titles, but since the Arabic texts in question have not (yet) been edited and presumably may be in the not distant future, it seems preferable to operate on the basis of the Latin names for the time being and to wait until the Arabic titles can be stated with certainty. The purpose of the present exercise is simply to survey the extent of this corpus, and for that the Latin names suffice.

Alonso (1979, 115) summarizes his own survey as containing "a total of 13 various finds—including the treatises *De fundamento Ecclesiae* and *De essentia Dei veneranda* but excluding the parchment discovered in the Torre Turpiana. There came to light 18 treatises, with a total of 229 tablets, 219 of which bore writing. The tablets which had turned up at early stages in the digs, and which announced the presence of the alleged relics, have not been enumerated."

Any discrepancy between the total given in this passage quoted from Alonso and figures that may occur elsewhere arises from two circumstances: first, Alonso points out that there are mentions of three other treatises: a *History of Saint James* written by Tesifón, a second part to the book *De fundamento Ecclesiae,* and *The Transit of Our Lady* by

Saint Cecilius. It is uncertain whether these were simply never written, or written and somehow never picked up during the excavations, or perhaps picked up surreptitiously but never handed in by someone who might have hoped to sell what he had found (Alonso 1979, 114). I would add that in Granada there are still rumors—that I am in no position to substantiate—of "plomos" (lead tablets) at present in private hands. It is not entirely unlikely that when the bulk of the discoveries were carried off for evaluation in Madrid and then Rome, some items may have been kept back, out of local piety or for whatever other reason.

A second circumstance to bear in mind is that it may not always be clear what is to be counted as a separate work and what is merely a subsection of another work (as in the case of *De fundamento Ecclesiae II* above). For present purposes, it may suffice us to know that there was a corpus of a score or so lead books, in textual terms perhaps of the same general order of magnitude as the Acts of the Apostles themselves within the New Testament.

The Books Listed

1. *De fundamento Ecclesiae/De los fundamentos de la ley* (Hagerty 1980, 63)

2. *De essentia Dei/De la Esencia de Dios* (Hagerty 1980, 69)

3. *Oratio et defensivum Iacobi/De Oración de Defensorio de Jacobo* (Hagerty 1980, 89)

4. *Liber modi [celebrandi] Missam a Iacobi Apostolo/De la Misa de Santiago* (Hagerty 1980, 73)

5. *Liber excelentis beati Apostoli Iacobi/Libro del Excelente Bienaventurado Apóstol Jacobo* [=Catecismo Mayor] (Hagerty 1980, 79)

6. *Planctus Petri* (should perhaps be included under the precedent)/*Llanto de Pedro Apóstol* ... (Hagerty 1980, 87)

7. *Liber bonorum actorum Domini nostri Iesu et Virginis Mariae* ... / *Libro de los actos de Jesús y María* (Hagerty 1980, 91)

8. *Pars prima assequibilium divinae potentiae et clementiae* (on original sin)/*Libro del conocimiento del Divino Poder: primera parte* (Hagerty 1980, 257)

9. *Pars altera assequibilium* ... (see no. 8)/*Libro del conocimiento del Divino Poder: segunda parte* (Hagerty 1980, 269)

10. A book on twelve tablets, title not stated

11. *Liber historiae signis Salomonis/Libro de la historia del sello de Salomón* (Hagerty 1980, 285)

12. In this case and in that of no. 13 Alonso tells us that his Madrid source manuscript is defective. He does not explain where the Spanish titles he cites are to be found.

Relación de la casa de la paz y de la venganza y de los tormentos.

13. De la naturaleza del ángel, y de su poder (Also Hagerty 1980, 295)

14. *Liber sententiarum erga legem et directionem/Libro de las sentencias acerca de la ley* (Hagerty 1980, 185)

15. *Liber Certificationis Evangelii* (the so-called *Mute Book*)/Certificación *del Evangelio* (Hagerty 1980, 317)

16. *Liber historiae Certificationis Evangelii/Libro de la historia de la Verdad del Evangelio* (Hagerty 1980, 119)

17. *Liber colloquii Sanctae Mariae Virginis/*Libro del coloquio de María (Hagerty 1980, 147)

18. *Liber donorum remunerationum Certificationem Evangelii credentibus/*Libro de los dones de galardón que se ha de dar a los que creyeren la verdad del Evangelio (Hagerty 1980, 131); a text of this is the book was found by al-Hajari in Tunis. Another copy, in the British Library, London, is translated below.

19. *Liber mysteriorum magnorum quae vidit Iacobus Apostolus in Monte Sancto/Libro de los misterios grandes* (Hagerty 1980, 253)

20. *Pars prima* and *Pars seguna* of *Libri actuum [sic] Iacobi Apostoli* (these two parts were hidden by somebody and only handed over in 1606)/*Libro de las acciones de Jacobo* (Hagerty 1980, 205)

Numbers 10 and 12 of my list do not appear in Hagerty (1980). One item listed by Hagerty (1980; *Libro de la Relación del Don del Lugar de la Paz,* no. 289]) does not occur in chapter 7 of Alonso (1979).

An Arabic Text Excavated from the Sacromonte Hill Near Granada in 1595

British Library Harleian MS 3507

Translating any part of the Arabic lead books that were found on the Sacromonte near Granada is not easy. This is in the first place because the forgers who created these apocryphal Christian scriptures did not intend them to be easy to read. The intention must have been to puzzle and to mystify. A second and quite different factor creating difficulties for those approaching these writings in modern times has been that until very recently it has not been possible to secure access to the originals, to the lead disks on which the texts were inscribed. Yet the multiple textual problems posed by these forgeries mean that those striving to interpret them constantly need to check and investigate the readings provided by the various transcripts. The "books" were preserved in the archives of the Holy Office in Rome, although there are indications that now, after nearly four hundred years, they may be accessible, in which case advances in their study are to be expected, although not overnight. For present purposes, material already accessible in libraries, especially on the Harleian manuscripts in the British Library, has had to suffice. In addition, the early translations into Spanish and Latin (made either in Granada before the discoveries left Spain, or later in Rome in the course of the protracted investigations into these texts carried out by the Church authorities) have been taken into account.

One method employed by the forgers to make these works difficult to read was to write them in an unusual Arabic script. This is not the place to enter into a full technical description of this distinctive writing system. Suffice it to say that the only parallels for this angular form of writing are to be found on certain astrolabes (and possibly on early tombstones: see *EI* (2d. ed.), s.v. "kitabat," plate 6). All Arabic scripts in normal use at the relevant time (and still nowadays) are cursive and depend heavily on a system of subscripted and superscripted dots (*nuqat*). The Sacromonte script is only vestigially cursive. The distinguishing dots are written only sporadically and erratically. To provide a simple example of the ambiguities that may result from these features, we may take *ı*, a character almost exactly identical to the undotted modern Turkish letter *ı*. If it does carry a superscripted dot, it represents in this script *n* (in nonfinal positions), but if the superscripted dot is not present, then the same basic letter form could equally well be a *t* (two dots), *th* (three dots), *b* (one underdot) or *y* (two underdots), not to mention *p* (one dot with a gemination [*tashdid*]). If a number of such letters with "missing" dots occur within a triliteral word, the possible permutations, and so the possible number of words that can be read from the same outline, rapidly become dauntingly large. If it were not for the fact that composition is highly formulaic, translation would be virtually impossible. Small wonder, then, that first the church in Granada, and then the Vatican authorities in Rome itself found it difficult to recruit translators, did not know whom to trust, and clearly commissioned a number of versions to allow for cross-checking.

What I present here is an attempt at a translation of just one of the Sacromonte texts. It is found in the British Library (MS Harley 3507), although account is also taken of two other sources. The British Library manuscript is in my opinion by far the superior textual witness. It was written in Italy by the Franciscan Arabist Bartolomeus a Pectorano (Bartolomé de Pettorano), one of the translators appointed in 1642 to study the lead books after they had arrived in Rome. Bartolomeus a Pectorano appears to have executed his task with care and to have had direct access to the lead originals. His transcription seeks to be a facsimile and to imitate the strange forms of the letters; where he was in doubt about a reading, he was honest enough to give us a mere dotted outline.

In the course of my initial preparations for this translation, I did not make a full collation of this London manuscript with the text given in al-Hajari's *Kitab nasir al-din 'ala qawm al-kafirin* because al-Hajari was not at that time available. Only where the Harleian manuscript poses major difficulties have I had recourse to the recent al-Hajari edition (in Arabic with an English translation), by van Koningsveld et al. (1997). I have already made copious use in chapter 8 of the work of these Leiden scholars, and I am much indebted to them, although my translation is for the reason just stated independent of theirs. What follows in fact remains largely unchanged from the text submitted as part of an appendix to Harvey (1958). The *Kitab nasir al-din* (al-Hajari) does not have the same authority as a witness to the text as the Harley manuscript has. It is not merely that al-Hajari (or his copyist) has to leave scores of words blank whereas the text in the Harley manuscript is relatively complete; it is also that in terms of textual transmission it is clear that the source from which al-Hajari was copying in Tunis was much further separated from the actual lead tablets than is the Harley manuscript. All the same, al-Hajari is at times of invaluable assistance, and it would be quite wrong to ignore his book, if only because, at the request of the archbishop Pedro Vaca de Castro, he had actually as a young man been able to work directly on the lead tablets. However, the text he gives in his travel book does not stem from transcriptions made during that period of his life but from a much later visit to Tunis. Al-Hajari reports a statement he found in a book by Ukayhil al-Andalusi (van Koningsveld et al. 1997, 248–49): "The total number of the books was twenty-one," and he sets out a chain of textual transmission from earliest times up to him as follows: the Archangel Gabriel revealed green chrysolite tablets to Mary; Mary sent the texts to Spain copied in her own handwriting; Saint James and his disciple Tasfiyun (both of them Arabs) wrote out the books dug up on the Sacromonte (*Khandaq al-janna*), which were copied (in the sixteenth century) by al-Ukayhil, from which a further copy was made by Yusuf Calvo al-Andalusi and taken by him to Tunis, from which al-Hajari makes the copy included in his book. One important feature of the al-Hajari text is that it is fully provided with conventional diacritical dots. This is obviously very helpful and makes reading much easier, but of course it presents us with only one possible interpretation of the consonantal outlines among many possible ones. One has to guard against it becoming a dangerous influence.

The Harley text dates back to about the time of al-Ukayhil's copy, according to the chronology established above, much closer to the source text than al-Hajari: Bartolomeus a Pectorano had the benefit of direct access to the lead texts themselves.

In addition, account is taken here of a third, even if indirect, textual witness: the Spanish translation printed by Hagerty (1980). This, as he explains (51 n. 27), is basically the seventeenth-century Spanish translation made by Adán Centurión, marqués de Estepa, but with corrections and emendations introduced by Hagerty from a number of manuscript sources not always specified. To avoid misunderstandings I have referred to this invaluable composite production as "Hagerty (1980)."

No attempt is made here to reconstruct any original text. That will be the task of those who eventually come to edit the lead disks themselves. What follows is simply an interim English version of a book that clearly has enormous interest for students of Morisco history.

The London Manuscript: British Library MS Harley 3507 (f.27ff)

Book of the Graces Bestowed on Those Servants of Allah[1] Who Believe in the Truth[2] of the Gospel

There is no god but Allah, the Messiah is the Spirit of Allah. The whole book is the truth of the Messiah Jesus.
The book of the graces bestowed on those servants of Allah who believe in the Truth of the Gospel, and in acting, when the last days come, according to its teachings; also a declaration of how accursed are those who stand out against it.

(It contains eight questions addressed by Peter[3] to the Blessed [Virgin] Mary[4] in the assembly of the disciples, and her replies, without which it

1. I hesitated a long time over the question of whether to leave the divine name here as "Allah" or to translate it as "God." "Allah" emphasizes the Islamic provenance of these texts, but in Granada readers of the first translations felt them as Christian. To gauge the initial impact of the texts in the 1590s, "Allah" should therefore perhaps be transposed to read "God," etc.

2. Van Koningsveld et al. (1997) render *haqiqat al-injil* as "the Essence of the Gospel." *Haqiqat* in its primary sense is "truth," and I prefer to preserve that word. We presumably have here the title of the book usually referred to as *El Libro Mudo,* "The Mute Book."

3. MS Harley 3507 (31r et passim) reads *Y-d-r-h*, and so, according to van Koningsveld et al. (1997), does the text they edit. I feel justified in interpreting the Arabic-character text here as reading Pedroh, i.e., Pedro. I suspect that the initial *ya* (i.e., two underdots) must be a misreading at some level of *ba* (one underdot) with a gemination (which was the Morisco way of representing *p*). I translate Peter throughout. I note that van Koningsveld et al. (1997) are in agreement with me (250, n. 4 of their translation).

4. MS Harley 3507 always has *al-saliha Maryam,* "Holy Mary"/ "Saint Mary." I do not know why English usage is so much more complicated than that of other languages

will be impossible for anyone to comprehend completely the meaning of Histories[5] of the Truth of the Gospel. Written at her command by James the son of Samech, [known as] the one who in religion came next,[6] by the hand of his disciple and scribe Tesiphon[7] Ibn 'Attar the Arab.

James the Disciple said, 'The Blessed Virgin Mary assembled the twelve disciples in her house after the *Truth of the Gospel* had been revealed to her and told us that we should obey it. She preached to us and addressed us, so that our understandings were captivated and our souls filled with contentment. She brought calm to our hearts by humbling them in those ways in which it is fitting to show humility, namely, prayer performed with care, the good deeds of a righteous man, and obedience to Allah.

She then addressed us on the subject of mighty secrets such that may not be mentioned in this book, although I will say that her address was sufficient to make the angels in heaven and mankind on earth stand up to magnify Allah. In it were marvels for those who would listen.

We have never seen a sweeter soul, a purer tongue, or greater wisdom than hers apart from our Lord Jesus. What she communicated was concerning the everlasting *Truth of the Gospel,* and yet without revealing to us its [inner] secret.

When she had brought her sermon to an end, the Vicar (*khalifa*) Peter said to her: "Thou hast illuminated our hearts, O Our Lady, with the light of Allah's great mercy, on the subject of the Truth of the beloved Gospel, thanks be to Him for that benefaction, but I beseech thee out of thy

---

in this one respect, but it is. Whereas "Saint Mary's" is quite common as the name of a church, some formula such as the one adopted here is perhaps more idiomatically acceptable in such a context as this when referring to Mary herself.

5. MS Harley 3507 has *t-]w-rikh*: van Koningsveld et al. (1997) opt for the translation "dates." With some hesitation I adhere to the rendering "histories" (or "stories"). Presumably they are thinking of some esoteric numerological content to *The Mute Book*. Obviously, if ever access to this book can be secured, it might be possible to resolve this doubt.

6. MS Harley 3507 has *'-q-b-at al-din*, which I rendered in Harvey (1956) as "the narrow pass into the Religion" *('aqaba*). Van Koningsveld et al. (1997) have "the outcome of the Religion," indicating that they vocalize the outline as *'aqibat*. That reading is perfectly possible, although I am not sure I understand it. I suspect that this epithet is simply intended as an echo of the triliteral root of the Arabic form of the name James (Ya'qub) and perhaps we should not probe too far into its sense.

7. MS Harley 3507 has Tis'un. I do not know which of the translators first decided that Tesifón (Thesiphon?) was the correct equivalent. Tesifón is so well established by now in the Sacromonte literature that there is little point in changing it, but the original reading should be noted.

power and bounty that thou shouldest answer for us eight questions about the granting of His graces, and about those who are resolute in acting according to it [the Truth of the Gospel], and those who follow it in faith, and of the reward that those who speak of it will receive at the end of days in the accounts of the faithful and, on the other hand, the damnation and punishment that will inevitably befall those who contradict it, in order that our Council (*j-m-h-r-na*) and the worshippers who come after us may thereby acquire light and knowledge and find repose at the end of days."

So she said to Peter, "Put to me the first question."

He said, "Inform us of the Truth of the Gospel and its special graces, O Our Lady."

She said, "The truth of the Gospel is the Spirit (*ruh*) of the Gospel, which is one of the treasures in heaven (*al-'arsh*) and is a joy for all believers. There is no worshipper who believes in it sincerely, with a pure intention, unalloyed with any sort of doubt, and who dies in that state, but Allah will decree him to be free from [hell]fire and pardon him all his sins, even if they be without number. There will be no believer who arrives at knowledge [or "wisdom"] thereby, after it has been explained to the faithful, but Allah will raise him to a high station in Paradise. But if anyone opposes it, he will have no forgiveness; Allah and His angels will curse him a thousand times a day. He will be subject to the wrath of Allah and will dwell forever in the fire of Gehenna, unless he repent completely and return to Allah.

Then she said to Peter, "Tell me what is the second [question]."

He said, "Tell us about the excellence of the Arabs, who are to be those who aid religion at the end of days, and tell us about their reward, and of the superiority of their language over all other languages, O Our Lady."

She said, "The Arabs will be those who aid religion in the last days. The superiority of their tongue over all other languages is as the superiority of the sun over the stars of heaven. Allah has chosen them for this purpose and has strengthened them with his victory. The excellence of those who believe is great in the sight of Allah, and their reward is copious. No believer who prays to them (*sic ilayhim*) for victory and aid after Allah has revealed the Truth of the gospel in the holy place in which it was buried will fail to be granted a clear victory by Allah. Allah will indeed register him as a worshipper who follows His will, as a righteous adherent of His true religion. Those who persist in evil opposition will be cursed by Allah and His angels a thousand times each day and be subject to his wrath unless they turn back to Allah in sincere repentance."

Then she said, "What is your third question, O Peter?"

He said, "Tell us about the holy priest (*faqih*) through whom Allah will reveal the truth, and about his reward, O Our Lady."

She said, "Verily the holy priest will be a believer in what of his perfect word Allah has brought into existence in the blessed Gospel, for the Spirit of Jesus dwells in him, and [he will be a believer] in the Truth of His Spirit hereafter, without any doubts or [heretical] opinions. It will be the assembly of the church of the true believers. This holy man will be wise and illuminated by the light of faith and mercy. The succession (*khilafa*, "Caliphate") of Jesus will be entrusted to him, as will be the power of forbidding and of commanding, of loosing and of binding, because that Truth sets out a pattern [*barnamij*, perhaps "program"] of what is right, and what is His light, and it provides a source of joy for all believers. No other illumination comes from Him in any other way, not for anybody in this world or the next (*al-'alamin*). There will be none of the faithful who believe in this with sincerity and truth, in obedience to Allah, without any trace of doubt, and who urge the speedy resolution of the question of the Truth in the Great Council which will take place on the island of Sapar[8] in the eastern regions of the Venetians; there will be nobody who explains it to the worshippers so that they may thereby enter the Religion of Allah, but it shall be recorded as to the credit of the holy priest, and of a group (*'asaba*) arising from that Council and its holiness. He will place round his neck the chain of His protection, and look upon him with the eye of His aid, and wrap him in the lap of His mercy. Should he spend for that purpose one good dirham of his own money in Allah's service, Allah will forgive him all his sins, and will gather him into His good grace, and will grant him in heaven reward such as what was merited by the alms that built the temple (*masjid*) of that Prophet of Allah Solomon, the son of David, for [the priest] has been singled out to erect with the alms he has received the temple of those who believe in Allah and in the Last Day. On the other hand, no worshipper into whose hands the story [ms.*t-w-r-kh* might either mean "history"/"story" or "date"] has come who has kept knowledge of it to himself, and who has had doubts about it, and

8. MS Harley 3507 has *S-b-b-r*. The Latin translation by Bartolomeus a Pectorano gives this as "Cyprus," and that interpretation has been widely accepted. It must be borne in mind that in this script final *r* and final *n* are easily confused. Since in Morisco usage geminate *b* is a way of writing *p*, this outline could equally well signify "Span." Was the aim to have the Sacromonte finds resolved at a council of the Church held in Spain? On the other hand, since Cyprus had just fallen to the Ottomans, a council intended to bring a settlement of conflicts dividing Christendom and Islam might best be held in the East, on Cyprus. The word "island" does not really help us here, because in Arabic the same word may cover both "island" and "peninsula." On the other hand, only Cyprus could be said to be "in the eastern regions of the Venetians," so if we are to exclude Cyprus, we would have to suppose that these words were some later gloss, and there is no evidence for that at all.

who wishes to defer the affair, and is content to hide it and hide the story [or "date"] of it, and hide this book, for however short a space of time, from that Council [*j-m-h-r*], and from the Succession to Jesus (*khilafat al-yasu'iyya*), and from the Arabs who are helpers, and from the Conqueror who lives in the East, and from the Kings of the Earth, and from those worshippers of Allah who follow His will to win the reward of the Truth that has been granted out of His bounty, [there is none such] but Allah will drive him out from that Congregation, and from its holiness, and will cut him off from His fellowship (*'asabiyya*), and will remove the chain which He hung round his neck, and will inscribe in the hidden record [kept concerning him] that he is an enemy to Him and an opponent of His will. He and His angels will curse him a thousand times each day. This is a curse that is incurred immediately by anyone who receives this My word, and the story [or "date"] of acting in accordance with its truth, whoever he may be, ["and does not act upon it"?]: He will make him to be like a niche for a lamp with no lamp in it, and will make him sit in the fire of Gehenna, condemned, banished forever in the torment of Hell, so long as His reign shall last, unless that person should truly repent and be pardoned by Allah."

Then she said, "Tell me, what is the fourth, O Peter."

He said, "Tell me about the conqueror who lives in the East and about the rewards he will receive, O Our Lady!"

She said, "The Conqueror is one of the Kings of the Arabs, but he is not an Arab. He dwells in the Eastern lands of the Greeks, and is a great enemy of the non-Arab (*'ajam*[9]) peoples, and their communities and beliefs and differences in matters of religion. He will have the laudable intention of obeying Allah and of securing victory for His righteous religion. Allah has strengthened him with His victory and placed the victory of the Truth of the Gospel within his power. He has set the banner of the Religion in his hand, strengthened him with victory, and given him dominion, among all created things, over all peoples at that time. He has filled him with light and with obedience to Him in this matter. He will remain unaware of these words until the time when the contents of the Truth shall reach him where he is. Allah, exalted be He, who leads aright whomsoever he wills, has foreknowledge of this. In the realms of this king there is nothing contrary to his will, nothing contrary to his

9. The word *'ajam* is here difficult to interpret. If we are geographically in the East, one might incline to give the word its primary sense: "Persian." At the time of the "discovery" of the Sacromonte texts, the Ottoman Turkish sultan ("the king of the Arabs who is not an Arab") was coming into conflict with the Shiite Safavid rulers of Persia.

command. His reward with Allah is great, and he will be set in a high station in Paradise. Any believer who prays for his victory and who either assists him himself or spends money for that purpose, and who dies in that condition, will have all his sins forgiven by Allah, who will grant him in Heaven the reward of those who have died as martyrs for the faith. Whosoever desires the contrary will be cursed by Allah and His angels a thousand times a day, and will be driven out from His mercy, unless he repent truly.

Then she said, "Tell us, what is the fifth, O Peter?"

He said, "Tell us about those whose hearts are inclined to the Great Assembly, and about their reward, O Our Lady."

She said, "Those who incline their hearts to the Great Council are those whose hearts turn toward Allah and submit themselves to Him. Their attention is turned towards the blessed Gospel and to the Truth, and to those, whoever they may be, of all races (*min jami' al-ajnas*) who have faith in the Truth that is brought together therein. They are also those who make contributions of alms thereto, and are eager to be present there themselves, and encourage others to be present as far as they are able, or at least to wish to do so. There shall be nobody among the worshippers of Allah who does that, and makes a contribution toward that work in the service of Allah, either himself or by way of alms, with [a sound] intention and sincerely, and who then dies believing in what he has done, but Allah will forgive him all his sins, even if they are numberless. Allah will inscribe him among those whose hearts are inclined to Him; and if [such a one] if present there, and believes in the Council, Allah will set him down as safe from [hell]fire, and accord him the reward that is granted to martyrs for the Religion. As for those who oppose [the Council] and who warn worshippers away from being present there, there is no doubt but that they will remain in the fire of Gehenna forever, suffering its great torment, unless they turn to Allah in true repentance.

Then Mary said, "Tell us what is the sixth question, O Peter."

He said, "Tell us about those who will make translations, and about those who write commentaries, and about the reward they will receive, O Our Lady."

She said, "The only ones who are truly translators are the translators of the book which contains the Truth of the Gospel, and the commentators on the Truth of the Gospel after it has been expounded[10] to the

---

10. The term translated as "commentator" is *mufassir*, "to expound" is here rendering *sh-r-h,* and clearly *sharh* is thought of as a stage preceding *tafsir. Tafsir* must here imply a more detailed type of explanation than *sharh.*

worshippers in the Great Assembly. Allah will send them at that time to be lamps for the peoples of Creation, so that they may bring light, the light of the knowledge and the light of the Law (*fiqh*) that has been granted them. When they enter the land of Sapar [see n. 7 above] Allah, out of His generosity, will increase[11] them in power and knowledge of the languages of men.[12] The translation and the above-mentioned commentary is so that some may rely on others. What they have to say to the peoples will explain His righteous religion and establish it in obedience to Him. Yet their number among the people will be small to publish Allah's miracle[13] to heaven and earth. The chief of them will be the most humble of His creatures, the commentator on the Truth, obedient to Allah and to the Vicariate (*khilafa*) of the Church (*masjid*[14]) of those who believe in Allah and in the last day, with complete faith in this belief and in the confederation sent by Allah ('*asaba*) that will arise from His Assembly at that time, enlightened to that end by wisdom and Law and mercy, just as I have described to you. Allah has assembled them all under the protection of the kings and nobles:[15] Allah hates sinners who are ignorant and loves holy men who are scholars; the reward in the sight of Allah of those of them who are believers will be great: a considerable recompense and a lofty station in Paradise. There will be no king, no noble, no worshipper of Allah who performs a good deed for them, or who is helpful to them with the business of the Great Council mentioned above, or with the exposition of the Truth or the commentary and translation of the [other] books with it, but Allah will forgive him all his sins, and he will be inscribed among the martyrs for the faith. For every sound

11. The ambiguity of this script means that this outline might be read as either *yaradduhum* or *yaziduhum*. It is the context alone that makes me think this must be the latter.

12. I amend *alsan* ("tongues") to *insan* ("men," "mankind" [an emendation affecting one letter only]).

13. It is perhaps relevant to bear in mind that the Koran itself is in Islamic theology a miracle. Is this text boldly laying claim to the same miraculous status?

14. *Masjid*, "mosque," is, of course, not in any normal usage to be interpreted as "Church," but from the days of Talavera and of Pedro de Alcalá onward in Granada Christian usage had sought to appropriate to itself what elsewhere were, and are, specifically Islamic terms.

15. In 1956, I could not read the Harley manuscript clearly at this point. My reading, *mutarif* (?), was speculative. Van Koningsveld et al. (1997) read *mutarabbin* and translate "overseers." I remain puzzled and cannot exclude the possibility that we have to do here with *matarib* [in this script final *b* and *f* are not far apart: both have a single underdot] as a plural of *matraba*, "poverty." However, on reflection, I adopt

dirham of his own money he spends to that end, Allah will raise him one degree in Paradise, and those who wrongfully make a stand against it, or contradict it, Allah and his angels will curse them one thousand times each day, and they will be deprived of Allah's mercy, unless they repent wholeheartedly and turn back to Allah.

Then she said, "What is the seventh question, O Peter?"

He said, "Tell us about the humblest of Allah's creatures, who will be the one who explains (ms. *sharih*) the Truth of the Gospel to the Great Assembly, and about his reward, O Our Lady."

She said: "Allah has a special place for him in His mercy. He instructs whomsoever he wishes of those who worship Him in the right interpretation [*t-w-l*, presumably *ta'wil*], and this worshipper is one of those singled out, one of those to whom hidden truths are revealed. Allah's bounties to him will be great. His mercies and the miracles [perhaps "signs of favor"] shown to him will be manifest to those who sincerely worship Him, for it is Allah's wish that through His grace they should be illumined. However, their number in this world and the next will be small.

His lineage will be noble, he will be a pure Arab, for it is not fitting that victory be accorded to any but an Arab and a conqueror[16] in those days. He will be outstanding in all branches of learning, as was My[17] own son Jesus. He will not be lacking in understanding of how to answer those who question him; he will be illuminated by the light of goodness and mercy; his intentions will be pure. His learning, granted to him by Allah, will be great; there is none like him among all the believers.

He will be of average height,[18] and on his face will be a smile. He will be a man who can say a great deal in few words. His knowledge will be great; he will be confident that Allah has sent him [at a time] of great overweening pride in an out-of-the-way place (*sanabik al-ard*). There He will instruct him in prayer (*dhikra*) in order that he, the most humble of His creatures in the world, may be the sharpest of those who reprove those who have gone astray, those who are apostates, evildoers, and hypocrites, those who are not in agreement with the blessed Gospel

---

van Koningsveld et al.'s reading, *mutarabbin*. Alongside "kings," it makes better sense (although I render it as "nobles" rather than their "overseers").

16. MS Harley 3507 has *nasir*. I do not follow the logic: of course a conqueror is victorious.

17. The text in general speaks of the revelation in the third person but, occasionally, it disconcertingly slips into the first person. Do we have what are presented as the actual words of God? And is this then an admission of the doctrine of the divine sonship? Perhaps my reading is mistaken.

18. MS Harley 3507 has *n-sh-y-ta marbuta*, which I interpret as *nsh'a*: "growth."

or its Truth (*bi'l-shahud al-manqub murattab fi manzila Sabar*[19]). He will be long-suffering in enduring poverty and hardship, ready to condemn pride and haughtiness. He will long to earn the reward of submission to Allah's will. He will turn aside from what is unlawful and what is hidden; he will be truthful in what he says and in what he promises. He will remember the faith and not forget to worship Allah, fear of whom is in his heart, nor to pray to him for a single moment. If ever any offense should touch him, he will overcome it by contrition and receive pardon and forgiveness from Allah. Great will be his guerdon from Allah, and mighty his reward, in proportion to his intentions and his faith and his works and his obedience to Him. Allah will increase his reward out of His bounty, for He does not decrease the reward of those who do good.

Allah has granted to him the interpretation (*sharh*) of the hidden truth of the blessed Gospel, and has set knowledge of it in his understanding, and its interpretation in his memory. He has illuminated his heart with faith in Him, and He has caused him to enter under the shelter (*kanaf*) of His mercy, and regarded him with the eye of His aid. What he already has knowledge of within himself, he will, when it is Allah's will, explain in that Council in obedience to Him. He will not be a prophet, nor an overseer of the worshippers, but Allah will convince[20] them through the Truth. Allah has endowed the Truth with the wisdom (*hukma*) that is requisite at that stage (ms. *maqam*), and it cannot be disputed. He through it will deliver a warning to those who worship Him and are forgetful of it, right up to the day His promise is fulfilled.

No faithful worshipper who prays and says:

"O Allah, my Lord, watch protectively over the humblest of Thy creatures, over him who interprets the Truth of the blessed Gospel in the Great Council. Smooth the way for him, and make me believe in the Truth contained in it that he will expound. Cause me to learn it by heart, and to act in accordance with what Thou hast commanded therein, for in the blessed Gospel obedience [is due], Thou hast power over all things."

[There will be nobody who prays thus] but Allah will look upon him mercifully, and protect him from all want. Anyone who is opposed will

19. This phrase defeats me. In my opinion *s-b-r* is likely to be the place name Sapar (?), already encountered twice (see n. 8). I note that both Hagerty (1980; "perseverancia del sufrimiento") and van Koningsveld et al. (1997; "patience") must be reading *Ar. sabr*, and do not take this as a placename as I wish to do. Neither of their versions convinces me at this point.

20. In the Arabic text, the root (*n-b-w*) of the noun *nabuwa* ("prophethood") is picked up by a cognate verb, here rendered as "convince."

be cursed by Allah and his angels a thousand times each day, and will incur His wrath, unless he truly turns in repentance to Allah for all he has done.

Then she said, "What is the eighth question, O Peter?"

He said, "Inform us of the blessedness (*baraka*) of the place in which the Truth is buried, and of the reward of the believers who go there on pilgrimage, O Our Lady."

She said, "An indication of the blessedness of the holy place in which the Truth and the Books are buried is that it was chosen[21] for that purpose, and that is sufficient. If any pure spotless believer goes there on pilgrimage with a pure and sincere intention uncontaminated by doubt concerning the blessed Gospel and the Truth (*haqiqa*) of His blessed Spirit,[22] and the Truth (*haqq*) of the books that are with it, prays to Allah after they have been revealed in that place, and says:

"O Allah, my Lord, I have truly believed in Thy full word that Thou didst reveal to the Spirit Jesus, and in the Truth of Thy blessed Gospel the text (*naskh*) of which Thou hast brought to light in that holy place, and in the true and certain book (books?) that are with it. I beseech Thee by Thy mighty name and by Thy might, majesty and mercy to all the worshippers that Thou shouldest raise up there through it [the Truth] and through him the standard of Thy righteous religion above all religions, and strengthen through it and him Thy Holy Church (*masjid*) of believers, and purify its holy assembly (*jumhur*) so that thanks to it and to him those who believe in Thee may be placed under the protection of Thy mercy and the veil of those who oppose it may be torn aside, for Thou hast power over all things.

[No one will pray thus] but Allah will forgive him all his sins, even if they are without number, and if he has given alms, for every honest dirham that he gives in that place to prepare for the aforementioned business, Allah will raise his station in Paradise in accordance with his intentions and to his good works.

I say to you that all this is in obedience to Allah, and to please Him, heaven forbid that it should ever be forgotten, for indeed he loves those who do good and are obedient to him. There is nothing to fear from enemies, for Allah does not guide aright the wiles of evildoers, and He

---

21. Van Koningsveld et al. (1997) translate "I have chosen it," etc. The undotted Arabic outline certainly permits this interpretation, but I find the theological difficulties inherent in that wording considerable.

22. MS Harley 3507 has *ruhihi* (=Jesus).

causes His peace to dwell (*sakana*) in the hearts of all believers, and His mercy is on those that worship Him, in order that they may attend to the explanation (*sharh*) of the Truth there. Out of His almighty bounty He will guide aright those among them whom He will."

When she had finished speaking thus, a voice was heard, coming from the direction of the Truth (*qiblat al-haqq*):

> "O thou to whom has been granted the Succession (*khilafa*) and the power of Jesus to forbid and to command, to release and to bind, according to that power, give thy word of confirmation to him to whom have been accorded mercies and graces and rewards as has been stated by the Virgin Mary in the answers to the Eight Questions. Confirm the sentence of cursing and excommunication from the body of the holy Church of those believers against whom cursing and excommunication has been mentioned already in that account. The rewards and the grace will never be revoked, but as for the cursing, it behooves nobody to set it aside after me except where there is sincere repentance for those sins.[23]

When she had finished speaking thus, the house shook, and the upper hangings were opened, and a hand came out that we could see as far as the wrist. It was writing upon the lines of Solomon's Seal inscribed in the middle of the wall: six lines. After completing what it had written, that hand departed from us, and the aforementioned hangings closed.[24]

Thereupon the blessed Virgin Mary turned to me[25] and said, "James,[26] set down the whole account, with what was written on the lines, and preserve it with the Truth in the holy place, so that those who worship may know the truth and know the sure word of obedience to Allah, so that my Word may be understood and so that they may profit from the graces and bounties granted through the Truth of the Gospel as described in the Eight Questions in the last days."

Then, in the assembly (*jumhur*), Peter asked a question, and said, "O Our Lady, what is the meaning of the writing on the lines of the seal?"

23. In van Koningsveld et al. (1997), and also in the translation edited by Hagerty (1980, 142), it is the "Vicar" speaking at this point, whereas the Harley manuscript omits the speech. From this point onward, the three texts, which have been in substantial agreement, show some divergences.

24. At this point in the text there is a drawing of Solomon's Seal, that is, the Star of David, inscribed with certain indistinct letters.

25. Van Koningsveld et al. (1997) have it the other way round: "I turned to the Holy Mary." Hagerty agrees with my interpretation: "volviose a mí." I feel it to be unlikely that James would be depicted as *initiating* a conversation with the Virgin.

26. He is given the epithet *'-q-b-t al-din* (see above, n. 6).

She replied to him, "It is an obligation of you all to fear Allah, this is no time to give an explanation, for Allah will reserve that [task] for the interpreter of the Truth of the Gospel at the end of time."

Then Peter said, "Tell us more of the date[27] when the time of revelation of the Truth will come, and what will happen after that, O Our Lady."

So she said, "When people study knowledge (*'ilm* but produce no sound works, and when people obtain high positions and dignities without obeying Allah, when they exploit unjustly the sweat (*'iraq* of those who worship in a way that is wrong, and take pride in their cunning frauds, and not in Allah, when all women live for is pride, and what men are devoted to is fornication, and people make a display of their clothing of black silk, when speaking in the form of indirect allusions (*kunya*) and deceit prevails, when both righteous and sinners are buried together in the churches (*masajid*), when Allah's word has been repeated to the believers without it making any impression in their hearts, then Allah will withdraw his benediction from the earth, and at that time will He reveal the Truth and the Books in the holy place, and this discovery will be the precursor to its declaration a short time later in the Great Council. And Jesus the Spirit of Allah will come back on earth (*ila'l-ujud,* "into existence") with his clear[28] (*fasih*) praiseworthy religion. As a sign the False Messiah will come, and his sign will be that the sun rises in the West.

The end of the book by my hand. All the book is the Truth of the Messiah Jesus.[29]

27. Here I think *t-w-r-y-kh* must be interpreted as "date."

28. The point here is presumably that, according to Islamic teaching, the Christian gospels in use by the churches are textually corrupt. Before Judgment Day, so this book appears to be telling us, Jesus will restore religion to its uncorrupted state.

29. The book closes with another version of Solomon's Seal, with more distinct but still mysterious lettering: apparently *k, h, ',* the *h* being emphatic.

Appendix IV

GÓNGORA ON THE SACROMONTE
In this sonnet on the Sacromonte by the poet Góngora, he compares and
contrasts the Sacromonte with Mount Etna. Under that volcano, according to classical mythology, there lay the giant Titans, who once had risen
in revolt against the Olympian gods and now were crushed underground.
Under the Sacromonte, in Góngora's day covered with crosses set up by
pilgrims, there lie the remains of the Christian martyrs (spiritual Titans)
whose bones should be venerated by those who undertook the pilgrimage
to the summit.

"Al Monte Santo de Granada" (1596)
Este monte de cruces coronado,
cuya siempre dichosa excelsa cumbre
espira luz y no vomita lumbre,
Etna glorioso, Mongibel sagrado,
trofeo es dulcemente levantado,
no ponderosa grave pesadumbre,
para oprimir sacrílega costumbre
de bando contra el cielo conjurado.

Gigantes miden sus ocultas faldas,
que a los cielos hicieron fuerza, aquella
que los cielos padecen, fuerza santa.
Sus miembros cubre y sus reliquias sella
la bien pisada tierra. Veneraldas
con tiernos ojos, con devota planta. (Góngora 1969, 224)

"To the Holy Mount of Granada"
Crowned with crosses, this hill, the ever-blessed peak from which/there
breathes out not fire but light,/is a glorious Etna, a holy Mongibel;/it

is a monument gently raised up to celebrate a battle won,/rather than a heavy burden pressing down/to crush the sacrilegious ways/of a conspiracy against Heaven.

The Giants who lie hidden in its slopes/imposed their will through the only strength that can prevail against the heavens:/the power of holiness./ Their limbs are covered and their remains lie sealed/under the well-trodden earth. Show them veneration/with your tender gaze and with your reverent feet.

Appendix V

Since Spain in the seventeenth century was very far from being a unitary state with one coordinated system of legislation, and since the operation of expelling of the Moriscos extended over the years 1609 to 1614, it is not surprising that a considerable variety and number of documents and other texts were produced in connection with the Expulsion. The Crown in the first place issued its orders to the various local commanders and authorities, and then at the local level those entrusted with putting orders into force drew up the texts of various proclamations which they might in some cases arrange to have printed. In all, there is a very considerable body of materials, although what has survived is no more than a chance selection. There could be no question of providing a comprehensive coverage of such sources here. The three texts that follow aim to do no more than provide some specimens of the ways in which Spanish officialdom set about drafting documents of such momentous importance.

Text A is a proclamation (*bando*) dated January 1610 and containing orders dated by the king in Madrid December 9, 1609. He directs the marqués de San Germán to carry out the explusions from Andalucia, Granada, and Hornachos. This text is of the relevant proclamation issued in Seville on January 12, 1610 (Bleda 1618, 1038–40).

Text B, dated January 13 of the same year, was printed in Seville and contains the instructions issued to the marqués del Carpio instructing him to draw up inventories of property left by Moriscos because such items became the property of the Crown (private library, Madrid).

Text C is dated Aranda [del Duero] July 10, 1610, and was drawn up by the secretary Antonio de Aroztegui. It affects Moriscos in Old and New Castille, in Extremadura and La Mancha. This proclamation states that all Moriscos are to be expelled with out exception, but goes on to clarify several: women married to Old Christian men were exempt from expulsion, as were converts to Christianity of North African origin and also various other categories including priests, friars, and nuns. Whereas up to this point those expelled had not been allowed to take valuables, they were now allowed to take money and jewels on condition that they handed one half over to the Crown (copy, private collection).

For ease of reading, I have partially modernized the orthography of the documents reproduced below.

Document A

Don Juan de Memdoça [*sic*] marqués de San Germán Gentilhombre de la Camara de su Magestad, de su Real Consejo de la Guerra, y Capitán General del Artillería de España.

Por quanto su Magestad a sido servido de mandar despachar por su Consejo de Estado una cédula refrendada de Andrés de Prada su Secretario del, sobre la expulsión de los Moriscos desta Provincia del Andaluzía, Reino de Granada y villa de Hornachos, la qual es del tenor siguiente: **EL REY** Por quanto la razón de bueno y christiano govierno obliga en conciencia expeler de los Reinos y Repúblicas las cosas que causan escándalo [y] daño a los buenos súbditos, y peligro al Estado, y sobre todo ofensa y desservicio a Dios nuestro Señor, aviendo la experiencia mostrado que todos estos inconvinientes a causado la residencia de los Christianos nuevos Moriscos en los Reinos de Granada y Murcia y Andaluzía, porque demás de ser y proceder de los que concurrieron en el levantamiento del dicho Reyno de Granada, cuyo principio fue matar con atrozes muertes y martirios a todos los Sacerdotes y Christianos viejos que pudieron de los que entre ellos bivían, llamando al Turco que viniesse en su favor y ayuda. Y aviéndolos sacado del dicho Reino, con fin de que, arrepentidos de su delito, biviessen Christiana y fielmente, dándoles justas y convenientes órdenes y preceptos de lo que devían hazer, no solo no los han guardado, ni cumplido con las obligaciones de nuestra Santa Fe, pero, mostrado siempre aversión a ella, en grande menosprecio y ofensa de Dios nuestro Señor, como se ha visto por la multitud dellos que se han castigado por el Santo Oficio de la Inquisición. Demás de lo qual, han cometido muchos robos y muertes contra los Christianos viejos, y no contentos con esto, han tratado de conspirar contra mi Corona Real y estos Reinos, procurando el socorro y ayuda del Turco, yendo y viniendo personas embiadas por ellos a este efecto. Y esta misma diligencia hizieron con otros príncipes, de quien se prometían ayuda, ofreciéndoles sus personas y haziendas: y milita contra ellos la vehemente presumpción y sospecha de todos los dichos delitos, pues no se halla que ninguno de los susodichos aya venido a revelar en tantos años ninguna cosa de sus máquinas y

conspiraciones, antes las han siempre encubierto y negado, que es clara
señal de que todos han sido de una misma opinión y voluntad, contra el
servicio de Dios y mío, y bien destos Reinos, pudiendo imitar a muchos
caballeros de los suyos de esclarecida sangre, que han servido y sirven a
Dios, y a los señores Reyes mis progenitores, y a mí, como buenos Christianos y leales vassallos. Considerando, pues, todo lo sotodicho [*sic*] y la
obligación precissa que yo tengo de poner remedio en ello, y procurar la
conservación y augmento de mis Reinos y súbditos: Y desseando cumplir
con ella, me e resuelto, con parecer y consejo de muchos doctos hombres,
y de otras personas muy Christianas y prudentes, zelosas del servicio
de Dios y mío, de expeler de los dichos Reynos de Granada, Murcia y
Andaluzía, y de la villa de Hornachos, aunque esté fuera de los límites de
los dichos Reynos, todos los Christianos nuevos Moriscos que en ellos ay,
assi hombres como mugeres y niños. Como quiera que quando algún grave
y detestable crímen se comete por algunos de algún Colegio o Universidad, es razón que el tal Colegio o Universidad sea disuelto y aniquilado,
y los menores por los mayores, y los unos con los otros, sean punidos: y
aquellos que pervierten el bueno y onesto bivir de las Repúblicas, y de sus
ciudades y villas, sean expelidos de los pueblos, porque su contagio no se
pegue a los otros, por tanto en virtud de la presente [p. 2] ordeno y mando
que todos los Christianos nuevos moriscos, sin exceptar a ninguno, que
biven y residen en los dichos Reinos de Granada, Murcia y Andaluzía y
la dicha villa de Hornachos, assí hombres como mugeres, de qualquier
edad que sean, tanto los naturales dellos como los no naturales, que en
qualquier manera o por qualquier causa ayan venido y estén en los dichos Reinos, excepto los que fueren esclavos, salgan dentro de treinta
días primeros siguientes, que se cuenten desde el día de la publicación
de esta cédula, de todos estos mis Reinos y Señoríos de España, con sus
hijos y hijas, criados y criadas y familiares de su nación, assí grandes
como pequeños, y que no sean osados de tornar a ellos, ni estar en ellos,
ni en parte alguna dellos, de vivienda ni de passo, ni en otra manera
alguna. Y les prohibo que no puedan salir por los Reinos de Valencia
ni Aragón ni entrar en ellos so pena que si no lo hizieren y cumplieren
assí, y fueren hallados en los dichos mis Reinos y Señoríos de qualquier
manera que sea, passado el dicho término, incurran en pena de muerte y
cofiscasción de todos sus bienes para el efecto que yo les mandare aplicar,
en las cuales penas incurran por el mismo hecho, sin otro processo, sentencia ni declaración. Y mando y prohibo que ninguna persona de todos
mis Reinos y Señoríos, estantes y abitantes, de qualquier calidad, estado
y preeminencia y condición que sean , no sean osados de recebir ni re-
ceptar ni acoger ni defender pública ni secretamente, morisco ni morisca,
passado el dicho término para siempre jamás en sus tierras ni en sus casas

ni en otra parte alguna, so pena de perdimiento de todos sus bienes, vassallos y fortalezas y otros heredamientos. Y otro si, pierdan qualesquier
mercedes que de mi tengan, aplicados para mi Cámara y Fisco. Y aunque
pudiera justamente mandar confiscar y aplicar a mi hazienda todos los
bienes muebles y raizes de los dichos moriscos, como bienes de prodic-
tores de crimen de lesa Magestad Divina y Humana, todavía, usando de
clemencia con ellos, tengo por bien que puedan durante el dicho tiempo
de treinta días disponer de sus bienes muebles y semovientes, y llevarlos,
no en moneda, oro, plata ni letras de cambio, sino en mercaderías no
prohibidas, compradas de los naturales destos Reinos, y no de otros, y en
fruta dellos. Y para que los dichos Moriscos y Moriscas puedan durante
el dicho tiempo de treinta días disponer de sí y de sus bienes muebles y
semovientes, y hazer empleo de ellos en las dichas mercaderías y fruto de
la tierra, y llevar los que assí compraren, porque las raízes han de quedar
por hazienda mía para aplicarlos a la obra del servicio de Dios y bien
público, o que más me pareciere convenir: declaro que los tomo y recibo
debajo de mi protección y amparo y seguro Real, y los asseguro a ellos,
y a sus bienes, para que durante el dicho tiempo puedan andar y estar
seguros, vender, trocar y enagenar todos los dichos sus bienes muebles y
semovientes, y emplear la moneda, oro, plata y joyas (como queda dicho)
en mercaderías compradas de naturales destos Reinos y frutos dellos, y
llevar consigo las dichas mercaderías y frutos libremente y a su voluntad,
sin que en el dicho tiempo les sea hecho mal ni daño en sus personas
ni bienes contra justicia, so las penas en que caen y incurren los quer
quebrantan el seguro Real, Y assí mismo doy licencia y facultad a los
dichos moriscos y moriscas para que puedan sacar fuera destos dichos
mis Reinos y Señoríos las dichas mercaderías y frutos por mar y tierra,
pagando los derechos acostumbrados, con tanto que como arriba se dize,
no saquen oro ni plata, moneda amonedada, ni las otras cosas vedadas
por leyes destos mis Reinos en especie ni por cambio, salvo en las dichas
mercaderías y frutos que no sean cosas vedadas. Pero bien permito que
puedan llevar el dinero que huvieren menester assí para el tránsito que
han de hazer por tierra como para sus embarcación por mar. Y mando a
todas las justicias destos Reinos, y a los mis Capitanes Generales de mis
galeras y armadas de Alto bordo que hagan guardar y cumplir todo lo
susodicho, y no solo no vayan contra ello, pero dan para su ayuda y breve
execución todo el favor y ayuda que fuere menester, so pena de privación
de sus oficios y confiscación de [p. 3] todos sus bienes. Y mando que esta
mi cédula y lo en ella contenido se pregone públicamente para que venga
a noticia de todos, y ninguno pueda pretender ignorancia.

Dada en Madrid a nueve de Diziembre de mil y seiscientos y nueve.
YO EL REY.

Andrés de Prada. Por tanto, para que venga a noticia de todos, ordeno que se publique este vando en la forma acostumbrada en todas las villas y lugares de la jurisdicción desta ciudad de Sevilla, y porque, estando como están tan cerca [text:cercr], y aviendo de ser en ella las embarcaciones de los dichos moriscos, y por algunas otras causas justas del servicio de su Magestad, y otras consideraciones que a ello me mueven, en virtud de las órdenes que suyas tengo para hazerlo que más convinere, en el tiempo que se les señala para salir, no concedo a los dichos moriscos de las villas y lugares desta ciudad más de veinte días para que salgan dellas, sin embargo de que el vando les concede treinta, los quales han de empeçar a correr desde la publicación del dicho vando, y durante este tiempo no han de poder salir de las dichas villas y lugares donde tuvieren su abitación y casa, so pena de la vida, sin que para ello tenga licencia de los Alcaldes mayores y justicias que el señor marqués des Carpio, Assistente desta dicha ciudad, nombra en cada villa o logar, y a donde no las nombra, de las justicias ordinarias dellos, y conduzidos por las personas que los han de guiar al embarcadero, y esta pena se ha de executar irremisiblemente, en la qual desde luego les doy por condenados lo contrario haziendo.

Dada en Sevilla a doze de Enero de mil y seisceintos y diez años.

Don Juan de Mendoça

Document B

Don Luis Méndez de Haro y Sotomayor, Marqués del Carpio,
Señor de las villas de Sorbas y Lubrín, y del Castillo y Playa de San Andrés de la Carbonera, Alcaide de la ciudad de Mojácar, Assistente desta ciudad de Sevilla y su tierra, y Capitán General de la gente de guerra de la Milicia della, por el Rey N. S. &c.

Primeramente con mucho cuidado y diligencia como de la vuestra se confía, procuraréis saber y entender si los dichos Christianos nuevos Moriscos al tiempo que salieren de esta dicha villa para su viaje dexan ocultados, encomendados o en otra manera qualesquier bienes, assí muebles, semovientes, como dineros y joyas, y hallándolos; por ante escrivano haréis inventario dellos, y los pondréis en depósito en poder del depositario general de esta dicha villa, y no lo aviendo, en persona abonada a vuestra satisfación y riesgo.

Item, atento a que los bienes Raizes de los Moriscos quedan por hazienda de su Magestad, haréis inventario ante escrivano de todos ellos, haziendo que se recojan las escrituras, títulos y demás papeles que tinen por donde les pertenezcan y toquen. En lo qual pondréis muy particular cuidado, de forma que se escusen los fraudes y engaños que puede aver, o las escrituras supuestas que se podrían fingir. Item, luego que se aya publicado el dicho vando, haréis particular diligencia en saber el número de moriscos que ay en esta dicha villa, quantos hombres, quantas mugeres y quantos niños, alistándolos por vuestras propias personas, ante el dicho escrivano. Item, atento a que su Magestad les concede licencia a los dichos Moriscos para que se puedan ir a las tierras que quisieren, sabréis dellos a las partes que quisieren ir, para tenerles prevenidas las embarcaciones y bastimentos necessarios, advirtiéndoles que las dichas embarcaciones han de ser por el río desta ciudad. Item, estaréis advertidos que si los dichos moriscos quisieren traer quien los gue quando se vinieren a embarcar, para que tenga cuidado que no se les haga mal ni daño, nonbraréis tres o quatro Christianos viejos, personas confidentes y honrados, y de quien los mismos moriscos tengan satisfación y a los que nonbraredes, compeleréis a lo suso dicho, encargándoles mucho les hagan buen tratamiento, y tengan particular cuidado dellos, y que no los prohiban que hablen con [p. 3] quien quisieren. Item, no daréis lugar a que a los dichos Moriscos se les haga mal tratamiento de obra ni de palabra, a ellos ni a sus mugeres y hijos, y que se les dé buen passaje, de suerte que no reciban daño alguno. Item, que si en razón de lo susodicho o en quebramiento del dicho vando, algunos delitos se cometieren por qualesquier personas, assí de los moriscos como de los Christianos viejos, de esta dicha villa, haréis información y prenderéis culpados, y sustanciadas las causas y conclusas para sentencia, las remitaréis originalmente al Señor Marqués de S. Germán, para que provea justicia. Item, se os advierte que todos los autos y diligencias que hizieredes tocantes a la expulsión de los dichos Moriscos, las avéis de hazer en virtud de la comisión que el dicho Señor Marqués de San Germán tiene de su Magestad para conocer privativamente dellas, la qual su Señorío tiene dada en forma a vos los dichos Alcaldes para todo lo referido. Y porque como en el dicho vando se declara, los bienes muebles y semovientes de qualquier calidad que sean, su Magestad les concede que puedan hazer dellos lo que quisieren, no les impidirés que lo hagan, ni que los empleen en mercaderías no prohibidas, y compradas de naturales destos Reinos, y en frutos de la tierra, en conformidad del dicho vando, y sin exceder del tenor del, advirtiendo que los gastos de las embarcaciones y bastimentos an de ser a su costa, y si vosotros hizieredes algunos, a de ser por la misma cuenta, y de las que hizieredes, y dinero tomaredes de los Moriscos para este efeto, tomaréis certificación, y me la embiaréis, y si uviere algunos moriscos tan pobres que no puedan salir del lugar, ni proveerse de los bastimentos y demás cosas necessarias para su embarcación y viaje, se les ha de cargar lo que fuere necessario para salir de a[h]í a los más ricos, y avisarme de los que fueren para que haga lo mismo en las embarcaciones.

Y todas las diligencias, imbentarios, listas y autos que en cumplimiento de lo que se os manda hizieredes originales, las embiaréis al dicho seññor

Marqués de San Germán, y le daréis toda cuenta, para que provea y mande lo que más convenga al servicio de su Magestad, y a mi me embiaréis testimonio el mismo día de san Antón de como se ha publicado el dicho vando, haziendo propio para ello. Lo qual hazed y cumplid, so pena de privación perpetua de oficio de justicia, y de perdimiento de bienes para la Cámara y fisco de su Magestad, en que luego os doy por condenados lo contrario haziendo. Dado en Sevilla a 13 de Enero de 1610 Años.

Item, mando su Señoría por segundo pregón que qualquiera Morisca de Sevilla y su tierra que tuviere criaturas criando de la cuna, las buelvan dentro del dicho término.

Item, se embargaron todos los navíos y barcos que no lleven morisco ninguno a ninguna parte sin licencia de su Señoría.

El Marqués del Carpio

Con Licencia de su Señoría, impresso en Sevilla en casa de Bartolomé Gómez a la esquina de la Cárcel Real, año de 1610.

Document C
EL REY
Por quanto, aviendo yo mandado expeler todos los Christianos nuevos, moriscos, hombres y mugeres, habitantes en los mis Reinos de Valencia, Andaluzia, Granada, Murcia, Cataluña y Aragon, por las causas y razones contenidas en los vandos que sobre ello mandè publicar: y aviendo assi mesmo permitido y dado licencia para que todos los de la dicha nacion que habitan en los Reinos de Castilla la Vieja y Nueva, Estremadura y la Mancha que quisiessen salir destos mis Reinos y señorios de España a vivir fuera dellos, lo pudiessen hazer, se ha entendido por diversas y muy ciertas vias que los que hasta agora no han usado desta permission estan muy inquietos, y van disponiendo de sus haziendas con fin de salir tambien destos Reinos, de que se infiere su animo y intencion: y sabiendose demas desto que assi los moriscos que se han echado de los dichos reinos de Valencia, Andaluzia, Granada, Cataluña, Murcia y Aragon, como los que han quedado en los demas de España, han sido, y son todos, de una misma opinion y voluntad contra el servicio de Dios, y mio, y bien destos Reinos, sin aver aprovechado las muchas diligencias que por largo discurso de años se han hecho para su conversion, ni el exemplo de los Christianos viejos, naturales destos dichos Reinos que con tanta Christiandad y lealtad viven en ellos, y que en efecto han perseverado los dichos moriscos en su obstinacion y dureza, y tratado de conspirar contra mi Real Corona y estos [p. 2] dichos mis Reinos de España, solicitando el socorro del Turco, y de otros Principes de quien se prometian ayuda, ofreciendoles sus personas y haziendas, y aunque por muy doctos y piadosos

hombres se me ha representado la mala vida de los dichos moriscos, y quan
ofendido tenian a nuestro Señor, y que en conciencia estava obligado al
remedio, assegurandome que podia sin escrupulo castigarlos en las vi-
das y haziendas, porque la notareidad y continuacion de sus delitos, y la
gravedad y atrocidad dellos los tenian convencidos de Hereges, Apostatas
y proditores de lesa Magestad divina y humana, y que por lo dicho podia
proceder contra ellos con el rigor que sus culpas merecian, no he querido
usar deste expediente, sino de piedad: pero considerando que la razon de
bueno y Christiano govierno me obliga en conciencia a expeler de mis
Reinos y republicas personas tan escandalosas, dañosas y peligrosas al
estado y a los buenos subditos, y sobre todo de tanta ofensa y deservicio
de Dios nuestro Señor, desseando cumplir con mi obligacion en procurar la conservacion y seguridad de mis Reinos, y de los buenos y fieles
subditos dellos, despues de averse encomendado a Dios nuestro Señor
este negocio, por lo que importa a su honra y gloria, me he resuelto, con
parecer de los de mi Consejo de Estado, Prelados, y de otras muchas personas doctas, Christianas y prudentes, zelosas del servicio de Dios y mio,
de expeler de los dichos Reinos de Castilla Vieja y Nueva, Estremadura
y la Mancha todos los Christianos nuevos, moriscos, Granadinos, Valencianos y Aragoneses que ayan en ellos, assi hombres como mugeres,
y niños , como quiera que quando algun grave y detestable crimen se
comete por algunos de algun Colegio o Universidad,[p. 3] es razon que
el tal Colegio o Universidad sea disuelto y aniquilado, y los menores
por los mayores, los unos por los otros, sean punidos, y aquellos que
pervierten el bueno y honesto vivir de las republicas y de sus Ciudades
y Villas, sean echados de los pueblos, porque su contagion no se pegue
a los otros. Por tanto, en virtud de la presente, o de su traslado signado
de escrivano publico, **Ordeno y mando** que todos los dichos Christianos
nuevos Moriscos, Grañadinos, Valencianos, Catalanes y Aragoneses, sin
exceptar ninguno, que viven y residen en estos dichos Reinos de Castilla
Vieja y Nueva, Estremadura y la Mancha, assi hombres como mugeres
de qualquier edad que sean, que en qualquier manera ò por qualquier
causa ayan venido, y esten en los dichos Reinos, salgan dentro de sesenta
dias primeros siguientes, que se cuentan desde el dia de la publicacion
desta mi cedula, de todos estos mis Reinos y Señorios de España con sus
hijos, hijas, criados, criadas y familiares de su nacion, assi grandes como
pequeños, y que no sean osados tornar a ellos ni entrar en ellos ni en
parte alguna dellos, de vivienda ni de passo, ni en otra manera alguna,
advirtiendo que no se ha de entender este vando ni han de ser expelidos,
los Christianos viejos casados con Moriscas, ellos, ellas, ni sus hijos, ni
los Moros que de su propia voluntad huvieren venido de Berveria a con-
vertirse, ni los descendientes de los tales, ni los que de la nacion de los

Moriscos fueren Clerigos, Frailes y Monjas, ni los que fueren esclavos, ni los Moriscos esclavos que quedaron de la rebelion de Granada, y prohibo a los dichos Moriscos que ansi han de salir, que no lo puedan hazer por los Reinos de Valencia, Aragon ni Castilla, sino solo por los puertos de mar de los Reinos de Murcia, Granada y Andaluzia [p. 4] ni buelban a entrar en mis Reinos, so pena que si no lo hizieren, y cumplieren assi, y fueren hallados en los dichos mis Reinos y Señorios, de qualquier manera que sea, passado el dicho termino, incurran en pena de muerte, confiscacion de todos sus bienes, para el efeto que yo les mandare aplicar, en las quales penas yo les doy por condenados por el mismo hecho, sin otro processo sentencia ni declaracion, y declaro que ayan de incurrir y incurran en las mismas penas todos los moriscos que bolvieren de los que se han echado de los dichos mis Reinos de Valencia, Andaluzia, Granada Murcia, Cataluña y Aragon. Y mando y prohibo que ninguna persona de todos mis Reinos y Señorios, estantes y habitantes, de qualquier calidad, estado y preeminencia y condicion que sean, no sean osados de recibir ni recetar ni acoger ni defender publica ni secretamente morisco ni morisca passado el dicho termino para siempre jamas en sus tierras ni en sus casas, ni en otra parte ninguna, so pena de perdimiento de todos sus bienes, vassallos y fortalezas y otros heredamientos. Y otrosi pierdan qualesquier mercedes que de mi tengan, aplicados para mi Camara y Fisco. Y aunque pudiera justamente mandar confiscar y aplicar a mi hazienda todos los bienes muebles y raizes de los dichos moriscos como bienes de proditores de crimen de lesa Magestad divina y humana, todavia, usando de clemencia con ellos, tengo por bien que puedan, durante el dicho termino de sesenta dias disponer de sus bienes muebles y semovientes, y llevarlos, no en moneda, oro, plata ni joyas, ni en letras de cambio, sino en mercadurias no prohibidas, compradas de los naturales destos Reinos, y no de otros, y en frutos dellos. Y para que los dichos moriscos y moriscas puedan [p. 5] durante el dicho tiempo de sesenta dias disponer de si, y de sus bienes muebles y semovientes, y hazer empleos dellos en las dichas mercadurias y frutos de la tierra, y llevarlos que assi compraren, porque las raizes han de quedar por hazienda mia para aplicarlos a la obra del servicio de Dios, y bien publico, que mas me pareciere convenir, declaro que los que tomo y recibo debaxo de mi proteccion, amparo y seguro Real, y los asseguro a ellos, y a sus bienes muebles y semovientes, para que durante el dicho tiempo puedan andar y estar seguros, vender, trocar y enagenar todos los dichos sus bienes muebles y semovientes, y emplear la moneda, oro, plata y joyas, como queda dicho en mercadurias compradas de naturales destos Reinos, y frutos dellas, y llevar consigo las dichas mercadurias y frutos libremente, y a su voluntad, sin que en el dicho tiempo les sea hecho mal, ni daño en sus personas, ni bienes, contra justicia, so las penas en que caen y incurran los que quebrantan el seguro Real. Y assimismo doy licencia y facultad a los dichos moriscos y moriscas para que puedan sacar fuera destos dichos mis Reinos y Señorios las dichas mercadurias y frutos por mar y por tierra, pagando los derechos acostumbrados, con tanto que, como arriba se dize, no saquen oro ni plata, moneda amonedada ni las otras cosas vedadas por leyes destos mis Reinos en especie, ni por cambio, salvo las dichas mercadurias y frutos que no sean cosas vedadas. Pero bien permito que puedan llevar el dinero que huvieren menester, assi para el transito que han de hazer por tierra como para su embarcacion por mar. Y declaro que sin embargo de que les este prohibido por leyes destos Reinos, si alguno, ò algunos, de los dichos moriscos quisieren llevar los dichos sus bienes en dinero, plata y joyas [p. 6], lo puedan hazer, con tal que ayan de registrar y dexar la mitad de todo ello para mi hazienda, en la parte donde se embarcaren en poder de la persona que estuviere nombrada para recebir semejantes cosas, como lo han hecho otros Moriscos que han salido, pero en este caso no han de sacar mercadurias. Y mando a todas las justicias destos dichos Reinos, y a los mis Capitanes Generales de mis galeras y armada de alto bordo que hagan guardar y cumplir todo lo susodicho, y no solo vayan contra ello, pero den para su buena y breve execucion todo el favor y ayuda que fuere menester, so pena de privacion de sus oficios, y confiscacion de todos sus bienes. Y mando que esta mi cedula, y lo en ello contenido, se pregone publicamente, para que venga a noticia de todos, y ninguno pueda pretender ignorancia.

Dada en Aranda a diez de Julio de mil y seiscientos y diez años.

YO EL REY

Antonio de Aroztigui

Appendix VI

THE MORISCOS OF THE CANARIES AND THE *GUANCHES*

The history of the "Moriscos" of the Canary Islands in the sixteenth century differs radically from that of all the other categories of Morisco in other parts of the Spanish realms at that time, and it would appear that what happened in the Atlantic archipelago contributes nothing directly to our understanding of the history of the Moriscos of the Iberian Peninsula. However, in the light of the title of this volume and since the Canaries are part of Spain, something needs to be said about this category of "Moriscos."

Although there is surprisingly little firm information on the aboriginal inhabitants, known as *guanches*, who were living on the islands when the first European explorers and settlers arrived, the Canaries themselves were not unknown, even in ancient times. They figured on early maps (indeed the zero meridian shown on some Ptolemaic maps runs through them). In the Middle Ages, they were visited by Muslim traders, but if we are to judge from the reported consumption of pork by the natives at the time of the Christian conquest, Islam does not seem to have attained much of a foothold. The violent campaigns that established Spanish rule in the islands in the course of the fifteenth century reduced the population of native pagan *guanches* to a remnant of only a few hundred. These people were not Muslim. In the 1520s, the Inquisition in the archipelago looked carefully into the state of religious instruction of various minority groups. The local Christianity was regarded as suspect, and the records of these interrogations provide us with some facts about the population.

Anaya (1996), in his study of this documentation, focused mainly on those individuals under suspicion because of their Jewish background, but he does also mention briefly two categories of Muslims relevant to the present study. Following the classifications employed by the Inquisition, he calls them *moriscos* and *negros*, and it is the former term that may give rise to confusion, of course. Numbers were very low: in 1525 there were only 190 *negros* and *123 moriscos*. The exact sense of the latter term in this context is unclear. The inquisitors found almost all of them to have been baptized a few years before, mainly in the Canaries, but some (a dozen or so) in Spain itself. Does this mean that this small group of 123 was made up of two quite distinct subsets? Did those baptized in Spain belong, not to the category *morisco* (2); ("Spanish Morisco") but *morisco* (1) (i.e., North African)? Or were they perhaps some third category: pagan slaves from the Canaries, taken to serve their masters in the peninsula, and baptized while they were there and before they were shipped back home? And were they called "Moriscos" because of their swarthy complexion, rather in the way that "Morisco" was in use in some parts of the New World for some people of mixed blood? (Any such "Moriscos" in the Americas, of course, fall entirely outside the purview of this study.) I incline to think most of those referred to in this Canarian documentation as "Moriscos" must have been people of ultimate North African origin, but I have no facts to back up that supposition.

We may guess that if the Inquisition in the Canaries made a distinction between the two groups, Moriscos and blacks, such a distinction would be based on little more than skin pigmentation. We might hope for more information about the way of life of the aboriginal inhabitants of the Canaries and of any Muslims who may have lived there, if and when archeological research is undertaken into the late medieval period. Study of burial customs might yield useful data.

Appendix VII

THE LITERATURE OF SELF-JUSTIFICATION AFTER THE EXPULSION: A SPECIMEN

Father Pedro Aznar Cardona, *Expulsión Justificada de los Moriscos Españoles y Suma de las Excelencias Cristianas de Nuestro Rey Don Felipe El Católico Tercero Deste Nombre* **(The Justified Expulsion of the Spanish Moriscos; Huesca, 1612)**

Aznar's anti-Morisco tract is among the most outrageous of the several books that appeared just after the Expulsion. All these works in this genre set out to demonstrate that the measure had been justified. A short extract is given here as a specimen in order to convey some of the attitudes to be found among some Christian Spaniards at this time. This piece of propaganda is put forward as an example of an extreme position, not as typical of ecclesiastical attitudes in general. (If used with care and discrimination, however, the book does serve as a valuable repertoire of information both on Morisco customs and on Old Christian prejudices.) Not infrequently, we find Aznar blaming the Moriscos for things that have actually been inflicted on them and for which they carry no responsibility. Some readers may be amused to read that the Moriscos were condemned in the early seventeenth century for favoring a diet very much like what is strongly recommended by most dieticians in the early twenty-first century.

From a Section Headed "On the Condition, the Behavior, the Dress, Food, Occupations, Vicious Ways and Contagious Pestilence of the Moriscos" (fols. 32–36)

> Having spoken of their nature, their religion and their heretical beliefs, what remains for us to deal with now is what they were like and how they behaved. In this respect they were the vilest of people, slovenly, and in

no way given to those helpmeets of virtue, noble letters and sciences. In consequence, they were far removed from all urbane, courteous, and polite manners and customs. They brought their children up to run wild like brute beasts, giving them no rational teaching or instruction for salvation, except what was forced upon them, and what they were obliged by their superiors to attend, because they had been baptized.

Their sentences were clumsy, their discourse bestial, their language barbarous, their way of dressing ridiculous. In general, they went about wearing hose of light linen or some other cheaper material, rather like what sailors wear. Their undergarments were cheap, and willfully ill-matched. Likewise, the women went in a colored bodice and just a skirt, with a yellow green or blue lining. Whatever the weather they wore light clothing that was not cumbrous; it was almost as if they were in a shift, but in the case of the young women, their hair was carefully combed, and they were washed and clean. In their meals they were coarse. They always ate on the ground (they were that sort of people) with no table or any other piece of furniture that might smell of other people. In the same way they slept on the ground, on cushions that they called *almadravas*, or on their kitchen stools or on benches alongside, and that was so as to be the more ready for their acts of self-indulgence, when they got up for their nighttime snacks; they took their sensuous pleasure (*refocilarse*) whenever they woke up. What they ate were vile things (in this a heavenly judgment has caused them to suffer here below), as, for example, vegetable rissoles (*fresas*) made from various sorts of ground pulses, lentils, beans, buckwheat, millet, and bread made from the same things. With this bread those who had the means combined raisins, figs, honey, grape jelly, milk, and fruit in season, such as melons, even if they were green and no bigger than one's fist, cucumbers, firm peaches (*duraznos*), and whatever else, even if it was not properly ripe, so long as it was fruit. After this they took the air, and they would not leave an orchard wall intact.[1] [All year round they ate fruit, fresh and dried (they would store it until it had almost gone bad), and just bread and water, for they would not drink wine, nor buy meat or game killed by dogs or caught in snares or shot by guns (*escopetas*) or in nets, nor would they eat it unless the animals had been slaughtered according to the rite of Muhammad, so it will be seen they spent very little, whether on food or on clothing, although they had large amounts to pay out in dues to their lords. Any game or meat that had not been slaughtered according to their rites was called by them *halgharaham* [i.e., *al-haram*], which means "accursed" or "forbidden." If

---

1. This puzzles me. Are the Moriscos being accused of stealing from orchards, or just breaking down enclosures so as to wander freely?

one argued with them, querying why they did not drink wine or eat bacon, what they would answer was that different sorts of people like different sorts of food, and that not all stomachs can manage the same food. Thus they hid the way that they observed their religion, for that was the real reason why they did what they did. I had the following exchange of words with Juan de Juana, a Morisco who was said to be the *alfaqui* of Epila [a Morisco village in Aragón not far from Almonacid]. He, not in the least abashed, was claiming that they were being expelled without cause, and said to me: "They should not throw us out from Spain. You will see us eating bacon and drinking wine yet!" I replied to him: "What is getting you thrown out is not the fact that you don't drink wine and don't eat bacon. It is that you don't do so because of the religious principles of your accursed sect. That's heresy, and that is what condemns you. You are a great dog. If you did it out of love for the virtue of abstinence, that would be admirable . . . but you do it for your Muhammad, as we know full well. We see how much you ill-use your own little children when you find out that in some house belonging to an Old Christian family they have been offered a bacon sandwich and have eaten it. It was because they were not yet capable of understanding your underhand tricks. What I ask is this: 'If the child were to eat it, would it cause the stomach to ache?' No. Why do you make such a public fuss if a child of four or five eats a piece of bacon? Believe me, the monkey finds it hard to hide behind his tail (*Se cubre mal la mona con la cola*).'"[2]

They were very fond of jokes, stories, boastful tales (*berlandinas*). As is shown, by the fact that they were so well provided with bagpipes, castanets, and drums, they were above all else extremely fond of dances, songs, dawn serenades, parading round gardens and fountains, and all those sorts of bestial entertainment that lead vulgar young lads to go about the streets shouting noisily. They boasted about being such great dancers, being so good at *pelota,* at pitch and toss, at bowls, and at running the bulls, and other such rustic pursuits. They were much given to trades not requiring gross physical exertion, such as weavers, tailors, ropemakers, makers of plaited straw goods, potters, shoemakers, horse doctors, quilters, gardeners, muleteers (*recueros*), retail sellers of oil, fish, honey, raisins, sugar, cloth, eggs, chickens, slippers, woolen garments for children. They undertook domestic service, which gave them an excuse to wander everywhere, poking into everybody's business. Thus they were usually idle vagabonds, stretched out in the sun with their water jar beside them in winter, under the porch in summer, except for those few hours when they were working away at their trades or in their vegetable plots, for they had this strong

2. That is obviously a proverb of some sort, but I do not grasp its relevance!

drive to gather fruit, green vegetables, or root crops. Few, or very few, of them had trades that entailed working metal or iron or stone or heavy wooden beams, although they did have some blacksmiths for their general use, because they took great care of their blessed mules, and wanted to avoid having dealings with us Christians, because of the great hatred they felt for us. In the handling of arms they were like raw recruits, in part because for years arms had been forbidden to them, and as Ovid says, lack of practice deprives one of skill, but in part because they were cowards and effeminate.[3]

3. One does not need to point out the contradictions here: Moriscos are accused at the same time of being too fond of running with the bulls and of being cowards, etc.

Appendix VIII

POPULAR REACTIONS TO THE EXPULSION

There is no way for us to gauge with any accuracy what the reaction of the Christian populace to the execution of the Edicts of Expulsion was. The following piece of doggerel verse is proof of nothing beyond the fact that some folk took perverse pleasure in the Moriscos' misfortunes. It is a naive ballad broadsheet of the sort that was hawked in market places by itinerant peddlers and others. Many would claim such texts as these ballads (*romances)* are among the most authentically popular forms of expression of Hispanic culture, but then others would dispute such an essentially Romantic glorification of the Volk.

In 1612, in Granada, a doggerel eight-sheet cheap ballad (*pliego suelto)* appeared of which the title will have been the chief selling point: "An Amazing Tale of the Cunning Strategam Adopted by a Discreet Woman against Three Devils ... etc." (Gracioso cuento y ardid que tuuo vna discreta muger para engañar a tres demonios). To this fantastic tale there is appended, to fill up the space, several makeweight pieces, including a "Ballad of the Advice Given by a Soldier to the Moriscos, Telling Them How to Use Their Money to Their Best Advantage" (Romance de los consejos que dio un Soldado a los Moriscos cerca de emplear sus dineros para aprouecharse). Such broadsheets most frequently circulated with no indication of the identity of the author (indeed, its anonymity, its ability to speak for and to the unnamed Legion, is what persuades many critics of the virtues of the genre). This "amazing tale" is in fact in this case attributed to a named individual, one Francisco de Aguirre, but I have so far been unable to identify him further.

The point of these verses is to mock the Moriscos who were at that time being forced out of Spain by telling them how to make money out of their expulsion. The humor extracted from the jolly situation arises from the fact that the advice given is invariably unsound: how to take coals to Newcastle, as it were. So a commodity is to be shipped back to its place of production, or it is to be taken where its unpopularity may be safely predicted. To say that making fun in this way of the dire misfortunes of others is in execrable taste is to pass a twentieth-first-century judgment on a doggerel whose author was clearly quite untroubled by what was being done to Spain's Muslims, who, indeed, rejoiced in what he seems to have regarded as condign punishment visited on irredeemably wicked folk:

> Descendents of Ishmael, disinherited from God's succor in beauteous Spain by divine inspiration and sacred Providence because God in His own country (en su patria) will have none of those who have displayed such stubborn attachment to their own rites and apostasies... There are two well-founded reasons for the confiscation of your possessions and for turning them to ashes—because you are traitors and because you are heretics. You are leaving Spain, because, ungrateful folk that you are, you decided after eight hundred years to pay your dues. And since your reward is to be obliged to make what you can from your livestock (this being granted to you as a concession), I, as your friend, (in the way that a cat is friend of all rats), am writing this memorandum for your sakes: after all, we do share the same fatherland. It will help you to know which commodities are most in demand, for you are going into foreign lands. My advice, then, is, if you go to France, invest your fortune in linen; Rouen and Holland, cloth; and if to England, you should know that there is great demand for woolen cloth, baize, and friezes.

The advice continues in the same vein of heavy humor: "take tons of syringes, needles, bells, and flutes to Flanders, take armour and harquebuses to Milan"—the Low Countries and Northern Italy were manufacturing centers of those days—"take tobacco and hides to Puerto Rico, take cinnamon, cloves and peppers to the [East] Indies"—all places that would have plenty of such goods already. In a variant form of bad advice, the Moriscos are told to take some goods to places where nobody would want to make use of them at all: "take fur robes to Guinea, or books and dramatic works." Our "poet" then tires of thinking up distant destinations: "why not choose somewhere nearer to hand? Try taking breeches and hose and lace ruffs to Barbary, your old home? Or high-heeled shoes and fancy skirts for the ladies? Or lives of the saints and crucifixes?"

His final remarks leave me in some slight doubt. In all probability they are to be interpreted as charged with the same heavy would-be irony and sarcasm as imbues the rest of the piece, but I am not entirely certain:

> Many people say that as soon as you cross over the straits, you will say you are on holy ground... and that you will straight away become renegades,

and then having become pirates, your Morisco ships will land on our shores. I say you will do no such thing, for I am confident that you will die for our God, for I have given my word to many people that many of you are Catholics, so do not cause me to be proved wrong. But may people who have always been dogs inside this Spain of ours, be even more so where there is no Christian law.

The doubt that remains with me arises from the possibility that some allusion may be intended to another theme of anti-Morisco polemic, which was that the worst of the sufferings inflicted on the Morisco refugees were the responsibility of their coreligionists, who robbed, despoiled, and even murdered them as they made their way into exile in North Africa. How such atrocities committed by others, if they did occur, could justify what was done in Spain, is difficult to understand, but in any case the ballad is probably simply closing with a clumsy attempt to make the point that the Moriscos were not good Catholics (the "soldier" is presented as consistently wrong in everything else he says and so is presumably to be taken as wrong in saying, "I have given my word that many of you are good Catholics").

Extracts from a *Romance de los Consejos Que Dio un Soldado a los Moriscos Cerca de Emplear sus Dineros Para Aprouecharse*

Descendientes de Ismael, / ya que de la bella España / por inspiracion de Dios / y su Providencia sacra: / De su auxilio os desedera, / porque no quiere en su Patria, / quien en ritos y apostasias / tenga tal perseuerencia. / Ya que el tercer Filipo / crisol de la casa de Austria, / a quien el cielo a otorgado / de Rey Catolico Palma, / en todo el Reyno a mandado / por sus Cedulas y Cartas / que como Señor de todo / todo lo gouierna y manda, / que por traydores y Herejes, / dos bien legitimas causas / para confiscar sus bienes / y conuertillos en brasas. / A España desocupeys, / porque como gente ingrata / despues de ochocientos años / quisistes darle la paga. / Ya que por premia os obliga / a que lleueys empleada / la semouiente hazie[n]da / pues os la dexa de gracia. / Yo, que vuestro amigo soy, / como el gato de las ratas / os hago esta memoria / porque, al fin, soys de mi Patria. / Por esta podreys saber / los generos de importancia / en que podreys emplear, / pues vays a tierras estrañas. /

Digo, pues, que el que saliere / para los Reynos de Francia / que auenture su caudal / en crea, ruan y olanda. / El que fuere a Inglaterra / sepa que ay mucha demanda / de paños, vayetas, frisas, / y de estambre medias calças. / Si para Flandes salieres, / lleuen muchas toneladas / de xeringas, y alfileles, / de caxcaueles y flautas. / Los que fueren a Milan / compraran telas riçadas / cosseletes y arcabuzas / porque ay mucha falta de armas. / Si fletaren para Guinea, / lleuaran ropas de Martas, / pelfas, libros y comedias / porque gustan de ver farsas / .... lleuen para Puertorrico / tabaco y cueros de vaca, / y agengibre, porque se / que a auido muy gran falta..... (*The writer of the romance eventually grows tired of trying to think up silly things for them to export, or silly places for these people to go.*) No se donde podays yr / que el juyzio se me cansa / pensando en vuestro prouecho / aunque no os pido la paga. / *Where then are they to go then?* E sabido que soys Moros / porque uno de vuestra casta / me lo dixo, que el traydor / aun sus secretos no guarda. / Y por esta cofusion / digo, que es cosa muy sana, / passaros a Berberia / que fue vuestra antigua Patria, / Frontero de Gibraltar / en tres leguas de distancia / Berberia esta tan cerca, / que se ven sus luminarias / y assi con poco trabajo / aquel estrecho se passa / comiendo reziente el pan, / carne fresca y fresca el agua. / Para alla podeys lleuar / chapines, mantos, y sayas / arandelas, verdugados / que alla lo gastan las Damas ... y para gente deuota / deuotisimas estampas / Cruzes, y algunos Rosarios, / libros de Santos, y santas. / ... y si perdierdes en ella / todo por mi cuenta vaya. / Llegareys entre los vuestros, / hablareys en vuestra usança / digo vuestra algarabia, / que fue imposible olvidarla. / Alli, si quereys ser moros / no ay quien a la mano os vaya / no ay temor de Inquisicion / ni capisayo con franjas. / Dizen que en passando alla / direys que la tierra es santa. / pues que en ella Mahoma / puso sus pessimas plantas, / que luego renegareys / y que ya hechos piratas / uestros moriscos baxeles / tocaran en nuestras playas. / Yo digo que no hareys tal, / que tengo firme esperança / que aueys de morir por Dios / con firmissima constancia. / Todos mirad, que yo tengo / dada a muchos la palabra / que soys Catolicos muchos, / no me hagays caer en falta. / Mas quien siempre an sido perros / de dentro de nuestra España / que mucho lo sean alla / adõde no ay Ley Cristiana. (Bauer n.d., 180)

Bibliography

In a study such as this, which is intended in the first place for English-speaking readers, but which inevitably contains very many Spanish names, it is perhaps desirable to explain how Spanish surnames will be alphabetized. Standard practice with Spanish names is to give the surname of a person's father first in order, and to follow it by that of his or her mother (second). This practice is adhered to here. Such names are ordered under the surname of the author's father, exactly as is done with English and other names, but that means of course that Spanish names will be alphabetized under their penultimate element, and not the last one. Thus Luis Alberto Anaya Hernández will be listed under *A* and not *H*. I am aware that Anglophones (and their computers) may be rendered unhappy by this practice, but that does not seem sufficient reason to flout it, especially since if there is a brief one-name reference to such an author, it will be to the father's surname: in this instance, Anaya. We therefore need to be able to look him up in the bibliography under *A*.

Some Spanish families (very few nowadays, the usage is in decline) link the two elements of their double surnames by "and" ("y" or "i" in Catalan names). From this usage uncertainty can sometimes arise. Are we dealing with two authors or one? In the present volume, if the English word "and" occurs between two names, they will be the names of two different people, but where "y"/"i" stands between two names, then we are dealing with one person only. Thus Ribera and Asín (1912) will refer to the important catalog *Manuscritos árabes y aljamiados de la Biblioteca de la Junta* published under the direction of the two great scholars Julián Ribera y Tarragó and Miguel Asín Palacios, whereas Corral y Rojas (1613) refers to the *Relación del [sic] rebelión y expulsión de los moriscos del reyno de Valencia,* which Antonio de Corral y Rojas published in Valladolid.

Acién Almansa, Manuel

1978. "Un ejemplo de repoblación señorial, la Serranía de Villaluenga." In *Actas del I Congreso de Historia de Andalucía, diciembre de 1976*, 2: 449–58. Córdoba.

Alarcón y Santón, Maximiliano A., **and Ramón García de Linares**

1940. *Los documentos árabes diplomáticos del Archivo de la Corona de Aragón.* Madrid and Granada.

Alba, duque de et al.

1952. *Documentos inéditos para la Historia de España*, 7. Madrid.

Albarracín Navarro, Joaquina

1985. "Unas 'alguacías' de Ocaña (Toledo), en el marco de convivencia de las Tres Culturas." In *Actas del II Congreso Internacional: Encuentro de las Tres Culturas*, 9–108. Toledo.

1987a. "La Qubba de Salomón en un manuscrito árabe de Ocaña (Toledo)." In *Homenaje al Prof. Darío Cabanelas O.F.M. con motivo de su LXX aniversario*, 2: 163–76. Granada.

1987b. *Medicina, farmacopea y magia en el "Miscelánea de Salomon."* Granada.

Alcalá, Angel

1995. "Tres cuestiones en busca de respuesta: Invalidez del bautismo 'forzado,' 'conversion' de judíos, trato 'cristiano' al converso." In *Judíos, Sefarditas, Conversos: La expulsión de 1492 y sus consecuencias; Ponencias del Congreso Internacional celebrado en Nueva York en noviembre de 1992.* Ed. Angel Alcalá, 523–44. Valladolid.

Alcalá, Angel, ed.

1995. *Judíos, Sefarditas, Conversos: La expulsión de 1492 y sus consecuencias; Ponencias del Congreso Internacional celebrado en Nueva York en noviembre de 1992.* Valladolid.

Alcalá, Pedro de

1505. *Arte para ligeramente saver la lengua araviga and Vocabulista arávigo en letra castellana.* Granada.

Alcocer, Pedro de

1554. *Hystoria, o Descripción de la imperial cibdad de Toledo.* Toledo.

Alonso, Carlos

1979. *Los apócrifos del Sacromonte (Granada): Estudio historico.* Valladolid.

Álvarez Millán, Cristina

2004. "Un corán desconocido de don Pascual de Gayangos en la Real Academia de la Historia." In *La memoria de los libros: Estudios sobre la memoria del escrito y de la lectura en Europa y América*, 2: 367–83. Madrid.

Álvarez Rodríguez, J. R.

1983–84. "La Casa de Doctrina del Albaicín: Labor apostólica de la Compañia de Jesús con los moriscos." *Cuadernos de la Alhambra* 19–20: 233–46.

Anaya Hernández, Luis Alberto

1996. *Judeoconversos e Inquisición en las Islas Canarias (1402–1605).* Las Palmas de Gran Canaria.

Andrés, Juan (Andrea, Giovanni d')

1515. *Confusión de la secta mahomética y del alcorán.* Valencia.

1537. *Opera chiamata confusione della setta maometica.* Seville.

1652. *The Confusion of Mohamed's Sect.* Trans. J[oshua] N[otstock]. London.

Andrés de Uztarroz, Juan Francisco

1663. *Anales de la Corona de Aragón: Segunda parte.* Zaragoza.

Anglería (Anghiera), Pedro Mártir de

1953. *Epistolario.* Ed. and trans. by José López de Toro. Vol. 1. Vol. 9 of *Documentos Inéditos para la Historia de España.* Madrid.

Anonymous

1853. "Leyes de moros." *Memorial histórico español* 5: 11–246.

Aranda Doncel, Juan

1984. *Los moriscos en tierras de Córdoba.* Córdoba.

Al-Arnaut, Muhamed Mufaku

1994. "Islam and Muslims in Bosnia, 1878–1918: Two *hijras* and Two *fatwas.*" *Journal of Islamic Studies* 5: 242–53.

Asin, Palacios, Miguel

1909. "Un tratado morisco de polémica contra los judíos." In *Mélanges Hartwig Derenbourg,* 246–73. Paris.

Atkins, William

1622. *A Relation of the Journey from St. Omers to Seville.* London.

Ayala, Martín de

1566. *Doctrina christiana en lengua araviga y castellana.* Valencia.

Aznar Cardona, Pedro

1612. *Expulsión justificada de los moriscos españoles.* Huesca.

Barceló Torres, María del Carmen

1984. *Minorías islámicas en el País Valenciano. Historia y dialecto.* Valencia.

Bauer Landauer, Ignacio

[1923?]. *Papeles de mi archivo. Relaciones y manuscritos (Moriscos).* Madrid.

Benítez Sánchez-Blanco, R., and E. Císcar Pallarés

1979. "La Iglesia ante la conversión y expulsión de los moriscos." In *Historia de la Iglesia en España.* Ed. R. García Villoslada, 4: 208–31. Madrid.

Ben Jemia, M. N.

1987. *La langue des derniers musulmans de l'Espagne.* Tunis.

2001. "Los moriscos en pos de una lengua sagrada." In *Mélanges Luce López-Baralt.* Ed. and with an intro. by Abdeljelil Temimi, 2: 415–22. Zaghouan.

Bernabé Pons, Luis F.

1988. *El cántico islámico del morisco hispanotunecino Taybili.* Zaragoza.

1992. *Bibliografía de la literatura aljamiado-morisca.* Alicante.

1996. "Zur Wahrheit und Echtheit des Barnabasevangeliums." In *Wertewandel und religiöse Umbrüche.* Iserlohn.

1998. *El texto morisco del Evangelio de San Bernabé.* Granada.

Bernard-Maître, Henri

1956. "Saint Ignace de Loyola mystique et les anciennes traductions espagnoles de l'*Imitation de Jésus-Christ.*" *Ons geestelijk Erf* 30, no. 1: 25–42.

Birriel Salcedo, Margarita María

1989. *La tierra de Almuñécar en tiempos de Felipe II: Expulsion de moriscos y repoblación.* Granada.

Bleda, Jaime

1618. *Corónica de los moros de España.* Valencia.

Boronat y Barrachina, Pascual

1901. *Los moriscos españoles y su expulsion.* 2 vols. Valencia.

Bosch Vila, Jacinto

1957. "Dos nuevos manuscritos y papeles sueltos de moriscos aragoneses." *Al-Andalus* 22: 463–70.

Boswell, John

1977. *The Royal Treasure: Muslim Communities under the Crown of Aragon in the Fourteenth Century.* New Haven and London.

Bouzineb, Hossain, and Gerard Wiegers

1996. "Tetuán y la expulsión de los moriscos." In *Titwan khilal al-qarnayn 16 wa-17.* Titwan.

Bovill, E. W.

1968. *The Golden Trade of the Moors.* 2d ed. Oxford.

Bramón, Dolors

1981. *Contra moros y judíos.* Barcelona.

Braudel, Fernand

1972. *The Mediterranean and the Mediterranean World in the Age of Philip II.* 2 vols. London.

Bravo Caro, Juan Jesús

1995. *Felipe II y la repoblación del Reino de Granada: La Taha de Comares.* Granada.

Brockelmann, Carl

1937–49. *Geschichte del arabischen Litteratur* 2 vols. and 3 suppl. vols. Leiden.

Bunes Ibarra, Miguel Angel de

1983. *Los moriscos en el pensamiento histórico: Historiografía de un grupo marginado.* Madrid.

Cabanelas Rodríguez, Darío

1965. *El morisco granadino Alonso del Castillo.* 2d ed. Granada. 1991.

1952. *Juan de Segovia y el problema islámico.* Madrid.

1981. "Intento de supervivencia en el ocaso de una cultura: Los libros plúmbeos de Granada." *Nueva Revista de Filología Hispánica* 30: 334–58.

1987. *Homenaje al Prof. Darío Cabanelas O.F.M. con motivo de su LXX aniversario.* 2 vols. Granada.

1993. *La incorporación de Granada a la Corona de Castilla.* Ed. Miguel Angel Ladero Quesada. Granada.

Cabrillana, Nicolás

1982. *Almería morisca.* Granada.

Cardaillac, Louis

1971a. "Morisques et protestants" *Al-Andalus* 36: 29–623.

1971b. "Le passage des morisques en Languedoc." *Anales du Midi* 83: 259–98.

1977. *Morisques et chrétiens. Un affrontement polémique, 1492–1640.* Paris.

1979. *Moriscos y cristianos: Un enfrentamiento polémico.* Trans. Mercedes García Arenal. Madrid.

2001. "Felipe II y los Moriscos." In *Mélanges Luce López-Baralt.* Ed. and with an intro. by Abdeljelil Temimi, 2: 169–182. Zaghouan.

Cardaillac, Louis, ed.

1983. *Les Morisques et leur temps.* Paris.

Caro Baroja, Julio

[1957] 1976. *Los moriscos del reino de Granada: Ensayo de historia social.* Madrid.

Carrasco Urgoiti, Soledad

1956. *El moro de Granada en la literatura.* Madrid.

1969. *El problema morisco en Aragón al comienzo del reinado de Felipe II.* Valencia.

1976. *The Moorish Novel: "El Abencerraje" and Pérez de Hita.* Boston.

2001. "En la frontera entre literatura e historia." In *Mélanges Luce López-Baralt.* Ed. and with an intro. by Abdeljelil Temimi, 1: 197–204. Zaghouan.

Case, Thomas E.

1993. *Lope and Islam: Islamic Personages in His Comedias.* Newark, Delaware.

Casey, James

1999. *Early Modern Spain: A Social History.* London and New York.

Castillo, Alonso del

1852. "Sumario e recopilación de todo lo romançado por mí." In *Memorial histórico español,* 3: 2–164.

1994. *Recopilación de refranes andalusíes.* In *Recopilacón de refranes andalusíes de Alonso del Castillo.* Ed. Federico Corriente Córdoba and Bouzineb Hussein. Zaragoza.

Castries, Henri de et al.

1905–65. *Sources inédites pour l'histoire du Maroc.* 26 vols. Paris and Leiden.

Centurión y Córdoba, Adán

1706. *Relación breve de las reliquias que se hallaron en la ciudad de Granada en una torre antiquíssima y en las cavernas del monte Illiputano de Valparayso.* Lyons.

Cervera Fras, María José

1987. *La plegaria musulmana en el "Compendio de al-Tulaytulî": Transcripción del manuscrito de Sabiñán (Zaragoza).* Zaragoza.

Chejne, Anwar G.

1974. *Muslim Spain: Its History and Culture.* Minneapolis.

1983. *Islam and the West. The Moriscos: A Cultural and Social History.* Albany.

Circourt, Albert de, comte

1846. *Histoire des mores mudejares et des morisques, ou des Arabes d'Espagne sous la domination des chrétiens.* Paris.

Císcar Pallarés, Eugenio

1975. "Prestamistas moriscos en Valencia." *Cuadernos de Historia* 5: 89–94.

1993. *Moriscos, nobles y repobladores: Estudios sobre el siglo XVII en Valencia.* Valencia.

Colas Latorre, Gregorio

1988. "Los moriscos aragoneses y su expulsión." In Institución Fernando el Católico, *Destierros Aragoneses,* 1: 189–216. Zaragoza.

Colas Latorre, Gregorio, and José Antonio Salas Ausen

1982. *Aragón en el siglo XVI: Alteraciones sociales y conflictos políticos.* Zaragoza.

Colin, G. S.

1955. "Un projet de traité entre les Morisques de la Casba de Rabat et le roi d'Espagne en 1631." *Arabica* 2: 17–26.

Colección de documentos inéditos para la historia de España

1842–95. 112 vols. Madrid.

Contreras, Alonso de

1982. *Vida del capitán Contreras.* Barcelona.

Corral y Rojas, Antonio del

1613. *Relación del rebelión y expulsión de los moriscos del reyno de Valencia.* Valladolid.

Corriente Córdoba, Federico

1977. *A Grammatical Sketch of the Spanish Arabic Dialect Bundle.* Madrid.

1990. *Relatos píos y profanos del MS. aljamiado de Urrea de Jalón.* Zaragoza.

Corriente Córdoba, Federico, and Hussein Bouzineb, eds.

1994. *Recopilacón de refranes andalusíes de Alonso del Castillo.* Zaragoza.

Cortés Peña, Antonio Luis, and Bernard Vincent

1986. *Historia de Granada. 3: La época moderna, siglos XVI, XVII y XVIII.* Granada.

Cruces Blanco, Esther

1987. "Ensayo sobre la oligarquía malagueña." In *Estudios sobre Málaga y el Reino de Granada en el V Centenario de la Conquista.* Ed. José Enrique López de Coca Castañer, 199–214. Málaga.

Danvila y Collado, Manuel

1889. *La expulsión de los moriscos españoles.* Madrid.

Davis, Charles

1987. "Tacitean elements in Diego de Mendoza's *Guerra de Granada.*" *Dispositio* 10: 85–96.

Dedieu, J. P.

1983 "Les morisques de Daimiel et l'Inquisition." In *Les Morisques et leur temps.* Ed. Louis Cardaillac, 493–522. Paris.

Deyermond, Alan, ed.

1996. *Historical Literature in Medieval Iberia.* London.

Domínguez Ortiz, A., and Bernard Vincent

1978. *Historia de los moriscos. Vida y tragedia de una minoría.* Madrid.

Dressendörfer, P.

1971. *Islam unter der Inquisition: Die Morisco-Prozesse in Toledo, 1575–1610.* Wiesbaden.

Drost, Gerrit Willem

1984. *Die Moriscos in de publicaties van Staat en Kerk (1492–1609).* Valkenburg.

Duggan, Joseph J., ed.

1975. *Oral Literature: Seven Essays.* Edinburgh and London.

Echevarria, Ana

1999. *The Fortress of Faith: The Attitude towards Muslims in Fifteenth-Century Spain.* Leiden, Boston, and Cologne.

Edwards, John

1987. "La religión en la comarca de Málaga." In *Estudios sobre Málaga y el Reino de Granada en el V Centenario de la Conquista.* Ed. José Enrique López de Coca Castañer, 215–20. Málaga.

1996. *Religion and Society in Spain c. 1492.* Aldershot.

1999. *The Spanish Inquisition.* Stroud.

Elliott, John H.

1973. *Spain: A Companion to Spanish Studies.* Ed. P. E. Russell. London.

1986. *The Count-Duke of Olivares: The Statesman in an Age of Decline.* London and New Haven.

1989. *Spain and Its World, 1500–1700.* New Haven.

Epalza, Míkel de

1963. "Sobre un posible autor español del *Evangelio de Bernabe.*"*Al-Andalus* 28: 479–91.

1971. *La Tuhfa: Autobiografía y polémica islámica contre el Cristianismo de'Abdallah al-Taryuman (fray Anselmo Turmeda).* Rome.

1982. "Le milieu hispano-moresque de l'Evangile islamisant de Barnabé (XVIe–XVIIe siècle)." *Cahiers de Tunisie* 26: 35–52.

1992. *Los moriscos antes y después de la expulsión.* Madrid.

1998. "Los moriscos y sus descendientes: Después de la expulsión." In Fundación Bancaja, *La Expulsión de los Moriscos (14 de octobre de 1997–9 de junio de 1998),* 43–74. [Valencia].

Epalza, Míkel de, and R. Petit

1973. *Études sur les moriscos andalous en Tunisie.* Madrid and Tunis.

Expulsió dels moriscos: Conseqüèncias en el món islàmic i el món cristià, L'.

1994. Collecció Actes de congressos, 4. Barcelona.

Fernández, Paz

1988. *Repertorio bibliográfico sobre moriscos. (=Cuadernos de Información bibliográfica F. M. Pareja 1988).* Madrid.

Fernández de Navarrete, Martín, et al.

1842–95. *Colleción de documentos inèditos para la historia de España.* 112 vols. Madrid.

Fernández Nieva, Julio

1983. "El enfrentamiento entre moriscos y cristianos viejos: El caso de Hornachos." In *Les Morisques et leur temps.* Ed. Louis Cardaillac. Paris.

1984. "Un pleito entre el lic. Cuenca y los moriscos de Hornachos en Extremadura, 1606–1609." In *Religion, Identité et Sources Documentaires sur les Morisques Andalous.* Ed. Abdeljelil Temimi, 2: 213–44. Tunis.

Fernández y González, Francisco

1866. *Estado social y político de los mudéjares de Castilla.* Madrid.

Ferrer, Pau

1994. "Los moriscos en la ribera del Ebro, las encuestas informativas, 1610–1613." In *L'Expulsió dels moriscos: Conseqüèncias en el món islàmic i el món cristià.* Collecció Actes de congressos, 4. Barcelona.

L

Fierro, Maribel

1994. "Mahdisme et eschatologie en Al-Andalus." In *Mahdisme: Crise et changement dans l'histoire du Maroc.* Ed. Abdelmajid Kaddouri, 47–68. Rabat.

Fletcher, John

1976. "The Spanish Gospel of Barnabas." *Novum Testamentum* 18, no. 4: 314–20.

Fonseca, Damián

1612. *Iusta expulsión del los moriscos de España.* Rome.

Fonseca Antuña, Gregorio

1983. "Sumario de la Relación y Ejercicio Espiritual sacado y declarado por el Mancebo de Arévalo en nuestra lengua castellana." Ph.D. diss., University of Oviedo.

Fournel-Guérin, Jacqueline

1979. "Le livre et la civilisation écrite dans la communauté morisque aragonaise, 1540–1620." *Mélanges de la Casa de Valázquez* 15: 241–59.

Fundación Bancaja

1997. *La Expulsión de los Moriscos del reino de Valencia.* Valencia.

1998. *La Expulsión de los Moriscos (14 de octobre de 1997–9 de junio de 1998).* [Valencia].

Fuster, Joan

1968. *Poetes, moriscos i capellans.* Barcelona.

Galán Sánchez, Ángel

1982. *Los moriscos de Málaga en la época de los Reyes Católicos.* Special issue, *Jábega: Revista de la Diputación Provincial de Málaga* 39.

1987. "Poder cristiano y 'colaboracionismo' mudéjar." In *Estudios sobre Málaga y el Reino de Granada en el V Centenario de la Conquista.* Ed. José Enrique López de Coca Castañer, 271–90. Málaga.

1991. *Los mudéjares del Reino de Granada.* Granada.

n.d. *Una visión de la "Decadencia Española": La historiografía anglosajona sobre mudéjares y moriscos (siglos XVIII–XX).* Málaga.

Gallego y Burín, Antonio, and Alfonso Gámir Sandoval

1968. *Los moriscos del Reino de Granada según el Sínodo de Guádix 1554.* Granada.

Galmés de Fuentes, Álvaro

1955. "Influencias sintácticas y estilísticas del árabe en la prosa medieval castellana." *Boletín de la Real Academia Española* 35: 213–75, 36: 65–131, and 36: 255–307.

1967. *El libro de las batallas (narraciones caballerescas aljamiado-moriscas).* Oviedo.

1970. *Historia de los amores de París y Viana.* Madrid.

1977–78. "Sobre un soneto barroco de un morisco." *Archivum* 37–38: 200–17.

1981. "Lengua y estilo en la literatura aljamiado-morisca." *Nueva Revista de Filología Hispánica* 30: 420–40.

1993. *Los moriscos desde su misma orilla.* Madrid.

1998. *Los manuscritos aljamiado-moriscos de la biblioteca de la Real Academia de la Historia (legado Pascual de Gayangos).* Madrid.

2000. *Romania Arábica: Estudios de literatura comparada árabe y romance.* Madrid.

Galmés de Fuentes, Alvaro, ed.

1978. *Actas del Coloquio Internacional de Literatura Aljamiada y Morisca (Oviedo, 1972)*. Madrid.

García Ballester, Luis

1977. *Medicina, ciencia y minorías marginadas: Los Moriscos*. Granada.

García Cárcel, R.

1980. *Herejía y sociedad en el siglo XVI: La Inquisición en Valencia, 1530–1609*. Barcelona.

1998. "Los moriscos y la Inquisición." In Fundación Bancaja, *La Expulsión de los Moriscos (14 de octobre de 1997–9 de junio de 1998)*, 145–68. [Valencia].

García y García, Luis

1947. *Una Embajada de los Reyes Católicos a Egipto, según la "Legatio Babylonica" y el "Opus Epistolarum" de Pedro Mártir de Anglería*. Valladolid.

García Villoslada, R., ed.

1979. *Historia de la Iglesia en España*. Madrid.

García-Arenal, Mercedes

1975. *Los moriscos*. Madrid.

1978. *Inquisición y moriscos: Los procesos del tribunal de Cuenca*. Madrid.

1983. "Últimos estudios sobre moriscos: Estado de la cuestión." *Al-Qantara* 1983: 101–14.

1998. "Los moriscos granadinos en Castilla." In Fundación Bancaja, *La Expulsión de los Moriscos (14 de octobre de 1997–9 de junio de 1998)*, 169–90. [Valencia].

García-Arenal, Mercedes, and Ana Labarta

1981. "Algunos fragmentos aljamiados del proceso contra Yuçe de la Vacia (1495)." *Nueva Revista de Filología Hispánica* 30: 127–42.

García-Arenal, Mercedes, and Béatrice Leroy

1984. *Moros y judíos en Navarra en la baja Edad Media*. Madrid.

García-Arenal, Mercedes, and María Jesús Viguera, eds.

1988. *Relaciones de la Península Ibérica con el Magreb (siglos XIII–XVI)*. Madrid.

Garrad, Kenneth

1954. "The Original Memorial of Don Francisco Núñez Muley." *Atlante* 2: 168–226.

1956. "La industria sedera granadina en el s. xvi, y en conexión con el levantamiento de las Alpujarras." *Miscelánea de Estudios Arabes y Hebráicos* 5: 73–104.

1965. "La Inquisición y los moriscos granadinos, 1526–1580." *Bulletin Hispanique* 67: 63–77.

Garrido Aranda, Antonio

1980. *Moriscos e Indios: Precedentes hispánicos de la evangelización en México*. México.

1984. "El morisco y la inquisición novohispana. (Actitudes antiislámicas en la sociedad colonial)." *II Jornadas de Andalucía y América* 1: 501–33. Sevilla.

Gayangos, Pascual de

1839. "The Language and Literature of the Moriscos." *British and Foreign Quarterly Review* 8: 63–95.

Geddes, Michael

1702. *Miscellaneous Tracts*. 2 vols. London.

Gil Grimau, Rodolfo

1999. *La política y los moriscos en la época de los Austria: Actas del Encuentro diciembre 1998*. Sevilla la Nueva.

Godoy Alcántara, José

1868. *Historia crítica de los falsos cronicones*. Madrid.

Góngora, Luis de

1969. *Sonetos completos*. Ed. Biruté Ciplijauskaité. Madrid.

González Palencia, Angel

1915. "Noticia y extractos de algunos manuscritos árabes y aljamiados de Toledo y Madrid." In Centro de Estudios Históricos, *Miscelánea de Estudios y Textos Árabes*, 117–45. Madrid.

1942. "El curandero morisco del s. xvi Román Ramírez" In idem, *Historias y leyendas: Estudios literarios*. Madrid.

González Rodríguez, Alberto

1990. *Hornachos, enclave morisco: Peculiaridades de una población distinta*. Extremadura.

Gozalbes Busto, Guillermo

1988. *Al Mandari, el granadino, fundador de Tetuán*. Granada.

1992. *Los moriscos en Marruecos*. Granada.

Griffin, Nigel

1981. "'*Un muro invisible*': Moriscos and Cristianos Viejos." In *Mediaeval and Renaissance Studies on Spain and Portugal in Honour of P. E. Russell*. Ed. F. W. Hodcroft et al., 133–54. Oxford.

Grima Cervantes, Juan

1993. *Almería y el Reino de Granada en los inicios de la modernidad (s. xv–xvi): Compendio de Estudios*. Almería.

Guevara, Antonio de

1956. *Epístolas familiares*. Madrid.

Guevara Bazán, Rafael

1966. "La inmigración musulmana a la América española en los primeros años de colonización." *Boletín histórico* [Fundación John Boulton, Caracas] 10: 33–50.

Guillén Robles, Francisco

1886. *Leyendas moriscas*. 3 vols. Madrid.

1889. *Catálogo de los Manuscritos Arabes existentes en la Biblioteca Nacional de Madrid*. Madrid.

Gutwirth, Eleazar

1995. "Reacciones ante la expulsión: Del siglo XV al XVIII." In *Judíos, Sefarditas, Conversos: La expulsión de 1492 y sus consecuencias; Ponencias del Congreso Internacional celebrado en Nueva York en noviembre de 1992*. Ed. Angel Alcalá, 195–218. Valladolid.

Hagerty, Miguel José, ed.

1980. *Los Libros Plúmbeos del Sacromonte*. Madrid.

Haïdara, Ismael Diadié

1993. *El bajá Yawdar y la conquista saadí del Songhay (1591–1599)*. Cuevas del Almanzora.

al-Hajari, Ahmad Ibn Qasim

1987. *Kitab Nasir al-din 'ala'l-qawm al-kafirin.* Ed. Muhammad Razuq. Casablanca.

1997. *Kitab Nasir al-din 'ala'l-qawm al-kafirin.* Ed. P. S. van Koningsveld, Q. al-Samarrai, and G. A. Wiegers. Madrid.

Haliczer, Stephen

1990. *Inquisition and Society in the Kingdom of Valencia, 1478–1834.* Berkeley.

Halperin Donghi, Tulio

1980. *Un conflicto nacional: Moriscos y cristianos viejos en Valencia.* Valencia.

Hamadi, 'Abdallah

1989. *Al-muriskiyyun, 1492–1616.* Tunis.

Hamilton, Earl J.

1934. *American Treasure and the Price Revolution in Spain, 1501–1650.* Cambridge, MA.

1948. *El florecimiento del capitalismo y otros ensayos de historia económica.* Madrid.

1978. "Las consecuencias económicas en Andalucía de la expulsión de los moriscos." In *Actas del I congreso de Historia de Andalucía, diciembre 1976.* Vol. 2, *Andalucia medieval,* 69–84. Cordova.

Harvey, Leonard Patrick

1956. "Yuse Banegas: Un moro noble en Granada bajo los Reyes Católicos." *Al-Andalus* 21: 297–302.

1958a. "Un manuscrito aljamiado en la Biblioteca de la Universidad de Cambridge." *Al-Andalus* 23: 49–74.

1958b. "The Literary Culture of the Moriscos (1492–1609): A Study Based on the Extant Manuscripts in Arabic and Aljamía." D. Phil. diss., Oxford University.

1959. "The Morisco Who Was Muley Zaydan's Interpreter: Ahmad ben Qasim . . . al-Hajari al-Andalusi." *Miscelánea de Estudios Árabes y Hebraicos* 8: 67–96.

1962. "A Morisco Manuscript in the Godolphin Collection at Wadham College, Oxford." *Al-Andalus* 28: 461–65.

1963. "A Morisco Reader of Jean Lemaire des Belges?" *Al-Andalus* 21: 231–36.

1964a. "Crypto-Islam in Sixteenth-Century Spain." In *Actas del Primer Congreso de Estudios Árabes e Islámicos (Córdoba 1962),* 163–78. Madrid.

1964b. "A Morisco Prayer-book in the British Museum." *Al-Andalus* 29: 373–76.

1967. "Castilian Mancebo as a Calque of Arabic 'abd." *Modern Philology* 65: 130–32.

1971. "The Arabic Dialect of Valencia in 1595." *Al-Andalus* 36: 81–115.

1973. "Textes de littérature religieuse des Moriscos tunisiens." In *Études sur les moriscos andalous en Tunisie.* Ed. Mikel de Epalza and R. Petit, 199–204. Madrid and Tunis.

1974. *The Moriscos and Don Quixote.* London.

1975. "Oral Composition and the Performance of Novels of Chivalry in Spain." In *Oral Literature: Seven Essays.* Ed. Joseph J. Duggan, 84–100. Edinburgh and London.

1978a. "El mancebo de Arévalo y la tradición cultural de los moriscos." In *Actas del Coloquio Internacional de Literatura Aljamiada y Morisca (Oviedo, 1972).* Ed. Alvaro Galmés de Fuentes, 20–41. Madrid.

1978b. "The Survival of Arabic Culture in Spain after 1492." In *La signification du Bas Moyen Age dans l'histoire et la culture du monde musulman: Actes du VIIIème Congrès de l'Union européenne des arabisants et islamisants, 85–88.* Aix-en-Provence.

1981a. "La leyenda morisca de Ibrahim." *Nueva Revista de Filología Hispánica* 30: 1–20.

1981b. "The Thirteen Articles of the Faith, and the Twelve Degrees in which the World Is Governed." In *Mediaeval and Renaissance Studies on Spain and Portugal in Honour of P. E. Russell.* Ed. F. W. Hodcroft et al., 15–29. Oxford.

1984. "When Portugal Converted Its Muslims." *Portuguese Studies* 1: 54–60.

1986a. "The Terminology of Two Hitherto Unpublished Morisco Calendar Texts." In *Les actes de la première table ronde du C.I.E.M. sur la littérature aljamiado-morisque: Hybridisme linguistique et univers discursif.* Ed. Abdeljelil Temimi, 70–83. Tunis.

1986b. "Pan-Arab Sentiment in a Late (A.D. 1595) Granadan Text." *Revista del Instituto Egipcio de Estudios Islámicos en Madrid* 23: 223–33.

1986c. "Aljamía portuguesa Revisited." *Portuguese Studies* 2: 1–4.

1988. "The Moriscos and the Hajj." *Bulletin of the British Society for Middle Eastern Studies* 14: 11–24.

1989a "A Second Morisco Manuscript at Wadham College, Oxford." *Al-Qantara* 10: 257–72.

1989b. "A Morisco Collection of Apocryphal *Hadiths* on the Virtues of Al-Andalus." *Al-Masaq* 2: 25–39.

1989c. "Los moriscos y los cinco pilares del Islam." In *Las Practicas musulmanas de los moriscos andaluces, 1492–1609: Actas del III Simposio Internacional de Estudios Moriscos.* Ed. Abdeljelil Temimi, 93–97. Zaghouan.

1989d. "In Granada under the Catholic Monarchs: A Call from a Doctor and Another from a "Curandera."" In *The Age of the Catholic Monarchs: Literary Studies in Memory of Keith Whinnom,* 71–75. Liverpool.

1989e. "Límites de los intercambios culturales." *Actas de las I Jornadas de Cultura Islámica, Toledo, 1987,* 89–94. Madrid.

1990a. "El alfaqui de Cadrete, Baray de Reminjo." In *Actas de las II Jornadas Internacionales de Cultura Islámica, Teruel, 1988.* Madrid.

1990b. *Islamic Spain, 1250 to 1500.* Chicago.

1994. "The Moriscos and Their International Relations." In *L'Expulsió dels Moriscos: Conseqüències en el món islàmic i el món cristià.* Barcelona.

1996. "Chronicling the Fall of Nasrid Granada: Kitab nubdhat al-'asr fiakhbar muluk Bani Nasr." In *Historical Literature in Medieval Iberia.* Ed. Alan Deyermond, 105–20. London.

1998. "Los moriscos y sus escritos." In Fundación Bancaja, *La Expulsión de los Moriscos (14 de octobre de 1997–9 de junio de 1998),* 75–90. [Valencia].

Hawkins, J. P.

1988. "A Morisco Philosophy of Suffering: An Anthropological Analysis of an *aljamiado* Text." *Maghreb Review* 13: 199–217.

Hegyi, Ottmar

1981. *Cinco leyendas y otros relatos moriscos.* Madrid.

Hess, Andrew

1968–69. "The Moriscos: An Ottoman Fifth Column in Sixteenth-century Spain." *American Historical Review* 74: 1–25.

1970. "The Evolution of the Ottoman Seaborne Empire in the Age of the Oceanic Discoveries, 1453–1525." *American Historical Review* 75: 1892–1919.

1973. "The Ottoman Conqest of Egypt (1517) and the Beginning of the Sixteenth-Century World War." *International Journal of Middle East Studies* 4: 55–76.

1972. "The Battle of Lepanto and Its Place in Mediterranean History." *Past and Present* 57: 53–73.

1978. *The Forgotten Frontier: A History of the Ibero-African Frontier.* Chicago.

Hodcroft, Frederick W. et al., eds.

1981. *Mediaeval and Renaissance Studies on Spain and Portugal in Honour of P. E. Russell.* Oxford.

Hoenerbach, Wilhelm

1965. *Spanisch-islamische Urkunde aus der Zeit der Nasriden und Moriscos.* Bonn.

Holt, P. M.

1990. "Al-Nasir Muhammad's Letter to a Spanish Ruler in 699/1300." *Al-Masaq* 3: 23–29.

Holy, Ladislav

1991. *Religion and Custom in a Muslim Society: The Berti of Sudan.* Cambridge.

Hopkins, J. F. P.

1982. *Letters from Barbary, 1576–1774: Arabic Documents in the Public Record Office.* Oxford.

Hourani, Albert

1991. *History of the Arab Peoples.* London.

Hurtado de Mendoza, Diego

1970. *Guerra de Granada hecha por el rey de España don Felipe II contra los moriscos de aquel Reino, sus rebeldes.* Ed. B. Blanco-González. Valencia.

'Inân, Muhammad'Abdallah

1966. *Nihâyat al-Andalus.* Cairo.

Institución Fernando el Católico

1988. *Destierros aragoneses. I, Judíos y moriscos.* Zaragoza.

Jaffar, Ghulam Mohammed

1992. "The Repudiation of Jihad by Indian Scholars in the Nineteenth Century." *Hamdard Islamicus* 15, no. 3: 93–100.

Janer, Florencio

1857. *Condición social de los Moriscos de España: Causas de su expulsión, y consecuencias que esta produjo en el órden económico y político.* Madrid.

Jayyusi, Salma Khadra, ed.

1992. *The Legacy of Muslim Spain.* Handbuch der Orientalistik, 1, no. 12. Leiden and New York.

Jedih, Iça [Shadili Gidelli]

1853. "Suma de los principales mandamientos y devedamientos de la ley y çunna." *Memorial histórico español* 5: 247–449.

Kamen, Henry

1991. *Spain, 1469–1714: A Society of Conflict.* 2d ed. London and New York.

Kendrick, T. D.

1960. *Saint James in Spain.* London.

Kontzi, Reinhold

1974. *Aljamiadotexte: Ausgabe mit einer Einleitung und Glossar.* Wiesbaden.

Kriegel, Maurice

1995. "El edicto de expulsión: motivos, fines, contexto." In *Judíos, Sefarditas, Conversos: La expulsión de 1492 y sus consecuencias; Ponencias del Congreso Internacional celebrado en Nueva York en noviembre de 1992.* Ed. Angel Alcalá, 134–69. Valladolid

Labarta, Ana

1987. *La onomástica de los moriscos valencianos.* Madrid.

Ladero Quesada, Miguel Ángel

1987. "Nóminas de conversos granadinos." In *Estudios sobre Málaga y el Reino de Granada en el V Centenario de la Conquista.* Ed. José Enrique López de Coca Castañer, 291–312. Málaga.

1988. *Granada después de la Conquista: Repobladores y Mudéjares.* Granada.

Ladero Quesada, Miguel Angel, ed.

1993. *La incorporación de Granada a la Corona de Castilla.* Granada.

Lapeyre, Henri

1959. *Géographie de l'Espagne morisque.* Paris.

Lapiedra Gutiérrez, Eva

1997. *Como los musulmanes llamaban a los cristianos hispánicos.* Alicante.

Latham, J. D.

1957. "Towards a Study of Andalusian Immigration and Its Place in Tunisian History." *Les Cahiers de Tunisie* 5: 203–52.

Lea, Henry Charles

1890. *Chapters from the Religious History of Spain Connected with the Inquisition.* Philadelphia.

1901. *The Moriscos of Spain: Their Conversion and Expulsion.* London.

1990. *Los moriscos españoles. Su conversión y expulsión.* With an intro. and notes by Rafael Benítez Sánchez-Blanco. Alicante.

Lewis, Bernard

1982. *The Muslim Discovery of Europe.* London.

Longás, Pedro

1915. *Vida religiosa de los moriscos.* Madrid.

López-Baralt, Luce

1980. "Crónica de la destrucción de un mundo: La literature aljamiado-morisca." *Bulletin Hispanique* 82: 16–58.

1983. "Las problemáticas profecías de san Isidro de Sevilla y de Ali Ibn al-Feresiyo en torno al Islam español." *Nueva Revista de Filología Hispánica* 29: 343–67.

1985. *San Juan de la Cruz y el Islam.* México and Puerto Rico.

1989. *Huellas del Islam en la literatura española: De Juan Ruíz a Juan Goytisolo.* Madrid.

1992. *Un Kama Sutra español.* Madrid.

2001. *Mélanges Luce López-Baralt.* Ed. and with an intro. by Abdeljelil Temimi. 2 vols. Zaghouan.

López de Coca Castañer, José Enrique

1987. "Los moriscos malagueños, ¿una minoría armada?" In *Estudios sobre Málaga y el Reino de Granada en el V Centenario de la Conquista.* Ed. José Enrique López de Coca Castañer, 329–50. Málaga.

López de Coca Castañer, José Enrique, ed.

1987. *Estudios sobre Málaga y el Reino de Granada en el V Centenario de la Conquista.* Málaga.

López-Morillas, Consuelo

1982. *The Qur'an in Sixteenth-Century Spain: Six Morisco Versions of Sura 79.* London.

1984. "Copistas y escribanos moriscos." In *Religion, Identité et Sources Documentaires sur les Morisques Andalous.* Ed. Abdeljelil Temimi, 71–78. Tunis.

1994. *Textos aljamiados sobre la vida de Mahoma: El Profeta de los moriscos.* Madrid.

Lovett, A. W.

1986. *Early Habsburg Spain, 1517–1598.* Oxford.

Lugo Acevedo, María Luisa

2001. "Simbología mística musulmana en el *Libro de las luces.*" In *Mélanges Luce López-Baralt.* Ed. and with an intro. by Abdeljelil Temimi, 2: 451–60. Zaghouan.

Luna, Miguel de

1592. *La verdadera historia del rey don Rodrigo.* Granada.

2001. *Historia verdadera del rey don Rodrigo.* Facsimile ed. with an intro. by L. Bernabé Pons. Granada.

Lynch, John

1969. *Spain under the Habsburgs.* Vol. 2, *Spain and America, 1598–1700.* Oxford.

Magnier, Grace

2001. "Pedro de Valencia, Don Quijote's Advice to Sancho and the *Tratado acerca de los Moriscos de España.*" In *Mélanges Luce López-Baralt.* Ed. and with an intro. by Abdeljelil Temimi, 2: 461–72. Zaghouan.

Magraner, Rodrigo

1975. *La expulsión de los moriscos, sus razones jurídicas y consecuencias económicas para la región valenciana.* Valencia.

Manzanares de Cirre, Manuela

1973. "El otro mundo en la literatura aljamiado-morisca." *Hispanic Review* 71: 599–608.

al-Maqqari, Shihab al-Din Ahmad bin Muhammad

1939–42. *Azhar al-riyad fi akhbar 'Iyad.* 3 vols. Cairo.

1949. *Nafh al-tib min gusn al-Andalus al-ratib.* 10 vols. Cairo.

Mármol Carvajal, Luis del

1600. *Historia del rebelión y castigo del los Moriscos de Granada.* Málaga.

1991. *Rebelión y castigo de los Moriscos.* Málaga.

Márquez Villanueva, Francisco

1991. *El problema morisco (desde otras laderas).* Madrid.

Martínez Ruíz, Juan
1972. *Inventarios de los bienes moriscos del reino de Granada (s. XVI).* Madrid.

Medina, Francisco de Borja
1988. "La compañía de Jesús y la minoría morisca." *Archivum Historicum Societatis Iesu* 57: 3–134.

Melón y Ruiz de Gordejuela, Amando
1917. *Lupercio Latrás y la guerra de moriscos y montañeses en Aragón a fines del siglo XVI.* Zaragoza.

Mendes Drumond Braga, Isabel
2001. "Fontes documentais portuguesas para o estudo dos Mouriscos." In *Mélanges Luce López-Baralt.* Ed. and with an intro. by Abdeljelil Temimi, 2: 523–28. Zaghouan.

Menéndez Pidal, Ramón
1952. *Poema de Yúçuf: Materiales para su estudio.* Facsimile ed. Granada.

Menéndez Pidal, Ramón, general ed.
1958–. *Historia de España.* 41 vols. Madrid.

Menéndez y Pelayo, Marcelino
1956. *Historia de los heterodoxos españoles.* 2 vols. Reprint. Madrid.

Meyerson, Mark D.
1991. *The Muslims of Valencia in the Age of Fernando and Isabel: Between Coexistence and Crusade.* Berkeley, Los Angeles, and Oxford.

Miletich, J. S., ed.
1986. *Hispanic Studies in Honor of Alan D. Deyermond: A North American Tribute.* Madison.

Mills, Kenneth
1994. "The Limits of Religious Coercion in Mid-Colonial Peru." *Past and Present* 145: 84–121.

Monroe, James
1966. "A Curious Ottoman Appeal to the Ottoman Empire." *Al-Andalus* 21: 281–303.

Montaner Frutos, A.
1988. *El recontamiento de Al-Miqdad y Al-Mayasa.* Zaragoza.

Monter, William
1990. *Frontiers of Heresy: The Spanish Inquisition from the Basque Lands to Sicily.* Cambridge.

Moral, Celia del, ed.
2002. *En el epílogo del Islam andalusí.* Granada.

Murphy, Martin, ed.
1994. *William Atkins, a relation of the Journey from St. Omers to Seville, London.* In *A relation of the journey of 12 students from the English College at St. Omers in Artois, to the English College of Sevill in Spaine Ano Dni 1622, stylo novo,* 191–288. Camden Fifth Series, vol. 3. London.

Nadal, Jordi
1984. *La población española. Siglos XVI a XX.* 2d ed. Barcelona.

Narváez, María Teresa

1978. "Los moriscos españoles a través de sus manuscritos aljamiados." *Cuadernos de la Facultad de Humanidades de la Universidad de Puerto Rico* 1: 51–65.

1981. "Mitificación de Andalucía como 'nueva Israel': El capítulo 'Kaída del-Andaluziyya' del ms. aljamiado la Tafçira del Mancebo de Arévalo." *Nueva Revista de Filología Hispánica* 30, no. 1: 143–67.

1984. "Más sobre la Tafçira del Mancebo de Arévalo." In *Religion, Identité et Sources Documentaires sur les Morisques Andalous.* Ed. Abdeljelil Temimi, 2: 123–30. Tunis.

1986. "El Mancebo de Arévalo frente a Jesús y María: Tradición y novedad." In *Les actes de la première table ronde du C.I.E.M. sur la littérature aljamiado-morisque: Hybridisme linguistique et univers discursif.* Ed. Abdeljelil Temimi, 109–15. Tunis.

1988. "La Tafsira del Mancebo de Arévalo." Ph.D. diss., University of Puerto Rico.

1989. "Nozaita Kalderan: Partera y experta en el Corán." In *Las Practicas musulmanas de los moriscos andaluces, 1492–1609: Actas del III Simposio Internacional de Estudios Moriscos.* 139–50. Zaghouan.

1990. "El Mancebo de Arévalo lector morisco de *La Celestina.*" In *Métiers, vie religieuse et problématiques d'histoire morisque.* Ed. Abdeljelil Temimi, 267–278. Zaghouan.

2001. "Notas a la presencia de Ibn al-'Arabi en la obra del Mancebo de Arévalo." In *Mélanges Luce López-Baralt.* Ed. and with an intro. by Abdeljelil Temimi, 2: 529–34. Zaghouan.

Narváez, María Teresa, ed.

2003. *Tratado. Tafsira.* Madrid.

O'Malley, John W.

1993. *The First Jesuits.* Cambridge, MA, and London.

Pastor Campos, Pilar

1978. "La conversión de los moriscos granadinos." In *Actas del I Congreso de Historia de Andalucía, diciembre de 1976,* 375–85. Córdoba.

Peinado Santaella, Rafael Gerardo

1987. "La repoblación de la tierra de Granada." In *Estudios sobre Málaga y el Reino de Granada en el V Centenario de la Conquista.* Ed. José Enrique López de Coca Castañer, 363–82. Málaga.

Pelorson, Jean-Marc

1972. "Recherches sur la *comedia* 'Los Moriscos de Hornachos.'" *Bulletin Hispanique* 74: 5–42.

Perceval, José María

1997. *Todos son uno: Arquetipos, xenofobia y racismo. La imagen del morisco en la Monarquia Española durante los siglos XVI y XVII.* Almería.

1998. "Todos son uno: La invención del morisco que nunca existió." In Fundación Bancaja, *La Expulsión de los Moriscos (14 de octobre de 1997–9 de junio de 1998),* 13–40. [Valencia].

Pérez Bustamente, Ciriaco

1951. "El pontífice Paulo V y la expulsión de los Moriscos." *Boletín de la R. Academia de la Historia* 129: 219–33.

1983. *La España de Felipe III.* 2d ed. Vol. 24 of *Historia de España,* Ramón Menéndez Pidal, general ed. Madrid.

Pérez de Culla, Vicente

1695. *Expulsión de los moriscos rebeldes de la Sierra y Muela de Cortes.* Valencia.

Pérez de Hita, Ginés

1998. *La guerra de los moriscos (Segunda Parte de las Guerras Civiles de Granada).* Facsimile of Madrid 1915 ed. Preliminary study by Joaquín Gil Sanjuán. Granada.

Plou Gascón, Miguel

1988. "Los moriscos de Letux y consecuencias de su expulsión." In Institución Fernando el Católico, *Destierros aragoneses: Judíos y moriscos,* 291–301. Zaragoza.

Prescott, William H.

n.d. *History of the Reign of Philip the Second, King of Spain.* London and New York.

Quinn, David B.

1973. *Raleigh and the British Empire.* Harmondsworth.

Rabadán, Mohamed

1868–73. "The Poetry of Mohammad Rabadán Arragonese." Ed. H. E. J. Stanley, third Baron Stanley of Alderley. In *Journal of the Asiatic Society of Great Britain and Ireland* n.s. 3 (1868): 81–104, 379–413; 4 (1870): 138–77; 5 (1871): 119–40, 303–37; 6 (1873): 165–212.

Ravillard, Martine

1979. "Bibliographie commentée des Morisques. (Sources imprimées de leur origine à 1978)." Cyclostyled Diplôme d'Études Approfondies, University of Algiers.

Razûq, Muhammad

1989. *Al-Andalusiyyûn wa-hijrâtuhum ilâ al-magrib khalâl al-qarnayn 16–17.* Al-Dâr al-Baydâ'.

Redondo, A.

1979. *Antonio de Guevara (1480?–1545) et l'Espagne de son temps.* Geneva.

Reglá Campistrol, Juan

1964. *Estudios sobre los moriscos.* Valencia.

Ribera, Julián and Asín, Miguel

1912. *Manuscritos arabes y aljamiados de la Biblioteca de la Junta.* Madrid.

Russell, Peter E., ed.

1973. *Spain: A Companion to Spanish Studies.* London.

Saavedra y Moragas, Eduardo

1889. "Escritos de los moriscos..." In *Memorias de la Real Academia. Española* 6: 140–328.

Sacy, Antoine Isaac Silvestre de

1799. "Notice de deux manuscrits arabico-espagnols." In *Notices et extraits des manuscrits de la Bibliothèque nationale.* Vol. 4, 626–47. Paris.

1827. "Notice d'un manuscrit espagnol écrit pour l'usage des Maures d'Espagne" In *Notices et extraits des Manuscrits de la Bibliothèque du Roi.* Vol. 11, 311–33. Paris.

Salmi, Ahmad

1956. "Le genre des poèmes de nativité (*mawludiyya-s*) dans le royaume de Grenade et au Maroc." *Hespéris* 43: 335–435.

Salvador, Emilia

1975. "Sobre la emigración mudéjar a Berbería. El tránsito legal a través del puerto de Valencia durante el primer cuarto del siglo XVI." *Estudis* [Departamento de Historia Moderna, Universidad de Valencia] 4: 39–68.

Santa Cruz, Alonso de

1951. *Crónica de los Reyes Católicos.* Ed. Juan de Mata Carriazo. 2 vols. Seville.

Sarnelli Cerqua, Clelia

1966. "La fuga in Marocco di As-Sihab Ahmad al-Hagari." *Studi Maghrebini* 1: 215–29.

1970. "Al-Hagari in Andalusia." *Studi Maghrebini* 3: 161–203.

1989. "Al-Hagari en France." In *Las prácticas musulmanas de los moriscos andaluces, 1492–1609: Actas del III Simposio Internacional de Estudios Moriscos.* Ed. Abdeljelil Temimi, 161–66. Zaghouan.

Sicroff, Albert A.

1985 [1960]. *Los estatutos de limpieza de sangre: Controversias entre los siglos XV y XVII.* Madrid.

Suárez Fernández, Luis, and Manual Fernández Álvarez

1969. *La edificación del Estado y la política exterio.* Vol. 17, part 2 of *Historia de España,* Ramón Menéndez Pidal, general ed. Madrid.

Surtz, Ronald E.

2001. "Maurofilia y maurofobia en los procesos inquisitoriales de Cristóbal Duarte Ballester." In *Mélanges Luce López-Baralt.* Ed. and with an intro. by Abdeljelil Temimi, 711–22. Zaghouan.

Szmolka Clares, José

1978. "Los comienzos de la castellanización del reino de Granada (1492–1516)." In *Actas del I Congreso de Historia de Andalucía, diciembre de 1976,* 405–12. Córdoba.

Tapia Sánchez, Serafín de

1991. *La comunidad morisca de Ávila.* Ávila.

Temimi, Abdeljelil

1975. "Une lettre des morisques de Grenada au Sultan Suleiman al-Kanuni en 1541." *Revue d'Histoire Maghrebine* 3: 100–5.

1989a. *Le Gouvernement ottoman et le problème morisque.* Zaghouan.

1990. *Métiers, vie religieuse et problématiques d'histoire morisque.* Zaghouan.

Temimi, Abdeljelil, ed.

1984. *Religion, Identité et Sources Documentaires sur les Morisques Andalous.* 2 vols. Tunis.

1986. *Les actes de la première table ronde du C.I.E.M. sur la littérature aljamiado-morisque: Hybridisme linguistique et univers discursif.* Tunis.

1989b. *Las prácticas musulmanas de los moriscos andaluces, 1492–1609: Actas del III Simposio Internacional de Estudios Moriscos.* Zaghouan.

1993a. *Études d'Histoire morisque.* Zaghouan.

1993b. *Le Ve Centenaire de la chute de Grenada, 1492–1992.* 2 vols. Zaghouan.

2001. *Mélanges Luce López-Baralt.* With a preface by Abdeljelil Temimi. 2 vols. Zaghouan.

Thompson, B. Bussell

1986. "La Alhotba arrimada (o el Sermón de Rabadán) y el mester de clerecía." In *Hispanic Studies in Honor of Alan D. Deyermond: A North American Tribute.* Ed. J. S. Miletich, 279–89. Madison.

Torre, Antonio de la, ed.

1966. *Documentos sobre Relaciones Internacionales de los Reyes Católicos.* Vol. 6. Barcelona.

al-Turki,ʿAbd al-Majid

1967. "Watha'iqʿan al-hijra al-andalusiyya al-akhira ila Tunis." *Hawliyyat al-jamiʿa al-tunisiyya* 4: 23–82.

Valero Cuadra, Pino

2000. *La leyenda de la doncella Carcayona.* Alicante.

Van Koningsveld, P. S., J. Sadan, and Q. al-Samarrai

1990. *Yemenite Authorities and Jewish Messianism: Ahmad ibn Nasir al-Zaydi's Account of the Sabbathian Movement in Seventeenth-Century Yemen and Its Aftermath.* Leiden.

Van Koningsveld, P. S., Al-Samarrai, Q., and Wiegers, G.A., eds.

1997. *Kitab Nasir al-Din ʿala'l-qawm al-kafirin.* Madrid.

Van Koningsveld, P. S., and G. A. Wiegers

1996a. "The Islamic Statute of the Mudejars in the Light of a New Source." *Al-Qantara* 17: 19–58.

1996b. "Islam in Spain during the Early Sixteenth Century: The Views of Four Judges in Cairo." *Orientations* [Yearbook of the Dutch Association] 4 (1996): 133–52.

1999. "An Appeal of the Moriscos to the Mamluk Sultan and Its Counterpart to the Ottoman Court: Textual Analysis, Context and Wider Historical Background." *Al-Qantara* 20: 66–98.

Vassberg, David E.

1984. *Land and Society in Golden Age Castile.* Cambridge and London.

Vera Delgado, Ana María

1978. "La revuelta mudéjar de 1501–2 : El destino de los vencidos." In *Actas del I Congreso de Historia de Andalucía, diciembrede 1976,* 405–12. Córdoba.

Villanueva Rico, María del Cármen

1966. *Casas, mezquitas y tiendas de los habices de las iglesias de Granada.* Madrid.

Vincent, Bernard

1978. *Historia de los moriscos. Vida y tragedia de una minoría.* Cowritten with A. Domínguez Ortiz. Madrid.

1998. "El río morisco." In Fundación Bancaja, *La Expulsión de los Moriscos (14 de octobre de 1997–9 de junio de 1998),* 125–44. [Valencia].

Wiegers, Gerard

1988. *A Learned Muslim Acquaintance of Erpenius and Golius. Ahmad b. Qasim al-Andalusi and Arabic Studies in the Netherlands.* Leiden.

1991. *Yça Gidelli (fl. 1450), His Antecedents and Successors: A Historical Study of Islamic Literature in Spanish and Aljamiado.* Leiden.

1993a. "Diplomatie et polémique anti-chrétienne: Naissance et influence de l'oeuvre de Muhammad Alguazir (vers 1021/1612)." In *Le Ve Centenaire de la chute de Grenada, 1492–1992*. Ed. Abdeljelil Temimi, 747–56. Zaghouan.

1993b. "The 'Old' or 'Turpiana' Tower in Granada and Its Relics according to Ahmad B. Qasim al-Hajari." In *Sites et Monuments disparus d'après les témoignages de voyageurs*. Ed. Rika Gyselen. Res Orientales, 8. Bures-sur-Yvette.

1993c. "A Life between Europe and the Maghrib: The Writings and Travels of Ahmad b. Qasim al-Hajari al-Andalusi." In *Orientations* [Yearbook of the Dutch Association] 1 (1993): 87–115.

1994. *Islamic Literature in Spanish and Aljamiado: Yça de Segovia (fl. 1450), His Antecedents and Successors*. Leiden.

1995. "Muhammad as the Messiah: A Comparison of the Polemical Works of Juan Alonso with the Gospel of Barnabas." *Bibliotheca Orientalis* 52: 245–91.

Zayas, Rodrigo de

1992. *Les Morisques et le racisme d'état*. Paris.

Index